Praise for *Tomorrow is Another C*

'A gripping, fast-paced, author mostly secret negotiations that brought South Africa's bitter conflict to its near-miraculous end. Sparks' description of these talks sometimes brings a lump to one's throat. He shows how the participants' deep mutual suspicion was gradually replaced by excitement at the prospect of making a momentous agreement – and also by the dawning realization that the people on the other side were human beings, perhaps even decent human beings.'
– Adam Hochschild, *New York Times Book Review*

'A splendid and original history ... Sparks' skillful weaving of myriad strands – Mandela's secret sessions with the committee, the clandestine talks in England between the African National Congress and the government, the back-channel communications between Mandela and the ANC in exile, the trepidation of Botha and the apparent transformation of his successor, De Klerk – possesses the drama and intrigue of a diplomatic whodunnit.'
– Richard Stengel, *Time*

'Sparks offers many reasons for hope, but the most profound of them is the story this book tells.' – Jacob Weisberg, *The Washington Post*

'The most riveting of the many [accounts] that have been published about the end of apartheid.'
– *The Economist*

Praise for *The Mind of South Africa*:

'Former editor of the Johannesburg *Rand Daily Mail*, and now a correspondent for US and UK newspapers, Sparks here writes one of the most sensitive and best balanced histories of relationships among South Africa's Dutch, English, Indian and indigenous peoples.'
– *Publishers Weekly*

THE SWORD
AND
THE PEN

SIX DECADES ON
THE POLITICAL FRONTIER

ALLISTER SPARKS

For Pranav

With best wishes

[signature]

RIVONIA
4/8/16

JONATHAN BALL
JOHANNESBURG & CAPE TOWN

To my grandchildren
Dylan, Victoria, Jonathan, James, Yann and Emil

Published in South Africa in 2016 by
JONATHAN BALL PUBLISHERS
A division of Media24 Limited
PO Box 33977
Jeppestown
2043

Reprinted once in 2016

ISBN 978-1-86842-559-4
ebook ISBN 978-1-86842-560-0

Twitter: www.twitter.com/JonathanBallPub
Facebook: www.facebook.com/JonathanBallPublishers
Blog: http://jonathanball.bookslive.co.za/

Cover by Michiel Botha
Author photograph by Gallo Images/Beeld/Cornel van Heerden
Design and typesetting by Martine Barker
Set in Baskerville 12/14.4pt

Printed by **paarlmedia**, a division of Novus Holdings

Contents

PREFACE

I WAS BORN on the frontier. Literally. The border of our eastern Cape farm was the Black Kei River near its confluence with the White Kei to form the Great Kei, which flowed into the Indian Ocean some 75 km north of the port city of East London and itself formed the border between the white settlement region of Britain's old Cape Colony and the large 'native reserve' of Transkei. It was thus the first fiercely contested frontier between white and black in South Africa — between the white settlers who had been moving up the east coast since landing at the southern tip of the continent in the mid-seventeenth century and the indigenous black Africans who had been drifting southwards for centuries in slow rhythmic shifts of generational expansion. It was an encounter that was to become the quintessence of all our history. And thus, too, of my life.

The encounter on that frontier was violent and tragic, and indeed laden with dreadful misfortunes, for the native Xhosa people. In the century before I was born, nine wars were fought over that territory. And there were many rebellions besides, including one that gave our farm its name: Hotfire. It was not so named, as many thought, because of the family name of Sparks, or even the heat of its climate in an encircling bowl of rugged mountains, but because of a fierce battle fought there in what became known as the Gungubele Rebellion of 1878. As the Ninth Frontier War drew to a close, Gungubele, heir to the chieftaincy of a sub-tribe called the Amatshatsha, made a deal with a white farmer to return to his ancestral land near the newly established town of Queenstown. He made a down payment but, when he could not come up with further payments, the farmer repossessed the land. When the farmer rejected Gungubele's demand for a return of the down payment, the young chieftain raised a force and crossed the Black Kei to fight for his money. A colonial commando engaged him, and there on the land that was later to become our family farm the sharp engagement took place, with gunfire on both sides. Casualties were heavy. As a child, stumbling through the thick thorn bush trying to hunt small game with my .22 rifle, I sometimes came upon cairns of stones marking the resting places of fallen fighters.

Truly, the soil of my birthland was soaked with blood after what had effectively been a Hundred-Year War between the black and white inhabitants of a country we are today trying to mould into a single, unified nation.

Blood and treachery. Britain was at the height of its imperial power during those Victorian years and Albion's traditional perfidy was fully at play. It tricked and cheated the bewildered Xhosa chiefs at every turn. Most of the governors and military commanders Britain sent to the Cape were veterans who had marched with the Duke of Wellington in the Peninsula War. They were heavy-handed and arrogant. None more so than the swashbuckling Sir Harry Smith, whose most noted achievements were a stunning military victory at the Battle of Aliwal in India in 1846 and his marriage to a 14-year-old Spanish beauty, Juana Maria de los Dolores de Leon, freshly out of a convent and only four days after rescuing her from his rampaging troops after they had stormed the walled city of Badajoz near Spain's border with Portugal.

Smith arrived first as Chief of Staff to Governor Sir Benjamin D'Urban, then returned some years later as Governor himself. It was during his first term that he became involved in one of the most shameful acts of the colonial period.

Soon after his arrival, Smith was caught up in the Sixth

Frontier War under the overall command of the frustratingly indecisive D'Urban. The war had broken out between the white frontiersmen and the Gcaleka and Rharhabe tribes, which formed part of the larger Xhosa kingdom. As tended to happen in all these engagements, the tribal warriors, armed only with spears, shortened assegais and a few guns, withdrew into the dense thorn scrub and ravines of the Amathole Mountains from where they waged guerrilla attacks that disrupted and confused the better-armed colonial units.

Frustrated by this hit-and-disappear harassment, D'Urban decided, to the impulsive Smith's increasing irritation, to bypass the main theatre of war and march through more open land nearer the coast to the Great Place of the Paramount Chief of all the Xhosa, Hintsa, which was across the Great Kei near the mission-ary town of Butterworth, well inside what became known as the Transkei. There he encamped and sent word to Hintsa to come to the British camp under an assurance of personal safety to discuss the war situation. Hintsa hesitated at first, as his counsellors warned that they mistrusted the British and feared they would kill him. But eventually Hintsa accepted the invitation.

He entered D'Urban's tent, a tall, muscular man of dignified bearing, dressed in his full regalia, with a splendid leopard-skin cloak denoting his royal status. He was warmly received, given food and coffee and plied with presents. But after a while D'Urban began reading out a list of charges, accusing the king of failing to prevent the Gcaleka and Rharhabe from launching an unprovoked attack on the colonists and of showing ingratitude towards the colony, which the Governor claimed had helped Hintsa. D'Urban then set out his conditions for peace: Hintsa was to hand over the Rharhabe and Gcaleka chiefs, deliver for execution certain tribesmen D'Urban claimed were responsible for the murder of two settlers, and pay compensation of 50 000 head of cattle and 1 000 horses to the frontier settlers who had been attacked.

When Hintsa demurred, he was told bluntly, despite the assurance of safe passage, that he was under arrest and would have to order his followers to pay a ransom of 25 000 cattle and 500 horses for his release. Shocked and bewildered, Hintsa haggled a while longer, and then purported to agree — but instead dispatched a messenger to order his people to drive their cattle deeper into the Transkei.

Smith gave Hintsa dinner in his tent that night, entertaining him royally, and the next morning set out with the king and a force of troops ostensibly to find and bring back the ransom cattle and horses. For two days they marched, then early in the morning of the third day Hintsa suddenly spurred his horse and broke away, racing ahead of the column. With a cry of rage Smith gave chase, and for a time the two presented a scene that must have resembled a Western movie. Smith drew a pistol to fire at Hintsa, but it jammed and he flung it away, then drew another which also jammed. Gradually he closed in on Hintsa, who tried to stab his pursuer with his assegai but Smith was already too close for that. The derring-do soldier lunged at Hintsa, grabbed him by the throat and flung him off his horse.

A trooper, George Southey, coming up fast behind, saw Hintsa fall and fired two shots at him, hitting him in a leg and in the back. Hintsa managed to scramble into some bushes beside a river, while Southey dismounted and searched for him. Moments later the wounded king hurled his assegai at Southey but missed, and the young trooper, turning, saw Hintsa standing up in the water where he called out several times in isiXhosa: 'Mercy!' Southey, who spoke the language fluently, must have heard him, but he took aim and fired, shattering Hintsa's head.

Other members of Smith's posse rode up and two of them cut off Hintsa's ears: earlier, Smith had told his men he would buy a round of drinks for any who could bring him a Xhosa chief's ears. One of the medics in the posse tried to prize out some of Hintsa's teeth with his knife to keep as souvenirs. Smith himself sent some of the chief's bracelets to his wife to add to his collection of memorabilia.

'Thus died Hintsa, king of the Xhosa, for trusting the honour of a British Governor,' wrote Jeff Peires, the distinguished historian of the Xhosa people, in his classic work, *The House of Phalo*.[1]

By today's reckoning the action would have to be classified as a war crime, twice over: once for violating the assurance of safe passage in wartime for purposes of peace negotiations, and the second for cold-bloodedly shooting an enemy trying to surrender. But chivalry was not part of these frontier wars. Instead of being demoted or cashiered, Harry Smith was honoured with a knighthood and a doctorate from Cambridge University, then sent back to the Cape as Governor. Today he has the rare distinction of having an important South African town named after him, and there are two named after his Spanish-born wife.

Yet in the end it was not the wars, nor even the murder of their king, that destroyed the Xhosa kingdom. Each of the nine wars ended in a kind of negotiated truce that saw the Xhosa driven back a bit further, forfeiting more and more of their ancestral land, but they never surrendered.

What finally broke them was not the guns and superior mobility of the colonial armies, but a strange act of mass self-destruction that can only have been induced by the relentless pressure, social disruption and state of confused desperation that these hapless people came under. It is not unknown for societies facing desperate circumstances that they can neither deal with nor understand to seek refuge in psychic delusion and spiritual fantasy – and that is what happened here.

It was an epidemic of lung-sickness, a form of contagious bovine pneumonia, that triggered the disaster. The disease, unknown to the Xhosa and probably introduced by the importation of European cattle, was devastating herds in the Transkei and in the Cape Colony and nobody knew the cause or what to do about it. Witchcraft was suspected.

It was in this atmosphere that a 14-year-old Xhosa orphan girl named Nongqawuse went to fetch water with a younger friend, Nombanda, in the Gxara River, a narrow stream with many rock pools a little east of the Great Kei. Nongqawuse claimed she heard the voices of ancestors calling to her from the bushes along the river. She made repeated visits on subsequent days, reporting to her guardian and uncle, a Xhosa spiritualist named Mhlakaza, that the ancestors' voices had ordered her to tell the community they should slaughter all their cattle because they were 'bewitched' and 'unclean'. They should also burn all crops, and then dig new grain pits and build new, much larger cattle enclosures and houses because new cattle, new crops and 'new people', including dead warrior heroes, would arise to bring new hope and wealth to the Xhosa nation.

If they did this, the spirits told Nongqawuse, the white settlers would be driven back into the sea whence they had come.

Nongqawuse faithfully reported all this to her uncle, who hastened to spread the word among the Xhosa chiefs. There was scepticism at first, but there can be no doubt that the continuing ravages of lung-sickness, along with Mhlakaza's reputation as a spiritualist, gave the messages increasing credibility. As Nongqawuse's contacts continued, including some blurred visions of the ancestors themselves — among them her late father, Mhlakaza's brother — the message was expanded. On a given day the sun would rise blood-red, move to its noonday zenith, and then return to set in the east — at which point the sky would become pitch-black and new livestock, crops and people would appear to great rejoicing by everyone.

The day duly arrived and, of course, no such things occurred. But instead of disillusionment, Nongqawuse reported to the community that the spirits had told her it was because many unbelievers had not heeded their message and had failed to slaughter their cattle and burn their crops. This set off a wave of bitter, often violent conflicts between those labelled 'believers' and 'unbelievers'. The worst of the tragedy might still have been avoided had not the Paramount Chief of all the Xhosa, Sarhili — the much-admired son of Hintsa — who had prevaricated through much of the year, eventually come down firmly on the side of the believers. This swelled their ranks rapidly, causing many unbelievers to flee for their lives, and leading to a national catastrophe.

As the crisis deepened, fighting broke out between believers and unbelievers, while mass starvation decimated the black population of the frontier region. In the two years of the cattle-killing, their numbers declined from 105 000 to 38 500, or by nearly two-thirds. The lands thus made available were surveyed into 317 white farms of about 2 000 acres each. This increased the white population of the region sixfold, from 949 to 5388.

At the turn of the eighteenth century, shortly before my ancestors landed at Algoa Bay with the 1820 Settlers, the Xhosa people were a proud and independent nation, self-sustaining and self-confident. Their outlying chiefdoms reached westward to the Sundays River, near present-day Port Elizabeth, and their hinterland northward to the headwaters of the Kei. By the end of the Hundred-Year War they had been driven back across a series of shrinking boundaries, the Bushman's River, the Fish River, the Keiskamma River and finally the Kei, expelled from a great swathe of territory known first as the Province of Queen Adelaide, then as British Kaffraria, all of which then became an additional expanse of white-owned farmland.

It was a shrinkage that changed the lives of the Xhosa people and the fabric of their societies. The sons of chiefs could no longer move out of the parental kraal and establish chiefdoms of their own; game was shot out; grazing lands were cropped bare so that storm waters gouged the soil into jagged dongas; carrying capacity was reduced − all of which meant the shrinking land could no longer support the population. Men had to leave their homes and families to work on white farms and in white towns and, from the mid-nineteenth century onwards, increasingly on the diamond fields of Kimberley and gold mines of the Witwatersrand. They were sucked inexorably into the vortex of the white colonial economy, where their social fabric gradually disintegrated and their self-esteem broke down as they became an exploited working class locked into that condition by the forces of economic greed and pervasive race prejudice.

But I knew none of all this as I spent a happy childhood on the farm, hiking in the hills, shooting game, fishing for eels in the Kei and playing with the children of the black farmhands. The white folk of our region, my parents included, never spoke of the past. They, too, were born after the Hundred-Year War, and history was not a subject that interested them. The lives that they led, segregated from the black workers on their farms and in the towns and cities, seemed to be the natural order of things. Black folk knew their place and stayed there. And in such a state there was harmony, even a degree of paternalistic friendship. Nearly all the whites in the frontier region spoke isiXhosa and knew the black workers on their farms and their families.

That is how I spent my childhood, accepting the naturalness of it all in these exceedingly unnatural circumstances. I had no siblings: an older brother and a sister had died before I knew them. The nearest white kids my age were some miles away. I spent my days with the black kids on the farm, all related to the headman of the farmhands, Mbhuti Lavisa, who became a sort of surrogate father to me when my own father went off to war in 1939. The boys became friends: Ncweniso, Tintele, Pogoqwana and others, all part of Mbhuti's extended family. They never came in the house, of course; they knew their place. But they were friends. Outdoor friends.

Then there was Daisy, the housemaid, a mature woman of great warmth who pampered me with tidbits from the kitchen; and No-Me, a wizened woman of uncertain age and weirdo mind who functioned as a sangoma, or traditional healer, and who told me strange stories of a little spirit called the *tokoloshe* as I sat with her and Daisy while they ate their lunch and puffed their long pipes under a peach tree in the garden; and Wasvrou, the washerwoman, who was married to Mbhuti and was the matron of the extended Lavisa family. Dear people all, who fussed over me when, in later years, I came home for holidays from boarding school, but whom we never considered to be our equals. The relationship was warm but essentially feudal.

Thus my birthland. My personal frontier where, in the century before my birth, my ancestors fought and died and extracted the teeth of the Xhosa nation. And where in the century of my life — the most terrible century in all of human history, which saw Hitler and Stalin, Mussolini and Franco, the Holocaust, the Gulag, Hiroshima and Nagasaki — the frontier of my birthland transmuted into the struggle of liberty against the racist crime of apartheid.

That frontier is what framed my life. What follows is the story of my part in that struggle, in which I participated not with the sword of my ancestors but with a pen.

It is the story of how, as a journalist, I watched and chronicled and participated in my country's unfolding drama for more than 60 years, covering events from the premiership of DF Malan to the presidency of Jacob Zuma, witnessing at close range the rise and fall of apartheid and the rise and crisis of the new South Africa.

From those years of early rural isolation, with little exposure to events beyond our narrow valley, I joined my first newspaper at age 17 and was pitched headlong into the vortex of South Africa's stormy politics. Ten years later I was political correspondent of the country's largest morning daily and boldest anti-apartheid challenger, the *Rand Daily Mail* of Johannesburg; later still I became its editor; and, after being fired from that hot seat, as world interest in the intensifying anti-apartheid struggle surged, I become a foreign correspondent reporting on my country for some of the world's leading publications.

It has been a journey that transformed me as an individual even as my reportage played a role in transforming my country. Journalism became my education and my intellectual salvation even as my country transformed from a racist police state to a non-racial democracy. It is not often one has the opportunity to be part of such a historic event in the life of one's country.

This, then, is the story I have to tell. My *bildungsroman*, the memoir of one journalist's life and times through an extraordinary passage of events.

CHAPTER ONE

The Sword

MAYVILLE HOUSE at No 77 Prince Alfred Road, Queenstown, was a daunting place for a five-year-old to visit. Its south-facing front entrance was covered with creeping ivy that shaded the red brick walls, giving the impression of a damp and chilly reception. Press the bell and after a while you would hear a hesitant shuffling of feet and there would be the figure of Aunt Kate standing in the doorway, an eternally ancient and skeletal Miss Havisham dressed in a pink padded dressing gown with pink pom-pom slippers, staring at me through thick-lensed cataract spectacles that made her eyes look large and owlish.

My mother used to take me there periodically to pay duty calls, for Kate and her two sisters, Lillian and Millicent, were her aunts, three elderly spinsters who had lived together in Mayville House for most of their lives. They were the three youngest siblings of Henry Thomas Lloyd, who had arrived in South Africa at the age of six together with his father, Henry James Lloyd, a London worsted weaver. When displaced by the industrial revolution, he decided to join the legendary 1820 Settlers and seek a new life on the war-torn eastern Cape frontier with his wife Rebecca.

Six-year-old Henry Thomas Lloyd, one of eight siblings, grew up into a sturdy young frontiersman who fought in the frontier wars of 1835, 1856 and 1847. He was rewarded with a

1

government grant that he used to build himself a large home-cum-inn called Travellers' Rest, just across the Great Kei River near the mission settlement of St Marks. There he sired 21 children in his 82 years – seven by his first wife, Ann Ulyate, and 14 by his second, Maria Godfrey – of whom 18 survived. Maria was my mother's grandmother, a strong Scots woman with blazing red hair that she bequeathed to several of her descendants, including one of my four sons. My mother, Bernice Constance Godfrey, who was named after her, cited her often in tones of deference. 'Beware of women with red hair,' she enjoined me. 'They can be difficult.' Welshmen, she declared, referring to Henry's family tree, were all horse-thieves. She was a woman of emphatic views.

On Maria's death, so the family story goes, Henry James informed his three youngest daughters that they should not marry but rather stay at home to care for him in his old age. Which, being dutiful Victorian maidens, they did.

And so it came about that my mother visited the 'Aunties' to give them some much-needed company. With me in tow. The gloomy entrance to Mayville House led through a passageway into a wide sitting room with ornate oak furniture and heavy maroon velvet curtains at the windows. Stern ancestral faces glared down from the walls and the place was cluttered with china ornaments and other Victorian bric-a-brac. This was not a happy playground for a small boy.

But the Aunties would cluck over me during those visits. How to entertain me, of course, was the problem during those few hours of serious adult conversation about the doings of distant and departed relatives about whom I knew nothing.

'What about Walter's old sword?' Aunt Kate, the imaginative one, suggested.

'Ah yes, I'll get it out,' responded Aunt Lillie, the eldest, as she took my hand and led me into another dingy room. There she opened a cupboard drawer and withdrew a long object wrapped in an old military blanket. Carefully, almost reverently, she carried it across the room, laid it on a bed and slowly unwrapped it.

There it lay. Not a shiny ceremonial sword, but an old battle sword rough-sharpened for use and sheathed in a battered metal

2

scabbard, rusted and darkened with age. Hardly a toy, of course, but no matter. The impact on me was immense. I was allowed to unsheathe it. And hold it. I stared at it, at the heavy brass hilt and at the strange inscriptions on the blade partly obscured by old stains. Were those bloodstains? How many men had it decapitated? There can be no end to the mind-games of heroism and derring-do that a small boy can play with an old battle sword in his hands.

It became a ritual. On every visit to the Aunties, once every six months or so, the sword would come out and I would be allowed to wage my imaginary battles with it.

Aunt Millie, the last to go, collapsed and died when she was 97. When the will was read, I found she had left me the sword.

* * *

FOR YEARS IT lay untouched at the back of a cupboard of my own, its novelty as a small boy's plaything long expired. It had no ornamental value, so it was simply stashed away along with life's other useless collectables, its provenance and story undisclosed.

And so it might have remained but for my first visit to the United States where, during a year of study at Harvard, I came upon WJ Cash's literary masterpiece, *The Mind of the South*, a vivid portrait of that colourful but cruelly bigoted region and its tempestuous history. It awakened in me an awareness not only of the importance of well-presented history in understanding the idiosyncrasies of different human societies but also, to my journalistic mind, the great stories buried in the past, waiting to be exhumed.

I had done well in history at high school, scoring decent grades, but how dull it had all been: a catalogue of dreary dates, drearily presented, as uninspired teachers and even more uninspired textbooks dragged us, year after year, through the same tedious sequence of dates, grievances, conflicts, wars, peace agreements and yet more grievances. The groaning wagons of the Great Trek, the repetitiveness of the battles, the treachery of the tribal chiefs, the heroism of the white settlers and the meddlesomeness of the missionaries and the Colonial Office in London who didn't understand the true nature of the natives. It was biased and it was boring.

Now here was I consuming it greedily in a foreign land. My mind went back to those dreary schooldays and I realised what a travesty had been committed by the South African education system, what great drama had been smothered, what tragedies of human misconception in that century of frontier warfare between different cultures and value systems, what epic endurance and heroism in the task of hauling ox-wagons and whole families a thousand kilometres over the great Dragon Mountains to the plains of the highveld that stretch all the way up Africa, the agony of what was effectively a civil war between the Boers and those of British ancestry that killed thousands and scorched the earth and poisoned relations between the two white race groups. The thought struck me that if there had been a Hollywood in South Africa, the dramatising of our history would have far outshone the story of the opening up of the American West.

That is when I began a new phase in my life of returning to the history of my country, of trying to revive and write about the vividness of it, of rediscovering and bringing to life its great stories. And so ultimately also to pondering the roles of my own family members in all this. They had all been 1820 Settlers, on both my father's and my mother's side — all except one, that is, but more of him later — so they must have been players in the whole tableau, with untold stories of their own to be unearthed.

So my mind went back to the old sword. Who was Walter?

A little research revealed that he was one of Henry Thomas Lloyd's 21 children, the eldest of his second marriage to Maria and thus the Aunties' big brother. He had obviously bequeathed the sword to them on his death in 1921, but how it had come into Walter's possession took longer to discover.

My first clue came from a distant cousin, Margaret Lloyd, who told me Walter had ridden in a military commando under the leadership of an officer named Von Linsingen, who was killed in a battle in the Transkei — and that the sword had belonged to Von Linsingen. This sent me to the provincial archives in Cape Town, where I found the death notice on one Ernst von

Linsingen, aged 16. It was dated 14 November 1880 and was signed by his mother, Bertha, who had filled in the space to describe cause of death: 'Fell on the field at Snodgrass.' There was a ring of pride in that wording, together with what must have been the agonising grief of a bereaved mother. Clearly a military family, I thought, all straight-backed and stiff-upper-lipped. But the lad was still a schoolboy, obviously not the commander of a military unit. But I had the curious name of the battlefield, Snodgrass, so I went to see the country's leading expert on the history of the Eastern Cape, Jeff Peires.

'Ah yes, Snodgrass's Café,' Peires replied. 'An interesting place. A trading store, once run by a man of that name. Thembu rebels used it as a kind of base during a rebellion in the nineteenth century, then guerrilla fighters used it again during the recent anti-apartheid struggle. It's still there, you know …'

And so the story unfolded, beginning with the discovery of the Kimberley diamond fields in the 1870s. That watershed event led, together with the rush of rapacious immigration, to a flood of illicit guns into the country. Fearful that this would compound problems on the frontier, the Cape Colonial Parliament, recently granted representative government, enacted a Gun Law prohibiting black people from owning firearms.

By a twist of constitutional fate, the Basutoland Protectorate, homeland of the Basotho people – who had sought refuge in their mountain kingdom from the ravages of Zulu King Shaka's wars of conquest – was at this time briefly incorporated into the Cape Colony. So the Gun Law applied to the Basotho as well. Furious at this outside interference in what they regarded as their sovereign right to defend themselves, as well as a slight to their national pride, the Basotho rebelled.

Tribal boundaries being porous, the Gun Law rebellion soon spilled over into the adjoining Transkei, where it was taken up by restless members of the isiXhosa-speaking Thembu tribe, the same tribe that a century later was to give us Nelson Mandela. The rebellious Thembus attacked several small Transkei towns, killing the white resident magistrate of Qumbu, Hamilton Hope, and his two lieutenants, besieging the magistrate of Maclear, Mr

Thomson, locking the magistrate of Tsolo, Mr Welsh, in his own jail, putting the magistrate of Ngcobo to flight and briefly seizing control of the town. As panic rippled through the colony, Prime Minister Sir John Gordon Sprigg ordered a commando to be raised on the frontier to engage with the rebels and restore order.

The commando was duly mobilised under the command of Colonel Wilhelm Carl von Linsingen, a former Prussian officer who had settled in South Africa at a time when the Colonial Office was eager to encourage immigrants with military experience to strengthen white settlement on the frontier. Von Linsingen was serving as governor of the prison in East London at the time, but as a professional soldier he answered the call unquestioningly.

His 16-year-old son Ernst asked, and was granted, permission to ride with his dad as a cadet. My great-uncle Walter, living in Grahamstown and at some point its mayor, joined the unit. Together they rode out to Snodgrass's café, a known trouble spot not far from Ngcobo.

Today the café is an old rectangular mud-daub building with a red corrugated-iron roof and a dilapidated front porch that is no longer a refreshment station but serves as a busy store for the local community. It is located at the foot of two exquisite little conical hills bearing the Xhosa name of *Mabele Nthombi* (a young maiden's breasts).

It was there that Von Linsingen's posse rode in search of the Thembu rebels. And it was there that they came under attack as the rebel group charged through the cleavage between the two hills, taking the commando by surprise. Von Linsingen gave the order to withdraw, but as his unit wheeled about one of the men was unhorsed, and as he fell broke a leg. Seeing that the man could not remount, Von Linsingen turned back to help him, followed by Ernst. Both were hit by gunfire from the attackers. Ernst was killed instantly and the colonel mortally wounded. Walter Lloyd galloped back to try to help Von Linsingen, but the dying colonel ordered him to save himself, asking him to 'Take my sword and my horse and give them to my parents in Port Elizabeth.'

In fact the horse, a prized Basotho pony, was also dead, so Walter sliced off a piece of hide with the sword, mounted his own horse and rejoined the unit. When later he visited Von Linsingen's family in Port Elizabeth to give them the sword and the piece of horse's hide, they were so touched that they presented him with the sword as a reward for his compassion and heroism.

And so it came via those old maiden aunts to me. A war hero's weapon and a child's plaything. But above all a symbol of the blood and tears and courage and folly of the frontier on which I was born. I have now retrieved it from that dark cupboard and given it a place of honour in my home.

I travelled to the Transkei in the summer of 2011 to see Snodgrass's Café and the battlefield where Von Linsingen and his son had fallen. There I met the new owner, Bambo Qongo, a minor regional chief who told me that he and his two brothers had befriended the black manager who ran the store for its white owner and used it as a refuge during the liberation struggle. He and his brothers were members of the Pan Africanist Congress's armed wing, Apla, and they had shared the refuge with members of the African National Congress's military wing, *Umkhonto we Sizwe* (Spear of the Nation). Though the two guerrilla groups were bitter rivals politically, Qongo said they had developed a comradeship of their own in their shared safe house. 'We were all fighting the same struggle and we got to know each other well,' he told me. After liberation he had become so attached to the place that he bought it from its white owner.

To my surprise, Qongo knew the story of the battle in which Colonel von Linsingen was killed and has an account of it framed and mounted in front of the rickety old trading store. He was enchanted when I told him the story of my great-uncle Walter's involvement in that battle and showed him the sword, which I had brought with me.

'So you were in the struggle too, weren't you, Mr Sparks?' he murmured reflectively as he fondled the blade of the sword, mentioning with a small smile that he had read my political writings over the years.

'Yes,' I replied, 'but that was with a pen.'

CHAPTER TWO

Man Without a Face

MY MATERNAL grandfather, Thomas Alfred Stephen, was the alpha male of our extended family. He was stern and authoritarian, a man of strong views that would brook no contradiction. He was known throughout the valley as 'Poppy' Stephen, more through deference to his age and acknowledged intelligence than to anything resembling affection. He was not popular, but he was respected. He could be abrupt. His manner of greeting family members as they called to visit him was often along the lines of: 'Hello. When are you leaving?' His nine children and their spouses quaked before him — all except my mother, Bernice, the oldest daughter who had brought up her siblings after her mother, Sarah Jane, had died. She took over the maternal role at the age of 18 and was the only one who could deal firmly with him. She was a trained nurse and he needed her. In some ways she was rather like him, strong-willed and somewhat didactic. There are some who suggest I may have also inherited a few of those genes.

But for all his forceful character and domineering ways, a strange secret hung over Poppy Stephen, one that remained long after his death at age 84. Who was his father? Where had he come from? Perhaps my mother and her oldest brother, Cecil, knew, but if so they took the information to their graves. We, the cousins of the third generation, knew nothing about him. We knew at least the name of our great-grandmother, Charlotte Stracey, and that she had married a man named Jonathan Heath after her first husband died. But who that first husband, our great-grandfather, was, where he had come from and what had become of him, none of us knew. No one ever spoke of him. There was no gravestone to his memory in the local cemeteries as there were to other family ancestors. He was a man without a name, without a face. He had been airbrushed out of the family history.

My maternal grandfather,
Thomas Alfred Stephen

We were a close-knit extended family in the farming valley where we all lived. Homesteads were within horse-riding distance of each other, so interaction during the early days tended to be intimate. Everyone knew everyone else's business, and marriages verged on the incestuous, with brothers of one family marrying sisters of another, resulting in what in the American South are called 'double cousins'. My own double cousins, Raymond and Wilfred Sparks, both older than me, lived on a neighbouring farm called Turnstream on a bend in the Black Kei River. To get there from Hotfire we had to drive five kilometres on a rutted farm track over a precipitous hill in our 1924 ragtop Buick with a bulbous rubber horn that one had to squeeze by hand. Family gatherings were jolly affairs at which our parents would regale us with reminiscences of how they would pack their finery and their nightgowns in saddlebags and ride together over the mountains to attend a dance in another valley. There they would dance till late in some farmer's woolshed as an elderly aunt would thump out the popular tunes of the day on an upright piano, then catch a few hours' sleep before riding back home next day. Romance was a collective activity.

We cousins knew our paternal family tree, unlike the mystery that shrouded Grandpa Stephen's parentage. We were proud of the fact that they were all members of the 1820 Settlers, as was my mother's maternal line, the Lloyds. We knew that Henry Sparks, Snr, a carpenter from Plymouth, had married a young woman named Mary Tassler, who had signed their marriage certificate with a cross showing herself to be illiterate, and that they sailed to South Africa with their five-year-old son, Henry, Jnr, aboard the settler ship *Aurora*.

Life was an impossible struggle for the settlers. Henry was given a five-acre plot of land in what was really ranching country, and left with a few wooden tools to build his own mud-daub cottage. The colonial authorities forbade stock farming because they believed it would encourage cattle rustling by the neighbouring Xhosa people. Henry and his fellow settlers were supposed to become agriculturalists in a region with a schizophrenic climate, halfway between the winter rainfall area of the Western Cape and the summer rainfall regions of the interior. Moreover, the nearest urban market for whatever fresh produce they grew was in Cape Town, about a month's trek by ox-wagon.

What the settlers had not been told, and had not guessed for themselves, was that the real purpose of the settlement was not agricultural but military. The British government wanted to ease the unemployment problem caused by the depression that followed the end of the Napoleonic wars, while at the same time strengthening the white population on the eastern Cape frontier, thus cutting the cost of the frequent frontier wars.

The inevitable result was that the farming settlement scheme effectively collapsed within two years, with most of the settlers going off to build the small towns of the eastern Cape and return to the crafts they had practised back in Britain. The few who showed an aptitude for farming bought up the plots of those who left, so forming holdings of economically viable size where they eventually turned to sheep farming and flourished.

Henry Snr built himself a home and a carpenter's workshop in the main street of Grahamstown, where he made a decent living until his death there at age 82. His widow Mary, younger than him, established an inn to eke out a living until she suffered a ghastly death, murdered by a tenant for her modest intake of the month's rent. She was 68.

Henry Jnr did a lot better, although he, too, came to an untimely end. He became a prosperous farmer on a holding called Haddon's Post near the village of Adelaide, where he married a woman named Mary Knott and with her produced ten children, of whom the oldest son, Henry George Tassler Sparks, in turn produced Henry Percival Sparks, who was my paternal grandfather.

As Henry Jnr gained some status in his community he drifted into politics, first becoming mayor of Adelaide, then, when Britain granted responsible government in 1853, a Member of the first Cape Parliament. But he remained an MP for only one term before going off to seek his fortune on the Kimberley diamond fields. It was there that he met his death. The official record says he died of a heart attack, but family legend has it that it was a practical joke by a friend that triggered the fatal seizure. The story is that Henry was gazing, fascinated, into the depths of Kimberley's famous Big Hole, still the diamond city's most popular tourist spot, watching the ant-like figures working far below, when a friend stole up quietly behind him and pretended to give him a push.

I knew my grandfather Percy well when I was a child. He was a kind and gentle man, creased and burnt a mahogany brown from years of toil under the kiln-hot sun that scorched our valley. He lived up the valley from us on a farm called Anta, site of the grave of an important Xhosa chief of that name, an older brother of the great King Sandile but of the lesser right-hand house that removed him from the line of succession. Chief Anta had been one of the senior disbelievers at the time of the great cattle-killing. This marked him as a rebel at the time but later led to his being revered for his wisdom and compassion so that pilgrims would periodically visit his gravesite on the farm.

'Boss' Percy, as we cousins affectionately called our grandfather, married yet another settler descendant, May Crout, a woman of seemingly endless afflictions requiring constant sympathy and a great variety of medications. She had a morbid fear of growing old and insisted that we youngsters call her 'Aunty' May rather than 'Granny'. Boss Percy doted on her and did his best to comfort her, but as it turned out he was the first to die in his early sixties, of neglected prostate cancer whose discomforts he had never mentioned and which had gone untreated. Aunty May finally ran out of ailments and died at age 97.

I was closer to my Grandpa Stephen, thanks to my mother's ministrations and her protection from his temperamental moods, but the others tended to shrink from him. He took a liking to me and over time I came to realise his crabbiness was partly due to the constant pain of rheumatoid arthritis, which kept him confined to a wheelchair.

But his tempestuous moments were theatrical. These occurred most dramatically when it came to starting his car, a 1928 Falcon Knight. It was a magnificent vehicle, solid and stately, its interior upholstered with a luxurious beige velvet cloth. The car weighed a ton and it had sleeve valves, something I still don't really understand but which made it a devil to start. On the rare occasions that Grandpa needed to go to town, to attend to some farm business and perhaps play a game of chess with Mr Chavannes, the butcher, he would order the car brought out and made ready. That was when the show began.

On winter mornings especially, the engine was too cold and stiff for the self-starting mechanism to turn it over. It was too heavy to start with the hand crank. Boiling water would be poured into the radiator to see whether that would ease things a little, but when it didn't help the entire staff of black farmhands would be called out to push-start the car. That would involve much heaving and chanting and cries of encouragement, to get the cumbersome old battleship to the top of a long downward slope. From there a rolling start was theoretically possible. Grandpa would be there, directing operations from his wheelchair. When the downhill roll began, he would rise unsteadily from his chair, brandishing his walking stick in the air and shouting instructions to whoever was at the controls. As often as not this procedure didn't work either, and as the Falcon Knight rolled to a stop at the bottom of the slope my grandfather's agitation would rise along with the decibels of his voice as he bellowed to the staff, now nearly half a mile away, to go fetch a span of oxen to haul it back and try again. Between the explosions of his orders one could hear the words 'Damn fools!' muttered under his breath.

Grandfather Stephen's last journey to his death was in keeping with his eccentric personality. He had long suffered from diabetes, and when complications set in soon after his 84th birthday – which he insisted was his 85th since he always counted the day he was born as his first – my mother, together with his second wife, Elizabeth, my 'Aunt Betty', decided he should be hospitalised in the nearest big town, Queenstown, some 75 km away. He was duly admitted there. But a few days later Aunt Betty phoned my mother with the disturbing news that he had discharged himself, called a taxi and driven away. Several hours passed and we heard nothing, and then a resident of our local town, Cathcart, phoned to report that he had seen a taxi speed past on the national road to East London with a white-haired man in the back, his chin resting on a bentwood walking stick.

He checked in to the Glenwood Nursing Home near the East London beachfront, where he died two days later. It was on my 11th birthday. He was buried in the old Cathcart cemetery beside his first wife, Sarah Jane, where he took the secret of his father's identity with him. I feel sure my mother and Aunty Betty knew, but in matters concerning my grandfather the family motto apparently was: Don't ask, don't tell.

* * *

PICTURE THE scene. It is a grey autumn morning, the trees just beginning to shed their damp leaves onto the cobbled streets of the old East Anglian town of Colchester. There, lined up at the door of the old Garrison Church, a large, white clapboard structure between Old Heath Road and Military Road in the centre of the town, are 44 young men dressed in smart black uniforms. Beside them are an equal number of young working girls, many of them from Brown and Moy's big silk factory in Dead Lane, down beside the River Colne. They are in their Sunday best, even though it is a weekday – Thursday, 19 October 1856.

Some of these young men and women have never met before. Others are only fleetingly acquainted, for these mercenary soldiers have been based here only a few months. Nor can they communicate very well, for the young men are Germans and the girls English and they know only a few words, if that, of each other's language.

Yet they are here to be married, these 44 young men and their hastily chosen brides. Some of the men, according to local historian Andrew Phillips, had only popped their proposals right there at the church door. It is to be a single ceremony, a mass marriage, conducted by a German Lutheran pastor, the Reverend Wilmans.[1] These young couples were about to board ship to sail halfway round the world to start new lives together in a new country about which they knew nothing: British Kaffraria, on the eastern Cape frontier of South Africa.

Other mass marriages like this one followed soon afterwards. In a fortnight in that busy month Pastor Wilmans solemnised no fewer than 150 marriages between German soldiers based in a tented camp alongside the Garrison Church and local English girls – all in mass ceremonies. Some of the mercenaries, based at other camps in England, were married on board ships lying in Plymouth harbour, including one batch of 56 couples married aboard HMS *Britannia* on 16 November 1856.[2]

It was that first ceremony, on 19 October, that gripped my attention. For among the black-uniformed figures before the altar on that day was a stocky young man, five feet six and a half inches tall, blond and blue-eyed. His name was Otto Oswald Robert Stephan and he was just 20 years old. He was, as I have only recently discovered after two years of searching through the archives of three countries, my maternal great-grandfather. My

14

The tented camp in Colchester, East Anglia, where the German mercenary unit, which included my great-grandfather, Robert Otto Stephan, was billeted in 1856. In the background is the Garrison Church where the mass marriages took place. (This picture is a photographic rarity, processed by a wet-plate collodion method invented in the 1850s.)

The Garrison Church in Colchester where a German Lutheran pastor solemnised 150 marriages between German soldiers and local English girls in mass ceremonies in October 1856, before the couples sailed for South Africa. Today the church serves members of the Russian Orthodox Church in England.

15

Many of the brides who hastily wed the German legionnaires were workers at this silk factory, which once stood on the banks of Colchester's Colne River. I believe my great-grandmother, Charlotte Stracey, was one of them.

16

Grandpa Stephen's father, who had anglicised the spelling of his surname from Stephan to Stephen on being given British citizenship when he landed at the Cape, but who had nonetheless been removed from our family history to conceal his ancestry. The sad and still largely mysterious man without a face.

And among those excited and no doubt tremulously anxious girls from the silk factory, about to head into the unknown with an unknown man as her husband, was my great-grandmother, Charlotte Stracey, at 19 still a legal minor. I suspect Charlotte was an orphan, for although she knew her mother's name, which was the same as hers, the records show she was uncertain of her father's, which she thought was either Thomas or Alfred — so she gave her first-born both. Her second son, born a year later, she named Otto Robert Stephen, after her husband. But the proud father barely had time to appreciate the honour, for within ten months of that happy event he was dead, in strange and still unfathomable circumstances, leaving behind a 24-year-old widow with two small children on a wild and war-torn frontier.

Great-grandfather Stephen's tragically short life, ending at age 26 in what I can only imagine was some sort of accident, on a stranger's farm far from home, just three weeks after his regiment was disbanded and his pay of three pence a day stopped, was no doubt one reason why we of the third generation knew nothing about him. Our parents were born a whole generation after his death. Nevertheless, the totality of his elimination by a family that knew and spoke so much about its other ancestors suggests there must have been more to it than that.

Did he desert his family in a moment of despair when his army pay stopped? Was it a failed marriage anyway between a couple who were strangers to begin with and never managed to find each other under the stresses of frontier life, so that when the second baby arrived and the money stopped Robert couldn't face it any more and just walked away from them to die an anonymous death?

His death notice, written in Dutch and signed by resident magistrate M Kannemeyer in the Western Cape town of Montagu, more than 800 km from where Robert had left his wife and children, states simply that he was a mason who died on 22 April 1861 on the farm Kruis owned by a Mr JJH Viktor. His place of birth is given as England. Parents: *Onbekend* (unknown). Marital status: *Ongehuwd* (unmarried). Occupation: *Metjelaas* (mason). Age: *Omtrent 36* (about 36). His employer, who may have hired him for a temporary building job only a day or two before, obviously knew nothing about him. Nor, apparently, did anyone else in the community. As for the magistrate, he seems to have been uninterested in what he may have thought was a passing vagrant, for he never bothered to enter the cause of death on the official death notice, still neatly filed in the archives in Cape Town.

So the last days of Otto Oswald Robert Stephen's life remain shrouded in mystery, as do the reasons for the family's silence about his very existence. Did they disown him, seeing him as a deserter who had shamefully abandoned his young family in a parlous situation?

There were indeed several instances of those German settlers abandoning their hastily chosen wives and returning to Europe when life in British Kaffraria became tough. But there is no evidence that Robert did that. Historian ELG Schnell notes that some of the legionnaires dispersed as far afield as Graaff-Reinet, Prince Albert, Wellington and even Cape Town in search of work after their regiments were disbanded, so it seems likely that is what Robert did.[3]

No, I believe the main reason for the family's obliterating him from memory was because both my generation and that of my parents lived between the two great world wars when Germany was the feared and hated enemy.

I grew up with Winston Churchill's voice ringing in my ears about Hitler, the Nazi 'jackal', and with dread in my heart that my father, all my uncles and one older cousin, who had joined the South African Army to go off to fight the Germans, might be killed and never come home.

News of the war and the dread of it filled my childhood. I can still hear Hitler's ranting voice coming over the radio my father installed in our farmhouse before he went off to the army, and the ringing of a bell by the Third Reich's Radio Zeesen at six o'clock every evening to announce the number of Allied ships sunk by

German U-boats that day. Ours was not a religious home, but I remember that I prayed a lot in those days that the wicked Germans would be overwhelmed and destroyed. More particularly, I remember my perplexity as a child when my cousin Raymond did eventually come home from the battlefront and showed me a German army belt he had brought as a souvenir. 'GOTT MIT UNS' read the slogan on the buckle. But how could that be? God, I had firmly believed, was on our side.

There was no way any of we children could have faced the fact that Grandpa Stephen's dad was a German, that in fact Grandpa himself was half German, that even we had German blood in our veins. So we were never told – and poor Robert died a second death, the more dreadful one of being erased from all memory.

Finding Robert and resurrecting him from his death of obliteration became an investigative journalism assignment that I set myself, a task that has rekindled my awareness of the insanity of war and the twin evils of racism and nationalist zealotry.

The search began in the Western Cape archives. I had little information to begin with, other than knowing my great-grandmother's name to have been Charlotte Stracey, a name that reappears several times in the family tree. All I knew about her, though, was that she had been widowed young and had married again to a man named Jonathan Heath, whom she had also outlived, but not before raising two daughters.

I also established that Grandpa Stephen was the only one of our family not descended from the 1820 Settlers, but that he and his brother, who I never knew but whom my mother referred to as 'Uncle Otto', had both married into the large settler family of Lloyds. Uncle Otto had moved to the Free State province and started another branch of the family there, but when I visited them none knew anything about his origins.

There were dead-ends aplenty. Grandpa's death notice as well as his will, instead of revealing who his parents were, simply stated that both were 'deceased'. There were no birth certificates or marriage certificates available; those, the archivists told me, were kept at the churches where the baptisms and marriages had taken place.

Finding where those churches were was a painstaking task, but eventually I discovered that Henry Thomas Lloyd and his large family had lived for a time at a home-cum-inn called Travellers' Rest just across the Kei River in the Transkei, and that Tom Stephen had married Sarah Jane in the nearby Tsomo mission church.

I found the church easily, an exquisite little stone building at the end of a rutted dirt road on a hillside some distance from the hamlet of Tsomo. It was quite early on a Sunday morning, 2 January 2011, and as I drove up I saw that the place was somewhat dilapidated. The windows of the little church were broken and the roof looked like it was about to collapse. There was an abandoned schoolhouse nearby and the shell of what had once been a girls' hostel, according to a sign above the broken door.

To one side was a sprawling bungalow with a few outbuildings beside it, and some chickens clucking and scratching in the dirt outside. This had to be the parson's house. I knocked tentatively on the front door and after a while a child opened it. 'Is this the *mfundisi*'s house?' I asked

'Yes,' the child replied.

'And what is his name?'

'Tandixolo Sikotoyi,' the child replied. An appropriate name for a parson, I thought, for it means 'Peacemaker'.

I asked the child please to call the Reverend Sikotoyi, to tell him there was a visitor who needed his help. After a while a lean, handsome man, relatively young, arrived, still adjusting his clerical collar, and asked politely how he could help me.

'My grandfather was married in your church 127 years ago,' I explained, 'and I believe you may have his marriage certificate here. I would very much like to see it if possible, because I'm trying to find out more about my family history. You see, we all came from these parts, from the old frontier.'

He looked briefly disconcerted. 'I may be able to help you,' he said, 'but you've come on a bad day. We're having a meeting of our local circuit of 30 Methodist societies and it's my turn to host them at a special service this morning.'

I had driven a long way and wasn't prepared to forsake the opportunity of finding a vital clue. So I asked if I could attend the service. 'I'd love to take the Sacrament in the church where my grandfather got married so long ago,' I said, knowing that would please him – which it did.

As we gathered for the service the good Peacemaker introduced me to the congregation, explaining that I was a child of the Eastern Cape and had come back home to seek out an ancestor who had lived here. This drew an explosion of applause and murmurs of approval. That a white man should come here to pay his respects to an ancestor was unusual and cause for acclamation. The applause merged into singing and the service was seamlessly under way. There was no organ, no piano, no instrument of any kind. Just voices. African voices, singing in lilting harmonies to the accompaniment of women beating time with their hands against the leather covers of their hymn books, with an occasional piercing ululation cutting through the harmony.

Then came the sermons. All nine of them. All delivered in strikingly different preaching styles – but none of them brief. There were chatty, conversational-style sermons, others were more revivalist, and one in particular that can only be described as passionately theatrical. The preacher began at a moderate level, recounting the story of Moses and the burning bush in a soft voice, then in tones of rising passion he began exhorting his audience to nurture that holy flame and never allow it to die out. With sweat flying from his brow he implored them with increasing urgency to 'Keep that flame burning … Never put out that flame … Never let the flame die … Don't even let the flame's own ashes put it out,' with each exhortation eliciting cries of approval from the congregation.

It was a fascinating cultural tableau, but my goodness it was exhausting. Pleading weariness after the four-and-a-half-hour service, the Reverend Sikotoyi asked if I could return the following day to look for my grandfather's details.

Next morning things moved a little more briskly. Sikotoyi invited me to accompany him to a quaint stone building some distance from the house. He fumbled through a thick bunch of keys, tried several, and eventually opened the door leading into a small, dusty cabin. It looked as though it had not seen daylight for years; an ancient, glass-fronted bookcase stood against one wall, several of its panes cracked and its shelves thick with dust. The bookcase was stacked with files but there were gaps, indicating that some were missing.

I had given Sikotoyi the approximate dates of when I thought the marriage had taken place, and after a while he reached inside and pulled out an old dog-eared file. We returned to the house and took it into his study, where carefully, breathlessly, we turned the brittle pages, yellowed with age, until − bingo, there it was! The entry of the marriage record of Thomas Alfred Stephen and Sarah Jane Lloyd, conducted by the Reverend AB Warner. And, most precious of all, in the space for the name of the father of the groom was clearly written − R Stephen.

There were no other clues to my puzzle, but this was enough for the moment. R Stephen was the name of the man without a face. I had established that he was not one of the 1820 Settlers, and since I kept recalling my mother's references to an 'Uncle Otto', I began wondering whether he might perhaps have been of German origin. There had, I knew, been a contingent of German military settlers in the eastern Cape.

A trip to the Amathole Museum in King William's Town, once the capital of British Kaffraria, revealed that there had indeed been a Robert Stephan among those settlers, and that he was married to one Charlotte Strey. That surname flummoxed me for a while, but then it struck me that in the haste of military registration and the confusion of translation, or perhaps just some illegible handwriting, all that had happened was that two letters, 'a' and 'c' had been left out or conflated. The name was obviously Charlotte Stracey, and so this was confirmation that my missing great-grandfather was indeed a member of the British German Legion that had gone to South Africa in 1857.

* * *

BUT WAIT, I am running ahead of myself. How all of this came about was because of a war on the far side of the world that had nothing whatsoever to do with South Africa. A war involving

Britain, France and Russia, the three major military powers of the day. The Crimean War.

It was a foolish war, a contest between these major powers for influence over territories of the declining Ottoman Empire. What distinguished it from previous European wars was, firstly, the incompetence of the commanders, for this was still an age when officers could buy their commissions. The second distinguishing feature was that this was the first media war. The advent of the electric telegraph meant that first-hand reports from the frontline could reach audiences back home in hours rather than weeks. William Howard Russell, the correspondent for *The Times*, immortalised himself with his vivid reports of the dreadful conditions that British troops had to endure in the Crimea.

Not surprisingly, the War Office soon found itself having difficulty raising sufficient volunteers to keep its frontline forces up to strength. So it was decided to raise a mercenary army on the Continent. For help it turned to a colourful Prussian officer with whom it had worked before, Baron Richard Carl Gustav Ludwig Julius von Stutterheim. The baron had been a lieutenant in a hussar regiment in Düsseldorf but had fled to England after killing a comrade in a duel. He had helped raise a unit to fight against Napoleon in the Peninsula War, so now the British turned to him again. He was contracted to recruit troops from the Germanic states and get them to the North Sea island of Heligoland, where they would be signed up as members of the British Army. Von Stutterheim required a fee of £10 per head for his services and ultimately recruited some 10 000 troops.

For the recruits it was a high-risk venture. Some had deserted regiments at home for the higher pay the British were offering, which meant they risked severe penalties, even execution, if caught. But all the German states were in severe economic recession, and so there were plenty of young men willing to take the risk.

Robert Stephan was one of them. He was a casual labourer in a small village outside Dresden, where his father, Johann, ran some kind of trading store. The recession aside, these were turbulent times in Saxony. The Paris uprising of February 1848 had triggered a wave of revolution across Europe, including the 39 independent states of what was then the German Confederation. The turmoil began in Frankfurt, then reached its climax in Dresden, the capital of Saxony, when the forces of monarchical reaction reasserted control.

There is no evidence that Robert himself was involved in the revolt, but the turmoil that roiled on for several years was almost certainly a factor in persuading him to leave and seek a new life elsewhere. How he made his way to Heligoland is not known, but the easiest and probably the safest route would have been by barge along the Elbe to the river's mouth. From there Von Stutterheim's organisation would have ferried him to the island and signed him up as a private in the 2nd Jägers regiment. He would also have been required to take an oath of allegiance to the British flag and the Queen before the regiment was transferred to Colchester for training.

It was while he was in England that the next big thing happened in Robert's life. A sudden peace treaty ended the Crimean War, posing a problem for both the German recruits and the British government. Having sworn allegiance to the Union Jack and Queen Victoria, the soldiers could not return to their homelands, which in any case many had left illegally. For Britain the problem was simply what to do with some 10000 young men whom they had to pay in terms of their contracts, but whose services were no longer required.

At this point the Queen herself intervened. She had a personal interest in the welfare of these German soldiers, of course, because she was married to a German and had numerous German relatives. 'Many of these poor men,' she wrote to the Secretary for War, Lord Panmure, had now lost their nationality and it would be 'very bad policy to act ungenerously towards them'.[4]

Meanwhile, far away in Cape Town the colonial Governor, Sir George Grey, was anxious to have more white settlers on the eastern frontier to fulfil his grand dream of opening up the territory to economic activity so as to draw in the Xhosa people as workers. Over time, he believed, the adoption of British social and cultural values would 'civilise' them. At the same time he needed to strengthen the colony's military capabilities to keep the Xhosa at bay and prevent more costly wars. To this end, with his eye on a tight budget, he proposed an immigration scheme that would involve bringing out 5 000 retired British army officers, family men who could fulfil both functions – establish themselves on the land and remain on call to perform a military role if necessary.

The Colonial Office reported back to Sir George that only 100 army pensioners had shown any interest in the offer. But then word reached the Colonial Office about the German mercenaries stuck in East Anglia. It was an opportunity to solve two problems at a stroke, pleasing both Her Majesty and the increasingly influential Governor.

Sir George was delighted. He had only one query: Were these German soldiers married? Young single men would not settle down to be stable frontier farmers; he wanted family men. For Lord Panmure and the bureaucrats at the Colonial Office, a little lie seemed quite justifiable. The majority of the men were indeed married and had children, Lord Panmure wrote back, and those who were not yet married would be quite prepared to become engaged.

Hence the scramble to get as many of the young legionnaires as possible married before the settler ships were due to depart. As an incentive to the young women, they were offered free passage to the Cape. But the numbers fell far short of anything Sir George had in mind. In the end only 2 362 men accepted the offer to go to British Kaffraria, instead of the 8 000 the Governor had been promised, and of these only 361 were married.

Nor were all the marriages as secure as the Governor would have liked. Some of the couples swapped partners in the course of the two-month-long voyage to the Cape, according to Bertha von Linsingen, wife of Captain Wilhelm von Linsingen – he of the sword – who was second in command of the legionnaires under Baron von Stutterheim.

Bertha von Linsingen was nearly 100 years old when she recounted her experiences of the settlement to her granddaughter, Mrs BE Rennie. 'Bertha von Linsingen told me she had seen the soldiers lined up opposite willing country girls in a kind of mass marriage ceremony,' Mrs Rennie wrote in a private note of the conversation. 'It must have been a risky business. Bertha certainly told me with a little giggle that there had been some exchanges on the voyage out.' To which Schnell adds a titillating detail, gleaned from a conversation with the elderly Reverend H Gutsche of King William's Town, who told him: 'It is doubtful whether a number of the settlers eventually lived with their rightful wives. Certainly some were by no means sure.'

Finally the settlers were assigned to the sites of various villages that had been laid out for them in the eastern Cape, all with German names such as Berlin, Hamburg, Frankfurt, Wiesbaden and of course Stutterheim. Each was given a building plot plus an acre of garden ground outside the village. They also had rights to pasture their stock on a village commonage. Officers were given allotments double that size.

Robert and Charlotte Stephen were settled first in the village of Berlin, but moved later to another called Dohne, close to the main settlement of Stutterheim, which today is a substantial town. It is from the home he built for his family in Dohne that Robert drifted off so mysteriously four years later to die on a stranger's farm 800 km away.

* * *

MY VISIT TO Robert's birthplace in Germany was really a pilgrimage. I needed to touch base with him, if only as a gesture of recognition after so many years of oblivion.

His military papers gave his country of origin as Saxony and his place of birth as Bergishleben. His next of kin, the papers recorded, was Johann Stephan of Dresden. However, my letters to the state archives of Saxony drew a blank: there was no such town as Bergishleben anywhere in Germany, they informed me. Again it turned out to be a translation error. The British recruiting officer in Heligoland had obviously misread Robert's handwriting in Old German script and given a distorted rendering of the charming village of Berggießhübel, located in a region of wooded hills known as Swiss-Saxony some 35 km outside Dresden. So eventually I headed there, accompanied by a German friend, Monika Sommer, to help me with navigation and translation.

This is a sleepy part of Europe's most highly industrialised country. Berggießhübel itself lies in a narrow valley with a mountain stream running through it. There were formerly some tin mines here, but today it is basically a farming village with a handful of small industries. Its centrepiece is a spa, and nearby is what was once a castle that housed the Baron of Friesen Leysser. Total population 5 671 – in Robert's day probably about 700.

Monika and I headed for the lovely stone church on a steep slope near the centre of the town, for village churches are the repositories of local history. In the churchyard we found the gravestones of three men with the surname Stepan – Gustav, Alfred and Berthold – and one woman. We also tracked down 65-year-old Bernard Stepan, the son of Alfred and the grandson of Gustav, who told us he was now the only Stepan living in Berggießhübel but that his family had moved into the village long after Robert's departure.

Finally it was back to the church, where the truth lay, awaiting discovery. Pastor David Lamprecht went to his carefully preserved files, returning with two volumes covering the dates I had given him, which he laid on a table. Solemnly I opened the first volume, and there, on the very first page the third entry seemed almost to leap out at me: Otto Oswald Robert Stephan, born at 11 am on 20 February 1836, baptised on the 25th. Only the third baby born in the village that year. Father: Johann Gottlieb Stephan. Mother: Selma Laura Flemming, who, it was noted, was Johann's second wife and this was her first child. The entry went on to name two godfathers, Friederich David Jungmichel of Reinholdshaim and Karl Adolph Hering, who was described as the administrator of the baronial castle in the village. Robert's godmother was given as Mrs August Flemming, presumably Selma's mother.

I still find it difficult to describe my feelings at that moment. Yes, there was a sense of achievement at having found him at last after such a long search, but that was quickly overwhelmed by a strong sense of relationship, an awareness that this was indeed my flesh and blood, and yet so alien in this distant, foreign place. There followed a huge sense of sadness, tinged with anger, that his life had been so short, his death so lonely, and the family's abandonment of him so harsh. What a poor, lonely, forgotten soul this was. And then, suddenly, I felt a sense of relief, almost of joy. I had resurrected him! I had saved him from that terrible second death of oblivion and given him back his living place within the family.

Energised by this success, I resolved to tackle the mystery of Robert's death. Some months after my return to South Africa I drove to Montagu, 190 km northeast of Cape Town. I found the farm Kruis with ease, tucked away in the Langeberg fruit-growing valley. A gravel driveway led up to a handsome gabled Cape Dutch homestead with a grapevine pergola out front and the date 1858 – just three years before Robert's death – engraved on the gable.

There I met a handsome young couple, Pieter and Marthie Venter, the latest occupants of the home and members of the Jordaan family, who have owned Kruis for the past two centuries. Sadly they knew little of the farm's history beyond the length of the family's ownership of it, but Pieter recalled that his Ouma (granny), Yvonne Bussel (née Jordaan), had written a family history shortly before her death at the age of 97. A scramble through the bookshelves yielded the 79-page booklet, written in Afrikaans and privately printed in December 2000.

The text was mostly about who had married whom and borne which children in the course of the family's long occupancy of Kruis. And there, on page 8, I learned that one JJH Viktor had married one of the Jordaan girls, Maria Paulina, and that the family had allocated the young couple a part of the large farm called Onderkruis – or Lower Kruis – and that Viktor had set about building his bride-to-be a new home, which had been finished some time after their wedding.

'Where,' I asked Pieter when he returned from farm chores to find me still reading Ouma's book, 'is the house at Onderkruis?'

'You're sitting in it,' he replied.

I gasped. Here, right here, was the house in which great-grandfather Otto Robert Stephen had died – as the death certificate in the Western Cape archives had said: 'In the house of Mr JJH Viktor on the farm Kruis near Montagu.'

I read on. 'Viktor bought all the building materials (for the house) in Wellington,' Ouma Yvonne wrote, 'and brought them here by ox-wagon.' A considerable task in itself, and obviously the building must have taken a considerable time to complete. My construction of what probably happened is that Robert pitched up, a mason looking for work, and Viktor engaged him to help build the house and several other outbuildings that Pieter Venter told me were erected about the same time, and that soon afterwards, before Viktor had got to know anything about his background, Robert had an accident – perhaps a fall from the scaffolding – and died in the house.

I cannot be certain of the facts in all their detail, but what matters to me is that I have found the place of birth and of death of this ancestor who had disappeared from our family history. This man without whom I would not have existed, who gave me life, and who I have now been able to repay at least partly in kind. I have bracketed his life, given him an identity.

CHAPTER THREE

Boyhood

I CAME INTO the world with difficulty. My mother was 39 years old and it was not an easy birth. The kindly Dr A Hay Michelle, the only GP in small-town Cathcart, had to haul me into existence with forceps, resulting in the left side of my face being partly paralysed for the first 18 months of my life — and permanently somewhat skewed. But the cranial contents appear to have survived the ordeal relatively intact.

It was also an inauspicious time to make my arrival. March 1933 was the very nadir of the Great Depression, and just 39 days after Adolf Hitler was sworn in as Reich Chancellor. It was also the time when a flamboyant right-wing politician-cum-lawyer named Tielman Roos, who had opposed the formation of the Union of South Africa in 1910, stepped down as an Appeal Court judge and set the domestic political scene alight by boarding a train and riding south on a crusade to force the stubborn Prime Minister, Barry Hertzog, to abandon the gold standard and let the South African pound float. It was a dramatic act that rescued South Africa from economic ruin, but it also split the ruling National Party, as Hertzog saved his skin by forming a 'fusion' government with General Jan Smuts through the establishment of the United South African National Party. That in turn was a prelude to disaster as Hertzog's hardliners broke away to join

*Me, aged three, on my tricycle in front of a palm tree my
father planted the day I was born. And ... the palm
tree 80 years later. I have asked the present owners
of the farm to alert me the day the tree falls.*

DF Malan, a theologian turned politician of formidable oratorical power who had established the 'Purified' National Party, which went on to craft the policy of apartheid.

For my father it was the toughest year of his life. Hotfire had always been a marginal farm in its hot and arid bowl ringed with towering mountains, but now, along with other farmers, he found himself hit hard as commodity prices collapsed. With his wool cheque bringing in a derisory £29 for the entire year, he couldn't even afford the licence fee for our 1924 Buick, so he put the car on blocks and faced the prospect of surviving the year as a subsistence farmer.

The following year, just to rub in the hardship, my brother died at age four of pneumonia. Medical science had not yet produced the miracle drug, penicillin, which would assuredly have saved his life. I, for good measure, contracted diphtheria at the same time – but I survived.

These harsh times left their mark on me, I guess. Having lost an earlier child, a girl, at birth, my parents, particularly my mother, became excessively protective of me. At the slightest breeze she would require me to put on a jersey or wrap myself up with a scarf. Whenever I stepped outdoors I was enjoined to 'watch where you walk' to avoid treading on the farm's many snakes. I loved my parents dearly, but I found this cosseting irritating and embarrassing, so that I often erupted angrily at her, which, I fear, left me with an irritable streak even towards those I have loved. Certainly the Great Depression left me, as I suspect it did everyone who was ever touched by that extirpating experience, with a lifelong awareness of the stresses and tensions that come with poverty. I watched it eat into my father's soul and into his lean, dried-out body.

My father was a gentle man, but he was a worrier. He worried about the weather, the droughts, the sudden devastating hailstorms, the sick cattle, the missing sheep lost in the mountains. When strangers asked him what kind of farming he specialised in, my father would reply drily: 'With aloes and stones.' It was rough, exhausting farmland, its only asset the river running through it, which was sometimes a tumbling torrent of tawny floodwater and sometimes a bone-dry bed of sand.

'You can choose whatever career you like, my son,' he would say, 'except farming. It's a mug's game.'

Yet I had a happy childhood on the farm. Lonely, yes. It was excruciatingly lonely being an only child in such an isolated place. I longed for that older brother I had never known and more than once begged my mother to adopt a playmate for me. Yet I also learned to keep my own company. One might say the experience instilled in me a certain schizophrenia — a hatred of loneliness coupled with a longing for spells of reflective isolation. I read a lot, as did my mother, who devoured books from the small Cathcart library and also ordered children's periodicals for me, which arrived by post and had to be collected at the Cathcart post office 35 km away. But no newspapers. There was no home delivery for any of the regional papers, so the future journalist never grew up with the culture of a morning paper at the breakfast table. In fact, I never became a regular newspaper reader until I worked on one.

Occasionally my parents would drive me over the steep Hotfire Hill to spend a day playing with my cousin Wilfred. And then, of course, there were the children of the black farmhands who were my most consistent playmates. I had an air gun that shot pellets and I would go bird-hunting with them, rambling through the bush or along the riverbank. Ncweniso Lavisa was the oldest and shrewdest of my black pals. He could make a noise like a cluster of birds agitated at the presence of a snake, which would bring the birds in chattering droves to the tree under which we were sitting, and I could pick them off with ease.

Sheepshearing time was another occasion that would interrupt the solitude. Teams of shearers would file across the river from the Transkei, each heading for farms where they had worked in previous seasons so that over the years we came to know them individually. The farmhands would collect our flocks, camp by camp, always a harrowing business for my father, who fretted over the missing numbers as he counted the sheep, two by two, as they dashed and leaped past him in erratic surges. I could never fathom how he managed it. But the number would be religiously entered into the stock-book and staff members would be sent out again to seek the missing animals.

The family trio, 1940. My soldier father was home on leave and I was age seven.

My parents, Bernice and Mont, seated on the lawn at Hotfire.

The shearers were skilled workers. Their shears would sweep around the sheep's body, clipping the wool within millimetres of the animal's skin, only occasionally snipping a tiny wound. They would toss the fleeces expertly onto a sorting table, where my father would grade the quality, sort out the fringe bits and place the wool in appropriate bales. The shearers were also men of the world. They had been to Johannesburg, the place of gold, to work in the mines and savour life in the big city, and their bantering conversation as they clipped away was meant to impress the local farmhands, especially the women, with their worldliness. As a small kid with big ears I would listen avidly to their tales, often from inside a big wool bale where my job was to tramp the wool down until the bale was tightly packed. I guess I learned more about black cultural life in those years than I could have acquired through any anthropology course.

But there were also long hours of solitude, of playing with my toy cars or inventing imaginary war games, building model aeroplanes and sailing boats.

Solitude is a strange condition. You can have a great fear of it and also feel a desperate need for it. It can be painful but it can also be comforting. And, of course, it can be creative. Priests seek solitude to meditate and find God; Archbishop Desmond Tutu, who still goes into solitary meditation for a week at a time, once described it as being like sitting beside a warm fire in winter. Aldous Huxley contended that the more original the mind the more it inclined towards what he called 'the religion of solitude'. Goethe regarded it as essential for creative writing. For my part, I think it's tougher when you are young than when you are more mature. Children need playmates. I certainly felt the pain and frustration of loneliness on the farm, but I do think perhaps it taught me to be reflective.

Solitude and silence. There was no traffic noise at Hotfire. If we saw the dust of a car coming over the hill, maybe once a fortnight, we knew we had a visitor. The rest was the stillness of Mother Africa, broken only by the small noises of nature – the lowing of the cows at milking time, the bleating of sheep at shearing time, the bark of a baboon in the mountains, the crickets and the cicadas at night and the croaking of frogs in the fish pond. Sometimes the alarmed cry of a nightjar. Otherwise nothing.

Bedtime was even more isolating and I resisted it, as all children do. My mother would tell me stories, wonderful, imaginative tales that I wanted never to end. But the moment came when she would tell me it was time to 'blow out the candle' and for her to go make the bread so that the yeast could rise overnight for baking in the wood-fired oven the next morning. There was no electricity at Hotfire so we lived by oil lamps and candles. Blowing out the candle became the ritual bedtime goodnight, leaving me in the dark with the sounds of the night outside my bedroom window at the back of the house. Sometimes, as I lay there with my private pre-sleep thoughts, I could hear the soft murmuring of voices from the small village of huts where the black staff and their families lived, on a plateau about two kilometres away. Occasionally, too, on a Saturday night there would be the sound of drumbeats and singing when the staff had a celebratory party with home-brewed beer made from fermented mealies. For this they required a written permit from my father to avoid arrest should the police from Cathcart come by. Black people were prohibited by law from consuming so-called white liquor, but could make their own traditional beer if granted written permission by their employer.

I would visit there sometimes with my black playmates. It was a busy place, with laundry hanging out to dry, open fires going, pots boiling, toddlers playing, babies crying, scrawny chickens scuttling about and sometimes a piglet awaiting its turn in the pot. The huts were round, mud-daub structures with thatched roofs, dung floors, often windowless and, in winter, with dung fires flickering in the centre, which made them smoky and dim. It was a world apart, and yet the people living there were close to us. They all knew me and I knew them, and my mother, the nurse, had helped deliver some of those babies.

Behind the plateau, the mightiest of the encircling mountains rises steeply to an apex capped by two conical krantzes. In my childhood imagination these became 'Sheba's Breasts', the twin peaks in H Rider Haggard's *King Solomon's Mines*, which formed the gateway to his lost world of Kukuanaland where Twala the one-eyed lived with his evil sangoma, Gagool. It was in one of those peaks that the odious Gagool kept watch over the hidden treasure of the biblical king. And so those twin Hotfire peaks have remained in my memory to this day, the welcoming maternal mounds that come into view whenever I reach the crest of Hotfire Hill. The landmarks of home.

* * *

MY FATHER was known throughout the valley as Mont Sparks. Outsiders thought that was short for Montgomery and called him Monty, but they were wrong and he would correct them. He was Mont. No 'y'. His full first names were Harold Montmorency. On how this struggling sheep farmer with only a farm-school education came to have such an aristocratic-sounding name hangs a tale.

The Hon Raymond Harvey Lodge Joseph de Montmorency was a dashing young man, the eldest son of the third Viscount de Montmorency, Knight Commander of the Order of the Bath and a representative peer of Ireland, which made him a member of the British House of Lords. The third Viscount was also a major general in the British Army. Truly a blue-blooded family, but it was young Raymond who was the star. He had won the Victoria Cross during the Battle of Omdurman in Sudan in 1898, when he was only 31, then gone on to form his own unit, the Montmorency Scouts, which performed heroic feats during the Anglo-Boer War, culminating in a clash at a place called Stormberg.

Located just north of Molteno, Stormberg was a strategic junction where the railways from Port Elizabeth and East London joined the main line between Cape Town and the Witwatersrand. The Boers seized Stormberg in December 1899, and the newly arrived commander of this sector, General William Gatacre, decided on an immediate counterattack to recapture it. But the counterattack was bungled and the British forces were routed.

This was the first of three serious defeats suffered by the British in what became known as Black Week. The others were at Magersfontein on the Cape line and Colenso on the Natal line. Suddenly the British and colonial forces were on the back foot in a war they had expected to be a walkover. One can imagine that my father's family, living on a farm only some 150 km south of Molteno and with my grandmother heavily pregnant, were in a state of anxiety. The Boer commandos were within easy raiding range of their farm, Anta.

At that point the daring Captain De Montmorency rode to the rescue with his scouts. His job was to scout the terrain and recommend the tactics for a new attack to recapture the Stormberg junction. With this in mind, he and two of his scouts rode to the top of a koppie on a farm called Weltevreden — where a small band of Boers from the nearby Free State town of Rouxville, who were concealed in the bushes on the koppie, opened fire and killed all three.

The date was 23 February 1900. News of the death of this glamorous figure probably reached Cathcart and Anta the next day, the 24th, which was the day my father was born. The news must have been shattering, which is why they decided to honour Montmorency by naming my father after him. So Mont Sparks he became. No 'y'.

My childhood memories of my father come in two categories: the stressed and overworked farmer and the enthusiastic sportsman. He was two different personalities in those roles. He was not a demonstrative man but he was affectionate. He planted a cotton-palm tree on the lawn in front of our house to mark the day I was born. It grew with painful slowness during the years of my childhood, but the last time I visited Hotfire it had miraculously leaped up to some 25 metres. A symbol of my life, one might say, and in an emotional sense something of an umbilical cord reaching skyward. I have urged the present owners of the farm, Patrick and Jennifer Fletcher, to notify me urgently if the southeaster should ever blow it over, so that I can call a priest to administer my last rites.

I didn't appreciate it at the time, but looking back I realise my father must also have been a wonderful farmer. Shaped by the Great Depression, he turned himself into a multiskilled handyman. If you couldn't buy things, you made them yourself. Or invented them. He made the bricks to build the farmhouse and the woolshed, the dairy, a garage for the car and two rondavels in the garden as extra guestrooms. He moulded the bricks from clay on the farm and built the kiln to fire them, with Mbhuti chopping wood for the firing. He did all the building work himself, from the flooring to the ceilings to the corrugated-iron roofing and even the thatching of the little round garden cottages. With the help of the farmhands, he fenced the whole farm and the kraals and built dipping tanks for the sheep and the cattle.

With no electricity on the farm, he made a food cooler for my mother, a contraption with cinders packed tightly between two layers of bird-netting on all four sides, the front being a hinged door, the whole lined with hessian kept moist from a slow-leaking bucket on top. It was less than a refrigerator, but it kept butter, milk and vegetables fresh for days.

My father even became something of a veterinary surgeon in the absence of a professional anywhere in the district. Apart from the regular farming jobs of tailing, ear-marking and castrating lambs and calves, he developed his own treatment for cattle that sometimes broke legs on Hotfire's rocky mountain slopes. It was a crude process but it worked — to the amazement of vets who much later witnessed some of his work.

But it was my father's passion for sport that bonded me closest to him. He was a fine tennis player, lean and agile, and self-taught. As a boy, he had spent hours hitting against a wall at Anta, where the lack of a decent ground surface had sharpened his skills on the volley.

Yet it was cricket that was his greater passion. He was not a great player but a decent middle-order batsman and a medium-paced seamer with the ball. His own best achievement as a cricketer was in his very last match, when he ended the opposing team's innings by taking two wickets with successive balls, both clean-bowled, to conclude the last over he ever bowled. Above all, Dad loved the game and spent many hours teaching me the funda-mentals. It began when I was about three; he made me countless plank bats from old tomato boxes and tossed tennis balls at me to teach me the forward and back defensive strokes. As I grew he made me bigger bats and eventually we graduated to a proper bat and leather ball. Dad would bowl to me in the driveway in front of our house and I would be forgiven for any broken windows – provided the stroke had been properly executed. He talked cricket, regaling me with stories about Don Bradman, Dave and Dudley Nourse, the Timeless Test and the bodyline menace of Harold Larwood and Bill Voce. The lore of the game was infused into me and has remained all my life. When later I became a decent opening batsman, making first team at school and earning a junior provincial cap after that, my father was always there to watch me, taking vicarious pride whenever I did well. Looking back, I guess he was my best playmate in that only-child early life. It was a close and happy relationship that lasted until shortly after I turned six, when suddenly he had to go away.

* * *

I CAN STILL hear the sonorous voice of a BBC newsreader announcing over our newly acquired radio on the one o'clock news that 'Britain and Germany are at war now'. It sounded formidable, and of course it was. It was a Sunday, 3 September 1939, and we had visitors who were clustered around the radio that my father had hastily acquired as the war clouds gathered, installing a wind-charger on the garage roof to charge a six-volt battery, which he carried to the house and connected to the cumbersome new instrument. He had also assembled a towering 40-foot aerial pole in the garden to capture the crackly radio relay from Grahamstown.

While the adults listened to this portentous news, I played happily on the floor with my toy cars, not realising that the news flash heralded the first big turning point in my life.

The next day, after a short but furious debate in Parliament, the South African government voted by a majority of 13 to go to war alongside Britain. It was a decision that split the government, with General Jan Smuts taking over from Barry Hertzog as Prime Minister and Hertzog rejoining DF Malan in opposition. Some members of the National Party, including John Vorster, who later became Prime Minister of South Africa, and Hendrik van den

Bergh, who became his tough security chief, were members of the pro-Nazi *Ossewa-Brandwag* (Ox-Wagon Sentinels), who carried out acts of sabotage against Smuts' government.

Within a few weeks, my father, my Uncle Claude and several other relatives had joined the army and were swept off by troop train to their first training camp as members of the First City, a Highland regiment named after the Grahams of Montrose, who were involved in the founding of Grahamstown. Later my oldest cousin, Raymond, was to sign up too, at the tender age of 16, to become a dispatch rider carrying messages by motorcycle between commanders on the battlefronts of Italy.

Suddenly we were alone on the farm, my mother and I. There were other 'grass widows' in the valley, too, and the crippling thing was that none could drive the cars their husbands had left with them. Realising the dilemma they faced, Sammy Meyer, the sympathetic official in charge of conducting driving tests in Cathcart, gave these stranded women licences after the flimsiest of examinations. That solved the problem at a theoretical level, but the practical results were scary. For the next few years travelling on any of the corrugated dirt roads in our district was an alarming fairground experience of weaving dodgem cars, crashing gears and spinning wheels as these amateur automobilists wove their way to town and back.

My mother was the worst. She was both terrified of driving and incapable. She had to navigate Hotfire Hill, which overwhelmed her with fear the moment she installed herself behind the wheel. It was, to be fair, a daunting drive – steep, narrow and rutted with big storm-water drains. Worse still, the new car we had acquired, a 1936 Chevrolet, had a nasty habit of jumping out of low gear on the climb, raising the prospect of it hurtling backwards down the hill if the gear suddenly sprang into neutral. To prevent this from happening, I had to become something of a co-driver, holding on to the gear lever as Mother, body taut and eyes bulging, ground her way up the hill to the gate at the top. This brought another nervous moment, for I had to leave her alone in the car while I opened the gate and watched her drive through and park on the precipitous downslope.

The truth is, at the age of six I knew more about driving than my mother did. My doting father had allowed me to sit on his lap and steer the car, even to change gears while he managed the clutch. So the journeys to town had me calling instructions to my mother, on how to turn inwards to a dry skid, not to brake on a sharp turn, and so on. Some years later, when I was 12, my father suffered a severe angina attack while we were on holiday in Durban. A doctor advised that he shouldn't drive, so the question arose of whether my mother should take the wheel for the homeward journey. By family consensus it was agreed she should not, that I should drive us home along the unfenced dusty roads of the Transkei. It was illegal, of course, but the family decided that was the less risky option. I had to sit on a cake tin to see over the high dashboard of the 1936 Chev, and the only advice I got from my father, as he lay prone on the back seat, was to beware of livestock wandering into the unfenced road: 'And whatever you do, son, don't hit a pig. That's like hitting a rock.' My mother stayed anxiously beside me all the way, but I completed the 800-km journey without mishap.

I had started school in January 1939. It was at a farm school on my Uncle Claude's farm, Turnstream, on the far side of Hotfire Hill, which meant I had to be driven there each morning and fetched in the afternoon. There were 12 children in the school, at different grades, with one teacher funded by the Cape Education Department, a Miss Venables. How she managed to cope simultaneously with so many different syllabi is hard to imagine, but she certainly taught me the ABC and simple arithmetic, while launching older kids into the complexities of long division and the conjugation of verbs. But with the onset of war came budget austerity, which meant we lost Miss Venables and the school had to close.

For the rest of that first year my mother taught me at home, using a round, thatched dairy my father had built near the cattle kraal as a classroom where we sat, together with my cousin Cynthia Stephen as the only other pupil, among the milk cans, a butter churn and a large, ungainly cream separator. The place smelled permanently of lactating cows, but it served its dual purpose. My mother seemed to enjoy the fresh challenge in her humdrum life, but she soon realised it was not a long-term proposition. I would have to go to the Cathcart High School. How to do that was the problematic question. My grandfather, Tom Stephen, owned a wood-and-iron building across the street from the school. It was a curious structure, long and narrow with interconnecting rooms but no passageway. One simply went through a series of doors from one room into the next. We called it the Rabbit Run. My mother asked whether we might use it, which led to a typical outburst of eccentricity from Grandpa Stephen.

'Why do you want to send the boy to school?' the old man demanded. He was self-taught, why could I not be taught at home? He had all the books I would need. What's more, he thought it ridiculous that my mother should continue to live at Hotfire now that Mont was in the army. She and I should move to his farm, Braemar, and live there with him, the unspoken corollary being that my mother could then attend to his medical needs while I got on with the business of acquiring an education from his library of old books. It was a tough contest but my mother, who was always a match for him when it came to tenacity, eventually prevailed and we moved into the Rabbit Run, sharing it with another grass widow, Alice Kemp, and her two children, Graeme and Ann. And so it was that at the age of seven I went to a proper school for the first time.

* * *

IF YOU WERE to ask me for a single word to describe that first school, I would say: 'Tough!' As I stepped into the playground for the first time I was confronted by the Kemp twins, Robert and Freddy.

'Are you *bang* [scared] for me?' barked Robert in a colloquial mix of English and Afrikaans as he stood in front of me, feet astride and fists clenched. He was a sturdy lad and his manner was aggressive. In my bewilderment I didn't know how to respond.

'No,' I murmured tentatively.

'Then you must fight me,' he declared, pointing to the town's power station building across the street. It dawned on me that this was a challenge to have a fistfight with him behind the building, out of sight of the school staff.

'No,' I replied. 'You've done nothing to me. I don't want to fight you.'

Now it was his turn to look bewildered. I was breaking the school code. I wasn't acknowledging that he had the beating of me, but I wasn't prepared to fight him to settle the issue. Robert turned to his buddies, now gathered in a pack, as though to seek advice on how to handle the situation, but they looked equally baffled.

'Are you not *bang* for anyone?' he demanded, and when I again said no, he sneered: 'Not even your father?'

That, for me, was quite unfathomable. I couldn't imagine ever being afraid of Dad. He was a gentle man who had never beaten me in his life, and now he had gone off to the war and the only fear I had was for his safety. I found the incident intimidating and bewildering, but at least I had stood my ground and the bully had backed off, bemused at my idiosyncratic response to his challenge. I settled in to the school somewhat better over time, even to the point of befriending Freddy Kemp and inviting him to the farm some weekends. But it was tough, a crash course in socialisation.

This was all in pre-apartheid time, under the wartime Smuts government, but racial segregation was the norm as it had been since the earliest settlement days. Although all the pupils at the school were white, there was a clear class distinction. Some of the pupils were the offspring of prosperous farmers and traders, but others were from the families of white workers employed on a major rail construction project, involving two long tunnels, taking place on the line to East London. These families were housed in corrugated shacks just outside the town, disparagingly known as 'tin town'. Mostly Afrikaners, they were classified as 'poor whites' in the terminology of the day, the victims of the Great Depression, which had ravaged the Afrikaner community. To ease their plight, they were given low-paid employment of last resort on the state railway system.

The children of these poor families arrived at the school with ragged clothes and some with no shoes. Few spoke English, the predominant language at the school, which made them doubly 'the other' and meant they were subjected to cruel mockery and taunts. I recall one small, particularly grubby girl, about the same age as me, sobbing at the taunts and ugly names being hurled at her and with no one willing to share a desk with her. When eventually the desperate teacher made an appeal for a volunteer, I raised my hand. Perhaps I sensed a fellow outsider. Perhaps, too, it was my first act of liberalism.

But if these first years of school were a crash course in socialisation, so, too, were they academically. I found the going tough, partly because of a general sense of alienation in a crowded classroom but mainly because Smuts, in his eagerness to build English-Afrikaner unity, had decreed that state schools had to use both official languages as media of instruction. I knew no Afrikaans, which meant I struggled in the subjects in which it was the language of instruction: mathematics, geography and, of course, the Afrikaans language.

My parents, I must confess, nurtured strong anti-Afrikaner prejudices, inherited from having grown up in the antagonistic atmosphere of the Anglo-Boer War. Both spoke fluent isiXhosa, as did all the rural white folk in that frontier region, but neither spoke a word of Afrikaans. This reached a point of absurdity when my father had to communicate with the owner of a neighbouring farm, Willem Oosthuizen, who spoke no English, doubtless for the same reason. My father and Mr Oosthuizen had periodic disagreements over shared water rights, which resulted in acrimonious arguments over the party-line telephone system – all conducted in isiXhosa.

As it turned out, my lack of Afrikaans seemed to evoke antagonism rather than sympathy from the Afrikaans teacher, a lean, athletic man named Frikkie Eloff, who was also the star flyhalf in the local rugby team. Eloff came to class armed with a *kweperlat*, a cane cut from a quince tree. He would hover over any hesitant student struggling to enunciate a sentence clearly, or failing to end it with the verb, and down would come the cane: Whack! Somehow it seemed to scramble my brain rather than clarify it, so I became a frequent beneficiary of Eloff's teaching technique. He adopted the same technique in his role as our rugby coach. He had me playing in the centre of the scrum as hooker, a singularly inappropriate position for my tall, spindly physique. As the scrum went down he would enjoin us to '*Stoot, jong, stoot!*' as he delivered a series of whacks to those he thought were not shoving hard enough. It goes without saying that I didn't like Frikkie Eloff and I blame him for my having failed as a rugby player. But thanks to his ministrations and my playground communication with the kids from 'tin town', I did learn the language, which was a huge asset in my later career when Afrikaans became the dominant language in our national affairs.

It was during my second year at the Cathcart school that my father suffered a series of severe attacks of angina pectoris and was discharged from the army. He was devastated that he never got to the front line, while I felt both relief that he had escaped that danger and fear that he might have a fatally defective heart. His unexpected return meant another shift in my life, as my mother left the Rabbit Run to return with my father to Hotfire, where he could convalesce and take control once again of the farm's precarious finances. At the age of nine I became a full-time boarder with the Reverend and Mrs Hill, and in fact never really went home again except for school holidays and occasional weekends.

The Reverend Hill was the rector of the Anglican Church in Cathcart, a classical scholar with a master's degree who loved chess and taught me to play the game. His wife, Vivienne, was a dab hand with watercolours who loved to paint small landscapes as gifts for friends. My mother adored them both; they had comforted her through the trauma of her four-year-old son's death, so it was to them that she entrusted me, her precious survivor. I could not have been in more caring hands, but still I found the separation from my parents at such a young age painful beyond words. Going to that tough school each morning made me so nervous that I could not eat breakfast. Dear Mrs Hill would try to encourage me to at least have a plateful of bread and milk, and not wishing to disappoint her I would stuff my cheeks full of the pulpy mixture like a hamster, and then hurry to the outside bucket-toilet to eject it. Whether she was aware of my charade I know not, but I kept up the routine for at least a year before I could actually eat the stuff.

The move also brought me closer to the reality of the war, for the Hills had taken in an English evacuee, a boy named Colin Mallows who was some three years older than me. His father was a London policeman and Colin had been shipped to South Africa to escape the Blitz. Otherwise the war was a distant factor which, but for the absence of my father and uncles, didn't touch my life. The closest it ever came in any real form was when we had to undergo a bizarre air-raid scramble at school. It was explained to us that we should prepare for the possibility that German bombers (of some unimaginable long-range capability) might attempt to raid a British airbase at nearby Queenstown, where pilots were being trained, and should the German planes be driven off they might jettison their bombs on little Cathcart. In preparation for such an eventuality, we had to learn to dive under our desks and bite on a piece of cork that was helpfully provided to each of us, and which, we were told, would prevent the bomb blasts from bursting our eardrums.

The only other personal proximity to the war I experienced was during weekends spent at Hotfire when I would occasionally hear the drone of the slow, twin-engine Avro Ansons flying down the Kei River gorge as those trainee British pilots practised their navigation skills. But the plight of poor Colin Mallows was much more tangible. He was lonely, an intellectual who found himself in what can only be described as an intellectual desert. He read incessantly and had a habit of sucking his thumb while doing so, which drew taunts of the cruellest kind at school. He escaped the playground as swiftly as possible each day, hurrying home to his beloved books in his isolated room. He also listened intently to the war news on the radio and to a weekly programme of messages from British parents to their evacuated children in distant Commonwealth countries. I pitied him but was never able to draw close to him or relate to his intense introversion; the life the war had inflicted on him drove home the message of its devastating impact on both body and soul.

* * *

FROM THE SHALLOW to the deep end. My next move was to a major boarding school, Queen's College, in Queenstown. A rugger-bugger school in local parlance, renowned for its prowess in all sports, and which has produced the likes of Tony Greig, who became England's cricket captain, and Daryll Cullinan, a star South African batsman who holds the record as the country's youngest player to score a first-class century, at age 16. It also has the distinction of holding an unbeatable sporting record – set during my time there – when, in a first-team match against one of our great rivals, Selborne College, our opening bowler, Wynton Edwards, took all ten wickets for no runs. Selborne were all out for nine. Rugby, of course, was the glamour game that command-ed the passions of the whole school body when teams from the under-14s to the stars of the first XV competed with our regional rivals on great gala days of songs and war cries.

Queen's, too, was no place for sissies, and again I found it tough, especially since I had to go first to a private hostel then to one of the major houses on campus, which meant I served two successive years as a fag, or 'skunk', which denoted the lowest form of animal life in that environment. The routine was that of a British public school, with cold showers every morning – even during the bitter Queenstown winters – a strict hierarchical order and bells that de-noted the dispositions of the day. It was all part of a British imperial model aimed at building character and inculcating a manly spirit.

But I survived, thanks mainly to the sporting abilities that my father had instilled in me. In fact, such skills constitute essential survival kit in a school like Queen's. They win you acceptance and, if you are lucky, even respect. And so after those first two years of skunking I blossomed, both socially and academically. I made runs and I made friends. My academic achievements were less impressive, for, if truth be told, this was not an academic hot-house. In my matric year, I was one of only five in a large class to achieve a first-class pass.

I was 12 years old, in grade seven, when the war in Europe ended, an event which brought a number of active young men home to rejoin the school's teaching staff. They returned as instant heroes in our eyes, particularly as some, including my housemaster, Dennis Scott, had been decorated for valour in the desert war. Scott, who had been a major in the First City, my father's regiment, and my history teacher, Donald 'Hoffie' Hofmeyr, who had been a tank commander, had both been awarded the Military Cross. Seldom can teachers have been in a better position to command the respect of their pupils. Both played a hugely influential role during my years at Queen's – Scott as a model of leadership with his ability to assert discipline simply through the force of his presence while at the same time exuding an easy camaraderie with the boys in his care, and Hofmeyr, who awakened in me a lifelong fascination with the drama of history.

Until Hoffie walked into my class, history had been the dullest of subjects, a catalogue of dates and conventions to be memorised like multiplication tables. But this returned soldier brought the action behind those dull dates to life as he took us through Napoleon's invasion of Russia, playing war games on the blackboard to demonstrate the strategies employed by the French emperor and his stubborn old opponent, General Mikhail Kutuzov. 'Always remember the name, Cut-us-off,' Hoffie enjoined us as he chalked out the route of the Russian's strategy of scorched-earth retreat. It was vivid stuff, like a movie serial that had us all sitting on the edge of our seats waiting for the next instalment. This was great teaching and it certainly stimulated this student, to the point where I got a distinction for history in matric and won the school prize for it.

Yet there were gaps, unforgivable great holes, in the subject matter we were taught about our own country. Here we were living in the eastern Cape, the old frontier, with all its drama of a hundred years of warfare, and in our time the very crucible of a re-emergent black intellectual leadership that was to change the adult lives of us all – and we knew nothing, absolutely nothing, about it. The institutions where this new leadership was beginning to blossom, Lovedale College and the University of Fort Hare, were barely a hundred kilometres from us, yet they might as well have been on the far side of the moon; we barely knew of their existence. There was no interaction with them whatsoever. While we learned about British monarchs and the doings of Napoleon and Bismarck and Garibaldi, our syllabus contained nothing about the founding of the African National Congress in 1912 or the emergence, so close to us at Fort Hare, of African figures of such huge future significance as Nelson Mandela, Oliver Tambo, Govan Mbeki, Robert Mugabe, Mangosuthu Buthelezi, Robert Sobukwe and others.

On reflection, perhaps it was not so surprising, for Queenstown had been built as a small outpost on that old war-torn frontier and the school had been established in 1858 to serve what was a rural frontier society, with all the vulnerability, cohesion and prejudices that go with such societies. Those are its roots and the culture remains little changed. The great paradox of the region is that, while its farming communities are probably the most closely interlinked in the whole country, both linguistically and physically, the whites of the Eastern Cape have always been – and remain – among the most politically conservative.

One small incident during my schooldays at Queen's burnt this paradox into my memory. It was during my senior year there, and I recall the headmaster, Dr Howard Quail Davies, a tall, athletic figure of a man who had won a silver medal for South Africa as a hurdler at the 1930 British Empire Games in Canada, telling us it had come to his attention that some old school blazers had fallen into the hands of black children in the town. This was unacceptable, he said. It was demeaning the school colours, and we were on no account to allow our own blazers to fall into black hands when we had outgrown them. Moreover, should we see a black child wearing a Queen's College blazer, we were to approach the boy and buy it from him, whereupon he, the headmaster, would reimburse us. Alternatively, should we not have sufficient pocket money to make the purchase we should escort the black child to the headmaster's house and he would buy it.

And so it came to pass that on a certain Saturday morning, not long after this improbable lesson in frontier tradesmanship, as we, the white boys of proud Queen's College, strode through the streets of Queenstown in all our sartorial finery – white first-team blazers, straw boaters and all – preening ourselves before the boarders from the Girls' High School, the word went around in that mysterious telepathic way that occurs in groups of school-boys, that a black boy had been seen in a Queen's College blazer.

Something akin to a foxhunt followed as the black boy was spotted darting down side streets and alleyways with half the school body in pursuit. Now Queen's had a proud reputation in the field of athletics, having won the regional inter-school shield eight years in a row, but we were no match for this nimble urchin as he jinked his way through the back alleys of Queenstown and eventually disappeared in the direction of the segregated black township.

Years later, when as a journalist I came to know Thabo Mbeki, the ANC star who became Nelson Mandela's successor as President of the new democratic South Africa, we once fell into conversation about our early lives in the eastern Cape, and Mbeki told me how his parents, Govan and Epainette Mbeki, fearing they might both be imprisoned because of their political activism, had sent him at the age of nine to stay with an uncle in Queens-town who lived on the edge of that black township. As I listened to his account I felt my blood run cold. 'Oh my God,' I thought, 'was that the future President of South Africa that we chased through the streets that day?'

A quick check of dates showed it couldn't have been him. But then again, for all we knew it might have been …

CHAPTER FOUR

The Pen

I BECAME A journalist by accident. It must have been around September of my last year at school that I fell into casual conversation with a close friend, Kenrol French, as we wandered across the playground. The spring holidays lay ahead, a short break of about two weeks, then it would be back to school for the start of the dreaded matric exams. 'What are you going to do when you leave school?' Ken asked me suddenly, interrupting the usual theme of our conversations – photography. That was Ken's passion and he had talked me into buying a good camera, which he was trying to teach me to use with some degree of skill.

'Oh, I'm going to Rhodes next year,' I replied. 'I haven't decided yet whether to do a BA or a BSc. I want to be a teacher and I guess it will have to be either English and history or science. Those are my best subjects.'

What I didn't tell my friend was that the real reason I wanted to be a teacher was that I had inherited my father's passion for sport. I had made first-team cricket and tennis and loved them both, so that I pictured myself becoming a sports coach in addition to my teaching duties, perhaps even coming back here to my old school to become the first-team cricket coach. I couldn't imagine anything more satisfying. Moreover, while the other boys of my age proclaimed loudly that they couldn't wait to escape

I knew deep down, though I never dared say so openly, that I'd been happy at Queen's. After my lonely early years on the farm it had given me a social life, companionship, perhaps even a little intellectual nourishment. So why not carry on doing what I had enjoyed?

We walked on in silence for a while as Ken weighed what I had said. 'Well, if I could write like you,' he responded at last, 'I'd become a journalist.'

I was taken aback. 'What,' I spluttered, 'does that involve?' A dumb question, to be sure; of course I knew that journalists were people who wrote for newspapers, but never having been a regular newspaper reader, the thought of working for one was so far from my imagination that I was thrown off balance.

'My grandfather owns a small paper in Cathcart,' Ken said. 'Why not come with me when we're there on holiday and you can have a look around? It's very small, but there's something about a newspaper office that may just interest you.'

So that is what I did. I cannot say it was a Damascene experience; the establishment was more of a commercial printing works than a newsroom, and the little news-sheet it produced each week was too small to be called a newspaper. But it was fascinating to watch the deft compositor put the handset lettering in place and run them through his flatbed press. There is something magical about the printed word. It is so simple and yet so powerful; it has been the greatest liberator in the history of humankind, striking fear into the hearts of priests and potentates alike, and stripping them of their medieval powers by informing and educating the people. I was not yet enough of an idealist for this thought to be decisive, but I did find it intriguing. Words, news, knowledge, freedom.

When I mentioned Ken's suggestion to my mother, she was ecstatic. 'What a wonderful idea,' she exclaimed. 'I would have loved to have been a journalist. You should do it.'

But I was still hesitant. I knew my mother well enough to realise that her enthusiasm may have stemmed more from her frustration at the intellectual aridness of being a farmer's wife than from any real enthusiasm or knowledge about the profession.

So the matter went into cold storage for the rest of the school holidays. I decided to discuss it with my English teacher when I got back to Queen's.

RN 'Bud' Rosseinsky, the English and Latin teacher, was a scholarly man with a dry sense of wit. He was head of the Literary and Debating Society and looked older than his years. A Mr Chips with a slightly hesitant manner of speech and an unsteady gait, which earned him the nickname among my group of 'Speedwobbles' – a typically thoughtless schoolboy calumny given that Rosseinsky had once been a rugby star, a wing three-quarter who had played at provincial level. Rosseinsky had encouraged me with my writing and given his approval to my thoughts about becoming an English teacher, so he looked a bit taken aback, even a little disapproving, when I asked him what he thought about journalism as a career. 'I don't know anything about it,' he replied shortly. 'Why don't you go and ask the people at the Rep?'

The *Daily Representative* was a remarkable publication, a broadsheet daily that ran between six and eight pages of world, national and local news in a town with a population, in the early 1950s, of about 12 000. This led to the boast, albeit unverified, that Queenstown was the smallest town in the world with a daily newspaper. Sadly the paper has now shrunk to a weekly tabloid and so forfeits that proud status.

The Rep, as it was popularly called, began life as a weekly, owned and edited by Frederick von Linsingen, none other than the sole surviving son of the original owner of my sword. The paper was later acquired by a canny Scots immigrant, AK McPherson, and it was he who turned it into a daily. It was a bold move, given a circulation of barely 1 000 a day, but in a busy country town he scooped up all the retail advertising that was going, which, combined with employing members of his family as editor and advertising manager, and paying derisory salaries to two or three trainee reporters, managed to turn a healthy profit. It also made him a citizen of note in the town.

The Rep was housed in a small, two-storey building sandwiched between a café and a car dealership on the main street, Cathcart Road. It sported the name, *Daily Representative*, in grand

Old English lettering on its facade. The advertising department was downstairs, the editorial upstairs. The 'Works', consisting of two Linotype machines for setting lines of type and a compositor's stone for making up the broadsheet pages, was behind a glass partition on the upstairs floor.

It was there that I ventured one day early in my final school term after making an appointment to see Mr McPherson. I was shown into one of three offices on the editorial floor, the others being for the editor, son-in-law Derek Gill, and the advertising manager, son-in-law Frank Green. Their wives, the proprietor's daughters, were at desks in the main room working as proofreaders. A secretary and a single reporter completed the editorial staff complement.

McPherson was an elderly man, small but stocky. He spoke with a broad Scots accent, and, as I was to discover, was a man of few words and a strong mind.

'What can I do for you?' he asked bluntly.

I began rather long-windedly explaining that I was interested in becoming a journalist and wanted to know more about it. What was involved and what were the career prospects? I was writing good essays at school and getting good marks, and my English teacher had advised me to come to the Rep to learn more about what journalism entailed and what its career prospects were.

'It's a fine career,' McPherson growled back, 'but it's not about writing essays, it's about gathering news. When can you start? First of January?'

'Oh no,' I responded, more than a little bewildered. 'I've got to go to Rhodes first, and that will take three years.'

'Don't do that, son,' he shot back, his voice deepening and his accent becoming more gravelly to add emphasis, 'they'll rruin ye. I'll teach ye all ye need to know. I'll pay ye twelve pounds a month.'

I muttered something about that not being very much, to which he replied curtly that, 'Ye're damn lucky not to be paying me to teach ye!'

As a callow 17-year-old I was ill-equipped to deal with such a steamroller. He pressed me on the starting date, and I told him that I had been invited to go on a cricket tour in January.

'Make it the first of February, then,' he replied, with a wave of the hand to indicate the door.

That left me in a quandary. I was all set to go to Rhodes but here was this man my English teacher had advised me to see telling me it was unnecessary, indeed that it might be harmful — presumably because he thought it might turn me into a pompous egghead instead of a hard-nosed newsman. What should I do? It was not as though I felt going to Rhodes was essential: 60 years ago, going from high school to university was not seen as a natural progression as it is today, but rather as a necessary step only for entry into one of the professions. Particularly not in a rural community such as the one in which I had grown up. None of my relatives and few of my classmates were doing so. Moreover, there were no journalism courses at any South African university in those days, so I had no idea which subjects to study if my career was going to be journalism. I had registered at Rhodes only because I had intended becoming a teacher, and now that was in doubt. The idea of becoming a journalist was beginning to loom larger in my mind.

I telephoned my parents for advice. It was a difficult call to make because I was painfully aware that my father, struggling on Hotfire, was going to be hard-pressed to come up with my university fees, which made it unfair to expect him to be objective. My mother was emphatic; she thought journalism was the right career for me and that I should follow McPherson's advice. After all, he had spent his life in the business and he should know. My father, as I expected, was non-committal. He assured me he would somehow manage to find the money to pay my Rhodes fees if that was the way I wanted to go, but the choice had to be mine. He was a simple farmer; this was not part of his world.

It was a tough call, but in the end I decided to go according to the only solid advice I had.

* * *

SO IT WAS that on 1 February 1951 I took my seat in a newsroom at the age of 17, to begin a career as a journalist that has now extended to 66 years. I often think back with resentment to that peremptory advice AK McPherson gave me not to go to Rhodes. It is obviously in every individual's interest to further his or her education if the opportunity exists; it is inconceivable that education could 'ruin' anyone. Worse than that, it was wicked for an adult to project his anti-intellectual prejudices on an impressionable youth who had called on him for advice. But most of all I am angry with myself for having allowed him to intimidate me into such tame submission. I know I was university material and would have benefited enormously, both socially and intellectually, from the experience. Watching my children flourish from it made me, well, I suppose, jealous.

And yet, and yet … The truth is, I have had a wonderful career and a wonderful life as a result. I have enjoyed every moment of it. The route I took was that of an apprenticeship, which is a perfectly good way to learn any craft or trade. For the rest, the job itself, the way it exposed me to the rockface of life in all its vicissitudes, became my education, or my substitute for an education, and moulded me into the person I am, whatever that may be. And when I look back I must confess that if I had my time again I would not want to change it in any substantial way. Such are the crossroads of life, those determining moments of decision that define who and what you are going to become. Just ten minutes in AK McPherson's office did that for me. Yet I still resent him for it.

On reflection, the advice the old Scrooge should have given me − which over the years I have given to many young aspirants − was to go to university first to broaden your mind, then come back and do your apprenticeship. And the university subjects he should have recommended were those of the basic Oxford PPE course − politics, philosophy and economics − with English literature thrown in. Yes, McPherson was right, journalism is not about writing pretty essays, but an acquaintance with the treasure house of great literature is a useful addition to one's armoury of expression. I recall my long-time friend, Joseph Lelyveld, a wonderfully expressive writer who became executive editor of *The New York Times*, once telling me I should read more fiction. He was right. Fine journalists draw telling analogies from fine fiction − and good movies.

The Daily Rep was indeed a great training ground, as McPherson had assured me it would be. Not that he ever gave me a single lesson himself, having boasted he would teach me all I needed to know. The only lesson I ever had was from the editor, Derek Gill, who on my first day took me on to the small balcony outside his office and, pointing across the street, told me to imagine a sign hanging outside a shop there which read: 'Fresh Fish Sold Here'.

'What's wrong with that sign?' Gill asked me.

'Nothing,' I replied after a moment.

'Well, do you think they're selling the fish somewhere else, not in their shop?' he asked.

'No, I suppose not.'

'So you don't need the word "here". And do you think they're selling rotten fish?'

'No.'

'And do you suppose they're buying fish? We're a hundred miles from the sea.'

I was silent by now. 'So you see,' Gill concluded, 'all you need on that sign is "Fish". Journalism is about getting rid of unnecessary words. Cut the clutter and keep it simple. But to do that you have to understand what it is you're writing about. That's the hard part.'

That was the only formal lesson I have ever had in journalism, and I reckon it was about as good as any beginner could have. For the rest, life at the Rep was a matter of learning on the job, and for that my fellow reporter, Anthony Rider, who had been working there for a year before I came, was my chief mentor.

Tony was a sturdy young man. He had been a rugby player at my rival school, Dale College in King William's Town, and he took long strides as we sped between the many assignments we had to cover each day, so I almost had to run to keep up with him. He was a fine reporter, quick to spot the one or two news items in a pile of bureaucratic bumf that would be dumped before us at town council or hospital board meetings. He taught me the importance of building a network of contacts throughout the town: which policeman to touch base with at the 'cop shop' as we did the daily crime round; which hospital official would tell us of accidents; which court official would help us get an early glimpse of the day's roll. He taught me court procedure and the key aspects of libel and other newspaper laws. He taught me basic newswriting and how to edit copy, write headlines and lay out pages.

We worked hard, Tony and I, while the editor, Derek Gill, who was too occupied in selecting and editing copy and writing the day's editorials to have time to direct the news-gathering operation, left us to do that for ourselves as well. It was an afternoon paper with a 2.30 pm deadline, which meant the mornings were a rush to get the paper out. It also meant we often had to work at night, covering meetings and writing up the reports so that the copy would be ready for editing and typesetting next morning. That often meant 12-hour, sometimes even 18-hour, days, with sport to be covered at weekends and written up on Sunday nights for publication on Monday. All for £12 pounds a month, of which £9 went on board and lodging (happily, my father subsidised me to the tune of £5 a month). I stayed at a modest boarding house called Nuffield Hall, which was a haven for young working people and thus also the hub of an active social life.

Life in those days revolved around work and play – not very different, I suppose, from the first years at university. I joined a sports club, Greydeane, run by an energetic sports-lover called Aidan Green, whose wife ran Nuffield Hall. I played cricket for the club and spent hours on its tennis, squash and badminton courts. But cricket was my main passion, and in those years I hit the best form of my short career, playing not only for the club but for Queenstown in the province's inter-town league, heading the league averages as an opening batsman in my second season and being selected for the under-23 provincial side. I also wrote a cricket column for the Rep and became secretary of the Queenstown Cricket Union.

Work, sport and girls. Life at boarding school had been severely restricted on the gender front. Although the Queenstown Girls' High School was just across the road from Queen's College, the headmistress, Miss Dankworth, so feared for the virtue of her charges in the vicinity of so much burgeoning testosterone that she restricted formal contact with the boys to two dances a year and occasional mixed tennis at first-team level. That left us panting teenagers with Saturday mornings in town as the only opportunity for female contact. That and letters. The volume of literary production that flowed between the two schools in the years I was there far exceeded anything written in the classrooms. They included letters of proposal; to be 'booked' to a girl at GHS, who then became your 'wife' and you her 'husband', between whom there would then flow a voluminous exchange of love letters, which was the primary object of the exercise. But to my shame I must confess that I was too inhibited by the barriers and far too shy to participate.

However, the proximity of life at Nuffield Hall and at the Greydeane sports club was another matter, and I did my best to redeem myself. Yet these were the strait-laced 1950s, a whole decade before the advent of the Pill, so that caution remained the watchword in relationships between the sexes. Still, we had fun with dances and sports expeditions and braaivleis parties and sometimes quite heavy petting sessions. I fell hopelessly in love at least three times in just over two years, but none was ever consummated.

In many ways it was a hedonistic life, but then slowly, incrementally, almost subliminally, I began to experience a political awakening.

* * *

AS FEBRUARY CAME around again, completing my first year as a journalist, Derek Gill decided to take his annual holiday, which meant I was thrust into the role of acting editor. Tony Rider had left by then and a new junior reporter, Doris Jackson, daughter of the car dealer next door, had just joined the Rep, so I was now the senior reporter with a new pay cheque of £25 a month.

It was heady stuff at the age of 18 to find oneself in editorial control of a daily newspaper. And the Rep was a rare thing in country newspapers in those days. It was not the kind of local rag filled with parish-pump chatter that you find in small and medium-sized towns around the world. It was a proper news-paper, a serious daily broadsheet punching well above its weight. It was served by the big news agencies, the South African Press Association (Sapa) and London-based Reuters, and it carried a spread of carefully selected local, national and international news as well as editorials commenting on major current affairs. We pretentiously imagined it to be in competition with the *Daily Dispatch* in East London and *The Friend* in Bloemfontein.

For me, this was deep-end training at its most extreme. I had to direct Doris in choosing which events she should cover, do some of the reporting myself as well as all the copy-editing and page layouts. The most challenging part was choosing which news items to place where in the paper, which should go on the front page and, above all, which should be the front-page lead. That meant having to weigh up the relative importance of the hun-dreds of news items clattering in on our telex machine each day.

It was a formidable task, and the kid from the farm who had never read a newspaper regularly until he came to the Rep was frankly out of his depth. But there is nothing like deep water to teach one to swim in a hurry. I found myself treading water in a flood of major national as well as global events. The Nationalist government was enacting a torrent of ferocious legislation at the time: the Group Areas Act, specifying which race group could live where throughout the country, the Population Registration Act, which defined every individual's race group, and, most controver-sially at that moment, the Separate Representation of Voters Act, which stripped the coloured people in the Cape of their voting rights. All these were generating intense public debate.

The big world stories were equally formidable. There was Churchill's disclosure that Britain had a nuclear bomb, Dwight Eisenhower's landslide victory over Adlai Stevenson to make him President of the United States, together with the Korean War and Britain's campaign against 'terrorists' in the jungles of Malaya. There was Stalin's death. General Mohammed Naguib had over-thrown King Farouk in Egypt, only to be overthrown himself by Colonel Gamal Abdel Nasser.

Nearer home there were reports that Kwame Nkrumah was going to become Prime Minister of the Gold Coast, while in Kenya Jomo Kenyatta went on trial accused of instigating the Mau Mau rebellion against white settlers. But the story that really captured the salacious interest of white South Africans was Chief Seretse Khama of Bechuanaland's marriage, in 1948, to an English secretary, Ruth Williams. There had been an outcry in the Western world over the apartheid regime's outlawing of mixed marriages and sex across the colour line, but to the delight of white South Africans, English and Afrikaner alike, Tory attitudes in Britain seemed little different. Bawdy jokes abounded. The Secretary for Commonwealth Relations, Lord Salisbury, announced that Khama could never be allowed to become chief of the Bamangwato tribe in his homeland. Salisbury offered him a government job in Jamaica instead, but Khama declined it – whereupon he was peremptorily banished from Bechuanaland for five years.

How was I to cope? How was I to judge the relative news value of all these events? Fortunately I had done enough copy-editing during my first year to get me a bit beyond the level of that vacuous farm boy. Fortunately, too, I was fortified by the bravado of youth. As the American humorist Garrison Keillor put it in one of his radio shows, when you are on the frontier and they ask you whether you can do it you reply, 'Yes,' and by the time they find out you can't, you can. And so by the time Gill came back from his holiday, I could actually do his job.

What really saved me was that, six days after moving into my exalted position, a story broke that was so big not even the rawest rookie could fail to recognise its importance. This was the death of King George VI, Britain's beloved wartime monarch. And since Queenstown was in the heart of royalist country, the story was seismic.

Inconveniently for me, the news broke at lunchtime – the nightmare of any journalist working on an afternoon paper. I had finished making up the front page and had slipped out for a bite of lunch when I heard the news. I leapt on my bicycle and raced back to the office, where I had to work frantically to edit the news agency copy and remake the front page with a screaming banner headline. With the help of a marvellous young compositor, Trevor Rankin, we got the front page off stone just on the 2.30 deadline.

The task then was to start preparing immediately for the next day's issue, with all the tributes and sidebar details that readers want after a big story has broken. Painstakingly I laid out a double-page spread of royal pictures with some suitably saccharine text, across which I appended the headline in Old English typeface: 'The King is Dead — Long Live the Queen'. I still wince at the mawkish triteness of it, but I've no doubt all those royalist readers loved it.

The rest of my acting editorship passed relatively smoothly, but it was a relief to get back to the more familiar task of daily reporting. My taste of editorship had been enough to make me aware of how fraught it could be with stress and anxiety, something I was to experience in full measure in later life. But, as I was soon to find out, it could be action-packed at the reporting level as well.

* * *

AS I SET OUT on my round of contacts on the morning of 26 June 1952, it seemed like just another ordinary day. There was a touch of winter chill in the air and frost on the ground. 'Nothing much to report today,' said the friendly information officer at the police station. 'Only a bit of trouble in the township last night. Some Natives were arrested. They should appear in court today.'

So on to the magistrate's court I went to check on how many had been arrested and what the trouble had been. I slipped in to the courtroom, took my place at the press table and waited for the day's proceedings to begin. The prosecutor entered, followed by chief magistrate BH O'Connor, but no sooner had they done so than a commotion erupted outside, with much screaming and shouting. O'Connor hastily adjourned the court, and I ran out to see what was happening. There I beheld for the first time something I was to witness again many times in the years ahead: the police baton-charging a crowd of protestors.

It was a sizeable crowd in a cramped courtyard with a narrow entrance gate that made it difficult for the protestors to flee as the police charged them with swinging batons. They were still singing as they tried to run, a lilting Xhosa song, '*Senzenina*', 'What have we done, we the African people', which I was to hear many times again as one of a new genre of freedom songs. As the police waded in, the flight turned into a stampede and I saw one old woman fall to the ground. As she lay there in the dust, a tangle of skirts and shawls with a *doek* wrapped around her head, I saw a white policeman pause in his charge and lash out at her with his boot. He was a man I knew, a Sergeant Ashburner, one of the contacts I called on frequently and always found to be amiable and helpful, even kindly. But in that moment he was seized with a viciousness that was beyond himself. Again it was a sight that was to become familiar, a spasm of fury that seized white officials when they came into contact with black political protestors. It was, I came to suspect, driven by a deep-seated fear on the part of the apparatchiks of an oppressive system when they came face to face with the front-line challengers of a majority population they subliminally knew would overwhelm them one day.

It was my first sight of the racial conflict that has coloured all our history, and it left an indelible impression. It was also an important turning point in that long conflict. Until then the African National Congress (ANC), always strongly rooted in the eastern Cape, had been a moderate organisation, restricting its activities to politely petitioning first the British Colonial Office, and then the South African government, for a better deal. But the post-Second World War years brought a change: the Allies had claimed the war was fought against racism and tyranny, while some of the major European imperial powers – France, the Netherlands, Belgium – had been ignominiously humiliated, which meant their colonial subjects were no longer disposed to submit to their authority when peace returned. A new liberatory spirit began to infuse the colonies.

Inspired by this, and weary of the ANC's ineffectual petitions in the face of ever more restrictive government policies, a new group of charismatic young ANC members formed a Youth League and began campaigning for more militant strategies.

Led by Anton Lembede, a brilliant young lawyer who tragically died at age 33, other members of the group included Nelson Mandela, Walter Sisulu, Oliver Tambo and Robert Sobukwe. The Youth League's aim was to function as a pressure group within the ANC, and at the organisation's annual conference in 1948 it successfully pushed through a commitment to adopt a new Programme of Action.

From this document, which was broadly conceptual rather than specific, the Youth Leaguers eventually extrapolated a more precise action plan, having in the meantime succeeded in replacing Dr AB Xuma, whom they regarded as too 'gentlemanly' and effete, with the more militant Dr James Moroka, as president of the ANC, and with one of their number, Walter Sisulu, as secretary-general. Another half dozen Youth Leaguers were elected to the national executive committee, making the league the effective driver of ANC strategy from 1950 onwards. The 'young lions' then set about putting their Defiance Campaign into action.

Moroka and Sisulu wrote to Prime Minister DF Malan demanding that he repeal six particularly onerous apartheid laws by 29 February 1952, failing which the ANC would embark on a campaign of defiance of those laws throughout the country. Not surprisingly, Malan responded with a blunt refusal and a warning of tough action should demonstrators break any laws. The ANC in turn decided to launch their campaign of defiance on 26 June, which was the day I wandered unknowingly to the court for my first witnessing of a conflict that was to dominate my journalistic career.

The Defiance Campaign continued for the rest of the year, when it died down after a series of bloody riots and much violence. By then some 8 000 black people had been sent to prison for defying apartheid laws, 70 per cent of them in small eastern Cape towns. It was the longest campaign of non-violent resistance ever launched in South Africa. It was also a turning point in the history of our race conflict, when the black resistance turned from moderation to militancy.

But the appalling thing was that I, the young trainee journalist, was taken totally by surprise. I had been in the job for just over a year, yet I knew nothing about the black resistance. Or that Queenstown, where I was living and working, was a particular hotspot of ANC activity. In fact I knew nothing whatsoever about the lives of the black community in the town that I was supposed to be covering as a reporter; neither about its politics nor its cultural life, including the fact that it was famous for its music through composers and performers who had evolved what was known among black cognoscenti everywhere as 'the Queenstown sound'. The terrible thing is that black people were not news. I had learned nothing about them, their culture and history or political institutions and personalities at school, and there was no call for me to report anything about them now in the newspaper for which I was working. It was an astonishing situation: here were two national groups occupying the same space but living in different worlds. This indeed was the essence of the South African malaise.

Of course these thoughts dawned only dimly on my teenage mind at the time, but they were to amplify with time. So, too, did the realisation that whites didn't know what was going on in the black world because they didn't want to know, and that the system of enforced racial segregation made it easy for them to avoid that uncomfortable knowledge. The only way to penetrate that wall of studied avoidance lay in my own hands, those of the reporter.

* * *

THE FOLLOWING year, 1953, was an election year. DF Malan's National Party had been in power for five years, having scraped in on a minority vote in the country's first post-war election. The Nats, as they were commonly called, had won only 40 per cent of the vote but, thanks to changes made to the boundaries of many parliamentary constituencies, and to a late alliance with the small Afrikaner Party, came to power with a majority of five seats.

The Nats' narrow victory in 1948 was attributed to post-war exhaustion, the slow demobilisation of South African troops who had fought in North Africa and Italy, and poor electoral organisation by Prime Minister Jan Smuts' United Party (UP). Smuts himself, having acquired a global reputation as a member of

66

Winston Churchill's War Cabinet, remained involved in grand international affairs, such as writing the preamble for the charter of the United Nations, to the neglect of matters in his own back yard. The UP's defeat in 1948 was therefore considered something of an aberration, not unlike Churchill's in 1945, and the English-speaking community, especially in the conservative eastern Cape, were looking forward to the election date, 15 April, with considerable optimism – even though their hero, Smuts, had died three years before, at age 80. His private secretary, JGN Strauss, was now leader of the UP and would surely lead it to victory.

It was in the early run-up to that election that I had the opportunity to have a one-on-one interview with a new figure in the National Party, Hendrik Frensch Verwoerd. He was not yet a Member of the House of Assembly, Malan having appointed him a Senator – a modest, unelected position in South Africa – and made him Minister of Native Affairs. Verwoerd was little known at the time and 'Native Affairs' was not yet the centrepiece of our politics, which still hinged mainly around English-Afrikaner relationships, but local Nats told me he was considered something of an intellectual and that I should see him.

So it came about that, at the age of 19, I went to interview the man who in time was to become the central figure of South Africa's racial notoriety, vilified as the architect of apartheid and therefore the quintessence of evil. However, I always regarded him as the Lenin rather than the Stalin of apartheid, who not only refined the ideology but set about trying to implement it with disastrous humanitarian results. Stalin came later in the form of the brutish John Vorster, Verwoerd's Police minister and successor.

I met Verwoerd in the Hexagon Hotel, located on Queenstown's centrepiece feature of that name. Verwoerd invited me to his room, where he sat on the only chair and I perched on the old iron bedstead. He was the epitome of courtesy, with a warm welcome and a grandfatherly patience as he set about explaining to his young visitor his concept of separating the races through what he called 'separate development' rather than apartheid, a word which itself simply means 'separateness'. He sounded altogether benign.

Towards the end of his rather convoluted explanation, which

I had difficulty following, I asked him whether he could sum it up more crisply. 'Yes,' he replied, after pausing a moment for thought. 'There won't be peace in this country, my boy, until the black man has his own countries.'

I had my punchline, but I was baffled as I left. What could he be talking about? How on earth could black people 'have their own countries' when they were here, all around us in racially mixed South Africa? It was a simple rhetorical question that a raw teenager asked himself, but it went to the heart of the fatal flaw in the whole Verwoerdian philosophy.

That evening I listened to Verwoerd expound on his thesis in a speech in the Town Hall, which I reported in the next day's Rep. He accused the United Party of having no colour policy, deriding it for fatuously wanting to remove the colour issue from the political arena when in fact it was the most pressing issue facing the country and was rapidly worsening. There were currently some 8 million Natives and two-and-a-half million whites, he said, and in 50 years time there would be 19 million Natives and about 6 million whites.

'Unless there is a strong policy to control them, the Natives will flood out the Europeans,' Verwoerd said. By contrast, the Nationalist policy of apartheid would provide the Natives with their own countries 'where they could live happily and independently', but which would be so located that labour could still be drawn from them. He explained that the implementation of this policy would take some time: so-called black spots in white areas had first to be removed, as did white spots in black reserves such as the Transkei, which consisted mostly of individual traders and small administrative towns. These people would not be forced out, but by a gradual natural process they would find that they had to move and then they would receive state assistance.

Verwoerd's vision was not yet official National Party policy, and would not become so until he became Prime Minister five years later. So this may well have been the first public exposition of what was to become the central feature of South Africa's notorious race policy.

* * *

COVERING THE 1953 election from my base at the Rep was an acrid experience. The historic polarisation of the country's two white communities had been deepened by emotions stirred up during the war years, when many Nats openly sided with Germany. Some, including Vorster and his eventual security chief, Hendrik van den Bergh, had been confined in internment camps, while thousands of our troops faced the rigours of five years of war in North Africa and Italy. Many of those who had joined up to fight were Afrikaners loyal to Smuts, adding the special sharpness of *broedertwis*, or brotherly discord, to the conflict.

One such was Group Captain Adolph Gysbert 'Sailor' Malan, who as a member of the Royal Air Force had been one of 'The Few', a decorated Spitfire pilot during the Battle of Britain. He returned after the war to join an ex-servicemen's organisation called the Torch Commando, formed to campaign against what they saw as fascist tendencies within the Nationalist government. Sailor Malan was soon elected president of the Torch Commando as it plunged into the election campaign against the Nats, adding a new edge to the acrimony.

The immediate pretext for the Torch Commando's intervention was the Separate Representation of Voters Act (1951), which disenfranchised 50 000 coloureds living in the Cape Province. They had been given voting rights under colonial rule and these rights, at Britain's insistence, had been entrenched in the new constitution establishing the Union of South Africa in 1910. The constitutional entrenchment stipulated that this could be changed only by a two-thirds majority at a joint sitting of both the House of Assembly and the Senate, but lacking such a majority the Nats had simply gone ahead and passed the new law with simple majorities of the two houses sitting separately.

On the face of it, the Torch Commando's resistance could be seen as an early campaign by the white opposition against apartheid, and some latter-day exculpatory attempts have been made to present it as such. But the truth is most opposition whites of the day cared little for coloured people's qualified franchise rights beyond the fact that they might be critical in a handful of swing seats. The real political issue, as it was articulated at the time, was over the only other entrenched clause in the constitution, which established both English and Afrikaans as official languages of the Union. Tearing up the constitutional entrenchments was seen as a threat that the Nats might scrap the official status of English, which greatly raised the emotional temperature.

The Supreme Court of Appeal struck down the Act as unconstitutional, but the government overcame that obstacle by enlarging the Senate chamber, which gave it the required two-thirds majority. Prime Minister Malan protested that the sovereignty of Parliament, as representing 'the people' and which of course his party controlled, should trump the Appeal Court. As he told *Time* magazine, the Appeal Court was no more than 'a few judges appointed by the government ... The struggle for [Boer] freedom has been reopened. No compromise is possible.'[1]

My first encounter with the intense hostility of that election campaign was at a political rally in the town of Aliwal North, located on the Cape provincial border with the Orange Free State but which fell within the Queenstown parliamentary constituency. The purpose of the rally was for the sitting MP, CM van Coller, who was Speaker of the House of Assembly, to announce his retirement and hand over the United Party's candidature to a young medical doctor and farmer, Johannes van Aswegen Steytler. Van Coller was a venerable figure, respected by English and Afrikaner alike, but here, in his declining years, perhaps for the only time in his life, he was subjected to voluble abuse. Local Nats had packed the town hall and yelled insults at him, drowning out his frail and faltering voice. Meanwhile members of the *Jeugbond*, the National Party's Youth League, headed at the time by one PW Botha — later to become President of South Africa — had clambered on to the corrugated-iron roof of the hall clad in army boots and carrying heavy rocks, which they rolled from the apex to the eaves, where colleagues retrieved them to cross over and repeat the process in successive relays for the duration of the rally. The noise inside the hall was deafening. Jan Steytler was later to become a significant political figure, leading a left-wing breakaway from the United Party that was to realign our political landscape, but although I could claim to have attended his first political meeting, I didn't hear a word he said.

Fists and stones flew freely across the country, particularly at Torch Commando rallies. Bailey Bekker, Sailor Malan's deputy in the organisation, embarked on a tour through the rough country of the Free State *platteland*, ending up in the small town of Rouxville, not far from Aliwal North, where he was told the National Party had booked out the town hall for the whole month. A local farmer, a *Bloedsap*, or diehard Smuts follower, offered Bekker his storage shed for a meeting. There, as Bekker began addressing a small group by the light of oil lamps, a posse of Botha's Jeugbond arrived armed with iron fence-poles and bicycle chains. They waded in, lashing out at people and overturning the oil lamps, which set fire to bales of lucerne stacked in the shed. The blaze gutted the shed and Bekker emerged from the melee with a broken arm. In Pretoria, the UP's most potent orator, Marais Steyn, was in full cry addressing a packed rally in the City Hall when a woman in one of the front rows stood up and hurled a stone at him, striking him on the forehead. Steyn was stunned for a moment, but recovered to continue his speech with blood streaming down his face. Pictures of the bloodied politician were splashed across the front pages of every daily paper the next morning.

Back in Queenstown I attended the last rally of the Nat candidate, Cornie Vorster, who concluded his speech with the bold declaration that Afrikaner Nationalism was on the march and would rule the country for the next 25 years. Hoots of mock laughter greeted this outrageous statement. UP confidence was at its peak. When the election results were announced two days later, the Nats had increased their majority from five to 29. They were to rule South Africa for the next 41 years.

CHAPTER FIVE

New Frontiers

I AM NOT by nature an impulsive person. A bit headstrong perhaps, but not the sort to take wild, impetuous decisions without considering the possible implications. Yet I suppose we all have our moments of madness. Which is what befell me one balmy autumn evening just after the 1953 election as I sat sipping beer with friends around a braaivleis fire at the sports club.

The conversation turned to someone somebody in the circle knew who had just driven from Europe through Africa in a Land Rover. What a fabulous experience, everyone agreed. Overseas travel, adventure, was surely something all young people ought to do. It was not yet fashionable just eight years after the war, but the idea moved like an electric charge through our little group.

'I think I'll do it,' said one member of the group, a burly fellow with a big motorcycle whom I barely knew and whose name I no longer remember. 'I'm going to go to the UK and have some fun.'

'I'll come with you,' I chipped in without a second's thought.

'Okay,' said the motorcyclist. 'Let's do that.'

So the decision was made. Just like that. And it was not the beer that did it, for when I awoke next morning, stone-cold sober and clear-headed, I was still firmly resolved to go ahead with the proposition. I had no money, of course, so I telephoned my indulgent father to check whether, maybe, he could help. He told me things had looked up a little, and, with the price of wool having gone up quite nicely, this trip to Britain, well, he might be able to help. But only a little.

A call to the Union-Castle Mail Steamship Company established that the cheapest available one-way fare to Britain was £69. With the £100 cash my father said he could give me, I made a reservation aboard the *Winchester Castle*, departing from East London, and handed in my notice to the Rep.

A week later my would-be companion crashed his motorcycle, injuring himself badly. He phoned to tell me he would not be able to make the trip. I decided to go ahead on my own anyway.

The *Winchester Castle* was an elegant old lady of 20 001 tons, long and sleek with the signature lavender hull, gleaming white superstructure and red-and-black funnel of the company's fleet. The Union-Castle Line had been granted a charter at the turn of the century to carry the royal mail between Southampton and Cape Town. In those days before air travel, these mailships were the standard means of overseas passenger travel. They were in fact floating hotels, providing their fortunate passengers with a splendid holiday even as they were transported between continents.

I boarded the *Winchester Castle* at East London and my parents drove from Hotfire to wave me goodbye. Other than those who had gone 'north' as soldiers during the war, I was the first member of my extended family to head abroad since our 1820 Settler forebears and poor Robert Stephan. Yet I was doing so in the most blunder-headed manner imaginable: I had no money other than my father's £100, no job to go to, nowhere to stay, no contacts to help me settle in, indeed no ideas whatsoever of where I was going or what I was going to do when I got there. Just the hazy notion that I wanted to expand my horizons and have an adventure.

My cabin was the cheapest on board – a cramped single-berther at the stern with a laundry chute passing through it. That meant I was in for a rough ride if the seas got up, for the stern and the bow of a ship do the worst of the pitching in heavy seas.

The voyage around the coast was pleasant enough, with a stop in Port Elizabeth and several days in Cape Town, during which

I effectively had a free hotel berthed in the harbour. Then came the great adventure. The Cape rollers make for some of the most uncomfortable sailing on all the seven seas. One leaves Cape Town running broadside on to the notorious southeasterly winds, which can sometimes reach gale force. This means the ship takes the worst of the weather on the beam, which makes it roll sickeningly. For three days I lay on my bunk wishing I could die, the standard experience of seasickness victims. Gradually I began to acquire my 'sea legs' and life began to seep back into my wracked body.

The rest of the voyage was pure hedonism. The further one sails towards the equator, the calmer the sea becomes. This is playtime. There were plenty of young people on the passenger list and a busy entertainment programme. There were films and dances and games and a fancy-dress party with prizes; there were deck and card games, bingo and quizzes and races with a tote betting system. Sport, too, with table tennis and even cricket played in an on-board net with a test match between teams representing the crew and the passengers.

I slipped into a sweet relationship with a girl named Selena Higginson, whose parents invited me to join them at their table in the dining saloon. We danced and cuddled and watched the flying fish and flashes of fluorescence leap from the bow wave in the warm and balmy evenings. The voyage passed in a seamless haze of jollification and gentle romance, so that I gave nary a thought to what I should do when the ship finally docked at Southampton.

The teeming hubbub of disembarkation. Crowds milling, reunited families hugging, taxis honking, newspaper vendors shouting. I was lost and confused in the melee. Reality at last.

Suddenly Mr Higginson's face appeared out of the mob. 'What are you going to do, Allister? Where are you going?'

'I don't know,' was my lame reply. 'I suppose I'll take the boat train to London and work it out from there.'

He looked quizzically at me. 'You mean you've made no plans?'

'No, I'm afraid not.'

'You'd better come with us, then,' was his remarkably generous response. The Higginsons' relatives were gathered around, hugging and chatting animatedly so there was no time or opportunity to introduce the rather bemused young stranger. I wasn't part of it and so didn't quite know how to handle myself, until I was bundled into one of the cars that had called to collect the family. We stopped at Winchester for tea, and again I sat on the edge of the jolly family group, this time gazing silently across the square at the city's great cathedral.

What a magnificent sight. I have never been a person of faith, but there is something about the architecture of a great cathedral that induces awe. I was with time to become fascinated by the cultural language of ecclesiastical architecture, but here, for the first time, sitting shyly on the edge of the kindly Higginson family group, I found myself looking in wonderment at that monument to the depth and richness of my own cultural heritage. It didn't strike me at the time, but this was the start of my voyage of self-discovery.

We drove on towards London and there, as we entered the outskirts of the great city, I was to experience my next sensory awakening. This was only a few years after the end of the war and extensive bomb damage was still evident. Amid all the activity of reconstruction was a man operating a pneumatic drill in the street. A common enough sight on any building site, to be sure, except for one thing. He was white.

It is difficult, even today, to explain the visual jolt I felt on seeing him. How does one explain the discomposure one feels at seeing something your rational mind knows is normal yet your instinctive reference point is of the abnormal? For the kid from the eastern Cape farm, from small-town South Africa, this was black man's work. Whites didn't do manual labour. Of course I knew perfectly well that job reservation laws were unique to South Africa, yet the sight of that white man operating a jack-hammer in a London street startled my sensory system. And it must have done so with some psychological force, that sudden awareness that my instinctive reference points of normality were actually abnormal. It puts me in mind of Archbishop Desmond Tutu's oft-repeated account of the emotional elation he felt when, shortly after arriving in London, a woman teller in a bank admonished an impatient white man for trying to jump ahead of him in the queue; and his sense of wonder whenever a London policeman addressed him as 'sir', to the point where he and his wife, Leah, used to stop bobbies in the street to ask for directions even when they knew perfectly well where they were.

The kindly Higginsons took me to their relatives' home in Finchley, North London, where they gave me a bed for the night. Next day they got on the phone and found me affordable accommodation with Marjory Warne, a motherly Cornish spinster, at 47 Fox Lane, Palmers Green. Here I met up with Australians Gregory Chesher, who was to become my cultural mentor and lifelong friend, and the attractive, vivacious Lorraine Lyons, with whom I promptly fell in love.

For the next two years this became my base and those my companions, and the farm boy from Hotfire settled into life in one of the world's greatest and most cosmopolitan cities, where he underwent a transformative experience that proved the celebrated philosopher of the Enlightenment, Jean-Jacques Rousseau, to be dead wrong.

Rousseau's ideal of human freedom and self-fulfilment was of the simple peasant farmer, master of his own domain, doing his own thing, but then this free and simple soul underwent a shrinking of his individuality as he entered an urban environment and began to see himself more and more through the eyes of others and to seek their approval as essential to his self-esteem. He thereby lost his sense of self and his personal freedom.

Modern psychologists may identify grains of truth in all this, but my personal experience is that Rousseau not only got it wrong but also got it backwards. My experience is that it was the stimulating environment of the great city over those two years that gave me my personal autonomy, that liberated me from the narrow vision of farm and small-town life, especially in a prejudice-ridden country such as South Africa. True personal freedom requires liberation from one's own prejudices as well as from the diminution of the freedom of others to whom those prejudices are directed.

* * *

LIFE AT 47 Fox Lane quickly settled into a bustling routine. Gregory, newly graduated as a pharmacologist from the University of Sydney, slipped easily into a job at Allen & Hanburys, the pharmaceutical company, based at Ware in Hertfordshire. He used to delight in responding to anyone who asked where he worked with a simple 'Yes'. Lorraine got a series of part-time jobs, sometimes as a model for nearby fashion houses. Then there was Paddy O'Dwyer, a middle-aged Irish pharmacist with a laconic wit who would navigate every weekday with a stolid and unchanging routine, then undergo a personality change on Friday evening. At that point he would return from work with his salary packet to pay Miss Warne his rent for the coming week – a prudent precaution for a true Irishman – before heading off to the dog races. We would usually not see him until Sunday morning as we awaited Miss Warne's Sunday lunch. This would consist of the household's weekly meat ration – wartime meat rationing did not end until July 1954 – followed by Cornish dumplings, which O'Dwyer irreverently referred to as 'Miss Warne's depth charges'. An Indian tenant, a tall and handsome man whose name I cannot recall, completed our modest household. He had little to say but seemed to observe our youthful activities with an amused tolerance.

And then there was me. By now I was clear about exactly what I intended doing. I was going to break into Fleet Street. The mystique of that thoroughfare, the domain of British journalism for half a millennium, captivated me the first time I walked its length from Temple Bar, where the City of London meets the City of Westminster, to Ludgate Circus. Here, on either side of the road, stood the offices of Britain's great national newspapers – *The Times, The Daily Telegraph, Daily Mirror, Daily Express, Daily Mail, The Guardian, The Observer* – and those of Reuters, the world's first news agency, which had pioneered modern communication by bringing news from continental Europe with homing pigeons. There they all stood, pantheons of my profession. And here, tucked back in alleyways, were the taverns and coffee shops where the great journalists, literary giants and political figures of the past had met to exchange views on the state of the nation and the news of the world. Pubs such as Ye Olde Cheshire Cheese, the oldest of them all, dating back to 1665; The Old Bell, which opened on to the back of Christopher Wren's exquisite St Bride's Church and where the journalists from Reuters would adjourn for their pints; The Feathers, the White Swan, and many others. The shades of Samuel Johnson, Edmund Burke, Oliver Goldsmith, Charles Lamb, Alfred Tennyson, Sir Arthur Conan Doyle, Charles Dickens and for a time that peripatetic American, Mark Twain.

And, of course, Samuel Pepys. The great diarist, perhaps the greatest journalist of them all, was born in Salisbury Court, just off Fleet Street. Pepys recorded, with extraordinary objectivity and frankness, the daily details and foibles of his own personal life and that of his family and friends, leaving posterity the most valuable primary record of everyday life during the Restoration period. His vivid accounts of the Great Fire of London and the Great Plague are surely some of the greatest on-the-spot report-age in the history of journalism.

All this I absorbed like a sponge. I spent hours walking that street, lingering in those taverns and coffee shops, hoping to bump into some of the big byline names of the day, dreaming of working there. It became more than an ambition; it became an obsession. I just had to get a job in The Street. Back at 47 Fox Lane I spent my days typing out letters applying for a job somewhere, anywhere, in that street of aspiration. Some elicited pro forma replies telling me there were no vacancies; others simply disap-peared into the ether. I joined the National Union of Journalists to get its magazine, *The Journalist*, to scour for job advertisements, but there were never any for Fleet Street jobs. I came to real-ise that not only was there serious unemployment in Britain but also that The Street represented the pinnacle of every British journalist's ambition and that only the best and most experienced got there. A kid from 'the colonies', as we were disparagingly referred to, stood little chance. Still, I kept trying.

Two brief responses sent my pulse racing. The first was from the *Daily Express*, the glamour paper of the moment, inviting me

Pub-crawling with Lorraine Lyons during my first sojourn in London.

to come in for a chat. It was then under the editorship of Arthur Christiansen, who had become a living legend as the pioneer of modern newswriting and presentation during his 24-year incumbency. I went for the interview charged up with excitement, only to meet a junior editor who told me the paper was interested in Commonwealth affairs and would like to chat to me about what was happening in South Africa. This I did, after which he thanked me, shook my hand and bade me farewell.

The second was from the Press Association, asking me to come in for an assessment. Again I sped in, adrenaline surging, to meet a desk editor who talked to me out of one side of his mouth as he barked instructions to a staffer out of the other side, simultaneously thrusting a bunch of telex copy in my direction with a muttered: 'Gimme three paras on that.' News agencies are frenzied places.

I took the copy, found an empty desk, and did my best to cobble together a three-paragraph news report. I handed it to the desk editor. He glanced at and shot back: 'Not bad, kid, but too slow. Go to the provinces for a coupla years then come back.'

Well, I had no intention of going to the provinces. London was too fascinating, too absorbing, and I could almost feel myself growing with its nourishment. So began another dimension of my urban education. There were theatre shows with Lorraine and classical concerts and art exhibitions with Greg Chesher. In time I think Lorraine and I saw everything of note in the West End, from Agatha Christie's record-breaking whodunnit, *The Mousetrap*, to *Hamlet* at the Old Vic (with Richard Burton as Hamlet and John Gielgud as Polonius).

Gregory introduced me to music. And art. He was passionate about both and shared his knowledge enthusiastically, accompanying me to concerts and inviting me to his room to listen to records from his extensive collection. Until then my musical awareness had been limited to the croonings of Bing Crosby and Frank Sinatra and the popular dance numbers I had twirled to in Queenstown. Now I was introduced not only to Beethoven, Schubert and Mozart but also to the more exotic modern classics of Igor Stravinsky, Dmitri Shostakovich and Sofia Gubaidulina. Likewise with art: it was the Impressionists, Expressionists and Abstractionists that fascinated him most. He was in all respects a modernist − and politically a socialist. We got on well together and have remained in touch for more than 60 years.

So it was that, in addition to the theatre, I began visiting the art galleries and concert halls of London, discovering Van Gogh, Gauguin, Chagall and Picasso and, at the Royal Festival Hall, encountering Stravinsky's stupendous ballet music, *The Rite of Spring*, which caused the audience to riot when it was first performed in Paris in 1913. I was blown away by the sheer power of the music and have been a Stravinsky enthusiast ever since.

There were more conventional activities as well. While it was still late autumn I went to the Middlesex Cricket School at Alexandra Palace, where a resident professional bowled off-breaks at me to try to polish my batting. With the onset of summer I made a pilgrimage to Lord's Cricket Ground, the sport's holy-of-holies, to watch a Test match between England and the West Indies. Then there was Wimbledon. Another pilgrimage with its strawberries and trim grass surfaces and that venerable Centre Court. There I watched immortals such as Jaroslav Drobný, Lew Hoad and Ken Rosewall, as well as, proudly, my own countrymen: Gordon Forbes, whom I had encountered at school tournaments in the eastern Cape, and his partner, Abe Segal. For a long time Forbes and Segal were ranked among the top doubles teams in the world, and two years after I saw him play at Wimbledon Forbes won the French mixed doubles with American Darlene Hard. He later also became South African singles champion, and later still a delightfully witty columnist for a newspaper I was editing.

But the great spectacle of the year was the coronation of Queen Elizabeth II on 2 June 1953, just over a year after I had excelled myself in getting the story of the death of her father, King George VI, into the Rep·before deadline. The long gap between Elizabeth's ascension to the throne and her coronation was to provide appropriate time for mourning the king's passing.

Three million people were expected to line the eight-kilometre route the Queen would take from Buckingham Palace through Admiralty Arch to Westminster Abbey and back, so Gregory, Lorraine and I set out the night before to select our chosen vantage points and settle down there to await the great day. Then the rain came. It poured all night and the next day, but the vast crowd endured the discomfort in a mood of high good humour, with much singing and cheering and quaffing of sustaining beverages. I chose a spot on a small grass bank in St James's Park on the south side of The Mall and settled down for an uncomfortably sodden but emotionally exhilarating night. With the dawn came a new wave of excitement: New Zealander Edmund Hillary, and his Sherpa guide, Tenzing Norgay, had conquered Mount Everest. The expedition was led by John Hunt and was the ninth British expedition to the world's highest mountain, so this was a day of double celebration for Britain. As the *Daily Express* trumpeted in what is still regarded as one of the all-time-great newspaper posters: 'All this and Everest Too.'

When it comes to pomp and pageantry, there is no doubt the British are best. And so it was on this day. Indeed even by British standards it reached new heights of grandeur and organisational excellence, for this was the first international event to be broadcast live on the new medium of television, with the renowned Richard Dimbleby as commentator. An estimated 27 million people watched it in Britain; satellite TV had not yet arrived so the rest of the world did not see the broadcasts. For those of us in the crowd, of course, the long and elaborate ceremony in the Abbey was out of view, yet it was enough simply to be there, to be part of such an occasion.

There were 8000 celebrities and invited guests at the coronation, which included all top government representatives of the 40 member states of the British Commonwealth. South Africa was represented in the persons of Prime Minister DF Malan and our High Commissioner at the Court of St James, Gerhardus Geyer. I felt pleased that my country was part of this great multinational event, which was part of my personal heritage, but resentful that it was by way of two men who represented a political movement that despised that heritage and whose triumph at the racist election I had just covered back in South Africa foretold trouble for my country. I felt a strong sense, too, as I watched Winston Churchill ride past in his carriage, of how inappropriate it was that these men, who had opposed my country's participation in the war and actively hoped for a German victory, should be there as honoured guests alongside him. So what did this make me? A patriot or a traitor? A rebel or just a dissident? It was a quandary I have never been quite able to resolve. I knew that I felt passionately about my country and all its people, but also that I despised all the racially focused governments it had ever elected, while at the same time being aware that in truth a country gets the government it deserves. So was I part of the collective to blame for the apartheid system? Years later I was to write that patriotism was a sentiment

I had never experienced until I was there in the amphitheatre of the Union Buildings in Pretoria, watching Nelson Mandela being sworn in as the first President of a democratic South Africa, but even that has not survived subsequent disappointments as Mandela's ideals have faded from the national scene. Perhaps journalism makes patriotism impossible, for it compels one to examine one's own country with a critical eye. Then again, perhaps that is what true patriotism really is, being a vigilant watchdog. But whatever the truth of this conundrum, beware the frequent invocation of patriotism: as Samuel Johnson warned, it is the last refuge of the scoundrel.

As I was soon to realise, Britain was by no means free of racism at this time. When it began to dismantle its empire, dark-skinned immigrants from countries such as Pakistan and the West Indies began arriving in numbers, and notices declaring 'No Coloureds' began springing up on the walls of boarding houses and bed-and-breakfast establishments. Apartheid, I thought to myself. But not quite, for although this was blatant racism it was not legally entrenched, which is what made the South African system so distinctive. Still, it was becoming an issue, both socially and politically.

It was around this time that I found myself at a party in a disco bar in Notting Hill, an area of London experiencing a rapid influx of coloured immigrants at the time. The music was loud and the party noisy, but it was a fun occasion during which I fell into conversation with a journalist who introduced himself as a reporter from the *Daily Express*. Naturally I was intrigued; here was surely a possible contact. But as the conversation progressed I found myself increasingly at odds with him, especially as it turned towards political events in South Africa. It emerged that he had visited the country and decided Malan's party had the racial issue just about right; blacks and whites were surely incompatible both socially and politically, so obviously the best thing to do was to separate them. I disagreed, and as the conversation heated up other partygoers drifted from the table. Except for one, a trim white woman in her thirties who sat there saying nothing but listening attentively. I was trying to explain the impossibility of separating the races and the fact that this would inevitability lead to ever-increasing racial oppression, which I felt was unacceptable.

But my adversary would have none of it. With his face slightly flushed, for by now we had both had quite a bit to drink, he turned to the silent woman at our table and addressed her directly. 'It may sound crude,' he said, 'but when all is said and done it boils down to the old question: Would you like your daughter to marry a black man?'

The woman was silent for a while, then in the softest of voices replied: 'My daughter is black. That's her over there' − pointing to a chocolate-skinned teenage girl jiving energetically with a white boy.

* * *

AS THE DAYS of the English summer lengthened, our thoughts at 47 Fox Lane turned to further exploration. I hitchhiked to Scotland, the land of my red-haired grandmother, and experienced the glories of Edinburgh and the grittiness of Glasgow. But back in London, grander plans were afoot. Lorraine had already left on a hitchhiking tour of Scandinavia, but Gregory and a university friend, John Sainty, newly qualified as a veterinary surgeon, had linked up with another Australian, Trevor Powell, and planned a hitchhiking tour of continental Europe. They asked me to join them and I agreed. What followed was an unforgettable adventure that took us through France, Spain, Italy, Austria, Switzerland, Germany and finally back to London.

Arriving in London, I found to my alarm that the bus fare from Wood Green tube station to Fox Lane cost me the very last coin I had, a sixpence. I was flat broke, which meant I would have to get a job immediately. So early the next day I made my way to the nearest labour exchange bureau. It was not an encouraging experience. All the jobs on offer were menial and poorly paid. I took a job as a labourer at a factory that manufactured screws. It didn't specify what sort of labouring was required, but the factory was conveniently nearby and the pay was £7 and ten shillings a

84

week, enough to cover my rent to Miss Warne and leave me with £4 spending money per week.

My job was to wheel a solid metal trolley, the shape of a supermarket trolley, around the lathes and, using an ordinary garden shovel, to scoop up the metal shavings beneath them and load them into my trolley. When the trolley was full I had to wheel it to the mouth of a furnace and tip the shavings in for them to be melted and moulded into new rods. To do this I had to wear heavy rubber overalls and thick gloves to protect myself from the sharp shavings and also from an oily substance that was sprayed on to the point of friction and created an oily mist around the machines.

It was heavy work. And boring. The only variation was an alternating of days – one day on the steel machines, the next on brass. The hours were from 7 am to 6 pm, with an hour's break for lunch and half an hour each for morning and afternoon tea. As winter set in it was dark when I came to work and dark when I got home. But the experience did instil in me an appreciation of the bleakness of a labourer's life. There is no such thing as job satisfaction in such an occupation; one has to put one's brain in neutral and freewheel through the day.

The months slipped by and I found I was losing weight. The motherly Miss Warne stepped in to admonish me. 'You've got to change your job,' she said sternly. 'You're getting too thin and you're going to get sick.' It sounded like an order, so I slipped away dutifully that weekend to the Strand, close to my beloved Fleet Street, where I got a job as a waiter in a Lyons tea shop. It paid only £6 a week and I had the expense of a bus and a Tube ride each way, but the work, which mainly involved collecting dirty dishes from the tables and putting them in the washing machine, was easier and the working days shorter. That kept me going for a few more months until I found a better-paid and even easier job as a clerk in a wholesale hardware store in Old Street.

Meanwhile I kept on writing: the endless letters of application for jobs in Fleet Street, which elicited the equally endless negative replies; a few feature articles which I posted back to the *Daily Dispatch* in East London and which some years later helped me land a job there; but mostly letters home. From my earliest days at boarding school it had been compulsory to write a letter home each Sunday evening, and this had become a habit. I diligently wrote to my parents each week, trying to use this as a way of practising my journalism with descriptions of what I was seeing and experiencing. These my mother diligently kept in a locked trunk in her bedroom.

Years later, after her death, I asked my father if I might have that trunk of letters. He looked blankly at me for a moment.

'You mean those old letters? Oh no,' he replied, 'I burnt them when your mother died.'

I was aghast. 'How could you do a thing like that?' I exploded.

My poor father looked puzzled. 'But they were old …' he stammered.

I could have wept. My whole life had gone up in flames. But I checked myself. I could see the look of horror on my father's face as it dawned on him that he had done something terrible. My father was a farmer, not a writer; how could he have known the value of those letters to me? I loved him dearly and couldn't bear to see that look of distress.

'It's okay, Dad,' I said as gently as I could. 'You're right. They were old.'

As winter merged into spring I received a letter from home informing me that the wool price had gone up, some decent money had come in, and so my parents had decided they, too, would like to visit England. They would be coming with my Uncle Les Stephen, one of my mother's brothers, and his wife. So would I please buy a second-hand car and be their chauffeur and tour guide when they arrived in the northern summer.

What a joy! The money arrived and, with the help of a friend of Miss Warne's who was in the second-hand car business, I chose a 1939 American-built Hudson, a big, bulbous, brown beast of a car that I reckoned could do the job. The immediate benefit of this new acquisition was that I could now romance Lorraine a little more effectively. The privacy of a parked car is useful that way. We still went regularly to theatre shows together but now when I could afford some petrol I could also drive her around occasionally.

Come March it was time for my 21st birthday, which required

special celebration. My parents had booked an overseas telephone call to me, a rarity in those days, and for three minutes we spoke on a crackly, indistinct line. We could barely hear each other but it was a great thrill nonetheless. That evening I took Lorraine out dining and dancing to Latin American music at Edmundo Ros's Coconut Grove in Regent Street. It was a deliciously extravagant and romantic evening.

My parents duly arrived, along with Uncle Les and Aunt May, and I drove them around England and continental Europe. It was a pleasure to be able to repay my parents in that way for their help in enabling me to have one of the most memorable and formative experiences of my life.

Then it was time to sail home with my parents, and to bid farewell to Miss Warne, Greg and Lorraine. I found it particularly difficult and emotional to leave Lorraine. We had drawn close in the nearly two years we had been together; there had clearly been affection between us but we had kept it private and chaste. Now we had a final night out together to say goodbye. I did not expect ever to see her again. She had a boyfriend waiting for her back in Australia and they would surely marry and she would disappear from my life. I agreed to write to her from South Africa, but we both knew that would fizzle out with time.

Yet I did see her again. Twenty years later, I received an unexpected invitation to deliver the keynote address at a ceremony for the presentation of the Australian Journalist of the Year Award. I seized the opportunity and took some leave to spend a little extra time in Sydney, to visit Greg, now married to his delightful wife, Terry, and with a young family, as well as to look up Lorraine, who was then working as Secretary of the Royal Sydney Golf Club. I discovered that she had indeed got married, not as expected to the old boyfriend, but to another man from whom she was now divorced.

Lorraine and I dined out together several times to catch up on our separate lives, then she drove me for a weekend into the Blue Mountains outside the city, an enchanting World Heritage Site of sandstone cliffs and deep dissecting gorges, all covered with a vast forest of eucalyptus trees. Oil from the leaves of those trees refracts the light to bathe the whole area in a soft blue vapour, giving the mountains their name. We toured the region, talking, reminiscing, and appreciating the beauty of the place. Come evening we stopped at an inviting-looking inn where we dined and wined sumptuously, only to learn afterwards that they had no vacancies to accommodate us for the night. However, by then we had befriended the proprietors, who told us there was a log cabin belonging to the establishment nearby where we could stay if we wished.

They gave us blankets and pillows and there, in that log cabin, deep in the forest, we at last consummated our youthful love affair in a night of delicate eucalyptus mist.

CHAPTER SIX

Return of the Wandering Son

DIPLOMATS ARE warned when they embark on their first foreign postings that the worst culture shock they will experience is not when they land in the alien societies where they will live for the next few years, but when they return home after that assignment. You expect to have to adjust to a different culture when you go abroad, but it comes as a shock to discover on your return that what you expected would be familiar and comfortable is in fact surprisingly disorientating.

The majestic spectacle of Table Mountain and the Twelve Apostles as they hove into view from aboard the *Athlone Castle* warmed my heart. But the jarring sights of my apartheid homeland hit me in the face the moment I stepped ashore. Right there in the immigration hall the ubiquitous signs, 'Europeans only' and 'Non-Europeans', proclaimed humanity's inequality in this land. One had barely noticed them before; they were simply part of the national scenery. But now they fairly leapt from the walls to command attention.

From that moment on my awareness of the injustices of my country seemed to grow by the day. What had been familiar before now appeared obscene. The separate facilities and entrances everywhere, for buses and trains, post offices and liquor stores, restaurants and hotels and parks and beaches, even the very city itself, which was in the process of being proclaimed for whites.

And just as the sight of that white man operating a jack-hammer on a London street two years before had disorientated my sense of normality, so now I found myself equally discomposed by the common enough sight in apartheid South Africa of a team of black roadworkers wielding their pickaxes while a portly white supervisor sat in his pick-up truck parked alongside, chain-smoking and sipping from a flask of tea.

Cape Town is a wonderfully colourful and cosmopolitan city, but through my fresh eyes it struck me as being stifled by ambiguity. Its streets were vibrant with all the polyglot hues of humanity, white people and black people and brown people and yellow people, Hindus and Muslims and Christians and Jews, descendants of slaves from Asia and the descendants of indigenous Khoi and San, and all the mixtures in between. But apartheid had advanced significantly in the two years I had been away, and all were now being systematically classified into specific racial categories. Categories that would determine where they could live, whom they might legally love and marry and, most important of all, what sort of work they could do. For apartheid was making every job colour-coded.

The mixed-race Cape coloured people, artisans and tailors, raucous flower-sellers and newspaper vendors with their vivid use of the Afrikaans language laced with bits of English and racy words of their own spontaneous invention. Linguistic gymnasts. The Cockneys of Cape Town, full of character and wit, but being psychologically crippled now with the humiliation of race classification, with pencils being run through their hair to check its texture and the colour of their fingernails examined in a crude form of pre-DNA testing to establish their racial identity and prevent them from crossing the frontier of freedom by 'trying for white'.

Then there were the fairest Cape's oak-lined avenues and gracious old Dutch gabled mansions, five-star hotels, great wine estates and fruit orchards. And slums. Run-down townships for the hapless sub-groups on the sandy flats outside the city, cold and drenched during the winter rainfall season.

Thus the beloved country. Welcome home.

As the ship lay berthed in Cape Town before sailing up the coast, I took the opportunity to call on the two local English daily newspapers, the *Cape Times* and the *Cape Argus*. A job on either would have been the cherry on the top of my great adventure, for Cape Town was my first choice of a city in which to settle and build my career. But alas, it was not to be. Both papers told me they had recently topped up their staffs with journalists more ex-perienced than I. However, the editor of the *Cape Argus*, Maurice Broughton, gave me a form to fill in which he promised to circu-late through the extensive network of the Argus Company to see whether any of its other papers might have a position to offer me.

So I sailed on, downcast once again and by now in danger of developing a rejection complex. The *Athlone Castle* made its leisurely way up the east coast, to Port Elizabeth then East London, from where we drove back to Hotfire. There life seemed to have frozen in time: Mbhuti, Daisy, Ncweniso, Tintele, No-Me, all the people of my childhood were still there, older now but still brim-ming with warmth as they welcomed the now adult 'Baas Allister' back home.

But it was an uncomfortable time. I needed a job. I wanted desperately to get back into journalism, but how was I to do it? Remote Hotfire was hardly a satisfactory base from which to con-duct a nationwide job-hunting operation. And then one day there arrived in the post a letter for me from the Argus Company. Maurice Broughton had been true to his word. The letter informed me that the Rhodesian Printing and Publishing Company, a subsidi-ary of the Argus Group, could offer me a job as a reporter on *The Chronicle* in Bulawayo, Southern Rhodesia. It was a country that had barely featured in my mind in any form, least of all as a place in which to live and work. But I accepted with alacrity.

* * *

AS THE TRAIN clattered northwards, I warmed to the idea of working in Southern Rhodesia. Although I had paid little attention to it at the time, a whole new country had been established in that part of central Africa while I was in Britain. The British colonies of

Southern Rhodesia, Northern Rhodesia and Nyasaland had been drawn together into what was called the Federation of Rhodesia and Nyasaland, with the aim of enabling it to move gradually towards majority rule and eventual independence by way of a qualified franchise system based on property and income.

The idea excited me. Here surely was a rational alternative to South Africa's apartheid system. If one confronted Verwoerd's contention that there were only two ways to end racial discrimination in South Africa, either through total separation or full racial integration, then the Federation was a possible third way – a Fabian process of overcoming white resistance by allowing integration to take place gradually. It would be fascinating to work in the new country and watch that process evolve.

I was wrong, of course. The Federation turned out to be a political disaster and I was not long into my stint at *The Chronicle* in Bulawayo before I found out why. The whites of Southern Rhodesia, nearly all migrants from Britain, were too stubborn and every bit as racist as the Afrikaners of South Africa, whom they condescendingly despised in a parallel strand of intra-ethnic prejudice, while the blacks, fired up by the spirit of African nationalism being fanned by Kwame Nkrumah in West Africa, were too impatient. In that atmosphere gradualism didn't stand a chance.

This, then, was the turbulent new country into which I plunged at the age of 22. It had been established only a few months before my arrival after three years of tough negotiations. It was to last only ten years before it disintegrated, breaking up into three separate countries – Northern Rhodesia becoming Zambia and Nyasaland becoming Malawi, while Southern Rhodesia tried to cling to its system of white minority rule with snail-paced black evolution for as long as possible.

My new employers had booked a room for me at a comfortable downtown hotel called the White House, but I soon rented a room at a more affordable sum from the fashion editor of *The Chronicle*, Eileen Simpson, a vivacious, thirtysomething woman who lived in a sprawling bungalow with her older husband. And I bought a car, a new Morris Minor.

Thus equipped, I settled into my new job at what was a

remarkable newspaper. Bulawayo was the second largest city in Southern Rhodesia after Salisbury, the capital of the Federation, but it was hardly what one would call a bustling metropolis. It had a frontier feel about it, as though it had recently been carved out of the African bush, which is precisely what it was. Bulawayo was established in the 1840s by King Lobengula of the Ndebele people, whose father, Mzilikazi, had founded the Ndebele nation after breaking away from King Shaka's mighty Zulu empire in South Africa and taking his warrior followers up over the Dragon Mountains to the highveld, where the Afrikaner Great Trek leader, Hendrik Potgieter, in turn drove him further northwards across the Limpopo River. Forty years later, troops of Cecil Rhodes' British South Africa Chartered Company, thrusting northwards in their visionary boss's great imperial quest, drove Lobengula out of Bulawayo during the Ndebele War of 1863 and established an initial colonial capital there.

Aside from a statue of Rhodes commanding the central city square, the layout of Bulawayo exudes the pioneering spirit that established it. Its streets were laid out wide enough for a span of 12 oxen, harnessed in pairs and drawing a four-wheeled wagon, to negotiate a U-turn. Strikingly, too, the streets have no gutters or underground drainage system, only sweeping dips at each side and across each intersection, which prove hopelessly unable to cope with the floodwaters disgorged by Bulawayo's torrential summer rainstorms. It became an annual feature in those days for *The Chronicle* to publish a front-page picture of a staff member swimming down Main Street after a November afternoon thunderstorm.

I did not find Bulawayo a stimulating city. The complex politics of the newly established Federation were fascinating, certainly, but I found the city itself provincial and dull. To be fair, for a young man returning from two hyper-stimulating years in London, just about anywhere I might have landed would have left me feeling decompressed. There were no theatres, music halls or art galleries, and precious little in the way of simulating conversation with people my own age. In later years I was to become deeply interested and involved in the region's convulsive politics, both personally and journalistically, but back then I guess it was a case of being in the wrong place at the wrong time. For me it was a social desert. In the year I spent in Southern Rhodesia I made no friends of my own age. I never had a single date.

My life at the newspaper, however, was altogether different. Not only was it wonderful to get back into my career as a journalist, but I also found my colleagues at the paper to be at a level well beyond my expectations. One doesn't expect to find a cracker-jack staff on a paper the size of *The Chronicle* in a two-horse town like Bulawayo, but the very factors that had made my job-hunting efforts in London so frustrating had resulted in a skills boom here. Experienced journalists who had been unable to find jobs in Fleet Street and even the major provincial papers in Britain's depressed post-war economy had migrated in considerable numbers to the 'colonies', mainly Australia, Canada and New Zealand, but some to Southern Rhodesia as well. So ironically I found myself here in the bush of Central Africa working alongside some of the talent I had so longed to encounter in London.

Chief among these was George Bishop, a Reuters veteran in his mid-forties who had worked as a war correspondent through-out the North African desert campaigns, then decided after the war to seek a more relaxed lifestyle in remote Rhodesia. But it didn't last. Bulawayo was ultimately too parochial for George. He began to hanker after the more vibrant atmosphere of the Reuters newsroom in London – the greatest engine room of news in the world at that time – but not before he had spent a year as my friend and mentor.

The only weak spot was at the top, in the form of an insipid editor named Ralph Peckover, whose only merit was that we seldom saw him. He was so overshadowed by his staff that he wisely kept out of the way and left them to get the paper out each day. My first encounter with Peckover was when I was taken to meet him on my arrival. He welcomed me and promptly informed me that in terms of company rules I could not be promoted nor receive a salary increase until I presented a shorthand certificate showing I was capable of taking notes at 120 words a minute. That is verbatim speed, required of *Hansard* recorders in most par-liaments. A tall order, and it came as a bit of a shock to me since there had been no mention of such a requirement in the letter offering me the job. But I said nothing. I enrolled in a shorthand class and over the next six months spent many hours each day practising the craft in my off-hours, hating every minute of it but in the end feeling grateful for a skill that serves me well to this day, the advent of tape recorders and other electronic gadgetry notwithstanding. When eventually I presented that damn certificate to the management I received a pro forma congratulatory note from Peckover informing me that I would receive an increase of £10 to put me on a salary of £40 a month, and that I would now be transferred to the sub-editors' room – where, of course, shorthand is not required.

Looking back on my Federation days, a handful of reporting assignments come to mind. The most vivid was of a Sunday when I was the only reporter on duty and George Bishop was acting news editor for the day. George was an obsessive vintage car enthusiast and he had spotted a magnificently restored 1920s Bentley parked in the street that morning. I sat there in the newsroom listening raptly to him extolling the merits of this British automotive masterpiece. George was a great raconteur and it was absorbing stuff, to the extent that both reporter and mentor failed to watch the clock or check the news diary, which would have reminded us that the Archbishop of Canterbury, Geoffrey Fisher, was to preach in the pro-cathedral that morning. It was already 11 am. In our preoccupation with George's obsession we had missed it. The Archbishop was the supreme prelate of the Anglican Church throughout the world. This was like a journalist in a Catholic country forgetting to report a papal visit. Surely a career disaster.

George, as always, was unflappable. 'Find out where he's going next,' he said, 'that'll be the real story.'

Feeling mortified, I hastened to the pro-cathedral where I found a kind clergyman who gave me a text of the Archbishop's sermon. I spotted a passage in it about the miracle of the Gadarene swine, about which I knew nothing but which the clergyman told me had been the central theme of the sermon. 'It was very good. Very appropriate,' he said. I decided to look up the biblical text later, but to hurry now to catch up with the prelate who I was told had gone to one of the city's black townships.

I found him there, in a dust-blown street among the rickety township shacks, with chickens, piglets and children scurrying around him. And dogs. The scrawny, unidentifiable mongrels that seem to inhabit every township throughout the African continent. His Lordship, in his grand clerical outfit, looked incongruous in this jam-packed place of poverty, smoke and dust, yet he seemed at ease. He chatted with the locals, asked the children about their schooling and ignored the chickens as they scratched in the dirt at his feet. I followed him for about an hour gathering as much local colour as I could, and then hurried back to the office to compose a news report as best I could.

I don't remember precisely how I knitted that desperate story together, except that I took the theme of how the supreme prelate of the Church of England, who only a year before had crowned the new Queen of this new country, had spent the day in Bulawayo communing across the full spectrum of its people, from the city notables in the pro-cathedral to the poorest of the black masses in the townships, symbolising the fact that the future of both depended on their being able to come together into a single nationhood. I then suggested, rather presumptuously I fear, that the Archbishop's message to both was the same, embodied in that parable about the Gadarene swine – which, on my hasty reading of the text, was about spreading the spirit of compassion and of Christian unity. Following George's advice, I then spiced up the story with as much detail about the township as I could and handed him the finished product.

George ran his expert eye over it swiftly. 'Nice job,' he murmured with a wry smile as he pushed it through to the sub-editors' room. Next day it was the paper's front-page lead.

Not long after this, and still before I was transferred into the subs' room, I was assigned to the paper's regional bureau in the Midlands town of Gwelo (now called Gweru) for two months. The most notable event during my two months in the Midlands was a meeting with the redoubtable Ian Smith, Rhodesia's nemesis who became first the hero of the country's white resistance to black rule then, inevitably, the agent of its downfall. He was a farmer in the Selukwe district, which fell in my large parish, and had won the Midlands seat in the Federal Parliament in the new country's first general election a few months earlier, having previously been a member of the Southern Rhodesian Legislative Assembly. Smith was a tall, lean man with a slightly scarred face, having been shot down twice as a fighter pilot with the Royal Air Force in the Second World War. He was just 35 years old. I drove to Selukwe (now called Shurugwi) to hear him deliver his first report-back speech to his constituents. It was an unmemorable speech: Smith was never a great orator, nor a great intellect, despite the adoration he was able to evoke from his white settler followers as a result of his implacable determination and, let it be acknowledged, considerable courage. He was a man prepared to stand up against the world. But all I remember of that first encounter these many years later was the ugly intonation of his flat vowels.

The most curious feature of my sojourn in Southern Rhodesia was that I never met Smith's diametric opposite, Sir Garfield Todd, who was Prime Minister of the territory at the time, nor his doughty daughter, Judith, who was later to become a journalist, a friend and something of a political collaborator in the affairs of our neighbouring countries. Of course Judy was only 12 years old at the time, the family was based in Salisbury, and one doesn't readily bump into prime ministers in the street. I knew all about Todd, of course, and admired him greatly. Indeed I think he was arguably the most progressive and imaginative white leader ever to step onto an African political stage. Which meant, of course, that the white Rhodesians considered him a dangerous radical.

Todd was born in New Zealand and immigrated to Southern Rhodesia as a Protestant missionary at an early age. Judith was born there two years later. Todd and his wife, Grace, a teacher, promptly built a school at their Dadaya Mission where together, over the following years, they delivered babies, tended to the sick and laid the foundations of what, to this day, is still the best education system in the whole of sub-Saharan Africa. Todd was obsessed with the importance of education as the basis for building a successful society, something the new South Africa has still not recognised more than 20 years after liberation. Scores of black Zimbabwean leaders were graduates of the Dadaya School and a network of others that the Todds established.

Todd became Prime Minister of Southern Rhodesia in 1953 when the long-serving Sir Godfrey Huggins moved up to become the Federal premier. It was in that role that Todd showed his true liberal colours, doubling the number of black schools in the territory and giving government grants to missionary-run schools to introduce secondary schooling and pre-university courses for blacks. He also ensured elementary education for every black child, allowed multiracial trade unions and introduced land husbandry in the black tribal trust lands. The deeply conservative white Rhodesians objected to this, and their resentment reached a peak a few years later when Todd proposed a revision of the franchise qualification to allow an additional 6000 to 10000 blacks onto the voters' roll. Although this would still have been only a fifth of the number of white voters, Todd's Cabinet resigned *en bloc*, forcing him from power. He was succeeded by the tentative Edgar Whitehead, who in turn went on to lose the premiership to the hardline Ian Smith who, as the Federation headed for collapse, had formed the right-wing Rhodesian Front.

The rejection of Todd goes to the heart of why the Federation project failed. Fewer than 450 African electors participated in the new country's inaugural election in December 1953 compared with nearly 50000 whites, making Todd realise that unless more Africans were able to participate in the political process, especially in the white bastion of Southern Rhodesia for which he was responsible, the federal experiment would never be able to withstand the mounting pressure for black-ruled independence in the two northern territories. They would feel they were being held hostage by the white south. But such was the hostility to black advancement among the white Southern Rhodesians that they found Todd's modest proposal too outrageous even to be considered.

When I paid my first visit as a journalist to the South African Parliament in the same year Todd was dumped by his party, the doyenne of white liberals in that legislature, Margaret Ballinger, put an interesting hypothetical point to me in conversation. Noting that Smuts' United Party had been defeated by the narrow margin of only five seats while gaining a majority of the overall national seats in the 1948 general election, she suggested that had the marginal vote gone the other way, with Smuts winning by a mere five seats, South Africa might never have been subjected to the odious policy of apartheid. Because, she conjectured, the wake-up call would have prompted Smuts to open South Africa to large-scale post-war immigration, especially from Britain, at a time when settlers could acquire full citizenship and voting rights in two years. The Afrikaner majority would have been swamped, Ballinger contended, and the National Party would never have achieved power to implement its apartheid policy.

An interesting speculative point, to be sure, but I begged to differ with the redoubtable Ballinger. From my experience in the Federation, I told her, I didn't believe there was any material difference between the English whites of Rhodesia and the Afrikaners of South Africa when it came to resisting black political advancement. The terminology they used might be different and the word apartheid might never have gained currency, but the results would have been the same. I noted that the United Party's declared policy was 'white leadership with justice' and that its leaders spoke of treating black people 'more fairly', but 'fairness' in no way meant 'equality'. White leadership meant precisely what it said.

My stint in Bulawayo came to an abrupt end when, after a trip to the Victoria Falls and up the Zambezi Valley over the Rhodes and Founders long weekend in July 1955, I contracted malaria. The small party I was with slept in the open, thinking it safe because this was mid-winter, but the dreaded *Anopheles* mosquito got me nonetheless. For three weeks I was seriously ill, with temperatures ranging up to 105 °F, accompanied by shaking, chills, heavy night sweats, horrible headaches and spasms of severe vomiting. I was a skinny fellow in those days and by the time the fever passed I was positively skeletal. My doctor prescribed a month's holiday before resuming work, which the paper readily granted. So with due care and many rests, I drove my little Morris Minor the 1 750 km back to Hotfire.

It was while I was recuperating on the farm that my caring mother, backed up by the family doctor, suggested it might be wise for me to leave Southern Rhodesia since another attack of malaria come the summer might be permanently harmful. Why not try getting a job at the *Daily Dispatch* in nearby East London? I have no doubt my parents' main motive was to get me nearer home, but since I had not really been happy in Bulawayo I decided to give it a shot. So I phoned the Dispatch and made an appointment to see the editor, Vernon 'Jock' Barber.

Barber was a crusty Yorkshireman, tough and gregarious, with a taste for fine whisky, which he was sometimes inclined to over-indulge. He was also a fine writer, producing some of the most lucid editorials I have read anywhere. He greeted me warmly, expressed appreciation for some of the articles I had sent the paper from Britain, told me he thought I would do well on the Dispatch, and offered me a job as a sub-editor at £80 a month − exactly double what I was earning on *The Chronicle*. I was taken aback but obviously delighted, and accepted on the spot. He wanted me to start right away, but I told him I had first to return to Bulawayo to work out a month's notice, to which he reluctantly agreed.

The drive back to Bulawayo was tedious, the arrival a shock. I typed out my letter of resignation and went to hand it to Peckover personally and thank him for what had been a stimulating year on his paper. But instead of wishing me well he exploded with rage. Literally shaking with fury, he accused me of abusing his generosity in giving me sick leave by going off job-hunting. When I protested that I felt I had every right to accept another job at double what he was paying me, and that in any case I had been given medical advice to leave Southern Rhodesia and not risk contracting another bout of malaria, he called me an 'impudent young puppy' for arguing with him. I became flustered and tried to apologise, assuring him I would work out my month's notice as required by my contract, but he told me bluntly that I should rather leave immediately and he would make sure I never worked for any Argus newspaper again. It was one of the most bewildering, and I still think most disgraceful, encounters with a superior I was to have in all my long career.

* * *

MOVING TO East London was really a homecoming. Back to the eastern Cape, to the familiarity of the old frontier with its flat-vowelled accents and the clicks of the isiXhosa language. Comfortable after the years of wandering. And it was only a 250-km drive back to Hotfire, so I was able to go home for occasional weekends.

I slipped back easily into the regional lifestyle, meeting up again with old school and sporting friends. Mike Wild, an old chum from the Greydeane Cricket Club in Queenstown, had made it into the Border provincial team and persuaded me to join his Bohemians' Club, which I did. Oswald 'Ossie' Dawson, who had been in Allan Melville's first post-war Springbok team to tour England in 1947 and Dudley Nourse's the following year, was our captain, a wonderfully fluent batsman and medium-paced bowler. Ralph 'Ricey' Phillips, a hard-hitting left-hander who had been the Border team's star batsman for years, was also a member. I became a regular opening batsman in the club's first team, but never quite recovered my earlier form: night work, which my job at the *Daily Dispatch* involved, is not conducive to sporting performance. Still, it was great to be back in the game I loved so much.

With my enlarged salary inducing a sense of affluence, I rented a neat bachelor flat in a seafront suburb near the city's premier beach and set about expressing my new-found interest in modern art, painting copies of an amoebic Joan Miró and Georges Rouault's *The Old King* as murals. Not great works of art, to be sure, but they certainly were colourful and I felt they added a Bohemian touch to my abode.

My social life also underwent a revival after the year of drought in Rhodesia as I reconnected with old friends and quickly built a new network. In those years social life for the young, in what might be euphemistically described as a low-pressure city with a high percentage of retirees, was the Windsor Bowl, a dance hall and restaurant in the beachfront Windsor Hotel. That is where the young couples, particularly from the many sports clubs, gathered on Saturday evenings to dine and dance to a fine five-piece band.

And so it came about that one Saturday morning, soon after my arrival, Mike Wild made a portentous proposal. 'Let's go look for some girls,' he suggested, noting that there was a speedboat regatta on the Buffalo River that afternoon and we were sure to meet up with some possible partners to go dancing at the Windsor Bowl that night.

Being a man of some experience in such matters, he turned out to be on target. At the riverbank we soon came upon two girls, one of whom I knew: Ann Thomas, a keen cricket follower and herself a member of the provincial women's cricket team. With her was a friend, Mary Rowe, a blonde woman with a strong, handsome face and a wicked sense of humour, to whom I was immediately attracted. So began, slowly at first, a two-year romance that marked my sojourn on the *Daily Dispatch* as the happiest and most carefree of my youth, culminating in Mary becoming my wife and joining me as an enthusiastic partner in an eventful, stimulating phase of our lives.

* * *

THE *DAILY DISPATCH* is a venerable institution in the Eastern Cape. It was founded as a weekly in 1872, a year before East London became a municipality, so the paper is actually older than the city it serves. Around the turn of the century, as the Anglo-Boer War ended, it was acquired by the scion of a British military family, Sir Charles Crewe, who bought it in partnership with some colleagues, then established the Charles Crewe Trust that effectively controlled the paper and influenced its character for the next three-quarters of a century. Sir Charles was a protégé and close friend of one of South Africa's most controversial figures, Dr Leander Starr Jameson, who instigated the botched Jameson Raid of 1895-96, one of the triggers of the Anglo-Boer War.

This history left its mark on the paper. When I arrived there to take up my new job half a century later there was still a whiff of jingoism in the corridors. The paper still flew only the Union Jack from its flagpole, and there was a distinct air of bellicose excitement in the newsroom during the Suez Crisis of 1956, when Britain and France occupied the Canal Zone after the upstart Colonel Gamal Abdel Nasser had nationalised the Suez Canal – and concomitant dismay when the United States forced the old imperialist powers to withdraw. Still, Rhodes had lent the paper some money to buy printing equipment on condition it maintained a policy of 'fairness to all races', probably a gesture of token paternalism at the time but which proved useful in a later phase of the paper's evolution.

It was a staid newspaper when I entered its sub-editors' department. Until a few months before, it had carried only advertisements on its front page, perhaps the last substantial daily in the world still to do so, with the main news, mainly international news with a bias towards British affairs, carried on what was called the cable page, opposite the leader page deep inside the newspaper. Its typography was also old-fashioned. But there were some fine journalists on the staff, all working under varying degrees of frustration, and an array of colourful characters.

The chief sub-editor, George Farr, my immediate boss, was a warm, intelligent man given to moments of excitability under stress, which tend to be frequent at that production end of the newspapering process. He was a veteran of the Second World War and a decorated hero, having been awarded the Military Cross for gallantry during the fall of Tobruk in June 1942, when the mainly South African garrison of the Libyan port city was overwhelmed and surrendered to Erwin Rommel's Afrika Korps. During his years as a prisoner of war, George found himself 'in the bag' with Sir De Villiers Graaff, later to become the long-serving leader of the opposition United Party. Graaff was the tall, good-looking scion of a wealthy, politicised Afrikaner family who had studied law at Oxford and Leiden and played cricket for Western Province. George found him an inspirational figure in the prison camp and became a devoted supporter, which strengthened the Dispatch's natural inclination to support the United Party in its opposition to apartheid but its profound confusion, shared by most English-speaking South Africans, about what to put in its place.

Another of George's compatriots 'in the bag' was the *Daily Dispatch*'s printing works foreman, Ossie Kershaw, a rough-voiced character with blunt mannerisms. Ossie had been a sergeant, and so retained a measure of military deference in his dealings with George, always addressing him as 'Mister Farr', or even 'Sir', even though there was traditionally some tension between printers and sub-editors when it came to getting the paper out on time. This was aggravated when the editor sometimes imbibed a little too much of his favourite beverage and ran late with his leading article, which compelled Ossie to appeal to George for help in getting the editor to deliver.

So it came to pass one memorable evening when, with the leader page already well past deadline, Ossie entered the subs' room in his ink-stained overalls and came to attention in front of George Farr's desk. 'Mister Farr,' he said in a voice of parade-ground formality. 'We have a problem, sir. The editor has puked on the leader and we can't read it. Can you please write us another one.'

True to his military discipline, George rose silently from his desk, asked his deputy to take charge for a while, and left the room to find a typewriter, think of a subject and knock out a leading article as fast as he could. A real trooper, one might say. His reward came years later when, at a tempestuous time in the paper's history, he became editor himself and held things together until his retirement after half a century of service.

My relationship with Mary steadily deepened during my two years at the Dispatch. She was attractive and lively and we had a lot of fun together. Her parents, Jim and Edith, had emigrated from Cornwall to join an older brother of Jim's and establish a general trading store in the rural northern town of Schweizer-Reneke. There they had prospered until taking early retirement to settle in East London. Schweizer-Reneke being a solidly Afrikaans-speaking *platteland* town, Mary had gone to an Afrikaans-medium primary school, then completed her education at an English-medium secondary school in East London. As a result she was fluently bilingual, which made her an ideal civil service employee. When I met her she had a senior position in the East London branch of the South African Revenue Service. I found her fluency in Afrikaans and her circle of Afrikaner friends helpful in developing my own competence in the language, which

*Donald Woods and I with our girlfriends, Wendy Bruce and Mary
Rowe, at the Windsor Bowl nightclub in East London. Donald
and I were both working on the* Daily Dispatch *at the time.*

*Mary and I cutting our wedding cake,
East London, December 1957.*

was to prove invaluable when I later became a political correspondent covering a Parliament where debates and interviews were predominantly in Afrikaans.

Our courtship was joyful and conventional and although we were still young – both 24 – we decided to get married. The plan was to set sail immediately for England, where I could meet Mary's Cornish relatives, whom she had encountered only once before, and then head for London where, with greater experience under my belt, I was determined to break into Fleet Street.

Before we left, though, two more figures who were to play major roles in our lives joined the staff – John Ryan and Donald Woods. John was one of the finest writers of the English language I have encountered in any newsroom and a man I was later to engage as an assistant when I became an editor, while Donald was the most kaleidoscopically talented individual I have known, a gregarious, light-hearted entertainer who became a deadly serious political player. He could have made a living as a virtuoso stage performer, a mimic and stand-up comedian who wrote and published his own scripts, and sang his own satirical songs in a Victor Borge style to his own piano accompaniment. Yet he chose the serious profession of journalism after dropping out of law school and making a quixotic run for Parliament as a candidate for the diminutive Federal Party while still in his early twenties. Donald's career on the Dispatch was meteoric. He became its political correspondent in his third year and its editor at age 31. In his 12 years as editor, Donald transformed the staid old frontier paper into one of the most dynamic and progressive in the country, ultimately to the point of activism that pitched both it and himself into a head-on collision with the apartheid government, bringing them both pain and international acclaim. Donald was banned and went into exile in Britain with his family, where he continued his anti-apartheid campaigning and Queen Elizabeth II awarded him a CBE for his courage.

He was a vivid personality who became a lifelong friend and confidant, and who exercised a major influence on me with his daring.

CHAPTER SEVEN

Realising a Dream

MY SECOND VISIT to London was very different from the first. This time I went with a focused ambition: to get that job in a major Fleet Street newsroom. And this time I made it, though not immediately. It was different, too, in that the only child who had so longed for a companion now had one in his wonderfully warm and attractive new wife. There can be few things more romantic than a sea-cruise honeymoon, so Mary and I arrived in London in the glow of young love.

First we took the train to Cornwall for me to meet Mary's relatives in the quaint farming village of Perranuthnoe, near Penzance, where Mary herself was born after her mother had returned home for the confinement. We spent two cheerful weeks there, meeting her cousins and aunts and doing the tourist thing.

While there I also bought a 1939 MG hardtop, a handsome beast of a car, black with big silver headlamps and a throaty exhaust. Its engine suffered from the weariness of age and it had difficulty reaching 60 miles an hour, but the look and sound of it made me feel sporty, so I bought a tweed cap and scarf to go with it. We drove back to London in this proud new acquisition where we joined the Overseas Visitors' Club, run by an enterprising South African named Max Wilson, which found us a bedsitter in Earl's Court.

Mary, with her civil service contacts, quickly landed a good job at South Africa House, our country's High Commission on Trafalgar Square, while I searched for suburban newspaper jobs, having decided this time to establish myself first on one of them and only then to resume the task of pounding on Fleet Street doors. The search brought me in contact with the Richards brothers, Derek and James, who had inherited a small grocery store from their parents in the London suburb of Uxbridge. They decided to turn the building into a newsroom to produce a chain of papers covering Uxbridge and the neighbouring suburbs of Hillingdon and Ruislip, and as far as Heathrow Airport.

Derek had worked on the *Daily Express* and James on the *Daily Mirror*, so both were steeped in the culture of Fleet Street and sought to bring its slick style of prose and layout to the local scene. That meant trying to pack the maximum amount of punch into mundane local events. James in particular was forever striving for a front-page attention-grabber – what he delicately called a 'holy shit!' headline – that would stop the passing reader in his tracks. Thus I recall one bleak week when the staff of the *Ruislip Post* had failed to come up with anything that would support such excitation.

'Call the ambulance and fire station people one more time,' James ordered in exasperation.

The reporter did so. 'Still nothing, sir,' he responded. 'The fire station says there've just been a few false alarms. Small fires in dustbins, that sort of stuff.'

'Okay, thanks,' said James, settling himself purposefully behind his old Underwood typewriter and beginning to hammer away at the keyboard. The story that flowed out stitched together an alarming tale of the remarkable number of fires that had erupted over the past week in the suburb's public dustbins, giving at least some semblance of substance to the arresting banner: 'Is there a firebug in Ruislip?'

Yet there is always something new to be learned wherever you are. One of the more intriguing features the Weekly Post papers ran was to pick a suburban street at random, then to interview everyone living there and write a feature about who they were and what they did. It was a striking lesson in discovering that just about everyone on this earth has a fascinating story to tell. Thus I discovered the designer of the Vulcan delta-wing bomber, used by the Royal Air Force at the time, living as a pauper in a shack in someone's backyard; and a philosophical young mother grappling with the fact that she had just discovered her baby was born blind.

Our social lives revolved around friends old and new. Donald Woods and John Ryan arrived from the *Daily Dispatch* a few months after we had settled in, and they quickly turned our bedsitter into a base where they could cadge a drink and a meal. Roy Instrell, a colleague from *The Chronicle* in Bulawayo, had returned to the *Bournemouth Times*, where he was welcomed home as something of an elder statesman. Through him, Mary and I met a trio of his young protégés who had come to London competing with each other to see who could be the first to break into Fleet Street. The winner was a wild, heavily accented young Scotsman named Gordon Williams, who landed a job on *The Boy's Own Paper*. The other competitors, Michael Clayton and Ian Wooldridge, sniffed at this, not least because they reckoned their friend, who was something of a Brendan Behan character, was hardly an appropriate figure to be working on a paper whose declared purpose was to urge its young readers 'to lead clean, manly and Christian lives'.[1] But despite his bacchanalian habits, Gordon went on to outshine his Bournemouth colleagues, becoming the author of more than 20 novels.

Not that his friends did badly. Michael Clayton was the antithesis of Gordon Williams in every way – tall, very English-accented and with the aloof air of a country squire. He became a hard-news reporter on the London *Evening News*. In those pre-digital days this was one of the toughest jobs in journalism, since beating the opposition in getting the news out fast through rapidly sequenced editions was the key to survival. That meant dictating reports over the telephone directly into the production system, rather than taking the time to write and polish them.

Ian Wooldridge's passion was sport. When I first met him he had just made his breakthrough to become a cricket writer for the *News Chronicle*. He was to rise meteorically to become one of

Britain's leading sportswriters, receiving the British Sportswriter of the Year Award five times.

These men became the core of our social group during this second visit to London. Ian Wooldridge's wife, Veronica, became a close friend of Mary's, so we saw a lot of each other in carefree circumstances. Then I learned that George Bishop had also returned from Bulawayo. It was a happy reunion – and an opportune one. George had returned to Reuters, where he held a position of some influence.

'Are you working here in London?' he asked casually.

'Yes, I've got a job at the *Uxbridge Post*,' I replied.

'What the hell is that?' It wasn't so much a question as an exclamation. And then: 'Why don't you come to Reuters?' Just like that, as though it was simply a matter of popping around and finding a seat.

But as the old adage goes, it's not what you know but who you know that matters. After all those months and years and hopes and frustrations, my entry into Fleet Street was as smooth and easy as if George had simply opened the door and invited me in. He phoned me a week later and told me to go to the Reuters building and see the head of the newsroom. Which I did – to be promptly offered a job. No trial, no test, nothing. As I made the move, Donald Woods and John Ryan moved seamlessly into jobs on the Weekly Post. Easy when you know how.

* * *

IT WOULD BE difficult to exaggerate how pleased and fulfilled I felt as I caught the Tube to Blackfriars Station that first day and made my way up that fascinating street to the broad marble portals of the Reuters building. The lift to the fourth floor and there I was, in the heart of one of the world's great newsrooms. A wide space occupying the entire floor; a news desk for every continent; the world in one room with the ceaseless chatter of hundreds of telex machines. There was an atmosphere of orderly urgency, for this was a place where time mattered all the time; every minute, every second, was deadline time somewhere in the world. A place that never slept, night or day, high days or holidays, wartime or peacetime – all were the same as shifts came and went, keeping the news cycle going.

I was shown to the central desk, the hub where the news flowed in from all parts of the world to be selected and edited and distributed to all the papers in Britain, including Fleet Street itself. That was where I was to work for the next 18 months, working in shifts, sometimes from midnight to 8 am. It was an invigorating place, with a sense of global wakefulness. It was also rigorous. Reuters had, and still has, an obsession with accuracy and objectivity. I still aspire to both, although I believe the latter is not strictly achievable since every individual views events through an inbuilt cultural and personal prism, which is bound to influence one's judgment on the relative importance of events. Still, it is a good injunction to pin up on newsroom notice boards, although I believe the most one can realistically hope for is fairness. *Audi alteram partem*, or 'hear the other side', is the old Roman requirement for a fair legal hearing. It is an appropriate slogan for journalists too. As for accuracy, Reuters was equipped with what must surely be the most remarkable news library ever compiled. In this pre-Google era it was a place where a copy editor, such as I was, could phone through, ask for a fact check, and have it provided almost immediately. For more complex inquiries, a relevant file would be sent to you by hand within minutes. I never found the likes of it again, but the principle of the rigour it underpinned has remained with me ever since.

Reuters is also a venerable place, rich in its own history as well as that which it records day by day. It was the world's first news agency, founded by a German, Paul Reuter, in 1851. Reuter, who lived in Berlin, began by sending financial news from continental Europe to London by homing pigeon. Later he installed the electric telegraph. In the annals of my profession, Reuters was the first to report news scoops from abroad, the most famous being the assassination of Abraham Lincoln in 1865. The story, as told to me, was that Reuters' New York correspondent chartered a tug and raced out into the East River to fling his dispatch aboard the mailship as it was pulling out of its berth for its voyage to Britain. The result was a weeklong scoop on the story in Britain.

Part of the fascination of that desk was finding myself working alongside correspondents who had returned home from foreign postings for a year or two before being given another posting. So I would find myself chatting to correspondents back from Washington, Bonn, Paris, Rome, Tokyo and, most exotic of all, Peking and Moscow. It triggered romantic notions of possibly heading in that career direction myself one day.

One of the closest friends I made at that time was Don Dallas, who had been Reuters' correspondent in Moscow during the toughest years of the Stalin dictatorship and the Cold War. He gave me an autographed copy of a book he had written about his experiences in the Soviet capital, titled *Dateline Moscow*, describing the problems Western journalists faced in trying to squeeze information out of Soviet officialdom. Don was passionate about the skills required to circumvent state censorship, and later became involved in training programmes to impart those skills to young journalists working in Africa and Asia. He could talk endlessly on the subject of Kremlinology: 'You must understand the ideology thoroughly,' he told me, 'and then listen for small deviations which may offer a clue as to what is happening in the secret conclaves where the decisions are made.' It turned out to be invaluable advice for me after I returned to become a political correspondent in South Africa, listening intently for any new shades of meaning in Verwoerd's long ideological perorations. I called it 'Apartheidology'.

The range of stories I found myself handling on all manner of subjects from all parts of the world fascinated and educated me. As I graduated to the lead-writer's slot on some of my shifts, I found myself handling running stories on major events that made the front pages of the leading Fleet Street dailies. One of these was about the revolutionary war in Cuba, where Fidel Castro and his guerrillas were fighting to overthrow the dictator Fulgencio Batista. The war had been bubbling away on inside pages for the better part of five years but had not yet gripped the public imagination in Europe. There had been the story of Castro's epic journey, accompanied by his brother Raul and their friend

Che Guevara, together with 81 revolutionaries, from Veracruz in eastern Mexico to Cuba in a leaky yacht called the *Granma*. Upon landing in a mangrove swamp they came under heavy attack from Batista's military and were forced to flee into the jungles of the rugged Sierra Maestra. When the remnants of the revolutionary army, calling itself the Fourth of July Movement, reassembled there Castro found he had only 19 men left. It was a miniscule beginning for a revolution that was ultimately to have global impact.

In April 1958, I handled the story of the turnaround battle in the Sierra Maestra that was to last several days before the outcome became clear; it was like a serial thriller. Batista surrounded the mountain hideout with a force of 10000 men and began bombarding villages suspected of aiding the rebels, who at that point numbered only 300. Castro and his guerrillas naturally avoided open confrontation with the government army, a pattern of struggle that was to become familiar throughout the post-war world, from Vietnam and Algeria to South Africa. As the reports coming to me quickly revealed, it was the brutality of the Batista forces that led to their gradual undoing. The bombing of the villages caused many of the locals to join Castro, while the imprisonment and execution of reluctant fighters in the government forces led to defections from the military as well.

The reports from the front made it clear that Castro's popularity was surging, until eventually I received a dispatch stating that an entire battalion of Batista's forces had defected. From that point Castro went on the offensive. It was only a matter of time before Batista fled into exile, and after a short interlude Fidel Castro became President of Cuba.

Years later, I was to meet the bearded Castro when both of us were invited guests at Nelson Mandela's inauguration as the first President of the new South Africa in the amphitheatre of the Union Buildings in Pretoria. I still have his autograph.

Another running world story I handled at Reuters was the United States' first attempt to fire a rocket to the moon. Smarting from having been beaten in the space race by the Soviet Union's successful launching of Sputnik I on 4 October 1957, the Americans decided ten months later to try to go one better. The idea was to launch an unmanned multi-stage Pioneer rocket that would either orbit the moon or crash into it. Either way, it would be the earth's first close-up contact with a celestial body. The build-up to the launch was intense and, as the desk editor assigned to the story, I found myself handling stories not only about the engineering and scientific aspects of the probe but also the ancient mythology attributed to the moon. It was Jules Verne stuff and I loved it. Then came the big day, with all the tensions and excitement of an anticipated moment in history. The telexed reports came to me from a team of reporters at the scene and I had to knit them into 'prelim' stories for newspapers whose deadlines would arrive before the launch. Then came the countdown – and the launch itself. The great letdown. Only 77 seconds after liftoff, a mere 16 km from the launch pad, the giant rocket exploded in a sea of flame. A spectacular failure, making a story almost as dramatic as a successful launch might have been. Again I had to scramble to package the whole story into a single lead story, which indeed made the page-one lead in many British newspapers.

Social life trotted along enjoyably. Mary and I were blissfully happy, and we began talking about the future. Should I aim at becoming a foreign correspondent? We discussed the idea with George Bishop, who encouraged us to think in that direction. Fascinated by Don Dallas's anecdotes. I even attempted the daunting task of trying to learn Russian.

But it was not to be. Inevitably there came a delicate moment when Mary told me, softly, a little hesitantly, that, well, she had missed a period. We waited another month, and when it seemed clear she had missed another she went to the nearest National Health Service clinic and received the confirmation. She was pregnant. As all young couples know, if marriage is a life-changing experience, the arrival of that first baby is an even bigger one.

Simon Patrick Sparks was born at St Mary Abbot's Hospital in Kensington, once a workhouse with a chapel attached. There were 18 new moms in the maternity ward, of all nationalities and races, with their squalling babies in cribs attached to the foot of each bed. Our new arrival behaved impeccably in the hospital, but perversely on his first day home announced himself to be a colicky baby. He slept all day and screamed in distress all night. We were rookie parents and didn't know what to do, until some of my mature colleagues at Reuters introduced us to the work of Dr Benjamin Spock, to whom I shall be eternally grateful.

But it was clearly decision time. We obviously couldn't continue living in our bedsitter; the idea of becoming a foreign correspondent faded. We decided to go back home. I sat myself down and wrote job application letters once again. This time most of the papers I wrote to responded positively, but the *Rand Daily Mail* in Johannesburg offered me £2 ten shillings a month more than the *Natal Mercury* in Durban. More enticingly, the managing editor, Ivor Benson, enthused in his responding letter about the exciting changes being made at the *Rand Daily Mail*. 'We have a new leadership here,' he wrote, 'and we don't pay stab rates. We want to hire the best staff available and we are prepared to pay to get them.'

It sounded good. I wrote back accepting. And so Mary, Simon and I set sail on the maiden voyage of the *Pendennis Castle*, with ships on all sides blasting their hooters to wish the new ocean liner well as we made our way down Southampton Water into the English Channel.

CHAPTER EIGHT

In the Engine Room

MY FIRST ENCOUNTER with the *Rand Daily Mail* was inauspicious. I had driven from Hotfire to Johannesburg, where I stayed with friends while searching for suitable family accommodation. On the last day of the month, before I was due to start work, I decided to pop in to the office to introduce myself, so I called at 47 Main Street and asked to be directed to the sub-editors' department.

I caught the lift to the first floor and made my way, as directed, to what in those days of hot-metal printing was the engine room of any newspaper. A tall, thickset man greeted me with a broad smile, introduced himself as George Davies, the chief sub-editor, and asked how he could help me. I shook his hand and gave him my name, expecting some response of recognition. There was none.

'I'm due to start work here tomorrow in your subs' room,' I explained. Another blank.

'I've just come back from London, where I was working for Reuters,' I went on, feeling that would surely trigger his memory.

'I'm afraid I know nothing about that,' Davies replied with a look of puzzlement. 'Nobody's told me anything about a new sub joining.'

'Oh, but I've got a letter of appointment from the managing editor, Mr Benson,' I replied, pulling the letter from my coat pocket.

At which point Davies burst out laughing. 'Oh, you'll find

him upstairs attending his farewell party,' he spluttered between guffaws. 'He's been fired. If you hurry you might get a drink.'

I was hardly amused, but I stumbled up the stairs where I found a small gathering in the Financial News department gathered around a lean-faced man who was thundering away about what a wretched paper this was, how it was doomed if it didn't get in line with the political mood of the country, and how he was only too glad to get away from it to involve himself in reality. Hardly encouraging stuff for an eavesdropping newcomer.

Anyway, I decided not to confront him with the problem of my appointment since he seemed unlikely to be in a position to help. So I went back to Davies. What should I do? I asked him.

He recommended I go down the passage to see the editor, Laurence Gandar. Which I did. I spoke to his secretary, a frail and protective woman called Daphne McMaster, who told me with equal puzzlement that she, too, knew nothing of my appointment to the staff. She told me the editor was busy on the phone, and would I please wait.

I felt both anxious and annoyed. Here I was, having given up the prospect of an exciting alternative career as a foreign correspondent for the world's greatest news agency, and now I was sitting here waiting like a beggar at an unknown editor's door. Damn!

When finally I was ushered into the editor's office, Gandar greeted me with a wintry smile. He told me that unfortunately he knew nothing about my appointment to the staff; Benson had never mentioned my name to him. He then began to ask me some questions about my previous experience, which I found annoying. I had set all this out in my letter of application and Benson had obviously exercised his judgment on it in making me the offer. Moreover, I had turned down several other job offers to accept this one, then travelled halfway round the world to be here. Now it seemed I was back at square one, being interviewed for a job I had already accepted. Choosing my words carefully, I hinted as much to Gandar and asked him delicately whether he thought I had a legal right to a job on his paper or not. He paused for what seemed like an eternity, then replied in a slightly dismissive way: 'Well, I suggest you come back tomorrow and we'll see whether we can fit you in somewhere.'

As it turned out I didn't see Gandar the next day, or indeed for several weeks after that. I simply walked into the subs' room, where Davies greeted me, told me to take a seat at the subs' table and start work. He said he had not heard anything from the editor but presumed I was on the staff.

Over time I was able to piece together the remarkable story of Ivor Benson's sudden demise that had so discomfited my arrival at the Mail. Gandar had known Benson some years before when both had worked on newspapers in Durban and had admired his technical skills as a copy editor and layout specialist. On being headhunted for the editor's job after spending some years out of journalism, working in the public relations department of Anglo American Corporation, Gandar decided he needed a number two who could complement his own skills as a political and public affairs analyst. So he offered Benson the job.

What he didn't know was anything about Benson's political views. It came as a shock, therefore, when he went on leave and handed over control of the paper to his managing editor for the first time, to read an editorial in the Mail extolling the insightful wisdom of the British Fascist leader, Sir Oswald Mosley, who was then visiting South Africa. Here, the editorial contended, was a highly intelligent man who had the right ideas for dealing with South Africa's vexed racial problem; the country should take serious note of the speeches he was delivering on his important visit.

Horrified, Gandar cut short his leave and hurried back to the office, where he discovered that Benson was not only an admirer of Mosley but also was actually hosting the Fascist in his own home and acting as his publicity manager. It was cause for instant dismissal.

It was a serious lapse on Gandar's part not to have checked out the viper he was clutching to his bosom. It turned out Benson had long been a disciple of Mosley, who had a notorious record as the founder of the British Union of Fascists.

How ironic that such a man should have been responsible for

bringing me to what became the most liberal paper in the country, where I was to spend the most challenging and formative phase of my life. It was a wonderfully fulfilling time, working with the best team of journalists ever assembled in South Africa, a time during which my first chilly encounter with Gandar gradually evolved into a close collaboration with him and then into a warm personal friendship. At a small memorial ceremony after his death I described Gandar as 'my intellectual father'. I was fascinated by his ability to cut to the nub of complex issues and analyse them in hard-hitting, forthright prose. He was a role model. But he was also a complex, paradoxical man – an intensely private public intellectual, a polemical journalist who made a major impact with his writing but hated the public limelight into which this inevitably thrust him. He was the greatest editor I ever worked for, perhaps the greatest South Africa has ever seen, certainly the bravest and most intellectually insightful, who elicited a passionate loyalty from a staff from whom he remained strangely remote.

In his 11 years at the helm of the *Rand Daily Mail*, Gandar transformed what had been a moderately good daily newspaper into an excellent one that won international acclaim for its bold opposition to apartheid and exposure of human rights violations by an abusive police state. By his example he also transformed the entire South African press, which in turn contributed to the remarkable transformation of the country from the outrage of apartheid to the hopefulness of a non-racial democracy. Gandar inspired a whole younger generation to follow in the tradition he had established for the next 20 years – at which point a management and board of directors, bereft of insight or imagination, closed the paper down. It was just four years before its moment of triumph, when all it had said and done over nearly four decades was vindicated in a single transformational speech by President FW de Klerk.

Yet Gandar did all this without any shred of what might be called charisma. Publicly and even within the office he was generally considered cold and reclusive. A dispassionate analytical brain. But behind that controlled exterior beat a warm heart that cared greatly about injustice and smouldered at the arrogance of authoritarianism. This side of his personality revealed itself only to a relatively small circle of friends, mostly fellow journalists, politicians and academics with whom he felt a close intellectual affinity and to which I fortunately found myself admitted fairly early in my career on the *Rand Daily Mail*. In that company Laurie Gandar would transform into an altogether different personality, along with his naturally more extrovert wife, Isobel.

* * *

I SPENT MY first two years at the *Rand Daily Mail* in the sub-editors' room, which, while being the engine room of a newspaper, is not its battlefront. It is where the thousands of reports flowing into the operation each day and deep into the night are tasted, selected, fact-checked, headlined and finally moulded into the publication that rolls off the giant presses into the delivery vans each morning. It is an exacting place, but the action is with the reporters and the specialist correspondents who work at the rockface where the news breaks.

So it turned out that I was not physically at the scene of any of the astonishing sequence of events that were to take place during those two years, setting the country on the road to a potentially catastrophic race war and dividing it politically in a way that was to challenge its people as few nations have been challenged before or since. It was a challenge to which the *Rand Daily Mail*, under Gandar's leadership, responded early and decisively and, in my view, played a pivotal role in averting that catastrophe. But in doing so it was able to triumph only posthumously. I regret not having been at the scene of the action during those momentous two years, not having met the likes of Nelson Mandela and Oliver Tambo before they went into prison and exile. But being in the engine room at the time enabled me to gain an overall perspective on what was happening and a sense of its unfolding importance. I was also fortunate to be in the engine room of a paper that was itself undergoing a historic change.

The *Rand Daily Mail* had a colourful history with some dashing editors at the helm, but it had never shown any real insight into the complex nature of the society in which it was operating. On the race issue, so glaringly the looming problem of the future, it conformed to the prejudices of its time. Black people didn't exist in its philosophy except as units of cheap labour who were both useful and a threat to white workers. The paper was literally born out of the passions of the Anglo-Boer War, and so politics was exclusively a matter of trying to reconcile the erstwhile white antagonists and of encouraging the Boers, the Afrikaners, to acknowledge the magnificence of the British Empire.

Its founding editor was a flamboyant English writer, Edgar Wallace, who had come to South Africa to report on the war, first for Reuters and then for the *Daily Mail*. Wallace made his name by achieving one of the great scoops of wartime journalism when he broke the story of the Treaty of Vereeniging a full day before it was officially announced.[1] Wallace had made a number of army friends when he first arrived at the Cape, and by chance learned that one of them would be guarding the marquee where Britain's Lord Kitchener and Lord Milner were negotiating with the Boer generals, Louis Botha and Christiaan de Wet, amid conditions of strict secrecy. Nothing was to be leaked before the release of an official statement on the outcome.

Young Wallace cut a deal with the guard, giving him three coloured handkerchiefs — one red, one white, one blue — and arranged that the man would wave one to Wallace as he rode past the camp by train between Johannesburg and Vereeniging each day. Red meant 'nothing doing', blue meant 'making progress', and white 'treaty definitely to be signed'. Wallace also devised a code, together with the *Daily Mail* office back in London, so his reports could get past Kitchener's censors. So it was that after several red handkerchiefs there came one day a blue one, then, hey presto, a white one. Wallace filed his story immediately. 'Peace absolutely assured', the *Daily Mail* trumpeted next morning. Rival papers sneered at the report, but they had to eat humble pie as the Treaty of Vereeniging was officially announced 24 hours later.[2]

Wallace returned to London to be given a hero's welcome and a lavish celebratory banquet at the Savoy Hotel by the grateful editors of the *Daily Mail*. But not before he had been collared by a wealthy financier in Johannesburg, Harry Freeman Cohen, who had decided somewhat impulsively to launch a new daily newspaper there and offered Wallace the job of editor. Wallace, just 27 years old, had never actually been inside a newspaper office, but here he was, the founding editor of a new daily newspaper destined to become the second largest in the country, at a salary of £2 000 a year, six times what the *Daily Mail* had paid him. The *Rand Daily Mail* was duly launched from a decrepit building at the corner of Rissik and Commissioner streets on 22 September 1902 – and nearly failed to complete its very first print run when a furnace powering the steam-operated press ran out of fuel. The day was saved when staffers scrambled around the shabby old building and found wooden crates which they broke up and fed into the fire.[3]

Four years later a sister paper, the *Sunday Times*, rolled off the same press, and from the start became a money-spinner that was able to cross-subsidise the *Rand Daily Mail*. But from the start, too, it was the fact that the *Rand Daily Mail* carried the bulk of the production costs for six days of the week that helped the *Sunday Times* become so profitable – a matter of contention in later years when the *Rand Daily Mail*'s trading position came under pressure.

Wallace did not stay long in his glamorous new job, in fact only nine months. As aggressive as he was as a newsman, he was equally profligate as a manager. Cohen soon became alarmed at the fat fees Wallace was paying his writers. The two men fell out and Wallace returned to the *Daily Mail* in London before devoting himself fully to writing best-selling novels. Apart from his glamorous launch, Wallace left little imprint on the *Rand Daily Mail*. When much later I found myself in that seat he had inaugurated, however, I was proud of the fact that the first editor of the paper had got the job by defiantly circumventing the censorship laws. It was a tradition I tried to uphold.

Only once in his many dispatches from the war did Wallace mention the majority population of black South Africans. Not only was this because all attention was focused on the British and Boer combatants, but also because, in the Eurocentric outlook of the time, black people did not feature in any political or intellectual context. They were merely part of the landscape. To that extent, Wallace's mere recognition of them as a potential political factor was noteworthy.

His dispatch was headlined 'The Intervening Black', and was published in London on 3 July 1901. 'Do not think that because the native has remained quiet during the war,' he wrote, 'that he has done so from ignorance of the power of his possibilities. He knows ... that he has but to issue that mystic summons to his young men; his fires are but to blaze from hill to hill; his long wail to arms has but to be shouted from kraal to kraal and the great Boer War of 1899 will be as nothing compared to the great rising of 1901 ... So far he has proved himself a worthy member of the great British household, but he has great power − and he knows it.'[4]

However, there is no record of Wallace ever having touched on the race issue in the *Rand Daily Mail*. Nor over the following 55 years did any of his successors deal with the subject in any insightful way. Indeed they emphatically endorsed the principle of segregation. When in 1909 the National Convention produced its first draft constitution to unite the two British colonies and two defeated Boer republics into a single country, the *Rand Daily Mail* strongly opposed the retention of the qualified franchise − which included a few black and coloured people who met the qualifications − that had existed in the Cape Colony since 1872. Not only did the paper object to the principle being introduced into the Transvaal province, where the *Rand Daily Mail* was published, it also insisted that the provision be scrapped in the Cape as well, to prevent the demand for it being spread to the other provinces.

When a leading Cape liberal, WPR Schreiner, warned against the new constitution drawing a vertical line separating its people on the grounds of colour into a privileged class on one side and an inferior class on the other, the then editor of the *Rand Daily Mail*, Ralph Ward Jackson, responded in a trenchant editorial warning that black and coloured people would see the concession as 'half a loaf', which would inevitably lead to a demand for the whole. 'We feel strongly,' Ward Jackson wrote, 'that the principle of discrimination between black and white is an absolutely essential principle of any successful policy for the peaceful governing of South Africa.'[5]

In the end the qualified franchise was retained in the Cape but not extended to the other three provinces.

Ward Jackson also championed what he called a 'white labour policy', a precursor of the job reservation legislation introduced years later by the apartheid regime. It meant giving preference to white workers over blacks and mixed-race people in all sectors of employment, especially skilled work, which eventually became a legalised white preserve. Ironically, this racist stance coincided with the *Rand Daily Mail*'s becoming a supporter of the new socialist Labour Party, which was also intent on safeguarding white jobs. The paper was seen as being on the side of the workers in labour disputes, with the result that when violent strikes broke out on the gold mines of the Witwatersrand the rampaging strikers burnt down *The Star* newspaper, which was perceived as being on the side of the bosses, but left the rival *Rand Daily Mail* untouched.

Even the notorious Natives' Land Act of 1913, which I have described as the 'original sin' of South African racism in that it prohibited blacks from owning land anywhere in the country, drew not a peep of criticism from the *Rand Daily Mail* or any other mainstream newspaper. This venal law was passed at a time when black agriculturalists were beginning to establish a degree of economic independence after the many disruptive wars they had faced. Its purpose was to force them off the land to provide the mass labour force needed to work the gold mines of the Witwatersrand without depriving the white farmers — a vital political constituency — of their own cheap labour demands. At a stroke, the Land Act destroyed the black peasantry and turned the entire black population into a vast labour reservoir of unskilled workers that white South Africa's nascent industrial revolution could draw on at will. The consequences of turning the country's peasantry into a mass lumpen proletariat living in shantytowns remain with us to this day.

There was a brief glimmer of light 23 years later when, after Prime Minister Barry Hertzog and General Jan Smuts had merged their rival parties under pressure of the Great Depression, Hertzog moved to use the two-thirds majority now available to him in the new United Party (UP) to amend the Cape franchise clause in the Constitution. His amendment did this by removing blacks from the common voters' roll and placing them instead on a separate roll, where they could elect three white representatives to the House of Assembly. It was a grotesquely retrogressive and illiberal act, and, although it easily passed, it inspired a passionate and prescient warning from the single most significant liberal voice of the day, Jan Hendrik Hofmeyr, who was then Minister of the Interior.

Declaring that he knew perfectly well that he was speaking against the feeling of the overwhelming majority of the House and against the feeling of the great mass of the people of the country, and that he knew his words would be dismissed as quixotic and unrealistic, Hofmeyr went on: 'This Bill says that even the most educated native shall never have political equality with even the least educated and the least cultured white or coloured man. This Bill says to these educated natives: "There is no room for you, you must be driven back upon your own people." But we drive them back in hostility and disgruntlement, and do not let us forget this, that all that this Bill is doing for these educated natives is to make them the leaders of their own people, in disaffection and revolt.'[6]

It was a courageous one-man stand in protest against the laying of another cornerstone in the edifice of apartheid that was to be raised in the decades to come, and the *Rand Daily Mail* wrote a leading article applauding it without actually endorsing it. The editorial was written by assistant editor George Rayner Ellis, an erudite man who became one of the paper's more distinguished editors. Ellis described Hofmeyr's speech as 'an utterance all compact of courage and generations yet to come will hold his name in honour because of it. The making of such a speech in such an atmosphere was an exhibition of intellectual and moral integrity that has probably not been exceeded in South Africa in our time.'

Yet Ellis withheld open support for Hofmeyr's standpoint. With a reluctance to break free of the prejudices of the age and give a moral lead to public opinion, he retreated into a mealy-mouthed ambiguity on the race issue that typified the stance of the press generally throughout the first half-century of the new country's existence. After his fulsome praise of Hofmeyr's courage, Ellis's editorial meandered on to say that because the parliamentary decision was a *fait accompli* there was 'little purpose to be served by going into the rights and wrongs of the issue now … This is a question which must be left to the future to decide.' Only to end his leader with the kicker line: 'But we have a sort of belief that history will be on the side of Mr Hofmeyr.'[7]

A sort of belief! Strong stuff for its time, I suppose, but it was to be two decades before anything more emphatic was to appear in the opinion columns of the *Rand Daily Mail*.

* * *

LAURENCE GANDAR took over the editorship of the *Rand Daily Mail* in October 1957. There was nothing in Gandar's previous record as a journalist to indicate that he might break with the stolid conformity of his predecessors on the race issue. He had been an assistant editor and a political columnist on the *Sunday Tribune* in Durban, but while he had shown himself to be a clear thinker and lucid writer there had been no spark of political fireworks.

However, Gandar's arrival at the *Rand Daily Mail* happened to be just seven months after Ghana had become the first African colony to be granted independence. The new editor, who had been an intelligence officer in the South African military during the Second World War, was finely attuned to reading the implications of shifts in the global political landscape. He had read the signs of changed political perceptions within the colonies. The humbling of the imperial powers during the war meant there was no inclination among their colonial subjects to return to the pre-war status quo. Across Africa and Asia, the mood gained momentum for a shift from colony to nation – and the independence of Ghana brought that mood to our doorstep.

Kwame Nkrumah was its African champion. He was a remarkable man who had been educated in a Roman Catholic school in the Gold Coast, and at Lincoln University and the University of Pennsylvania in the USA. Influenced by the seething environment of post-war black American politics, and by the black nationalism

126

and pan-Africanism of the influential Jamaican intellectual Marcus Garvey, Nkrumah returned to the Gold Coast, where he founded the Convention People's Party and began campaigning for independence, which Britain finally granted, to the new country called Ghana, on 6 March 1957. That in turn triggered a burgeoning of African nationalist movements throughout the continent, to the point where, in a single momentous year, 1960, 17 countries attained independence, including five in southern Africa − Malawi, Zambia, Botswana, Lesotho and Swaziland.

Gandar sensed the implications of Ghana's independence immediately, and soon after taking his seat at the *Rand Daily Mail* began preparing the paper to address developments in South Africa's own black community, which had been almost totally ignored by all newspapers until then. He was not himself a hard-news man, but had that vital leader's talent for picking the right people to put in the right slots, while he himself concentrated on his own strength of writing insightful and penetrating leading articles and an occasional personal column. It was in these analytical articles that the first signs of a shift in the paper's policy became evident.

It emerged in the first of a series of articles Gandar wrote on the state of the nation in the run-up to the April 1958 election. Writing under the byline of his middle names, Owen Vine, he bewailed the fact that, although the rest of Africa and the world at large were undergoing a period of dramatic changes in many fields, from nuclear science to space exploration, and with the emergence of new nations and new alliances of nations stirring the minds of people everywhere, here in South Africa the election campaign had been bereft of any fresh thinking. It had revealed a 'calcification of political attitudes'.

In a second article Owen Vine cut loose in language more biting than anything that had been said before about government policy. 'Apartheid is meaningless,' he wrote, 'because it cannot, on the highest admission, bring separation to the economic sphere. Apartheid is unrealistic because it is geared to a timetable that will be surely and completely overtaken by events. Apartheid is a sham because there is no evidence of any willingness to face the sacrifices it involves. Apartheid is unworkable because it is set to run counter to the massed forces of world opinion and the tides of contemporary human progress.'

The news team at the *Rand Daily Mail*, arguably the strongest ever assembled on any South African newspaper, was soon to follow the same trend, not only beating the opposition repeatedly on hard-news stories but also introducing more and more reports about stirrings in the black community. The team consisted of news editor Harry O'Connor, a veteran journeyman who had been close to Smuts and later served as a war correspondent for the South African Press Association; night editor Raymond Louw, a young go-getter who had served six years on newspapers in Britain; night editor Aubrey Sussens, who had been a star political correspondent for the *Cape Times*; and Rex Gibson, soon to become a highly talented chief sub-editor. All except Sussens, who left journalism to become a successful businessman, were subsequently to become editors of newspapers in the company.

As a key part of his newsroom reconstruction, Gandar also appointed a full-time 'African Affairs Correspondent' to specialise in reporting on all aspects of black politics and everyday social existence under apartheid. It was the first time any mainstream South African newspaper had done this and it sent out a clear signal of the new editor's intentions. The reporter he chose for the job, Benjamin Pogrund, had been involved in left-wing student politics and had become a member of Alan Paton's Liberal Party before turning to journalism. Pogrund, a dedicated and energetic reporter, had acquired a wide range of contacts in the black political world, particularly in the African National Congress, and his outpouring of news items soon began transforming the political colouration of the newspaper.

Coinciding with this, Gandar also made a small terminological change that startled all of us with the strength of its negative impact and drove home a warning message of just how deeply racist the *Rand Daily Mail*'s predominantly white readership was. The change was simply to stop using the word 'native' and replace it with 'African'. It triggered a furious reaction, a flood of protest letters and the biggest drop in circulation the paper had ever experienced. As the angry letters revealed, the word 'African' was emotionally loaded, particularly among Afrikaner readers, for seemingly containing an implication that black people had a proprietary right to the continent, that it was theirs and that white South Africans were outsiders, non-Africans. It was a hypocritical attitude, since whites had long taken pride in regarding themselves as 'Europeans' and the country was littered with signs at every public facility proclaiming them to be either for 'Europeans only' or 'Non-Europeans'. Despite the fuss and the cancelled subscriptions, Gandar stuck to his guns and the storm passed. But the opening up of the *Rand Daily Mail*'s columns to more and more news about black people was steadily to change perceptions of the paper by both race groups, and with that its readership profile.

Pogrund's first big scoop on his new beat came in November 1958 when he attended an ANC conference in the Orlando Communal Hall in Soweto to discuss how best to resist the intensifying application of apartheid restrictions. It was a time of turmoil in black politics as Nkrumah's pan-Africanist ideas captured the imagination of many in South Africa. The ANC itself had always been committed to the ideal of non-racialism rooted in its 1955 Freedom Charter, which boldly declared that 'South Africa belongs to all who live in it, black and white'. The ANC had formed an alliance with Mohandas Gandhi's old Indian National Congress, as well as with the predominantly white Congress of Democrats – a cover name for the outlawed Communist Party of South Africa (CPSA). Now this non-racial concept was being challenged by the more radical strain of Africanism that Nkrumahism had ignited. There had long been a trace element of Africanist thinking in the ANC, advocated initially by a charismatic Youth League leader, Anton Lembede, who believed black people should campaign on their own for their freedom before linking up with other race groups. But Lembede had died young and the idea had faded. Now it came roaring back in the light of Nkrumah's enhanced image. It did so under the leadership of a black intellectual and university lecturer, Robert Sobukwe, who was at pains to stress that the concept was not racist. As he explained: 'We aim, politically, at government of the Africans by the Africans for the Africans, with everybody who owes his only loyalty to Africa and who is prepared to accept the democratic rule of an African majority being regarded as an African.'

However, behind this bland exculpation lay a more substantive factor. The Africanists resented the influence that the white communists seemed able to exercise on the ANC. Not only were these members of the banned CPSA better educated and more politically sophisticated than the ordinary ANC members, but also they regarded themselves as the 'vanguard party' of the liberation movement and were perceived to be overly assertive in trying to impose their views. African intellectuals such as Sobukwe resented this attitude of superiority on the part of a political ideology they regarded as foreign, not African. So the rupture occurred at that conference in Soweto, with the Africanist wing breaking away from what had been the country's main black political voice for nearly half a century. Pogrund, finding himself almost the only journalist present, got his scoop. His story made the front-page lead in the *Rand Daily Mail*, jolting the competition into realising they had better respond to his monopoly of such a neglected news beat. Some months later, Sobukwe's group formed themselves into a separate party, the Pan Africanist Congress (PAC), resulting in a phase of black political rivalry that was to catalyse a turning point in the whole South African story.

* * *

WHILE I WAS still at Reuters, Johannes Gerhardus (JG) Strijdom, who had succeeded the retired Malan as Prime Minister after the 1953 election, died of cancer and was succeeded by Hendrik Verwoerd. Strijdom, who went by the nickname of 'The Lion of the North', was known even within his own National Party as an extremist. I recall some of the editors at Reuters asking me what this new chap Verwoerd was like. Would he be better or worse than Strijdom? I cast my mind back to that extraordinary interview I'd had with Verwoerd in Queenstown when I was just 19 years old to try to find an answer, remembering his words to me: 'There won't be peace in this country, my boy, until the black man has his own countries.'

'He's very charming,' I replied cautiously. 'And intelligent. He was a professor of applied psychology. But frankly I think he's an apartheid extremist to the point of living in a dream world of his own.'

Now here I was, back in South Africa putting together the parliamentary pages of the *Rand Daily Mail* each night, and as the new session began in Cape Town in February 1959, Verwoerd rose to deliver his first parliamentary speech as Prime Minister. It became known as his 'New Vision' speech, in which he spelled out an altogether new concept of where the apartheid policy should lead the country. It was a vision of a new South Africa in which there would be no 'horizontal segregation', as he put it, in which whites would dominate blacks in perpetuity, but instead a 'vertical segregation' in which each of the races would develop alongside one another, each along its own traditional lines to the utmost of its own ability, in its own territory. This was to be achieved by enabling each of the country's nine major black tribes, which Verwoerd now euphemistically referred to as 'national groups', to become self-governing in its own tribal reserve area, now referred to as Bantustans – Verwoerd having reacted to our use of the word 'Africans' instead of 'natives' by ordering the government to use the anthropological term 'Bantu', for the indigenous people of east and southern Africa. Clearly a terminological cleanup was part of the 'New Vision'.

These Bantustans, Verwoerd explained, could be developed to the point of full independence, leaving the core part of South Africa to be 'the white man's country'. There would be no more racial discrimination. Thus it could be seen that 'separate development', as he now called apartheid, was really a policy of liberation, not domination. Here, then, was what he had meant by the black man getting 'his own countries'.

It all sounded too good to be true; there had to be a catch – which of course there was. As Gandar had noted earlier, there was no way the government could bring about separation in the economic sphere, since the economy was already racially integrated, with the black population providing the vast bulk of the working class. That omelette could not be unscrambled. Gandar now also expressed doubts about whether the government had the political will to spend the vast sums of money that would be needed to develop those reserve areas into viable national states — without which the whole grand vision would be meaningless, an illusion.

Nonetheless, he was intrigued by what he saw as an important shift in the ruling party's ideological thinking, an attempt, however unrealistic, to come to terms with the intellectual challenge presented by the implications of Ghana's independence. He began writing editorials and columns cautiously welcoming Verwoerd's speech, saying that, although he had grave doubts about the practicability of the new vision the Prime Minister had spelled out, it reflected a recognition, at least in theory, that racial domination was no longer sustainable and that South Africa had to come to terms with the reality of its demographics.

At the same time Gandar expressed some cautious criticism of the United Party for its failure to respond to the reality of a changing Africa. The United Party, under the leadership of Sir De Villiers Graaff, had assailed Verwoerd's 'New Vision' as a plan to carve up the country and give away valuable parts of it to the blacks. The UP, Graaff said, remained firmly in favour of maintaining the geographic unity of South Africa and pursuing a racial policy of 'white leadership with justice' — in other words a milder form of apartheid. Gandar accused it of being in an ossified state of mind, bereft of any new ideas in a changing environment. It also, of course, carried more than a hint of racism, with the suggestion that the NP was gifting good land to the blacks.

Both the UP leadership and some powerful members of the company's board of directors, completely misreading the essence of Gandar's analysis, were horrified at what they saw as a shift towards the National Party by a newspaper that had always shown the UP unquestioning loyalty. Graaff, new in the job of Leader of the Opposition, complained to Gandar but to no avail, so Graaff went to see the most powerful man on the board of directors, Clive Corder, chairman of a trust company called Syfrets, which represented the majority shareholders. Corder was a close friend of Graaff's, having been best man at his wedding, so he took up the matter at the next board meeting, asking that Gandar be reprimanded. But Gandar had two strong supporters in the managing director, Henry Kuiper, who had headhunted him, and Leycester Walton, the general manager, who was an experienced newspaper executive and former journalist. So the storm passed. But it was the first sign of what was to become a long-running conflict that the paper was to face for the rest of its life.

I saw more and more of Gandar around this time. He would periodically call me into his office, sometimes to his home, to discuss the unfolding political scene. He wanted the sub-editor handling the political news to be aware of his thinking so as to have a clearer idea of which issues he regarded as important. I found these sessions fascinating as I gained insight into the workings of a fine analytical mind. I learned, too, why he regarded Verwoerd's New Vision as so important despite its impracticability. The National Party's recognition that racial domination was no longer tenable was a game-changer, he explained, in that it would eventually confront the NP with precisely the same challenge it habitually threw at the UP – that there were only two possible answers to the South African race issue: either segregation, in the form of fair and equitable territorial partitioning, or racial integration. Once the Nats discovered for themselves that fair partitioning was impossible, it would have to turn to the only alternative the party had itself defined.

Our job as a newspaper, Gandar told me, was therefore to study what he called 'the arithmetic of apartheid', meaning the pattern of future demographic trends, together with the financial cost and social upheaval that would be required to consolidate the envisioned Bantustans and make them economically viable. This should be juxtaposed with the increasingly indispensable role of black labour in the economy of so-called white South Africa. Those should be the focal points of our political news coverage and commentary.

The only trouble, Gandar reflected gloomily, was the United Party. As long as it shrank from acknowledging the inevitability of racial integration, however gradual, there would be no electable opposition to push for the only alternative. The Liberal Party embodied a number of fine, idealistic people, but its call for immediate majority rule rendered it unelectable in the foreseeable future.

But a shift on that front, too, was already in the making. There had long been a ferment of discontent on the left flank of the UP, where a group calling themselves the 'progressives' were chafing at the old guard's entrenched conservatism. Graaff himself was a charming and elegant man, but, as an anglicised Afrikaner, 'Div', as his supporters called him, remained convinced his people would never accept integration, that the only hope of ever unseating the National Party government was to offer them a milder, gentler form of apartheid.

It was Graaff and the old guard's immovable stance on this issue that galled the 'progressives'. The UP's stasis in the face of the rising clamour for independence in Africa and Verwoerd's headline-catching New Vision speech brought matters to a head. At the UP's annual congress in August 1959, 12 of its 53 MPs resigned from the party, led by Johannes van Aswegen Steytler, the MP for Queenstown, whom I had watched having his maiden political speech drowned out by PW Botha's rowdy Jeugbond thugs in Aliwal North five years before. Three months later the 'Progs', as they became known, announced the formation of the Progressive Party, advocating a new federal constitution and a qualified franchise for all races based on set standards of education and income. In other words, a policy of gradual integration. Cautious, but still a vital breakthrough in the direction of the only realistic alternative to apartheid. It opened up a new phase in the white political debate and the role of the South African press.

CHAPTER NINE

A Tipping Point

NINETEEN-SIXTY was a momentous year in which both South Africa and the world changed dramatically — in opposite directions. A wave of liberalism and social change began to sweep the globe, while the decolonisation of Africa accelerated dramatically. Meanwhile South Africa retreated into a laager of ever-increasing reactionary conservatism and global isolation.

The new trends appeared early. On 3 February, British Prime Minister Harold Macmillan arrived in Cape Town at the tail end of a six-week tour of Africa that took him first to independent Ghana, then to Nigeria and the Federation of Rhodesia and Nyasaland. He was, rather surprisingly, the first British Prime Minister to visit South Africa and it coincided, as he put it in an address to a joint sitting of both Houses of Parliament, with 'what I might call the golden wedding of the Union'.

But the purpose of Macmillan's visit was much more than that. He had come to indicate a shift in British policy both towards its sub-Saharan colonies, where the clamour for independence was intensifying, and towards South Africa, with its policy of apartheid. Macmillan had the mannerisms of a Tory grandee, yet he was more liberal than many of his younger colleagues in the Conservative government. He was elegant, affable and famously 'unflappable'.

Macmillan's speech to the South African Parliament, which became known as the 'wind of change' speech, was a carefully weighed package that lasted 50 minutes, long even by the standards of the day. Most of it, in the words of Douglas Hurd, writing much later, was 'wrapping paper', but 'inside were two messages', and it was those two messages that made the speech a watershed event in the history of both Africa and South Africa.[1]

One made it clear for the first time that Britain acknowledged that black people had the right to rule themselves and that Britain had a responsibility to help create societies in which the rights of all individuals were upheld. The second made it equally clear that Britain could never support South Africa on the issue of apartheid.

His words were clear and emphatic: 'The wind of change is blowing through this continent, and whether we like it or not, this growth of national consciousness is a political fact. We must all accept it as a fact, and our national policies must take account of it … That means, I would judge, that we've got to come to terms with it.'

The second message, about Britain distancing itself from apartheid South Africa, was equally clear though courteously phrased: 'As a fellow member of the Commonwealth it is our earnest desire to give South Africa our support and encouragement, but I hope you won't mind my saying frankly that there are some aspects of your policies that make it impossible for us to do this without being false to our own deep convictions about the political destinies of free men to which in our own territories we are trying to give effect.'

Macmillan had declined to give Verwoerd a draft of his speech in advance, which angered the South African Prime Minister because it left him in the uncomfortable position of having to give an impromptu response to this brace of bombshells. But Verwoerd was no intellectual slouch himself. His off-the-cuff reply, though brief, remains as crisp an outline of his vision of apartheid as he was ever to give.

'The tendency in Africa for nations to become independent and at the same time do justice to all,' he said, 'does not only mean being just to the black man of Africa but also to be just to the white man of Africa. We call ourselves Europeans, but

136

actually we represent the white men of Africa. They are the people not only in the Union but through major portions of Africa who brought civilisation here, who made the present developments of black nationalists possible. By bringing them education, by showing them this way of life, by bringing in industrial development, by bringing in the ideals with which Western civilisation has developed itself.

'And the white man who came to Africa, perhaps to trade, in some cases perhaps to bring the gospel, has remained to stay. And particularly we in the southernmost portion of Africa, have such a stake here that it is our only motherland. We have nowhere else to go. We settled a country that was bare, and the Bantu came to this country and settled certain portions for themselves, and it is in line with the thinking on Africa to grant them there those fullest rights which we also, with you, admit all people should have. We believe in granting those rights in the fullest degree in that part of southern Africa which their forefathers found for themselves and settled in. But similarly, we believe in balance. We believe in allowing those same full opportunities to remain within the grasp of the white man who has made all this possible.'

Verwoerd's followers were delighted. In their eyes he had given every bit as good as he got from Macmillan. Even many of his opponents conceded it was a worthy performance, given that he'd had no time to prepare. But it was based on a fundamental falsehood, just as his whole vision of dividing the country into a series of separate states – giving 'the black man his own countries' – was a chimera. The falsehood was the myth propagated by the National Party for years that 'we settled a country that was [empty]'; that white and black settlers had occupied different parts of the country at more or less the same time. This was a myth not unlike that propagated by early Zionists about Palestine being 'a land without people for a people without land'. In both cases the objective was to legitimise the settlement as having taken place without the displacement of anyone; there had been no original sin of disinheritance.

It was a gross untruth, as the *Rand Daily Mail* hastened to disclose at the time, for there was plenty of archaeological evidence that black people had penetrated deep into the Transvaal, Natal and as far south as the Kei River about AD 800. The paper also pointed out the relatively well-known fact that there were remains of an Early Iron Age settlement to be seen right in the heart of Johannesburg, on a hillock known as Melville Koppies, dating as far back as 500 000 years, as well as the remnants of the kraal walls of a Late Stone Age settlement about 1 000 years old. Nevertheless, successive National Party governments continued to propagate the myth for at least another two decades, together with the idea that apartheid would reverse the flow of black people from their 'own' tribal homelands to the so-called white industrial cities. The tide was supposed to turn in the magical year 1978 – by which time, of course, it had become a flood.

I well remember the sense of being present at a historic turning point as the text of Macmillan's speech reached us in the sub-editors' department of the Mail. Aubrey Sussens, the night editor, was the first to rip the 'takes' off the chattering telex machine as they arrived. 'This speech will go down in history,' Sussens remarked as he handed copies to the chief sub-editor and to me, the parliamentary sub. 'Note that wind of change quote,' he muttered to me, 'that's gotta be the headline.' And so it was, in banner type.

As it turned out, Macmillan's speech had as strong an impact in Britain as it did in South Africa, and even more so among the British settlers in the African colonies, who vociferously denounced what they saw as 'Britain's abdication in Africa'. Some in Macmillan's own party feared Britain would appear weak on the international stage after a mass decolonisation. They formed a pressure group, the Conservative Monday Club, to give voice to the dismay and distrust felt within the country and among the settler communities. Many settlers, especially in Kenya, began packing their bags and moving south – soon to be joined by large numbers from the Congo as that unhappy land also became independent and promptly slid into chaos. All this contributed to a growing sense of angst among white South Africans, which caused a steadily increasing number of English-speakers to give their support to Verwoerd and his predominantly Afrikaner government.

* * *

I WAS PLAYING golf the day South Africa's race problem changed and became a civil war. Since we worked mostly at night, a group of Mail sub-editors had formed a Monday Club of our own to play 18 holes each Monday morning on a different course. So it was that I found myself lining up a putt on the 10th green of the Germiston Country Club on the morning of Monday 21 March 1960 when a flight of half a dozen Harvard aircraft screamed overhead at treetop height. It was a startling sight and should have alerted our four-ball of newshounds that something unusual was taking place, but we completed our leisurely round, dallied a little at the 19th hole, then made our way to the office – to discover that a war had broken out.

Today, 21 March is a public holiday in South Africa, commemorating the Sharpeville Massacre – the killing by police of 69 unarmed pass-law protestors. The events at Sharpeville and elsewhere led to Verwoerd's declaring a state of emergency and to the banning of all black political movements. In turn, it led both the ANC and PAC to make the fateful decision to shift from peaceful to violent resistance, forming armed wings and going underground with operational headquarters in exile. It was a tipping point in our history.

It all began with the planning of a campaign of passive resistance against the pass laws, the regulations used to control the influx of black people into the industrial cities. The only black people allowed permanent residence in the 'white' urban areas were those who had either worked there continuously for 15 years or for the same employer for ten years. All others could legally be there only if they were currently employed; to lose one's job meant to lose one's right to be in the city. Every black person, therefore, had to carry a pass indicating his or her state of employment, and thus the legal right to be in any urban area. These passes had to be produced on demand to any policeman of any rank, otherwise the individual would be arrested immediately and taken to prison to await trial before a special pass court. Pass-law arrests at the time of Sharpeville were averaging 18 000 a day and were the single most hated feature of the apartheid system. So it was that Chief Albert Luthuli, president of the ANC, announced at the organisation's national conference in December 1959 that 1960 was going to be 'The Year of the Pass'.

By the time the new year dawned, however, the Africanist wing had already broken away from the parent body to form the PAC, and so the element of political rivalry entered black politics for the first time. When the ANC announced that its campaign against the pass laws would be launched on 31 March, Robert Sobukwe decided to pre-empt that by launching the PAC's campaign ten days earlier. In doing so, Sobukwe was at pains to emphasise that the campaign had to be disciplined and peaceful. As he put it in a public announcement: 'My instructions are that our people must be taught now and continuously that in this campaign we are going to observe absolute non-violence.'

The strategic objective of the campaign was simple. Black people all over the country would leave their passes at home and march peacefully to their nearest police stations and hand themselves over for arrest. This, Sobukwe contended, would over-whelm the whole system and render it ineffective. It would swamp the jails and the courts and the regime would have no choice but to abandon the pass law system. However, Sobukwe and the ANC leaders, who had decided to climb aboard and join the PAC campaign, had reckoned without the ruthless determination of Verwoerd and his police force.

Sobukwe himself set out with a group of fellow PAC leaders early on that bright, crisp autumn morning to walk the eight kilometres to the Orlando police station, where they handed themselves over and were duly arrested without incident. But in another black township 70 km to the south things turned out differently. Crowds began gathering early on a field outside the police station at Sharpeville, in the heavily industrialised Vaal Triangle, embracing the cities of Vereeniging, Vanderbijlpark and Sasolburg. Michael Zondo, a middle-aged Sharpeville school teacher who was in the crowd on that fateful day and whom I interviewed some years later, takes up the story.[2]

'There had been some trouble over the weekend,' Zondo

recalled. 'I had heard some shooting on Sunday night and there was this talk about an anti-pass-law protest at the police station. I was worried about my students because my school is close to the police station, so I took my bicycle and rode over there. The school was closed, but I saw people moving up Seiso Street towards the police station. I followed them, pushing my bicycle. I'm not really political but everyone was going that way so I wanted to see what was happening.'

When Zondo arrived at the police station, a sizeable crowd had already gathered, chanting and singing and pressing up against a high security fence surrounding the squat red-brick building. A number of policemen were already lined up inside the grounds and, just 30 paces from where Zondo was standing with his bicycle, there were two Saracen armoured cars with machine guns mounted on their turrets.

The crowd thickened as the day wore on. A rumour went around that someone important was coming to address them. Was he going to announce the scrapping of the pass laws? Anticipation rose. More people arrived. The noise and the pressure on the fence increased.

'I don't know exactly what happened then,' Zondo told me. 'I remember the time. It was exactly ten to two when there was a disturbance at the gate, over to my right. I couldn't see what was happening, but I think there was a fat woman who got bumped by a police car as it tried to get through the gate. Then while I was looking over there I suddenly heard this rat-tat-tat noise in front of me.'

First one, and then both the Saracens had opened fire with their machine guns.

'Brains,' Zondo murmured to me, shaking his head in a vague way that conveyed a sense of disbelief still, all these years later. 'I just saw brains. Skulls were bursting open in front of me.'

He fell, spread-eagled over his bicycle. Bodies fell on top of him. He was facing one of the Saracens and he could see a tongue of flame turning into a white haze 'like hailstones in a storm' coming from its barrel as it raked back and forth across the crowd. It stopped and there was silence for a moment, then it started again.

141

'Then there was silence. Everything was still. People started to get up and I heard some sobs and cries. I woke up. I looked around. If you Doom flies you know how they lie down,' Zondo said, using the trade name of an insecticide spray. 'That's what it looked like. I got up and started to walk away. I saw some kids from my class. They started shouting, *"Tichara othunswe! Tichara otunswe!"*, which is siSotho for "Teacher has been shot." I was shocked. I thought, am I dead? I remembered magazine stories I had read as a child, of King Arthur's soldiers in battle who kept running after they had been beheaded and I wondered if that had happened to me. But then the children pointed to my leg, and I looked down and saw that my left calf had been shot away. I collapsed.'

Sixty-nine people were shot dead at Sharpeville that day and 180 were wounded. Michael Zondo spent three months in Soweto's Baragwanath Hospital recovering from his wound. When it had healed he was arrested and charged with incitement and public violence, along with 74 others. He was acquitted after a 15-month trial but never got promoted in the state-run education system that employed him.

Meanwhile, back at the Mail, the subs' room was abuzz with the biggest story in years. But the excitement of handling a big running story was tinged with anxiety about what was happening in the country. Reports were coming in of clashes with the police in townships across the land. From our office windows we could see the evening sky glowing red over Soweto, where angry protesters had set buildings ablaze.

This tense atmosphere raised a touchy ethical point. A senior Mail photographer, Warwick Robinson, had been in the thick of the gory events at Sharpeville together with the paper's chief crime reporter, Harold Sacks. Robinson had returned with a series of graphic pictures of the bodies strewn across the field in front of the police station with the Saracens facing them. Aubrey Sussens looked at them briefly and shuddered. 'Jeez what pictures!' he exclaimed, before handing them to Gandar, who had come in to see how we were handling the story. Gandar studied the pictures gravely and I could see his brow furrow. He asked Sussens and the chief sub-editor to accompany him to his office, where he was joined by the news editor, Harry O'Connor, and two assistant editors, Lewis Sowden and AB Hughes.

Sowden later described the tough decision-making process that took place there. 'It was dusk when six of us gathered in the office of Laurence Gandar to see Warwick Robinson's photographs,' he wrote eight years later. 'We passed them around in silence for some minutes. They seemed to require no comment. They were the best news photographs ever taken in South Africa. They showed a field littered with dead and two policemen with rifles looking on. They were large full-plate prints, each nearly half the size of a page of the newspaper, and they recorded a stillness charged with atmosphere.

'Very soon, as we passed them round, it became clear that we would not use these photographs. Gandar's face, normally grave, became darker in scanning them. Without saying it, we all knew that it would be no more than ordinary newspaper practice and courage to print these photographs; but more important than courage at that moment was responsibility. In that orderly, wood-panelled office, hung with etchings and modern paintings, we knew the temper of the half-million black population which surrounded this white city of Johannesburg, and we could not print those photographs without being aware of their potentially inflammatory effect.'[3]

There were gasps of dismay around the subs' room when Sussens returned to give us the editor's decision. Robinson's face went red. He had risked his life taking those amazing pictures and here was his editor, a man already acquiring a reputation for boldness, saying we couldn't use them. He couldn't believe it, and he was livid. The following week we saw that *Time* magazine had bought one from him and splashed it across their cover page. But Robinson was still not placated and resigned from the Mail.

Much as I admired Gandar, I thought his decision was wrong – and more than half a century later I still do. We knew, even as we stood there that night, that we were dealing with one of the great news stories of our time, a landmark event in the history of our country, and that, as Sowden said, we had perhaps the greatest news pictures ever taken in South Africa to illustrate it. We knew, too, that there is truth in the old cliché that a picture tells a thousand words. No reportage could possibly capture the impact of what had happened as eloquently as those photographs. As for the contention that the pictures might inflame black passions and lead to more violence, black passions were already inflamed, as the fires in Soweto testified, and no newspaper picture was going to inflame them more than the reality of what they already knew had happened.

No, the real importance of those pictures lay not in their possible impact on the paper's black readers, but in the effect they may have had on its white readership. In the cellular nature of apartheid society, where whites lived in total isolation from the realities of life in the black townships and rural areas, it was they who needed to be shocked into a full awareness of what had happened. As was often noted at the time – and in fact is still the case – the white citizens of Johannesburg were far more familiar with New York, London and Paris than with the huge dormitory suburb of Soweto adjoining them, which few had ever entered. They lived inside a cocoon that apartheid had spun for them. So the really important audience for Warwick Robinson's pictures that Gandar and his headquarters staff failed to recognise that night was not black but white South Africans. It was they who needed to be made vividly aware of what had been done in their name.

Yet, in retrospect, I can sympathise with Gandar for making the decision he did, even though I believe it was an error of judgment. As I was to discover later, and eventually experience myself when I occupied that same seat, he was already under pressure from a deeply conservative board of directors. Clive Corder, as the most powerful figure on that board, was already on Gandar's back for being 'too liberal' and for criticising the United Party. It's a tricky thing to be a courageous editor if you don't have the backing of your board. I suspect that part of Gandar's thinking that night was that Corder and his liegemen would doubtless regard publication as 'against the national interest' and thus a bridge too far. Such are the subtle, and sometimes subliminal, influences that can lead to self-censorship.

* * *

THE SWITCH FROM protests to armed struggle was not immediate. The ANC and the PAC tried to continue their protest campaigns, but found it increasingly difficult. Then a few days after Sharpeville another confrontation occurred that alarmed the government even more. With a spontaneity that took even the vigilant security services by surprise, a crowd of some 30 000 black people emerged from the sprawling flatlands outside Cape Town and began marching in a silent, orderly procession towards the city. At the head of this vast column was a young man dressed like a schoolboy, in short pants and no socks. His name was Philip Kgosana, only 20 years old, who for just a single day was to play one of the most remarkable roles in the whole anti-apartheid struggle before disappearing from it again forever.

As the white citizens of Cape Town quaked at the sight, Kgosana led his formidable procession along the broad De Waal Drive motorway into the heart of the city towards the Houses of Parliament. It was, as *New York Times* correspondent Joseph Lelyveld was to observe, 'an hour in which the Bastille might have been stormed in South Africa, and wasn't'.

It wasn't because young Kgosana and his followers felt bound by Sobukwe's stricture to avoid violence. He had warned his followers that any violent confrontation would provoke retaliation that would alienate the black masses from their objective, which was to fill the jails. 'We are not leading corpses to the new Africa,' Sobukwe had told them. So Kgosana halted his marchers as they neared the precincts of Parliament and he saw a helicopter hovering overhead and armoured cars with police units surrounding the area. He ordered the vast crowd to sit down, and they obeyed him.

Kgosana stepped forward to speak with the police commander in charge of the defending units. The youngster in his short pants demanded to see the Minister of Justice so he could hand him a petition protesting against the pass laws. The police commander told Kgosana the minister was at lunch, but offered the young man a 'gentleman's agreement' that he would arrange a meeting later in the day if Kgosana would first send his people home.

Naively, but mindful of his leader's injunction to avoid violence, Kgosana agreed. Then followed another astonishing display of discipline and authority as the youngster turned back and faced the massive crowd and told them to about-turn and go home. Which they did.

When Kgosana returned to Parliament that afternoon, he did not see the Minister. Instead he was arrested and charged with 'incitement'. So much for the 'gentleman's agreement'. But Kgosana didn't go to jail. He skipped bail and disappeared into exile, not to be seen or heard of again until his unannounced return four decades later to a transformed homeland where he now lives quietly as an old man and an unsung hero.

The government moved swiftly to crush the resistance after Kgosana's great march. Eight days later it announced a state of emergency and declared both the ANC and PAC to be 'unlawful organisations'. That meant not only that both the main black organisations were outlawed but also that it would be a criminal offence for anyone to further any of their aims or objectives. At a stroke, all of black nationalism was criminalised. The movements became unmentionable in the press and, as factors in the South African public debate, they ceased to exist — except as images that the apartheid government could demonise as 'terrorists' to alarm whites into supporting ever-tougher security legislation.

The ANC made one last forlorn attempt to keep functioning under these crippling circumstances. With its leader, Chief Luthuli, also banned, it sent secretary-general Oliver Tambo abroad to lobby for support and made Nelson Mandela leader of a National Action Council to organise continuing protest activity. Working underground, Mandela wrote a letter to Verwoerd calling on him to convene a national convention of all races to draft a new con-stitution for a non-racial South Africa, warning that if he did not do so there would be a three-day nationwide work stoppage. Verwoerd did not deign to reply. Instead he threw a cordon of steel around every black township and warned that anyone who went on strike would be endorsed out of the urban areas, meaning they and their families would starve. The strike flopped and after two days Mandela called it off.

It was at that point that the ANC decided its strategy of non-violence alone was futile. If it could not organise and campaign legally, and if naked force was to be used to crush every peaceful demonstration, it would be impossible to make progress. Mandela and a handful of others who had managed to escape detention, met secretly and decided to form a military wing, *Umkhonto we Sizwe*, the Spear of the Nation. This amounted to a declaration of war and marked the start of South Africa's 30-year guerrilla struggle.

* * *

SATURDAYS WERE special in our little family. I worked a five-night week in the Mail subs' room, so Saturdays were the only day Mary and I could count on being completely free and able to plan an outing with Simon, then a lively two-year-old. We were intending to do just that on this particular Saturday. It had been a strenuous couple of weeks at the office, what with the Sharpeville Massacre, the emergency declaration and the spate of detentions that followed, so I felt in need of a break. We were about to leave our one-bedroom flat on a ridge overlooking an expanse of Johannesburg's northern suburbs when the phone rang. I picked it up a little irritably.

'Hello, is that you, Charles?' asked an excited voice.

'Sorry, wrong number,' I replied.

I was about to replace the receiver when I heard the man's voice again. 'Never mind,' it said breathlessly, 'I've got to tell someone. Verwoerd's just been shot.'

'What!' I exclaimed incredulously.

'Yes, I'm here at the Showgrounds and a white man just walked up to Verwoerd and shot him in the head.' With that there was a click. The anonymous voice had ended the call.

I was dumbfounded as I stared at Mary and told her what the man had just said. Could it be true? Was it a hoax? A white man, and in a crowded arena in the heart of Johannesburg? Surely not. Yet the man hadn't sounded like a hoax caller; he was agitated and had dialled a wrong number.

I called the *Sunday Times* and was put through to the news desk.

No, they hadn't heard anything and they sounded as though they thought I was a hoax caller. But even as I was telling the news editor about the call I had just received, I heard him splutter: 'Here it is. The flash has just come through from Sapa.'

That was the end of our outing plans. No journalist can stay away from a newspaper office when a big story is breaking. After quick apologies to Mary and Simon, I leapt in my car and raced to the newsroom of our sister paper. I was just a spectator there, along with several other Mail journalists who had responded as I had. We helped out here and there, but the reason we were there was simply to be there, to be in the thick of the intoxicating buzz of a newsroom when history is unfolding.

As the details rolled in we learned that a wealthy business-man and trout farmer, David Pratt, who was a member of the Witwatersrand Agricultural Society, which held a big agricultural and industrial show at Milner Park in central Johannesburg each year, had been seated in the members' stand at the opening of the show. This year the show was special, labelled the 'Union Exposition' to mark the jubilee of the Union of South Africa, so the Prime Minister had been invited to deliver the opening address. He had just completed it and resumed his seat when Pratt shouldered his way forward and shot Verwoerd twice in the head at point-blank range with a .22 pistol. The president of the society, Colonel GM Harrison, who had been seated next to Verwoerd, had slapped the pistol out of Pratt's hand and, with the Prime Minister's bodyguard, wrestled the farmer to the ground. Pratt was arrested and taken to police headquarters in Johannesburg.

Reports were that Verwoerd had been taken, still conscious, to the nearby Johannesburg General Hospital, where the first medical reports were encouraging. It was revealed that the first shot had pierced his cheek and the second his ear. It was the second one that was life-threatening, because although Pratt's pistol was only a light calibre, the bullet that had pierced the ear was close to the brain.

As it turned out, Verwoerd not only survived but also recov-ered rapidly. Within two months he was back in public life. He had been transferred from Johannesburg to a hospital in Pretoria, where the neurosurgeon who treated him described his escape as 'absolutely miraculous'. I was later able to establish, through medical contacts who had studied the case, that Pratt's second bullet had missed Verwoerd's carotid artery by one millimetre on one side, and his spinal cord by one millimetre on the other side. Miraculous indeed.

Certainly the notion that a miracle had occurred infused the minds of a number of Nationalist parliamentarians. Afrikaners are a deeply religious people of a Calvinist faith and their politicians were disposed to exploit this. Verwoerd himself had done so in his inaugural speech on becoming Prime Minister, implying none too subtly that he believed himself to have been God's choice and that he would therefore be open to divine guidance in fulfilling the role of leading his people. This had prompted a talented *Cape Times* cartoonist, David Marais, to portray Verwoerd regularly thereafter as carrying a telephone with a line leading up to a celestial figure perched on a heavenly cloud.

But there was nothing humorous about the ecstatic welcome Verwoerd's supporters gave him on his return to Parliament. It verged on the devotional. For the simpler members, here was a chosen leader whose life had been saved by miraculous intervention. For the more intellectual among them, Verwoerd was no less a hero. Here was a man who was giving their party's policy of crude racism, necessary for regaining power and 'getting our country back' from the British imperialists, an overlay of intellectual respectability and moral acceptability. From then on Verwoerd, never really a man of the people, was nonetheless revered as a prophet who would surely lead his *volk* to the Promised Land.

There was a curious coda to the story of the assassination attempt on Verwoerd. After being held at police headquarters for some weeks, Pratt was committed to a mental institution for observation. While he was there a maverick *Sunday Times* reporter, Desmond Blow, decided on a highly original strategy to try to reach him for an interview. After buying a trout from a fishmonger, Blow went to the mental institution, where Pratt was under strict medical surveillance, and managed to convince the staff on duty that he was one of Pratt's workers and that he had brought his employer a trout from the farm to cheer him up. Blow was escorted

149

to Pratt's ward, where he presented the prisoner with the fish and got his interview. It didn't reveal much, but that didn't matter. It was the scoop of getting to the would-be assassin that made the story not only a front-page lead but also a journalistic legend.

Eventually Pratt appeared in court for a preparatory examination, where a magistrate had to decide whether the case should go to a High Court trial. Pratt testified, saying simply that he had shot Verwoerd because he regarded him as 'the epitome of apartheid'. Pratt was a highly educated man, a Cambridge graduate, but the medical evidence from five psychiatrists portrayed him as a manic depressive who at times imagined himself to be a 'saviour of the world' and at others plunged into a state of suicidal depression. He didn't go on trial, but was committed instead to a mental institution where some months later he committed suicide by garrotting himself with a bedsheet.

Soon after these dramatic events, Gandar decided that, as the sub-editor processing the news from Parliament, I should have some first-hand exposure to the institution. So I was sent to Cape Town for a month, ostensibly as a temporary assistant to the political correspondent, 'Bunny' Neame, the son of a former editor of the Mail, but mainly to become acquainted with the rules and lore of Parliament and its main newsmakers. By that time I had received enough warm words about my work to have a hunch there might be something more to it than that, but for the moment it was enough just to go there and revel in being at the heart of what was rapidly becoming one of the world's most controversial stories.

It was an enlightening experience, opening my eyes to the banality of most of the debates in the House of Assembly but also giving me insight into the inflexibility of mind that prevailed there. Here was a House full of white people talking most of the time about black people, assuming they knew all about them, their wants and wishes and traditions and what should be done *for* them, never *with* them, while it was clear even to this newcomer that their 'knowledge' was based purely on stereotyped assumptions rather than real information. With isolated exceptions, these putative representatives of our nation had no idea what they were talking about. It was clear that few had ever had a conversation with an educated black person outside the master-servant relationship. Yet they thought they knew all there was to know about them. It was an alarming case of a community living in a closed intellectual space, isolated from the experiences and perspectives of the vast majority of people whose lives they controlled.

It was also an experience that gave me an opportunity to write my first major story for the *Rand Daily Mail*, with a report of the first parliamentary clash between the 12 breakaway members of the Progressive Party and the United Party. Bunny Neame had taken advantage of my presence to knock off early one day, asking me to keep an eye on the evening sitting, which he didn't expect would produce anything newsworthy. He was surprised to see my report as the paper's front-page lead next morning.

After I returned to Johannesburg, Gandar called me aside one evening to tell me he would like me to take over as political correspondent the following year. It was an important promotion, for 1961 was to be an election year. It was also the year South Africa changed its Constitution, became a republic and left the Commonwealth, so withdrawing ever deeper into isolation.

CHAPTER TEN

In the Belly of the Beast

THE OLD House of Assembly is an elegant chamber of perfect proportions designed in the 1920s by that master of colonial architecture, Sir Herbert Baker. Its elegance is crowned by panelling in dark stinkwood, the country's most prized hardwood. The Members' desks are of that same noble timber. Yet when I first took my seat in the Press Gallery there, I thought the atmosphere a little dark, a little gloomy. But perhaps that was subliminal, given the chamber's role as the venue of our fierce historical conflicts.

Paradoxically it was also lily-white. Not a dark face to be seen, not even among the messengers, dining-room waiters, or kitchen or cleaning staff. My first session there was also the first at which there was no representation whatsoever for the country's African majority. The long constitutional struggle over this had ended with the National Party triumphant: the positions of the three white MPs representing the country's 8.5 million Africans had been abolished at the end of the 1960 session. Eight years later, the four whites representing the Cape coloured population were gone as well. Thereafter the national Parliament represented only the country's white population, less than a quarter of the whole. Whites only, talking endlessly about the destiny of all those who were not there.

It was also a session that was cut in half, with each half

operating under a different constitution. When I began my first session early in February, it was still under the old constitution of the Union of South Africa. But a year earlier, Verwoerd had called a referendum to decide whether the country should realise the long-held Afrikaner dream of becoming a republic. The referendum was held on 5 October and the pro-republicans won by 52 per cent of the vote – a majority of only 74 580 votes. The new constitution, which replaced the Queen as head of state with a non-executive State President, came into effect on 31 May 1961.

From my perch in the Press Gallery, I found myself looking directly down at the top of Hendrik Verwoerd's head. He was Prime Minister and would remain so under the new constitution, but he was now at the very apex of his power, hero-worshipped to the point of reverence after miraculously surviving the assassination attempt and at the point of being able to deliver to the Afrikaner *volk* their longed-for dream. Yet I remember thinking how vulnerable he looked, sitting there alone at his desk – all other MPs shared desks – directly beneath me. How easy simply to drop a poisoned dart on that scalp.

A fantasy moment, of course, yet a mere five years later a parliamentary messenger – one serving the Press Gallery, what's more – was to walk up to the Prime Minister as if to hand him a message but instead stabbed him to death with a dagger right there, in that seat. Many national leaders have been assassinated over the years, but I know of none killed literally in the seat of power. That, too, is now part of the ugly history of Sir Herbert's elegant chamber.

Surrounded by all the trappings of power and the ancient rituals of parliamentary procedure inherited from Westminster – from the solemn entry of the robed Sergeant-at-Arms bearing the Mace to its stand in the House of Assembly, with the Gentleman Usher of the Black Rod performing the same in the Senate, to the Members bowing to the Speaker as they entered and left the chamber – I felt daunted at first by the responsibility of my job as the representative of the biggest morning newspaper in the country. I was just 28. But I soon slipped into the routine, absorbed into a collective life in a bubble of its own, self-contained within itself and largely cut off from the outside world. Rather like being aboard an ocean liner.

What surprised me was the ease with which one had contact with the most powerful figures in what was a harsh authoritarian regime. In the lobby one could chat with ministers, including the Prime Minister, sometimes even reaching a level of familiarity with them. So it was that I was able several times to engage with Verwoerd, asking him to elaborate on points of policy. This he always did with great readiness; he was an evangelist for his cause, always courteous and avuncular. His manner was that of a patient professor trying to help his student understand. He was never impatient or irritable, not even when confronted with blunt questions. I once asked him whether he was aware of the pain and suffering the implementation of his policies was causing in the black communities being forcibly removed from so-called black spots in 'white' South Africa. 'Yes of course,' he replied. 'It is unfortunate, but it is necessary in the interests of the country and of the Bantu people themselves. They must have their own freedom in their own areas otherwise we shall never have peace in this country.'

His speeches in the House were long and tortuous, two-hour perorations delivered mostly in Afrikaans, which his supporters listened to in silent reverence. It was as though he was bringing the tablets of political truth down from Mount Sinai. Any interjection from the opposition side would bring howls of outrage. It was not great oratory, more in the style of extended lectures. We in the Press Gallery had to listen intently throughout, for in the midst of the sermon, just as you were dozing off, there might be a hint of some new twist in the apartheid labyrinth that would be tomorrow's front-page lead. There was no simultaneous translation, so note-taking became a special skill. My Afrikaans was good enough but I had only English shorthand, which meant having to do my own simultaneous translation in my head and get it down in shorthand script at verbatim speed. Not easy, especially as Verwoerd's concepts were often very convoluted.

Verwoerd would expound, over and over again, on his philosophy of ethnic nationalism, the need to have pride in your own national language, culture and identity, all derived from your own struggle history and literature and grounded in the soil of your own nation-state, which was a God-given right for the existence and survival of any *volk*. To lose it to the black majority would be national suicide. But to claim that right for yourself meant you had also to grant it to the other *volke* (nations) living here in South Africa. It was all redolent of the age of German Romanticism, of Herder and Fichte and *Blut und Boden* (blood and soil), with some touches of Calvinist theology thrown in – remember his father had been a missionary. But in Verwoerd's mind it was a practical political programme, not just a philosophy of life.

Granting these rights to black South Africans, whom Verwoerd regarded not as one national entity but nine, would be difficult, he conceded. It would require white people to become less reliant on black labour and to do more manual work themselves. When business leaders, including some Afrikaners, spoke out that this would retard economic development, Verwoerd was unmoved. 'If I have to choose between being rich and multiracial or poor and white,' he said more than once, 'I will choose to be white.'

I never heard Verwoerd raise his voice, not even in the stormiest debates. He spoke with the confidence of absolute certitude, didactic and dogmatic. Rykie van Reenen, a leading Afrikaans journalist, once wrote of Verwoerd's revealing response when she asked him in an interview whether he could sleep at night, given the heavy responsibility of implementing his policies. 'I sleep very well,' Verwoerd replied. 'You see, one doesn't have the problem of worrying whether one could perhaps be wrong.'[1]

In fact, it was precisely this certitude that was the undoing of the Afrikaner cause. It rendered Verwoerd inflexible. He was wrong in many instances, but he could never recognise or rectify it. And the worst of it was that he so dominated his party for so long that none of his successors was able to depart from the course he had charted until very late in the day.

Verwoerd was wrong, hopelessly so, in his home-grown demographics, which were based on amateurish projections by a Stellenbosch University think tank that the black population would reach 19 million by the year 2000. Verwoerd calculated that 10 to 12 million would be accommodated in the Bantustans, or 'homelands' as he preferred to call them. He reckoned the white population would then be 6 million, with only 5 to 7 million blacks remaining in 'white' South Africa, bringing the race groups close to equilibrium. To Verwoerd, this ratio, coupled with regulations to restrict the influx of black workers into the industrial cities, would be a sustainable situation.

But anyone acquainted with the homeland areas knew Verwoerd's projections were pure fantasy. Even I, having lived at Hotfire, knew that the territory across the Kei River, by far the most viable of the putative Bantustans, was being ecologically ravaged, with too many people and animals on too little land. There was no way its carrying capacity could be significantly increased. As it turned out, not only were Verwoerd's projected figures hopelessly wrong – the black population was 35 million by 2000, almost double his projected figure, while the numbers in the homelands had increased only fractionally – but also the white population remained almost static. The implications of his mis-calculation were fatal to his entire political project. It meant that after half a century of apartheid, whites were more outnumbered than ever in 'white' South Africa.

Verwoerd was wrong again in prohibiting outside investment in the homelands, which would have been the only way to absorb more people and reduce the flow of migrant labourers to the cities. But he was adamant that black people had to create their own economic development in these arid and off-the-beaten-track regions. In his view, outside investment, particularly by white South Africans, would amount to economic colonialism, diluting the purity of black people building their own national states according to the utmost of their own abilities and in accordance with their own traditions and cultures. That was his mantra.

He was wrong, worst of all, in insisting that education for young black people should be prescribed to equip them to serve their own people in their own areas according to the needs of those areas, and not to equip them for careers in 'white' South Africa. This was the cornerstone of the notorious Bantu Education Act of 1953. Verwoerd has been accused of proclaiming that blacks should not be trained for careers above their station, that their proper role was to be 'hewers of wood and drawers of water', but in fairness I must say I never heard him say that, nor have I found a quote of his approximating such a statement. I believed then, and still do, that his Bantu education policy was determined primarily by his fixation on the perceived needs of his misbegotten ideology. Not that the results were any different in terms of the human damage inflicted.

But on one issue Verwoerd was unfortunately not wrong in his foresight. As he pressed ahead with implementing the Group Areas Act, which involved the forced removal of millions of black, coloured and Indian people into separate living areas according to their race classification, he urged his people never to let up on this heartless programme. 'We owe it to the future generations of our people,' he said, 'to take this policy so far that no one will ever be able to reverse it.' Regrettably, this goal was largely achieved. The human geography of the new South Africa still represents a patchwork of racially segregated areas, with the poorest of the black people living in townships and informal settlements at the greatest distance from where they work. The emerging middle classes can afford to move in to the formerly whites-only suburbs, but even the new housing complexes being built for the poor are forced by the cost of urban land to be located at ever greater distances from the town and city centres.

These were the issues I found myself focusing on in my reportage of the government's activities. I would have a telephone conversation at six o'clock every evening with Laurence Gandar, during which we would exchange views on how the political scene was evolving, what insights could be gained from the debates, and which issues required deeper elaboration or investigation. I would then send to the news desk my diary of what stories I would be submitting for the next day's paper, so that their placement could be decided at the evening news conference. I found those quite lengthy conversations with the editor hugely instructive, a daily interchange between the reporter on the spot and the commander-in-chief whose job was to analyse and interpret and set the editorial policy line for the paper. It was stimulating and exciting, for these were extraordinary times as the *Rand Daily Mail* moved further and further ahead of the pack in its trenchant criticism of government policies.

Verwoerd intrigued me. His obsessive attention to dogmatic detail reflected a lack of flexibility. Everything had to be done strictly in accordance with the ideology as he was enunciating it; no deviations were allowed. Pragmatism was a strategy totally alien to him. '*Hy dink konsekwent*,' his colleagues would explain. 'He thinks logically.' Any departure from the prescribed doctrine would lead to a chain reaction of catastrophic consequences. I remember listening, bemused, to his explanation in Parliament of why his government couldn't allow the New Zealand Rugby Union to include a Maori wing three-quarter in its team that was about to tour South Africa. 'You see,' Verwoerd explained, 'if we allow this black man into the country, we will have to let him play on sports fields meant for whites only. We will have to let him stay in white hotels, go with his team-mates to white bars and restaurants. How can we then say to our own black people you can't do those things, you can't stay in white hotels or go to white restaurants? And how will we be able to say to our black people that you can't play in our national sports teams? It will be the end of apartheid, and that will be the end of the white man in South Africa.'

I wrote a column at the time ascribing Verwoerd's ideological rigidity to his Dutch ancestry. The boy with his finger in the dyke, knowing that if he took it out the water would gush forth and sweep all before it. A nice metaphor, but perhaps a little unfair to the Dutch who, at that time, were the most liberal people in the world and among the most vocal critics of apartheid.

Piet Cillié, editor of *Die Burger* and one of the Afrikaner community's leading intellectuals, shared my theory that Verwoerd's Dutch ancestry was partly responsible for his dogmatism, but put a different slant on it. 'Historical evidence shows that the foreign immigrant absorbs the prejudices of his adopted nationalism in distilled form,' Cillié once expounded to me in an illuminating conversation. 'Napoleon was a Corsican, Hitler was an Austrian and Verwoerd was a Hollander.' Which I guess is another version of the zeal of the convert.

The irony, of course, is that it was precisely this ideological rigidity of Verwoerd's that produced the consequences he so feared. It led to the international sports boycott of South Africa, perhaps the most painfully felt by white South Africans, and from there to a series of other, much more damaging boycotts that ultimately helped to bring apartheid to its knees.

Yet I still have a slightly different view of Verwoerd from the standard one as the consummately evil racist. He was an intellectual who gave a veneer of moral respectability, however delusional, to a policy which until then had been expressed in the crude Afrikaans slogan, '*Die kaffir op sy plek en die Koelie uit die land*' (The nigger in his place and the Coolie [Indian] out of the country). Verwoerd used to explain, with painstaking patience, that the 'black man' could not be held down forever, that he would inevitably demand full political rights and the only choice would be to do so either through separate development, the Bantustans, or through racial integration, which would result in black majority rule.

I used to watch him make poor Sir De Villiers Graaff, leader of the United Party opposition, squirm in his seat as he demanded: 'If you are opposed to separate development, you must be in favour of one-man-one-vote.' As Graaff insisted he was not, knowing that to concede the point would be suicidal given the deeply conservative character of the whites-only electorate, Verwoerd would come back at him: 'If you don't believe in separate development or integration, that means you can only be in favour of permanent racial domination. The black man can never have his freedom under your policy. So you are the racist, not me.' It was devastating stuff, and was in fact the argument that convinced me at an early age that full racial integration was the only possible future for South Africa.

More important, for all its impracticality Verwoerd's relentless theoretical logic had an electrifying effect on the young Afrikaner intelligentsia. As the distinguished Afrikaner historian Hermann Giliomee has written, they responded enthusiastically to Verwoerd's ideas, which seemed to offer a new way out of the country's racial dilemma, with some hailing him as 'a man with a sense of calling and a vision'.[2] It is my contention that Verwoerd's veneer of morality, thin though it was, coupled with his insistence that the choice lay starkly between apartheid and integration, sowed the seeds for the future emergence of the *verligte*, or enlightened, movement in the National Party that was a key factor in the constellation of events that led President FW de Klerk to embark on the transformative process he announced on 2 February 1990.

Even as the international pressures increased, Verwoerd's confidence never flagged. I recall listening one long afternoon in the House as he expounded on a thesis that there was no need to worry about these pressures for they would all prove temporary and would inevitably recede. It was an observable feature of history, he explained to his avid listeners, that political ideas moved in cycles in which each new idea would gain momentum, and then gradually generate its own reaction. Multiracialism was the current vogue, but be assured that in time, as individual groups began to feel their national and cultural identities coming under the threat of being swamped by the influx of alien elements, there would be a reaction against it. Humanity would revert to a recognition of the need to protect their cultural identities in their own homeland areas. They would then come around to realising that South Africa had been right all along, that apartheid was the only stable way for the ordering of global society. So all we had to do in the face of these rising international pressures was to hang in there, stick to our principles and wait for the reaction to set in and for the world to come around to our way of thinking.

There was just enough Hegelian logic in his thesis to make it seem credible, and I remember being struck by the man's political skills as I watched the serried ranks of Nationalist MPs soak it all in with expressions of relief and gratitude. For Verwoerd, the applied psychologist, had touched on the very core of Afrikaner angst, the fear of cultural swamping and the loss of *volksidentiteit* that lay at the heart of their racist responses to the black majority. And he had told them to relax, have no fear, for I have the answers. No wonder they idolised him.

Ironically, another South African President to recognise the depth of that Afrikaner angst and make it central to his political strategising was Nelson Mandela. During his long years in

Parliamentary Press Gallery group, 1962 — all white and all male. I am back row centre; Stewart Carlyle at my right shoulder; Donald Woods second last row far left; Tertius Myburgh, then of The Star, *third row second from left; Donald Prosser,* Eastern Province Herald, *front row far right. We formed a close anti-apartheid group.*

prison, Mandela set about studying the mentality of the warders guarding the political prisoners' section on Robben Island. As he explained to me in our many conversations later, he was puzzled by the warders' wanton brutality. What made them hate black people so much? Carefully he set about trying to engage them individually, asking about their personal circumstances. He soon found most of them were in difficulties, facing financial problems and turbulent domestic lives. Being a lawyer, Mandela was able to offer them advice and so, over time, establish warmer relations with his jailers.

'It was then,' he told me, 'that I discovered that their aggressive attitude towards us was because they feared us. They feared that if we ever took over control of the country, we would turn on them with vengeance. You see, these were people at the lower economic end of the Afrikaner community and so they feared that they would be the first to lose their jobs if we took over. They looked at us, the political leaders, and they were afraid of what we were fighting for, and so they hated us. I realised then that if we ever ended up at a negotiating table, I would have to neutralise that fear.'

Hence the policy of racial reconciliation that Mandela pursued with such energy and skill after his release.

This underlying existential threat was something I encountered again and again in conversations with Afrikaner journalists in the Press Gallery. It was all very well for me, an English-speaker, to adopt a liberal stance, they would argue, because if things went wrong under majority rule I could always flee to any part of the great English-speaking world and still be culturally secure. For them it was different. It was a theme spelled out most eloquently at the time by the doyen of Afrikaner journalists, Schalk Pienaar, in a small volume co-authored with a leading critic of apartheid, Anthony Sampson, who later became Mandela's authorised biographer. The essence of Pienaar's argument was that Afrikaners, through 300 years of history and struggle, had won the right to be regarded as a nation. Faced with the pressure to submit to a rising black nationalism, their only option was to refuse. According to Pienaar, 'the Afrikaner has nowhere else to go. For him there is no Britain and no Holland to return to; for him no central shrine of national existence to survive the death of the outposts. On the soil of Africa he, and with him his history, culture and language, stay or perish.'[3]

As a liberal journalist working for a liberal newspaper, I had to come to terms with these issues. My nightly phone calls with Laurence Gandar had us going beyond simply discussing the day's news from Parliament; we had to discuss the larger issues involved, which meant recognising both the crudity of apartheid's racism and the validity of the Afrikaner dilemma. How to position the paper's editorial line to take account of both?

The answer was to go back to Gandar's original theme, which was that there were only two ways out of such a dilemma:

either through a fair partition, a two-state solution, or through integration into a single, multiracial state.

That became the *Rand Daily Mail*'s editorial line. If a fair partition of South Africa into nine geographically coherent and economically viable black states capable of accommodating the great majority of the black population were feasible, fine. We would accept that, even though it would not be our first choice because, as Gandar put it, 'it would involve a shrinkage of the human spirit'. But if it were not feasible, then the country would have to face up to the only alternative that Verwoerd had spelt out to his own people – the single-state solution of a racially integrated South Africa. The paper's policy would be to hold the apartheid government's feet to the fire on that clear-cut issue of Verwoerd's own defining.

In fact, Gandar was already writing powerful columns and editorials pointing to the sheer impossibility of Verwoerd's vision. Drawing on a five-year study prepared by a government commission under the chairmanship of a leading Afrikaner academic, Professor FR Tomlinson, Gandar laid out what he called the 'arithmetic of apartheid' to demonstrate that the policy's own advocates could not envisage it ever achieving a meaningful separation of the races. The Tomlinson Report, presented in 1956, was effectively the blueprint for Verwoerd's policy of 'separate development' – and in Gandar's opinion was its most damning condemnation.

The report, comprising 18 volumes in its original form, endorsed Verwoerd's contention that South Africa faced only two possibilities – either the progressive integration of the black and white races into a single homogeneous society, or their separate development each in its own areas. Since, according to the report, the first alternative envisaged the disappearance of the Afrikaner nation, it strongly advocated the second, but warned that if nothing was done to upgrade the productive capacity of the black areas, the white population, then numbering 2.6 million to the blacks' 8.5 million, would become increasingly outnumbered in 'white' South Africa. By the year 2000, it warned, the blacks in those mainly urban areas would number 21 million, to between 4.5 million and 6 million whites.

Tomlinson therefore advocated a massive development programme for the black areas, to consolidate them and boost their productivity. If this programme were fully implemented, he predicted, the Bantustans could hopefully be able to accommodate nearly 15 million black people. But, as Gandar pointed out, that would mean there would still be about 17 million blacks to 4.5 million or 5 million whites in 'white' South Africa.

'After all that effort, all that expenditure and all that human disruption over the next forty years,' he wrote, 'the National Party will have solved nothing. Whites will still be outnumbered two-to-one in what is supposed to become the white part of the country.'

According to Verwoerdian mythology, the tide of black migration to the cities was supposed to turn in 1978. Why that year was chosen no one ever explained. In fact, it turned out to be the year when black numbers began to swell way beyond Tomlinson's prediction. By February 1990, when President FW de Klerk finally threw in the towel and still ten years short of the turn of the century, the total black population had swelled to 37.5 million, with only 5 million whites. More than seven to one.

Yet when that moment of capitulation finally came, Afrikaans journalism's most celebrated intellectual, Piet Cillié, offered what must surely be the most pathetic attempt at exculpation yet offered for all those years of black suffering. 'We had to try apartheid,' he said, 'to prove that it couldn't work.'

* * *

WHILE GANDAR was spelling out apartheid's unworkability on the evidence of the government's own projections, my task as political correspondent was to underpin his editorial arguments by looking closely at the implementation side of the policy. What were the facts on the ground? How much was the government actually spending on Bantustan development? How did it measure up to the Tomlinson Commission's recommendations? And what was the pattern of labour demands and influx into the cities?

It was not long before the budget allocation for Bantustan

development received a sudden surge, accompanied by much trumpeting on the part of the Afrikaans press. Here was the government's answer to the sceptics, they crowed; Verwoerd was clearly serious about building up the carrying capacity of the black 'homelands'. It was a claim that required closer examination. So I sought out the blue books that had been tabled after the Budget speech and began the task of churning my way through the dense prose and long columns of statistics. It was some days before I came upon the details of the Bantustan development allocation, but when I did it was like striking gold. Three-quarters of the total allocation was devoted to purchasing a finger of land to be attached to the Ciskei 'homeland' in order to form a corridor that would take the Bantustan to within about ten kilometres of East London. Another significant sum was allocated to the cost of relocating the inhabitants of East London's black township of Duncan Village to a new township, called Mdantsane, to be built for them at the tip of that corridor.

It was a blatant scam. This was not Bantustan development at all. It was simply the relocation of an urban black township, almost the entire workforce of East London, and their artificial attachment to the putative Ciskei, a wedge of land covering 5 300 square kilometres (about 3 294 square miles), or a quarter the size of Wales, that was destined for future independence. Having grown up in the eastern Cape and worked on the *Daily Dispatch*, I was able to describe the arid landscape of the region, with its low carrying capacity and complete lack of natural resources. My story made a front-page lead and provided material for more scathing Gandar editorials.

Moreover, it provided the basis for future case studies of not just the futility but also the deception of the Bantustan programme. The Ciskei was never developed to increase its human carrying capacity. It became the dumping ground for 350 000 black people – half the original population – who were evicted from so-called black spots in 'white' South Africa and literally dumped in settlements whose names became international symbols of apartheid notoriety – Dimbaza, Sada, Thornhill, Zweledinge, Ilinge and

Potsdam. I went back there years later with South Africa's finest photographer, David Goldblatt, to do a colour magazine feature for *The Observer*. Television teams followed.

Far from East London's black workers benefiting from being resettled in their own 'homeland', they were infinitely worse off. Whereas before they had been able to walk to work from Duncan Village, now they had to catch and pay for buses for the 20- to 30-km round trip from Mdantsane, which, with the huge influx of resettled families, soon became the second-largest black township after Johannesburg's Soweto. Bus boycotts, strikes and rioting became endemic. Unemployment reached 35 per cent, while the 1 400 000 Ciskeians living in the rest of South Africa lost their citizenship rights and became deportable aliens. Professor Jan Lange of the University of South Africa calculated at the time that the average Ciskeian would be 465 per cent better off if he went away to work illegally for six months in a city in 'white' South Africa, and paid a penalty of six months' imprisonment on his return, than if he stayed at home.

This was a far cry from Verwoerd's long expositions about 'separate freedoms' that I listened to in the House of Assembly. But then he, like the vast majority of white South Africans who kept voting for him in increasing numbers, never saw the gap between theory and practice. They lived in a bubble.

* * *

THREE MONTHS before the new republican constitution was due to come into force, Verwoerd flew to London to negotiate South Africa's continued membership of the Commonwealth. He had assured South Africa's English-speaking community during the referendum campaign that this would be a mere formality, but I doubt he could genuinely have expected that. Harold Macmillan's speech the year before had forewarned him that apartheid had become a contentious issue among the growing number of black member states. Julius Nyerere, President of the soon-to-be-independent Tanganyika, had already made a speech ahead of the Commonwealth summit warning that 'To invite South Africa in is to vote us out.' Kwame Nkrumah of Ghana and India's Jawaharlal Nehru had also spoken out publicly ahead of the conference, and once it got under way further objections were raised by Archbishop Makarios of Cyprus, Tunku Abdul Rahman of Malaya and even Canada's Conservative Prime Minister, John Diefenbaker. Faced with the certainty of defeat, Verwoerd withdrew the republic's application for membership and flew home.

A crowd of thousands greeted him as a hero as he landed at Johannesburg airport. It was clear that, far from having suffered a humiliating defeat in London, he had struck a popular chord with his supporters at home. He received an equally enthusiastic accolade in the House. For the most part, the English-speaking community's reaction was one of passive disappointment, except in Natal, where there was a blossoming of Union Jacks and mutterings about secession by 'the last outpost of Empire' that no one took seriously. Verwoerd was on a high and he seized the moment to announce that he would seek a new mandate at a general election on 18 October.

There were a few expressions of dissent from the opposition in the House, both the United Party and the new Progressive Party expressing their concerns about the economic and diplomatic im-plications of losing Commonwealth membership. One passionate protest sticks in my mind. Douglas Smit, an ardent Afrikaner royalist from East London, who had served the Smuts regime as a supporter and civil servant for most of his life, delivered a speech choked with emotion that was a cameo of personal pathos. In those days, for reasons I never understood, MPs were not allowed to read their speeches in the House; they had to speak extem-poraneously. But on this occasion Smit, whom we in the Press Gallery had nicknamed 'Chalkie' after the gaunt schoolmaster in the Giles cartoons, rose with a wad of notes in his hand, osten-tatiously removed his hearing aid, and proceeded to read in his thin, reedy voice. It was a catalogue of Britain's glorious imperial achievements, of its compassion towards the defeated Boers, and above all of the wondrous advantages of the Commonwealth as-sociation. The Speaker repeatedly called Chalkie to order, but he was deaf and his hearing aid was switched off, so he churned on.

167

There was no stopping him. The Nationalist MPs laughed and hooted with derision, but then gradually the laughter subsided and even the Speaker fell silent out of a kind of reluctant respect as Chalkie reached the climax of his eulogy with tears streaming down his face. 'And all this,' he sobbed, 'you have exchanged for a mess of apartheid pottage.' Douglas Smit never spoke in Parliament again and he died soon afterwards.

A more explosive outburst came from a Press Gallery colleague, Donald Prosser, who was political correspondent of the *Eastern Province Herald* in Port Elizabeth. Donald, too, was an ardent royalist. As the news of our withdrawal from the Commonwealth reached us in the parliamentary press corps, he rose in a fit of uncontrollable anger, burst open the door leading into the Press Gallery benches above the assembled MPs, and in a voice choking with rage called out: 'You bloody maniacs!' Nothing like this had ever happened before. It violated all Press Gallery rules, and the rest of us quaked at what the consequences might be. Yet there were no repercussions, except that, four years later, after Verwoerd's assassination in Parliament, security police investigators called on Donald to interrogate him.

My own reaction was mainly one of indifference. My experiences of travelling abroad had made me value the fellowship that came with being a member of the Commonwealth, and I certainly felt that severance would be a loss for the country. But beyond that I felt nothing of substance had changed. The ending of the relationship with the Royal Family meant nothing to me. Neither my family nor I had ever felt any personal attachment to the royal connection. Our roots in South Africa went back too far for us to regard England as 'home', as many English-speakers did. What I did begin to recognise, however, was that I could not consider myself to be a true South African patriot. The National Party regime often accused people like myself of being unpatriotic, and, although I hated the accusation, at one level I knew they were right. Yes, I loved the country, its physical beauty and its people, all its people, the human texture they brought to its cultural mix. Yet I couldn't pass the litmus test of the true patriot, of 'my country right or wrong'. I could not accept the wrongs of my country;

they were too fundamental to my moral conscience. I was not prepared to die for my country. Nor to kill for it. I was not stirred by the sound of its national anthem, nor by the sight of its flag. Yet I felt deeply about the country and its future. At an intellectual level I could understand, and even sympathise with, the existential fear of the Afrikaners, the vulnerability of their national identity that had driven them to adopt the policy of apartheid. But I couldn't support them in that endeavour, nor condone it. I had seen the effects of that policy's implementation in its reality on the ground and it was too obscene, too inhumane. Surely no people had the right to build their nationhood on the basis of the deprivation of the human rights of others.

As I was to write later in response to that compelling piece by Schalk Pienaar: 'There is a duplicity in [Pienaar's] argument that lies at the bottom of this issue. He bases his case on the immutability of history and then ignores the greater part of it. Which is that history so decided, too, that the Afrikaner nation would arise in a country they would have to share with others; that South Africa was not theirs alone; that they would constitute only one-tenth of its population; that in no part of it, not in one single district, would they constitute a majority. The injunction of history is surely that the Afrikaners must come to terms with this truth. Yet they have defined their nationalism in terms that deny this … Defined as it is, the existence of the Afrikaner nation becomes contingent on the exclusion or oppression of the other people with whom it shares the country. Ultimately that can only be done by physical and institutionalised force, at which point Afrikanerdom loses its claim to legitimacy.'[4]

Where did this leave me? I was not an Afrikaner, but I was aware that a large number of my fellow English-speakers, perhaps a majority, quietly approved of the basics of apartheid while at the same time looking down upon the Afrikaners as being too rough, too unsubtle. There was an element of hypocrisy about some that I found contemptible. Racists without a cause, was my private label of derision, for they did not suffer from the Afrikaner's sense of cultural vulnerability. Then again, I wasn't black either. I could empathise with the oppression black people were suffering, but

I could not share it with them because I was born white, born privileged, inevitably part of the oppressor race. So who was I, what was I, living in this land whose very ethos I rejected but about whose moral challenges I felt passionate? The answer, of course, was that as a journalist I was a communicator between these conflicted elements of my country who lived separately from each other and therefore did not meet each other and were moving inexorably towards some terrible confrontation without speaking to each other, without hearing each other, without understanding each other, just filled with a fear turned to hatred of the other. Fate had cast me in that role. It was to be my identity. A journalist.

CHAPTER ELEVEN
A Fight for Survival

WITH THE TRIUMPH of the referendum and the inauguration of the republic already in the National Party's favour, the
outcome of the 18 October election was a foregone conclusion.
We knew, too, that the delimitation of parliamentary constituencies would give the Nationalists an extra edge, so an increased
majority seemed likely. Which meant the only real interest was on
the opposition side. It was obvious that one of Verwoerd's reasons
for calling the snap election was to try to eliminate the Progressive
Party before it could properly establish itself. He could live with
the softly critical me-tooism of the United Party, which had even
supported his watershed Unlawful Organisations Bill banning the
ANC, the PAC and all other black nationalist movements the year
before, but he couldn't tolerate a voice in Parliament that was
diametrically opposed to his policies. So the key issue in the
election was whether the Progressive Party could survive.

There was a lot loaded against it. Ineffective though the United
Party was in its opposition to apartheid, it remained embedded in
the conservative ethos of the English-speaking establishment. It
was still seen as the party of Smuts, the Afrikaner icon who had
stood by Britain through two world wars. Moreover his successor,
Sir De Villiers Graaff, was custom-built for the role: the handsome, titled scion of a wealthy Afrikaner family, who was himself

171

the godson of General Louis Botha, the leader of the Boer forces who had become South Africa's first Prime Minister.

Graaff was an articulate debater and an effective critic of the government's apartheid policy. His weakness was an inability to come up with an alternative policy, which left him unable to win over disaffected Nationalists, of which there were growing numbers. This was partly because Graaff realised how difficult it would be to sell the only real alternative to his party followers, but also because he himself could not countenance the idea of racial integration. He repeatedly suggested that, if treated 'decently', the 'natives' would naturally want to live separately from the whites, implying that some form of natural apartheid would take place if there were no attempt to enforce it. It was as unconvincing as it was wishy-washy, but it was enough to keep the majority of conservative English-speakers and the old Afrikaner *Bloedsappe* (diehard Botha-Smuts followers) happy – at least for the time being. It would obviously be difficult for the Progressives to break into such a loyal following, particularly since they would be vulnerable to accusations of splitting the opposition vote to the advantage of the Nationalists.

The other more serious disadvantage the Progressives faced was the flood of bad news from newly independent states to the north that gathered pace in 1961. Words of alarm echoed from Kenya when Jomo Kenyatta was released from prison, where he had served a term for allegedly being a leader of the Mau Mau resistance movement. Kenyatta assumed leadership of the powerful Kenya African National Union (Kanu) party and was flown to London to participate in independence negotiations. Meanwhile, just across our northern border, Kenneth Kaunda and the bombastic Hastings Kamuzu Banda were putting pressure on the Colonial Office to dissolve the Federation of Rhodesia and Nyasaland and grant independence to Northern Rhodesia and Nyasaland.

Worst of all, though, was the collapse of any semblance of law and order in the Congo. In June 1960, Belgium had precipitously granted independence to this enormous, mineral-rich slab of land straddling the heart of the continent. One week later, a rebellion broke out within the Congolese gendarmerie, the Force Publique, against its mainly Belgian officers. This ignited a wave of violence across the vast country, and horror stories of atrocities committed against whites, including the rape of nuns, filtered south. The situation grew worse as a regional leader, Moïse Tshombe, led a secessionist movement to declare his Katanga province independent – supported by the huge Belgian copper mining company, Union Miniére, as well as by the United States. Soon afterwards Tshombe had the newly elected Congolese Prime Minister, Patrice Lumumba, arrested, then executed by a firing squad.

None of this was conducive to the Progressive Party's message of racial integration. The Progs argued that these calamities were the result of delaying integration and political negotiation with the African nationalist parties for too long, and urged that South Africa should not make the same mistake. It was obviously a valid observation but it cut little ice in the face of the alarmist headlines appearing almost daily in South Africa. Fear trumps logic any day. The Progs were going to face an uphill struggle.

As Parliament went into recess at the end of June, Mary, toddler Simon and I drove back to Johannesburg. By then Mary was five months pregnant, but we gave little thought to how this might impact on my coverage of the election. Mary had become fascinated by the moral challenges of South African politics and soon after we had settled into a rented house in Johannesburg's Houghton constituency, she enlisted as a volunteer worker in Helen Suzman's campaign.

Soon after my return to head office, Gandar began a round of discussions with what he called his 'headquarters staff' – a quaint carry-over from his army days – to discuss the policy line the paper should take in the run-up to the election. This meant talking individually to his assistant editors and other senior staff members, including me as political correspondent. It soon became evident that he had made up his mind to commit the paper to supporting the Progressive Party, but wanted to make sure his own senior staff were behind him. Significantly, he did not speak to anyone on the board of directors, nor to the managing director, Henry Kuiper, or the general manager, Leycester

Walton. This was because Gandar was a strong believer in the principle of editorial independence, which holds that editors should not be subjected to pressure from managers or shareholders who might seek to interfere with news coverage, for personal, political or economic reasons. News decisions were meant to be the sole prerogative of the paper's staff of professional journalists working under the direction of the editor. It is a principle that has become sadly eroded in recent times as economic pressures on newspapers have intensified with the growth of the electronic media. But I believe it remains fundamental to the publication of any quality newspaper or other news media.

In Gandar's case, to have informed the board or the management of his intention to commit the *Rand Daily Mail* to supporting the Progressive Party would have effectively been to seek their approval. If any or all of them had objected, Gandar would have been in an invidious position. He would effectively have given them the right to veto his decision, in which case he would have forfeited his right as editor to be the final arbiter of how his newspaper should report the news and comment upon it. Such a lame-duck editor would have had no choice but to resign. So Gandar didn't tell them – a correct decision, but one that was to have repercussions for years to come.

Gandar duly published an editorial declaring the paper's support for the Progressive Party. From then on coverage of the election campaign went into high gear. My role was to cover all election meetings and events in the Johannesburg area, but also to write a series of 'Election Profiles' focusing on constituencies where the key contests would take place. This involved visiting the constituencies, getting a sense of the voters living there, the electoral history of each, and profiling the candidates. I eventually published 22 of these profiles, mostly covering constituencies where Prog candidates were running against UP candidates. This was a tricky issue for the Progressives as they faced the charge of splitting the opposition vote to the Nationalists' advantage. To lessen the damaging impression this was causing, they had to do some juggling, wherever possible putting up candidates in safe opposition seats that the Nationalists were not contesting. This meant several of their most senior members had to leave the constituencies they had served for many years and stand elsewhere; the most seriously disadvantaged case was their leader, Jannie Steytler, who had to leave Queenstown, where he had lived all his life and enjoyed strong personal support, and stand in Port Elizabeth, where he was little known.

Splitting the opposition vote was an issue that also troubled Gandar. He decided on a complex compromise: the paper would support Progressive candidates only where there was no risk of this benefiting the Nationalists, while at the same time it would support United Party candidates – and encourage Progressive and other liberal-minded voters to do likewise – wherever there was a real chance of defeating the Nationalists. It was a strategy that invited some ridicule from the United Party leadership, who described it as duplicitous, but it made pragmatic sense.

As the campaigning entered its final phase, Gandar upped the tempo of support for the Progressives. Over the final ten days he ran a countdown of powerful front-page editorials, emphasising the importance of sending signals to the restive black community and an increasingly critical world that there was a significant body of white voters in South Africa who were opposed to apartheid and willing to accept its alternative of integration. But he was privately worried that if the Progressives were wiped out, left with no voice in Parliament whatsoever, not only would the opposite signal be sent out but also, worse still, the promising movement would be stillborn. It had become clear that all the contests in which the Progressives were involved would be extremely tight, but the one where there was the best chance of success was in Houghton, where Helen Suzman was running. Gandar urged me to arrange an interview with her and write a special feature on her for publication in the week before polling day.

I made the appointment for 1 August, a Sunday, for lunch at 12.30 at her home. I woke early to prepare questions. It was going to be an important interview, perhaps decisive for the survival of the Progressive Party. As I was getting dressed I heard Mary, who was still in bed, give a sudden gasp. 'Contractions,' she muttered. 'The baby's coming.'

175

'Omigod,' I thought. 'Not today of all days.' But another gasp convinced me it was indeed the day of our new baby's arrival. I helped Mary pack an overnight bag and bundled her into our car. It was a long drive to the Marymount Maternity Hospital in Kensington, and Johannesburg's notorious traffic was already thickening. We seemed to crawl our way there, while Mary's contractions intensified.

Eventually we arrived at the Marymount and I helped Mary walk, with her contractions now coming strongly and continuously, into the hospital and up to the reception desk. There was no one there. Frantically I looked around to find someone, anyone, who could help us with the admission procedure. The place seemed deserted. I ran up and down stairs, searching. Eventually I found an African woman with a mop and pail of water cleaning a floor. Where, I asked, could we find someone to check in my wife. 'Oh, the nuns are all at Mass,' she replied nonchalantly as she continued to mop the floor.

'Please call someone to help,' I begged. 'The baby's coming.' She put down the mop and wandered off. I went back to the reception and waited. And waited. Time ticked by. It was nearing 12 o'clock. Helen Suzman would soon be waiting.

'Don't wait for me,' Mary urged. 'I'll be all right. Remember how long it took for Simon to arrive. I was in labour for 24 hours.'

'Yes,' I said, 'but I think second babies come faster. I can't just leave you here alone.'

Just then a nun arrived. Laboriously we filled out a stack of forms. It seemed to take an eternity. Eventually it was done and the sister took Mary's overnight bag and led her away. Mary turned and looked back at me just as they rounded a corner. 'Good luck,' she called. 'Give Helen my love.'

I looked at my watch and fled. It was 12 noon.

The interview went well. Helen was lively and provocative as always, and I headed back to the office to begin preparing my special feature, trying to capture something of her vibrant personality as well as covering some of the pertinent policy points I had prepared. I thought the article came out well. It was about 3.30 pm by the time I had finished. I thought it was time to call the Marymount to see how Mary was doing.

'Oh, Mr Sparks, we have been trying to reach you,' the duty sister replied. 'You have a son. They're both well.'

'When,' I asked, gulping, 'did he arrive?'

'At exactly 12.15,' came the reply.

Omigod, I thought again. Just 15 minutes after she was admitted. It can't be true.

'Yes it is true,' the sister replied. 'A very quick birth. Very easy.'

Thus did Michael Jonathan Sparks come into the world at record speed, bearing with him a shock of red hair as an inheritance from his Scottish maternal great-grandmother, Maria Godfrey. When I told Helen Suzman of his speedy arrival she laughed heartily and promptly nicknamed him '*Tweeling*', the Afrikaans word for twin, to denote his birth so close to her own moment of triumph.

The Progressive Party's final rally on the Saturday night before the Wednesday election was a dazzling affair, with 3 000 cheering people packing the Johannesburg City Hall. Steytler, the key speaker, was in fine form urging the crowd to ensure that South Africa had a party in Parliament that was ready and able to negotiate with the country's black leaders 'when the inevitable collapse of the *baasskap* [supremacist] government comes about'.

But the greatest applause, which brought the crowd to its feet, came when Steytler, having pledged that he would not force social integration on anyone who did not want it, declared: 'But by the same token, if I want a non-white as a friend, who dares deny me that right? If my friend, Chief Albert Luthuli, comes to Queenstown, my house is open to him. His people and my people have been in this country for hundreds of years. We don't need laws to keep our identity.'

Just the mention of the name of the leader of the banned ANC was a courageous act. Luthuli was living under virtual house arrest and it was a criminal offence to say anything that could be deemed as 'furthering the aims' of his organisation. But Steytler was on a roll and the big crowd was erupting with enthusiasm. He pledged to remove the pass laws and influx control regulations, which had resulted in 985 000 people going to jail the previous year. More controversially still, before a white audience, he pledged to remove the industrial colour bar and scrap job reservation, which prohibited black people from doing skilled work. 'No man must ask me to give him special protection just because he is white,' Steytler declared. 'I am not prepared to subsidise inefficiency.'

Finally, the Progressive leader enjoined the crowd: 'Come with me into a future of prosperity by helping me to release the vast human potential of our country from the bondage in which it is held today. South Africa can produce work and prosperity for all only if it uses all its people.' Looking back, this was bold stuff uttered from a political platform at the height of the Verwoerd era, three decades before the birth of the new South Africa – by which time Steytler and some of his key colleagues were already deceased. The Progressives, like Gandar, were accused of being ahead of their time, but they were people of foresight without whom I doubt a change in white thinking would have come about in time to save South Africa from a catastrophic race war.

Next day Gandar showed me the final editorial he proposed publishing on page one on election day. It was a historic document, the first time any mainstream newspaper in South Africa had called on the white electorate to vote for a racially integrated society after three and a half centuries of segregation. That in itself was a turning point that was to contribute, together with other related events, to a process that was to lead eventually to the birth of the new country.

The editorial, set double column on page one under a miniaturised masthead of the paper, was written in Gandar's crisp, clear style with key paragraphs italicised for emphasis. The final paragraphs starkly reiterated the Mail's stance over the past few years:

Two Choices

South Africa has reached a point in its history where two ineluctable choices confront it – either political separation accompanied by immense economic sacrifices; or economic integration accompanied by extensive political concessions. It is one or the other and there is no time left to prevaricate about it.

178

To suggest that there is a middle way whereby we can have the best of both worlds — enjoy the fruits of economic integration and ignoring the political obligations — is hopelessly unrealistic. It is worse — it is downright dishonest and dangerous.

That is why the 'Rand Daily Mail' has thrown its weight behind the Progressive Party. We believe that the country has got to face up to the alternatives in front of it — apartheid or integration, each with its proper consequences. It is the indecision, the timidity, that is killing us, for half-measures merely perpetuate the injustices that are the crux of our problem.

We have got to grasp the nettle and prove to ourselves and the world that we have the courage, the ability, the faith and the integrity to make this choice.

As the election results rolled in on Wednesday night, I felt a mixture of relief, disappointment and an overall sense of satisfaction. Relief because Helen Suzman won her Houghton seat, albeit by a mere 564 votes, which meant the Progressives would continue to have a voice in Parliament. In fact, Helen's remarkable 13 years as its sole representative enabled the party to gain traction later and eventually become the official opposition in Parliament. Disappointment because, in Gandar's vivid phrase, it had come 'damnably close' to winning another seven seats. John Cope lost Parktown by 87 votes and six other Progs by fewer than 1 000 votes.

The satisfaction was that the Progressives had polled a total of 60 000 votes in the 18 constituencies they had contested — a total exceeding the majority by which South Africa had voted to become a republic. A further encouraging factor was that Chief Luthuli put out a message stating that while he deeply regretted the increased support for the National Party, the support received by the Progressive Party was an encouraging sign. Similar messages of congratulation came from Joe Daniels, secretary of the Coloured National Convention, and Monty Naicker, president of the South African Indian Congress. So at least the Progressives' performance had made some impact on the black community, as Gandar had hoped it would.

That night the Nobel Committee announced in Oslo that it was to award the Nobel Peace Prize to Chief Albert Luthuli.

* * *

AS THE HEADINESS of the election campaign cooled down, Gandar suggested that I should expand my beat by getting to know more about what was happening in the rest of Africa. He proposed that, instead of spending the parliamentary recess months scouring news sources in Pretoria, as most other political correspondents did, I should spend the time visiting countries in Africa and reporting on what was happening there. Once again, it was a suggestion that revealed Gandar's sense of political relevance. What was happening in the newly independent African states was having a huge impact on attitudes in South Africa. But was the bad news all that was happening there? How were whites coping with the dramatic political changes taking place? South Africans needed to be better informed. The idea excited me, although I felt guilty at leaving Mary to cope alone with three-year-old Simon and baby Michael.

I flew first to Southern Rhodesia, my first return there since my stint on *The Chronicle* in Bulawayo. There was palpable tension in the air, for the winds of change had now reached southern Africa. Sir Edgar Whitehead, a decent but overly cautious man, had replaced the liberal Garfield Todd as Prime Minister, while Todd himself and his feisty 18-year-old daughter, Judith, had allied themselves to the black nationalist leader Joshua Nkomo. Todd had gone so far as to appeal to the British government to suspend Southern Rhodesia's colonial constitution.

Whitehead had amended the franchise qualification terms to admit more blacks to the voters' roll, and he had relaxed a number of segregation laws, so that when I reached my hotel in Salisbury, the capital, I found it racially integrated. The mixed dining room and bars injected an atmosphere of change, even excitement, but as I chatted to black people in the hotel I soon sensed that the reforms were not placating them. On the contrary, they saw the token reforms as a weakening of the white regime's resolve and that more pressure was now needed to achieve full equality. This set me thinking about the Progressive Party's qualified franchise policy. Would it be sustainable, or would Verwoerd be proved right in his argument that any reform would simply invite more pressure?

My next stop was Lusaka, where I was able to have a long, private discussion with Kenneth Kaunda, then at the peak of his independence campaign. I found him to be warm, friendly and remarkably well-informed on the state of South African politics. As the putative future president of his country, he had established a relationship with the managers of Anglo American, which had big operations on the Northern Rhodesian Copperbelt, and they were obviously keeping him in the picture. He asked probing questions, told me of his solid support for the ANC, and expressed his admiration for the *Rand Daily Mail*'s role in the recent election. I left feeling that I had established a firm relationship.

In Nyasaland, which would achieve independence in 1964 as Malawi, I found the nationalist leader, Hastings Kamuzu Banda, to be a different proposition. I had heard from Anthony Delius, the veteran *Cape Times* political correspondent who was also an Africa specialist, of a bizarre encounter he had once had on meeting Banda in Britain some years before. Banda, a medical doctor, was practising in the English Midlands at the time, and had taken exception to some questions Tony had asked him in an interview. 'He chased me out of his surgery with a hypodermic syringe,' Tony told me. My meeting with the future President also ended with a freakish touch. I was accompanied to his office by a young local journalist, Aleke Banda (no relation), where I encountered Banda sitting in a darkened, heavily curtained room, wearing dark sunglasses. I could only presume he had a problem with bright lighting, but I wondered how he could see anything at all in such gloom. The interview consisted mainly of a lecture on his mistrust of journalists and his determination to break up the federation and to run the country his way. He was clearly no democrat, as he was later to demonstrate by declaring Malawi a one-party state and himself President-for-Life. Indeed he was to preside over one of the most authoritarian regimes in Africa, which regularly tortured and murdered political opponents. He also introduced some strange laws, such as banning miniskirts – for tourists as well as his own people. But he did introduce a good education system, the centrepiece of which was an elite boarding school, Kamuzu Academy, modelled on Eton.

I left Banda's office after about half an hour and was on my way to hail a taxi when I heard the pounding of footsteps behind me. Turning, I saw Aleke Banda running after me. 'The President wants to see you again, please,' he panted. Puzzled, I made my way back. Banda asked me to be seated as another person was ushered into the room, a young white guy who was introduced to me as a journalist from Reuters. Turning to me, Banda explained: 'This young man has written a very bad story about our new stadium, and I want you to see how I deal with journalists who do that sort of thing.' Then followed a tirade of abuse and threats that went on for about 20 minutes, at the end of which Banda stood up and, turning to me, said: 'You may go now.'

The flight from Blantyre to Dar es Salaam, in an ancient Canadair Argonaut, was the most uncomfortable I have ever made. The aircraft was slow and apparently unable to climb higher than about 9000 feet, which meant it bumped and bucked sickeningly for about four hours before reaching its destination. But the journey was worth it. Julius Nyerere remains one of the most thoughtful, perceptive politicians I have ever met — and I count myself fortunate to have made his acquaintance before he became President of Tanganyika and was still easily accessible. It meant I was able to establish a relationship with him, as I had with Kaunda, that was to endure after he reached high office. We had several one-on-one discussions during the week I was in Dar. I found him sensitive to the Afrikaners' fear of having their national identity swamped, but he insisted that black majority rule was the only way for South Africa to go and said he was sure the ANC leaders, whom he knew well, would also be sensitive to the Afrikaners' fears.

Nyerere was a socialist. He gave me a copy of a book called *Ujamaa*, his own doctrine of 'African socialism', which he told me would be the centrepiece of his policy when Tanganyika became independent. It involved gathering rural communities together into farming villages where they could cultivate the land and herd livestock collectively, which he believed was in line with African traditionalism. When I read the book I had my doubts. Having seen the disruption caused by the apartheid regime's attempts at 'black spot' removals, I had come to the conclusion that any such attempt at social engineering could only cause hardship. That indeed turned out to be the case when Nyerere tried to implement Ujamaa, but when he realised it wasn't working as he had intended he dropped the programme – something Verwoerd could never bring himself to do.

I returned to Johannesburg a great deal wiser about the realities of politics in southern Africa. I realised that the transitions taking place in the countries to the north were problematic at many levels, and that those of us advocating change in South Africa should recognise that it would not simply be a matter of overcoming race prejudice and implementing 'sensible' Western political systems. We needed to understand African cultural and political issues much better. In particular, I returned convinced that the Progressive policy of a qualified franchise was a non-starter for African nationalists everywhere. Majority rule was their bottom line, and sooner or later we would have to come to terms with that. I discussed this with Gandar, warning that Verwoerd, with his relentless logic, would surely harp on this weakness in the parliamentary session to come and we would have to come up with convincing answers. Gandar agreed, but felt it was too soon for the Mail to make waves for the fragile Progressive Party, with its single MP.

There was, however, one curious sequel to the *Rand Daily Mail*'s electoral stance. United Party MPs in Parliament now shunned me. They no longer sought me out in the Press Gallery offices and they pointedly snubbed me in the lobbies. It was both childish and pointless, for with its declining representation the United Party was in desperate need of publicity. As for me, it mattered little, for they were not the newsmakers; the government members were, especially Verwoerd and his Minister of Bantu Administration and Development, the bumbling Daan de Wet Nel. So was Helen Suzman, as the only representative of a party offering a clear alternative to apartheid. I was also finding that more and more of the contacts that interested me were outside Parliament, in black organisations. If the United Party did not want publicity through the *Rand Daily Mail*, that was its problem, not mine. I then discovered that Helen was being shunned in the same way, particularly in the Assembly dining room, where United Party Members pointedly avoided any table where she was sitting. To avoid this minor unpleasantness, she decided to have her lunch sent to her parliamentary office each day, and on hearing that I was being similarly avoided, she invited me to join her. Lunch breaks became stimulating interludes, for Helen was both a delightful and a highly intelligent companion. I recall one key early exchange between us, when she expressed concern about how she would be able to get meaningful publicity for her party when, as its solitary representative, she would get only ten minutes' speaking time.

'Don't worry,' I remember telling her. 'You can make a lot of impact in ten minutes if you use them right. Just focus on a single issue in each speech. These scattergun speeches that Div Graaff makes drive us mad; all those little pellets dealing with lots of different issues leave us with nothing to get our teeth into. There's no coherent story. Give us a single bullet rather. Oh, and make sure you include a headline, you know, just a short catchy phrase.' What I didn't realise was how spot-on my advice was. South Africa did not yet have television, so I had not yet been introduced to the concept of the sound bite – today the very cornerstone of a successful speech. Helen grabbed at the idea and made it a hallmark of her public speaking. She never forgot my little contribution to her success. At her 90th birthday party she embraced me and in her forthright way said: 'That was the best damn bit of advice anyone ever gave me.'

Our shared lunch breaks had another unexpected sequel. After about a month we began to hear a few rumours and notice a few winks and nods. United Party Members were spreading a rumour that we were having an affair. Helen heard it first and erupted with fury – and I must say there are few things to be feared more than a furious Helen Suzman, who had a tongue like a whiplash. She put what she called her 'sleuths' on to the issue, and they came back with a report that they believed the rumour had been started by a new and intensely ambitious young MP from Natal, Michael Mitchell, who fancied himself as a debater and to whom

Helen had taken an instant dislike. She gave him the sarcastic nickname of 'The Younger Pitt'. I don't know whether Helen ever confronted Mitchell on the issue; I didn't bother. But if I needed any further evidence of the inevitability of the United Party's decline into pettiness, this was it.

Fifteen years later, the party disbanded. Its surviving MPs had a group picture taken, with poor Div Graaff sitting in the centre, on an ice rink at Johannesburg's Carlton Centre. They had been frozen in time since the death of Smuts.

CHAPTER TWELVE

My Camelot Year

ON MY RETURN from Parliament at the end of the 1962 session, night editor Aubrey Sussens greeted me with the news that he had nominated me for a Nieman Fellowship at Harvard University and that I had been accepted. I should leave with my family for the United States towards the end of August, to be at Harvard in time for the start of the fall semester.

It was exhilarating news. I knew the Nieman Fellowship was one of the most prestigious journalistic awards in the US. At that time 15 young Americans considered to be especially talented were chosen annually from around the country to spend an academic year at Harvard studying whatever they wished. They would have access to all that great university's resources and facilities to immerse themselves in a feast of intellectual nourishment. They would have the status not just of registered students but also of faculty members, including membership of the Faculty Club, which meant they would have access to some of the greatest minds in US academia, including several who were, or had been, senior White House advisers. The only restrictions were that they could not work as journalists while on the fellowship, particularly not for their own newspapers, and that their studies would not count towards degrees. This was meant to be a sabbatical year of total intellectual self-indulgence.

The fact that I, a South African, was able to join this group was due to the founding curator of the Nieman Foundation, Louis M Lyons, who was a quiet evangelist in combating racism. Each year he sought out two or three talented journalists from the American South to participate in his programme, with the obvious intention of helping them make a difference in the fight against racial segregation in that part of the country. This prompted a like-minded American Quaker, Frank Loescher, who was director of an organisation called the United States/South Africa Leadership Programme (USSALEP), to persuade Lyons to accept a South African on his programme each year. Sussens had been the first. I was the fourth, and am now the doyen of 46 survivors of a proud group of 58 who have received the fellowship.

Nor was it only Harvard that made this a special year in my life, for this was the peak of the Kennedy administration, when the White House became Camelot, a place of glamour and style and intellectual brilliance, inhabited by a handsome young war-hero President with his beautiful wife and their two delightful small children – the perfect all-American family. It was also a time of drama and danger as the United States faced off against the Soviet Union during the Cuban Missile Crisis, bringing the world the closest it has ever been to an all-out nuclear world war. Moreover, Harvard was at the nub of this glitter and drama, for three of the four Kennedy brothers, John, Robert and Edward, had graduated from there.

This was the dawn of the Swinging Sixties, the decade of the great youth rebellion, a time of hedonism and optimism, which seemed to match the image of the Kennedy White House, with its vision of a new frontier. In the US it was also the time when the Civil Rights movement approached its emotional peak. The months before my arrival had been marked by the crisis over the admission of an African-American student, James Meredith, to the whites-only University of Mississippi – 'Ole Miss' as it was known in the Deep South. President Kennedy and his Attorney-General brother, Robert, ordered the deployment of federal troops and US Marshals to enforce Meredith's admission. It was a pivotal moment in the civil rights struggle.

* * *

CAMBRIDGE, MASSACHUSETTS, is a modest-sized town on the banks of the broad Charles River, which separates it from Boston. This is a cerebral place, home to two of the world's greatest centres of learning, Harvard University and the Massachusetts Institute of Technology, generally known as MIT.

When we arrived at Harvard, Mary and I and our two children settled in a modest two-bedroom house near the university. With the help of Louis Lyons and his wife-cum-assistant, affectionately known as 'Totty', I began to plan my study courses. It was like being confronted with a huge smorgasbord of goodies. The problem was, which to leave out? Eventually I narrowed the choice to my three main areas of interest: political theory, race relations and the economic, social and political problems facing the emerging states of Africa.

In the first area I found a galaxy of great names, such as Henry Kissinger, Carl J Friedrich, Louis Hartz, Stanley Hoffman and Samuel Beer. Kissinger had just returned from a stint as an adviser at the Kennedy White House and later, of course, achieved fame as Richard Nixon's Secretary of State. He was teaching a fascinating course called 'Nuclear Diplomacy'. Friedrich – like Kissinger, born and educated in Germany – was teaching a course on public opinion and propaganda and was working on a radio project in the Greater Boston area to stress the importance of fighting totalitarianism to preserve democratic institutions. Hoffman was a specialist in the political thought of Charles de Gaulle, while Beer focused on the political history of Great Britain. All fascinated me and I dropped in periodically to lectures by all of them, especially Kissinger, but in the end I focused on Louis Hartz because I felt his course on 'Eighteenth Century Political Thought' would be more useful in broadening my general understanding of politics. I was not wrong.

My second field, race relations, was to become my most important area of study. Again I was richly blessed. The course I chose was run by Professors Gordon W Allport and Thomas Pettigrew. At the time, Allport, a psychologist, was the leading authority on

Mary and I with our two youngest sons, Simon, aged three, and Michael, one, while we were on my Nieman Fellowship year at Harvard University, 1962-63.

race studies in the US and his book, *The Nature of Prejudice*, was re-garded as the definitive work on the subject. I still regard it as the best I have ever encountered. Pettigrew was himself a Southerner, a Virginian, so the two of us were able to establish a warm mutual understanding that was to last for many years.

My third field of special interest was less well blessed. The New Africa was indeed exceedingly new, and the academic world had difficulty keeping up to date with all the changes that were occurring. Still, I managed to find some useful courses and also attached myself to the Africa Studies programme at Boston University, where a highly experienced South African, Jeffrey Butler, was a professor.

Over and above all this intellectual activity, the Nieman Foundation provides a series of special seminars and dinner-meetings for the Fellows, with members of the faculty and leading public figures, both American and foreign, as invited guests. Thus in the course of my year we were able to meet and interrogate Willy

Brandt, then mayor of embattled West Berlin and later Chancellor of West Germany; Robert Kennedy, the President's brother and Attorney-General; Henry Kissinger; Ralph McGill, legendary editor of the *Atlanta Constitution*, the South's most liberal newspaper; and, most memorably, three senior Soviet journalists who were touring the US at the time.

It was at the peak of the Cuban Missile Crisis, the tense 13-day period in October 1962 when the Cold War came closer than at any other time to turning into a nuclear war. The confrontation also gave birth to the doctrine of Mutually Assured Destruction, or MAD, which held that if each side had enough nuclear weaponry to destroy the other side totally, neither would be likely to attack first because it knew the other would retaliate with equal force and both would be utterly destroyed. Thus MAD was supposed to ensure a tense but stable peace. It was my first, and indeed my only, real-life experience of living in the very epicentre of a potential global apocalypse. I remember wondering, as I went to bed on the first night of the crisis, whether one would even know that the Russian rockets were on their way, or would one be atomised before the news arrived?

It so happened that our Nieman group were having lunch with the three Soviet journalists on the day news broke that Soviet air defences had shot down an American U2 reconnaissance aircraft over Cuba, killing the pilot. The Russians were warm, friendly folk and we slipped into easy conversation with them about our respective journalistic experiences. There was palpable tension in the air, however, and I felt sorry for our visitors. How awful, I thought, to feel you might die at the hands of your own people in the enemy's country. But the subject was studiously avoided.

Then, just as the main course was being served, a sudden cacophony of alarm bells and wailing sirens filled the air. Everyone leapt from their seats and rushed to the windows on the far side of the room, the pale-faced Russians in the lead. This was surely it! Air-raid sirens. The thought that at least we were getting a warning flashed through my mind.

Never can a serious fire have been so welcome. New England, with its many wooden clapboard buildings, is prone to fires and this was obviously a bad one, a 'twelve-alarmer' as they call it in those parts, with every available fire engine racing to the scene. We waved to the firefighters as though they were the bringers of peace.

* * *

I MADE ONE major investment during this magical year. I bought a used car — a 1955 Buick convertible with a powerful eight-cylinder engine. It was so large we could place a full-size baby's cot on the back seat where we could install the children as though they were in a playpen. I bought it from a graduating student for all of $300, and sold it at the end of my year for the same sum. In between it took us to Canada for Christmas and to the Deep South, all the way to New Orleans.

The trip to the Deep South was one of the major experiences of the year, both journalistically and for its personal insights into the American civil rights struggle. It began in Washington, DC, which many don't realise is a Southern city as well as being the federal capital. Its population is 51 per cent black to 38 per cent white. But it was in journalistic terms that I struck gold here, first meeting Alfred Friendly, who was managing editor of the *Washington Post* for 42 years, then Ben Bradlee, at the time Washington bureau chief of *Newsweek* and a buddy of President Kennedy. He later became the *Washington Post*'s legendary executive editor, presiding over the exposure of the Watergate scandal, and for whom I eventually worked as a correspondent covering South Africa for 13 years. He was the most dynamic journalist I have ever known.

From Washington our journey took us through Virginia to North Carolina, where in a later phase of my life I was to spend much time teaching and writing, then through South Carolina to Atlanta, Georgia, where we made a major stopover. At that time Atlanta was effectively the capital of the civil rights struggle. It was the home base of the Reverend Martin Luther King, Jnr, founder of the Southern Christian Leadership Conference (SCLC) and the principal figure in the whole US civil rights struggle. Mary and I decided we simply had to attend a church service at King's Ebenezer Baptist Church. I had heard him preach in the Harvard Chapel during the fall semester, but now I wanted to meet him personally.

The church itself is a large but elegant structure with a simple redbrick facade and beautiful stained-glass windows. It has an indoor balcony so it can accommodate some 800 people. It was packed the Sunday we attended the morning service, having stowed the children in the church crèche next door (where, with delightful spontaneity, they proved beyond doubt that there is nothing inherent in race prejudice). We were the only whites attending the service. As it happened, King's plane, bringing him back from his endless campaigning across the country, was running late, so we were treated to a sermon of considerable gusto from his father, Martin Luther King, Snr, but generally known as 'Daddy' King, while the service was periodically interrupted by progress reports from the airport. Eventually the great man arrived in time to deliver a brief coda to his father's sermon. He was greeted with enthusiastic cries of, 'Preach it, brother, preach it!' from the congregation. It was my first experience of an African-American church service in the South – an experience not to be missed. They are rich in audience participation, with congregants leaping to their feet with cries of 'Yeah, yeah!' or 'Praise the Lord!' clapping their hands, stamping their feet, always urging the preacher on to greater oratorical heights. King was a master performer in this arena, working the emotions of his audiences up to fever pitch with the rich cadences of his baritone voice and his effective use of repetition to drive home his key points, as in his landmark 'I have a dream' speech in Washington a year later.

After the service he and 'Daddy' King mingled with the congregants, enabling Mary and I to meet briefly with him and shake his hand. He seemed pleased to hear that we were from South Africa and urged us to 'Carry on the struggle against apartheid there.' It was a moment to cherish, and it acquired poignancy a few years later when the news reached us in South Africa of his assassination. King was shot in the head by a white racist named James Earl Ray as he stood on the balcony outside his motel room in Memphis, Tennessee. The assassination triggered a wave of rioting across the nation. Ray was eventually arrested at London's Heathrow Airport while trying to board a flight to Ian Smith's white-ruled Rhodesia. He confessed to the crime and was sentenced to 99 years in prison, where he died.

Another prominent civil rights campaigner we met in Atlanta was Julian Bond, a dynamic young man who had helped found the militant Students' Nonviolent Coordinating Committee (SNCC, or 'Snick', as it was called) that joined forces with the SCLC in organising sit-in demonstrations and freedom rides. I found him an engaging intellectual who was making his mark as a writer. He later became one of the first black members of the Georgia House of Representatives after the passage of the Civil Rights Act of 1964 and the Voting Rights Act of 1965. After serving several terms there he became a member of the state Senate, where he served six terms. A real pioneer of black emancipation in the US.

In Jackson, Mississippi, we met a striking young activist named Medgar Evers, who had been an adviser to James Meredith in his fight to gain admission to Ole Miss. It was a case that had turned Evers into a national figure. He was a remarkable man who at the age of 20 had fought at the Normandy landings in 1944. On his return to civilian life he encountered the hostility of white fellow countrymen for whom he had put his life at risk. I found him warm and thoughtful, one of the most impressive young people we had met in the South. But sadly, not long after our meeting he was assassinated — shot in the back with a rifle by a white racist as he stepped from his car in the driveway of his own home carrying a pile of T-shirts with the slogan: 'Jim Crow must go'. Evers was taken to the local state hospital, where he was initially refused entry because of his skin colour, but was later admitted only to die shortly afterwards. The murder, and the assassin's subsequent trial, caused a national furore. Evers was given the status of a hero and the honour of a funeral attended by thousands in Arlington National Cemetery in Washington, DC, where American military heroes and statesmen are buried.

However, it was in the state of Alabama, in Birmingham and the capital, Montgomery, that I encountered the most rabid white racists I have ever met. The hostility towards black people was palpable everywhere. My first experience of it was on walking into a bar in Birmingham. A group of imbibers who, on hearing I was from South Africa, fell upon me with much handshaking and backslapping. Here was an emissary from the imagined pantheon of their prejudices, the keeper of their ungodly faith. In all my global travels I had grown accustomed to being looked at askance, like some pestilent-ridden outcast, whenever I mentioned my land of origin. It never troubled me, for I was comfortable with the knowledge of my own beliefs. But this was different. I found being identified so instinctively and enthusiastically with an ideology I despised was disconcerting, like being upturned in a judo throw. They wanted to congratulate me on how we white South Africans were standing up to the tyranny of the liberal world. Worse still, they wanted me to join with them in the liturgy of their racist loathing. The jokes, the anecdotes, the assumption that 'niggers' were inferior, don't anyone tell me otherwise, and how imperative it was that they be kept in their place. And don't you agree? Of course you do, you're down there doing the right thing by them – have another drink. There was no euphemistic Max Factor-ising of segregation here, as I had grown accustomed to in South Africa. No Verwoerdian sweet talk about separate development or separate freedoms or helping blacks develop to the utmost of their own abilities in their own areas. Here the white racists wore their views openly, like badges of honour.

It happened also to be celebration time in Alabama, for the primary champion of the segregationist creed, George Wallace, had just been sworn in once again as Governor of the state, and had done so in melodramatic fashion. He had taken the oath of office standing on a gold star marking the spot where, 102 years before, Jefferson Davis had been sworn in as President of the Confederate States of America as the Civil War loomed. Speaking words for which he was to become known, Wallace declared: 'In the name of the greatest people that ever trod this earth, I draw a line in the dust and toss the gauntlet before the feet of tyranny, and I say segregation now, segregation tomorrow, segregation forever.'

Well, forever is a long day. Wallace was a persistent man who served for two consecutive and two non-consecutive terms as Governor of Alabama – 12 years altogether – and ran four times for the US presidency. He earned the sobriquet of 'the most influential loser in American politics'. He survived an assassination attempt that left him paralysed and wheelchair-bound, but still he kept going. Then, to everyone's astonishment, this life-long racist announced in the late 1970s that he was a born-again Christian and now accepted racial integration.

We kept meeting individuals who had undergone similar conversions, from passionate supporters of segregation to equally committed advocates of integration, some even joining the civil rights struggle. One such was an elderly Atlanta architect named Henry Toombs, who told us he was born in the 'Black Belt' of south Georgia and grew up with all the entrenched attitudes towards race to be found in that part of the world. Then, at age 62, he underwent a double metamorphosis: he became an ardent integrationist and, at the same time, set out for Florence to launch himself on a career as a sculptor.

The contrasts intrigued me. While the expressions of racism were vehement and openly uttered, often tinged with a sense of imminent violence, we kept encountering brave white liberals dedicated to the civil rights struggle. Certainly such contrasts existed among whites in South Africa, too, but in the US they were markedly more extreme, the threat of violence more overt, and the liberal responses more confidently expressed. As I pondered this I had recourse to a marvellous book, prescribed in my Allport-Pettigrew class at Harvard, called *The Mind of the South*, written by a journalist from North Carolina named WJ Cash back in 1941. The South has produced many great writers over the years; according to Pettigrew this is because of the rich rhetoric of the King James Version across the 'Bible Belt' that spans the Southern States. Cash was in this tradition. He had spent most of his life writing for small-town Southern newspapers before quitting his journalism job to work on what has been called a socio-historical, intuitive exploration of Southern culture – in other words, a vivid description of the folkways of the people he had lived with all his life and of whom he was one. It became an

instant classic and has remained so. I became so riveted by it that
I resolved one day to try a similar journalistic analysis of my own
South African people, which I eventually did.[1]

To understand the South, Cash contends, it is necessary to
come to terms with two correlated legends, those of the Old and
the New Souths. He then proceeds to outline the legend of the
Old South in his mellifluous Southern style:

> It was a sort of stage-piece out of the eighteenth century, where-
> in gesturing gentlemen moved soft-spokenly against a back-
> ground of rose gardens and duelling grounds, through always
> gallant deeds, and lovely ladies, in farthingales, never for a
> moment lost that exquisite remoteness which has been the dream
> of all men and the possession of none. Its social pattern was
> manorial, its civilisation that of the Cavalier … They dwelt in
> large and stately mansions, preferably white and with columns
> and Grecian entablature. Their estates were feudal baronies,
> their slaves too numerous ever to be counted, and their social life
> a thing of Old World splendour and delicacy. What had really
> happened here, indeed, was that the gentlemanly idea, driven
> from England by Cromwell, had taken refuge in the South and
> fashioned for itself a world to its heart's desire: a world singularly
> polished and mellow and poised, wholly dominated by ideals of
> honor and chivalry and *noblesse* – all those sentiments and values
> and habits of action which used to be, especially in Walter Scott,
> invariably assigned to the gentleman born and the Cavalier.
>
> Beneath these was a vague race lumped together indiscrimi-
> nately as the poor whites – very often, in fact, as the 'white trash.'
> These people belonged, in the main, to a physically inferior
> type, having sprung for the most part from the convict servants,
> redemptioners, and debtors of Virginia and Georgia, with a
> sprinkling of the most unsuccessful sort of European peasants
> and farm labourers and the dregs of the European town slums.
> And so, of course, the gulf between them and the master classes
> was impassable, and their ideas and feelings did not enter into the
> make-up of the prevailing Southern civilisation.[2]

But, Cash goes on, in the legend of the New South, the Old South
was supposed to have been destroyed by the Civil War and its

aftermath, as industrialisation and modernisation swept away these stereotypes. Not true, he contends. Certainly much has changed, but there has been a synthesis between the two so that the South remains significantly different in body and mind from the rest of the United States, which he goes on to expound upon with more rich metaphorical language.

> The South, one might say, is a tree with many age rings, with its limbs and trunk bent and twisted by all the winds of the years, but with its tap root in the Old South. Or, better still, like one of those churches one sees in England. The facade and towers, the windows and clerestory, all the exterior and superstructure are late Gothic of one sort or another, but look into its nave, its aisles and its choir and you will find the old mighty Norman arches of the twelfth century. And if you look in to its crypt, you may even find stone cut by Saxon, bricks made by Roman hands.[3]

In other words, the past lives on, and in many ways, as Cash contends, in terms of the mind, of social attitudes, it is the past that dominates. The past becomes revered, its grievances nurtured. This, I realised, as I travelled through the region in its time of travail, was true of South Africa as well. The grievances of the abolition of slavery at the Cape, of the travails of the Great Trek, of the Anglo-Boer War (there is surely nothing that fires up group nationalism more than to lose a war heroically), the deaths in the concentration camps, all compounded by the pain and humiliation of a great economic depression. All those similarities between the Southerners and the Afrikaner Nationalists of my own country struck me as I travelled the South with Cash's vivid descriptions in mind.

But there was something else as well. Why was racism, the hatred of black people, much more vividly and openly expressed here in the South than in South Africa, and why had it always been infused with so much violence? Yes, there was a lot of violence accompanying the enforcement of apartheid, such as the bulldozing of Sophiatown and Cape Town's District Six and the forced resettlement of other communities, as well as the torturing and deaths in detention of political prisoners. But we had not experienced such shocking public brutalities as the mass gatherings at the lynchings of black people and the assassinations of black leaders that had taken place in the South and were still occurring at the time of my visit. Our worst brutalities in South Africa were committed by the instruments of the state; here they were committed by ordinary citizens of the land. Why the difference?

The answer soon came to me. In South Africa, the state, backed by its apartheid laws, performed the role of the oppressor on behalf of the white citizens of the country. The state committed the racial cruelties in the name of the law and on behalf of the white population, the majority of whom passively and gratefully accepted it and voted again and again for its continuance. Whereas in the US the Constitution, and therefore ultimately the law, made race discrimination illegal; therefore the white racists of the South sought to enforce segregation themselves. They could not rely on the law to do it for them. True, they could initially, because state laws in the Southern states provided for segregation in schools, buses, lunch-counters and the like, but when the US Supreme Court struck these down all that changed.

I found it a sobering thought that the laws of my country required me to be a racist. To fight actively for integration required me to break the law, to be a criminal, to risk imprisonment and shame. Here in the South it was, or was soon to become, the other way around: for a white Southerner to act as a segregation-ist was to be a criminal; to fight for integration was lawful and honourable. Was that why I kept encountering these encouraging cases of former hard-liner segregationists undergoing a change of heart and accepting, sometimes even becoming activists for, integration? Was it because people have a natural desire to be law-abiding and not lead a criminal life, so that as the law began changing in the South through Supreme Court decisions it put psychological pressure on former segregationists to change their ways and so eventually their views?

It was an encouraging thought that exercised my mind as we drove back to Harvard for the start of the spring semester. If we could change the law in South Africa, attitudes would follow.

* * *

THE NEW YEAR brought news from South Africa of increased rumblings of political violence. James Brewer, an academic analyst, reported that 47 actual or attempted acts of sabotage and violent clashes between police and activists had taken place in the ten-week period covering October and November 1962. This seemed to indicate the first attempts by the underground black nationalist movements to get their violent revolution under way, which set me pondering a conundrum: why did ruling elites seem never to see coming the revolutions that threaten to topple them? Why did they wait until it was too late before introducing reforms that could have saved them from the firing squads and guillotines? I discussed this with my closest Nieman buddy, Saul Friedman, then of the *Houston Chronicle* (he was later to become a distinguished White House correspondent and a lifelong friend), who suggested I should spend my second semester studying this intriguing subject and write a dissertation on it.

I liked Saul's idea, so I consulted Professor Pettigrew and found him enthusiastic. He directed me to a pile of psychological literature on dissonance theory, which deals with the tension that arises when a person is confronted with two conflicting beliefs, for example, between ingrained race prejudice and a religious teaching that all humans are created in the image of God and are therefore equal. This condition reaches its apex when a person is confronted with two options that are equally unacceptable, such as reform and revolution, if you believe that giving the vote to the lesser classes would lead to anarchy. The inclination is to avoid both, which can result in a refusal to recognise the reality of the conflicting threats. Or what psychologists call 'a cognitive withdrawal from the situational reality'. It is also known as an 'avoidance-avoidance' syndrome or, more simply, 'a derailment of the understanding'. People shut their minds to the situation confronting them and render it invalid to their lives.

Pettigrew also introduced me to the work of Crane Brinton, the Harvard historian whose masterpiece, *The Anatomy of Revolution*, analysed the common features of these recurring historical phenomena. Brinton, a specialist in the history of France, focused on the English Revolution (1640-1660), the American Revolutionary War (1775-1783), the French Revolution (1789-1793) and the Russian Revolution of 1917. As I read Brinton's work it seemed to me there were sufficient similarities to the situation in South Africa to make his analysis a useful tool for my purposes.

Brinton notes that in all four cases, the revolutions did not occur in societies that were economically retrograde but when their economies were on the rise. It is not the poor who revolt – they are too focused on survival – but rather groups who are beginning to prosper but feel the ruling authorities are hindering their progress. They become the stirrers, launching pressure-group action, protest rallies and dramatic riots.

Then comes a second phase when, although the society is enjoying economic progress, the government encounters fiscal ills and becomes chronically short of money. The lower orders, cramped and frustrated, become open to new ideologies. As the ruling class remains unyielding, these increasingly angry groups assume a more revolutionary character.

We then come to a feature that intrigued me, because of its echoes of South Africa: the apparent ignorance among the rulers of the real causes of the social turbulence. Working on the assumption that the turbulence is all the work of a few agitators, the rulers enact harsh laws to silence the agitators, while introducing some reforms to improve conditions for the subordinate groups.

The critical moment arrives when some incident, often quite minor, sets the tinder aflame. The rulers, caught by surprise, react sluggishly or not at all, and are overthrown, with a revolutionary government replacing them.

During the revolutionary phase, the new government soon finds itself confronted by the complexities of administration, for which it is ill-prepared. It cannot deliver on its promises. Moreover, as Brinton says, the moderates soon find themselves accused by the more extremist elements of betraying the revolution. That is when the first batch of revolutionary children get devoured, or go to the guillotine – only for the new incumbents to run into similar difficulties and face the same challenge from a yet more extreme group. Thus the fever works its way to a crisis with the hardliners, the most hardened, disciplined and fanatically dedicated of the revolutionary groups, who grab power and institute what Brinton calls 'a reign of terror and virtue'. This is followed, eventually, by a thaw.[4]

What was of chief interest to me, as I prepared for my dissertation, was the remarkable failure of the ruling elites to see the crisis coming. Clearly the elitists in each case feared the consequences of reform. They equated democracy with anarchy. The mobs had to be kept at bay, the agitators stirring them up dealt with forcefully. With the exception of the American Revolution, all the ruling elites analysed by Brinton were consumed in the reign of terror. As Brinton says: 'People never seem to expect revolution for themselves, but only for their children. The actual revolution is always a surprise.'[5]

My objective in all this, of course, was to see if I could get a sense of what caused this dulling of the ruling groups' recognition of the revolutionary threats facing them. The answer seemed to lie in the psychological literature about 'avoidance-avoidance' syndrome, when both the violence of the revolution and the anticipated anarchy of democracy seemed too ghastly to contemplate. So contemplation ceased. The elites opted out psychologically. My task then became to search for a historical case where this did not occur, where the ruling elite saw the revolutionary danger coming and acted in time to avoid it, when a transition to democracy took place by reform rather than revolutionary violence. Eventually I was persuaded that my best case study would be the stormy passage of Britain's Great Reform Act of 1832, which widened the electoral system in the face of bitter opposition from conservatives.

Although Britain was ruled by a parliamentary system, the country was still effectively under the control of a hereditary aristocracy. But the Industrial Revolution was rapidly changing the social structure of the country. A new industrial working class, or proletariat, was emerging in the cities and in the north. This was changing the balance of parliamentary constituencies, with some being depleted of voters into what were called 'rotten boroughs'.

The Industrial Revolution brought not only an unprecedented economic boom to Britain, but also wildly fluctuating prices and great social dislocation. New ideas spread, such as Jeremy Bentham's Utilitarianism and Robert Owen's Utopian Socialism, fired by William Cobbet's popular journalism. Riots, strikes, arson and bloodshed pit the pages of British history through these years. There were hunger riots in East Anglia, frame-breaking in the lace districts, and an attempt on the life of the Regent.

The unrest climaxed in 1819 when a huge crowd gathered at St Peter's Fields in Manchester to choose their own MP in defiance of the law. Troops were summoned and clumsily broke up the unarmed crowd, killing 11 and wounding several hundred. The 'Peterloo Massacre' prompted the government to strengthen the army and to pass laws drastically curtailing freedom of the press, the right of public meetings and the right to bear arms, and suspending *habeas corpus* and strengthening the laws against sedition.

In the face of the rising turbulence, the Tory government of the Duke of Wellington stubbornly refused to consider any kind of reform or expansion of the suffrage. Other Tory nobles such as Sir Robert Peel backed him. Moreover, far from the French Revolution driving home a lesson of the merits of timely reform, the fact that the British elite had seen the anarchic horrors unfolding across the Channel in France only intensified their fears. The word democracy, wrote historian JRM Butler, had become a bogey, conjuring up in aristocratic minds pictures of 'barricades, bad money and the guillotine'.[6]

A series of events followed more or less simultaneously to change the atmosphere. First the Tory Party split over whether Catholics should be admitted to Parliament. This was followed by the death of the bitterly anti-reformist King George IV, which necessitated a general election within six months. The Whig Party under Lord Grey came close to winning the election. Grey had also been opposed to reform, but even as the election campaign was under way events occurred in France to change his mind. In July 1830 a popular uprising against the new ultra-conservative government of the Prince de Polignac drove the French king,

Charles X, from his throne. However, the insurgents 'used their victory with moderation as admirable as it was astounding'. There was 'no dramatic vengeance taken, no breach was made in the national continuity, no dormant anarchy was released as befell 40 years before.'[7]

The impact in Britain was profound. Suddenly the fear of the consequences of reform was eased, the London *Morning Chronicle*, mouthpiece of the Whig Party, declared exultantly: 'The battle for English liberty has really been fought in Paris.'[8] Emboldened, Lord Grey's Whigs stepped forward to lead the demand for reform. The Tories, though weakened, continued to dig in their heels but the tide of public opinion had turned, so that when Wellington made an adamant declaration against reform it broke his party and the King asked Lord Grey to form a new government. On the evening of 26 March 1831, Lord John Russell rose in the House of Commons to move the first reading of the Great Reform Bill. But it took two more years for the Bill to become law.

My hypothesis suggested that the only way to break the psychological withdrawal from reality that occurred when ruling elites had to choose between reform or revolution would be if it could be demonstrated that one or other of the feared alternatives would not involve the expected degree of pain. The events in France in July 1830 had obviously provided that demonstration to enough people in Britain to enable the Great Reform Bill to pass. But it was equally clear that the role of Lord Grey, a noble himself with influence among the upper classes, in championing the cause of reform, was also critical.

But there was something else as well. I came across the work of a distinguished French philosopher and historian, Élie Halévy, covering this period of British history. Struck by the anarchy of economic life in Britain at the time, Halévy finds cohesion only in the country's religious life, particularly in the Methodist revival of John and Charles Wesley and George Whitefield. This, he contends, brought solace to the victims of the Industrial Revolution and taught the poor to endure hardship without despair. Unlike the militant Puritanism of the English Revolution, the Methodist movement tended to be conservative in politics. Fortunately for the

British aristocracy, Halévy notes that the new piety was strongest in just those elements from whom they had most to fear – the proletariat and the lower middle classes of England and Wales.[9]

This was the body of historical analysis that I sought to apply to the South African situation as it was in 1963, and attempt to project what might happen in my country as its intensifying racial conflict unfolded. What factors would be required to enable white South Africans to snap out of their refusal to recognise the real prospect of revolution and opt for reform instead, as Britain had done?

As I worked my way through the various features of South Africa's political condition, it became clear that pretty well all of the symptoms of cognitive withdrawal I had identified in the revolutionary societies I had studied were there: the stubborn determination of Hendrik Verwoerd and his followers to stick to apartheid; their belief that the country's black people were really content with their lot and that the protests were instigated by a handful of political agitators; that all advocates of racial integration were communists or fellow travellers; that tough security measures were required to deal with those troublemakers; and above all that racial equality, one-man-one-vote, would lead to chaos and anarchy and the collapse of all civilised society. Above all – and this was the toughest nut to crack – it would lead to the demise of the Afrikaner *volk*. It would mean national suicide for the Afrikaner, a factor that had not featured in any of my other case studies and was obviously a formidable one.

None of this made for an optimistic prognosis in the conclusion of my thesis. But I did make a few observations that, in retrospect, I think were propitious. One was to suggest that if some reassuring event were to occur in one of the newly independent African states, such as had happened in France in 1830, or from within the black liberation movement in South Africa, that might reduce the degree of fear of reform in the minds of our ruling elite and make a peaceful transition to democracy possible. Another, more speculative thought, derived from the social psychology literature Pettigrew had recommended. There I encountered studies of what was called 'the authoritarian personality', the result often of

204

being brought up with an authoritarian father figure. A society in which authoritarianism was common could become collectively inclined to follow the dictates of an authoritarian leader, a factor measured on what is called an F-scale. It seemed to me, from what I knew of Afrikaner society in general, that it probably rated pretty high on the F-scale.

This led me to write in my conclusion: 'A final possibility remains. Since psychological withdrawal is born of anxiety, it seems reasonable to suppose that its sufferers will react to a desire to re-discover the security of childhood. A father figure of charismatic quality, preferably thrown up from the heart of Afrikanerdom, might find a mass following ready to follow him on a road to reform – even though this would be against deep-held beliefs.'

It was, as things turned out, a prophetic suggestion.

Moreover, the entire American experience, from the trip through the South to my studies at Harvard, and particularly the readings and the writing to produce what Pettigrew told me was the equivalent of an MA thesis, helped shape for me a clearer frame of reference through which to view the South African race problem. I understood more about the nature of race prejudice, the influences of culture and upbringing and fear that gave rise to it, and the elements of dissonance theory that might put pressure on those ingrained attitudes. What issues might a journalist focus on to try to increase those pressures? Religion perhaps? The Afrikaners were a deeply religious people; was this not a field we should be focusing on more intensely and with a deeper understanding of the theological concepts involved? And what of the ANC's decision to launch an armed struggle? Would it drive home white awareness of the need to reform, or would it intensify the fear of black majority rule? What effect, if any, was our reporting of the injustices inflicted on black people having on the white electorate? Was it prodding their consciences, or pro-ducing an avoidance syndrome that closed their minds? And what of all the bad news coming out of Africa? Was it all that bad, or was there another side to be told by whites who had not fled the wind of change?

All this and more formed the subject of a series of intense

discussions with Laurence Gandar on my return. They did much to open new avenues for the *Rand Daily Mail* to explore. Not least they raised the issue of whether my beat as political correspondent was wide enough. New vistas beckoned, but much drama still lay immediately ahead.

CHAPTER THIRTEEN

The Great Escape

I RETURNED TO South Africa to find the country under the lash of a security crackdown. Balthazar Johannes Vorster, better known as John Vorster, the Minister of Justice, together with his security chief, Hendrik van den Bergh, were working in tandem to try to crush what remained of resistance to apartheid after the 1960 banning of the ANC and other black political movements. Both were tough, ruthless men, and they made a formidable combination: Vorster in the Cabinet, where he enacted laws empowering the security police to hold suspects in detention without trial, and Van den Bergh to order their ruthless interrogation. Vorster first enacted a 90-day detention law, which he later doubled to 180 days, with an additional clause allowing the order to be repeated until, as he once put it in Parliament, 'this side of eternity'.

Van den Bergh, known as 'Lang Hendrik' because of his height (196 cm), later founded an intelligence unit called the South African Bureau of State Security, which we in the press swiftly dubbed 'BOSS'. It became effectively a law unto itself with limitless snooping powers, from tapping telephones to opening mail and, with the very latest electronic espionage equipment, tuning in to private conversations almost anywhere. Van den Bergh commanded a veritable army of spies who penetrated every organisation suspected of having information about anti-apartheid activities, such as universities, religious organisations and, particularly, as we were to discover to our cost, newspaper offices. BOSS agents were literally everywhere.

Worst of all, Van den Bergh's men had what amounted to a free hand when it came to interrogating suspects. Detainees were held in solitary confinement for long periods, often several months, to soften them up. They were then subjected to interrogation, which might go on for days at the hands of different teams who worked in shifts while the detainees were deprived of sleep. Torture was routine, and sometimes extreme, with several detainees dying in detention. There was waterboarding and 'tubing', which involved asphyxiating a detainee by stretching rubber tubing across his face until he either lost consciousness or died. As one practitioner confessed: 'When they voided their bladders you knew they had gone to another place.' Some were held by their feet out of the windows of high buildings under threat of being dropped if they did not 'talk', a threat that was sometimes carried out to spread credibility among those still detained.

The crackdown had begun shortly after my departure for the US when Nelson Mandela, who had been operating underground for 17 months after returning from a trip abroad to undergo military training and seek support for the ANC's newly formed armed wing, was captured. He had travelled to Natal province to see the banned ANC leader, Chief Albert Luthuli, to report on his foreign activities, and was on his way back to the movement's secret headquarters outside Johannesburg when he was flagged down at a roadblock near Howick. He was thought to have been betrayed by a member of the Durban Indian community working as a CIA agent. Mandela, who was driving the car, with theatre director Cecil Williams in the back, tried to pass himself off as a chauffeur named David Motsamayi, but to no avail. He was too well known. He was arrested, taken to Johannesburg for trial, and sentenced to five years' imprisonment on Robben Island off Cape Town for leaving the country without a passport.

So began Mandela's 27-year 'Long Walk to Freedom'.

But the major crackdown came on 11 June 1963, only a matter of weeks after my return from the US, when a police unit raided a small farm called Liliesleaf outside the village of Rivonia, just north of Johannesburg, which was the secret headquarters of the High Command of Umkhonto we Sizwe, the military wing of the ANC. Ten members of the headquarters staff were arrested in that raid, and the remaining few were picked up soon afterwards.

It was a devastating blow for the liberation movement, yet it was more a matter of happenstance rather than the investigative brilliance of Lang Hendrik van den Bergh, as he later claimed. The security police were searching for Walter Sisulu, a key leader of the ANC and close friend of Mandela, and had received a tip-off that he might be at the Rivonia smallholding. A relatively small posse, 19 men and a dog, was sent to check this out, and they struck gold – leading not only to the capture of the entire ANC leadership, except for those who had already gone abroad with Oliver Tambo to establish an overseas base, but also to the seizure of an array of documents, duplicating machines and even a radio station. Most incriminating of all was their document-ed programme, called Operation Mayibuye, setting out plans for an armed campaign to overthrow the apartheid regime. It was incontrovertible evidence of treason, a capital offence.

* * *

IT LOOKED as though it was all over for the ANC. Yet just one month after the Rivonia raid, on 11 August 1963, came the startling news that two members of that headquarters staff, Arthur Goldreich and Harold Wolpe, had escaped from the security police cells at The Greys, located at police headquarters at Marshall Square, in central Johannesburg. It seemed scarcely believable, given the formidable reputation of Van den Bergh's security police.

Yet it was simple enough. The story soon emerged that the two detainees, together with two members of the Natal Indian Congress, Mosie Moola and Abdullah Jassat, who were in adja-cent cells, had bribed a young Afrikaner prison warder named Johan Greef to leave a back door leading to a courtyard behind the cells unlocked at midnight on 10 August. Greef, aged 18, was what Goldreich called 'a decent young man', who happened to confess to his prisoners that he disapproved of the principle of detention without trial. As their relationship warmed, he also confided that he was in some financial difficulty. He earned a paltry R50 a month and had recently borrowed a friend's car and 'buggered it up', causing damage he could not reimburse. That was the signal for his captives to try their luck. Moola, who had drawn particularly close to Greef, was assigned to seek a deal. After some bargaining with the young warder it was agreed that friends of the four detainees would arrange for him to be paid R4 000 after the escape.

Meanwhile, Wolpe had alerted his wife, AnnMarie, of the escape plan by concealing a note in his laundry. She in turn had alerted an ANC escape committee, which arranged for a car, with driver, to be parked at an agreed point not far from The Greys. To enable the escapees to identify the car, a hat would be placed in a visible position against the rear window. As a precaution, should there be a delay and the driver have to leave, a back door would be left unlocked with an ignition key under the hat. It was also agreed that should something go wrong and the escape have to be postponed, the car would be removed at 1.15 am.

Predictably, something did go wrong. Shortly before midnight a group of drunken revellers were arrested and brought to the police cells to be locked up for the night. They were in a noisy, fighting mood and Greef became involved with the night staff in having to subdue them. To the dismay of the four detainees, and of Greef, it took considerable time, so that it was well past midnight before Greef could whisper to his four escapees that the coast was now clear. Given the lost time, there was a discussion about whether the escape should be delayed because there would be insufficient time to carry out the agreed plan for Goldreich to knock Greef unconscious, take his keys and lead the escapees out. But Greef insisted they go ahead without further delay, saying he could hit his head against an iron bar in the corridor after they had left. It was a harebrained scheme, yet it worked – at least for the detainees, not for poor Greef. His knockout blow was not severe enough to convince the police medics, and he was sentenced to six years' imprisonment, of which he served two and a half before being released on parole, his prison service career at an end.

210

It was 1.10 am when four shadowy figures slipped out of that back door Greef had unlocked for them, then through another into a courtyard where a number of police cars were parked. All empty. Tentatively they tiptoed across the courtyard, and went through a gate into Main Street in the very heart of Johannesburg. It was an extraordinary moment. Here were these four men, two of whom, Goldreich and Wolpe, were facing the awful prospect of death sentences, walking away, free into the night. They felt a sense of exhilaration, quickly overtaken by resurgent fear. How long would it be before the alarm was raised and they were captured? They decided to separate: two Indians and two whites walking together would attract attention. So Moola and Jassat headed off to the Indian quarter of Fordsburg, where they merged inconspicuously into the local population and did not feature again in the dramatic escape story. Goldreich and Wolpe, the two primary escapees, went on alone.

They walked past a popular restaurant where the last customers had just left and the waiters were clearing up before closing. Still no alert. Goldreich was the first to spot the car and sprinted ahead. Then he stopped with an expression of dismay. A hat was there against the back window ledge, but there was no driver and all the doors were locked. Wrong car. Theirs had already left. What were they to do? It was nearing two o'clock in the morning, they were in the deserted heart of a big city, there was no public transport available, they had no money even for a call box, and their escape could be discovered at any moment.

They started to walk, not knowing where to go. They tried to avoid main routes as they made their way out of the city centre, up towards the inner suburb of Hillbrow with its many tall apartment blocks. It was a long uphill climb; time was passing. They began to tire and Wolpe was limping from an acute attack of gout. They stopped at one apartment block where an acquaintance lived and they knocked on his door, but there was no response. They hurried on, growing ever more desperate. Then, as they rounded a corner into a narrow, dark street they saw an old, battered Renault painted an extraordinary pink colour. It was double-parked, and, as they approached, its taillights came on and they heard the engine start.

'It's bloody Barney!' cried Wolpe, who recognised the rattle-trap vehicle of one of their closest friends, a writer, playwright and theatre producer named Barney Simon. The car started to move forward. Fortunately its aged engine gave it a slow take-off, so that Goldreich, summoning his last reserves of energy, managed to catch up and bang on the driver's window. 'It's Arthur,' he called out breathlessly. 'We've escaped. Harold's with me.'

'Well I never!' Simon responded. He was a taciturn man, not given to extravagant expressions. The escapees scrambled into the car and Simon drove them to his flat, only a few minutes away. He explained on the way that he had been visiting a friend and had stayed late, then soon after leaving found he needed to urinate urgently. So he had turned off into this quiet, dark street to pee unnoticed against a tree. It was sheer chance that he had been there when they spotted his car.

Goldreich and Wolpe spent the night at Barney Simon's flat, where members of the escape committee picked them up the following morning and for the next ten days spirited them to various other homes where they stayed in total obscurity while a frantic police search for them continued. The escape was front-page news almost daily; regular broadcasts on the radio were interrupted to issue appeals to the public to give any assistance possible that might lead to their recapture. A reward for information was offered. AnnMarie Wolpe was arrested and subjected to rough interrogation to try to extract information from her about where her husband might be hiding, but she was able to say truthfully that she did not know. It was days before the hullabaloo began to die down. Then began the next dangerous stage of the saga. The men were hidden and covered in the boot of a newly acquired second-hand car – along with a bag of oranges to sustain them – and driven 500 km through the night by a young man they knew only as Crawford, who managed to slip them across an un-watched section of the border into the small British protectorate of Swaziland. There they were given refuge at a mission station run by a priest, the Reverend Charles Hooper, where they lay low while a nationwide search for them continued in South Africa.

* * *

IT WAS a typical late winter's morning on the highveld, sunny with a crisp bite from the overnight cold. There was still frost on the ground, for I was on my way to the office early. I had a mid-morning interview appointment and needed to pick up some background documents I had left on my desk. There were no reporters in the newsroom as I walked in just before 7 am; morning papers tend to get under way late, and to operate late into the night. Only the early-duty news editor, Oscar Tamsen, was at his desk, with a phone to his ear. He was looking agitated.

'Christ!' he exploded, spotting me as he slammed down the phone. 'I can't find any bloody reporters. Nobody's answering.'

'What's happened?' I asked, puzzled by his agitation so early in the day.

'I've just had a call from Jack and Rica Hodgson,' Tamsen spluttered, referring to a left-wing couple who had recently fled to Bechuanaland. 'Goldreich and Wolpe have just landed there, in Lobatsi. They flew from Swaziland disguised as priests. Now they've set out for Francistown by road. They left at midnight and should be in Francistown by early afternoon. We're the first to know. We've got to get that story for tomorrow's paper; it's a cracker. I've managed to charter a plane and I've got Ernie Christie standing by as a photographer. But I can't find a bloody reporter anywhere.'

'Well, I'm a reporter,' I replied softly.

'But you're the political correspondent,' he muttered, clearly becoming confused in his agitation.

'Same thing,' I said. 'Where's the plane? Tell Christie I'm coming.'

So it was that by 9 am on 29 August 1963 I boarded a single-engine plane at Rand Airport, just outside Johannesburg, together with photographer Ernie Christie, to cover what turned out to be one of the most dramatic stories of my career.

Bechuanaland, later to become the independent Republic of Botswana, was one of three British protectorates that had been historically connected to South Africa before Union. Unlike the other two, Basutoland and Swaziland, both small and enclosed within South Africa, Bechuanaland was a vast expanse of arid flatland, roughly the size of France or Texas, wedged between South Africa and South West Africa (today's Namibia), with a population of barely 1 million. Its expanse and its emptiness made it an ideal escape route for political fugitives leaving apartheid South Africa, but its long, porous borders also meant Lang Hendrik's agents could penetrate it with equal ease. It was not a safe haven to linger long.

At the time of the Goldreich-Wolpe escape, three years before the protectorate's independence, its future capital, Gaborone, had not yet been established. The southern town of Lobatsi, though little more than a village, was the main commercial centre. Francistown, some 500 km to the north, was a sparse and dusty settlement with a single street, a population of about 250 and a hostelry that went by the pretentious name of the Grand Hotel. This establishment sported double bat-wing doors off the street into the bar, giving it a whiff of the Wild West. It was an isolated habitation, lying close to the Southern Rhodesian border to the east. To the north lay the South African-controlled Caprivi Strip. A tricky spot from which to make a further leap to freedom.

There was no proper airport, simply a landing strip in the bush that was used by South African mining companies to ferry mineworkers to the goldfields of the Witwatersrand. As we approached the landing strip, we saw a herd of elephants grazing on it, blocking our way. Our experienced bush pilot had to buzz the elephants several times before they reluctantly lumbered away and allowed us to touch down. From the airstrip we had to hike across the veld, carrying what little luggage we had brought, into the little town. The pilot agreed to wait another two hours before taking off on his return flight, to take back whatever rolls of film Ernie might have for publication in the next morning's paper.

'Do you have two men here named Arthur Goldreich and Harold Wolpe?' I asked the African receptionist at the Grand Hotel.

'Yes,' came the reply. 'There are three actually. There's an Indian gentleman with them. But they are very tired and I think they are all sleeping.'

I managed to squeeze their room number out of the hesitant receptionist, and made my way around the open veranda to knock on the door. No reply. I knocked again, more loudly. Still no response. So I pounded on the door, which brought the soft sound of bare feet approaching it. The door opened, just a crack, to reveal an Indian face.

'What do you want?' the face asked.

'My name is Allister Sparks. I'm from the *Rand Daily Mail*, and I want to talk to Arthur and Harold. I know they are here.'

The door closed again. More sounds of bare feet. Murmured voices. Then the door opened again and Arthur Goldreich stood before me, bearded, grubby and unkempt. 'Come in,' he murmured.

The conversation began cautiously. I had not met any of the escapees before, and they knew of me only through my connection with the *Rand Daily Mail*, which they respected as an outspoken anti-apartheid newspaper. But they were clearly nervous. As we talked it turned out their chief concern was not to expose any of the people who had helped them to further police harassment. I assured them I would do no such thing, that all I wanted was a broad outline of their escape and what their future intentions were. How were they going to get out of Francistown?

Gradually, as we sat in that darkened hotel room sipping beer together, Goldreich and Wolpe recounted the story of their escape while Ernie moved silently around the room taking pictures. Goldreich did most of the talking. He was a flamboyant figure, handsome and extrovert, and he became more and more animated as he talked. Goldreich was a talented abstract artist and designer, who in 1955 had been acclaimed the Best Young South African Artist. Even more formative, as far as his personality was concerned, was a close involvement in African theatrical productions, which had plunged him into the racy lives of Soweto's artistic community. He had been involved as the decor and costume designer for the hugely successful musical, *King Kong*, billed in 1959 as 'an all-African jazz opera', which featured some of South Africa's most famous musicians, such as Hugh Masekela and Abdullah Ibrahim, and launched the career of the singer Miriam Makeba. Goldreich was in his element in that community. At this our first meeting, I sensed a touch of the playboy adventurer about him.

Wolpe was more reserved and cautious, to the point of being ascetic. He was a lawyer and a sociologist whose legal work had been concerned mainly with political detainees, while his academic work had focused on evolving a theoretical analysis of the particular form of capitalism's exploitation of cheap labour in South Africa. He was the dedicated Marxist intellectual.

As for the third fugitive to turn up in Francistown, Ismail Bhana, he remained an enigma. He had not been part of the group arrested at Liliesleaf, nor had he featured in the escape from The Greys. As far as I could make out, he was an ordinary member of the ANC who had slipped across the border into Swaziland to escape arrest, and there found himself in the same safe house as Goldreich and Wolpe. When it came time for the organisation to arrange for its two escapees to fly to Bechuanaland disguised as priests, it was found there was a spare seat in the plane. So it was offered to Bhana. He was the hitchhiker of the trio.

After two hours of intense interviewing, I had enough material to make a blockbuster of a story. Ernie handed over several reels of film to the pilot, who set off across the veld back to the airstrip, while I ensconced myself in my hotel room to write my report. The words flowed easily; this was hot news and I knew I had it first, that I had a scoop. There was no phone in my room, but I had spotted a coin box on the open veranda, so I went there to book a reverse-charge call to dictate my story to a high-speed typist in the *Rand Daily Mail* newsroom. It had been a good day and I slept well that night, not knowing what the morning might bring.

* * *

AS IT TURNED out, the morning arrived early with a knock on my door just after 5 am. It was Ernie Christie, already dressed and with his camera bag on his shoulder. 'Hurry,' he said. 'They're leaving. We've got to get to the airstrip.'

I threw on a few clothes and rushed out. It was still dark, but I could see Goldreich, Wolpe and Ismail Bhana standing at the front porch talking to a tall white man, who introduced himself to me as Philip Steenkamp, the District Commissioner, which meant he was the regional representative of the British government.[1] 'Follow me,' Steenkamp said abruptly, without explanation, and we set out in single file along the narrow footpath that led to the airstrip.

'Apparently a plane has been sent to fly them out,' Christie told me. 'That's all I've been able to find out. I was awakened by the sound of them talking outside my door.'

I tried to engage Steenkamp to find out more, but he was in earnest conversation with Goldreich and asked me please to wait, that he would be able to give me more information once we reached the airstrip. So we walked on in silence. We crested a slight rise and began to descend towards the airstrip. Suddenly we stopped dead. There were gasps of astonishment.

Before us lay the smoke and ashes of a burnt-out plane. A Dakota, with the faint markings of East African Airways just visible on its smouldering fuselage. There was total silence for a moment, broken by Steenkamp's strangled voice. 'Oh my God!' he muttered. 'We'd better go back to the hotel.' Which we did, slowly and silently.

To say that Goldreich and Wolpe were shocked would be an understatement. They were ashen-faced. It was all too obvious that Lang Hendrik's agents were right here among us in this small community, perhaps even in the hotel, and that they had the capability to destroy an airliner. The prospect of assassination at any moment was vividly apparent.

Back at the hotel, Steenkamp whisked the three fugitives away in his Land Rover, while I headed for the phone booth to call the news editor, Raymond Louw, at his home to tell him I had a story worthy of a special extra edition of the Mail, and that if he could get staff to the office to get it out on time, I could dictate the story within half an hour. Which I did, asking the news desk at the same time to send an office car to Francistown because I was clearly going to be stuck there with a running story for some days. Goldreich and Wolpe were trapped and vulnerable.

Just how vulnerable emerged only many years later when a

Francistown resident, Betty Rundell, revealed that her husband, Ralph, who was in charge of security at the mining company's landing strip, had gone out to check on the Dakota about midnight on 29 August after its arrival late in the afternoon. The hostility towards the escapees among the white residents of the town, mostly white South Africans, was so intense he feared someone might try to sabotage the plane. All seemed to be well as he made his inspection, which ended with him checking on whether the cockpit door was locked. It was. Satisfied, Ralph Rundell went home to bed. About three hours later, a firebomb exploded inside the plane, destroying it. According to his wife, Ralph believed that by testing the door he had triggered a time bomb.

'Ralph believed the bomb was set to go off three hours after takeoff, when the plane was in midair,' Betty Rundell told an interviewer. 'So actually he saved their lives by setting it off early.'[2]

As the day wore on, the town and the Grand Hotel began to fill up as journalists from every news operation in southern Africa and many from abroad began to fly in to the little airstrip. Several diplomats arrived, too, including a young Australian first secretary and a Canadian whom I knew well and who arrived in a chartered plane flown by a veteran mercenary of the Congo wars who went by the name of Captain Excell. Several burly men with heavy Afrikaans accents also appeared in the bat-wing bar, mostly farmers and game rangers from the nearby Tuli Block, a wedge of land on Bechuanaland's eastern border between Southern Rhodesia in the north and South Africa in the south. Some locals arrived too. By evening the bar was crowded and noisy, with some of the locals raucously declaring their intention to 'get hold of those commie bastards' and return them to South Africa to claim the reward money. Others just wanted to 'bugger them up'. As I moved along the veranda, past the fugitives' room, I noticed they had tried to barricade themselves in by moving heavy furniture against the door and window. It struck me as being hopelessly inadequate.

In the bar itself some heated arguments flared up, too, between locals and journalists, whom the locals seemed to categorise collectively as a bunch of lefties. I recall one lean, frail, heavily bearded reporter from *The Star*, whose name I forget, becoming embroiled with a chunky, Mike Tyson of a figure clad in farm boots and khaki shorts, trying to lecture him on the ethics of democracy and the wickedness of detention without trial. Both had had too much to drink, as had just about everyone else in the bar. 'You're just pro-commie,' the big man barked. 'And you're just a racist,' came the response. At which point the big man raised his fist, and with eyes bulging moved to deliver the killer blow. But he paused as he looked at the wispy figure in front of him. 'Ag man,' he muttered as he lowered his fist, 'why don't you just get back on your cross?'

By morning the fugitives were gone. I met Ernie at breakfast. 'They're in the jail,' he told me. 'Steenkamp took them there late last night for security. Apparently he got a message that a second Dakota had taken off from Dar es Salaam to fetch them, but it turned back because the airline was scared it, too, would be sabotaged.' I told Ernie an office car was on its way. We would need it; with all the new arrivals, this was going to be a difficult story to handle.

Later that day, after I had filed a further story about the dangers now facing the fugitives, I met up with Ernie again. 'We're in luck,' he said. 'I went up to the jail and saw the jailer, who turns out to be an old school friend of mine. His name is Delville Knight. We both went to St Andrew's College in Grahamstown. He says he will let us in to see Goldreich and Wolpe, and they have both agreed that you and I can meet with them, but none of the other journos.'

It was an incredible scoop. We would have exclusive access to the central figures in this great escape drama for as long as the story ran. Ernie Christie, who wangled us that access, was one of those extraordinary individuals who seemed able to talk his way through closed doors and persuade obstructing police officers to get out of the way of his probing camera.

With the office car having arrived from Johannesburg, the two of us drove regularly to the jail to visit the fugitives. Days went by with no new developments, but I managed to file something each day to keep the story alive. The crowds in the bar thinned out a little, and Goldreich, Wolpe and Ismail Bhana relaxed somewhat.

Some evenings Ernie and I would take a few bottles and some snacks up to the jail to have a small party with them in their cell. The jailer, Delville Knight, would usually join us. Goldreich was the life and soul of these prison gatherings, at which he showed himself to be an entertaining raconteur. We provided him with drawing paper and pencils, and the artist sketched delightful cartoons and souvenir portraits for all of us. With tensions easing and our little cell parties generating a bond of friendship, Goldreich the extrovert even became bold enough to propose that I organise a soccer match between the waiting press corps and a prison staff team, which he said he would like to captain. It might even have taken place had District Commissioner Steenkamp not intervened to veto the idea in the interests of security.

After a full week in the jail, the morale of the fugitive trio suffered another heavy blow. It had been arranged for a small outfit called the Tanzanian Air Charter Company to send yet another aircraft, a twin-engined six-seater, to Bechuanaland to fetch them. But on the morning of 6 September the *Rand Daily Mail* office called me to say they had just received a news flash that the plane had crashed in southern Tanzania. One engine had failed and in the crash landing the plane was severely damaged, although the pilot was unhurt. The news was shattering for Goldreich and Wolpe, who immediately assumed that this plane had also been sabotaged. To them it meant no commercial aviation company would be prepared to touch them now. They were in a depressed state of mind and there was no party in the jail that night.

Early next morning I was awakened by a pounding on my hotel room door. It was one of the hotel staff to tell me there was a phone call for me. It was 4 am. I slipped on a dressing gown and made my way to the phone booth. It was Goldreich. 'Sorry to wake you,' he said, 'but would you mind having a look in the hotel's registration book to see whether someone by the name of Leo Baron has checked in there?'

I agreed and asked the night receptionist to let me have a look at the registration book, and there indeed was the name. 'Yes,' I said, 'he checked in yesterday afternoon. He's in Room No 2.'

'I'd like you to do something for us,' came Goldreich's response.

'Go to his room, wake him up and bring him here to the jail. We'll meet you in the kitchen.'

It was an extraordinary request. I had no idea who the man was, and it sounded as though Goldreich didn't either. But then this had been an extraordinary news assignment and Goldreich's tone of voice had sounded urgent, so I didn't hesitate. I located Room 2 and knocked loudly on the door. It opened to reveal a smallish man with a sleep-fogged face.

'Sorry to disturb you,' I began. 'I've just had a phone call from Arthur Goldreich and he asked me to drive you to the jail to see him right now.'

It was hardly the most conventional wake-up call to receive at four o'clock in the morning, but Baron seemed unfazed.

'Just give me a moment,' was all he said.

He emerged, dressed, a few minutes later and we got into my office car. We said little on the way, except that I was able to establish that Baron was a lawyer living in Salisbury (today's Harare) who had arrived in his own plane the previous afternoon to attend to some business in Francistown.

I parked the car, got out to ask someone in the murky pre-dawn dark for directions to the prison kitchen, then escorted my enigmatic companion to the door. I opened it to reveal a scene that remains vividly in my memory. There were a number of large black pots bubbling away on a long stove, with clouds of steam rising from them together with a pervading odour that I can only describe as repulsive – the prisoners' breakfast. Through the steam and the smell, on the far side of the pots, I could discern the figures of Goldreich, Wolpe, Ismail Bhana and Philip Steenkamp. It was certainly an unusual venue for the hatching of a conspiratorial escape plan.

Goldreich was the commanding figure in this exotic conference room. The entertainer I had come to know was gone; we were confronted by the commander of a unit of revolutionaries. I still don't know whether Baron was a member of that unit, but his responses in the exchanges that followed certainly seemed deferential.

Goldreich greeted him courteously, then went straight to the point.

'We have been approached by a man called Captain Excell, who is here now in Francistown and has offered to fly us out,' Goldreich began. At which point I pricked up my ears, for this was the charter pilot who had flown in my two diplomat friends and had struck me as looking a bit dodgy at the time, and particularly in the hotel bar afterwards with his stories of exploits as a mercenary in the Congo.

'We don't trust him,' Goldreich went on. 'We think he may try to trick us by veering off course and landing in South Africa to claim the reward money for handing us over. So here's what we want you to do. We want you to come with us and take a seat immediately behind this pilot. You are an experienced pilot so we want you to watch what he is doing. Watch his navigation. You will have a gun and if you see any indication that he is deviating off course you are to threaten him with it and order him back on course. If he refuses, or resists in any way, you are to shoot him and take over the controls yourself.'

There was silence in the room except for the bubbling of the pots and the soft hissing of steam. I don't recall Baron making any response; his silence struck me as being acceptance. My own reaction was one of shock and confusion. This was a helluva story, but how could I ever write it? I had stumbled into a compact born of desperation that might end up in a murder. I remember wondering whether I might be considered an accessory to such a deed. It was Steenkamp who broke the silence. 'There's still time for you to think this over,' he said, addressing Goldreich. 'Let's meet again tomorrow.' I drove Baron back to the hotel in silence. I did not see him again.

Next day I made my way to the jail once more. I was met by a beaming Delville Knight. 'The birds have flown,' he cried as I drew up beside him. But not with the dodgy Excell watched over by an armed Leo Baron. Knight told me another plan had been hatched in the intervening hours. A charter plane had flown in from Kasane, on the border between Northern Rhodesia and Bechuanaland, to touch down briefly at Palapye, some 200 km south of Francistown. The fugitives had been driven to meet it. Knight said the men had used a bedsheet to flag the plane down to a safe landing spot in a clearing in the bush. The three had scrambled into the plane, which had taken off immediately. No time had been wasted, for fear of another sabotage attack.

So the Great Escapers had got away at last. My assignment was over. It had yielded a remarkable number of scoops and special editions in the three weeks Ernie Christie and I had been there, thanks to our early arrival and the special access we had been given to the escapers in the Francistown jail. We had covered every angle of what had been one of South Africa's most dramatic running news stories — except for one. After careful thought, I decided not to publish anything about that dramatic night meeting in the prison kitchen. The professional code by which I live is to publish everything that is in the public interest, but in this instance I decided there were special reasons not to. Both Leo Baron and, particularly, District Commissioner Steenkamp, a British civil servant, who by happenstance had been privy to an escape plan that could have involved murder, would surely have been seriously compromised had I done so. And anyway, as it turned out, the plan had not been implemented. So this is the first time I have publicly disclosed the events of that night and the extent of Goldreich and Wolpe's readiness to act ruthlessly in their desperate situation.

All that remained, then, was to file my last story, get in the car together with Ernie and drive back to Johannesburg – where, on my arrival back at the office, I found that the pro-apartheid Afrikaans newspapers had made much of the fact that the *Rand Daily Mail*'s political correspondent had been sent to cover the escape story. It proved, they said, that the Mail was politically connected to the revolutionary underground and therefore a danger to the security of the state.

Several years later, the *Sunday Times* ran a bold front-page banner headline: 'How I Nearly Tricked ANC Fugitives'. It was an interview with none other than the boastful Captain Excell, in which he told how he had nearly fooled Goldreich and Wolpe into accepting his offer to fly them out of Francistown. He told the Times reporter he would have flown them across the border into South Africa and handed them over to the security police.

It would have been easy, he said, because they would not have noticed what he was doing until it was too late. *Ja-Nee*, as the marvellous Afrikaans expression goes, taking another for a fool can sometimes be foolish.

CHAPTER FOURTEEN

The Silencing of the Dissidents

THE OPENING YEARS of the 1960s were the most dramatic in the country's history, but as we moved deeper into the decade a pall of silence settled over the land. With the black political movements banned, and thus silenced, and the leaders of the ANC's armed wing captured at Rivonia, the repressive Vorster/Van-den-Bergh machine set about hoovering up the rank-and-file members of the black political organisations. ANC branch members and other figures of significance were served with banning orders, which restricted their movements, prevented them from attending gatherings (defined as more than one other person at a time) and from being quoted in the media or by anyone else. Smaller fry were simply jailed for their membership of what was now an illegal organisation.

The result was the silencing of any black voice in the national political discourse. The only voices of protest and opposition that continued to be heard were those of liberal white dissenters, notably Helen Suzman, the lone Progressive Party MP, her party colleagues, a few activist bodies such as the Black Sash and student organisations, some key religious leaders and the English-language newspapers, with the *Rand Daily Mail* foremost among them.

The last black voice had been that of Nelson Mandela, in his celebrated 10 000-word statement from the dock at the Rivonia

Trial on 20 April 1964, in which he outlined the aims and objectives of the ANC and explained unreservedly why he and his
fellow accused had decided to launch an armed struggle against
the apartheid regime. Two months later, Judge Quartus de Wet
sentenced the accused to life imprisonment.

Then the curtain of silence came down.

Using an archive they had captured at Rivonia, Van den Bergh's
security police first managed to pick up several members of the
new leadership who had not been at Liliesleaf at the time of the
raid. These included David Kitson, Mac Maharaj and eventually
Abram Fischer, the distinguished senior counsel who had led the
legal defence at the Rivonia Trial but was secretly leader of the
Communist Party of South Africa (CPSA). All were detained for
interrogation under the security laws, then tried and sentenced –
Maharaj to 12 years, Kitson to 20, Fischer to life.

Fischer is today honoured as one of the major heroes of the
anti-apartheid struggle. Nelson Mandela lauded him as having
shown 'a level of courage and sacrifice that was in a class by itself'.
He was of royal Afrikaner blood, the son of Abraham Fischer,
who had served as the only Prime Minister of the Orange Free
State Colony after the Anglo-Boer War, and then as a Cabinet
minister and Judge-President after the formation of the Union
of South Africa. But despite this pedigree, the younger Bram, as
he was known, rejected the racial prejudices of his people and
became an ardent anti-apartheid activist and member of the outlawed CPSA. Yet he remained a passionate South African patriot.
After he was arrested and charged with being a member of an
illegal organisation and of trying to overthrow the government,
Fischer, while out on bail, applied for permission to travel to
London to represent a client in a patent case. In his application
to the court he declared: 'I am an Afrikaner. My home is South
Africa. I will not leave my country because my political beliefs
conflict with those of the government.' Such was his status in the
Afrikaner community and reputation for integrity that, amazingly,
he was granted permission.

While in London, exiled ANC leaders tried hard to persuade
Fischer to estreat his £5000 bail, arguing that he could be of

much greater use to the struggle as a symbol of a white Afrikaner prepared to grant equal rights to blacks. But Fischer refused to break his pledge to return home. However, not long after the case against him began in Pretoria Fischer failed to turn up at the court one day, sending a note to his counsel, Harold Hanson, who read it in court:

> By the time this reaches you I shall be a long way from Johannesburg and shall absent myself from the remainder of the trial. But I shall still be in the country to which I said I would return when I was granted bail. I wish you to inform the Court that my absence, though deliberate, is not intended in any way to be disrespectful. Nor is it prompted by any fear of the punishment which might be inflicted on me. Indeed I realise fully that my eventual punishment may be increased by my present conduct …
>
> My decision was made only because I believe that it is the duty of every true opponent of this Government to remain in this country and to oppose its monstrous policy of apartheid with every means in his power. That is what I shall do for as long as I can.
>
> What is needed is for white South Africans to shake themselves out of their complacency, a complacency intensified by the present economic boom built upon racial discrimination. Unless this whole intolerable system is changed radically and rapidly, disaster must follow. Appalling bloodshed and civil war will become inevitable because, as long as there is oppression of a majority, such oppression will be fought with increasing hatred.

Fischer went underground and for the next ten months ran the CPSA clandestinely, keeping himself heavily disguised all the while. He was eventually captured and sentenced to imprisonment for life in Pretoria's maximum-security Central Prison – South Africa's hanging jail – but after 11 years contracted cancer. His last days were agonising. As his condition deteriorated he fell, injuring his neck in a way that paralysed him, rendering him unable to walk or to speak. Yet the prison authorities kept him in his cell for another three months before admitting him to a hospital, where he stayed a further four months before public petitioning prodded the government into allowing him to be transferred under

227

house arrest to his brother's home in Bloemfontein, where he died a few days later.

Thus the Afrikaner leadership's treatment of one of their own whom they saw as an ethnic traitor.

The security police dragnet was ruthlessly efficient. As it swept across the country hauling in ANC members large and small, news leaked out that many of the detainees were breaking under interrogation and torture, revealing not only details about the workings of the underground organisation but also the identities of nearly all its members. Torture had become routine under a Special Branch team headed by Captain Theunis Swanepoel, known as 'Rooi Rus' because of his red hair and ruddy face. So a constant stream of detainees passed through the torture rooms at police headquarters, as those who cracked were followed by those they had disclosed.

Nor was it only ANC members who were detained under the security laws, which empowered the police Special Branch to detain any suspect incommunicado for, first 90 days, then 180 days, later indefinitely, without charge or access to any lawyer or court of law. Some members of the Liberal Party and other legal organisations were detained. And in July 1964 the Special Branch pounced on 29 members of a group of mainly young white activists calling themselves the African Resistance Movement (ARM), which brought the crackdown much closer to home, for several of these were young journalists whom I knew. One, Raymond Eisenstein, was an economics reporter on the *Rand Daily Mail*; another, Hugh Lewin, a sub-editor on *Drum* magazine and *Golden City Post*, was close to Jill Chisholm, who as political reporter was my understudy on the *Rand Daily Mail*. David Evans, also a journalist, I had known at primary school in Cathcart. This personalised their incarceration for me.

Lewin gives a graphic account of his treatment at the hands of Rooi Rus and his team of interrogators in his powerful book, *Bandiet*, written after serving a seven-year sentence for his ARM activities. He was taken to The Greys, the security police head-quarters from which Goldreich and Wolpe had escaped, and escorted to an office on the sixth floor, where he met Swanepoel and four of his men. It was late afternoon but Lewin noted that Swanepoel had with him a picnic basket containing a thermos of hot coffee, a package of sandwiches and some fresh fruit. He realised it was going to be a long night.

One of the men drew a chalk circle on the floor and ordered Lewin to stand in it, never to step outside and never to sit down. There was no furniture near the circle to lean on. The questioning began quietly, persuasively. Why stay silent when others are talking?, Swanepoel taunted, as he read from telexed messages to show that was indeed the case. Other ARM detainees had broken and made statements. We already know all about you, Swanepoel went on, so why not save yourself a lot of unpleasantness by making a statement? Who is Tom? Who is Eric? But Lewin was intent on holding out for as long as possible to allow colleagues on the run time to cross the borders into Swaziland and Bechuanaland. That was when the interrogation began to intensify. Two other men joined the team, and as Swanepoel began to bark his questions at Lewin, first cajoling and then threatening, his men began circling him, stalking around and around, first one way then the other, until their faces became blurred in his tired vision. Hour after hour went by as Lewin's legs, feet, back and body ached unendurably. No violence, but it was a highly sophisticated form of torture that left no physical traces, while leading the exhausted subject eventually to break and talk. So Lewin, too, ultimately reached breaking point, but only after he reckoned, hoped, his escaping colleagues had made it to safety:

About three hours after midnight above the quiet streets and the room wasn't a room any more, not a room with chairs and desks and a couple of windows. It was a world with four faces, sometimes six, a world that was a void, moving around and around, swimming with faces and sheafs of paper, a talking pressing world where I was no longer standing because there was no need to stand because my legs were fixed into a solid mass of concrete covering my ankles and holding me up, pressing up into my back and forcing my shoulders forward, forcing my head to burst open, under the weight of a huge sheet driving the ceiling down, and down, heavy into the floor ...[1]

Once he had cracked and made his statement, Lewin was transferred to Pretoria Local Prison where he spent the next three months in solitary confinement under Vorster's 90-Day Detention Act. It was an experience, as he was to describe it, of prison life without any trappings: 'Just a cell, with nothing in it; nothing that could give you any semblance of control – no light switch, no windows that you could open or close, no taps to turn on or off, no toilet to flush, no pictures, curtains, carpets, no phones, no radios, no newspapers, and no handle on the inside of the door. Just a cell, with four walls, a floor and a ceiling; the bare essentials of clothing, furniture and bedding, with a spoon to eat with (no knife, no fork), a Bible to read (no other books) and nothing on which to write nor anything with which to write. And no contact at all with Outside: no private visits, no letters, no personal messages.'[2]

Ninety days. Alone. Incommunicado. A life so Spartan it tested the detainees' sanity. But there was a grim interruption in this soul-numbing solitude. On 24 July 1964 a member of the ARM, Frederick John Harris, a 27-year-old schoolteacher who had escaped detention because he had joined the movement late, decided in a fit of recklessness as he saw the organisation crumble around him to stage a dramatic demonstration of his own. He primed a bomb, placed it in a suitcase and left the case beside a bench in the whites-only section of Johannesburg's crowded railway terminal, Park Station. Harris then telephoned the railway police to alert them that the bomb was there, giving details of what it looked like, where it was placed and the time it was set to detonate. He also made two other calls, one to the Afrikaans newspaper *Die Transvaler* and the other to the *Rand Daily Mail*, which in turn alerted the police Special Branch.

What happened after that is a matter of conjecture. Either the police dismissed the warnings as false alarms, or, more likely, the warnings reached Van den Bergh, who saw it as an opportunity to entrap the anti-apartheid activists into committing a capital crime, so discrediting their cause and winning massive white support for Vorster's draconian security laws. Both the ANC and the ARM had committed themselves to the use of violence against 'strategic' targets that would avoid human harm. A

230

devastating bomb blast in a public place would give the lie to that. So the bomb went off at exactly 4.33 pm. It killed a 77-year-old woman, Ethyl Rhys, who was sitting on the bench, severely burned her 12-year-old granddaughter, Glynis Burleigh, scarring her for life, and injured 22 others. The public were appalled. Banner headlines splashed across all the newspapers. And the security police went berserk. Lewin and other detainees were bundled into cars and driven to the station to witness the carnage, and then taken upstairs at The Greys once again to be beaten up as the interrogators demanded more information about their movement. Lewin recalls that as they drew up at The Greys, one of his persecutors, a Lieutenant Van der Merwe, screamed at him: 'Your bomb! You're going to talk. No jokes tonight, Lewin. You'll shit yourself tonight. Tonight you'll die. Tonight, Lewin, I'm going to kill you.'³

Well, he didn't kill him, not quite, but it was a savage going over with fists and boots that left the tough, wiry Lewin groaning on the floor. And even as he lay there, bruised and bleeding, he could hear worse going on in the room above. The branch had pulled in Harris that same night and were busy kicking and battering him into a state of submission and confession. By morning Harris had a broken jaw.

Harris was duly tried and sentenced to death. In the seven months that followed I had my first close-up experience of the full horror of the gibbet that those close to a condemned person have to endure. We all know we are going to die some day, but to know exactly when and in what nightmarish circumstances is beyond comprehension to all but those involved in the execution of a friend or loved one. I didn't know the Harris family, but I did know Walter and Adelaine Hain, Liberal Party activists who had been regular contributors to the *Rand Daily Mail*'s opinion pages before they were banned, who were close friends of Harris and his wife, Ann, and of my colleague, Jill Chisholm, then Lewin's girlfriend. It was Lewin who had recruited Harris to the ARM. Through them I became caught up, albeit only peripherally, in the atmosphere of agony that pervaded the small community of ARM relatives and friends. It was an atmosphere devoid of

231

hope, for John's only moment of that had come and gone with the failure of his appeal. All that remained now was to wait for the day, the awful day, of the rope.

During the final days, Ann Harris's friends gathered around her, sitting vigil with her often late into the night, for sleep did not come easily. Jill Chisholm invited me to attend one of these. It was one of the most emotionally disturbing experiences of my life. How does one comfort a young woman who is about to be widowed in such a ghastly, calculated way, in the name of a society of which one is a part?

Ann Harris didn't speak much that night. Others spoke to her as she sat there, looking glazed. There was a terrible awareness of the clock ticking, of time passing. The execution was due at 6 am. I became involved in a conversation with one of Ann's friends who had become a frequent visitor. She told me how two members of the Special Branch had called at the Harris home a few days before. They had come to inquire whether John had a pair of swimming trunks and, if so, could they please have them. What for? The Special Branch men explained to her, relishing the detail, that when a person was executed by hanging, his bowels discharged and the swimming trunks would make it easier for the prison authorities to clean up afterwards. A nice touch of sadism.

John Harris went to the gallows with as much courage as any doomed human being could, singing the American Civil Rights song, 'We Shall Overcome', as the rope was placed around his neck. At the cremation that afternoon the Hains could not speak, for by now they were both officially banned and silenced, so their 15-year-old son Peter did in their stead. After a brief eulogy, the teenager recited from Ecclesiastes 3:3: 'A time to kill and a time to heal, a time to break down and a time to build up.' The Hains went into exile in Britain soon afterwards, where Peter went on to head the highly successful anti-apartheid sports and cultural boycott campaigns against South Africa. Later he became a Cabinet minister in the Labour governments of both Tony Blair and Gordon Brown.

Ten years later, soon after I had become editor of one of the Mail's sister papers, the *Sunday Express*, a member of my staff,

Gordon Winter, brought the 22-year-old Glynis Burleigh to my office to introduce her to me. Winter was an ambiguous character, an excellent reporter whom everyone suspected was also a security police agent, which eventually turned out to be the case. What we were not aware of at that stage was that he also had a close personal relationship with Hendrik van den Bergh. In retrospect I have no doubt that he brought Burleigh to me at Van den Bergh's behest, and that the purpose was to shock me. For the poor young woman was cruelly disfigured. I can only describe her face as looking like molten wax from the burns caused by Harris's bomb. We conversed for a while in Winter's company and I found her to have a gentle charm. But her life had been ruined. Inevitably she was painfully self-conscious and she spoke of how hard it was always to see people's reactions to her appearance. I felt deep sympathy for her but also a deep anger that she should have been brought to my office as a kind of human exhibit to influence me politically. Clearly Van den Bergh's objective was to try to counter my editorial criticisms of the government's security laws by showing me what wickedness he was up against. His effort was counterproductive because, although I have always felt Harris's demonstration was unforgivably reckless, it was in fact Van den Bergh himself who was primarily responsible for Ethyl Rhys's death and Glynis Burleigh's disfigurement, as well as for for John Harris's execution, because of the criminal failure of the unit he commanded to respond to the many advance warning calls made to them about the bomb.

* * *

IT WAS Mary Benson, the most indefatigable lobbyist and activist ever to have taken up the anti-apartheid cause, who tipped off Laurence Gandar about a series of political trials that were going unreported in small towns across the eastern Cape in mid-1964. Mary had heard about them through her wide network of lawyer friends and had travelled there to see for herself. 'You must do something about it, Laurie,' she told the editor in her soft and gentle voice that somehow came across as an imperative

233

command. One did not ignore Mary Benson's directives, for not only were they always soundly based but also they were delivered with an unspoken inference of moral obligation. It was clearly your duty to act.

I was summoned to the editor's office and told to travel to the eastern Cape and find out what was happening in these small-town court cases. Gandar told me to contact Benson, who was staying with the rising young actor-playwright, Athol Fugard, at his home in a windswept seafront settlement outside Port Elizabeth.

Thus began one of two related journalistic assignments that were to expose the brutality and abuse of legal processes by the apartheid administration to an extent that had not been publicised before. For as I headed off to the courts of the eastern Cape where small-fry members of the ANC and other banned political organisations were literally being railroaded to prison, my colleague Benjamin Pogrund was interviewing newly released political prisoners who were telling of the beatings and abuses that were taking place behind bars. Both were high-risk stories and we both knew it, as did Gandar, for our lawyer, Kelsey Stuart, had told us so. Benjie was up against a law called the Prisons Act, which was intended to prevent publication of anything that went on in the country's jails, while I was in danger of being charged with contempt of court for implying that the sentences being handed down were unjust. But Stuart, the country's finest media lawyer, believed we could navigate our way through those risks if we were meticulous in our reportage.

This was the kind of bold investigative journalism that was to define the character and role of the *Rand Daily Mail* in the years ahead, through four successive editorships. It was to make the paper internationally famous and win it and its staff members many awards, but it also made powerful enemies and led eventually to the paper's unseemly demise. Success does not always favour the brave.

Ironically Stuart believed my assignment was riskier than Pogrund's, because he believed he had spotted a chink in the protective armour of the Prisons Act. The law stated that it was illegal to publish false information about conditions in prisons without taking reasonable steps to ensure the information was true. The intention was obviously to compel journalists to seek confirmation of their information from the prisons authorities themselves, which invariably led to flat denials — thus sealing the prisons off from any public probing. But Stuart believed those key words, 'reasonable steps', gave us the opening we needed. He advised Pogrund to obtain sworn affidavits from all his informers — mostly political prisoners released after completing their sentences. In addition, Kelsey would himself subject those informants to rigorous cross-examination to satisfy himself, as an experienced trial lawyer, that their evidence was truthful. That, he reckoned, should satisfy any court that 'reasonable steps' had been taken.

But he was wrong. Not in his analysis of the law, but in underestimating the ruthless determination of the apartheid regime to nail the *Rand Daily Mail,* and in the vulnerability of criminal prisoners to deals in which they promised to give perjured evidence in exchange for early release or even just a few special privileges.

The eastern Cape political trials presented me with a simpler task. All that was required to recognise the blatant miscarriages of justice taking place was an understanding of the rules governing the powers of magistrates hearing cases in South Africa's lower court system. I knew from my experience covering magistrates' courts for the *Daily Representative* in the early 1950s that they were restricted to hearing cases that carried sentences of no more than three years' imprisonment. But here the charges were being split into several 'counts' relating to what was essentially the same offence, with the prosecution seeking three years' imprisonment on each count.

All I needed to do was state the statutory limitations applying to magistrates' court hearings early in my reports, then report straightforwardly what was actually happening in these cases, being careful not to relate the one to the other. That would leave readers able to relate the two aspects of the report for themselves without exposing me to a contempt charge for directly implying that the magistrates were cheating. It worked.

What hadn't worked from the state's point of view was that it had counted on getting away with these crooked trials, firstly because it believed the simple country folk it was bringing to court would not have legal representation, and, secondly, that by holding the trials in an array of small country towns some distance from Port Elizabeth, the provincial daily newspapers would not have the resources to cover them adequately. But they had not reckoned on the redoubtable Mary Benson, who alerted a British-funded body, the Defence and Aid Fund, which put up money to provide these ANC grassroots members with skilled advocates to defend them. Finally, she had alerted Laurence Gandar to ensure that the trials were publicised.

The first trial I attended was in Addo, some 75 km northeast of Port Elizabeth, a hamlet so small it consisted of little more than a railway station, a post office, the magistrate's court and a bridge. Even the court officials had to commute there each day. In the dock was a small black woman with bright eyes and an intelligent face named Zibia Mpendu. She was a nursing sister at the Provincial Hospital in Port Elizabeth and an active member of the eastern Cape branch of the South African Institute of Race Relations. A woman of note, visibly out of place in the dock of a criminal court.

Sister Mpendu's crime was that she had attended an ANC meeting after the organisation had been banned. She had been driven there by car with a group of friends. She had neither spoken at the meeting nor asked any questions. There was no suggestion she was even a member of the banned organisation. She had simply been there, an individual in the audience. But Zibia Mpendu faced three 'counts' under the Prohibition of Political Organisations Act – one for attending an illegal gathering, another for furthering the aims of an illegal organisation, and a third for contributing funds to a banned organisation. She had contributed half a crown (25 cents) towards petrol for the car that had transported her and friends to the meeting.

Mpendu had no real defence. She admitted attending the meeting. It was important for her, as a member of the community, to hear what was being said, she told the court. And she admitted paying the half crown towards the petrol. Her advocate, Michael Klotz, had objected to the splitting of the charge at the outset

236

of the trial, but the magistrate had overruled him, contending it was within the state's rights to do so. After the guilty verdict, Klotz pleaded strongly in mitigation of sentence, arguing that it was really a petty offence simply to have attended such a meeting as a non-participant, and that it warranted no more than a reprimand. But his words fell on deaf ears. The security of the state was of paramount importance in these dangerous times, the magistrate declared, and it was necessary to set an example to deter black people from joining these revolutionary organisations. He sentenced Mpendu to three years on each count. Nine years altogether.

I still remember the look of bewilderment on Zibia Mpendu's face as she was led away to the waiting prison van. Nine years in jail for going to a meeting. Unbelievable. Outrageous. But inescapable.

My next case was in Humansdorp, a more substantial farming town 85 km west of Port Elizabeth, where a young white activist, Sylvia Neame, was on trial. It was a repeat of the Addo case, the only difference being that Neame was a known member of the ANC and the CPSA. She, too, had attended a meeting of the banned ANC and she, too, had the charge against her split into three 'counts' — attending an illegal gathering, furthering the aims of a banned organisation and contributing money to the ANC. Her advocate, David Soggot, later to become one of the country's most distinguished civil rights lawyers, objected vehemently to the splitting of the charge — but again to no avail. So Neame, too, got nine years. Obviously an order had been handed down from the Department of Justice to overrule these protests from the defence lawyers, and the magistrates, vulnerable as government employees, were meekly complying despite their status as supposedly independent judicial officers.

And so it went on. I stayed in the eastern Cape for several weeks, covering case after case, which all followed the same pattern. After that, by keeping contact through Mary Benson and Athol Fugard, I followed the grim saga for two years, by which time nearly a thousand rank-and-file members of the ANC had been shunted off to prison. The aim was not merely to break the back of the organisation in the stronghold province where it had arisen, but to eradicate it root and branch. That, the regime hoped, would create a political vacuum in the black community and enable it to implant an alternative political culture based on compliant traditional chiefs who could administer its projected independent Bantustans.

My reports on this protracted violation of legal procedure attracted international attention. Both *The Guardian* in London and *The New York Times* ran lengthy articles on the trials, which in turn helped prompt the legal authorities to take a closer look at what had happened. The cases all went on review to the Supreme Court, which declared the splitting of charges to be illegal and lopped 2 000 years off the collective sentences.

Looking back over 66 years of journalism, I guess that should rank as my most creditworthy achievement.

* * *

FOR SOME TIME Benjamin Pogrund had been hearing through his extensive network of left-wing contacts about the abusive treatment of prisoners, especially black prisoners, in the country's jails. Now, with the surge in the prison population, more and more of these stories began to circulate. On a holiday trip to Durban in June 1965, Pogrund met Harold Strachan, who had just been released on completing a three-year sentence for instructing members of the ANC's armed wing on how to make bombs.

Strachan was a poet and humorous writer, who later made something of a name for himself as an artist. But he had been trained as a pilot in the South African Air Force during the Second World War, and, as he put it, that led his ANC colleagues to assume he knew all about bombs. In any event, he had been picked up early, sentenced, and served his full term. Now he was free and telling friends openly about the shocking things he had seen in Pretoria Local and Central prisons, where he had been incarcerated alongside members of the ARM. When Pogrund heard about this, he sought out Strachan, who agreed to tell all for publication.

So the stage was set for the most fateful piece of reporting the *Rand Daily Mail* was ever to publish.

Apart from the threat posed by the Prisons Act, Pogrund faced the risk that if the Special Branch got wind of his meeting with Strachan it could simply serve the released prisoner with a banning order, preventing the Mail from publishing anything he said. So speed was vital, adding to the risk. Pogrund tape-recorded Strachan's detailed account of what he had seen and experienced in prison, returned to Johannesburg to have it transcribed into a 35 000-word document, gave copies to Gandar and Stuart, then, on the lawyer's instruction, drove back to Durban to query a few points and for Strachan to sign the transcript as a sworn affidavit. That done, Strachan was flown to Johannesburg, where Stuart subjected him to several hours of rigorous cross-examination. Pogrund then condensed Strachan's testimony into three articles, which were published on successive days in June 1965. It was explicit stuff:

> We had a flush toilet in the cell, which was quite unusual as far as prisons I have been in. But an interesting thing about this toilet was that you didn't only defecate in it, you also washed in it, you brushed your teeth in it. They had sufficient bathroom facilities. They had a very spick and span shower room with hot water and everything laid on, but we weren't allowed to use it … It was kept clean for inspection.[4]

The articles described how warders hit and kicked black prisoners at random, lashed them with the straps of their truncheons and keys; drove them 'like animals' with sticks and leather straps from one section of the prison to another; and kept those needing medical attention waiting, standing naked and barefoot in the freezing highveld winter with frost thick on the ground from 6.15 in the morning until the doctor came around nine o'clock, or even later.[5]

The accounts were from first-person observation. 'I saw it from my cell window,' Strachan told Pogrund. 'We could see these men being hit with fists and open hands. We could see them coming in a column two-abreast, that is "two-two" as they put it in prison, and being thrashed as they rushed into the prison. We could see the same men rushing up the stairs and into the section above us with the same cries as we had heard in the yard and we could hear the blows following.'

The worst, said Strachan, was having to live in the hanging jail, where executions were carried out about every ten days. At that time South Africa was notorious for having the highest execution rate in the world.

> Days beforehand the condemned started singing, and being Africans most of them they can't help singing harmoniously ... The last two days they just sing right through. 'Nearer my God to Thee' and stuff like that. I never want to hear such hymns again. Then you would hear the condemned walking to the gallows singing hymns. You would hear the door shut. Later you would faintly hear the sound of the trapdoor opening. I would feel a tremble run through the part of the building where I was as the trapdoor fell.[6]

The response to these reports was explosive. Readers were appalled; journalists on other papers were astonished to read what they thought could not be published; and the government reacted in fury.

After the first article appeared, police called at Gandar's office demanding that he hand over all copy and photographs relating to the remaining two articles the paper had announced it would publish. Gandar took the police to Pogrund's office but the reporter wasn't there, whereupon they carried out a thorough search and triumphantly confiscated the copy. What they didn't know, however, was that Pogrund had already given the copy to the chief sub-editor, Rex Gibson, who had sent it through to the printers for advance setting. So the lead type was still there, safe in the printing department.

Nor was that the only attempt to stop publication of the Strachan disclosures. The night after the second article appeared, Gandar received a strange phone call at his home from Johannesburg's police chief, Brigadier Louis Steyn, begging him, 'as a personal favour', not to publish the third article. Steyn claimed he was not a supporter of the ruling National Party but of the opposition United Party, and told Gandar the articles were causing him great distress because of the harm they were doing to the country's image abroad. But there appeared to be a veiled warning as well, when Steyn mentioned that he was speaking on behalf of someone in high authority whom he wouldn't name. In retrospect, he may have been aware of the vicious counteroffensive Vorster was already plotting against the *Rand Daily Mail* and was trying to warn Gandar. Just hold off a few days, Steyn urged, so they could discuss it 'like gentlemen'. But whatever the reason for the call, Gandar ignored it and went ahead with publication.

Soon afterwards there appeared an unexpected backup for the Mail's campaign when its sister paper, the *Sunday Times*, ran an article in which a head warder named Johannes Theron, from the Cinderella Prison, east of Johannesburg, poured out a series of disclosures of his own that he said were burning his conscience. 'I have seen electric shock treatment being given to prisoners as a punishment and in order to make them talk,' he told the paper. 'Once a prisoner has had the treatment he is prepared to sign anything.'

Theron said conditions at Cinderella were the worst he had seen in 17 years of service, and that he had fought a running battle of protest against these abuses. 'I have seen brutality absolutely contrary to prison regulations,' he declared. 'Warders who have spoken out against these appalling conditions have been victimised.'[7]

Pogrund immediately sought out Theron and persuaded him to amplify the details of what he had seen for a further article in his series. Theron went further and introduced Pogrund to other warders at Cinderella, who confirmed what Theron was disclosing. One, Gysbert van Schalkwyk, said he was leaving the prisons service because he couldn't stand the maltreatment any longer. Another, Nooientjies van Rensburg, said if Theron landed in trouble he would support him. A black Mozambican prisoner, Filisberto Taimo, said he had been subjected to electric-shock torture, which he described as 'burning'. All were cross-examined by lawyer Stuart and all signed sworn affidavits that their testimony was the truth.

Gandar, feeling emboldened by all this corroboration of Strachan's statements, published a challenging editorial. 'Get

241

cracking, Mr Vorster. Evasion is impossible now,' he declared, calling for a full judicial inquiry into prison conditions.[8]

But he had not reckoned on the ruthlessness of Vorster and the Special Branch. Within days they struck. Strachan was banned and charged with perjury; ex-warder Van Schalkwyk was arrested and kept secretly in custody while the authorities claimed he had been released on bail, leaving the Mail to search in vain for him. Head Warder Theron was suspended from duty and ordered to stay at home, and several other young warders, friends of Theron, were also arrested. Van Rensburg and the Mozambican disappeared; they had simply been spirited into police custody.

When Van Schalkwyk resurfaced two weeks later it was to appear before a magistrate on a charge of perjury – to which he pleaded guilty. What followed was the travesty of a trial. Dr Percy Yutar, who had been the high-powered prosecutor in the Rivonia Trial, was assigned to lead the state in this relatively minor matter in a lower court – obviously because he was a master in the art of political smear tactics, and in this case the Mail was the primary target rather than the intimidated young man in the dock. The task was made easy for Yutar because Van Schalkwyk did not have a lawyer, and the Mail could not provide him with one because he had pleaded guilty, which meant the newspaper had no standing in the case. So Yutar's outrageous insinuations about the Mail's actions and motives could not be challenged; the newspaper was literally flayed in open court without having the opportunity to deny or reply to any of the prosecutor's false assertions. Van Schalkwyk had made his false allegations to the paper for financial gain, Yutar declared, claiming that 17 of the 18 paragraphs in the young warder's published statement were false.

Gandar wrote an overnight letter to Yutar denying there had been any financial inducement and giving the name of a witness who could testify to that effect. Yutar slyly twisted the intervention to suit his propaganda role. He told the court he accepted the paper's denial, but went on to declare that Pogrund had been 'the nigger in the woodpile' who had unscrupulously set out to hit the headlines at home and abroad with a story that had done 'irreparable damage' to the country's image.

The magistrate sentenced Van Schalkwyk to three years' imprisonment. The young man's family turned their backs on him, and his girlfriend broke off their engagement. Some time later Pogrund bumped into Van Schalkwyk, who was out on bail after lodging an appeal. Shamefacedly, the warder told him the security police had given him a blunt choice: he could either stand by his statement to the Mail and get a three-year jail sentence, or he could give the police another statement denying his published words and get a much lighter sentence, possibly even an acquittal. 'What else could I do?' he asked.[9] So he had not even been given the promised reward for selling his soul.

The Van Schalkwyk trial was accompanied by a tirade of political abuse and threats from the Afrikaans press, Nationalist politicians and Vorster himself, with accusations that the Mail was poisoning race relations at home and the country's image abroad. One Afrikaans editor went so far as to contend that the Mail's prisons series amounted to 'the final proof that South Africa has a growth in its midst that should be cut out' – an unprecedented call from within the body of South African journalists for the government to close down a major newspaper.

More trials followed: Taimo, Theron, Strachan and others. Taimo the Mozambican was quick to recant. He was particularly vulnerable. Not only had he faced an intimidating grilling by senior prisons officers, but he also had good reason to fear being deported back to Mozambique, where the PIDE, the notorious Portuguese secret police of the Salazar era, would doubtless have given him an even more severe going-over. So he parroted the answers the authorities wanted. No, there had never been any electric-shock torture; the machine was used only to treat prisoners with sore muscles. And no, there had never been any assaults. In fact, conditions at Cinderella were so congenial that the chief warder would often pick up a spade himself and happily join the prisoners in their work. The other charged informers tried to stand their ground, but were packed off to jail after trials conducted in a maze of lies from a procession of inmates who swore to the idyllic conditions under which they were incarcerated. Theron got four years, reduced to two on appeal.

With a relentless inevitability, the authorities then turned on Pogrund and Gandar. First they seized their passports, then came the news that they were to be charged with publishing false information about prisons without taking reasonable steps to ensure accuracy. This time they chose the country's most eminent senior counsel, Sydney Kentridge, to defend them – a man I was myself later to depend on in conflicts of my own with the apartheid regime. Kentridge was the right man for the job, calm yet forceful with a deep voice and polished in both the country's official languages. 'He speaks Afrikaans with a Knightsbridge accent,' wrote Gavin Young, one of *The Observer*'s finest journalists, who had flown from London to cover the case as Gandar's international reputation began to soar in the wake of the prisons series and his powerful anti-apartheid editorials. 'Thunderer Against Apartheid', *The Observer* had headlined him when he went to London to accept a gold medal from the British Institute of Journalism, while the American Newspaper Publishers Association had awarded the *Rand Daily Mail* its World Press Achievement Award. Foreign celebrities arrived for the case: Lord Devlin to represent the International Press Institute, the eminent British peer Lord Butler, and William Rees-Mogg, editor of *The Times* of London, who testified for the Mail on the role of a watchdog press in a democracy.

Then a funny thing happened on the way to the court. Gandar and Pogrund were called to the company's lawyers, where they were joined by the company chairman and senior management. There they were told that the lawyers had been informed by someone who purported to be speaking on behalf of 'people in high places', but whose identity could not be disclosed, that if the Mail apologised publicly for its prisons coverage the charges against them would be dropped. A tough call for people who had already been through so much and who by now had lost all faith in a judicial system the regime was so easily able to manipulate. But Gandar and his reporter were resolute. They were damned if they were going to renege on what they knew to have been the truth.

To the dismay of many of us on the Mail, the editor of the *Sunday Times*, Joel Mervis, decided otherwise. Mervis was the senior editor in the company, a lawyer himself with long journalistic experience, and the *Sunday Times* was the company's money-spinner. To him it was a matter of prudence over principle. Mervis knew the court cases were costing the company a ton of money, and by nature he was more of a pragmatist than a crusader. Very different from Gandar. So he published a grovelling apology for having been the first to run Head Warder Theron's disclosures, which meant he never went to court while Gandar and Pogrund did. Mervis's apology left the Mail badly exposed in the public eye.

What I always liked most about Kentridge was not only his knowledge of the law but also his shrewd insight into the judges before whom he appeared. Who was good, who was bad, who was independent and who was a political appointment. One therefore knew from the outset in any case of political significance whether one stood a chance of a fair trial or not. So when it was revealed that the case was to be heard by Mr Justice Piet Cillié, who had been appointed Judge-President of the Transvaal over the heads of more senior judges, we knew right away that the case was headed south.

For the next eight months the state produced more than a hundred witnesses — 'a small army', as Gandar called it — in a replication of what had gone before. A parade of perjuries. As Kentridge, at his pithy best, put it in his summing-up to the court: 'Nothing could have harmed the good name of the Prisons Department more than the sorry procession of plainly untruthful warders and officers who gave evidence … Not only were individual warders untruthful but they made concerted efforts to mislead the court by perjured evidence.'[10]

Judge Cillié was unmoved by this damning admonition. He delivered the predetermined guilty verdict, but in an attempt to soften the wave of negative reporting about the case in news media abroad, he sentenced Gandar to a paltry R200 fine and Pogrund to a suspended prison sentence of six months.

The case made a deep and lasting impression on me. I found it painful to watch this editor, whose brilliant analytical mind and courageous determination I so admired, sit there day after day enduring the indignity of such a charade. Yet he never showed the faintest flicker of emotion. He was the farthest thing from a showman it was possible to imagine, a figure of stolid dignity in the midst of this circus of clowns. He was an inwardly emotional man but with an iron discipline to contain it. He sat there silently, impassively, and at the end of the long day's session went back to his office to check over the day's news pages and read through the editorials his assistants had written, make a few changes here and there, then head home around midnight, where he had difficulty sleeping because of chronic asthma and the stresses of the day.

But the journalistic lessons of the prisons case burned themselves into me and were to serve as a guide for the rest of my career. I realised that when it came to investigative journalism in a country like South Africa, with a ruthlessly determined government that didn't respect press freedom, it was not enough to ensure to your own satisfaction that your reporting was accurate. You would have to make sure before publishing that you would be able to prove its accuracy in court, even a court that might be loaded against you.

In other words, you would have to prepare your court case even as you prepared your news report. That meant making sure all your informants would be available to testify as witnesses, and ensuring that none was vulnerable to pressure from the state, particularly from the security police. You should have more than one reporter on every investigative assignment, so they could corroborate each other's evidence in court afterwards, and it would be wise to keep a dossier of their progress in the investigation in a safe place away from the office. Above all, never be impatient. Never allow fear of a competitor beating you to the scoop to tempt you into publishing before you are ready to face the storm. These were lessons that stood me in good stead years later when I found myself occupying that same hot seat Gandar had endured.

CHAPTER FIFTEEN

Mahogany Row

IN THE MIDST of those drawn-out prison trials I received a call from the editor's secretary, Daphne McMaster. 'The editor would like to see you,' she said. So I made my way down the long passageway to his office, an oak-panelled private haven decorated with exquisite modern paintings, prints and sculptures by some of South Africa's finest artists. And equipped with a private toilet. For all his tough and fearless journalism, Gandar was an intensely private man, quiet and with refined tastes. He had once run a family art gallery, and collecting the works of his favourite artists was his greatest joy. He was sitting at his desk beside his ungainly old Underwood typewriter when I entered. 'Thanks for popping in, Sparks,' he said, with a quaint mix of formality and familiarity that was the beginning of an incremental transition to a close relationship.

'I wanted to talk to you about your future,' he said. 'I think it's time to promote you to the position of assistant to the editor.' I felt the blood rush to my face. It was a singular honour. I was just 31 years old and here I was being offered a job on the editorial executive staff of the country's biggest morning newspaper. I felt flattered − and appalled.

'I … I, thank you, Mr Gandar, but I'm not sure,' I stammered. 'I don't know that I'm ready for it. I mean, I'm enjoying what I'm

Laurence Gandar, my hero and mentor, captured here by the Rand Daily Mail's *iconic cartoonist, Bob Connolly.*

doing. I feel I'm just reaching my peak as a reporter. I don't want to interrupt that.'

At which point I got my wits together and came to the real point of my objection. 'I don't want to end up in Mahogany Row subbing letters to the editor,' I said.

A wisp of a smile crept across Gandar's tired face. 'I know what you mean,' he said, 'but there comes a time in everyone's life when he has to decide whether he wants to stay in the ranks for the rest of his life or join the headquarters staff. So think about it and let me know. Thank you.'

Brief. To the point. Always such an economy of words. And that little military touch, reflecting his wartime experience.

I was in a dilemma. As a young man with a wife, two children and another on the way, I needed the extra money that would come with the promotion. There was education to think about, a home to buy at some point. I couldn't consider staying 'in the ranks' for the rest of my life. Yet I was stimulated by the work I was doing as a reporter, covering major events in my country's racial conflict. I felt I was at the rockface, reporting history as it unfolded. I didn't want to be shunted into a fusty executive job.

Coupled with this was a professional objection I had developed to the way South African newsrooms were – and still are – constructed. My experience in Britain and with colleagues at Harvard's Nieman Foundation had convinced me that one of the things preventing South African journalism from reaching the fullness of its considerable potential, given the epic national story we were covering, was its failure to give full recognition to its best reporters. Good reporting is an exacting task. It requires a quick mind, a wide range of general knowledge, extensive contacts in many fields and, above all, an ability to render a complex issue into a fascinating story that is easy to understand. And to do all that quickly. My problem has always been that whenever a South African editor spots a really talented reporter able to do all that, his instinct is to promote him to an executive job in which he ceases to do any reporting. He becomes an assistant to the editor, then an assistant editor, gets paid more and is given an office of his own in what the rest of the newsroom staff mockingly refer to as Mahogany Row – a place where he is more of an administrator and an odd-job handyman than a journalist.

The talented young man or woman accepts, of course. Because of the money. South African reporters are poorly paid compared with their overseas counterparts. To get by on a reporter's salary if you have a family to support is difficult. The job is low on the social scale, too; one needs a title to have some social standing. The result is that South African newsrooms tend to be young and understaffed. Too many experienced reporters are either bumped up into Mahogany Row or leave for better-paid jobs outside journalism. In Britain and the US I had encountered reporters with many years' experience and great reputations who earned considerably more than some of the executives in their own newsrooms. It was their work that made their newspapers great. In South Africa the mature, well-rounded, 45-year-old reporter is a rarity. The result shows in the mediocre quality of our big metropolitan newspapers.

So it was that I went home that night in a disturbed frame of mind to discuss Gandar's proposal with Mary. She had been a tax specialist in the revenue service, and was an eminently practical person. 'What does this new job entail?' was her first question. I said I didn't really know, but that it usually involved some editorial writing, what we call the leading articles that are supposed to express the newspaper's collective view on key issues, sometimes putting together the 'letters to the editor' page and then a lot of ad hoc stuff that the editor doesn't have time to, or doesn't want to, deal with himself.

'If it's so undefined,' Mary responded, 'if it's like he just wants to promote you to develop you, why don't you work out what you'd like to do in such a job and put it to him as a proposal?'

It was good advice and I took it. So for the next few weeks I engaged with Gandar in a kind of creative negotiation about what we felt the paper needed and what I might do to help provide it.

Gandar began by outlining his basic needs. The prisons cases were taking up a lot of his time, both in court and in consultations with the lawyers and with management. He needed help with leader writing. The paper usually ran three leading articles a day, which required prior discussion and topic selection, and at that stage there were only two assistant editors, AB Hughes, who was Gandar's deputy, and Lewis Sowden who, with his wife Dora, were also the paper's art and theatre critics. So Gandar said he would require me to be on hand to write a leader whenever needed.

And, yes, he would like me to handle letters to the editor. Not pulse-racing stuff, but a necessary part of every newspaper. Beyond that, he was open to ideas.

I began by reminding him of our mutual agreement about the importance of reporting and analysing developments in the newly independent African states. I pointed out that the paper had already made a significant investment in my trips into the continent, where I had developed a network of valuable contacts, including some who had since become presidents of their countries. Surely we should capitalise on that investment. Gandar readily agreed, so part of the new job description was that I should continue to make regular visits to selected African countries, preferably arranged around the annual summit meetings of the Organization of African Unity (OAU), and write a weekly column on African affairs.

This drew the discussion to a broader project. Several senior staff members had become admirers of a new form of analytical reporting being developed by the serious British Sunday papers, particularly the *Sunday Times* and *The Observer*. The *Sunday Times* was being edited by Harold Evans, a Welsh train-driver's son who had become one of the most dynamic editors of the age. Evans introduced a crusading style of investigative journalism through an elite Insight team of reporters. *The Observer* was edited by a very different personality, David Astor, scion of an immensely wealthy dynasty, but who was painfully shy compared with the supercharged Evans, and despite his background had a passionate commitment to championing the causes of the disadvantaged — particularly the black people of apartheid South Africa. Indeed Astor's personality and passions were similar to Gandar's, and the two became mutual admirers and friends.

Out of our discussion about the merits of these two fine news-

251

papers came the idea that the Mail should establish its own modest Insight team, with one or two reporters who could focus on in-depth articles analysing some of the critical issues facing South Africa. These should be published on the editorial and op-ed spread of broadsheet pages in the Saturday edition. The leading article would then be moved to column one of the front page, giving it much greater impact. All this, Gandar felt, would boost the Saturday issue, which traditionally had the lowest circulation of the week and thus the least advertising support. It would also give the Mail a powerful new platform to put across its message of the urgent need to bring about radical changes in the political, economic and social life of the country.

Gandar wanted me to take charge of this project, working with one specialist reporter to begin with, maybe two or more if the venture proved successful. The pages would also carry Gandar's political column, my 'Inside Africa' column, a bitingly sharp column critiquing the Afrikaans press by night editor Harry O'Connor, a column by a rising young black journalist, Nat Nakasa, about his day-to-day experiences of life under apart-heid, a humorous column by the elegantly witty AB Hughes, and other items of fine writing culled from *The Observer* Foreign News Service.

As a package, it fulfilled my dream of the ideal job. I would still do some reporting on events as they unfolded. At the same time I would get some experience of editing, both in leader writing and in putting together a new section of the paper. I was filled with enthusiasm as I went home to express my thanks to Mary for her wonderful idea. I also decided then and there that I would never, ever accept a job without establishing exactly what it would in-volve – and if necessary to negotiate terms acceptable to me. Job satisfaction, not titles or monetary reward, has to be one's primary aim in life. That principle governed my 23 years of service at, and eventually my departure from, the *Rand Daily Mail*.

Of course there was a certain amount of derision among the staff about the new Saturday edition. Journalists are a cynical lot and they like to affect an image of hard-nosed anti-intellectualism. They quickly dubbed the Saturday edition the 'Egghead', and I have no doubt some sincerely believed it would not succeed. But the list of applicants wanting to work on it belied their scepticism. Eventually I chose Michael Cobden, a rising young star with a fluent writing style, as the key reporter on the team. Following Evans' example with his Insight team, I labelled those Saturday pages 'Inside Mail' — but the 'Egghead' sobriquet stuck among the staff.

Inside Mail was an instant success. From its inception, the circulation of the Saturday edition rose from being the worst of the week to the best, where it stayed for the remaining 21 years of the *Rand Daily Mail*'s life. Yet there was never a concomitant increase in its advertising content, an incongruity I can only attribute to ineffective salesmanship.

Above all, the section's success convinced me that, contrary to some common newsroom prejudices, quality journalism can be a circulation builder. I have done my fair share of pop journalism in my time, but as educational standards rise worldwide, I believe the survival of the print media, as it faces the challenges of the digital age, will depend on its ability to raise the standard of brightly written explanatory journalism that can help readers understand the increasing complexity of the world in which they live.

* * *

IT WAS SOON after Inside Mail was launched that Gandar wrote what I still consider the boldest and most insightful of all his columns, which now appeared under his own name instead of his *nom de plume*, Owen Vine. Indeed it was arguably the boldest political step ever taken by the editor of a mainstream South African newspaper, the more so since it came only three years after he had already rattled the white establishment cage by committing the paper to supporting the integrationist Progressive Party ahead of Smuts' United Party. Now he leapt further ahead of the Progs as well by declaring that white South Africans should recognise that black majority rule was the only possible future for the country. That meant accepting the dreaded 'one-person-one-vote' system demanded by the ANC and other outlawed black nationalist movements. Within white politics only the Liberal Party, headed by author Alan Paton, had advocated that and it was forced to disband when Verwoerd prohibited the existence of multiracial political parties.

To describe that column, written in April 1964, as leaping well ahead of the bulk of his newspaper's readership would be a massive understatement. Verwoerd was at the height of his power, Vorster was waging his repressive crackdown, and, with the Rivonia trialists about to go to prison, black resistance was at its lowest ebb. Helen Suzman's was the only liberal voice in Parliament, and even her party, the Progs, were advocating a qualified franchise to allow for a gradual extension of the vote to educated black people. It was to be another 13 years before the Progs came around to accepting the principle of universal franchise.

Gandar knew very well that he was ahead of his readership but it didn't deter him. He must have known, too, that this controversial leap ahead of his readership on such an emotional issue would not endear him to an already vexed management and board of directors. But that didn't deter him either. It was not that Gandar was pig-headed, as some were to say of him. Nor was he really a bleeding-heart liberal, driven by emotional idealism. No, Gandar certainly cared about injustice and human suffering, but what drove him was his own logical intellect.

In this, Gandar was not unlike Verwoerd, of whom his Afrikaner followers would say: '*Hy dink konsekwent*' ('He thinks logically'). Except that Gandar's was the flipside of such thinking. Verwoerd believed there could be only two outcomes to South Africa's racial conflict – either racial separation, his concept of 'grand apartheid' based on independent Bantustans, or racial integration. Since he rejected integration, which he said would lead to majority rule and thus to the 'national suicide' of the Afrikaner *volk*, apartheid was the only logical policy for the Afrikaners to follow.

Gandar agreed with the basic analysis, but not the prognosis. Yes, there could be only those two choices, but since apartheid was unachievable – the races were already too integrated economically ever to be physically separated – whites would have to come to terms with the inevitability of integration when eventually

254

they realised apartheid was going nowhere except towards disaster. That meant they should be made aware of this now, so they could begin to prepare themselves for the inevitable. Surely the role of a good newspaper, he reasoned, was to speak truth to its public, however reluctant they might be to hear it.

Gandar walked into my new office late on a Thursday afternoon and handed me the copy, typed with his old Underwood on the same sheets of newsprint that the reporters used. He paused for a while, looking out of the window as I began flipping through the sheets. 'I suppose that may cause a bit of a stir,' he murmured as he gave me another of those thin smiles before walking out again. I don't think he had consulted anyone else on the staff about the column. He certainly didn't ask for my opinion. But then it was his personal column, not an editorial.

I was riveted. Verwoerd had been hammering away at the Progs, and at the Mail for supporting it, ridiculing the party's qualified franchise policy. 'They think this will save the white man,' he mocked. 'But it won't.' No, he argued, if the Progressives ever came to power, the blacks wouldn't accept a qualified franchise. They would see the Progs as weak and that would increase their clamour for full power. Then they would take everything. You would have a black neighbour, the schools would be integrated, the whole country would go black. Now here was Gandar saying in effect: 'Yes, Hendrik, you are right. But we must do it anyway.'

I read carefully through the column, making all the necessary typographical markings for the typesetters, and then wrote the headline that sprang immediately to mind. I looked at it once more, then added a heavy underscoring for emphasis beneath one of the words.

I went to Gandar's office. 'I thought I'd better show you the headline I've written before sending it to the works,' I said. 'It puts your case rather bluntly.'

He glanced at it briefly, then gave a slightly warmer smile. 'It's fine,' he said.

The column, headlined 'Yes, it <u>does</u> mean the whole hog', laid out in compelling fashion the case for embracing change and embarking on the transition to a multiracial future. The final paragraphs summed up the challenge:

> Yet it is true that we might fail. It is true also that the process of adaptation will be extraordinarily difficult and painful, requiring of us the exercise of every ounce of patience, wisdom and tolerance we can muster.
>
> There could scarcely be a greater challenge, a more stimulating mission than this – the uplifting of one's own underprivileged peoples and sharing with them the rewards and values of Western civilisation.
>
> We should not shrink from this task because success is not assured. Does Christianity not teach us to be ready to suffer and, if necessary, to lose all for what we know to be right and just? Is it not preferable to serve our less fortunate fellow men than to hold ourselves apart from them, clutching our own privileges to our bosom? Apartheid is a contraction of the human spirit, an impoverishing act of self-concern, a retreat from life. Integration is meeting life and entering its stream.
>
> In the memorable words of Garfield Todd: 'Let us cooperate courageously and generously with the inevitable.'

Three decades after Gandar wrote that prophetic column, noting the futility of Verwoerd's multinational vision and urging acceptance of its only alternative, the last Afrikaner leader, President FW de Klerk, finally yielded to the political realities Gandar had noted way back then. As he did so Piet Cillié, the doyen of Afrikaner editors, was to declare that it had been necessary for the National Party to try to implement apartheid in order to discover its impracticability. Only by doing that, Cillié contended, could the Afrikaner people have been persuaded to accept multiracialism.

What weasel words! Such discombobulation adds insult to the gross injuries inflicted by apartheid. Cillié was an intelligent man, and as editor of the National Party's most important mouthpiece, *Die Burger*, he was in a uniquely influential position. He purported to be a *verligte*, a leading figure among the so-called enlightened Afrikaners who were supposed to be the intellectual pathfinders of their people. Yet throughout the Verwoerd years and after, he never raised a word of doubt about the fundamental impracticability of the doctrine of 'separate development'. As a journalist he must have read Gandar's many columns and leading articles dealing with what we at the *Rand Daily Mail* referred to as 'the arithmetic of apartheid', the devastating demographic facts culled from the government's own studies that exposed the policy's unworkability, yet never once did he deal with those facts.

Had he and others like him done so, had they used their influence within the tent to persuade the ruling party to follow the course Gandar urged so passionately in that column, what suffering might not have been averted; how many lives saved; how much bitterness avoided; how much easier it would have been to reconstruct the new South Africa we now have? Not least it could have led to a much earlier release of Nelson Mandela, that we might have had more than just one all-too-brief term of his remarkable talents as a conciliator to lay the foundations for a durable democracy.

* * *

NAT NAKASA'S column was an instant success. No mainstream daily had ever had a black columnist and it seemed clear to me that the liberal *Rand Daily Mail* should break new ground by hiring one. Someone who could present our readers with a perspective on life in the apartheid society from the wrong side of the colour bar. Preferably a young person with a fresh eye and a subtle mind who could hopefully go beyond the angry rhetoric of most black writers during those bitter years.

I spread the word and scoured the pages of the major black publications, *Drum* and *Golden City Post*, until someone suggested that Nat Nakasa might be the right person. He was doing some writing for those publications, but most of his attention was on a new magazine for black writers, called *The Classic*, that he had founded with the help of the writer Nadine Gordimer. I checked out some of his work, and then called Nat to make him an offer. He accepted eagerly, and so began one of the most profound relationships of my life. We worked closely together. I watched him blossom as a writer and reach the apex of his career on the Mail.

We became close friends. He was a frequent visitor to my home, often staying overnight, which was illegal in those days. As his column rapidly gained readership, particularly among our white readers, I realised that I had a rare talent on my hands. After two years I nominated him for a Nieman Fellowship at Harvard, and thereby sent him to his death. A twist of apartheid cruelty that haunts me to this day.

Nat was an anomalous figure in the South Africa of the 1960s. He was a black liberal, committed to non-racialism at a time when the apartheid regime was cracking down hardest on black resistance and black people were responding in kind by identifying with the nascent Black Consciousness movement, which spurned collaboration with white liberals. The result was that many of Nat's fellow black writers held him in a degree of disdain. He mixed with them and partied with them, but he was not really one of them. His writing didn't contain the sting of bitterness that they felt the intolerable conditions of black life under apartheid required. He was not a 'struggle writer' in the conventional sense. He was not angry enough for that. His columns were never polemical tracts. Nat achieved his objective with a deftly humorous touch, mocking rather than raging at the absurdities of apartheid and bringing his characters, from gangsters to angry intellectuals, to life as colourful human beings.

Nat dealt with the mild disapproval of his peers with a lightness of spirit that was the most endearing feature of his personality – and of his writing. He was confident in his own beliefs and he knew exactly what he was doing. In his Inside Mail columns, his target audience was the paper's predominantly white readership, even though its black readership was ballooning at the time.

Nat the humanitarian believed emphatically that white South Africans, including the Afrikaners who had devised the apartheid ideology, were not inherently evil. They did not, as he wrote in one of his columns, 'spend their time contemplating new and more effective ways of making scars on black skin'. No, he argued, the problem was that 'most white South Africans have simply never opened their eyes to the reality of there being other humans besides the whites in this country'.

His mission, as he saw it, was to open those eyes. To that end his columns focused on his everyday experiences as a black person living under apartheid, his observations, his difficulties, the personalities of township characters and their lifestyles, his personal thoughts and ideas and how the whole asymmetric system looked from a black perspective.

But perhaps his most seminal column was one in which he ruminated about his own identity in terms of apartheid's tortuous definitions. He was, he told his readers, supposed to be a member of the Pondo tribe, but he couldn't speak their isiXhosa language. He had been brought up in a Zulu-speaking home, but as a writer he couldn't express himself fully in that language either. Moreover, he lamented, he had never owned an assegai, the weapon of choice for the fierce Zulu warriors of yore. Nor could he claim to be an African, for he felt more at home with a white Afrikaner than with a West African, a Kenyan or a Tanzanian. But then whites considered themselves Europeans, even though many had never set foot in Europe. He notes that even the city of Johannesburg shared his identity problem, since it had been built by white technical know-how plus the indispensable cooperation of black labour, which meant neither could claim ownership.

'If I am right,' Nat concluded, 'therein lies my identity. I am a South African. "My people" are South Africans. Mine is the history of the Great Trek, Gandhi's passive resistance in Johannesburg, the wars of Cetshwayo and the dawn raids that gave us the treason trial in 1956. All these are South African things. They are part of me.'

That was as fine an exposition of the non-racial ideal of a new South Africa as has ever been expressed, written 28 years before it became reality. Its eloquence has led to speculation that it was the inspiration for Thabo Mbeki's renowned 'I am an African' speech, delivered on the day our new Parliament passed the South African Constitution Bill, 8 May 1996.

The impact on our white readers was striking. Nat's column quickly acquired a devoted following, which found expression in the letters pages of the paper. I believe Nat made a real contribution to the eventual birth of the Rainbow Nation through the many white eyes that he opened. He was a talented and lovable soul. And effective. Which is why I nominated him for that fateful Nieman Fellowship.

Nat was thrilled when he was awarded the fellowship. But then the cruel axe of the apartheid regime fell. The government refused to grant him a passport, which meant the only way Nat could accept the fellowship was by taking an 'exit visa' — a one-way ticket with loss of his citizenship and no return to the land of his birth. Nat was appalled. He loved his country despite apartheid. He loved it because it was *his* country; he loved it in all its physical beauty and inhuman ugliness; because he knew it, he understood its people, all of them, and because he could communicate with them in a way few have ever been able to across the colour line. That is what inspired him, gave him life. He didn't want to go. But I persuaded him to. Because he was so talented. I thought he would flower in freedom. Instead he died.

He died of frustration and disillusionment because he didn't find freedom in the United States as he had expected. He found racism instead, something he had thought was uniquely evil to South Africa. I don't know how this worked out on his conflicted emotions, for by then I had lost contact with him. Was it disillusionment with the whole human race? Was it the unspeakable thought that racism was endemic everywhere and that he, the committed non-racialist, was somehow the odd one out, that broke his spirit and left him unable to cope with the evil?

Whatever his thoughts, he must have felt driven to despair. Sometime after he had completed his course at Harvard I received a telegram from him, sent from a post office in New York City, saying: 'Please phone urgently.' But there was no phone number. No address. I phoned the Nieman Foundation, but no one there knew where he was. There was no way I could contact him.

Two days after sending that telegram Nat leapt to his death from the seventh floor of a New York apartment building. He was just 28 years old.

Nat was buried at a simple ceremony, attended by members of his family, at Ferncliff Cemetery in upstate New York. But in September 2014, almost 49 years later, after long and painstaking international negotiations, his body was returned for reburial near his childhood home, Chesterville, outside Durban. It was an elaborate ceremony, attended by a number of ANC dignitaries, in a heroes-acre section of the township's cemetery, with a headstone paying tribute to him.

I attended the funeral, both to honour his memory and to beg his forgiveness. I met members of his family there, to whom I made my confession. I told them how Nat had come to my home the evening before he was due to fly to the United States. 'I can't do this,' he said.

'You must, Nat,' I urged. 'You'll never reach your full potential here, and these bastards can't stay in power for ever. You'll come back one day.'

* * *

MEANWHILE, the other aspect of my new job, Africa, was growing rapidly in importance through the 1960s. By 1965 South Africa was still protected from direct confrontation with the black nations to the north by an arc of white-ruled colonies: Angola and South West Africa to the west, through Southern Rhodesia to Mozambique in the east. That meant the ANC's Umkhonto guerrillas could have no direct access to South Africa from their exile bases in the north. Even if they managed to traverse the white buffer, they had no lines of retreat, communication or supply. They were vulnerable. But how long could the white buffer hold? Guerrilla wars were rumbling in both Angola and Mozambique, the South West African People's Organisation (Swapo) had formed a military wing alongside that of the ANC, while the collapse of the Federation of Rhodesia and Nyasaland had left the whites of Southern Rhodesia isolated and potentially vulnerable. The British protectorates of Bechuanaland, Basutoland and Swaziland, all within the protective buffer, were the main escape routes for black South Africans wanting to leave the country to join the guerrilla forces. Independence movements were beginning to stir there, too, which meant these territories were also potential Trojan horses within the buffer zone.

With the growing importance of these developments, it was felt I should make another trip up north, focusing on West Africa since my previous journeys had been through the central and eastern parts of the continent. I was particularly keen to time the trip to coincide with the OAU summit meeting, to be held in Accra from 21 to 26 October. Not only would this give me insight into the extent of the OAU's support for the South African liberation movements, but I would also be able to make contact with key members of the ANC in exile who would be attending the summit as observers. A great opportunity to get in touch with an organisation that had been censored out of existence within South Africa.

But there was a major snag in the way of getting to Accra. President Kwame Nkrumah, who had played a major role in getting South Africa kicked out of the Commonwealth, announced early in 1965 that no South African would be granted a visa to enter Ghana unless the individual was prepared to sign a document declaring his or her opposition to apartheid. Stanley Uys, who by then had become London editor of our Morning Group[1] of newspapers, happened to be in the air on his way to Accra when Nkrumah made his statement. So Stan wrote a story for the *Sunday Times* breaking the news and revealing that he had had no compunction about signing the declaration on landing at Accra.

The Verwoerd government was outraged. It denounced Stan as a traitor and warned that it would strip any other South Africans who dared sign such a devilish document of their citizenship. So what was I to do? I was quite prepared to denounce apartheid publicly, but I was not prepared to forfeit my citizenship and become stateless.

The answer came when I was part of a group of political journalists on a tour of Basutoland. The mountain kingdom was due to become independent the following year and the British Colonial Office was taking us on an information tour. In the course of this I happened to fall into conversation in a hotel bar one evening with a Ghanaian who mentioned that he was soon to become his country's ambassador to the Congo. He was in Basutoland, he explained, to get a close-up view of South Africa, which he felt might be useful in his new diplomatic role. I promptly asked whether it might be possible for him, once he was installed in Léopoldville, to grant me an entry visa to Ghana on a loose sheet of embassy paper without my having to sign that damned anti-apartheid declaration. I knew that people visiting Israel could have their visas and entry stamps made on separate sheets rather than in their passports, so they could still travel to Arab countries. Could he not do the same?

'I don't see why not,' my new friend responded. 'We know what your newspaper is doing in the fight against apartheid and we don't want to keep people like you out. Why don't you call on me when you come through Léopoldville?'

So that is what I did, and duly got my loose-sheet visa.

Léopoldville, soon to be renamed Kinshasa, was the first stop on what was to become a six-week tour that covered four countries: Congo, Ghana, Nigeria and the Ivory Coast. In this teeming city on the banks of the broad Congo River, I met up once again with the *New York Times* correspondent, Joe Lelyveld, with whom I had worked on the eastern Cape trials. Joe had been to the Congo many times, covering the tribulations of that unhappy land, so he was able to link me up with some contacts.

The Congo of the 1960s was ground zero of Africa's multiple post-independence problems. Belgium's precipitate granting of independence in 1960 had plunged its huge former colony into three years of bloody civil war and led to the intervention of the United Nations. Now, as I landed, the local papers were splashing a story of an assassination attempt on Prime Minister Moïse Tshombe at a football stadium the previous day. Tshombe had led his mineral-rich Katanga province into secession two weeks after independence, triggering the civil war. A friend of mine, journalist George Clay, had been shot in the head while reporting the war. Now, miraculously, Tshombe had returned from exile and was back as Prime Minister, this time of the whole Congo, with his rival, Joseph Kasavubu, as President.

Was Kasavubu involved in the assassination attempt?' I asked a diplomatic observer.

'Oh no,' the man replied. 'We think Tshombe stage-managed it himself to try to discredit Kasavubu.' How convoluted can things get?

A week later Kasavubu fired Tshombe, who fled into exile once more, this time to Spain. After nearly two years there he chartered a private jet, presumably to fly back to Africa, but the plane was hijacked by a French intelligence agent and Tshombe ended up in an Algerian prison, where he died. Thereafter the turmoil in the Congo continued until it was eventually stopped by the iron fist of General Joseph-Desiré Mobutu.

Ghana was another story altogether. More settled and order-ly eight years after independence, but there, too, I soon became aware of problems lurking beneath the shiny front that had been put on for the OAU summit. It was an exciting personal experi-ence to see some of the key political figures I had only encountered in the news-service copy I had handled: Egypt's Gamal Abdel Nasser, with an army of adoring Arab journalists scurrying after him; Emperor Haile Selassie of Ethiopia; Sékou Touré of Guinea; the OAU's Guinean secretary-general, Diallo Telli; and of course Nkrumah himself – the Osagyefo, or 'Redeemer'. All legends in their own lifetimes, with some destined to come to sticky ends – the most ghastly being that of Diallo Telli, who was sentenced to death for allegedly supporting a Fulani plot in his country and executed by what was charmingly called 'the black diet', which meant being starved to death with neither food nor water.

The key issues at the OAU summit had to do with Nkrumah's two ideological goals: to commit Africa to a position of non-alignment and what he called 'positive neutrality' in the Cold War, which was then at its height; and to persuade his fellow national leaders to accept the principle of uniting the continent under a Union Government for Africa. The first was easily obtained, but the fanciful notion of creating a United States of Africa put him sharply at odds with many of his more practical fellow heads of state and government. Tanzania's Julius Nyerere in particular insisted that each nation-state had first to establish its own econo-my, institutions and nationhood, and this would take many years, perhaps generations. But Nkrumah was adamant. He wanted

264

immediate acceptance of the principle of a united government for Africa, and a commitment to begin immediately organising the African economy as a unit. Clearly he, as the 'Redeemer' of Africa, saw himself as the leader of this united continent.

Nkrumah's language, too, was elaborate and inflammatory. 'To say that a United Government of Africa is premature,' he declared, 'is to sacrifice Africa on the altar of neo-colonialism … A United Africa is destined to be a great force in world affairs.'

Nkrumah lost the vote heavily on the conference floor, and it marked the parting of ways particularly between himself and Nyerere. Nkrumah's resentment of Nyerere's opposition to his dream was so intense that, as it later emerged, he had had the Tanzanian leader's room bugged in the special hotel built for the conference delegates. Nkrumah fell out, too, with his Francophone neighbours, Ivory Coast, Niger, Upper Volta and Togo, scorning them as 'client states' of imperial France. It soon became clear to me that this man, so admired by African nationalists back home, was not the democratic liberator of their dreams.

Most of the summit proceedings were held behind closed doors, which meant we journalists had to ambush delegates and officials in the corridors to find out what was happening in the conference hall and committee rooms. It also meant we had a fair amount of downtime, during which I was able to engage with the sizeable group of ANC delegates who were there as observers and also couldn't attend the closed sessions. Delegates of the PAC were there too, and the rivalry between the two as they lobbied for support among the African delegations was intense.

But it was with the ANC group that I spent most of this spare time. Robert Resha, then the ANC's 'ambassador' in Algeria, was the main figure with whom I connected. He was a dozen years older than me but he was a lively fellow, always game for a party, and so it was that he and I, together with various groups of his colleagues, went out on the town a few evenings.

Transport was our only problem on these expeditions. The Ghanaian government had provided all the delegations with courtesy cars, but not the observer groups such as the ANC and PAC. However, Robert Resha, being a resourceful chap, persuaded the Deputy Chief Minister of the Bechuanaland Protectorate to join us, because he had a car. So it was that the young Quett Masire became our driver. He chauffeured us around on our pub crawls with all the deference of a hired hand. Masire was a small man who looked younger than his 39 years. He didn't participate much in our raucous partying, and he drank very little. He simply sat to one side listening to our political chatter, and occasionally as the night wore on he would nod off in a corner. When that happened Robert Resha would nudge him with a foot. 'Wake up, Chief Minister,' he would say mockingly, 'it's time to move on. There's another good place I know.' And Masire would dutifully rise and accompany us to his car.

We treated him like a kid, I'm ashamed to say. After all, to be Chief Minister of a poverty-stricken British protectorate didn't seem to amount to much in those days. It was just his car we wanted-ed. But a year later, the place became independent and Quett Masire was sworn in as Deputy President of the Republic of Botswana. Four years later, with the death of Sir Seretse Khama, he became President, a role in which he served for 18 years. He became the principal architect of mineral-rich Botswana's steady economic and infrastructural growth, to the point where it is now rated the most successful country in Africa. Three years after his retirement, Queen Elizabeth II knighted him. Today Sir Ketumile Masire is a highly respected elder statesman who, among other things, chaired the international panel of eminent persons that investigated the 1994 Rwanda genocide.

I met up again with Sir Ketumile many years later and reminded him of those days when he had served as our driver. 'Yes, I remember them well,' he said with a chuckle. 'We had a lot of fun, didn't we?'

Modest and gracious. The diametric opposite of Nkrumah. As I explored the city of Accra, I was astonished at the extent of the political symbolism extolling the merits of the great Osagyefo and his ideological vision. There were concrete obelisks glorifying his ideas at just about every traffic circle. There was a statue of him outside Parliament. There was the great Black Star Square on the waterfront where the President delivered his orations, the Black

Star State Shipping Line, the Black Star Hotel, Kwame Nkrumah Circle, Kwame Nkrumah Street, the Kwame Nkrumah Centre and the Kwame Nkrumah Ideological Institute.

Yet it was clear from conversations I had in the bustling marketplaces, where I went to buy some of the country's brilliantly coloured *kente* cloth, its national fabric, that the man was not popular at street level. I heard complaints that Nkrumah had not honoured his election promises and that he was becoming increasingly authoritarian. The cocoa producers, a major constituency that had brought him to power, were disillusioned because as the cocoa price boomed after independence, Nkrumah had appropriated the increase for the state's coffers. When the railway workers went on strike, he had their leaders thrown in jail without trial, then made all strikes illegal. And more recently, he had proposed a constitutional amendment to create a one-party state with himself as President-for-Life, which had been passed with an improbable 99.1 per cent of the vote.

Worse still, unemployment was increasing and there were acute shortages in the shops. Yet the government was spending vast sums on prestige projects, such as a large dam and hydroelectric project on the Volta River and, more visibly to the general populace, the extravagant new conference centre for the OAU summit I was attending, which included a special hotel for the heads of state and a banqueting hall. All built at breakneck speed at a cost of £8 million – a lot of money in those days.

I went back to the conference centre with my camera after the summit had ended. In my reports I had written that, while the summit had produced unanimity among African leaders to support the anti-apartheid struggle in South Africa, it had also exposed conflicts in its own continental affairs and revealed Ghana itself to be an ostentatious but unhappy land. Now I wanted to get pictures of that complex to illustrate my theme.

So it came about that as I wandered about the complex with my camera, a security officer approached me to ask what I was doing. I explained that I was a journalist covering the summit and that I was now taking pictures of the new complex to go with my reports.

'But the conference is over,' he said, looking suspicious. 'May I see your passport please?'

I handed him my passport, and saw him give a double take when he saw it was South African. He took out the sheet of paper with the Ghanaian visa. 'Where did you get this?' he asked.

'At your embassy in Léopoldville,' I said.

'But you're from South Africa. You'd better come with me.'

I followed the man with some trepidation to a police station within the complex. Only that morning I had read a report in one of the local newspapers about a German couple, both journalists, who had been arrested for being in the country illegally and sentenced to 12 years in prison.

At the police station there was some rapid conversation between the security man and a small group of police officers. A number of phone calls followed. There seemed to be a lot of confusion, but my questions as to what their problem was went unanswered. All the chatter was in a language I couldn't understand. Nearly an hour went by before an officer, who appeared to be in charge of the station, approached me and said in English: 'You will come with me please?'

'Where are we going?' I asked. He didn't answer, so I followed him out of the station to a police car parked at the back. A black Wolseley, looking very British. He told me to get in the back, while he slipped into the driver's seat and another cop joined him in front. We drove off. They didn't put the siren on, but there was an ominous silence in the car as the Wolseley wound its way through the city streets and eventually headed off into the countryside. I kept asking where we were going, but there was no reply. Eventually we arrived at some heavy security gates with a sentry on guard. Again there was an exchange of words I couldn't understand, the sentry opened the gates, and we drove through into what appeared to be some kind of military compound. There were soldiers everywhere.

After a while we came upon a platoon of guardsmen, complete with crimson tunics and black bearskin hats, standing stiffly to attention. They looked absurdly British in this land of vehement anti-colonialism. It occurred to me that we might be approaching

Christiansborg Castle, a fortress on a point called Osu, outside Accra. Built by the Danes in the seventeenth century to house slaves, it was now the seat of the Ghanaian government and Nkrumah's official residence.

We drew up short of the castle and I was ushered into a cluster of low-profile buildings, which struck me as probably some sort of security police headquarters. My two police escorts took me into an office where they handed me over to a stern-looking woman secretary, and left.

'Where am I?' I asked the secretary, as she asked me to take a seat. By now I was really feeling anxious.

'The commander will see you shortly,' was her only reply as she turned back to her typewriter.

The 'shortly' turned out to be about two hours, during which only one or two people came into the room, spoke briefly to the secretary, then left again. The secretary herself typed away and said nothing. I asked her several times when the commander might see me, and her reply each time was short and curt: 'When he is ready!' I wondered what complex inquiries he was making to take so long.

Then suddenly the door opened and in walked an elderly white man with a vaguely familiar face. 'My goodness, it's Allister Sparks, isn't it?' he said. 'I heard you were coming to Accra. How are you?'

I was flabbergasted for a moment until he jogged my memory and introduced himself. 'It's Hymie Basner.'

Basner, a member of the banned CPSA, had been a senator in the South African Parliament representing the black population before that miniscule political privilege was scrapped. I barely knew him; he had been before my time in the parliamentary Press Gallery, but I could have thrown my arms around him in welcome relief. Here surely was someone who knew me and could hopefully rescue me from whatever predicament I was in.

But Hymie Basner wanted to talk. 'Tell me what's going on in South Africa,' he insisted. Dammit, I thought, I don't want to talk about South Africa right now. I want to get the hell out of here. But Hymie was insistent. He had gone into exile after the banning of his party, had worked for a time for Julius Nyerere in Dar es Salaam, and was now a political adviser to Nkrumah. I realised

269

that the homesickness of political exiles was not to be denied, so talk of events in South Africa it had to be. 'Don't worry,' was all he would say when I asked him what kind of sticky mess I was in. 'I'm sure it will be alright.'

After some time Basner looked at his watch. 'I've got to go,' he said. I asked him once more please to help get me out of my predicament. 'Don't worry,' he said again as he waved and walked out.

I didn't have to wait much longer. Eventually the secretary's phone rang. 'The commander will see you now,' she said, getting up to open his door.

It was a vast office, with a large plate-glass window at the distant end, through which the setting sun cast a blinding light on a big desk with a small, black-suited man behind it.

The small man sprang to his feet and came bounding towards me, hand outstretched. 'Mr Sparks,' he cried, 'welcome to Ghana!'

I reeled back in astonishment before grasping his hand. 'Sorry about the confusion,' he said, pumping my hand vigorously. 'We heard you were coming and I have been looking forward to meeting you. Is there anything we can do to make up for this inconvenience?'

My recovery was quick. 'Yes,' I said, 'you can arrange for me to have an interview with the Osagyefo.'

His face clouded a little. 'That will be difficult,' he said. 'He's very busy, as I'm sure you realise. But I'll see what I can do. Give me the phone number of your hotel and I'll call you in the morning.'

The commander of the Special Branch of the Ghanaian Police Service did indeed call me the next morning to say sorry, the interview was out. But he would send me a special gift from the Osagyefo.

It arrived later that day. A book, *Consciencism*, by Kwame Nkrumah. Unsigned. I flipped through the pages. It was dense, abstruse stuff, choked with ideological jargon. Unreadable.

* * *

FROM GHANA I flew on, first to Nigeria, then to Côte d'Ivoire, the Ivory Coast. Both countries carried the footprints of their

270

colonial heritage, the one English-speaking, the other French. But the differences went beyond language. The Ivory Coast was the epitome of the French colonial policy of assimilation, whereby educated and culturally assimilated Africans could be accepted as French citizens. President Félix Houphouët-Boigny served six times as a minister in the French government and represented France at the United Nations. The capital, Abidjan, was like a city in Provence, with *boulangeries* and *pâtisseries*, and there were even some white French citizens in Houphouët-Boigny's Cabinet. Nigeria, on the other hand, was the product of Lord Lugard's policy of indirect rule. For Lugard, the idea of a black Englishman was inconceivable. For that reason, and for reasons of economy, this architect of Britain's colonial policy prescribed that traditional black leaders should administer their own territories as servants of the Colonial Office. The result was much less imperial acculturation of Nigeria than there was in the Ivory Coast.

On my return from this fascinating six-week venture into Africa, Gandar suggested that I write a colour piece on the three main countries I had visited. 'Our readers have no idea what these places are like,' he pointed out. So I wrote the article, feeling rather like a returned astronaut describing a distant planet, and titled it 'A Tale of Three Cities'. Of the Nigerian capital I wrote: 'In the entire continent there is no more completely African city than Lagos: crowded, cluttered, messy, gaudy — and pulsatingly alive. It is situated just where the continental bulge begins and it has been called the armpit of Africa.'

The article won me an award — my first — from the English Academy of Southern Africa. But what was far more important were the events that followed shortly after my return. First came Ian Smith's unilateral declaration of independence (UDI) for Rhodesia on 11 November 1965. At the time, I wrote that I believed he had killed forever the prospect of an incremental transition to multi-racialism, and had ensured that Rhodesia would end up with black majority rule of an aggressive kind. White intransigence, I wrote, had won out over Garfield Todd's orderly transition, and would likely be met in due time with a responding extremism.

The other major event, just three months later, was Nkrumah's overthrow in a military coup while he was on a state visit to North Vietnam and China. I was not surprised, as many others were. I had sensed the undercurrent of discontent in Accra. Nkrumah had lost contact with reality and with his own people. Destroyed by his own overblown ego – the first of many to suffer that fate in post-independence Africa.

Nkrumah was offered exile in Guinea by his friend Sékou Touré, where, until his death from prostate cancer at the age of 62, he continued to churn out literary diatribes against neo-colonialism, especially the policies of the United States, which had given him his education and his start in political life. He accused it of being complicit in his overthrow, and there may be some truth in that. But there can be no doubt he was not a popular man at the time. Angry Ghanaians had toppled his statue outside the Parliament building.

They have resurrected it now, in a fine monument to his memory on Nkrumah Square. I am glad about that. For all his faults, Nkrumah was a transformative figure in the history of our continent. Truly the Redeemer of Africa who started that wind of change.

* * *

THERE ARE FEW places on earth more exotic than Ethiopia, a land of faith and fable with a history that goes back to Old Testament times. It is the second most populous country on our continent; South African forces helped liberate it from five years of Italian occupation during the Second World War; it has housed the headquarters of the OAU (now the African Union), which was the nerve centre of the continent's political campaign against apartheid for 30 years. Yet most South Africans, particularly white South Africans, know next to nothing about it. Testimony to the isolation and insularity the apartheid system inflicted on us over so many years.

A year after my trip to West Africa, I embarked on another journalistic expedition into the heart of the unknown. It was an adventure that was to prove even more illuminating than the last.

I used the same visa strategy I had for Ghana. With the help of friends in the foreign press corps, I made contact with the Ethiopian Embassy in Kenya, then stopped over in Nairobi to collect the visa. As I took off on the second leg of the journey I found myself on the same flight as Colin Legum, *The Observer*'s veteran Africa correspondent. It was a fortunate encounter. Colin was a South African who had worked as a journalist there before moving to London. We were good friends and I was able to have a background briefing during the flight. Moreover, Colin had lots of government contacts throughout the continent, which I found comforting should I run into the same kind of difficulties I had in Accra.

We landed at Addis Ababa and I encountered no problems passing through customs and immigration. My passport was stamped and I walked on alongside Colin towards the luggage carousels. As we strode on, chatting together, I felt someone tap me on the shoulder. I turned to see two men, both in identical light grey suits and grey suede shoes with soft spongy soles.

'Your passport please?' one asked curtly.

'I've already been through immigration and my passport's been stamped,' I protested.

'I know. But I must see it,' the man insisted.

I handed him the passport. He flipped swiftly through the pages. 'South Africans are not allowed in this country,' he said. 'We have a law prohibiting it. This visa must be forged.'

Colin tried to intervene to explain that I was an anti-apartheid journalist who had been granted special permission to attend the OAU summit, but the man was unimpressed. I was also a little uncomfortable at Colin's labelling of me as a kind of political propagandist. I liked to consider myself a professional. But in a tricky situation like this one doesn't quibble.

'Come with me,' the man said as he and his colleague, obviously security spooks, turned to lead me away.

'Don't worry,' Colin called out to me. 'I'll see what I can do when I get into town.'

Ja well no fine, as we South Africans are wont to say when flummoxed. I'd heard that 'don't worry' bit before, but this time my situation seemed rather more ominous. Forging a visa was surely an extremely serious offence, and how on earth was I going to convince these men the visa wasn't forged? With Colin gone, I felt acutely lonely.

The security men took me to a small room in the terminal, locked the door and left me there, taking my passport with them. I waited, and waited, and waited. More than an hour passed before they returned, handed me my passport and told me I could go. No explanation. No effusive apology such as I'd had in Accra. They just walked away.

It took me some time to locate my luggage, to hail a taxi, and then to realise I had no idea where to go. I had counted on accompanying Colin and the other foreign correspondents who had been on the flight from Nairobi to wherever the press corps was going to be billeted. But here I was, alone, unable to communicate with my taxi driver, who spoke no English, while my understanding of Amharic was less than zero. After a painful exchange of sign language I managed to communicate that I was a journalist here for the summit and wanted a place to sleep. He drove off into the city, eventually pulling up at a school hostel, which turned out to be one of several such places that had been commandeered to accommodate people arriving for the summit. I asked him to wait while I dumped my luggage, and then returned for more sign-language conversation. I knew there was supposed to be a cocktail party somewhere to welcome the incoming media people, but I had no idea where it was. The sign language this time included gestures of handshakes and drinking, and the cab driver seemed to get the message. Smiling broadly, and saying something in Amharic that might have been 'Cheers!', he drove on.

It was dark when we arrived at a stately white entrance portal with two large ornamental lions beside the pillars. I felt relieved. This must surely be the right place. The one thing I knew about Emperor Haile Selassie was his full title: His Imperial Majesty, King of Kings, Conquering Lion of Judah, Elect of God, the Light of the World. The lion was the national symbol of His Imperial Majesty. This must surely be where the Emperor was welcoming the media. The cab driver nodded vigorously, pointing into the grounds where I saw a palatial white building with a large circular structure beside it from which I could hear music. Obviously this was the right place.

I entered the grounds, noting casually that there were no guards at the entrance, and walked towards the circular building. There were windows all around it covered with dark green curtaining, with open double glass doors in front. I stood there for a moment, blinking from the glare of the interior lighting. I saw people standing around with cocktails in their hands. I stepped inside, looking around for someone I knew. Straight ahead I saw a tall, gangly man with a beard chatting to a surprisingly short man who was also bearded. They looked vaguely familiar, and then the penny dropped: it was King Moshoeshoe II of Lesotho and Emperor Haile Selassie. I looked around further and spotted Julius Nyerere and Zambia's Kenneth Kaunda.

With horror I realised I had stumbled into a cocktail party for Africa's heads of state. There were no media people around. No officials. This was an exclusive gathering of monarchs and presidents. And here was I, a white South African with that damn passport still in my pocket. Any moment security guards would be all over me, an obvious assassination suspect from the land of apartheid.

What was I to do? I couldn't run for it, for that would attract attention. Nor could I just stand there looking conspicuous. At that moment I caught Kaunda's eye and he gave me a little wave of recognition, thanks to our interview meetings in Lusaka. In a flash I saw him as a guardian angel. I walked briskly up to him and he extended his hand in greeting. 'How are you?' he asked.

'Good evening, Mr President,' I stammered. 'I'm so sorry to interrupt you but I need your help. I'm afraid I've stumbled in here by mistake and when someone finds out I'm a South African I'll be arrested.'

Kaunda gave a hearty chuckle and put his arm around my shoulder. Walking slowly and chatting animatedly all the while, asking about what was happening in South Africa, he ushered me towards the entrance. Then he gave me a broad smile and shook my hand. 'I think you'll be alright now,' he said. I fled.

Back in my room at the boarding school I reflected on the fact that there had been no security guards either at the gates to the palatial grounds or at the entrance to the circular building. Had I indeed been an apartheid agent I could have wiped out the entire leadership of black Africa with a single bomb. I had exposed a security lapse of monumental proportions.

* * *

THIS OAU SUMMIT, in November 1966, was a more subdued affair than the one in Accra, firstly because Nkrumah wasn't there and secondly because of the shock of a double coup in Nigeria, Africa's most populous and potentially most important country. This had reduced the acrimony between the so-called Casablanca bloc that Nkrumah had led, calling for the establishment of a United States of Africa, and the more moderate Monrovia group in which Nigeria had been a leading member, together with most of the Francophone states. There were signs of a degree of disillusionment setting in because of the OAU's helplessness in the face of Nigeria's year of crisis and its inability to take effective action against Ian Smith's UDI in Rhodesia or South Africa's ongoing crackdown against anti-apartheid activists. Only 18 of black Africa's 32 heads of state were attending.

The summit produced some well-meaning resolutions but not much action. There were declarations of support for the liberation movements battling Smith and for the ANC and PAC. There were pledges to give them more weapons, training and military bases. All OAU states were enjoined to isolate South Africa by severing diplomatic, trade, transport, sport and cultural links. African harbours were declared closed to South African shipping and South African Airways was prohibited from flying over the rest of the continent. Unlike my reports from Accra, however, none of this was likely to make banner headlines back home.

CHAPTER SIXTEEN
A Time of Betrayal

THERE WAS A buzz of expectation in the air as the bells of the House of Assembly rang to summon MPs to their seats on a sunny day in Cape Town. It was 6 September 1966. Hendrik Verwoerd, the Prime Minister, was expected to make a major speech that day expounding further on his vision of grand apartheid as the solution to the country's race problem. No one knew quite what he was going to say, but there had been a lot of speculation in the Afrikaans press that it was going to be an important speech that would throw new light on how he intended implementing his vision.

The bells were still ringing when Verwoerd strode into the chamber with a broad smile on his face, pausing to shake hands with several frontbenchers. He had reason to feel pleased, for he was at the height of his powers.

As Verwoerd made his way towards his front-bench seat directly before the Speaker's chair, a parliamentary messenger threaded his way through the milling legislators coming into the House and made his way towards the Prime Minister's bench, as though to hand him a message. Instead, as Verwoerd was about to sit down the messenger drew a dagger from beneath his jacket and plunged it into his neck. Several more blows followed while there was a brief, stunned silence in the chamber. Then pandemonium broke loose as MPs rushed forward to grab the messenger and pull him away. Two members who were medical doctors tried desperately to apply artificial respiration to the stricken Prime Minister as blood spurted from his wounds. But they were too late. Verwoerd was certified dead on arrival at the city's military hospital.

It was surely as dramatic a political assassination as there has ever been. The National Party legislators and their followers were stunned. Some went hysterical. The Defence minister, PW Botha, who was eventually to inherit that seat of power himself, rushed across the floor of the chamber to confront the lone Prog MP, Helen Suzman.

'It's you, you and the liberalists – you are responsible for this!' he screamed at her.

'Control yourself!' was Helen's crisp response.

I was not present to see this epochal moment in my country's history, but the startling details were swiftly communicated to us back in the *Rand Daily Mail* newsroom by our political corre- spondent, George Oliver, who had witnessed it all from the Press Gallery directly above Verwoerd's bench. Moreover, George knew the assassin personally, a Press Gallery messenger named Dimitri Tsafendas, who turned out to be a mixed-race man of Greek paternity. A coloured man working in this ethnically cleansed, all-white Parliament. And a man with three aliases who was sub- sequently certified insane, unfit to stand trial, and who spent the rest of his life in a mental institution.

If nothing else, this told us something about the much-vaunted South African security system.

How to handle Verwoerd's assassination posed a problem for the *Rand Daily Mail*. To us he was the Amalekite,[1] the political enemy we had fulminated against because of the harassing raids he was conducting against poverty-stricken black communities to halt their migration to the cities and force them into the separate nation-states he was trying to establish. It is true Gandar had a reluctant respect for the man's intellect, but he was exasperated by Verwoerd's obscurantism in refusing to recognise the demographic facts of apartheid's impracticability that were there before his very eyes.

So how were we to present this news? It was obviously a huge

278

story. A blockbuster. For Verwoerd's devotees it was a national disaster. Many around the country were weeping openly. I have to confess that no one in our newsroom shed a tear, but we wrestled with the problem of how to report the death of our principal political opponent. We knew many of our readers in the black townships would be celebrating Verwoerd's death that night, but we knew, too, that those hostile to the Mail would be scrutinising every word in our pages next morning that might reveal a lack of sensitivity to the national loss. We couldn't in all honesty write a eulogy, but at the same time one does not speak ill of the dead. Moreover, what had happened on the floor of the House that day had been a dastardly deed and we had all been truly shocked by it.

In retrospect I think we went a little overboard in our concern not to show indifference. The *Rand Daily Mail* appeared next morning with a heavy black border around its front page. An expression of mourning or an insurance policy? Gandar wrote a double-column front-page editorial under the heading 'A Heinous Crime', in which he paid tribute to Verwoerd's 'exceptional powers of leadership, his unusual intellect, his prodigious energy, his steadfastness of purpose and his utter dedication to the vision of South Africa that he held before him'.

Gandar made it clear that we had serious disagreements with that vision, but he made it equally clear that he regarded Verwoerd as an exceptional individual. 'Much more than Dr Malan or Mr Strijdom before him,' he wrote, 'Dr Verwoerd came to be known, at home and abroad, as the chief architect of apartheid. And so it was, for it was he who took the crude concept of racial domination and *baasskap* and refined it into a sophisticated and rationalised philosophy of separate development. The policy of Bantu homelands ... and the distant goal of a confederation of independent and cooperating black and white states — these were the creation of his fertile brain though he had yet to prove them workable.'

In my own column two days later I wrote that part of Verwoerd's aura was his remoteness. He spent most days closeted in his office, seemingly keeping his own counsel, so that whenever he appeared in the lobbies of the House, where MPs gathered to chat during breaks, a hush would surround him as he shook the odd hand

and smiled benevolently to those he blessed with his presence. He appeared to have few confidants, no close advisers of whom we journalists were aware; intellectually he appeared to be sufficient unto himself. Perhaps because of this, I suggested, he exercised a mesmerising power over his followers. He was not a great orator: he had a high-pitched voice and a rather staccato delivery. Yet he dominated the House.

'Whenever he spoke,' I wrote, 'the benches were full and there was absolute silence. His own supporters especially listened in a state of transfixed reverence.'

The following Tuesday the Minister of Justice and Police, John Vorster, was appointed as Verwoerd's successor. A better orator, but in every other respect a lesser man. He got the job because he was the party's Enforcer. The hard-faced, unsmiling man who was responsible for the draconian security laws, for detention without trial, for the security police and their brutal techniques of interrogation. Vorster's closest associate was Lang Hendrik van den Bergh, the security police chief who had been with him in the extremist Ossewa-Brandwag movement. They were interned together during the Second World War for their Nazi sympathies. At one point my soldier father had guarded them in the internment camp.

Vorster's appointment was a clear indication that the ruling party was feeling nervous. With their guiding light gone, members felt lost and anxious as they found themselves isolated in a hostile world. So they wanted a tough guy at the top to keep law and order. The problem was that the man they chose had no ideas about how to deal with the hard demographic facts preventing the fulfilment of Verwoerd's ideological dream. Nor did he have the imagination or courage to back away from that vision. It was all the party had. As historian Hermann Giliomee was to write: 'The spell Verwoerd cast over Afrikaner nationalists was so powerful that for many years after his death there was no attempt to find alternative ways of reaching a more lasting form of political accommodation with blacks.'[2]

Would Verwoerd have made such an attempt had he lived? Giliomee thinks so; that he had the intelligence to adapt as the need to do so became more obvious. I disagree. Verwoerd was a man in whom I never saw the faintest hint of flexibility. He struck me as being the ultimate ideologist, with a fixity of mind and purpose that couldn't conceive of ever being wrong.

* * *

ASSASSINATIONS, of course, are not uncommon in the world of politics. They come in different forms, some, like Caesar's, at the hand of ambitious conspirators, others, like Verwoerd's, by seriously deranged individuals, and yet others who fall victim to corporate and political manipulation and treachery. So it was that only a few months before the prophet of apartheid fell, there was an attempt to cut down the prophet of the left, Laurence Gandar. Though not lethal, it was also malicious and underhanded.

As the scriptures tell us, a prophet is not honoured in his own country. Even as international honours were showered on Gandar and his newspaper, the knives were out for him here at home. As fellow editor Joel Mervis was to note in his history of the publishing company, by the time Gandar left the *Rand Daily Mail* 'he had possibly become the best known editor in the world'.[3] The British Society of Journalists had awarded him a gold medal, presented personally by Prime Minister Harold Wilson at a banquet in the City of London; the American Newspaper Publishers Association had awarded the *Rand Daily Mail* its prized World Press Achievement Award, and the Christian Council of the City of New York had honoured him at an enormous banquet in the New York Hilton.

In the midst of all this, Henry Kuiper, the managing director of South African Associated Newspapers (SAAN), the company that owned the Mail, had called on Gandar in his office to tell him the board of directors had decided that for health reasons it was time for him to relinquish the editorship of the paper. A trope for, 'You're fired!'

The assumed pretext for this decision was that the paper was losing readership. At least it was losing white readership. It was gaining more and more black readers, but the advertising sales staff claimed the black readers didn't count. Advertisers were interested in white readers only, they said, because that's where the purchasing power was. And the white readers were being put off by the paper's liberal stance, which the board felt was being overdone. Extensive coverage of the prolonged prisons trials in particular had angered them, implying that whites had no interest in how black prisoners were treated. That and what was crudely called 'black news', meaning news of special interest to the paper's black readers. Some white readers were purported to have been heard saying: 'I can't bear to have that paper at my breakfast table.'

Yet, as I was to discover much later, there was another, more covert reason behind Kuiper's mission. Indeed a degree of skulduggery, which may explain why Gandar found Kuiper to be visibly uncomfortable about the message he was bringing. Gandar put it down at the time to the fact that he and Kuiper were friends. It was Kuiper who had headhunted Gandar to take the job as editor of the Mail, and the two had developed a good working relationship. But the fact is that when Kuiper spoke to Gandar that day he did not tell him the whole truth, either because he couldn't bring himself to do so or because he had himself been kept in the dark.

In any large commercial organisation there is always one individual tucked away in the labyrinthine web of stockholding interests who, when the chips are down, really wields the power. In the case of SAAN, that individual was Clive Corder, a pillar of the Cape Town business establishment, who resided in the elite suburb of Constantia in a large estate that included a nine-hole golf course.

Corder was chairman of Syfrets Trust Company, which controlled the Bailey Trust and the administration of the estate of the mining magnate, Sir Abe Bailey, which in turn was the controlling shareholder of SAAN. This meant that Corder, although not chairman of SAAN or even a member of its board, was the power behind the scenes. He was also chairman of the *Cape Times*, one of South Africa's oldest newspapers, which was not part of SAAN but worked in a collaborative relationship with the *Rand Daily Mail* as part of the Morning Group. But for those of us on the staff of the Mail, Corder was a faceless figure. In my 23 years with the company I never once clapped eyes on him. Yet he was the man who ordered that Gandar be fired.

But I am running ahead of myself in this tale of corporate malfeasance. The crunch point in that uncomfortable conversation between Kuiper and Gandar came when Gandar asked the MD who the board proposed putting in his place as editor of the *Rand Daily Mail*. As Gandar later recounted the conversation, he was not too dismayed by Kuiper's initial message. 'I was prepared to go in peace,' he later told Joel Mervis. 'I had no particular wish to remain at the Mail if I wasn't wanted there; and it had been a bloody great strain, I can tell you.' But when Kuiper told him that the board was thinking of giving the job to Meyer (Johnny) Johnson, then editor of the *Sunday Express*, Gandar erupted. Johnson not only openly despised the Mail's liberal political line and its support for the Progressive Party, but he had also taken the Express, its smaller tabloid sister paper, in a diametrically opposite direction.[4]

Johnson was a moody, combative fellow who was vigorously championing the conservative 'Old Guard' of the United Party against the more reformist 'Young Turks' that Mervis's *Sunday Times* was supporting. The clash of political standpoints between papers in the same company had not only become a public war of words, but also personal relationships between Johnson and members of the *Rand Daily Mail*'s staff had become acrimonious. The prospect of Johnson becoming editor of the Mail appalled Gandar. As he told Kuiper: 'I'll have to use every bit of influence that I can to stop this because it is absolutely ludicrous. And in any event, I don't know how you chaps could take a decision of this nature at this time' – his point being that it would amount to a public admission that the board considered he was guilty and had done a wrong thing in publishing the prison torture reports.[5]

I was shattered when I heard what the board wanted to do. I knew I could never work for Johnson, so that would mean the end of my career on the Mail as well. I confided as much to night editor Rex Gibson, a close friend, who told me he felt as I did. Out of that grew the idea of a group of senior staff members making a demarche to the chairman of the board, Cecil Payne. It was a dodgy thing to do, since declaring one's support for a man the board was busy firing is hardly a career-enhancing move. Moreover, we knew nothing about Payne, who had only just been appointed – over the head of Kuiper, to the latter's great displeasure. But we felt so strongly about the issue that we went ahead nonetheless.

Before doing so, however, I suggested we should first check with Gandar; there would be no point in fighting for his retention if he didn't want to stay. The others agreed. Gandar happened at the time to have gone on a brief holiday to the Natal South Coast with his wife, Isobel, and schoolboy son, Mark, so I drove there to see him. He greeted me warmly, but when I told him of our plans he responded cautiously. He said he greatly appreciated our willingness to fight for him but he felt uncomfortable at the thought of working for a company that didn't want him. He wanted to think it over. In the meantime he suggested I join him and his son in nine holes of golf on the local course. It was a pleasant interlude, after which I joined the family for tea. As I was about to leave, Gandar accompanied me to my car, where at the last moment he gave me his answer in a hesitant tone. 'I don't think it will get you anywhere,' he said, 'but okay, go ahead and do it.'

I realised as I drove away that Gandar had not given his agreement out of his own self-interest, but because he had been touched by our loyalty and didn't want to let us down. Even more, he didn't want to let the *Rand Daily Mail* down. He knew Johnson would transform it into a right-wing sheet and he didn't want to let that happen unchallenged. But the element of reluctance was to remain with him.

Our group of the paper's six most senior executives – deputy editor 'Barno' Hughes, assistant editors Harry O'Connor, Lewis Sowden and myself, night editor Rex Gibson and political correspondent George Oliver – went to see Payne at his home one evening to tell him bluntly that we believed the idea of replacing Gandar with Johnson was a terrible mistake that would have a devastating effect on staff morale. We presented him with a memorandum setting out our views, which we had all signed. The memo

noted that the board's decision to fire Gandar appeared to be because it disapproved of his editorial policy, then went on to state
that board members should know that we, his senior staff, had fully
supported that policy and considered it to have been the right one
for the *Rand Daily Mail* to have pursued. Moreover, we believed
Gandar's direction of the paper had won it prestige and earned
respect both in South Africa and abroad. 'We therefore cannot,'
the memo concluded, 'allow the dismissal of Mr Gandar to pass
without recording our sorrow and our protest, and without urging
management to reconsider its decision and withdraw from an
error which will do the *Rand Daily Mail* and South African
journalism incalculable harm.'

It had been with some misgivings that we had gone to see
chairman Payne. But to our surprise he greeted us warmly, welcomed our interest in the matter and assured us he would convey
our feelings to the rest of the board. In the course of the amicable
conversation that followed, the six of us made clear our opposition
to Johnson's replacing Gandar as editor and told Payne that if
that were to happen we would all resign from the paper.

In time we came to learn that Gandar was fighting his own
rearguard action against Johnson's appointment and had proposed that Raymond Louw, the Mail's news editor, be appointed
instead. We let it become known that we not only agreed that
Louw would be a good choice, but also, given that his main journalistic strength was in hard news gathering, we believed it would
make sense for Gandar to remain in charge of the paper's political policy while Louw headed up its strong news team. Such a
division of roles was common in American journalism and we felt
it would be appropriate for the *Rand Daily Mail*.

Our next stroke of luck came from Jim Bailey, youngest son of
the eminent Sir Abe and something of a black sheep of the family.
Having founded the two black publications, *Drum* and *Golden City
Post*, Jim spent much of his social life, and a good part of his substantial inheritance, partying with its black staffers in township
shebeens. But he cared about newspapers. As a beneficiary of the
Bailey Trust, Jim Bailey was also a member of SAAN's board of
directors. And it was from Jim that we learned that Clive Corder

had never convened a meeting of the trust to discuss the dismissal of Gandar. He had acted on his own. Of course, as chairman of Syfrets, he had the power to impose his will on both the Bailey Trust and the SAAN board. But he had not gone through the proper procedures to exercise that power. The trust had not met, and so it had no proper mandate to exercise its controlling power on the SAAN board. Corder had assumed that, because everyone knew he had the ultimate power, he could simply go ahead and exercise it unilaterally. So in ordering that the country's most renowned newspaper editor be fired, Corder had acted *ultra vires*. Jim Bailey objected to this, which was enough to stall the process.

The eventual outcome was that Corder backed off. Kuiper left the company in a huff at not getting the chairmanship and handed over the chief executive's job to his easygoing number two, Leycester Walton. Under Payne's leadership the board endorsed the appointment of Gandar as editor-in-chief in charge of editorial policy, with Louw as editor in charge of news. Johnson, seriously aggrieved, was placated by the departing Kuiper, who told him he would assuredly get the editorship of the *Sunday Times* when Mervis retired. In due course that, too, was to cause a load of trouble.

* * *

ONLY MANY years later, after I myself had left the *Rand Daily Mail*, did the final piece of Clive Corder's shenanigans fall into place. I learned that he had written a book of memoirs, which he had published privately to distribute among friends, and I managed to locate a copy in the library of the University of Cape Town. There I found a passage in which he described his dealings with the newspapers that had been under his control.

'I did not at any stage interfere in the editorial policy of the newspapers,' Corder wrote, 'except on the occasion when it was necessary to curb the editor of the *Rand Daily Mail*, Mr Laurie Gandar. He had involved us in a direct confrontation with the Government over the so-called Prisons Act cases which cost the company a tremendous amount of money in legal costs and also made me firmly feel that Gandar's editorials and policy were not in the best interests of the country. I did not mind his attacking the Government but I felt some of his writing was not in the national interest.'[6]

There was a tacit admission in those weasel words that it was his decision, not that of the Bailey Trust or the board of SAAN, to break with the practice of not interfering in the editorial policy of the newspapers, and that the conflict with the government over the prisons cases and Gandar's political policy line 'made me firmly feel' (not the trust or the board) that Gandar's editorship was 'not in the public interest'.

That phrase, 'in the national interest', has, of course become, with apologies to Dr Johnson, the last refuge of the censor. No authoritarian figure has ever clamped down on free speech without claiming it to be necessary 'in the national interest', a phrase that means whatever its user wants it to mean. In my book, informing readers about the torture of prisoners – surely the most vulnerable of all citizens in any country – and warning the public about an impractical government policy that could lead to serious social upheaval, is about as strongly in the national interest as one can get.

Unless, of course, one has another agenda. Which brings me to an even more revealing aspect of Corder's actions. It turns out he showed the manuscript of his memoir to the editor of the *Cape Times*, Tony Heard, and to its deputy editor, Gerald Shaw, apparently for them to check the text. The upshot was that Shaw, in a book of his own about the history of the *Cape Times*, quoted verbatim from Corder's text about his role in the Gandar saga. With one striking insertion. Shaw's text reads: 'After being summoned by John Vorster and told "to do something about Gandar", Corder reached the conclusion that Gandar's editorials and policy were "not in the interests of the country".'[7]

In a footnote, Shaw cites as his source for this information JAB Cooper, then secretary of the Board of Executors, another big Cape Town trust company, and an associate of Corder's at Syfrets. Shaw says that Cooper told him that personally. If true – and neither Cooper nor anyone else has challenged the accuracy of Shaw's book – that means Corder acted at the behest of a man who was the apartheid government's most vicious assailant of the press and freedom of speech. On 19 October 1977, a date commemorated as 'Black Wednesday', Vorster banned 19 Black Consciousness organisations and their publications, killed two newspapers – *The World* and *Weekend World* – jailed their editor, Percy Qoboza, and his key assistants for months without trial, banned my closest friend, Donald Woods, so ending his editorship of the *Daily Dispatch* and driving him into exile, and silenced the brave Dutch Reformed Church dissident Beyers Naudé, who was producing a hugely important religious publication called *Pro Veritate*.

For Corder to have acted at the request of such a man must rate as one of the most deplorable acts ever performed by anyone involved in the proprietorship of the English-language press in South Africa.

Nor was that all. Firing Gandar was one thing, but choosing Johnny Johnson to replace him was another. Anyone with any knowledge of personal relationships within the SAAN building must have known that Johnson and the *Rand Daily Mail* staff were hopelessly incompatible. So why did Corder choose him? True, Corder was an outsider, 1 500 km away in Cape Town, but Johnson's open hostility to the Mail and the Progs, which he routinely referred to as the 'Phlops', dripped venom from the columns of the Express every Sunday.

It took me some time before I realised the obvious reason for Corder's decision. The central theme of Johnson's editorial policy at the Express, one he pursued obsessively, was to champion the conservative Old Guard leadership of the United Party against the reformist Young Turks. Most journalists at SAAN believed Johnson was doing this not so much out of personal conviction, but because of an ego-driven determination to pit himself against Joel Mervis at the much larger and more influential *Sunday Times*. Johnson was nothing if not competitive. But Corder obviously saw this rivalry in a different light. The United Party Old Guard were headed by Sir De Villiers Graaff, the leader of the party and of the parliamentary opposition, while the Young Turks were a relatively small group headed by a lawyer,

Harry Schwarz, who later led them into a merger with the Progs to form the Progressive Reform Party.

The key factor here is that Graaff and Corder were both members of the Cape Town social establishment. They were also close friends: Corder had been Graaff's best man at his wedding. Schwarz, meanwhile, was seen as an upstart, an outsider in those circles, a man who had been blackballed for membership of the Rand Club because he was Jewish. It must have been galling for Corder to see his friend the baronet being given a hard time by these troublesome rebels. My conclusion was that when it came to choosing Gandar's successor at the *Rand Daily Mail*, what more satisfying choice could there be for Corder than this aggressive champion of his friend Graaff? A double bonus. Get rid of Gandar to please the Nat government and get the Mail to switch its support from the Progs to Graaff's Old Guard UP.

Corder would have had no compunction about stripping the Progressive Party of its main media supporter. He made his dislike of the party quite clear in his memoir, in which he wrote that when people asked where his political loyalties lay, his reply was: 'I tell them I'm forty-nine percent Nat, forty-nine percent UP, and one percent Prog.' It was intended as a flippant claim to neutrality, of course, but his derisive dismissal of white liberalism was telling.

If I am right in my conjecture about why Corder wanted Johnson as Gandar's successor, it means his actions were not only in response to John Vorster's injunction to 'do something about Gandar', but also because he wanted to help his friend Sir De Villiers Graaff politically. No small degree of hypocrisy on the part of a man who proudly claimed to be apolitical and that he didn't interfere with the editorial policies of the newspapers he controlled.

Laurence Gandar was an exception, of course. Because, you see, curbing him was 'in the national interest'.

CHAPTER SEVENTEEN

A Roller-Coaster Ride

AS THE repressive 1960s closed out and we entered the even more turbulent 1970s, I began a new phase of my life. A switch-back phase of steep ascents and descents, of sudden turns and few straight lines, of successes and disappointments, triumphs and tragedies, of scaling the heights only to suffer a heavy fall – then to pick myself up and start again. A testing time. They say it builds character. I'm not so sure. It can also leave scar tissue.

It began smoothly enough. The dual leadership of Gandar and Louw had worked well. Louw injected a new energy into the newsroom, which soon became the most dynamic South African journalism had ever seen. He also realised that one of Gandar's few weaknesses, which had hurt the paper's public image, was his personal reclusiveness. He was an analyst, a thinker, not a public personality. He hated the limelight that editorship inevitably brought with it. He found attending public functions a chore, and it showed. There was no pressing of flesh or hosting of the country's movers and shakers. His social life was restricted to a few close friends, with whom he was warm, relaxed and a wonderful host. But beyond that the general public didn't know him. Which meant they saw him, and the paper he edited, in the stereo-typed imagery that his detractors painted of him, as a pro-black extremist out of step with society. And in those Manichaean days of apartheid, pro-black meant anti-white. So Gandar was perceived as an ethnic traitor.

Raymond set about rectifying this false perception. He was a man of immense energy, so despite his long hours overseeing the news operation, he launched himself into the social scene with gusto. He attended every function in town, seized every speaking opportunity to spread the gospel of what the *Rand Daily Mail* really stood for, organised new functions and exhibitions and competitions at which the paper's name could be emblazoned on banners and its personnel introduced to new sectors of economic life. In other words, a massive and well-run public relations campaign. How Ray managed it all amazed us, but he did and it soon produced results. The newspaper's circulation began to rise to heights never before attained, while Gandar kept its policy on track, building on its repu-tation as the first major newspaper in South Africa to champion the cause of the oppressed black population. And to show that morality and commercial viability were not incompatible if managed with commitment and competence.

Then, after two years of the dual leadership, Gandar left. Not fired this time, but by his own choice. That nagging feeling of discomfort at working for a company that had tried to get rid of him had never left him. He had great respect for Ray, and felt that by staying on the paper he was himself cutting Ray's job in half, which was unfair given Ray's role in putting the paper back in the black. Moreover, with the exception of Payne, Gandar had lost all respect for the board. So when his friend David Astor, owner-editor of *The Observer*, offered him a job to launch and head up a new foundation in London to study the plight of minority groups worldwide, Gandar accepted it.

I was dismayed. He had become my role model and chief mentor as well as a good friend. In fact he was to remain so for the rest of his life. So when he told me he was leaving I tried to persuade him not to go. But he was emphatic. He felt he had done his bit to save the Mail from Corder's folly, and when he told me he felt that by staying he was cramping Ray's style I accepted that and reconciled myself to his departure.

Gandar's leaving in fact led to my rapid advancement along

Mahogany Row. Louw, aware that he had been promoted over the head of the older and more experienced Harry O'Connor, and that O'Connor had been hurt by this, decided to maintain roughly the same dual leadership structure as before. He appointed O'Connor chief assistant editor and delegated him to run the paper's editorial pages. It was a token gesture, of course: Louw retained ultimate responsibility for editorial policy as well as for the paper's news content, and he would have to approve the leaders each day. But he wanted Harry to have a relatively free hand, a smart as well as a generous decision that smoothed Harry's ruffled feelings.

He promoted me to a full assistant editor, number three on the paper, where I would be Harry's sidekick as a leader writer. In practice that meant Harry and I decided on the leaders each day, wrote them, and then passed them on to Ray for approval. I was still heading up the Inside Mail investigative team and putting together the special Saturday pages, so it was a richly fulfilling job.

Then Harry left. The editor of the *Eastern Province Herald* in Port Elizabeth, Mac Pollock, father of South Africa's great cricketing brothers, Peter and Graeme, and grandfather of Shaun, retired. Harry was appointed to replace him. It was a well-deserved reward for one of South Africa's finest journalists, and I was pleased for him. It also meant that I became deputy editor of the *Rand Daily Mail*, number two to Ray Louw. And two months later Ray told me he was off to the United States on three months' long leave, one of the perks of editorship at SAAN that came around once every five years, and that I would have to take over while he was away.

So at the age of 37, I found myself acting editor of the biggest, most famous and most controversial morning newspaper in South Africa. The roller coaster was going full tilt.

* * *

MEANWHILE, back at the farm, my father had decided to retire. He had turned 70 and was finding that farming in the harsh conditions at Hotfire was becoming too much for him. My mother, six years older than him, had never liked it there. She yearned for a more intellectually engaging life and badly wanted to spend her final years nearer her only child, who had effectively left home when he went to boarding school at age seven. So Dad told me he wanted to sell up and move to Johannesburg, where we could both build homes and live in some proximity for the first time in our adult lives. This marked another major change in a different dimension of my life, that of me as a family man.

We found adjoining plots of vacant land going cheaply in Rivonia, then a small village on the outskirts of northern Johannesburg. We found a contractor with whom we cut a deal to build two homes on what had been a small farm subdivided into one-acre plots. So Mary and I moved with our three small children into the first home we had owned, with my parents as next-door neighbours.

The children's education was a matter that exercised our minds. I was still in touch with my old school, Queen's College, and had even been invited to deliver the valedictory address there one year. But as journalism exposed me to the realities of race discrimination in our country, I had become increasingly appalled at realising the lopsided education I had received there.

I didn't want my children to have that kind of education in a country that seemed to me obviously headed for a major challenge in having to integrate a multitude of races and cultures. Yet I believed in boarding school. An educational initiative started by some influential liberal friends seemed to offer an ideal solution to the kind of education we wanted for our children. This group were raising funds to start a private multiracial boarding school in Swaziland, an apartheid-free enclave in the midst of South Africa.

I loved the whole idea of the school, but the children were still very young: Simon was 12, Michael nine and Andrew at six had just moved from kindergarten to first-year primary school. Mary and I agonised over it, but in the end decided to enrol Simon in what by then was named Waterford-Kamhlaba School.

* * *

TAKING EDITORIAL control of the *Rand Daily Mail* at such a young age, and only two months after having been appointed

Louw's deputy, was a daunting task. I remember taking my seat on that first day and feeling incredibly lonely. I had never lacked in self-confidence, but the sense of being alone at the top was rather unnerving. It was such a big, important and difficult-to-run newspaper that I knew if anything went seriously wrong on my watch it would be disastrous. And I would be responsible. The flow of news from across the world was so immense, so relentless, and you, ultimately, were responsible for its orderly control, selection and publication, every day. You alone. Suddenly there was no older and more experienced journalistic sage above you to make the tough decisions; now you were it, the final decision-maker, and the buck stopped on your desk.

But it was also exciting, challenging, stimulating. I was young, ambitious, and I knew this was my great chance. I threw myself into the job with great energy and commitment. Family matters slipped into the background, for it was an all-consuming 24/7 job in which I had to be on top of the breaking news in time for the 10 am news conference, and up around midnight to make a final call to the night editor to check on how the major stories were being displayed in the paper, particularly on the front page.

In this adrenaline-charged routine, I barely noticed that my father had not been looking too well lately. He had suffered from angina pectoris for years and periodically had to visit his doctor to get his controlling medication adjusted. Mary told me as I left for work one morning that she would be taking him to our family doctor for a check-up. While she was there, she said, she would ask him to have a look at her right eyelid, which had started drooping a bit. It wasn't troubling her, but since she would be there with my father she felt she might as well ask the doctor to have a look at it.

I thought little about it as I drove off to work, but after the morning news conference I asked my secretary to phone the doctor for me so I could ask about my father. When he came on the line I heard him say: 'Good morning, Mr Sparks, I suppose you're worried about your wife.'

'My wife?' I spluttered. 'No doctor, I was worried about my father.'

'Oh your father's okay,' he replied, 'he just needs his blood-thinning medication adjusted. It's your wife I'm worried about. That drooping eyelid is called third nerve palsy; something is touching the nerve that controls the eyelid's movement and we'll have to find out what it is. I've booked her into the Garden City Clinic and I want a specialist to examine her.'

Seldom can a high-flying young ego have been brought to earth so fast. I asked Rex Gibson, then acting as my number two, to take charge of the day's paper while I raced home to see Mary. I found her in tears. Through sobs she told me she was sure it was a brain tumour. She had been worrying about that damn eyelid for some time because a friend of hers in East London had recently died of brain cancer. But she hadn't wanted to tell me about it because she didn't want to alarm and distract me when I was so involved with my new role at the Mail.

I was stricken with guilt. Here was I flying high, so preoccupied with myself and my challenging job that I had been unable to spot this signal of possible tragedy on the face of my own wife. How blindly self-absorbed can one get?

Next morning, as I drove Mary to the clinic, there was a heavy silence of anxiety in the car, which I tried to ease with a reassuring remark. 'I know you are terribly anxious, my love, but all of us who love you are equally worried. It's tough for us too.'

'Care to swap places?' Mary shot back with a wry smile.

The neurosurgeon who examined Mary, Dr Plotkin, was a top-ranking specialist. He decided immediately that Mary should have a brain scan. We waited a few anxious days while it was assessed, then came the joyful news that there was no tumour. The relief was so great that I took Michael and Andrew with me to Mary's ward for a little family celebration with a bottle of champagne.

But Plotkin wanted to do another test: an angiogram, a special X-ray procedure that can make a video of the blood flow in the vascular system – in Mary's case, her head. The picture showed clearly what the problem was: an aneurysm, a swelling caused by a weakness in a blood vessel, in a vein directly behind Mary's right eye. As the swelling had grown larger it touched the nerve controlling her eyelid, causing it to droop. At any moment the aneurysm could rupture and cause a fatal stroke. He would have to remove it as soon as possible. There were only two ways to do that, he said. One way was to cut an entrance through the top of Mary's skull and insert surgical instruments to cauterise the weak vein, which he said was difficult and high-risk. The other, simpler method was to cauterise the carotid artery on the right side of her neck, and let that dry up the whole vascular network on the right side of her head.

'Your wife has a wonderfully extensive cranial vascular system,' Plotkin told me, 'and I've no doubt that the carotid artery on the left side will supply all the blood her brain needs. I've no doubt that is the way to go.'

It sounded so simple I felt it was not worthwhile telling young Simon at Waterford what his mother was undergoing. Why distress him at boarding school when he could not be part of what was happening, and anyway his mother would be home in a few days.

The operation was performed two days later. When I accompanied Plotkin to his car afterwards, he told me it had gone well. No problems. 'The only real risk with this procedure,' he said, 'is that in rare cases when you tamper with the vascular system it can cause the rest of it to shut down.' For that reason Mary would not be allowed to sleep for the next 48 hours, because sleep slowed the heart rate, which could increase the risk of such a mishap. A nurse would be at her bedside throughout that time to keep her awake.

'But I don't think that's a risk worth worrying about in your wife's case,' Plotkin said, 'particularly because her problem is on her right side.' He went on to explain that the interaction between the brain and the body was inverse: the left side of the brain controlled the right side of the body, and vice versa. So the fact that Mary's surgery had been on the right carotid artery, he said, meant the risk of interaction would be on her inferior left side, and therefore lower.

'But doctor,' I said, 'Mary is left-handed.' I saw him flinch for just an instant. 'Oh, I'm sure she'll be alright,' he replied, and walked to his car.

I saw Mary in the intensive care unit that evening. She was at ease, told me the procedure had been painless and that she was feeling okay but a little drowsy. She kept dropping off as we spoke, but the nurse at her bedside would shake her awake again. I bade her goodnight and went home to tell the children everything had gone smoothly.

Next morning my bedside phone rang early. 'Mr Sparks,' the voice said, 'we think you should come to the hospital right away.'

The 45-minute drive to the clinic was a nightmare. I knew the news could only be bad, but I couldn't hurry. The morning rush-hour traffic was building up, and every red traffic light seemed to take an eternity to change.

When eventually I reached the clinic I ran up the stairs to the ICU. The scene that confronted me remains blurred in my memory to this day. Nature has a way of numbing the recollection of events too painful to relive. What I remember, as though through a gauze filter of time, is of a group of nurses surrounding Mary's bed trying to restrain her body, which was in a spasm of convulsions, arms and legs thrashing about, disconnecting a tangle of wires and tubes linking her to an ECG monitor and an oxygen supply, with the doctor standing over her trying to administer an injection. I remember Mary's eyes, bulging from her face, and her mouth trying to utter something. I thought I heard the thick, blurred words, 'I'm dying,' and the doctor's quick reply: 'No, you're not dying.' And then I collapsed in a heap of shuddering sobs. One of the ward assistants must have helped me away from the bedside to a spot behind a ward curtain. I must have asked somebody to phone my office and arrange for a company driver to come to collect my car and drive me home, where my aged nurse mother eventually gave me a sedative and put me to bed.

The clinic called me early next morning to tell me Mary had died. It was just four months before her 40th birthday.

Next was the agonising task of having to tell the children their mother had died. Of seeing them stricken with shock and bewilderment. How could it be? We had only just had that champagne celebration in her room. Little Andrew, aged seven, had difficulty taking it in. As he got out of bed next morning he looked at me with big, wet, worried eyes. 'Daddy, is Mommy really dead?' he asked. And Simon, oh poor Simon, away at boarding school and

I had never given him a full account of why his mother was in the hospital. Now a matron at the school had to break the dreadful news to him and then put him on a plane to Johannesburg. When I met him at the airport, he was in a state of great distress – and anger. 'You never told me,' was his admonition.

* * *

RAYMOND LOUW telephoned me from the United States to express his sympathy at Mary's death and to suggest that he cut short his long leave and return to relieve me at such a distressing time.

'Please don't do that, Ray,' I begged. 'I appreciate your offer, but I really think that to keep right on working here is all that is going to keep me sane. If I were to go and sit around at home with nothing to distract me from brooding over what a terrible thing has happened, I think I'd have a breakdown. So please carry on with your leave. I'll be alright.'

There was no braggadocio in that. I really felt that total immersion in my work was my only way of emotional survival. Some psychologists might regard that as an avoidance strategy that would repress my emotions and cause more future problems, that I would have done better taking time out to confront and deal with my grief, to work through it with counselling. Maybe. But I couldn't imagine myself sitting around at home wallowing in my miseries. That thought scared me.

So I did it my way, and I think it worked for me. My parents helped. They insisted that the children move in with them for a while, which helped the boys recover in a warm and loving environment. My father took on the role of driving them to and from school, while my mother insisted that I have dinner at their home each evening, which revived a degree of family life for us all. And believe me, there was still plenty of time for grieving. The nights alone in my home were hell, and I was relieved when morning came and I could slip away to work. That hot seat was a blessing.

I think I managed the three months of acting editorship reasonably well. There were no major confrontations with the

Vorster government to rock the boat. The main problems I had to deal with were within the staff, particularly the black reporters. They were a fine team of journalists, doing a great, often courageous, job of covering events in the townships, but they were also becoming involved themselves in the re-emergence of political activism in the black community and this was affecting the way they saw their role as journalists.

It was precisely at the turn of the decade that Stephen Bantu Biko emerged as a powerful new voice in black politics. He had been a medical student, but he quit his studies to found the Black Consciousness Movement (BCM), which quickly filled the political vacuum caused by the banning of the other liberation movements. Biko's movement caught fire, particularly among young black intellectuals, which included the journalists. Especially the *Rand Daily Mail* journalists, who were the best and had the biggest platform. And it was not long before that began to present me with some problems.

Biko's creed, drawn in part from black consciousness thinking in the United States, was that if black people were to liberate themselves they had first to slough off the insidious self-sense of inferiority that generations of racial oppression and apartheid had induced. They had to recover their sense of racial self-worth and pride in order to emancipate themselves from the submissive slave mentality that was contributing to their own oppression. To do that required acting on their own to build up the self-confidence and strength needed to liberate themselves. It had been the experience of the past, Biko asserted, that working with white liberals in the so-called non-racial organisations had resulted in the whites taking the lead in decision-making, and this was inhibiting the growth of the black members' own political maturity and effectiveness. Therefore they had to break with the non-racial organisations and form their own, separate organisations in a broad black consciousness movement. Hence the slogan: 'Black man, you are on your own.'

Many white liberals were hurt and confused by this. Some saw it as a form of reverse apartheid and were angered by it. But they were wrong. Biko was no black racist. He was a black strategist

299

and an insightful psychologist. His strategy made practical sense and his broader philosophy, which he expounded in writings and speeches until banning orders silenced him, sparked a whole new black political revival.

The way all this impacted on me at the Mail during those three months was that black staff members felt they had an obligation to activate this philosophy through their work. Now the concept of journalistic objectivity is a tricky thing, because no two people view the same event or interpret the same speech in the same way. Each has his or her own perspective and frame of reference. So the concept of objectivity is impractical and its pretence phoney. What is practical and should be the aim of all journalists is fairness: report the event as you see it through your own lens and from the perspective of the publication you represent, but do so in a context that is balanced and fair. Don't become a propagandist.

As Black Consciousness (BC) took off in the early 1970s, the black journalists at the *Rand Daily Mail* came under pressure from their affiliated branch, the Media Workers' Association of South Africa (Mwasa), to practise their craft in accordance with the BC credo. Only black journalists should report on Mwasa's and other BC affiliates' affairs, such as congresses. White reporters would not be accredited to cover such events. Moreover, Mwasa members should ensure that their publications referred to all 'non-white' people as 'blacks' and cease differentiating between Africans, coloureds and Indians – in accordance with Mwasa policy. For any editor, such demands were impractical and objectionable. One couldn't have all political organisations in the country dictating to news editors who should be assigned to report their events, certainly not that this could be done only by members of their own ethnic group or political persuasion. Moreover, it was essential for our political specialists to have access to all political movements to give them an overall sense of the state of the nation.

My difficulty was that I empathised with the broad objectives of the Black Consciousness Movement, and the last thing I wanted was for the *Rand Daily Mail*, with its strong identification with black grievances, to be seen getting into an ugly public confrontation with its own black staff. Not only would that seriously damage the image of the paper, exposing it to accusations of hypocrisy, but also internally it would be unpalatable and bitterly divisive. Our black staff were highly professional and very loyal to the paper. For them to get into an open fight with the editorial leadership of the paper would be terrible. I shared my concerns with some key members of the black staff. They were sympathetic but stressed that they had to show solidarity. It is at such moments that one realises the loneliness of the decision-maker at the top.

I decided the only way I could handle this awkward situation was to try to finesse it. I announced that henceforth the paper's style would be to use the term 'blacks' instead of 'Africans', and also to use it as a generic term when referring collectively to the victims of apartheid. However, we should retain the terms 'Coloureds' and 'Indians' when necessary for clarity. I then drew the news editor aside and asked him to make sure that Ameen Akhalwaya, one of our political reporters who was of Asian descent and a founder of Mwasa, was assigned to cover the association's up-coming congress and to keep focused on the association's affairs for the next month or two. I felt pretty sure the issue would fade after that – which it did.

I could have telephoned Louw in the US to seek his advice, or at least his approval, and on his return he said he felt I should have done so since it involved a change in the paper's stylebook. He had reason to be concerned, recalling the uproar that had followed Gandar's decision that the paper would refer to black people as 'Africans' rather than 'natives'. I was aware of that event, but I didn't phone Raymond. I felt the issue was so deli-cate as far as relations with the black staff were concerned, that he wouldn't be able to exercise his best judgment from so far away, with no direct feel for the sensibilities in the newsroom at the time. As it turned out, this time the change had no impact on circulation.

Raymond Louw duly returned and I decided to take a break. I drove alone to Durban to spend a week with my cousin Wilfred, who was working as a horticulturalist there. It was then that I nearly fell apart. My sense of decompression was so acute that I felt overwhelmed. All the feelings of grief, guilt, anger and solitude that I had shoved aside during the busy months as acting editor came sweeping back in waves of crippling despair. My cousin and his wife were kind and solicitous, and as the week advanced I began to feel a little better.

As I was having a pre-dinner drink with my cousin one evening, I received a call from East London. It was to tell me that Mary's mother had died. She had recently undergone surgery and had collapsed of a postoperative thrombosis while working in her kitchen.

My first thought was of my children. What a wicked double blow. They were particularly fond of their maternal granny, Simon especially. And now the poor boy, still struggling to come to terms with the death of his mother, was back at boarding school in Swaziland. I had to get to him, and quickly. But how? My car was with me in Durban, but my passport was in Johannesburg and I would need it to enter Swaziland.

At least I was back in action mode. Our Durban correspondent, JR Naidoo, was a good friend, which sparked an idea. I phoned him. 'Do you have a valid passport?' I asked.

'Yes,' he replied, 'where the hell do you want to send me?'

I told him of my dilemma. Would he be willing to accompany me on a drive to the Swaziland border and, leaving me there, use his passport to drive my car across the border to fetch Simon and bring him to me so that I could take him to East London?

'I'll do more than that,' was JR's response. 'I'll take my car and I'll drive, because you must be under a lot of stress. And you can bring your other children with us. That will be helpful for Simon.'

Such was the fellowship of *Rand Daily Mail* staff, then and through all the tough years that followed. We made the journey and collected Simon, so that we were able to be together for their granny's funeral. But I also realised it was time to consolidate my traumatised little family. Much as I admired what Waterford School stood for and what a great institution it was, I made arrangements for Simon to leave and come back home. I enrolled him in another new private boarding school, Woodmead, modelled on similar lines to Waterford except that, being in the land of apartheid, it could not be multiracial. But it was close to where I lived and we could see him often. That is where he went and that is where he eventually graduated.

CHAPTER EIGHTEEN

Road to Recovery

THE HUMAN SPIRIT is a resilient thing. It takes time, of course, as friends are wont to say when trying to comfort the bereaved, but it is true that there can be life after great bereavement. Having my parents next door was a major blessing, for they were able to provide emotional as well as practical support. The children spent their after-school hours, those problematic homework hours, with them, and then came home to me when I returned from work in the evening. How ironic that my parents' decision to leave Hotfire and come to live in Johannesburg was so that they could spend their evening years near me and I would be at hand to support them as they aged, yet here they were playing the supporting role while I was the one in need of help.

Friends and colleagues from the Mail rallied around, too, visiting frequently and bringing children to play with mine. Mary's newly married younger brother David and his wife, Pat, came as well, often accompanied by Pat's closest friend, Sue Matthey. I had come to know Pat and Sue through David, and now they started visiting quite regularly, especially on Sundays when I had to fill the editor's chair at the Mail while Ray Louw took the day off. They would take the children on outings to give my parents a break.

And so it was that as the months passed Sue gradually drifted into my life. She was a slightly built, delightful person with a bubbly

304

personality. She was 11 years younger than me, well-travelled and smart. I was attracted to her from the start, but our relationship developed slowly as my state of emotional turbulence gradually stabilised.

Sue brought a new dimension of vitality and fun into our lives. Her parents were Swiss, from the French-speaking canton of Vaud, and had immigrated to South Africa during the Second World War. Her father, André, a brilliant engineer, had founded a company manufacturing metal tubing that had been highly successful, but he was not satisfied with that. To him, true engineering success could be claimed only if he succeeded back in his homeland. So the day came when André Matthey announced to his family that he had designed a machine to manufacture stainless-steel tubing faster than any other process in the world, and that they were all to go back to Switzerland and work together as a family to prove his success in the only place where it really counted.

To his dismay, Sue baulked. 'I'm not going with you,' she told her father. 'I was born here, I'm a South African and I'm staying right here.' What put her back up particularly was that her father had sent her to the famous university city of Heidelberg to learn German, and she now realised his purpose had been to prepare her to head up the German sales branch of his planned enterprise. He had told her nothing of his plans for her at the time, but now she twigged – and rebelled. Dominating though André Matthey tended to be, he found he had met his match in his equally strong-willed daughter. So while the rest of the Matthey family, including her two brothers, duly returned to Switzerland, Sue remained in South Africa. She also made it clear she wanted no part in the new factory project. She didn't believe in family businesses, contending that family conflicts tended to spill over into the business, and vice versa, an observation that proved sadly prescient in this case. So although her father was a wealthy man, Sue chose to live a simple, almost Spartan, life. She worked as a schoolteacher, lived in a tiny suburban flat above a grocery store, and when she came to visit us in Rivonia it was in an old Peugeot the family had left behind that was so rusty and leaky that when it rained she opened an umbrella inside the car.

As our relationship deepened I began to feel a need to learn Sue's home language. It seemed the right thing to do now that I was becoming serious about her. Moreover, I had always loved the sentient intonations of French. So I enrolled for a course at the Alliance Française in Johannesburg. For a year I struggled with the problem of declining its verbs and, worse still, the illogicality of gender differentiation between inanimate objects. 'How the hell can a chair be feminine and a couch masculine?' I would demand of Sue as I struggled with my homework. She would just laugh at me. 'Don't quarrel with the language, just learn it,' she would say, adding that I was lucky not to be learning German, which has three genders for its nouns.

Towards the end of my year of this rather fruitless endeavour, Air France offered a free flight to Paris for Alliance Française students. I seized the opportunity and spent a whole month of total immersion in the language. I checked in to a cheap boarding house just off the Place de la Madeleine, having first ensured that no one there spoke English, then enrolled at the Alliance's main branch, which was within walking distance of my digs. I spent six hours every day in language classes, then chose a different *arrondissement* to explore each evening, stopping strangers to ask for recommendations of where best to dine. The one thing I soon discovered is that the easiest way to get into conversation with a stranger in France is to talk about food, a subject about which they are all both expert and voluble.

For a month I spoke not a word of English, and by the end of it I could undertake at least a rudimentary conversation in French. To such an extent that I was emboldened to propose to Sue in French. True to her teasing nature she pretended at first not to understand, complaining that I had a rotten accent, then threw her arms around me and accepted.

Again Sue encountered conflict with her father. He flew from Switzerland to try to persuade her not to marry me. Marrying an older man with three children was a foolish idea, he told her, not unreasonably. She brushed him aside with the rejoinder that it was her life to live as she chose. He knew better than to try to bend her to his will, and for her part Sue never resented her father's authoritarian ways. She loved and admired him, and he her. Two of a kind really.

Our marriage was a simple yet extraordinary affair. Sue was teaching French at St John's College in Johannesburg at the time, so we chose to have the service in the college chapel. And we chose as our priest the Afrikaner dissident, the Reverend Beyers Naudé, whose bitter conflicts with the apartheid government I had covered for the *Rand Daily Mail,* becoming a great admirer and friend in the process. There were two problems with our choice. One was that 'Oom Bey', as his admirers called him, had been defrocked by the Dutch Reformed Church for his denunciation of its theological support for apartheid, which meant he was no longer a licensed marriage officer. The other was that the government had served him with a banning order, which meant he couldn't attend any gathering of more than one other person at a time.

The first problem we solved by asking the school chaplain to perform the legal part of the marriage the previous evening. We called him out of a cocktail party and, standing in a passageway, he asked us one question: Did we know of any legal reason why we shouldn't marry? We replied that we did not, whereupon he said simply: 'I think that's all that's required.' He signed the marriage certificate and returned to the cocktail party. It was all over in less than a minute. So we were actually married the day before our wedding day.

As for the ceremony, it was rich in symbolism. Mary's brother and Pat were there, Sue's parents had flown out from Switzerland, and my three sons served as Sue's pageboys instead of bridesmaids. Oom Bey delivered a moving address about the importance of recovering from bereavement and wished Sue well in her partnership with what he called a 'crusading journalist'.

Then he asked the congregation please to remain seated while he left, explaining that his banning order enabled him to attend a church service but that he would be in breach of it, and liable to imprisonment, if he were to be in the company of more than one of them should we all leave the chapel at the same time. He apologised, too, for not being able to attend the reception. There was a round of applause from the wedding guests as this man of

Sue and I on our wedding day. There were no formal pictures; a Rand Daily Mail *news photographer took all the wedding pictures informally.*

The Reverend Beyers Naudé preparing to conduct the wedding service of Sue and I in the St John's College chapel, Johannesburg. Since Naudé had been banned by the government and defrocked by his Dutch Reformed Church, the ceremony had no legal status. But the school's friendly chaplain had earlier fixed that side of the marriage, so no one knew the difference.

such immense moral courage walked back down the aisle and out of the chapel alone.

* * *

MY MOST immediate aim now was to reconsolidate my family. And what better way to do that than by taking an extended holiday together to enable us to bond as a family unit. Now that I was a deputy editor, I qualified for long leave, and since Sue's parents were in Switzerland and I had many good friends in Britain, Europe beckoned. It was high summer in South Africa, school holiday time, so the five of us made our way to Cape Town where we boarded the SA *Vaal* and set sail for Southampton on Boxing Day 1973. Once again there was the pleasure and leisure of long days at sea, of sun and games and moonlit evenings. For Sue and I it was a honeymoon, while the children had endless fun. It was blissful, relaxing after the past two years of stress and pain.

During this time away, in London, I read voraciously and began drafting the outline of the book I had resolved while at Harvard to write one day, an analysis of South Africa modelled on WJ Cash's *The Mind of the South*. Sue and I would wander down to Hyde Park nearly every day, and walk along the Serpentine while I bounced ideas off her about the themes I should focus on and how the chapters should be organised. She was a great listener and a creative contributor of ideas. Back at the flat I would make notes of our discussions and even begin writing some passages when I felt the creative juices pumping.

It was to be another decade before I actually got down to writing that first book, for great challenges and dramas awaited me on my return to South Africa. When I did finally get down to writing *The Mind of South Africa*, which I regard as the best piece of work I have ever done, those conversations in Hyde Park and the notes made after them were invaluable.

* * *

MY MOTHER, then in her eighties, was lying gravely ill in her bed when she received an unexpected visitor. She had been dozing when she heard a slight sound, and on opening her eyes saw the figure of Mbhuti Lavisa, the old *induna* from Hotfire, standing at her bedside. 'Hello, Miss Beness,' he said softly, using the isiXhosa pronunciation of the Hotfire farmhands for her first name, Bernice. 'I have come to see you before you die.'

Just like that. No beating about the bush, no delicate euphemisms. To the rural people my parents knew so well, the facts of life and death are realities to be faced, not feared. There is a marvellous honesty about such frankness that sophistication has blurred with a pretence of sensitivity that is actually more embarrassing and hurtful. In fact Mbhuti's brief announcement to my mother that day was the culmination of an extraordinary, indeed a heroic, gesture of humanitarian concern by one elderly human being to another whom he believed to be on her deathbed. It epitomised the African concept of *ubuntu*, meaning the quality of being human.[1]

I say it was an extraordinary gesture because Mbhuti had never been in a city before. The only towns he had ever seen were Cathcart and a few villages in the Transkei, such as Qamata and Cofimvaba. Yet to see my mother he had, in his late seventies himself, embarked on a 700-km journey by train and on foot to the great, sprawling metropolis of Johannesburg to locate a small suburban cottage among a population of some 7 million people. How he did it still baffles me. When I asked him he said he had an address written on a piece of paper that he showed to people in the streets (he was illiterate himself) who told him which way to go. All to see and pay his last respects to the wife of his old master, who had paid him a pitiful wage but with whom he had formed a lifelong bond that defied all the stereotyped imagery of South Africa's harsh and repressive race relations.

My mother had gone to the Johannesburg General Hospital to seek a diagnosis of chronic chest pains and difficulty breathing, as well as badly swollen legs and ankles. She had been examined by some of the country's top pulmonologists, including the professor of pulmonology at the Wits Medical School, who eventually telephoned me to say there was nothing they could realistically do to save her. He thought she had lung cancer, but to take a biopsy in her weakened condition, he felt, would simply add to her distress. He advised that we take her home and make her as comfortable as possible. In other words, take her home to die.

This was the message my distressed father passed on to old friends in Cathcart, including Keith Snelling, an old school buddy of mine who had bought Hotfire from my father. That is how the news came to reach the ears of old Mbhuti Lavisa, prompting him to make his epic journey.

As it turned out, the diagnosis was wrong. I found it intolerable simply to watch my mother grow weaker each day and to do nothing about it. Eventually I telephoned Helen Suzman's husband, Mosie, once a specialist physician with a global reputation and by then deep into retirement. He spent half an hour with my mother, and then emerged smiling. 'Your mother's going to be fine,' he told me. 'She's got oedema, the tissue in her lungs and legs are full of watery fluid, probably caused by some defect in her liver or heart. Nothing to worry about. I've given her some diuretic tablets and she should be up and about in a few days.' Which she was. Mosie Suzman told me this had been the worst case of misdiagnosis he had ever seen, and that he intended writing a blistering report to the medical school about it.

Meanwhile Mbhuti was still with us, unfazed by the fact that his heroic moral mission had been unnecessary. Having undertaken the most astonishing adventure of his life, he decided to make a holiday of it. He stayed with us for a month, during which time he became surely the most enthusiastic tourist Johannesburg has ever known.

Sue became the tour guide, Mbhuti the tourist, and, since he spoke no English and Sue no isiXhosa, I became the interpreter. But it was an interpreting role with a difference, since I was then heavily involved in my job as deputy editor of the *Rand Daily Mail* and could not accompany them on their excursions. So the end of each day found the three of us, sitting under a tree in my garden, reliving the day's events, with me trying to reconstruct an interpretation of the events and impressions of the two people involved. It was a hilarious and hugely instructive exercise in merging the perceptions of the same events that two people of different cultures who could not communicate with one another had experienced.

* * *

I SAW MBHUTI for the last time several years later in distressing circumstances. He had become too old to work, which meant that, under apartheid's cruel laws, he could no longer stay on the farm, which was deemed to be in a 'white area'. Verwoerd's Bantustan policy decreed that black people could be in 'white South Africa' only if they were in full-time employment there. Dismissal or retirement meant they had to be relocated to the Bantustan, or 'homeland', designated for each particular tribe. This was the logic that led to the notorious forced removals, which inflicted untold hardship upon millions of black people.

In Mbhuti's case it meant he had to leave Hotfire, where he had spent his entire life, and be dumped in the Ciskei 'homeland' some 100 km away, a place he had never seen before.

When I learned of this I decided I had to try to find Mbhuti and see if I could help him. Sue and I drove from Johannesburg to the Ciskei. It was like seeking a needle in a haystack. There were dozens of what we on the *Rand Daily Mail* called 'dumping grounds', all teeming with bemused humanity living in mud huts and tin shanties and under plastic sheeting, with no prospect of employment. Where to find Mbhuti in all this confusion was a major challenge.

We navigated by word of mouth, trying to determine which groups had been moved from where. We eventually located a sector where people from the region around Cathcart had been dumped, and by talking to individuals we found someone who knew where Mbhuti was – a round mud-daub hut among an array of shanties. We made our way there. The door was open. We walked in. Mbhuti was sitting on the floor, his wife Wasvrou on the far side of the dark, windowless abode. 'Hello. I knew you would come,' was his laconic greeting.

His circumstances were dire. Mbhuti was supposed to receive

312

a small state pension, but the money wasn't coming through. The Ciskei was supposed to be an independent country, but no arrangements had been made for Pretoria to transfer its pension obligations to this new puppet regime. Moreover, to fight his case would have required Mbhuti to make his way to the Ciskei capital of Bisho, a journey he was incapable of making at his age. Eventually I was able to make arrangements for some payments to be conveyed regularly to him, while Keith Snelling was able to pull some political strings that enabled the old man and his wife to return to Hotfire.

Mbhuti died there not long afterwards, and on my most recent visit to Hotfire I made my way to his grave on a hillock above the farmhouse to pay my own last respects to him.

CHAPTER NINETEEN

A Weird Way to the Top

I WAS APPOINTED to my first editorship in a bizarre manner, something I was later to realise was a further symptom of SAAN's incoherent management, board and ownership structure, which had led to the disruptive attempt to fire Laurence Gandar. I learned of my appointment not from the managing director or chairman of the board, whose job it was to appoint me, but from my own editor, Raymond Louw, who had no hand in it at all.

The precursor to my appointment was a decision by Joel Mervis, editor of the *Sunday Times*, to retire in 1975. He had edited the *Sunday Times* for 16 years and had built the paper from a weekend addendum to the *Rand Daily Mail* into a hugely successful money-spinner with a circulation of more than half a million. It was the financial pillar that sustained the company, which gave Mervis himself significant influence within the company. That had enabled him to stay on in the job well beyond the normal retirement age of 65. The common belief among the company's journalists was that he had delayed his departure to prevent the *Sunday Express* editor, Johnny Johnson, taking over from him at the *Sunday Times*, as Johnson had been promised when we had successfully blocked him from replacing Gandar at the *Rand Daily Mail*. Mervis and Johnson had been at loggerheads for several years, as the aggressively competitive Johnson chose to challenge Mervis's support for the reformist Young Turks of the United Party by committing the *Sunday Express* to championing the party's Old Guard. This Johnson did in a mocking style that Mervis found offensive, and I have little doubt he was aware of the promise to Johnson and was determined to delay that for as long as possible.

He may even have gone further than that, for Joel Mervis was a canny operator who had qualified as a barrister before turning to journalism. Whether or not he had a hand in the decision I don't know, but the fact is that when Joel finally decided to step down the board didn't choose Johnson to succeed him. It decided that, since the promise had been made by acting chairman Henry Kuiper, who had since left the board, the board was no longer bound by it. Instead they chose an outsider, Tertius Myburgh, editor of the *Pretoria News*, owned by the rival Argus company, to be the new *Sunday Times* editor. Myburgh, an urbane and smoothly bilingual Afrikaner, was a friend of mine from our days together in the parliamentary Press Gallery. He and his wife, Helmien, had helped support me through Mary's death, often having my children spend weekends with theirs in Pretoria. He had also been the main speaker at the reception of my marriage to Sue. It was a controversial appointment, and Johnson was so outraged that he fell on his sword. He resigned from the company with immediate effect and bade farewell to no one.

That was how I became editor of the *Sunday Express*. It was a bizarre choice. I was known to be possibly the most liberal member of SAAN's senior editorial staff, yet here I was being chosen to assume the editorship of the most right-wing English-language newspaper in the country. Even more bizarre was the manner of my appointment.

Several days passed after Raymond Louw told me I was to be made editor of the *Sunday Express*, and I heard nothing from either the managing director, Leycester Walton, or the new chairman of the board, Ian MacPherson, who had succeeded the admirable Cecil Payne. I found this strange, but assumed it meant I would be taking over in a few months' time. But the very next Sunday the Express carried a long valedictory message from Johnson making it clear that he had already left. Puzzled, I telephoned Walton's

315

office on Monday morning, to be told I would have to wait for a meeting because Walton had left for Port Elizabeth to attend an *Eastern Province Herald* board meeting. My confusion began to turn into concern as I realised that the paper I was apparently going to be asked to take over had no leadership: the deputy editor, Bunny Neame, had retired several months before and had not been replaced. There was no assistant editor.

I telephoned Walton in Port Elizabeth and found him quite sanguine. He told me he would have to talk to MacPherson before meeting with me, and MacPherson was on holiday in Durban. But there was no need to hurry; we could talk later. I was appalled; he had obviously not read Johnson's farewell message in the previous day's Express. 'But Leycester,' I protested, 'Johnny's gone and there's no deputy editor. So who is going to bring out next Sunday's edition? If you want me to do it you'd better get me there in time.'

'Yes, I can see that,' Walton replied rather vaguely. 'I suppose the best thing would be for you to fly down here tomorrow and meet me at the EP Herald building.'

I must stress that Leycester Walton was one of the nicest, most affable, courteous and gracious human beings I have ever known. The ultimate gentleman. But he was not what one would call an action man. His critics said he was just 'too nice' to be effective in the tough world of business. There were certainly times when I found his lack of decisiveness exasperating, and this was one of them.

I flew to Port Elizabeth the next morning, arriving at the Herald offices at 11 am. I had to hang around for two hours until the board meeting ended. An embarrassing wait as old eastern Cape acquaintances saw me and asked what I was doing there. Had I told them I was waiting to see Leycester Walton, it would immediately have set the journalistic rumour mill abuzz, since everyone knew Johnny Johnson had quit in a huff. So I muttered something about just passing through town and wanting to see one of the board members when the meeting was over. When the meeting did finally end, Walton introduced me to all the other directors and invited me to join them for lunch, where, of course, it was not possible to hold a private discussion with him. After lunch Walton told me that unfortunately he had to go to another appointment, and he could give me only ten minutes.

Our brief talk was held in Walton's car as it drove round and round the block, during which time a tremendous thunderstorm raged, with flashes of lightning, crashings of thunder and torrential rain. Walton sat in front with the driver and I sat in the back. We could hardly hear one another above the roar of the storm and the swishing of the windscreen wipers as the car drove round and round the block. I told Walton I thought we ought to discuss the editorship of the *Sunday Express*, if it was true they wanted to appoint me, and he asked me what I thought about it. I told him it would be difficult because Johnny had run the Express as a UP Old Guard paper and I could obviously not follow such a line since, as he knew, I was strongly committed to the principles of the *Rand Daily Mail*. I told him I thought the best course would be for me to 'depoliticise' the Express and strengthen its news content. Walton said he thought that was a good idea.

As the ten minutes drew to a close, we agreed that I should write a leader setting out the future policy of the paper, and that Walton and I should meet MacPherson in Durban on Wednesday. The car dropped me off at the entrance to the *Eastern Province Herald* and Walton went on to his next appointment. I took a taxi to the airport and flew back to Johannesburg, still not knowing whether I was going to be the next editor of the headless *Sunday Express* or not.

I wrote my proposed 'Statement of Policy' at home that evening. In it I latched on to a statement in Johnson's farewell message that 'a newspaper is, in truth, a living organism' with a character of its own that made it larger than any single editor. I conceded that as a political columnist my own views had been expressed publicly over a number of years and were well known, but that any wise editor was bound to take the keenest cognisance of his newspaper's traditions and corporate personality, which Johnson had described as 'independent'. It was a false claim, I fear, because Johnson had been a blatantly partisan campaigner, but his assertion gave me the opportunity to lay claim to the label on behalf of the Express, which I said would report all viewpoints fairly and overtly champion none.

I went on: 'But political independence should not be mistaken for political impotence. Far from it. The *Sunday Express* will have views of its own and it will present them to the public. For its democratic function is not only to provide an arena for public debate, but to stimulate the action as well.' That, I hoped, would satisfy the conservative board while at the same time leaving the door open wide enough for me to run the paper in a manner that would be true to my own conscience.

I took the statement with me to Durban where I was to meet Walton and MacPherson for lunch at the elegant King Edward Hotel on the beachfront. It was my first direct encounter with MacPherson, a baffling choice by the giant Anglo American Corporation, now the majority shareholder of SAAN, since his knowledge of newspapers was minimal. Moreover, MacPherson was known to have close relations with the National Party. At that point he was sitting on at least 60 other boards. His image within the South African journalistic community was not flattering: they instantly nicknamed him 'The Greaser'.

Walton gave MacPherson a brief outline of our discussion in Port Elizabeth, whereupon I handed the chairman a copy of my 'Statement of Policy'. He glanced cursorily through it, gave a slight nod that I took to be of approval, then said to me: 'I hope you won't turn this paper into a *Rand Daily Mail.*' I was thrown completely off balance, and asked MacPherson what he meant, at which point he launched into a tirade of abuse of the paper. He told me he regarded the Mail as a left-wing, extremist newspaper with serious defects. He wasn't explicit, but he revealed an intense dislike of the paper and made it clear he didn't want me to run a paper anything like it.

It was an extraordinary discussion, and I became increasingly frustrated and angry. He was supposed to be interviewing me about my suitability to be editor of the *Sunday Express*, and here he was venting his spleen in a torrent of denunciation of the *Rand Daily Mail* of which, at that moment, I was still deputy editor and a loyal supporter of its editorial policy. What did he expect me to do? Denounce it in his presence? He went on and on and for the

318

next hour we became engaged in an acrimonious conflict over the merits of the paper I was presumably leaving without uttering a word about the one I was presumably soon to take over.

Eventually MacPherson glanced at his watch and announced that he had another appointment. He rose and left the room with a curt goodbye. As Walton and I stood up to see him go, I turned to the MD and asked: 'What the hell do we do now?' Walton had said not a word throughout the whole acrimonious exchange, yet he was quite unflustered. 'I guess we just carry on,' he replied.

'Do you mean I must take over as editor?' I asked.

'I guess so,' Walton replied.

So I flew back to Johannesburg, and the next day, Thursday, I walked into the Express newsroom, introduced myself to the staff and then went into my office to take my seat as the paper's editor.

I saw MacPherson again a few days later when he arrived at my office to tell me that a member of the SAAN board, Dr Frans Cronje, was so infuriated by my appointment as editor of the Express that he had resigned. I was not surprised. Cronje was one of Sir De Villiers Graaff's right-hand men in Parliament and a pillar of the United Party's Old Guard leadership. The impending loss of Johnny Johnson's support for that ossified group was obviously upsetting for him. But I could see that MacPherson was also upset by Cronje's peremptory departure. He asked me to fly with him to Cape Town to meet with Sir De Villiers and assure him that the *Sunday Express* would not change its policy of supporting the United Party.

I was flabbergasted. 'But I can't possibly do that, Ian,' I replied. 'I've already published my Statement of Policy, which you have seen, and which made it clear that the Express under my editorship would not declare its support for any party. I can't possibly go back on that now.'

MacPherson looked vaguely stupefied by my response, but didn't press the issue and he never raised it again.

* * *

IT WAS A bit of a scramble, but we managed to bring out that first issue of the *Sunday Express*. On my arrival I sensed that the

319

newsroom staff were in a state of confusion and no small degree of apprehension. Understandably so. They were all Johnson's people and when they heard I was going to take over they feared I was going to clear the decks and hire a new team more in harmony with my liberal ideas. Given those uncertainties, and given that there had been no newsroom leadership through the week, few news items had been prepared. But we made it and the paper came out on time.

There was a minor drama in the printing department that Saturday night – production night for all Sunday papers – when I approached Joel Mervis as he was putting the *Sunday Times* to bed. The printers stared in astonishment seeing the two of us together: the rivalry between Johnson and Mervis had been so intense that each had used his own selected Linotype operators and page compositors to prevent the other getting a glimpse of his scoop stories. Mutual secrecy had pervaded every aspect of the production process. As for two editors talking to each other in the works, that was unheard of. Unaware of this ridiculous protocol, I had simply walked over to where Joel was standing to chat with this veteran of Sunday journalism. He greeted me warmly.

'Joel, I've never worked on a Sunday paper before,' I told him. 'Can you give me just one tip on what has been the key to your success?'

Mervis looked at me quizzically. 'Oh, it's quite simple,' he said. 'You've got to go over Niagara in a barrel every Sunday.'

That was it. You had to have at least one story that would astonish the public in every issue. It was the briefest, most cogent lesson in the noble craft of journalism that I ever had.

My appointment had been such a muddled and disconcerting affair that, as I settled into my new seat, I realised I had given little thought to some of the problems I now faced. I was obviously not an easy fit at the Express. I knew few members of the staff well, and I was probably not in harmony with what I presumed was the paper's readership profile. How should I set about dealing with these problems? It was one thing to talk generally about 'de-politicising' the paper, but what did that really mean in practice? Should the paper be a lively pop tabloid, or a paper of serious news analysis? And what about its trading position? I knew it was running at a loss, which meant I would have to look closely at the figures and determine what could be done to improve its profitability — a new field of responsibility for me.

Not least of my concerns was about the ethics of some individuals in the newsroom. In short, I wondered whether, in some cases, the Express was their only employer. The Mail had suffered a few nasty shocks when some of its journalists turned out to be security police agents planted on the paper to inform on its operations and, worse still, on the activities of their colleagues. There were also some activists of the outlawed CPSA and black liberation movements working under cover as Mail journalists. Occasionally one would break cover, appearing in court to reveal himself as Police Major So-and-So and give testimony for the state. Or appear as an accused charged under the security laws. Identifying such undercover people was well-nigh impossible, because asking a direct question would inevitably bring a denial, and one couldn't fire an individual on the basis of suspicion.

Chief suspect on the Express was the mercurial Gordon Winter, who had a disconcerting habit of taking pictures of his colleagues and filing them in a locked cabinet beside his desk. 'You never know when they may appear in the news,' he would say cheerfully. Winter also had a remarkable ability to come up with scoop stories on the crime beat, particularly those dealing with the arrest of major political activists and the serving of banning orders. He made no secret of the fact that he had good security police contacts.

Another was our Durban bureau chief, Tim Clark. Among other things Tim was the official coach of the police rugby team in that city, and again his contacts delivered cracking good crime and security stories way ahead of our competitors. Obviously these scoops were most welcome from a journalistic perspective, but they were also a source of suspicion and anxiety among other journalists.

As I pondered these vexing issues I decided to drive to Durban that first Sunday and Monday — the Sunday journalist's weekend, since they work every Saturday — to seek the advice of Laurence

Gandar, who by now had returned from London and settled into retirement. He was still the wisest man I knew, and since I didn't yet have a deputy or assistant editor, I felt a need to have someone trustworthy with whom to consult. Sue came with me and it proved to be a delightful sojourn as well as an instructive one. Freed of the stresses of editing the *Rand Daily Mail*, Gandar was in a jovial mood, but he was still as incisive as ever.

He agreed wholeheartedly with the strategy of 'depoliticising' the paper, at least for a time, but cautioned that this should not mean ignoring politics. Instead Gandar advised me to find and engage a really smart and well-informed political correspondent who could analyse the political news informatively, while being careful to keep it balanced in party terms. He believed South African readers across the entire spectrum of viewpoints were passionately interested in politics and would appreciate good analysis. But there should be no polemical journalism. He advised me to put my own opinion column on hold for at least a year, then introduce it carefully before turning up the volume to the level it had reached on the Mail.

Gandar counselled that I should keep the entire newsroom staff, except for Johnson's political correspondent, who had mercifully resigned on the day I arrived. To fire any of them, he felt, would send out a message of alarm and trigger speculation in the pro-apartheid media that I was going to turn the paper into a liberal crusader. That could cause major readership defections, given that the paper had long been pitched at white conservatives. Rather try to win over the newsroom staff: be open with them, tell them I realised the change was probably making them feel awkward but that I respected their journalistic talents and intended using them to build what had been a controversial newspaper into a respected and successful one.

I returned to Johannesburg feeling a good deal more comfortable. I made three quick appointments. I asked Ray Louw if he would agree to the transfer of his most skilled design and production journalist, David Hazelhurst, to be my deputy. Ray was reluctant, for the multiskilled Hazelhurst was a jewel of a journalist, but when I pointed out that it would be a significant promotion for Dave within the company, he agreed. Ray was never one to stand in the way of an individual's career development. Next, I asked for my old friend John Ryan, one of the country's most brilliant writers, to join me as an assistant editor. Thirdly, I did a talent scout around the country and finally hired the highly recommended Martin Schneider, then on the *Sunday Tribune* in Durban, to be my political correspondent. Within the existing staff, I made one hugely important change. Kitt Katzin was the news editor and he was doing a good enough job, but in a one-on-one chat he confided that the one job he really longed for was to be a free-ranging investigative reporter. 'I know I can be the best,' he told me, eyes gleaming. I have always believed in backing passion, so I promptly gave him the job, appointing another senior reporter, Peter Bunkel, to replace him as news editor — a happy swap since both turned out to be stars.

Thus equipped, I was ready to go. But first I wanted to confront Gordon Winter. I asked my secretary to call him in to my office. 'Gordon,' I said, looking straight into his eyes. 'I'm only going to ask you this question once, and I don't suppose I can expect an honest answer if you are what most people in this building believe you are. Are you a BOSS agent?'

I saw Winter flinch for just a second, then he erupted with emotion. 'I'm not,' he declared. 'I swear to you I'm not. I know a lot of people think I am. I know Van den Bergh and I know a lot of people in the branch, but they are contacts. I am not one of them.'

At which point, his voice rising with emotion, Winter stood up, clapped his right hand over his heart, and said with the hint of a sob in his voice: 'I swear to you on my mother's grave that I am not a BOSS agent.'

'Okay, Gordon,' I replied. 'I'll accept that. But let me tell you that if I ever find that you've just lied to me, you'll be dead meat as far as I'm concerned.'

With that, Winter left my office, looking shaken.

Winter produced some great stories after that, some distinctly lurid thanks to his contacts among the police and the underworld. The most spectacular was to expose the fact that the mayor of Johannesburg's wife was having an affair with the mayoral chauffeur, which included having sex in the back seat of the official black Rolls-Royce, registration number TJ 1. It produced a loud front-page banner headline that indeed had us going over Niagara in a barrel.

Winter produced other startling stories, too, but I was always careful to keep him away from anything even remotely political. Then one day, when I was on leave, he resigned and left, never to set foot in the SAAN building again.

* * *

FAST FORWARD five years, by which time I had returned to the *Rand Daily Mail* as editor. As I drove home late one evening after another stressful day at that energy-sapping newspaper, Sue met me in the driveway. 'There's something very odd going on,' she said. 'Gordon Winter is here and says he wants to see you. He's behaving very strangely. He arrived here after dark on foot, telling me he had left his car up in Rivonia village. Then he pulled out all the telephone plugs and put cushions over the plugs in the wall. He won't tell me what it's all about. He says he'll only tell you, and it must be in private. He doesn't want me around listening to it, so I'm off to bed.'

I went into the house and found Winter sitting in the dining room, looking agitated. 'What's up?' I asked.

'I have to speak to you,' he said, and began sobbing, an unexpected sight in one usually so gung-ho. I offered him a drink to calm him down, and he gulped it gratefully. After a pause he went on. 'You are the only person who has ever treated me decently,' he said. 'You and Hendrik van den Bergh, and I have to tell you that I lied to you that day you asked me whether I was a BOSS agent. I have been all along, but now I've changed. Working for you made me see what is happening to black people in this country. It's opened my eyes and I can't go on with it. I'm going to leave the country and write a book about what BOSS is doing. They know that and they've already tried twice to kill me. I have to leave in a hurry but I had to come and see you first. I walked here so they wouldn't follow me, and I've muffled all the phone lines in this house in case they're tapping your lines. I know they're watching you, too, so I've got to be careful. When I leave here I'll walk back to my car, drive to the airport, abandon the car in the parking lot there and stay in hiding until it's time to board the earliest flight leaving Johannesburg in the morning. Then I'll disappear and write my book.'

For the next few hours Winter told me the story of his life. His mother, he said, had been a prostitute. He had never known his father, not even who he might have been. He had grown up as an urchin in war-torn London where he had mixed with criminal gangs and learned the skills of basic survival. At some point he had been taken in by one of the most notorious outfits, the Richardson Gang, who operated globally and used him as a smart kid who could outwit both the cops and criminal competitors. He had done a big job for them in Casablanca, then they had flown him to South Africa to help the gang 'take out' a rival gang leader who had fled there. In the course of their investigation the South African police had picked up Winter, who had driven the getaway car. Someone in the police force had spotted his remarkable street smarts and decided to bring him to the attention of Hendrik van den Bergh, my only rival, apparently, in Winter's estimation of people who had treated him decently. This was because Van den Bergh had instantly recognised Winter's unique talents, had employed him as an agent, and treated him with the respect those talents warranted in that line of work.

As dawn approached, Winter again became emotional. By that time we had both consumed quite a lot of my best wines, which released further confessions. He told me he'd had an affair with a young reporter on my Express staff, whom he identified, and they'd had a baby. He showed me a picture of Van den Bergh holding the little boy, with Winter and the child's mother standing either side of him. 'Van den Bergh is his godfather,' Winter told me proudly. He told me the arrival of his baby son had had a huge psychological impact on him. 'It has humanised me,' he said. 'I'm a different human being now.' He went on to tell me that in this transformed state of mind he had begun noticing for the first time the wretched circumstances in which so many black people lived.

'I went to buy some baby food in the grocery store the other day,' he said, 'and there was this black woman with a baby strapped to her back. I saw her buy some dog food. I asked her conversationally what it was for; did she have a dog? She told me no, it was for her baby. Just think of that. She was so poor she was feeding her baby on dog food. It made me realise what kind of system I had been working for.'

It was nearly dawn before Winter left, wishing me well and telling me that if ever I needed his help I should track him down and he would happily assist – an offer I was to take up some years later.

* * *

WINTER'S TALE was not the only startling revelation I was to encounter at the *Sunday Express*. Once I had been in the job just over a year, my relationship with the staff settled down comfortably. Our mutual suspicions had faded and most staff members started opening up to me. Katzin especially. He loved his new job and loved coming into my office to share some of his ideas and discoveries on his investigative beat.

It was in one of these candid moments that he confided in me about the suspicions and anxieties that had gripped the Express staff members when they heard I was going to be their new editor. Tim Clark, he told me, had arranged with his contacts in the Durban branch of the security police to monitor Laurence Gandar's home during the weekend of my visit there to seek his advice. Katzin told me the 'spooks' had given Clark a recording of every word that had been uttered in those exchanges, and that Clark had flown to Johannesburg the following Sunday and played the recording to the newsroom staff.

It was a shocking and deeply disturbing disclosure. An appalling invasion of privacy and the misappropriation of highly confidential information. It meant the whole staff knew exactly what I thought of them individually and collectively, which in itself was highly compromising for any chief of staff. I also had no doubt it was illegal. But what to do about it? I said nothing to Katzin, who had blurted all this out in a moment of friendly innocence. His purpose, he implied, was to let me know that staff members had been reassured by the recording. They had learned that none of them was to be fired.

I thought long and hard about this issue. I didn't consult anyone about it; I felt that might simply set the rumour mill running. I decided not to let the staff know that I was aware of what had happened, for that would reflect badly on Katzin for splitting to the boss about something that had obviously been kept as a group secret. Katzin didn't deserve that, for he had not intended to be malicious. Nor could I fire Clark for the same reason, although I felt his action had certainly been a firing offence.

But most of all I didn't want to stir up another hornet's nest in the newsroom, after all the care I had taken to build a good relationship with them and just as they were settling down so well. So I did nothing. I didn't even speak to Clark about it. But, as I had done with Winter, I kept a close eye on every story he wrote and remained keenly aware that his relationship with the security police must indeed be very close.

* * *

THOSE THREE YEARS of my first editorship were formative ones. The Express staff was tiny, only 36 journalists compared with about 140 on the Mail at that time. But a small staff can be flexible and innovative, and it is easier to build a good relationship and to energise them. This I set out to do, and I believe I succeeded. It became a happy little ship, and because of that an enterprising one.

Our first major success, derived from having the wonderful layout specialist, David Hazelhurst, in charge of the production end of the paper, was to win the Frewin Trophy for being judged the best-designed newspaper in the country. It was a singular achievement. I don't think the *Sunday Express* had won any major award before in its 38-year history.

Next, a young reporter, Ingrid Lewin, got her teeth into the story of a couple, Joe and Pam Higson, whose parents claimed their seven-year-old daughter, Gayle, had been stolen by a childless couple and taken to Australia. The Higsons, recent immigrants from Liverpool, told Lewin they had met the couple, John and Joan Bracebridge, at a hotel the government was using as a halfway house for arriving immigrants. Little Gayle had become friendly with the Bracebridges, who, after a while, had persuaded the Higsons to allow her to accompany them on a Christmas holiday in Australia. So off the Bracebridges went with the happy little girl in tow. But when, by April, the Higsons had heard not a word from the Bracebridges or their daughter, they understandably became concerned. This resulted in a small two-paragraph item in a suburban newspaper, which is where Ingrid Lewin spotted it.

The moment Lewin drew my attention to the story, all my news instincts lit up like a Christmas tree. This was one of those human-interest stories that hard-bitten journalists callously refer to as a 'tear-jerker'. It is gourmet food, especially for tabloid newspapers like the Express. We just had to make a meal of it.

Lewin wrote the story for the Express, then sent copies to a number of Australian newspapers, together with a picture of Gayle. This elicited a response from a reporter in Perth saying the Western Australian police had contacted him to say the Bracebridges had come forward with the child, but insisted they would not be returning her to her parents. This elevated the story to a much higher level. What were they − kidnappers? The story cried out for the Express to fly to the rescue, but we didn't have the budget for such a grand venture. However, the resourceful Kitt Katzin talked South African Airways into flying Lewin and Pam Higson to Perth on a 'humanitarian mission' to rescue little Gayle.

It turned out to be not that simple. The police in Perth told Lewin the Bracebridges were refusing to give up the child because they had legal guardianship and provided the documents to prove it. Lewin, now teamed up with the Perth reporter, briefed an attorney and prepared to take the case to the Supreme Court of Western Australia. But before the case could be heard, it was revealed that the Higsons, badly strapped financially, had sold the child to the Bracebridges for R500, and that the Bracebridges, for

328

their part, confessed to having falsely told little Gayle that Pam was not her real mother. Ingrid Lewin, in true Hollywood style, rose above her role as a reporter to reconcile everyone, so that all lived happily ever after.

It was a humdinger of a story, and it won Lewin South Africa's top prize for enterprising journalism – the first time this coveted prize had gone to a woman journalist, and the first time it had been won by a Sunday newspaper.

Addressing the *Sunday Express*'s trading problems was a bit trickier. Johnson, in his obsessive drive to compete with Mervis's *Sunday Times*, had insisted on the paper circulating nationally to boost its circulation figures at much as possible. He had managed to push the number of sold copies up to 200 000 a week, still way short of the *Sunday Times*'s half million, but a considerable achievement nonetheless. The trouble was the national printing and distribution costs far exceeded the advertising pulling power of that circulation figure. Therefore the Express was running at a considerable loss.

In the complex economics of the newspaper business, the selling price of the paper itself falls far short of covering the costs of gathering the news and printing and distributing the product. The difference has to be made up by the advertising the paper can attract, which in turn is related to its circulation and readership figures. The higher the circulation, the more attractive the publication is to advertisers and therefore the higher the rates it can charge them. The snag in all this is that local advertisers, such as a retail store in a particular town, are primarily interested in the number of papers sold in that particular area. If it is relatively small, the store will pay a high advertising rate based on the paper's national circulation figure, in which case it will do better advertising in the local paper with its much lower ad rate.

It was immediately apparent to me that the Express's poor trading position was due to Johnson's ego-driven obsession to compete with the *Sunday Times*. It made no financial sense, and as far as I could see it made no journalistic sense either. The Express's main income was derived from property advertising in the Pretoria-Witwatersrand-Vereeniging (PWV) triangle, where its circulation

329

was strongest and its advertising rate competitive. Once it went beyond that densely populated region, it began losing money hand over fist. After combing through the figures with two successive business managers, John Fairbairn and Ted Sceales, I decided to withdraw the *Sunday Express* from its national enterprise and turn it into a locally focused regional paper.

It was not an easy decision. No editor likes to shed readers deliberately, and had I felt that the Express served some vital national purpose, as the *Rand Daily Mail* certainly did, I would doubtless have felt differently about it. But its proper role, as I saw it, was to focus its small editorial staff on providing the country's densest population area with the best possible news coverage we could provide – rather than dilute its strength across a huge country our small staff could never cover adequately.

So it was that I repositioned the *Sunday Express*, shedding some readers as I did so, and it began making money for the first time in many years.

***

IF MY THREE years as editor of the Express were a great learning experience for me, so, too, were they for Sue. We were still really newlyweds when I got the job, which meant that to some extent she was thrust at the age of 29 into public life. But she was undaunted by the prospect. The day my appointment was formally made, she told me bluntly: 'I want you to understand that I'm not going to be the editor's wife. I'm going to go my own way and do my own thing. You are the editor and you are going to be dealing with big issues. I'm going to play my role, but I'm going to do it with small people. I believe in the power of one.'

I was delighted. Sue's feistiness and strong individuality were the finest features of her personality. I must confess, though, that I was a little worried about her lack of knowledge of the political personalities among whom we would obviously have to move. To put it bluntly, I knew her to be politically naive. But that, as I was to discover, was to change rapidly and radically.

Only a matter of days after becoming editor, I fell ill with chickenpox, a minor children's ailment that can be rather un-pleasant when contracted as an adult. It was quite serious, and the family doctor ordered me to bed for a week. It came at a particularly awkward time because the Express was running a Businessman of the Year Award – another of Johnson's ego-projects. The winner had already been chosen and I was due to attend the presentation that week. This was before the formali-ties of Hazelhurst's and Ryan's transference to my staff had been completed, so I still had no deputy or assistant editor to stand in for me.

I thought of defying the doctor and slipping out for an hour that evening just to put in an appearance. 'Don't do that,' Sue ordered. 'You'll just infect everyone else there, and besides you look terrible with that rash. Don't worry, I'll go in your place, present your apologies and explain why you can't attend.'

So that was what was agreed. The presentation was to take place at a dinner hosted by the Express, so John Fairbairn was there to welcome the guests and attend to the formalities. The seating arrangements had me between the wife of State President Nico Diederichs and the wife of the chairman of the board of the South African Broadcasting Corporation, Piet Meyer. Both men were big figures not only in the National Party but also in the pow-erful Afrikaner secret society, the *Broederbond* (Band of Brothers), of which Meyer was the current chairman, making him, in the opinion of many, the most powerful figure in the country.

Sue, it must be noted, had no idea of the pedigree of the two women between whom she was seated. She simply sat there chat-ting cheerfully to both of them in her usual bubbly manner. Nor did she notice that they were both pumping her for information about her husband, who, to everyone's surprise, had just been made editor of this right-wing, effectively pro-Nat, newspaper. Wasn't he very liberal? How did he get on with Johnson? How did he get the job? How was he going to run the paper?

To say Sue was cunning in dealing with this interrogation would be an overstatement, but her replies were so bland as to give nothing away. 'Oh yes,' she replied, he's very liberal, but he's a good journalist and I'm sure he'll do a good job.' And then, with the most innocent of smiles, she turned to Mrs Diederichs and asked: 'And what does your husband do for a living?'

But in the months and years that followed I watched my politically innocent young wife transform into a major activist as a member of the Black Sash.[1] From my vantage point as a journalist, I saw her join protest marches and demonstrations, saw white racists spit at her, watched her set up and run an advice centre in a black township, and saw her thrown into police vans and into a cell at security police headquarters for a night. She even played a role as a facilitator of some secret talks between black activists and Afrikaner reformists that formed part of the overall negotiating process that eventually gave us our democracy. All of this she undertook with an irrepressible spirit of *joie de vivre* that won over even her captors. Having snatched me from the brink of despair, she became the light of my life.

CHAPTER TWENTY

To the Stormy Summit

ONE EVENING in the spring of 1976, Rex Gibson, who had succeeded me as deputy editor of the *Rand Daily Mail*, called at my home to drop a bombshell. Had I heard, he asked, that the management was thinking of getting rid of Ray Louw as editor of the Mail and giving me the job?

I was dumfounded. 'That can't be,' I stammered. 'Ray's done a great job; he's saved the Mail. Why on earth would they want to get rid of him?'

'I know,' Gibson replied. 'The whole newsroom is upset about it. Of course nothing official has been said, but the word seems to have leaked out and I wondered whether they had said anything to you about it.'

I told him I had heard nothing, but then, given the bizarre way I had been appointed editor of the *Sunday Express*, I supposed anything was possible. What, I asked, was Ray doing about it?

'Oh, he'll fight back, you can be sure of that,' Gibson said. 'You know what Ray is like. He'll never take anything lying down.'

I felt conflicted. Obviously there was a sense of excitement at the prospect of taking charge of the country's most famous newspaper, but it was quickly quelled by a sense of foreboding. Why would they want to make this change? What was the motive behind such thinking? The timing was all wrong anyway. An attempt had just been made by Louis Luyt, a fertiliser magnate and prominent supporter of the government, to buy control of SAAN, with the obvious intent of radically changing the *Rand Daily Mail*. This had alarmed not only those of us working for the company but also many heavyweights in the English business community, particularly those well disposed to the Progressive Party. At the head of this group was the party's key political organiser, a stockbroker named Max Borkum, who was particularly close to its only MP, Helen Suzman. Borkum, a hobbit of a man with boundless energy and seemingly endless contacts, had swiftly raised money secretly from Harry Oppenheimer to form a trust, which he called the Advowson Trust, to buy out the Syfrets shareholding and so block Luyt's politically motivated bid. At which point Luyt had diverted the money to launch a rival morning newspaper, *The Citizen*, to challenge the Mail commercially. After a wobbly start, he had hired none other than Johnny Johnson to edit the new paper. This meant the Mail was now engaged in a direct circulation war with a new, well-backed rival, which struck me as being the wrong time to change editors.

Worse still, at this precise moment the country was going through its worst phase of racial unrest, with the massive youth uprising of 1976. Black students had revolted against a government decree that Afrikaans had to be used as a language of instruction in all black schools. The whole system of Bantu education, segregated and far inferior to the education white students were given, was grievance enough, but to require black schoolchildren to take half their subjects in a language few understood was a bridge too far. Besides which most blacks resented Afrikaans as 'the language of the oppressor'.

The uprising had begun on 16 June when thousands of Soweto schoolchildren set out to march to the Orlando Stadium, where they intended holding a protest rally. The police blocked their way, and when they started firing teargas canisters at the marchers, the youngsters hurled stones in return. Then the police opened fire with live ammunition. Among the first to die was 13-year-old Hector Pieterson. A picture of a fellow student carrying the dying Hector, with his weeping sister running beside them, went around the world as an iconic symbol of this youth rebellion, which was in fact a turning point in the whole black struggle against apartheid.[1] As the insurrection spread nationwide, some 600 young protesters were killed, thousands were detained without trial, and some 14000 escaped across the border to swell the ranks of Umkhonto we Sizwe.

When, much later, I asked the officer who had commanded the police unit in Soweto that fateful day, Brigadier Theunis 'Rooi Rus' Swanepoel, why he had ordered his men to open fire on the schoolchildren with live ammunition, his response was instructive. 'From my experience as a policeman,' he said, 'I had learned that the only way you can deal with the Bantu [black people] when they get out of control is to give them more violence than they can take.'

What troubled me was that the *Rand Daily Mail*, under Louw's editorship, had covered these turbulent events brilliantly. It was a hellishly difficult and perilous story to cover, given the maze of security laws through which Louw had to navigate his team. It was physically dangerous, too. Reporting any war is tough enough, but a civil war is the worst because there are no front lines and one can't be embedded in any side. We on the *Sunday Express* had never been able to get to grips with it fully, partly because it was a day-by-day breaking news story for the dailies, while all the Sunday papers could do was try to pick up special angles. Moreover, the *Sunday Express* did not have a team of black reporters who could gain inconspicuous access to the troubled township areas, as the Mail did.

The Mail's black journalists had done an extraordinary job, heroic and impactful. Gabu Tugwana once spent a whole night hiding in a coal box, watching events through holes in the box. When he emerged next morning he found three corpses near his hiding place. Peter Magubane, the paper's star photographer, had his nose smashed by a policeman who lashed him across the face with a baton while ripping the film from his camera. But they got the stories and pictures that kept the whole of South Africa and the rest of the world informed. Eventually 14 black journalists were imprisoned without trial, including four from the Mail:

Magubane and fellow photographer Willie Nkosa, as well as Tugwana and fellow reporter Nat Serache. Magubane set a world record by being kept in solitary confinement for 365 days, but he also won the cherished Stellenbosch Farmers' Winery Award for taking the year's most graphic news pictures. Their efforts aroused world awareness of the violence being used to suppress protests against apartheid. It marked the beginning of the wave of international outrage that was to lead eventually to the imposition of sanctions, which played a key role in forcing South Africa to change.

All this sent the Mail's circulation skyrocketing, especially in the black communities, pushing its monthly average up by some 40 000 to a record 166 000. In the face of such success, it made no sense that the board now wanted to fire the editor who had presided over it. Recalling Ian MacPherson's openly expressed dislike of the *Rand Daily Mail*, I felt suspicious. Why were they doing this? And why me, when I had made my feelings about the Mail's policy so clear to him?

After pondering all this, I sent a verbal message to Ray Louw telling him I'd heard nothing from management about their wanting me to replace him as editor of the Mail and therefore I couldn't get involved in the issue, but wishing him well in his fight-back. 'Tell him,' I said, 'that if he loses the battle and they come to me, I'll accept only if they give me firm assurances that they don't want me to change the paper's policy.'

* * *

SEVERAL MONTHS went by and I heard nothing, although the rumour continued to circulate. Then one afternoon I received a call from Leycester Walton's secretary asking if I could meet the following day with him and Ian MacPherson, together with the new deputy managing director, Clive Kinsley, at the chairman's home. This was obviously it. I braced myself.

The addition of Kinsley to the management team had come as a surprise. We journalists knew little of his background, except that he had come from the rival Argus company, which by then

336

had acquired a major stake in SAAN. He had headed the Argus's Rhodesian chain during the years when Ian Smith's UDI regime was applying press censorship, and he spoke with pride of his role in those difficult circumstances. Other views were less laudatory. Henry Kuiper, the former MD of SAAN, told me years later that Kinsley had been 'a disaster' in Rhodesia. He certainly turned out to be a disaster at SAAN. It was also contended by some that the Argus company had 'shunted him aside' by sending him to SAAN to take over from Walton, who was due to retire in a year. Kinsley was later to lend credibility to this by nurturing a smouldering hatred of the Argus general manager, Hal Miller, who was said to have been the one responsible for the sidelining to clear his own way to the top of the bigger company. Kinsley, a red-haired man with a florid face, would flush with anger at the mere mention of Miller's name.

I knew little about Kinsley when the four of us met at MacPherson's home that afternoon. I had chatted with him a few times and found him affable and friendly. He had shown interest in the fact that I had worked on the Bulawayo *Chronicle*, where he had once been manager, but beyond his frequently expressed pride in his role in Rhodesia I had little idea of where he stood politically or in terms of newspaper management. Nor did I feel much concern about that. It was MacPherson I was worried about. So I was on my guard from the outset, determined to make my position clear.

MacPherson began the discussion. 'We are thinking of appointing you editor of the *Rand Daily Mail*,' he said, 'and we'd like to hear what you feel about it.'

'Why do you want to make this change,' I asked, wanting to get directly to the nub of my concerns. 'And what is to become of Raymond Louw? Most people think he has done a great job at the Mail.'

'We think it's time for a change,' Walton chimed in. 'When Ray took the job I told him we felt he should be there only ten years. Now he's been there for 11, so we think it's time for a change.'

'Where will he go?' I asked.

'We're going to move him into management,' Walton replied.

'We're going to make him general manager.'

'But you've just got a new number two in management,' I said, pointing to Kinsley. 'There's Tony Fleischer as general manager and each newspaper has its own manager. How is this going to work?'

Walton, looking a bit uncomfortable, gave a vague reply. 'Oh, there's plenty to be done in management,' he said, 'don't worry about that, what with our change to the new computer technology that Ray has been involved in, and the arrival of TV last year. There're a lot of challenges and Ray is well equipped to help us meet them.

'Ray needs a break and this is a promotion for him,' he added.

Yeah, I thought to myself. Kicked upstairs.

I felt distinctly uncomfortable at this point. Clearly the board had decided to get rid of Ray as editor, and I had little doubt they wanted to remove him in order to change, or at least mute, the political stance of the paper. I suspected, too, that they were worried about a backlash from the paper's staff and loyal readers, and so they wanted someone with a liberal record to take over, someone who would be more malleable, easier to influence than the stubborn Ray Louw. Someone like me. And one could see why. Because I had 'depoliticised' the *Sunday Express* after Johnson's departure, they presumably felt I could be persuaded, or pressured, to do the same at the Mail.

I couldn't possibly allow myself to be used as their agent in such a manoeuvre. I had to disabuse them of that notion. Yet I didn't want to blow my chances of getting the job, not only because I obviously found the prospect of such a prestigious role appealing, but also for the sake of the paper I so admired. If they were getting rid of Ray and I turned down the job, who would they get to replace him? Would they find a really conservative editor somewhere else? Everything this great paper stood for would then be destroyed.

I had thought about this conundrum a good deal before the big moment came, but when the critical moment does come, when you have to declare your position, yes or no, decisiveness can sometimes desert you. The Hamlet syndrome.

But it didn't that day. Subtlety, I'm afraid, has never been my strong point. I tend to be forthright, often too forthright. And so I found myself setting out my position in no uncertain terms.

'Gentlemen,' I began, 'I want to make my position clear. I am greatly honoured that you should be offering me the editorship of the *Rand Daily Mail*. As you know, Mr MacPherson,' I said gesturing towards him, 'I'm a great supporter of its editorial policy. I was involved along with many others in shaping that policy under the editorship of Laurence Gandar, and I believe it has been well maintained by Raymond Louw. If you are wanting to make this change of editorship in order to change the Mail's editorial policy, then I must tell you I cannot do that. If that is what you want, you must find somebody else.'

I paused. There were nods and murmurs all round of, 'No, no, that's not what we want.' After a brief pause, I decided to press home the point.

'Gentlemen,' I said. 'I want this to be absolutely clearly understood, because I'm actually very happy to stay at the *Sunday Express*. The Mail is a hardship post, it's the toughest job in journalism, perhaps the toughest in the world, and I'm really very happy with what I'm doing.'

I pointed out that my wife had died not long before and I had remarried, which meant my new wife, still only 29, would have to cope with three young children. It was hardly an appropriate time for me to pitch into a hot seat.

What I didn't tell them is that Sue had expressed serious doubts about whether I should accept the job if it were offered. She was unsure whether she could cope with my fractious young boys and with my working long hours, which she knew the Mail job demanded. She certainly didn't relish the idea, and I suspect she even thought of ending our marriage if I accepted. She asked for time off on her own to think about it, so I drove with her to Durban where she checked into a hotel on her own while I went off to visit friends further down the coast. When I picked her up three days later, she put her arms around me and whispered: 'I love you too much, so I've made up my mind. I'll manage. Go ahead and accept. I know it means a lot to you.' Such a commitment demanded that I stand firm on my terms and not become a pawn in their hands.

'I must first get a clear assurance from each of you,' I told the group, 'that you are not offering me this job because you want me to change the editorial policy of the *Rand Daily Mail* to which you know I am committed.'

I then put the same question to each in turn, beginning with MacPherson, the man of whose motives I was so deeply suspicious. 'Is that clearly understood, Mr MacPherson? I want it from you personally that you do not require me to change the policies of the *Rand Daily Mail*.'

'That is correct,' he replied. Then I said: 'And you Mr Walton, and you Mr Kinsley.' I put it to each in turn, and got the same response. So I got it from them jointly and severally, in the most explicit terms, that the paper would continue unchanged in its editorial policy.

In his history of the company, Joel Mervis chastises the board for allowing me to 'decide the *Rand Daily Mail*'s future policy', to which they responded with 'docile deference'. He contends that they should have laid down their own forthright claim that 'the board, and the board alone, laid down newspaper policy', and that 'their meek acceptance of the Sparks ultimatum was astounding'.[2]

I dispute his contention that I decided the paper's future policy, or that I issued an ultimatum. That is unwarranted. The *Rand Daily Mail*'s policy had been firmly established and internationally acclaimed for the past 20 years. I certainly didn't decide it. All I did was to ask them whether they would require me to change it. Any potential employee has the right to ask what the terms of his employment will be, and to state whether he is prepared to accept them or not, which is what I asked for and which they gave me. As for issuing an ultimatum, that is absurd. An ultimatum implies a threat of retaliation and I had no way of retaliating beyond saying, 'No thanks.'

No, the only problem with that conversation is that they lied to me. All three of them.

When Mervis, while preparing his book, asked MacPherson why he had appointed me in spite of my 'ultimatum', the chairman replied that he thought I was 'putting on an act', and that he did not take me seriously.[3]

* * *

MY TRANSFER to the Mail was seamless. Ray organised a staff meeting in the newsroom and introduced me, which was hardly necessary since I knew nearly everyone and they knew me. It was a gracious gesture, and it gave me an opportunity to address the staff, telling them there were going to be no changes in editorial policy but that there would be some reshuffling of staff positions that I would announce soon.

Rex Gibson was replacing me as editor of the *Sunday Express*, so I would need a new deputy. I decided to offer the job to Benjamin Pogrund, who was then doing a sabbatical stint on *The Boston Globe* and whom I knew was thinking of settling in the United States following the bruising experience of the prisons case. I knew some members of the board blamed him for landing the paper in costly trouble over those reports, and that MacPherson in particular disliked him. But I knew him to be a good journalist with a lot of valuable contacts, especially in the black political community. He was a forceful personality with a passionate commitment to the Mail, and I felt I needed that kind of backup.

I wanted Dave Hazelhurst back with me as managing editor, to take charge of the engine room of the newspaper, and my old friend John Ryan to rejoin me from the Express as an assistant editor. We needed another assistant editor to replace Koos Viviers, whom Rex wanted to take from the Mail as his deputy. In a bid to redress the male dominance of senior staff that had prevailed since the beginning of time, I appointed Lin Menge, a former schoolteacher who had made a career switch and become a fine reporter, as an assistant editor. She was a strong personality with a critical mind who was always ready to challenge authority. Every leader needs that.

I also wanted to crack the colour bar at the senior staff level, which was difficult in the face of the apartheid laws. We had a number of good black reporters, but black people were not supposed to be in positions where they could give orders to whites. I managed to slip John Mojapelo, recently returned from a Nieman Fellowship at Harvard, on to the news desk as assistant news editor.

But my main focus was on the paper's political staff, which I wanted to structure in readiness for what I saw as the imminent emergence of a major shift in the political landscape. A revival of black politics was taking shape, encouraged by the rapid growth of Steve Biko's Black Consciousness Movement. It was this black political reawakening that had ignited the 16 June uprising.

But there were even more important stirrings on the black labour front. The South African economy had surged forward during the 1960s, a phenomenon that prompted a cynic to observe that South Africa advanced 'by political disaster and economic windfall'. The booming economy meant the country was running short of skilled labour. Underpaid black workers, sensing their power, launched a series of impromptu mass strikes, beginning among textile workers in Natal province in 1973, which swelled into a form of rolling mass action. The employers were in despair. Black trade unionism was forbidden under the apartheid system, and it was a crime for black workers to strike. But the police could not force these large numbers to go to work, and the employers had no way of persuading them. As one exasperated employer put it: 'How the hell do you negotiate with a mob on a football field?' They needed leaders with whom they could cut deals. And so Prime Minister Vorster found himself under pressure to appoint a commission to consider legalising black trade unionism.

He appointed Professor Nic Wiehahn of the University of South Africa to head the commission. I had met Wiehahn and found him to be an enlightened man. I had little doubt he would recommend legalising black unionism, because there was no other way out of the cul-de-sac in which the industrialists found themselves. And I saw those two factors – the revival of black activism and the empowerment of black workers – as pointing to the emergence of black political muscle at a level South Africa had never experienced before.

The Black Consciousness Movement was generating new political energy, and the power of strike action would give blacks real political leverage, a toehold in realpolitik. I reckoned that could make it a turning point in our history, and although it was still two years before Wiehahn was to deliver his report, I felt the Mail should prepare itself for a massive change in the political scene. The days of white politics were drawing to a close and a new phase of direct black-white political confrontation was about to hit us — with the business community caught in the crossfire. It didn't occur to me at the time that this latter factor was likely to exacerbate the Mail's political problems. I was simply making an editorial judgment about what the next big national story was going to be, and how we should start preparing our newsroom to handle it.

I set about reshaping the political team with that in mind. I negotiated with Gibson to bring Martin Schneider to the Mail as political editor, and appointed Helen Zille, who had shown herself to be a star in the company's training programme, to my old job of political correspondent, covering the all-white Parliament. At the same time I appointed the talented Indian reporter, Ameen Akhalwaya, who was close to the Black Consciousness Movement, as a political reporter specialising in political events outside Parliament.

My main innovation was to build a strong team covering labour affairs. Traditionally the mainstream papers had employed a single labour correspondent to cover the relatively minor affairs of the white trade unions. But now that I saw labour as the coming new factor in our politics I decided to strengthen that sector. I appointed three top-rate specialists to cover labour developments: Steven Friedman, who was later to become a professor and much-quoted public intellectual; Phillip van Niekerk, who later became editor of the *Mail & Guardian* weekly; and Riaan de Villiers, liberal son of a distinguished Afrikaner advocate and CEO of the big Afrikaans newspaper chain, Naspers. It was the strongest labour team ever assembled on any South African newspaper.

Zille was my most unconventional appointment, because of her youth and because women were a rare presence in the Press Gallery at that time. But I saw great talent in her. She had grown up in my suburb of Rivonia and had come to me as a schoolgirl to

In my office as editor of the Rand Daily Mail. *I still have the typewriter, which had belonged to Laurence Gandar.*

ask my advice about becoming a journalist. I remember telling her to take a basic arts degree in politics, philosophy and economics – I was not enamoured of journalism as an academic subject – to make herself fluent in Afrikaans, and to study shorthand. This she did, went through our training programme, which included a stint under me at the *Sunday Express*, and became an outstanding reporter. Zille later became leader of the main opposition party in the new South Africa, the Democratic Alliance.

In other words, one helluva team. And it bore results. The Mail's political coverage became by far the best in the country, both in its depth of analysis and in the spread of its reportage. But it was in our reporting of the emergence of South Africa's first organised black labour movement where we really took the lead. In 1979, the Wiehahn Commission duly recommended the legalising of black trade unionism, and the government had little option but to accept it. The new movement began cautiously, focusing only on so-called workerist issues to avoid provoking the regime into acting against it on political grounds until it had gained strength. The new formation called itself the Federation of South African Trade Unions (Fosatu), but it quickly morphed into an effective political pressure group and changed its name in 1985 to the Congress of South African Trade Unions (Cosatu), thus cleverly implying an affinity to the banned Congress movement.

There was one other appointment that was to play a significant role in my future – my secretary, Gina Pogorzelsky, whom I had hired while at the Express on Gordon Winter's recommendation when Johnny Johnson's secretary quit as he departed. She was young, stylish, super-efficient and I liked her. I negotiated with Rex for her to transfer with me when the changeover came. A big mistake.

The staff changes worked well and brought results. The strength of our political coverage, and particularly our strong focus on the emergence of the black labour movement, brought a rapid increase in our black readership. This was amplified by the closure of *The World*, many of whose readers switched to the Mail to get their news. In time our black readership equalled, then exceeded, our white readership. This made the Mail unique, the only paper in the country that reached across all race groups to the extent that we did. As I wrote in a memorandum to yet another commission appointed by the government to investigate the press: 'Apartheid South Africa is a cellular society in which each race group lives in a separate cell, completely cut off from any meaningful contact with all the other groups living in their separate cells. In this dangerous situation of mutual isolation the *Rand Daily Mail* is the only institution in the country that communicates across all the race groups, telling each in its cell something about the others.' I wrote that with pride. But it had consequences.

* * *

JUST FIVE MONTHS after I had taken over at the Mail, one of the seismic stories of the apartheid era broke. The news editor, Chris Day, dashed into my office just before the morning news conference on 13 September 1977 clutching a sheet of telex paper. 'We've just had a flash message, Steve Biko is dead,' he blurted out.

I was stunned. 'He was detained just the other day for breaking his banning order,' I said. 'That means he must have died in Security Branch custody.'

'Yes, that's right,' Day replied, 'but all we've got at the moment is this flash from Sapa. I'll keep you informed as the details come in.'

This was obviously going to be a huge story, my first big challenge as editor of the Mail. Stephen Bantu Biko was the hero figure in the black community at that moment, even outshining memories of the imprisoned Nelson Mandela and the silenced ANC. Biko had been served with a banning order silencing him and confining him to the magisterial district of King William's Town in the eastern Cape Province. But the Black Consciousness Movement, which he had founded in 1963 after breaking away from the multiracial National Union of South African Students (Nusas) to form the black South African Students' Organisation (Saso), had spawned a range of other community organisations across the country. The movement's philosophy, that blacks should liberate themselves psychologically and become self-reliant in

346

order to overcome their 'slave mentality', had captured the imagination of the black masses, the youth particularly, and re-energised
black politics.

Black Consciousness had driven the 16 June student uprising, which had still not fully subsided. It seemed obvious to me
that Biko's death in detention was going to trigger another mass
upheaval of black anger.

But worse was to come. At our morning news conference Day
informed us that the Minister of Police, James Kruger, had made
a statement in Parliament that Biko had died in custody 'as a
result of going on a hunger strike', the outcome of which, he added,
'leaves me cold'.

I called Donald Woods, editor of the *Daily Dispatch*, whose paper
was just a half-hour drive from where Biko was confined, and who
had been visiting him frequently. Donald had been telling me for
months how impressed he was with the young leader, how he
had come to accept that Biko's unwillingness to ally himself with
white liberals was not racist but was a strategy rooted in the belief
that black self-emancipation was an essential first step to national
liberation. They had become close friends and mutual admirers.

When Donald answered my call he was beside himself with
rage. 'Kruger's lying,' he exploded. 'Steve would never have gone
on a hunger strike. He'd been in detention several times before
and he's always relished challenging his interrogators because he's
brighter than them. This time the bastards have killed him. But
I'll tell you this, Allister. They'll pay for it. I'll make sure of that.'

This was not the Donald I knew. He was normally a light-
hearted fellow, witty and full of wisecracks, given to writing little
rhymes and songs full of puns and wordplays mocking the follies
of the apartheid system and its pompous legislators. Now he
was breathing fire and revenge, which left me shuddering at the
thought of what Biko's black admirers must be feeling.

Two days later I received a call from Dr Jonathan Gluckman, a
pathologist who was part of a group of liberal medical and legal
friends with whom I socialised. 'Won't you please come to my
home as soon as possible, I want to talk to you,' he said.

I drove immediately to his home in the upmarket suburb of

Parktown, where I found Gluckman sitting in his study. He was a tall, rotund man with a slightly pompous air that concealed a passionate humanitarianism that drove him into some of the darkest corners of the apartheid state — its mortuaries. He lived graciously, with a liking for fine French wines and Cuban cigars. I once asked him why, with his refined tastes and medical skills, he spent his time cutting up cadavers rather than healing the sick.

'Because,' he said simply, 'that's where the truth lies.' It was his passion for the truth that had prompted him to phone me.

Gluckman was in a state of agitation as we greeted each other. 'Thanks for coming,' he said. 'But let's not talk here. Come into the garden.' This was a common precaution in those days to avoid the listening devices used by the security police. So we walked into the garden and sat under a shade tree. Gluckman leaned closer to me and spoke in a barely audible whisper. 'The Biko family appointed me as their pathologist and I've just come away from the postmortem examination in Pretoria this morning,' he told me, 'and I can tell you that Kruger is lying. Biko didn't die of a hunger strike. He died of brain damage. He was beaten to death.'

Gluckman went on to explain the medical details of his finding. It was clear there had never been any hunger strike, he said, because Biko was not emaciated and there was food in his stomach at the time of his death. But the brain had taken a severe knock. It had inflicted what he called a 'contra-coup', which meant a heavy blow on the front of the head had caused the brain to jolt backwards and impact against the back of the skull, inflicting a traumatic brain injury. That is what had killed him.

Gluckman showed me the death certificate, signed by both himself and the state pathologist. There, in the space for declaring cause of death, was clearly written: 'Brain damage.' There could be no doubt about what had happened, and now I knew the incontrovertible truth. Biko had been killed by his interrogators and the Minister of Justice and Police had lied in Parliament to protect his men.

'It is important that you publish this as soon as possible,' Gluckman urged. 'I believe Kruger wants to brush the issue aside as a death caused by a hunger strike and there is therefore no need for an inquest. He mustn't be allowed to get away with that.

'But you can't use my name, and I can't give you a copy of this death certificate,' Gluckman added. 'Because I shouldn't have given you this information and if it becomes known that I did I won't be able to testify at the inquest.'

I gave Gluckman my pledge of confidentiality. It was a pledge I honoured until after his death 16 years later. I didn't mention it to anyone outside a small group of need-to-know senior staffers at the *Rand Daily Mail* and my lawyers. But talk about being between a rock and a hard place. I knew the truth with absolute certainty, and it was obviously in the most profound public interest that I publish it. But how, when I was bound not to reveal the source of my information? How could I prove the truth if challenged?

This is not a unique dilemma in journalism. It happens often. But never before in my career had the conundrum been so tightly drawn – the need to publish so imperative, the difficulty of doing that so great and the implications so dangerous in the prevailing authoritarian climate.

My first decision was that I had to publish, come what may.

We knew the truth, what we needed now was to try to find something to hang it on, since we couldn't disclose our primary source. The only possible source I could think of, other than Biko's interrogators, who would obviously give us nothing, were the state's doctors who had examined him in detention. They were, after all, physicians, not cops, with an ethical commitment to act independently in the interests of their patient. So I decided to target them.

My next decision was to call in Helen Zille.

She was young, but I already had a high regard for her level of accuracy, backed up by verbatim shorthand in both English and Afrikaans. This was before the days of light, portable tape recorders and we could not afford any mistakes or allegations of misreporting. We needed an accurate record of what was said as a backup. I also judged Zille to be determined and smart, with a political savvy that I thought would enable her to think on her feet in what was going to be a helluva tough assignment.

So Zille flew to Port Elizabeth to confront the 'Biko doctors':

Dr Ivor Lang, the district surgeon who was the first to examine Biko after one of the security policemen reported that he was behaving strangely and not responding to questions; Dr Benjamin Tucker, the chief district surgeon who was called in a day later and found Biko lying naked on a mat soaked with urine and complaining of pains in his head and neck; and Dr Colin Hersch, a specialist physician who had examined Biko in a prison hospital. Hersch had given him a lumbar puncture that revealed blood in the cerebro-spinal fluid — a clear indication of possible brain damage.

The first two were worse than uncooperative. Tucker refused to answer any questions, eventually slamming the door in Zille's face. Lang was simply abusive, cursing Zille and threatening to put his dogs on to her. Hersch was different. He invited Zille into his home, and was both apologetic and ill at ease. It was a dreadful case, he told her, and he was aware that a very serious situation existed, but he had been instructed not to talk about it. 'I felt quite a lot of empathy for him,' Zille told me. 'It was clear he knew the truth but he'd been ordered not to talk about it and was visibly grappling with his conscience.'

We felt Hersch's disclosure that he had been sworn to silence and his obvious discomfort spoke volumes. Even more important for our purposes, as we unpacked the information after Zille's return, was that none of the doctors had been prepared to confirm Kruger's hunger strike allegation when she put it to them. We took that as amounting to an admission that there was no such evidence, since they could not possibly have got into trouble with the authorities for confirming the minister's statement.

Zille and I composed a carefully worded report that began: 'An investigation by the *Rand Daily Mail*, which included interviews with doctors who examined Steve Biko in detention, has revealed that the Black Consciousness leader showed no signs of a hunger strike or dehydration.'

It went on to say that our investigation indicated that Biko had died of brain damage and that the facts we had unearthed contradicted Kruger's statements. It stated that, far from having died of a hunger strike, Biko was in fact slightly overweight when he died. His well-developed body weighed between 85 and 90 kg when it was delivered for burial. We published the report under a banner headline: 'No sign of hunger strike – Biko doctors.' We did not put the phrase in quotes, which we felt covered the fact that the doctors had not actually said that in so many words but had clearly implied it. And, of course, Gluckman was also a 'Biko doctor'.

Kruger was apoplectic. He protested that the report was false and demanded an immediate hearing that very day of the Press Council, a body set up by the Newspaper Press Union (NPU), the proprietors' organisation, in the face of threats by Prime Minister Vorster to pass a press control law if the newspapers did not 'discipline themselves'.

I refused Kruger's demand for an immediate hearing. The rules of the Press Council allowed an editor seven days to respond to a complaint and I didn't want to be bullied by Kruger into forsaking that right. I also felt there was a good chance of the facts of Biko's death becoming public during the week, now that we had opened this can of worms, and that this would force Kruger to drop his complaint. But the newspaper proprietors were in a panic. The president of the NPU came to see me, pleading with me to abandon my rights, saying they feared Vorster would use any delay as an excuse to claim the Press Council was ineffective, and he was therefore going to introduce statutory press control. Finally my own managing director, Leycester Walton, came to me saying our board was worried that if Vorster did carry out his threat, everyone would blame the Mail for having brought about press control.

Under this pressure from people I felt should be my supporters, I yielded. I should not have done so. In retrospect I have become convinced that when you face this kind of political blackmail in an authoritarian society it is better to stand your ground and challenge the authorities to do their worst – and to be seen to be doing so by all the world. The prospect of open confrontation might make them back off, but even if they don't it is better not to become complicit in their cover-up games. Let the public see what is happening. But the pressure from my own industry, particularly my own proprietors, tipped the balance and caused me reluctantly to agree. It was my first direct experience of the double whammy of government pressure and unsympathetic proprietors, which had driven my two predecessors from the editorial chair of the Mail, and which in time was to drive me out as well and eventually to shut down that great newspaper just as its moment of vindication was at hand.

So that night I appeared before the Press Council, constituted like a court with a retired Appeal Court judge, Oscar Galgut, presiding. I was represented by that superb advocate, Sydney Kentridge. Kruger, having lodged his complaint in writing, did not bother to attend.

As the hearing got under way it became clear that if the NPU feared a refusal to hold an urgent hearing would be unacceptable to Vorster, so too would an acquittal. Not being able to call Gluckman as a witness to cite the postmortem report made our case difficult to present, but even so it was evident that Kentridge's assurance that he personally knew the identity of our confidential primary source, and that he could vouch for his integrity, cut no ice with Galgut. He had a scalp to deliver on behalf of the NPU.

Even when Kentridge pointed out that the minister hadn't contested a single fact in the report but had simply claimed the headline didn't accurately reflect the body of the report, which Kentridge described as a matter of 'syntactical trivia' since the headline had not been a direct quotation, Galgut wasn't interested. He found in favour of Kruger, saying the report was 'misleading and tendentious', and ordered the Mail to publish a correction and apology on its front page next morning. Since it was already 1 am, it meant we had to stop the presses and do that in the early hours.

Kentridge was furious. I'll never forget Galgut's face as this legendary legal figure told him bluntly that his judgment was 'completely unacceptable' and that the newspaper reserved the right of review in court on the grounds that no reasonable tribunal could possibly have come to such a conclusion.

The case didn't go on review. The proprietors, relieved that the Press Council had been able to deliver the scalp to mollify Vorster and Kruger, were happy to let it go at that. So the verdict of

352

misleading and tendentious reporting in the Biko case still stands against me. Guilty of reporting the truth.

But the inquest duly took place, with Gluckman as the principal witness, revealing in all its hideous detail how Biko had been killed; how he had been beaten into a semi-conscious state, then chained naked and shackled to a grille in a crucifixion position for 12 hours; and how, when he was clearly dying, his torturers tried to wash their hands of him. They transferred him, still naked and shackled, in the back of a Land Rover on a 1 200-km journey through the night to a prison hospital in Pretoria, where he arrived with no medical papers specifying his condition. There he was placed on a gurney and left in a corridor, where he died unattended.

As all this poured out over the course of 15 days. Helen Zille and other reporters were there to give massive, almost verbatim coverage, day after day, telling it all to an appalled public. Yet even then the presiding magistrate tried to continue the whitewash with a shameful finding that while Biko had died of brain damage, no one could be held criminally responsible for his death. But we on the Mail had the satisfaction of knowing that the truth was out in the public domain. It provided the basis, in 1985, for the South African Medical and Dental Council (SAMDC) to strike two of the Biko doctors, Tucker and Lang, off the medical register.

There was a revealing coda to this shameful affair. Some years later Benjamin Tucker, the chief district surgeon who had slammed his door in Helen Zille's face, wrote to the SAMDC seeking reinstatement. His *mea culpa* offers some insight into how easily a totalitarian system can corrode the morality of those who work within it.

'I came to realise,' Tucker wrote, 'that over a period of ten years I had been working as a district surgeon, I had gradually lost the fearless independence that is required of a medical practitioner when the interests of the patient are threatened. I had become too closely identified with the interest of the organs of the state, especially of the police force, with which I dealt practically on a daily basis.'

* * *

POLITICAL UNREST continued to roil the black townships in the days following Biko's death and the huge funeral rally that took place near King William's Town on 25 September. Ten thousand people arrived from all parts of the country, and police armed with automatic weapons turned back thousands more at roadblocks. Thirteen Western countries sent diplomats. It was an occasion that fumed with fury and teetered on the edge of violence.

Three weeks later the Vorster regime dealt a legal death blow to the Black Consciousness Movement and all its affiliates, including the Union of Black Journalists. In what became known as Black Wednesday, 19 October, the government banned several black newspapers and jailed editors and journalists under its detention-without-trial laws. The Mail escaped, saved no doubt by its prominent international image.

Soon after this, Donald Woods arrived unexpectedly at my office. He looked tense and hurried as my secretary, Gina, ushered him in. 'I wanted you to be the first to know,' he told me in a low voice as he sat down. 'I'm flying to London tonight. I'm going straight to the airport from here. Nobody else knows about this outside of my family and now you. I'm going to speak to journalists and important political figures about Steve, what an important figure he was. The world must know what a tragedy his death is and that it was the state that killed him.'

We chatted on in this vein for a while, until Donald said he had to leave for the airport, I arranged for a company car to take him there, wished him well, and he left.

Some hours later I learned that the security police had arrested him at the airport. How they knew he was going there puzzled me, but I got the newsroom working on the story for the next day's paper. It turned out that Donald had been served with a banning order, bundled into a police car and driven off to East London. The banning order meant he could no longer leave the magisterial district of East London, be in the company of more than one other person at a time, address any gathering or enter any newspaper office, and that nothing he said or wrote could be published. Like Percy Qoboza, editor of the newly banned black newspaper, *The World*, the ban meant he could no longer work as a journalist.

But Donald was a resourceful fellow and not easily deterred. As he told me later, his mind was racing all the way on that long drive to East London. He chatted quite amiably with his captors. When they reached the border of the Cape Province after midnight, he had to be transferred to another police car for the rest of the journey. At which point he shook hands with the two men who had driven him that far, bade them farewell and asked them to deliver a personal message to Justice minister Kruger.

'Tell your boss,' Donald said sternly in Afrikaans, 'to remember the law of Transvaal.' The two men chuckled knowingly, for it was a well-known aphorism derived from the days of the old Boer republics. '*Kak en betaal, is die wet van Transvaal*,' which, delicately translated, means there'll be payback for this dirty deed.

And indeed there was. In spades.

Come December, my family and I drove back to my old stamping ground of the eastern Cape for our annual summer holiday. We stopped over at Donald's home in East London and, being careful not to meet him together, which would have constituted a criminal offence, Donald drew me aside and led me into the garden where we could talk one on one and hopefully out of listening-device range. He told me the security police kept a constant watch on his home from a building across the street and that he had been subjected to a good deal of harassment, with insults and threats daubed on his front door. Worst of all, his two-year-old daughter Mary had been sent what purported to be a gift parcel containing a toddler's T-shirt. It had been infused with a harsh skin irritant that sent the poor child screaming in pain.

'I'm going to skip the country,' Donald whispered to me in the garden. 'I've written a book about Steve and what they did to him, and I'm going to take the manuscript with me and get it published abroad. The world must know what these bastards have done.'

He didn't tell me how he was going to leave the country, since his passport had been withdrawn, and I didn't ask. The less one knows in such circumstances, the less one can disclose under

355

extreme pressure. What he did add, though, was that he planned to go on a speaking tour of the Western world, particularly Britain and the United States, to promote the book and call on the governments of those countries to apply sanctions against South Africa. International sanctions, he believed, was what would finally bring the apartheid regime to its knees. And he was not wrong. There is consensus today that international sanctions, combined with a massive uprising of township youth across the country, were the decisive pressures that persuaded the regime to abandon apartheid and release Nelson Mandela. And certainly Donald did as much as anyone to bring about those sanctions.

Donald's escape from the country was both courageous and hilarious. A friendly Australian diplomat helped smuggle him across the border into Lesotho, where he picked up temporary travel documents and flew out to London. When he landed, a British reporter asked him how he had managed to enter Lesotho. Always the humorist, Donald gave him the most outrageous answer. He was an ardent admirer of Winston Churchill and took delight in mimicking the great man's voice and appropriating his quips. Churchill had once claimed, tongue in cheek, that his famed escape from a Boer War prisoner-of-war camp in Pretoria had been achieved by crossing the 'mighty Apies River'. The Apies, as it happens, is a tiny brooklet any child can jump across. So Donald, who was obviously not going to compromise his Australian diplomat pal, told the reporter blithely: 'Oh, I had to swim the crocodile-infested Caledon River' – a waterway where no such reptile has ever been seen. That is what was printed, to the derision of Donald's enemies and delight of his friends.

During his 12 years in exile, Donald delivered 426 lectures in the United States alone, lobbied the governments of 37 countries on the need for sanctions, and became the only private citizen to be invited to address the United Nations Security Council. But his greatest impact came from the film *Cry Freedom*, which director Richard Attenborough based on Donald's book about Biko. The film was released in 1987 to international acclaim and won a number of awards. Its popular influence was immense.

Thus was the law of Transvaal applied.

CHAPTER TWENTY-ONE

The Mervyn and Myrtle Show

MERVYN REES was the mildest of men. Tall, lean and softly spoken, he was the last person one would expect to find occupying one of the toughest positions in any newsroom, that of chief crime reporter. He was as far as one could imagine from the Hollywood stereotype of the hard-bitten, hard-drinking, gung-ho newshound with a fedora pulled low over his brow, joshing it up with crooks and cops in some rowdy Runyonesque bar. Mervyn was always neatly turned out in suit and tie, and his drink of choice was Coca-Cola. At age 36 one could have mistaken him for a bank clerk. But he smoked. Pirellis. Sixty a day, which was the only indication of the stresses that went with his job.

How Rees managed to hit it off with members of the South African Police always baffled me. But he did. His network of police contacts was unmatched, and he always seemed to know exactly who to call on any case he was investigating. There was no other reporter in the country, except perhaps Kitt Katzin on the *Sunday Express*, who could touch him when it came to cracking the big crime and investigative stories.

What made Rees's performance even more remarkable was that the police, down to the most junior constable, loathed the newspaper he worked for. They were the front-line enforcers of the apartheid laws, which meant the liberal *Rand Daily Mail*, which was constantly exposing their heavy-handed excesses, was anathema to them. Yet Rees moved easily among them, taking notes as they gave him scoops.

There was no magic in this. It was simply professionalism. Mervyn Rees's main attribute was that he was unfailingly accurate and fair. Although passionately loyal to the Mail, he was himself pretty much apolitical, so he never allowed the image of his employer to get in his way. He had a quietly persuasive manner and, most important of all, over the years he had built up a reputation for absolute integrity. He knew and played by the rules of confidentiality; if he gave his word that an informant's identity would not be disclosed, that individual knew Mervyn would take that identity secret with him to his grave. As indeed he did with many such cases when, finally, the Pirellis laid him low with lung cancer.

Early in August 1977, Rees came to my office bearing what might be called a slow-fuse time bomb. He told me about a confidential meeting he had just had with a senior civil servant, to whom he had been introduced by one of his most trusted contacts. The man, whom he named only as Daan, was both troubled and nervous, seemingly fearful for both his job and possibly his life, but at the same time conscience-stricken because he had become aware of a massive scandal brewing in the government's Department of Information. Top government people were involved, he told Rees, and so was a great deal of money.

'This is not going to come out easily,' Daan had said. 'There's too much at stake.' Even he, with all his political contacts in Pretoria, knew only the barest details. He had also given Rees a chilly warning. Speaking to Mervyn's contact, Daan had added: 'If this man is a friend of yours, you'd better tell him to watch his back.'

The import of this tip-off was immediately apparent. I smelt a massive scoop in the offing, but how were we going to tackle it? The Mail's grim experience of the prisons case, and of the state's ruthless ability to bribe and threaten witnesses, came sharply to mind. Apartheid South Africa was effectively a police state, and if top government people were involved, as Daan had said, they would stop at nothing to clamp down on any newspaper threatening to expose their nefarious activities. The Vorster regime had already closed down several newspapers and banned two editors. I had no doubt that if the Mail were to make one false step, like publishing information from a confidential informant like Daan who could not be produced in court, they would shut us down too.

So Daan's warning to Rees to watch his back was not only pertinent to him in a personal sense, which was realistic enough, but also to the survival of the country's most important newspaper.

After pondering these daunting problems, I called Rees and assistant editor Chris Day to my office to discuss a strategy that was beginning to take shape in my mind. I told them I wanted them to take on this assignment as a team, full time, but that, given the experience of the prisons case, we could not simply approach it in the normal journalistic way of gathering the information needed to publish a story. We would simultaneously have to prepare for the court case, or series of cases, that might follow. That was why I wanted the two of them to work together, so that there would always be a primary and a corroborative witness for every fact we published.

More important still, since Daan had indicated that this was a wide-ranging story with many tentacles, it would be wise for us not to publish it piecemeal as we uncovered fragments of the whole, because that might prompt the regime to take action against us before we could get to the big story. Better to hold our fire until we had all, or most, of the total story, at which point we could drop a bomb so big that it would be too late to stop us. They would be thrown off balance and public opinion would be on our side. 'So let's wait until we can see the whites of their eyes,' I told Rees and Day.

It was a high-risk strategy, for it meant that, even if we got well ahead of our rivals in gathering the information, we could still be beaten on the story by someone else publishing a significant chunk of it first. But I felt it was a risk we would have to take. It was a decision that might well have outraged many hard-charging young reporters, but Rees and Day had the maturity to accept that it was the most sensible strategy to follow.

So began a journalistic operation that was to last more than two years and span four continents. The rivalry from other publications was intense, but in the end the *Rand Daily Mail* and the *Sunday Express* won hands down, the Mail trouncing its daily rival, *The Star*, and the Express overshadowing its much bigger and more expansively staffed sister paper, the *Sunday Times*. In his memoir, Joel Mervis was to describe the operation as 'perhaps the most brilliant exploit in the history of the Times Media group, carried out in the finest traditions of investigative reporting'.[1] To which I would add that it might be rated the finest achievement in the entire history of South African journalism – one that brought down a hardline prime minister and altered the course of political events in the country.

We began pretty cold on the trail. The only clue we had was that the scandal was centred on the Department of Information. This was a newly established government department headed by Dr Cornelius 'Connie' Mulder, who as leader of the National Party in Transvaal province was the most powerful figure in the ruling party after Prime Minister Vorster, and his most likely successor. We knew, too, that soon after his appointment to the Information portfolio, Mulder had gone on a world tour, accompanied by the department's secretary, Gerald Barrie, to study the relentlessly critical media coverage of apartheid South Africa. Mulder returned convinced there was what he called a highly organised and generously funded 'international propaganda offensive' against South Africa. He advised Vorster to allow his department to mount a counteroffensive, using covert means if necessary.

At the same time Mulder plainly considered Barrie to be too stolid and orthodox a personality to carry out the project he had in mind. He turned instead to the flamboyant young Eschel Rhoodie, who had served in the country's information service in the United States, Australia and the Netherlands, to replace Barrie, who he arranged to have kicked upstairs into the role of Auditor-General. Mulder then picked a young Afrikaner journalist, Lourens Erasmus Smit de Villiers, nicknamed 'Les' because of his initials, who had also represented the information service in the United States and Canada, as the department's deputy secretary. The two made an energetic and innovative pair.

Both Rhoodie and De Villiers had written books aimed at presenting South Africa in a better light. Rhoodie's book, *The Paper Curtain*, dealing with what he called the international media's misinterpretation of apartheid and its failure to highlight black atrocities in the rest of Africa, had attracted some attention. Around that time Rhoodie had also met a former CIA agent, whom he described only as a 'Mr Brown', who had told him that 'the only way to control the media is to own it, or to own some of the senior people in it'.[2] A sliver of advice that shaped Rhoodie's entire career.

These fragments indicated there was a likelihood that the big scandal Daan had talked about was somehow related to the recent attempt by Louis Luyt to buy South African Associated Newspapers (SAAN) and, when that was thwarted, to launch *The Citizen*. This line of thinking was strengthened by the fact that shortly before I took over the editorship of the Mail, my predecessor, Raymond Louw, had expressed doubts about *The Citizen*'s boast that it was selling 90 000 copies a day. With his thorough understanding of the newspaper industry, Louw reckoned that was simply not possible. So, enterprising journalist that he was, he organised a Mail investigation. A team of reporters, headed by then assistant editor Koos Viviers and including both Rees and Day, rented a big camper van, which they parked one night near *The Citizen*'s printing works. From there they watched copies of the paper being loaded into delivery vans. After the last of the vans had departed they waited until, some hours later, a large truck arrived, into which thousands more papers were loaded. The Mail team followed this later truck until it arrived at a farm, later identified as belonging to Luyt, where the papers were dumped.

The Mail team kept up this tracking operation for two months, by which time they calculated that up to 30 000 copies of *The Citizen* were being dumped each day without being put out for sale. Clearly the newspaper was being produced at a huge loss. Who was footing the bill? Luyt was a wealthy man, but not that wealthy, and he was certainly not known as a businessman with a lust for loss. It seemed likely some other source was bearing the costs.

* * *

REES SPENT WEEKS prowling around the clubs and haunts of Pretoria frequented by the capital city's half-million civil servants. It was a foreign maze to him: Rees had never worked in a political environment before, but he had a quiet charm that enabled him to engage easily in conversations. He soon picked up that the gossip of the moment was about the high-flying lifestyle of the new regime at the Department of Information, the way they were throwing money around, holding lavish parties, taking overseas trips and how the young and handsome Eschel Rhoodie was the glamour boy of the social scene. His Italian-Afrikaner wife, Katie, was always fashionably dressed and there seemed to be an endless array of attractive young secretaries around.

Rees met one of these, a young woman named Trixie, who had done some work for Rhoodie and spoke glowingly of his charm, his charisma and his passionate dedication to the role he believed he was playing for his country. 'He works and plays hard,' she told Rees, 'but he gets you to do the same for him. He's easy to get on with and he makes you feel important, so much so that you'll do anything for him.'[3] Trixie confessed to having been 'a little in love' with Rhoodie. There were tales of girlfriends and jiltings and quite a few broken hearts. Money and power, as Henry Kissinger once noted, constitute a powerful aphrodisiac.

All interesting stuff, but none of it publishable according to the strategy I had laid down. Time was passing and we were making little headway in gathering hard facts. Then came a galvanising moment. Gerald Barrie, in his new role as Auditor-General – and, possibly smarting from Mulder's having replaced him with Rhoodie – tabled a report in Parliament criticising two unnamed officials of the Department of Information (clearly Rhoodie and De Villiers) for making unnecessary trips abroad. Barrie also said the department had been using money without Treasury approval. This was followed soon afterwards by a Kitt Katzin report in the *Sunday Express* revealing that Rhoodie had flown a party of ten, including his wife, their daughter and a relative, as well as Les de Villiers and his wife, on a holiday trip to the Seychelles. It was ostensibly to enable Rhoodie to have talks with the President of the Seychelles, James Mancham, about landing rights for South African Airways, but it was patently also an extravagant holiday for Rhoodie and his friends on those playground isles.

Typically, this stung Rhoodie into an aggressive response. In a blazing press statement he accused Barrie of violating the Official Secrets Act by leaking documents classified as secret to the media, disclosing 'sensitive and even highly secret operations funded by secret funds under the control of the Information Department'. The department was undertaking these secret operations at the government's request, he said, 'as counter-action to the propaganda war being waged against South Africa'. For this, Rhoodie added, 'a secret fund was provided to the Department of Information but I do not intend, now or ever, to say how much or in what way it reached me.'

For us, it was an 'Aha!' moment. The disclosure that Rhoodie's department had secret funding for secret propaganda purposes pointed to the strong likelihood that this was the source of the big scandal Daan had spoken about, and that the attempt to buy SAAN and then launch *The Citizen* were part of it.

But how to get the proof? I called a meeting of our team. Now that we had the broad outline of the big picture, we reasoned, it was time to move from the periphery of our investigation to the centre. We had a lot of fragments from a wide range of informants; what we needed now was to find a contact closer to the heart of the scandal who could pull it all together. In other words, I said, recalling the *Washington Post*'s breaking of the Watergate scandal, we needed a 'Deep Throat' who could give us the big picture, even though that would almost certainly be someone who could not be quoted or produced as a witness in court.

We drew up a list of all the contacts the members of the team – which now included senior reporter Don Marshall – had encountered, trying to assess each one's potential. At that moment I had a prescient thought. The women. We had heard a lot about women being caught up in this Playboy scene and of some being jilted and hurt. Could we not find one who knew a lot and might be willing to talk?

363

We ran through the list of contacts again and Rees came up with the name of a young woman he had heard about, but never met, who was said to be close to the action but in a particularly vulnerable position. 'Try her,' I suggested.

That was easier said than done. Rees made the contact, but the woman was terrified to be seen speaking to anyone from the *Rand Daily Mail*. 'Are you mad?' she blurted out when he approached her. 'Leave me alone!'

But Rees was not easily deterred. He met her again, and again, and with his persistence and powers of persuasion eventually got her to agree to meet him at a secluded venue outside Pretoria. Rees sensed that the contact was both angry and afraid. She was at the hub of things and knew what was going on, which alarmed her because she felt sure the whole operation was bound to blow up one day and she would be in the midst of the wreckage. There were just too many rumours flying around, too much glamour and too much scandalous misuse of public money. It couldn't last. But she was locked into it and couldn't leave.

That was when Rees came into his own. He sensed that this troubled woman needed to unburden herself. She needed a confidant, so he gave his word that if she spoke to him, told him what she knew, he would never disclose her identity whatever pressures might be brought to bear upon him. He said he would have to tell his colleagues, Day and myself, but we would be as strongly bound by his pledge of confidentiality as he was.

She might have been forgiven for being sceptical about this kind of promise, given the underworld of deception and intrigue she was living in, but Rees's innate integrity shone through and she accepted his word. Mervyn Rees was not only a tough and hardened journalist, but his work on the crime beat had also sharpened his innate humanity. He had seen much violence and mendacity and the pain and suffering they caused, and it had imbued him with a strong capacity for empathy. He could see what this young woman was going through and he felt compassion for her. What followed was a remarkable two-year relationship that was as much therapy for the troubled subject as it was a massive vacuuming-up of information for the reporter.

Back at the office, we code-named this vital new contact Myrtle, after the children's book character Myrtle the Turtle, because as Day, who fancied himself as a quipster, put it, her cover was strong and she could keep her head down.

* * *

JOURNALISTS can't function in a publishing limbo. Like athletes, they must perform to keep in shape. Yet here was my investigative team meeting scores of contacts every day but getting nothing published in the paper. It was hugely frustrating and I realised I had to do something to ease their pain. So I required each member to prepare a memorandum after each encounter with a contact. This would not only help to keep them sane, it would also provide us with a carefully filed record of all data gathered that would be available for quick reference when the time came to publish.

Rees held scores of meetings with Myrtle, writing each one up for me to lock in a safe. It became a formidable portfolio, for Myrtle not only knew a great deal but was also able to direct Rees to other sources in a plot that seemed to grow more and more tentacles the more we gleaned from her. Rhoodie was nothing if not a man of extravagant vision and ambition. His aim was no less than to change how the world viewed apartheid South Africa.

He had, as it turned out, persuaded not only Mulder but also Prime Minister Vorster to give him a free hand in planning and carrying out one of the most ambitious propaganda projects ever devised by any government. It was initially designed as a five-year programme involving scores of underground agent-propagandists and more than a hundred secret projects, all controlled by just three men in their mid-thirties — Rhoodie himself, his brother Denys and De Villiers. The projects were to be funded with money diverted from a secret Defence Special Account, intended for the clandestine purchase of weapons in the face of the United Nations arms embargo on South Africa and therefore not subject to scrutiny by either Parliament or the Auditor-General. Vorster informed his Cabinet of these facts through a confidential letter that Rhoodie himself drafted.

It also became evident that Rhoodie was working hand in glove with General van den Bergh, the head of BOSS ('They are like twins,' one contact told us), which meant the country's formidable security apparatus was linked to the project. That was going to make it even more hazardous for us.

As Rees learned from Myrtle, the attempt to buy SAAN and then to launch *The Citizen* was but one of many projects. During his time in the diplomatic service, Rhoodie had encountered a right-wing Dutch publisher, Hubert Jussen, who had then been connected with the Dutch news magazine *Elsevier*. Rhoodie now persuaded Jussen to launch a similar magazine in South Africa, called *To the Point*, modelled on *Time* and *Newsweek*, funded and staffed by the department. Later a European version, *To the Point International*, was also launched, with some French staffers who helped establish links with leaders of Francophone African countries, notably President Félix Houphouët-Boigny of Ivory Coast. This helped Prime Minister Vorster launch what became known as his 'outward-looking' policy, aimed at establishing links with some of the more conservative African leaders, including Malawi's Hastings Kamuzu Banda, which caused a brief flutter of curiosity on the international front.

In the United States, De Villiers, too, had established contact during an earlier posting with a wealthy conservative publisher of a chain of local newspapers across the US, John McGoff. In line with the advice of 'Mr Brown', Rhoodie and his colleagues encouraged McGoff to make a bid for the *Washington Star*, the main local rival to the influential *Washington Post*. They gave McGoff $10 million to make a bid, but he was outbid by the immensely wealthy Sun Myung Moon, the North Korean-born founder of the Unification Church. McGoff thereupon used the money to buy one of his own papers, the *Sacramento Union*, in California, for Rhoodie's department. Rhoodie's project thus acquired a voice in the capital of a state where a man named Ronald Reagan was governor.

There were other daring newspaper ventures in the Rhoodie programme as well. When rumour had it that the *Financial Times* was thinking of selling off a sister publication, the *Investor's Chronicle*, Rhoodie persuaded two South African exiles he had roped into his team, David Abrahamson and Stuart Pegg, to try to buy it for them. Abrahamson had been a supporter of the Progressive Party and a buddy of Max Borkum, as well as of SAAN chairman Ian MacPherson. He had been involved with a publishing company, Hortors, in Johannesburg and had also made and lost a lot of money on a financial venture called the National Growth Fund. He had then moved to London and become associated with a big business publishing company, Morgan Grampian. His friend Pegg was a champion rally driver.

As it turned out, the *Investor's Chronicle* deal fell through, apparently because the *Financial Times* was tipped off about 'funny money' from South Africa and withdrew it from the market. Abrahamson and Pegg then made a bid for 50 per cent of the *Investor's Revue* instead, but that also failed.

Rather more successful were two advertising agencies that Rhoodie established in Europe. One, called the 'Club of Ten', consisted of a group of wealthy conservative British business-men with interests in South Africa. It was headed by an eccentric author, businessman and former Judge of the International Court of Bangkok named Gerald Sparrow. The other was called 'The Committee for Fairness in Sport', aimed at countering the growing movement to isolate South Africa from the Olympic Games and other international sports events.

Both produced advertisements punting South Africa's case that were placed in major newspapers, such as *The Guardian*, *The Observer* and the *Daily Telegraph* in Britain; *The New York Times* and *Washington Post* in the US; the *Montreal Star* in Canada; as well as a variety of papers in West Germany, Holland, Australia and New Zealand.

News reached us through our network of contacts, now con-stantly widening thanks to Myrtle, that Sparrow had become disillusioned with the operation and had quit. This prompted us to send Don Marshall to London to meet with him. That enabled us to break our first story of the Information scandal, about how Rhoodie's Department of Information controlled and financed a secret propaganda campaign to sell apartheid to the Western nations through some of the world's most respected newspapers. More than that, Marshall persuaded Sparrow to write a series of op-ed articles for the Mail. In these, he recounted his meetings with Mulder, Rhoodie, De Villiers and Vorster. Like everyone who ever met Rhoodie, he was struck by his personality, describing him as 'a man of lightning perception with great animation' and possessed of 'a quicksilver brain'. Yet he did not feel he was a man of judgment.

What had eventually disillusioned Sparrow was a trip to Soweto, where he and his Thai wife, Chauley (whom the government had granted special 'white status' for the trip), came face to face with 'the horrific consequences' of apartheid for black South Africans. The final straw was when Rhoodie objected to the content of an article in a new magazine called *Phoenix* that Sparrow had launched for the department. 'I replied that in England it was not possible to have the policy of a paper dictated from outside,' Sparrow wrote in his Mail article, 'and that I must retain the right to judge what should or should not go into *Phoenix*.' What irony from a man who had been an enthusiastic collaborator in a programme devoted entirely to public deception.

But there was more to the Muldergate scandal than media manipulation and deception. There was freeloading as well, to an outrageous extent. When eventually the chickens came home to roost, it was this more than the secret propaganda operations that outraged South Africa's white population. To lie for one's country was okay, but to make free with the white taxpayers' money was most certainly not.

Again it was Myrtle who led us to these extravagances. The trip to the Seychelles had not been the only holiday jaunt for department members with spouses and friends. There had been others to Europe, the United States and Canada. She told Rees of an apartment block that the department owned on exclusive Clifton Beach, in Cape Town; of property at the fashionable resort of Plettenberg Bay; of two luxury houses in Pretoria, another in London, one in Miami, Florida, and, paradoxically, one in Soweto. There were two apartments in France and a share in a South African farm. All ostensibly meant to accommodate and entertain influential guests, but also capable of generating considerable income to finance the department's high life.

It was clear that large amounts of money were involved, much of it moving in and out of the country. We learned that the centrepiece of the whole network was a registered company called Thor Communications, through which all transactions were channelled. Thor's 'offices' in Johannesburg consisted of a large, extravagantly furnished lounge, which Myrtle told Rees was used for secret meetings of the department's agents. She said it was bugged and had a hidden camera in the front door to photograph people.

By now I felt we had a fairly comprehensive picture of Rhoodie's operation and that all we needed was a breakthrough to a usable source who could corroborate the large amount of information we had. Then we could start publishing. But at that point our confidence took a knock. With rumours swirling that the Department of Information had provided Luyt with the money to launch *The Citizen*, Information minister Connie Mulder rose in Parliament on 10 May 1978 to make a statement. 'The Department of Information owns no newspaper in South Africa and runs no newspaper in South Africa,' he declared. 'The Department of Information and the Government do not give funds to *The Citizen*.'

Where to now? We had felt certain that the money for *The Citizen* had indeed come from the Information department, but surely a senior minister in line for the premiership would not risk his entire future by uttering a blatant lie in Parliament. Vorster, in failing health, announced his retirement as Prime Minister, to be given the nominal post of President just four months later. As it turned out, though, the rumours appeared to exert some influence, for to Rhoodie's surprise and dismay Mulder was narrowly defeated in the party's succession ballot by the bombastic Minister of Defence, PW Botha.

Just as we were reaching a nadir of frustration, Rees and Day heard that a Supreme Court judge, Anton Mostert, who had been appointed as a commissioner to investigate exchange control contraventions, had interviewed a friend of Rhoodie's – a director of Thor Communications. A month after the election of the new Prime Minister, Rees and Day went to see the judge in Pietermaritzburg. He greeted them warmly, but told them bluntly that he would not give them any information about his investigations. 'I've only agreed to see you because you told me you might be of assistance to my commission,' he said. At which point the two Mail men adopted a crafty approach. They told him they understood his position, but would like to discuss a problem informally with him.

Day explained that Rees had been investigating issues involving the Information department for many months, and much of what he had gleaned had been on a strictly confidential basis. Rees had also become aware that some of the contacts he had spoken to had also been questioned by Mostert. These people were now fearful that the confidentiality Rees had given them might be broken.

'What we want to know, Judge,' Day continued, 'is whether we could be of assistance to your commission. If so, would you demand to know the identity of these informants? If you did, it would mean that Rees would have to refuse in terms of his journalistic ethics and the consequences for him would be serious.

'If we did have information that might help you,' Day went on, 'could it not be off the formal record?'

Judge Mostert thought for a while, then answered cautiously that he could indeed accept information off the record initially, placing it on the record later if necessary. 'I understand and believe in the right of journalists to gather information on a confidential basis, and I would like to tell you gentlemen that I am not interested in squeezing information out of you, or throwing you into jail if you don't comply.

'But I won't barter with you,' he added sharply, wagging a finger at them.

With that Day proposed that Rees show the judge a comprehensive report that he had prepared for me a few weeks earlier, which contained nearly all the relevant facts the team had gathered in the course of its long investigations. Judge Mostert read it silently, then, looking at Rees, said: 'That's a remarkable piece of work. What do you intend doing with it?'

'That's up to my editor,' Rees replied. 'He decides.'

'You're not the first newspaper to speak to me on this, you know,' Mostert said quietly.

'Are we ahead, sir?' Rees shot in smartly.

The judge smiled in acknowledgment of the smart gambit. 'I'm not sure if that question falls under the section of bartering information, Mr Rees,' he replied, 'but yes, I would say you are well ahead.'

When Rees and Day reported back to me, I realised that this revealing encounter may well have put us in a position where we could now publish – at least the story about the government putting up the money to buy *The Citizen*. The judge would surely not have spoken as he did if Rees's text had been wide of the mark. But I hesitated. I was still haunted by the Mail's prisons case experience and anxious that if we did publish, *The Citizen* might bring a libel action against the Mail and we would be stifled by the *sub judice* rule from publishing all the other information we had about the department's clandestine operations. So I asked the team to try to flesh out the other aspects a little more so we could publish everything together.

A bad decision. It lost my team the scoop they so richly deserved.

* * *

THE BANNER headline on the front page of the *Sunday Express* of 29 October 1978 was a screaming admonition. 'THE CITIZEN SECRET REVEALED', it trumpeted over a report by Kitt Katzin stating that the tabloid newspaper, launched as a supposedly independent daily by Louis Luyt, had in fact been financed by public money channelled through a secret government fund. That meant the paper was effectively a clandestine organ of the ruling National Party. A fraud committed by the government on the people of South Africa.

It was also a stunning scoop for the small and thinly staffed *Sunday Express*. All the big newspapers in the country had been pursuing this story for months, yet this lean little outfit had got it first. As I learned later from its editor, Rex Gibson, reporter Katzin had also been in touch with Judge Mostert − something we had guessed at the time when the judge told Rees and Day they were not the only journalists to have met with him. When Katzin told his editor the previous Friday that he believed he had enough information to go with the *Citizen* story that Sunday, Gibson found himself in the same situation I had confronted. He could not produce a single witness or any proof if challenged in court.

He and his deputy, Koos Viviers, decided on a cunning strategy. They told Katzin to phone the judge, keep him on the line and get him to listen to the opening paragraphs of the story. On no account was he to ask the judge to confirm the story. He was merely to ask: 'Judge, if we publish this story, will we end up with egg on our face?' This Katzin did, with Viviers and Gibson sitting beside him listening anxiously. At the end of the call, Katzin hung up and looked silently at his seniors with a sombre expression. Their hearts sank. 'Well, what did he say?' they asked.

To which Katzin replied: 'He said: "What took you so long?"'

It was enough to prompt Gibson into taking the bold leap I had hesitated to take.

While the Mail had been beaten with this first story, we knew we had a great deal more information than the *Sunday Express* had published. And we knew that because the Express had published this initial item, we now had corroborative evidence available that could be produced in court if necessary, which meant we could publish everything. The Express had given us the green light we had been waiting for.

I met with the investigative team and other key staff members in my office that Sunday morning and gave the order to prepare to drop our stick of blockbuster bombs throughout the coming week, beginning the next morning.

But there were still risks. The government surely knew we had a lot more information than the Express had published, so with the appearance of our first big report on Monday morning they might still take action to prevent further disclosures by using any number of weapons in their armoury of security laws. There were

372

personal dangers, too. Rees had only recently experienced a fairly explicit threat when he met a specialist spook who had worked as an instructor with the intelligence services. 'Has it ever occurred to you that you might be travelling along a motorway one fine day and suddenly the wheels of your vehicle come off?' the man asked. 'You should think about that, Mr Rees. I do, because I taught some of them.'

We decided that Rees should leave home immediately. We booked him into a local hotel where he and Day could prepare the copy for the big story in the next day's paper, and arranged that they should travel together to Durban the next morning where they could prepare the rest of the week's copy and telex it to us from the offices of our partner paper there, *The Mercury*. Thank heavens, I thought, for all those regular contact reports I had required them to make. They would have all the information they needed readily at hand.

Our first bombshell came on Monday under the banner headline, 'MISSING MILLIONS'. The report stated that not only had *The Citizen* been funded with secret government money, as the *Sunday Express* had reported, 'but that an amount of R13 million "disappeared" en route to *The Citizen*'. Attempts to recover this money had failed because the money had been sidetracked to rescue an ailing private business, even though *The Citizen* was desperately short of funds at the time.

'The Mail can also disclose that the Department of Information was forced, because of this misappropriation, to raise a loan of millions of rands in Switzerland to continue to finance *The Citizen* operation.' The report went on to list other sums intended for secret Information department projects that had been misappropriated and funnelled into private operations.

'According to the Mail's informants,' our report said, 'the funding of *The Citizen* was so secretive that not even prominent people associated with the newspaper were aware of the true source of the funds … The Mail has been told that even senior Cabinet ministers were not entrusted with the knowledge of the secret project.'

The publication of these two reports by two newspapers in successive days sent a ripple of dismay through the ruling National

Party. Luyt promptly gave an interview to *The Star*, published that Monday afternoon, flatly denying that he had received any money from the government to launch *The Citizen*. To which I responded in a front-page editorial the next morning, saying equally bluntly that Luyt's denial was 'simply not true', that the evidence we had was 'irrefutable'. It was an open challenge to him to sue us for publicly calling him a liar. But he fell silent.

The editor of *The Citizen*, Johnny Johnson, was enraged. 'We dismiss with contempt the rotten smear by the left-wing *Rand Daily Mail* about the financing of *The Citizen*,' he wrote. 'The disgraceful attack on us proves one thing: The *Rand Daily Mail* is unable to compete fairly against *The Citizen*, newspaper against newspaper, in a battle of newsworthiness. It has resorted instead to the smear, but its dirty tactics will not halt *The Citizen*.'

I decided to shrug that one off, knowing what we still had to publish. I'd never liked Johnny, but he was in an unenviable spot.

Meanwhile Rees and Day paid another visit to Judge Mostert. What was he going to do with his report, they asked. The evidence given before his commission was still not available for publication, he said, then added intriguingly: 'I am, however, considering this in the light of the law and the public interest.'

That was enough to give us our banner headline for the next day – 'JUDGE MAY ACT'.

On Wednesday morning we carried the next blockbuster with details of the attempt to get McGoff to buy the *Washington Star* for Rhoodie's propaganda machine, and of how, when this was thwarted, McGoff diverted the South African government's money to buy the *Sacramento Union*. The front-page banner this time was 'INFO'S US PAPER BID'.

Thursday's banner was equally bold, 'FLOP YOU PAID FOR', over a story about how Rhoodie had channelled money to an American film director to make a thriller called *The Golden Rendezvous*, which had bombed badly.

By now the impact of our blockbusters was immense: the *Mail*'s daily circulation figures had rocketed from 130 000 to 190 000 over that week. The country was electrified by the scandal. Prime Minister Botha went on television to address the

374

nation, giving an assurance that the government would investigate the whole matter and appealing to the media to give it a chance to gather all the facts.

At the same time, Judge Mostert announced that he would see the Prime Minister on Thursday morning and hold a press conference afterwards.

The entire press corps, domestic and foreign, gathered on the steps of the Union Buildings in Pretoria the next day as Mostert, accompanied by Finance minister Owen Horwood, arrived to see Botha. They were smiling and joking as they entered the premier's office. Forty-five minutes later Mostert emerged alone, scowling. 'I'll speak to you at my offices at 2 pm,' he snapped at the journalists. 'I will have nothing to say until then.' It had clearly not been a congenial meeting with the bombastic Botha.

The air was crackling with tension as the press corps gathered in the judge's office. Mostert began by spelling out the law governing commissions of inquiry. Commissions would normally hear evidence in public, he explained, although the chairman had discretion to hear some or all evidence privately if he deemed that desirable. In this case, Mostert said, he had not exercised that discretion, so the commission's sessions had the legal status of public meetings. He referred to Botha's televised appeal to the media. 'The prime minister's appeal is entitled to serious consideration,' he said, 'but that does not release me from the duty of examining the cogency of the prime minister's arguments. I have endeavoured to discover what particular interest of the State is furthered by suppression rather than disclosure of the evidence. I have been able to find none.

'In such matters,' the judge went on, 'public interest is paramount and is usually best served by frank disclosure. Only reasons of great cogency will cause suppression or secrecy to be preferred to disclosure. I do not find such cogency in emotional appeals unsupported by valid considerations' – a not very subtle dig at Botha.

It was a brave and honourable decision by Mostert, an Afrikaner judge, deciding to put his ethnic and political loyalties aside and to defy his Prime Minister in a matter he regarded as being in the national interest — an act I paid tribute to in our editorial in the next day's paper.

There was a frantic rush back at the Mail newsroom as the production team cleared just about the entire newspaper to accommodate what was surely one of the most dramatic news stories in the country's history. Even as we worked, Botha made yet another effort to stop publication, issuing a warning to editors that if we did so it would contravene gazetted regulations forbidding disclosure of a commission's evidence. But Mostert issued a swift rejoinder, noting that these regulations applied only to 'a third person', not to the commission itself. So we went ahead, and under the blown-up banner, 'IT'S ALL TRUE', published our story, which began as follows:

> South Africa's biggest political bombshell burst yesterday when Mr Justice Anton Mostert made public startling evidence which has confirmed reports in the *Rand Daily Mail* and the *Sunday Express* of massive misuse of public money through the Department of Information secret funds.
>
> Judge Mostert released evidence which shows beyond doubt that *The Citizen* newspaper was financed out of state funds.
>
> And in evidence under oath, Louis Luyt named the former Prime Minister, John Vorster, Minister Connie Mulder and the head of the Bureau of State Security, General Hendrik van den Bergh, as key figures in the secret project to finance the newspaper.

This was in direct conflict with public denials on the issues made by Luyt, Mulder and Van den Bergh, who was appointed by Vorster to investigate secret projects of the Department of Information.

Two days later political editor Martin Schneider wrote an equally dramatic story showing how fast the impact of this massive scandal was rippling through the administration. In a single day, Connie Mulder resigned from the Cabinet, and Prime Minister Botha disbanded the Mostert Commission, announced the appointment of another judge, Rudolph Erasmus, to head a separate commission to investigate the Information department scandal, and convened a parliamentary select committee to probe the breaches of exchange control regulations exposed by Judge Mostert.

376

Eschel Rhoodie fled the country; Van den Bergh retired as head of BOSS; Anton Mostert stepped down from the Bench to return to the Bar and practise as an advocate; Les de Villiers, who had left the country earlier to join a New York public relations company connected to the Information department, decided not to return.

And six months later John Vorster resigned as President.

As all these chickens settled in their roosts, Rees received a call from Myrtle. 'Well, well,' she said, 'so you cracked it! But don't you think there's a lot more to come?' Rees agreed that there probably was. 'That's right,' she replied. 'Come and see me when you've had a little break.'

* * *

IT WAS NO time to rest on our laurels. Eschel Rhoodie had left the country a bitter man, threatening to play Samson and 'pull down the pillars of government'. In statements before leaving he had indicated that he considered himself a scapegoat, that the whole Information department project had been agreed to by the government, from Prime Minister Vorster down, and now that the secrets had been blown they were leaving him to take the rap. He was particularly enraged by PW Botha's claim that he had known nothing about the whole enterprise, even though, as Rhoodie pointed out, all the money for the projects had come from the secret Defence Special Account while Botha had been Minister of Defence.

So a whiff of revenge was in the air. It was obvious we had to go after Rhoodie to get the big follow-up story, but not even Myrtle knew where he was. Things became murkier still when the government revealed that it had cancelled the passports of both Rhoodie and his wife. As we pondered where to begin, Rees received a call from Ted Olsen, a *Cape Times* reporter who had worked with us earlier in the investigation. Olsen told Rees he had met someone they had encountered before who claimed he could put us in touch with Rhoodie. A meeting was arranged where this contact — whom they code-named Mike — told Rees and Olsen

that, while he didn't know where Rhoodie was, he had a telephone number in Europe he could call and leave a message at.
Rhoodie would phone back or get a message relayed.

I met with Olsen's editor, Anthony Heard, and we agreed that
Rees and Olsen should fly to Europe with Mike to see if they
could contact Rhoodie. They were to fly to Frankfurt, where Mike
would try to make the contact. After doing so, Olsen and Mike
returned to South Africa and Day rejoined Rees in Europe.

Meanwhile, an even stickier problem arose. Our deputy finance
editor, Hamish Fraser, had done a breakdown of *The Citizen's*
finances, which revealed that a total of R32 million of public
money had in fact been spent on the paper. We published the
story – and were promptly charged by Judge Erasmus with
contempt of his commission by anticipating its findings. It then
became clear why Prime Minister Botha had shut down the
Mostert Commission and established the Erasmus Commission
instead: it was to use the more compliant judge to prevent any
further publication of the scandal under the *sub judice* rule.

Judge Erasmus had spent many years as a legal adviser to the
National Party. He was also something of an eccentric. Even
though he was highly qualified, having been a Rhodes Scholar at
Oxford, he was a lugubrious and curiously inarticulate man with
a propensity for using mangled metaphors. When I telephoned
him to protest that his charging the Mail was a misguided act to
muzzle the press on a matter of great public interest, his response
was in character. 'Mr Sparks,' he said, 'your protest is like a duck's
water off my back. The law is the law.'

Later, during his commission's hearings, he was heard to
remark about Rhoodie's multiple secret projects, that 'this man
seems to have had a finger in every tart'. No doubt there were
some who considered that not to be an inappropriate observation.

Hamish Fraser and I duly appeared in court, defended once
again by the incomparable Sydney Kentridge. We appeared before the Chief Magistrate of Johannesburg, who found us guilty.
I was fined R50; Fraser was cautioned and discharged. A cameo
of intimidation followed. I was not allowed to leave the dock and
return to my office; instead police frogmarched me downstairs

378

to the holding cells, ostensibly until the formalities of paying the petty fine were completed, which seemed to take an eternity. So there I waited among an assortment of awaiting-trial prisoners sitting in cages like animals in a zoo, until the magistrate, learning of my illegal incarceration, ordered my release.

Kentridge was outraged at the magistrate's judgment and took the matter on appeal, where it was heard by a full bench of three Supreme Court judges. He delivered a powerful argument that the matter was of great importance to the proper functioning of democracy, and that a commission of inquiry was not a court of law and so the *sub judice* rule should not apply to it. The judges ruled in his favour, so I got my R50 back and the case, *State* vs *Sparks*, stands to this day prohibiting the use of commissions of inquiry to block public debate on matters of public interest.

That hurdle overcome, the way was open for us to continue with our quest for Rhoodie and his counterattack story. In February 1979, while I was in Cape Town attending the annual opening of the new parliamentary session, Raymond Louw sidled up to me at a cocktail party and murmured that I should go to his student daughter Fiona's flat at 2 pm next day to take a call from Chris Day. Another crafty attempt to avoid the ubiquitous telephone tappers. Surely no one would bother to bug a student's phone.

When I took the call I was astonished to learn that Rees and Day were in Quito, Ecuador. I hardly knew where the place was, except that it was high in the Andes. They were with Rhoodie, Day told me over the thin, crackling line. They had met up with him at Miami airport, from where Rees and Day had flown with him to Quito, while Olsen returned to Johannesburg. 'Rhoodie's angry and he's ready to talk,' Day told me, 'But he wants money.'

'No way,' I replied. 'Tell him we can't pay him anything, because if we do the word will get out and that will discredit everything he tells us. His enemies will say he embellished his story to push up the price.'

'We told him we knew that would be your response,' Day replied, 'but he says if he blows the whistle on everyone, from PW Botha down, they'll cut off his pension and he'll have nothing to live on.'

'Too bad,' I said. 'There's no way we can pay him. It would be a violation of journalistic ethics and taint everything we have done so far. Tell him the best I can do is put him in touch with some television broadcasters who might be prepared to pay him, and who can then share the story with us. In the meantime, see if he will agree to tell you everything on tape, with our undertaking to use the material only if he can find someone to give him the money he wants.'

Rees and Day spent days in a hotel room in Quito recording dozens of tapes giving Rhoodie's side of the story – leading to speculation in rival papers for months afterwards about mysterious 'Rhoodie tapes'. I got in touch with the BBC's David Dimbleby, who showed some interest in doing a deal with Rhoodie. There matters rested for another few weeks. Meanwhile, on my return to Johannesburg the day after the phone call from Quito, I bumped into the editor of the *Sunday Times*, Tertius Myburgh, in a corridor.

'I believe you guys have found Rhoodie,' he said. Tertius and I were old friends, but I was stunned by his words, which were uttered more as a question than a statement. How the hell did he know? I had spoken to no one about the call from Quito, and even if Fiona's phone had been tapped how could Myburgh have got the information? In my consternation, I lied. 'No,' I said hastily. 'No, we haven't.'

I walked away, deeply troubled. I didn't like the fact that I had lied to a colleague, but I was thrown off balance by the fact that this confidential piece of information had so quickly reached the ears of a competing editor, albeit of a newspaper in our own company. Something fishy was going on.

Day flew back to Johannesburg with the Rhoodie tapes, which he quietly set about transcribing at a rural resort well outside the city. He brought news that Rees was sticking with Rhoodie, who was planning to move to France. It appeared he had friends in key positions in many countries, as well as a variety of identity documents. Moving about without a passport seemed not to be a problem.

The next call was from Rees and his tone was urgent. 'Rhoodie wants to see you to discuss everything. He wants to know whether

380

you can leave right away, and if so you should check in to the Baur au Lac Hotel in Zürich and he'll meet you there.'

'Tell him yes,' I replied. 'I'll try to leave today, which will get me to Zürich tomorrow.' This story was still too big and I wasn't going to hesitate again. We were in the extraordinary position of having our prize victim in our hands, ready to become our prize informer. What story could be more dramatic than that?

I asked my secretary, Gina, to check the airline schedules and book me on whichever flight would get me to Zürich soonest. She told me there was a flight leaving in three hours, but it meant changing planes in London. 'Make the booking,' I said, 'then phone my wife and ask her please to pack some clothes for me and meet me at the airport.'

The overnight flight to London was comfortable enough, and I made a quick transfer to a Swissair flight for Zürich. I was seated in a front row with a vacant seat beside me. Just as the flight attendant was about to close the plane door, a late passenger burst in, a burly man red in the face from exertion, and who planted himself in the seat beside me. He looked like a rugby forward badly out of condition, for he was out of breath from running.

'You nearly missed the flight,' I said to him.

'Ja,' he replied. Then silence. Neither of us spoke again throughout the flight.

When we landed at Zürich I noticed that my neighbour had no luggage. Since I had only hand luggage, I bypassed the carousel and was heading for the taxi ranks when I noticed the burly man following me. I hailed a taxi. So did he. We took off for the Baur au Lac, and as I looked back I saw his taxi following. As we rounded a few corners, the burly man's taxi was still in sight.

I leant forward to speak to the taxi driver. 'There's a taxi following us,' I said. 'Please lose him.'

Suddenly we were in a B-rated movie. My driver, revelling in a moment of excitement in what I imagine is a rather dull occupation, stepped on the gas and began hurtling through a series of narrow side streets with tyres squealing. My tail tried to follow for a while, but soon realised this was making him conspicuous. So we cruised sedately up to the entrance of the venerable Baur au Lac.

As I gazed at its splendid portals, I winced at the thought of the bill. Rhoodie had tastes far in excess of my modest editorial budget.

For two days I waited in my room, having all meals sent up to me, for fear of being out when our quarry-cum-informer called. On the third morning there was a brisk knock on the door and in strode Rhoodie, smiling broadly. 'Aha!' he said, throwing himself casually into an armchair. 'So you were followed. Hendrik told me' – a reference to the erstwhile head of BOSS. 'They're pretty thick, some of these goons. I bet you had no problem picking him out.'

The equanimity of the man was astonishing. Here he was, on the run without a passport, slipping across national borders, facing arrest at any moment, but smiling and looking as relaxed as if he were on holiday. He told me he had been to Britain where he had tried, but failed, to get political asylum. At least he had met with David Dimbleby, who had interviewed him for the BBC. He didn't say whether Dimbleby had paid him, and I didn't ask. But he was now ready to agree to our telling his story.

'I wanted to see you to warn you that you are surrounded by informants,' Rhoodie said. 'I have told Mervyn which stuff you can use of the information I have given you, but you will have to be careful. Make sure you put those tapes in a safe place. They could be used against me. As I say, you are surrounded by informants. Tertius Myburgh of the *Sunday Times* is one. He kept Hendrik informed all the way along about what progress you were making with your investigation. But I have to tell you there is someone else as well, much higher up in your organisation. Very senior.'

I tried to probe Rhoodie further about who this individual might be, but he was adamant. 'No, I can't tell you that,' he said. 'I just wanted to alert you to be careful.'

With that he left. With much still left of the day, I checked out and headed for the airport. I had arranged through Stanley Uys, now our bureau chief in London, that I wanted to stop over there to meet with David Abrahamson. I called Uys to give him my time of arrival and ask him to send a car to fetch me and take me to the Abrahamson meeting.

On landing, our company driver, a long-serving Irishman inevitably known as Paddy, greeted me with a frown. 'What the hell's going on in this company?' he asked. 'I was supposed to pick up Sue Vos of the *Sunday Times* to take her to the airport, because her editor had told her to fly to Zürich where he said you were meeting with Eschel Rhoodie. I said to her: "That doesn't make sense, I'm on my way to the airport now to pick up Allister who's just landed from Zürich." At which point she burst into tears. She said she'd spent days tailing *Rand Daily Mail* reporters at her editor's request rather than getting on with news stories.'

Paddy drove me to the Hilton in Holland Park, where I met with both Uys and David Abrahamson. The businessman poured out his side of the story, expressing his regret at ever having become involved in the scandal. Rhoodie was very persuasive, he said, and by the time he realised what he was into he was too deep to pull out. As his anxieties rose, he said, General Van den Bergh kept assuring them all that he had an informer in Tertius Myburgh, who would keep them informed of the *Rand Daily Mail*'s progress with its investigation. If they felt the Mail was getting too close, they would take action to stop it.

When Rees later asked Rhoodie what this action would have been, would they have closed down the Mail, Rhoodie's reply was unhesitating. 'Oh no,' he said, 'that would have caused too much of an outcry. We'd just have banned Sparks.'

Uys recorded Abrahamson's statements on a tape recorder. He later passed the tape on to Raymond Louw, the newly appointed general manager who, shocked by what he heard, gave it to Clive Kinsley, the managing director. Kinsley later told Louw that he had confronted Myburgh with the contents of the tape, and Myburgh had denied emphatically that he was an agent of any sort. Kinsley did nothing further about the matter.

I flew back to Johannesburg to encounter an even bigger shock. Gina, my secretary, was no longer there. Other secretaries on the newsroom floor told me she had quit in distress, confessing to them that she had been a BOSS agent all along but had become stricken with guilt because she had grown fond of both me and my family. She didn't tell anyone where she was going. I never saw or heard of her again. But, looking back, I could have kicked myself for my naivety. Of course, she had been introduced to me at the *Sunday Express* by none other than Gordon Winter. What a fool I had been. She had known everything about my movements, my flight numbers, even the hotel bookings we had made for our investigative team to have what we imagined were confidential discussions away from our bug-filled office building. About the only thing she didn't know was Myrtle's identity, for we had never mentioned that even in private discussions.

Next shock in this drawn-out saga was that the French police arrested Rhoodie, who was by then relaxing on the Riviera, and locked him up in the bleak medieval prison in Aix-en-Provence. Rees was still there, together with Katie Rhoodie, and with my approval Rees arranged for the Mail to pay for decent restaurant meals, which Katie took to Rhoodie each day. The victim-cum-informant had now become a dependant as well. But soon Pretoria put pressure on the French government to have Rhoodie extradited.

He stood trial in South Africa and was sentenced to six years' imprisonment for fraud. But the sentence was overturned on appeal. The last time I saw Rhoodie he was still buoyant and bursting with big ideas. He was going to move to the United States, he told me, where he would write books about the Information scandal – and, he added conspiratorially, maybe a novel based on more dirty tricks perpetrated by the Vorster and Botha governments.

Rhoodie settled in California in 1983, where he duly published two books, and then wrote an unpublished novel, the manuscript of which he sent to Mervyn Rees, seeking his opinion. It was never published. Rhoodie died in the US in 1993, appropriately while playing tennis, a sport he was passionate about and which suited his style of athletic competitiveness. He was 60.

* * *

THIRTY-SEVEN YEARS later, as I was writing these memoirs in the relative calm of the new South Africa, I decided to seek out Myrtle, who had played such a pivotal role in my journalistic life. I knew her identity, of course, because Rees had been bound to confide in me, but I had been equally bound by his pledge of confidentiality. Could I, after all these years, now disclose her identity? Was there an ethical equivalent of the legal statute of limitations, the time after which a person cannot be charged with a criminal offence? I thought probably not.

As a journalist I had always regarded the pledge of confidentiality to a vulnerable informant as sacrosanct. Without it, investigative journalism would be impossible. In fact, several times in my career I faced the prospect of imprisonment for refusing to divulge the identity of informants.

But I was also mindful that the identity of 'Deep Throat', the *Washington Post*'s key informant in the Watergate scandal that had dethroned President Richard Nixon, had eventually been disclosed as William Mark Felt, Snr, deputy director of the Federal Bureau of Investigation (FBI). Felt was terminally ill when *Vanity Fair* magazine named him as the Post investigators' key informant. Felt himself then openly confessed that he had been Deep Throat, whereupon the *Washington Post* confirmed it.

We had kept the secret of Myrtle's identity for six years longer than the *Washington Post* had kept theirs, so I decided to seek out Myrtle to ask whether she would agree to disclosure. It took me a long time to locate her: I had no idea whether she was still living, where, or under what name. But when I did eventually track her down and ask her the question, she was horrified. 'No, please don't,' she begged. 'My life wouldn't be worth living if people found out.' So two decades into the new South Africa, the bonds of Afrikaner solidarity and the fear of being labelled an ethnic traitor were such that she was still fearful of disclosure. I did not press the matter further.

We chatted amicably instead. She spoke warmly of Rees. 'What a gentleman,' she said. 'I knew from the beginning that I could trust him absolutely.' He had given her an inscribed copy of the book he and Day had co-written about the Muldergate scandal. The inscription read: 'To a very special friend.'

'He was my special friend too,' she said. Then, with a wistful air, Myrtle added: 'So much has changed since then. I've even undergone a sex change. I used to be man, you know.'

385

At which point I recalled that in their book, Rees and Day had strengthened Myrtle the Turtle's hard cover by referring to her throughout in masculine terms. That much of her cover I have now peeled away, but for the rest her identity shall remain secret forever.

CHAPTER TWENTY-TWO

The Killing of a Secret

ROBERT VAN SCHALKWYK SMIT was a striking figure of a man, tall and muscular with a shiny bald pate and a dashing handlebar moustache. He had played rugby and water polo for the University of the Free State and was a fine tennis player to boot. Smit was also smart. He had graduated *cum laude* with a doctorate in economics from the UFS, then gone to Pembroke College, Oxford, on a Rhodes scholarship to pick up a DLitt. He had enjoyed a meteoric career in the public service, first as deputy secretary at the Treasury, then as South Africa's ambassador to the International Monetary Fund (IMF) in Washington, DC.

Now, aged 44, Smit had decided to enter politics. He was being tipped as South Africa's next Minister of Finance and had been made the National Party's candidate in the safe seat of Springs, east of Johannesburg, in the upcoming general election. But despite his impressive pedigree and the importance of the portfolio that appeared to be his for the taking, Smit's candidacy had attracted little media attention. He was a newcomer to the country's stormy politics, at the time dominated by mounting threats of international sanctions and boycotts over apartheid and the simmering issue of the Information scandal, which had not yet reached its explosive climax.

I was mystified, therefore, on arriving at the office on the morning of 23 November 1977, just seven days before the election, to learn from the news desk that they had just received a flash message that the National Party candidate for Springs, Dr Smit, was dead — and it looked like murder. The police had cordoned off Smit's house and reporters were being kept away and couldn't get any details. The news editor said they were trying to get Mervyn Rees to go to the scene, but he was baulking because he was working full time on the Information scandal.

South Africa was not unaccustomed to political assassinations, yet I found it difficult to imagine that the little-known Smit might have been targeted by ANC guerrillas. I doubted whether any of the ANC leaders even knew who he was. Nor was Springs a constituency of any real importance in the election. It was a shoo-in for the Nats whoever ran there, so why would anyone want to eliminate an obscure candidate in a seat of no electoral significance?

Still, the mystery was intriguing enough to warrant serious attention, so I ordered the news desk to tell Rees to drop his day's assignments and get to Springs as soon as he could. Two hours later he was on the phone to me. 'Something very strange is going on here,' he said. 'Smit and his wife, Jeanne-Cora, have been murdered and the police won't let anyone from the media near the place. They won't tell us what's going on, yet Gordon Winter of *The Citizen* has been inside the house since early this morning.'

That was enough to set bells ringing in my mind. This was still some months before Winter's strange night of confession at my home, yet the rumours about his alleged connections with BOSS, and particularly his personal relationship with Hendrik van den Bergh, were thick enough to raise the question of whether the security services were somehow involved in the murders. And if so, in what capacity: as investigators or perpetrators? What connection could there possibly be between the killing of this candidate and his wife and the general election in a few days' time?

The mystery deepened the next day when *The Citizen*'s front-page lead story was written not by Gordon Winter, their chief crime reporter, but by another *Citizen* reporter, a young woman named Rita Niemand. Her story was about how she had been the last to see Smit alive as he left for home after she had interviewed him at his election office in Springs.

There was not a word by Winter about what he had seen in the house, or what theories he had picked up from the police. What the hell had he been doing there? Why had the police let him in, alone among all the press corps?

The only item of news to emerge from the death house was that the killers had left a spray-painted slogan in red on the kitchen wall, and again on the refrigerator door, that read 'RAU-TEM'. There was a frenzy of newspaper speculation about what the lettering might indicate, but no one came up with anything that made sense.

The only other information to emerge from the police in the days that followed was that the receptionist at Smit's election office, Sarah Lombard, had revealed that he had told her he needed to be home by 8 pm to meet a Mr MacDougal, who wanted to discuss some political issues before deciding how to vote. The entry was there in Smit's diary: 'MacDougal, 8 pm.' Lombard said Smit had been running late, and his wife had phoned at 7.40 pm asking her to tell him that 'his guests are waiting for him'. Smit had left the office at 9 pm.

Next morning Smit's chauffeur, Daniel Tshabalala, drove up to the Smits' rented home in the fashionable suburb of Selcourt at 7 am to deliver the morning newspapers. He was surprised to find the front door unlocked and slightly ajar. He rang the doorbell, and when no one answered he pushed the door open and stepped inside – to stumble upon the corpse of his boss lying on a bloodstained carpet in the entrance hall. Robert Smit's skull was a shattered mess of blood and splintered bone, and his body looked as though it had been almost cut in half by a hail of bullets. In the passageway leading to the lounge, the driver found the body of Jeanne-Cora Smit kneeling beside the telephone, her head slumped forward on her knees. She had been shot in the head and stabbed in the back 14 times with a long stiletto knife. Mercifully, their two children, Robert, 15, and Lise, 13, were away at boarding school in Pretoria.

Days turned into weeks, weeks into months, and the supposedly crack Brixton Murder and Robbery Squad appeared to make no progress with the investigation. The general election came and went, with the National Party winning the biggest victory in the country's history, gaining all but ten of Parliament's 144 seats. The United Party had disbanded itself at a final congress before the election, having decided there was no political future in its efforts to find a middle way between apartheid and racial integration. The rump of what remained of the UP, calling itself the New Republican Party, was eliminated at the polls. The once-miniscule Progressive Party, which the Mail had supported since infancy, became the official opposition in the new Parliament.

* * *

JUST AS THE story of the Smit murders was fading into the background, two startling things occurred. First, General Van den Bergh gave testimony behind closed doors to the Erasmus Commission, which was investigating the Information department scandal. Word leaked out that the general had made some extraordinary statements to the commission but that these had been deleted from its report at his instance. But after a media outcry over the omissions, a final report of the evidence given to the commission was eventually published − and Van den Bergh's full statement was there in all its starkness:

> Mr Commissioner, I really want to tell you that I am able with my department to do the impossible. This is not bragging. I can tell you here today, not for the record, but I can tell you I have enough men to commit murder if I tell them, kill. I do not care who the prey is, or how important they are. Those are the kind of men I have. And if I wanted to do something like that to protect the security of the State nobody would stop me. I would stop at nothing. But that is such a damaging admission that, for the sake of the South African Government, you will be compelled to omit it from your findings.[1]

The other startling piece of information was conveyed to me by Mervyn Rees. One of his contacts had told him to visit a

Supreme Court judge, Joe Ludorf, at his home, unaccompanied and preferably at night. Judge Ludorf was a figure of note in the Afrikaner community. He had a reputation as an excellent judge and a fearlessly independent man, but he was also known for his conviviality.

Judge Ludorf met Rees at the front door with a glass of the finest malt whisky in his hand. He invited Rees in and offered him a drink, which the unconventional journalist politely declined. Then, settling into a comfortable armchair, the judge began recounting his story, pausing occasionally to refresh his glass.

An informant, whom the judge said he knew and trusted but declined to name, had recently called on him in a troubled state, he said, telling him he believed Smit had been killed because, while at the IMF, he had uncovered what he called 'a capital evacuation scheme' that involved leading members of the Afrikaner Nationalist establishment. Smit was 'taken out', the man believed, because those involved feared he intended disclosing the facts as soon as he was elected and could speak with the immunity of parliamentary privilege.

The financial scheme, according to the informant, stemmed from US President Richard Nixon's decision in August 1971 to cancel the direct convertibility of the US dollar to gold. Until then, all international monetary transactions were conducted in terms of the Bretton Woods system established towards the end of the Second World War. Under that system, all countries settled their international accounts in dollars that could be converted into gold at a fixed exchange rate of $35 per fine ounce, which was redeemable by the US government.

This meant the US was committed to buying every dollar overseas with gold. Other countries were fixed to the dollar, which was pegged to gold. The system had worked well in the immediate post-war years, stabilising international currencies, but in 1971 Nixon decided it was no longer working to America's advantage, nor indeed to those of other countries. So he instructed the Secretary of the Treasury, John Connally, to bring it to an end. Not only did this allow all currencies to float freely, it also unpegged the dollar price of gold.

According to Ludorf's informant, Dr Nico Diederichs, then South Africa's Minister of Finance (later to become State President), realised immediately that this would mean a huge bonanza for South Africa, then by far the largest producer of gold in the free world. In fact, in the course of that decade alone the price of gold shot up from $35 an ounce to $850 and continued rising thereafter.

Armed with this insight, the informant claimed Diederichs had travelled to Switzerland and done a deal with the Union Bank of Switzerland (UBS). The deal, the informant said, was to move most of South Africa's physical gold sales (as distinct from paper gold sales) from the London gold market to Zürich. There the gold would be sold by a process known as 'gold swaps', which involved the transfer of bullion to a dealer in exchange for currency, with an agreed forward price at which the gold would be purchased when the swap time came due.

The trick here, apparently, was that the agreed price could be variable. This, Ludorf's informant claimed, enabled Diederichs and the UBS to reach an agreement whereby a small percentage of each sale could be creamed off and kept in a secret numbered account at the bank – in this case, the informant claimed, for the possible future funding of some kind of government-in-exile for the Afrikaner Nationalist leadership should the ANC ever gain control of South Africa.

This, the informant contended, was the explosive secret Robert Smit carried with him – and for which he was eliminated.

When Rees recounted the story of his meeting with Ludorf to me, my first question was: 'Was Ludorf sober when he told you all this?' Rees hesitated a moment as he considered the question. We had both heard tales of the judge's convivial habits. 'Look, he had quite a few drinks while he was talking to me,' Rees said, 'but I'm quite sure he wasn't in his cups. He was very serious. Very concerned.'

Judge Ludorf had made no claim as to the truthfulness of what his informant had told him. He had said only that, on the face of it, the allegation was extremely serious and should be investigated. But if the scheme had indeed been set up at such a high level, it was obviously pointless to expect the security police to investigate it seriously. Nor could he, as a judge, do anything about it. Therefore it seemed to him the best thing would be to give the information to a newspaper like the Mail to investigate.

With that, Judge Ludorf gave Rees the number of the secret account at the Zürich branch of the Union Bank of Switzerland. And Rees gave it to me.

* * *

A FEW MONTHS later, as South Africa entered the fateful 1980s, Sue received news that her father, André Matthey, was ill, diagnosed with terminal cancer. It was time for an ingathering of the family, uncles and aunts and brothers and cousins from all parts of Switzerland, as well as Sue and I and our four-year-old son, Julian. A sad time, as family passings always are, but also one that would present me with an opportunity to test that haunting bank account number.

It was my fifth visit to Switzerland, the first three with Sue and then that extraordinary encounter with the fugitive Eschel Rhoodie in Zürich's Baur au Lac Hotel. Sue had worked for a year in Zürich after graduating from Heidelberg fluent in German. There she had stayed in the home of a family friend, a young Swiss journalist who had gone to the United States to broaden his experience. Now he had returned to take up the editorship of Switzerland's leading newspaper, the *Neue Zürcher Zeitung*, and bringing with him an American wife, also a journalist, who was a specialist in Swiss banking affairs. Sue introduced me to this couple.

That link established, I learned of the perils that Switzerland's bank secrecy laws posed for investigative journalists. It was a crime, I was warned, even to try to establish who had opened a numbered account, and who the beneficiaries were. So be careful. Be very careful. But at the same time I was able to learn the name of the man who had been chairman of the UBS in 1971. If Nico Diederichs, as Finance minister, had indeed cut a deal with the bank to cream off a percentage of South Africa's ballooning gold-sale profits, this man would surely have been involved. He would know.

With a bit more probing I also learned that the UBS chairman had recently retired and moved to a luxury home in an Alpine resort. And I had his telephone number.

Top priority, though, was to test that numbered account. So I went to the main branch of the UBS in Zürich's Bahnhofstrasse. There, with some trepidation, I filled out a deposit slip in my own name to place 50 Swiss francs into account number 187.613.LIE. I signed it and handed it with the money to a teller, who checked the slip, stamped a receipt and handed it to me without any expression of surprise on his face. Routine. Deadpan.

Emboldened, I returned to the bank the next day. Same routine, but a different teller. This time I boldly filled out the deposit slip in the name of Dr N Diederichs of Pretoria, and handed it to the teller with a 30-franc note – a silly little act of economising in the face of the steeply adverse exchange rate with the rand. Again the teller accepted it with equanimity.

What had I achieved? Maybe nothing. Except perhaps, I told myself, that a secret account with that number I had been given actually existed. Surely no bank would accept one's money for nothing, for a bank account its staffers knew didn't exist?

I then found a telephone and dialled the number of the retired UBS chairman. A gruff voice answered, confirming that he was indeed the man I wanted. I identified myself and asked whether I could travel up to his resort to meet with him.

'What do you want to meet with me about?' he asked, his tone softening to deep caution.

'I believe you had some discussions a few years ago with our then Finance minister, Dr Nico Diederichs, who is now our State President,' I said. 'I would like to talk to you about that.'

There was a long silence. Then the voice came back in an angry blast: 'Look here, I will not do anything to besmirch the name of my good friend Nico Diederichs. Goodbye!'

And he slammed down the phone.

* * *

I FLEW FROM Zürich to London, where I dialled the number – just a number, without knowing whose it was – that Gordon

Winter had given me as he left after that extraordinary night of confession at my Rivonia home. 'If you are ever in the UK, just call this number and leave a message for me and I'll get back to you.' Which is what I did. An anonymous voice answered, to which I gave my name and the phone number of the bed-and-breakfast establishment where I was staying.

Within the hour the voice called back: 'Gordon says you must fly to Dublin, check into an airport hotel there and he will get in touch with you.'

So it was that I made my first and only visit to the Republic of Ireland, the Emerald Isle of faith and fable, of which for two days I saw nothing but the bleak interior of an airport hotel. Winter arrived, looking pale and drawn. He was a fugitive, fearful of being tracked down. He told me he was keeping constantly on the move as he worked on his manuscript giving the inside story of BOSS, and he was certain its agents were out to stop him. It may have been paranoia or it may have been reality. Either way the hunter spy was looking hunted.

For two days we sat in my room and in the bar lounge, talking. I put my key question to him: What the hell was he doing in Robert Smit's house the day after the assassinations?

'General van den Bergh sent me there to clean up the place,' was Winter's deadpan reply, explaining that this involved re-moving all traces of evidence, fingerprints, scribbled messages, anything that could help the investigators trace the perpetrators of the crime. So while the police were there ostensibly to gather evidence, his job was essentially to remove it. Van den Bergh had been particularly concerned that he should 'clean up' Smit's car, which Winter said he couldn't understand since the car had been in the hands of the chauffeur, Daniel Tshabalala, throughout the night of the murders. But he had not queried this. His job was not to reason why.

Winter said he had also gone with the police to the mortu-ary, where he had seen the couple's naked and damaged bodies. Robert Smit's wounds, he said, showed clearly he had been shot by a professional assassin. He had been hit by a series of bullets from the head down. Winter explained that the proper way to shoot a victim is to raise your revolver — in this case a .38 Webley — above your head, holding it with both hands, then fire rapidly while moving the firearm downwards. That way the bullets will strike head, neck, chest and abdomen, ensuring that vital organs are hit.

Jeanne-Cora had been shot in the back of the head with a lighter-calibre pistol, Winter said, showing that at least two assassins had been involved in the killings. The head shot would have been fatal, which suggested the 14 stiletto stabbings might have been some sort of blood-lust ritual.

Winter had another intriguing theory. The postmortem examination, he said, had shown there was food in Robert Smit's stomach. This indicated that he had eaten a meal before returning home, leading Winter to speculate that he had dined out and had sex with a lover after being interviewed by *Citizen* reporter Rita Niemand, and finally returned home around midnight, not just after 9 pm as the police had originally assumed. Winter's theory was that the assassins had killed Jeanne-Cora first, shortly after her phone call to the election office, then sat waiting for Robert to arrive, at which point the professional gunned him down as he walked through the front door.

Who were the assassins? Winter professed not to know. Who had hired them, and why? Again he feigned ignorance. How much had Winter really known about the killings? I must confess my own uncertainty on that. Winter was a complex personality, distorted by his painful childhood and years in the espionage business. He was smart and there was a yearning within him for honesty and acceptance. But I never knew when to believe him. When his book on BOSS was finally published it contained many fascinating disclosures, but also a number of allegations and smears that I knew to be patently false.

* * *

FOR YEARS, RUMOURS ran rife about the motive for the Smit murders. One early version was that Robert Smit had visited Prime Minister Vorster at his holiday home near Cape Town, and during a walk on the beach had told him of his intention, once in Parliament, to disclose the existence of a $3-billion slush fund established at a Swiss bank for the benefit of government leaders in the event of a national emergency. Vorster, alarmed at the implications, had summoned General van den Bergh and told him to investigate the matter 'and do something about it'. At which Van den Bergh had taken it upon himself to eliminate the source of such a disclosure.

Another was that, while in Washington, Smit had worked clandestinely for an organisation called Santam International, created to circumvent the arms boycott of South Africa. Its finances were said to have come from the same secret fund that had been used for Eschel Rhoodie's projects. Kitt Katzin wrote a report in the *Sunday Express* saying Smit had been murdered 'shortly after he uncovered a foreign currency racket and made it known that he meant to expose the swindlers'. The *Sunday Times* quoted a woman named Emmarentia Liebenberg, a friend of Smit's, saying that five months before his death the candidate had told her he had decided to approach a senior Cabinet minister about a matter that would 'rock the nation' and go 'right to the top'.

The Afrikaans Sunday paper *Rapport* quoted Smit's brother Iaan as recalling a visit to him in Springs. When he asked his brother how his campaign was going, Smit had replied: 'Things are not right. There are things on the go that are improper [*onbehoorlik*] and that will shock the people. I am sorry but at the right time I am going to go public with it.' At much the same time a British publication, *Euromoney*, reported that rumours had circulated in Washington, when Smit was at the IMF, that he had become suspicious about money transactions taking place, and that on his return to South Africa he had uncovered 'a capital evacuation scheme'.

But by far the most intriguing explanation came from none other than Eschel Rhoodie. Shortly before leaving the country to start a new life in Atlanta, Georgia, Rhoodie called on me to say he was writing a book that would deal with the Smit murders. It was a novel, he said, but like a Frederick Forsyth saga it would stick close to the facts. 'It will lead to a lot of speculation,' he said with a grin, 'but only those who read it will know if it's true.'

Rhoodie duly wrote his book, but it was never published, and soon after completing it he died unexpectedly and prematurely. Twenty-two years later I stumbled upon the unpublished manuscript while arranging for Mervyn Rees's private papers, after his own untimely death, to be archived at the Institute for the Advancement of Journalism in Johannesburg. Rhoodie had sent it to Rees with a covering letter offering him 20 per cent of the proceeds if he could find a publisher. Obviously Rees failed to do that, but the request was in itself remarkable testimony to the curious bond that had developed between the flamboyant propagandist and the investigative journalist who had brought him down.

It was a racy book, laced with sex, glamour and political intrigue, which I thought more in the style of Ian Fleming than Frederick Forsyth. But there were intriguing touches. His main character, not very subtly named Robert Smit, had stumbled upon an immensely wealthy but shady Costa Rican businessman who had done a deal with a small Afrikaner super-elite, more exclusive and secretive even than the Broederbond, calling themselves The Puritans, who had managed to cream off money from a secret Swiss bank account and were using him as the middleman to invest the money in a Costa Rican entity called The Puritan Company. Again, the money was there for these select few to use should the ANC ever gain control of South Africa.

Rhoodie's manuscript names the hired assassins as two Swedes who entered South Africa through Swaziland posing as businessmen under the names of Sven Halforsen and Olaff Flaggstad. They brought with them a .38 Webley revolver and a .32 Beretta with specially adapted small silencers.

He links the assassins to a West German terrorist group called the Red Army Unit Ten (perhaps explaining the spray-painted 'RAU-TEM' slogan) that had killed two German financiers, Dr Jürgen Ponto and Dr Hanns Martin Schleyer, some years before. This passage, at least, was close to historical fact in that the killings of Ponto and Schleyer involved the militant left-wing Red Army Faction, also known as the Baader-Meinhof Group. But whether Rhoodie was correct in attributing the Smit killings to them is questionable, for 17 years later an investigation ordered by the government of the new democratic South Africa came to a different conclusion.

While stressing that its findings were not conclusive, the 1999 investigation reported that the Smits had most likely been murdered by a special BOSS 'Z-Squad'. The investigators named the probable assassins as Phil Freeman, a former British commando who had settled in South Africa after the Second World War, and one AFP 'Dries' Verwey, who had also joined BOSS's Z-Squad. Both were now dead. The investigators said there had also been a third member of the hit squad, whom they declined to name because he was still living in 1999, they believed in Australia, and therefore might still be subject to arrest.

There the case of South Africa's greatest unsolved political murder remains. All the principal figures involved are dead or disappeared, but the mystery itself remains alive.

* * *

FAST FORWARD again and you find me in the office of the gentle Dullah Omar, Minister of Justice in Nelson Mandela's government. I explain to him that I am still troubled by that secret account at the Union Bank of Switzerland where the tellers had happily accepted 80 Swiss francs from me over two days. Whose account was that? Who had profited from my meagre deposits? I suggested that the new government's cash-strapped Treasury might be able to ease its difficulties by as much as $3 billion if it made an assertive application to the bank to disclose information about the account.

I made this suggestion because I had recently read about a case in which the Supreme Court of Switzerland had ordered the UBS to release information to Scotland Yard about an account that had allegedly been used to deposit a $9-million ransom paid in an Irish Republican Army (IRA) blackmail scheme two years earlier. The bank claimed that providing the information would endanger the customers involved. But the Swiss court held that it was in the country's best interests for the bank to cooperate with the British government, although it ruled that the information supplied by the bank could be used only in prosecuting the IRA.

This precedent struck me as perhaps the start of a softening of the strictness of Switzerland's bank secrecy laws. A call to contacts in Zürich supported this notion. A few glaring cases of serious criminals escaping justice because of the secrecy laws had caused a public outcry in Switzerland. The country was being accused of protecting murderers for financial gain, and there was a possibility that the laws might be amended to enable a government to apply for bank details to be disclosed if it could show that a serious crime was involved.

The Smits had been murdered, I pointed out to Omar, so if the government could show that disclosing the details of the numbered account at the UBS could lead to the arrest of the assassins, an official application might be successful.

Omar liked the idea. He asked me to set out all the details in a document that he could show to President Nelson Mandela. This I did, in a letter dated 7 October 1997.

Time passed, and when I heard nothing I called on Omar again. 'I'm sorry,' he murmured softly, 'but the Old Man doesn't want us to open up this thing. He doesn't want to stir up old conflicts with the Afrikaners while he is working so hard to bring about racial reconciliation.'

So typical of Mandela. A man who, whatever the circumstances or temptations, always knew where his priorities lay. So there the matter rests. The numbered account, and my 80 Swiss francs, are presumably still there in the vaults of that Zürich bank.

* * *

I RETURNED to the Mail after the trip to Zürich and the meeting with Gordon Winter in Dublin. In 1981 the prestigious *World Press Review*, which monitors the performance of newspapers globally, named Rex Gibson and myself joint International Editors of the Year for our exposure of the Information scandal in the face of draconian press control laws. We were flown to Washington, DC, for the presentation, where we were also invited to address the Washington Press Club. I flew home from there to find a newly published book on my desk assessing the quality of what the authors considered to be the world's greatest newspapers. They rated the *Rand Daily Mail* among the top 12 in the world. It was the highlight of my career.

Four months later I was fired.

CHAPTER TWENTY-THREE

Fired

IT TOOK ME a long time to recognise the duplicity of the men who had appointed me editor of the *Rand Daily Mail*. Every editor is entitled to be given a clear policy mandate upon being appointed to such a highly responsible role, so closely associated with freedom of expression and the national interest, which is why I had gone to such lengths to ensure absolute clarity when I was interviewed for the job. I assumed those interviewing me took it equally seriously. I had accepted their sincerity and honesty when they told me they did not require me to change the policy the Mail had been following for the past two decades. I took that to be the mandate they had given me on behalf of the board of directors.

But I was wrong. They had deceived me. They did want a policy change, a 'new image' as they later put it, but they never had the courage to tell me so outright. It was a deception that led to my dismissal, then to the closure of the country's greatest newspaper just four years before everything it stood for was validated. A death its own chief assassin was later to admit had been a terrible mistake.

I knew Ian MacPherson didn't like the newspaper. He had made that clear enough during that extraordinary interview before my appointment to the *Sunday Express*. But I thought he understood that one could not radically change the image of a newspaper —

particularly one with such a strong image as the Mail – without doing grave damage to its reputation and readership. That was why I had moved with such caution in de-emphasising Johnny Johnson's aggressive right-wing racism on the *Sunday Express*.

I knew for certain that Leycester Walton, whom I had known and respected for many years, didn't want the Mail's policy to be changed. But Walton had retired by this time; this profoundly decent human being and fine newspaperman simply couldn't bear working under the chairmanship of the crass MacPherson, whose understanding of the industry was negligible.

It was Clive Kinsley I misread. I had found him warm and friendly, even charming, at first, and his strong support for us throughout the hugely expensive and risky Muldergate investigation was all an editor could have wished for. I was impressed and I thought we had built a good relationship. But bit by bit I became aware of another side to his personality. He was a deceptive man. He hated face-to-face confrontation, but he harboured dogmatic ideas. He was also paranoid about people he thought were plotting against him.

I first became aware of this when he would pop into my office, all warm and friendly, to raise some troubling aspect of the paper's trading position. He would offer a viewpoint, and sometimes I would disagree. A discussion would follow, usually ending in what I considered to be a reasonable and practical compromise – only to find a memorandum on my desk a few days later laying down his original viewpoint as a diktat. I would call on him to express my concern, saying I thought we had reached a compromise agreement – at which point he would apologise, saying he had acted in haste and would reconsider, only for another memo to arrive confirming the edict.

This kind of duplicity eroded our relationship. I began accusing him of not being open with me; he began accusing me of being difficult. Our first serious clash arose when he issued a memorandum to all four editors in the company insisting that we could not dispatch reporters outside our provinces without his permission. It was obviously a cost-saving exercise, but it was a clear intrusion into the editor's prerogative. Our job as editors was to assess the importance of news events and at the same time ensure that we remained within our allocated budgets. For a manager, a non-journalist, to assume responsibility for assessing the news value of a story assignment was to violate that principle. I understood Kinsley's concern about the Mail's trading position, but I felt this issue should have been discussed with me and my fellow editors. The instruction affected the Mail particularly; as a daily newspaper it had to move swiftly to get the news first. Speed and decisiveness are the essence of running a daily newspaper. Bureaucratic trivia get in the way.

I intended raising the issue with Kinsley, but the first crisis arose before I could do so. Tony Rider, our excellent Zimbabwean bureau chief, who had been the only South African journalist to call that country's independence elections correctly, phoned me at home one evening in November 1980 to tell me he had picked up reports of clashes between militia of President Robert Mugabe's Zimbabwe African National Liberation Army (Zanla) and those of Joshua Nkomo's Zimbabwe People's Revolutionary Army (Zipra) at Entumbane, outside Bulawayo, in the southern province of Matabeleland. Since these were the newly independent country's most important rival factions, Rider felt he should get there immediately. He wanted to leave right away.

Unsure whether this fell under the new diktat or not, I called Kinsley's home to ask him for authorisation, to be told he was attending a banquet in Durban. It took some time to establish where the banquet was being held, and once I had the number I phoned the venue and asked for Kinsley to be called to the phone. A message came back that he was occupied at the banquet and couldn't be disturbed. I asked to speak to the manager and asked him please to tell Kinsley that the editor of the *Rand Daily Mail* needed to speak with him.

When Kinsley eventually came on the line he was in explosive mood. 'What the hell do you mean by interrupting me at this function,' he yelled. I was completely taken aback. 'But Clive,' I protested, 'you've just put out a memo saying we have to get your clearance before sending any reporter across a provincial border. Tony Rider needs to—'

I got no further. My explanation seemed only to make him angrier. 'This is outrageous!' he cut in. 'I was in the midst of important discussions' – and he slammed down the phone.

I phoned Rider back. 'I'm sorry,' I told him. 'The MD won't authorise the assignment under a new rule he's just laid down.'

When Kinsley returned to his office a few days later, I went to see him. He was contrite, telling me he had been working late for weeks, that he was exhausted and worried about the paper's trading position. I left it at that. There seemed no point in irritating him further. But it was too late to get Rider to the scene. We missed the story.[1]

As it turned out, by failing to report the two-day Entumbane battle the *Rand Daily Mail* missed the first instalment of what over the next two years was to swell into the Gukurahundi massacres, in which an estimated 20 000 Ndebele people were killed by Mugabe's North Korean-trained Fifth Brigade. Many of them were shot in public executions, often after being forced to dig their own graves in front of their families. Sadly, Rider, who was badly put out by being blocked from going to Entumbane, never managed fully to catch up on the story as it spread, and then he was killed when his car collided with a military truck on Zimbabwe's narrow strip roads. And because the Mail, which was miles ahead of all other papers in its coverage of events in Zimbabwe at that time, stumbled on this one, the Gukurahundi massacres never acquired the global notoriety they deserved.

There were other differences, too, between Kinsley and I, almost invariably arising from those irritating edicts that arrived in memo form without prior discussion. I once tried to organise a meeting with my fellow editors to discuss them, which annoyed Kinsley immensely – and perhaps justifiably. But in the daily hurly-burly of bringing out newspapers in a society riddled with racial conflict and a despotic government constantly threatening to act against us, these were really minor irritants. What was more serious was that over time I became increasingly aware that there were fundamental differences of philosophy and strategy between my managing director and myself.

What made it worse was that he never alluded to them directly.

He never came out openly and said: 'Look, here is what you will have to do, and if you are not prepared to do it we shall have to part ways.' Nothing remotely like that. Instead we drifted along in a state of muted disagreement.

* * *

TWO FUNDAMENTAL ISSUES rendered the relationship between Kinsley and myself unworkable, and in the end led to the death of the *Rand Daily Mail*. Two simple issues. But all the king's horses and all the king's men in the management and board of SAAN and of the giant Anglo American Corporation, which was the ultimate owner of the newspaper, couldn't see them.

The first was Kinsley's inability to see that the *Rand Daily Mail*'s burgeoning black readership was of any economic value to the newspaper. Apparently after my departure he mentioned once or twice that black readers might be of value some time in the future, but not in the here and now. What he wanted were white readers, especially white women readers, who he felt made the key household purchases that interested advertisers. And we were losing those as our black numbers swelled.

My counterargument was that the Mail had an established image, which was strong both nationally and internationally, that we had a loyal readership and reputation across all racial lines, and that it would be fatal, both politically and economically, to shatter that image. We would lose credibility and surely advertising revenue with it. Moreover, as he well knew, I was not prepared to go that route. I had made that clear before they appointed me: if that was the route they wanted the paper to take, they should have found another editor. But even then I believed it would be fatal.

Kinsley's other key issue was a determination to centralise control upon himself. For years each newspaper in the group had had its own business manager, circulation manager, advertising manager and advertising staff. Soon after taking over as CEO, Kinsley abolished that system and established a central management team, with himself in command, to deal with all the publications.

My first inkling of what Kinsley really thought about the *Rand*

406

Daily Mail came in a casual remark he made after I had testified before a government-appointed commission of inquiry into the conduct of the South African media, chaired by Judge MT Steyn, a former administrator of South West Africa. I was a reluctant witness because it was by now commonly assumed by the opposition press that the government used these investigations to provide a legal peg on which to hang further constraints on our ability to cover the news. This was the third such commission to have been established by the apartheid regime, and Joel Mervis, editor of the *Sunday Times* and himself a trained barrister, had made an application *in limine* urging the commission members to resign rather than let themselves be used in this way. The commission had rejected his application, and Mervis had refused to testify. But I decided to go ahead and use the platform to present a case for the media in general and the Mail in particular.

In doing so I told the commission bluntly that I was certain my testimony would do nothing to deter the government's determination to further muzzle the press. I said I believed the Minister of the Interior, Alwyn Schlebusch, had already decided to act against the newspapers and was simply looking to the commission for a pretext so that it didn't look too crude. 'The Government hopes it will find something in the commission's report that will help it do this, something like a recommendation in favour of a register of journalists, for example,' I said.

'I may not be able to stop the introduction of such measures,' I added, 'but I and my fellow journalists can make sure that when such measures are introduced, it is on record that this was not done with the connivance or in accordance with the wishes of our profession [we believed this would lead to critical journalists being struck off the roll]. This, then, is the occasion for me, as editor of a newspaper that has been a prime target in the Government's anti-Press campaign for more than 20 years, to state what it is we are trying to do and why we are trying to do it.'

I then presented a memorandum. The judge interrupted me several times, asking questions and seeking clarification, but the core part of it was that apartheid had turned South Africa into a divided society whose members were isolated from each other to an unparalleled degree. The influence of apartheid had gone beyond the separation of white and black, and had created a 'honeycomb of cellular group ghettoes, full of ghetto attitudes of "us" and "them", and with little understanding of the other groups. Empathy is not a flourishing commodity in South Africa.' In such an extraordinarily divided society, the *Rand Daily Mail* provided the most significant channel of communication between all these segregated groups, 'telling each something of the attitudes and activities of the others. No other institution is able to do this on the same scale, not the churches or the cultural institutions or even the universities.' The memorandum continued:

> Most newspapers are also predominantly group orientated. *The World* and *Golden City Post*, which have both now been closed by the Government, were extremely important newspapers in that they provided black people with platforms of their own. But they did not tell whites about the black community because whites did not buy them on any significant scale. Nor did they tell blacks much about the white community because their reporting was devoted almost exclusively to black affairs. They operated within their own group cell and told blacks about the black community … Similarly the Afrikaans newspapers don't tell Afrikaners much about blacks or blacks much about Afrikaners. Several of the major English newspapers stretch across a wider spectrum, but none equals the *Rand Daily Mail* for its universality. Readership surveys show we have some 880 000 readers a day, a little more than half of whom are blacks. A quarter of our white readers are Afrikaners, the rest English-speakers. We also have substantial numbers of coloured and Asian readers.
>
> We believe this is the primary role we must try to play − to provide a channel of communication between all these segregated groups in a tension-ridden society. We also provide black people with just about their only opportunity to state their own opinions on national issues, and to express their aspirations and grievances, in a medium which brings them to the attention of the white ruling community.

As it turned out, the commission's report did everything Schlebusch could have wished for, and more. It didn't merely provide a pretext for action, it made a specific recommendation that a compulsory register of journalists be established, with a statutory press council (initially appointed by the government), which would have the power to strike journalists off the register. And no one would be allowed to employ a journalist who was not on the register.

It was grotesque. But thankfully it met with such a wall of opposition from the English-language press, backed up by a global outcry spearheaded by the International Press Institute, that the government flinched. It hesitated and delayed until it was eventually overtaken by events. The register was never established, although three decades later President Jacob Zuma's ANC government came up with a similar idea, and encountered the same opposition.

At the time of my presentation, I sent a copy of my testimony to Kinsley. A few days later he came to my office to congratulate me. 'I thought it was brilliant,' he said with a smile. 'Well done.' Then, still smiling, he added: 'But you realise, of course, that you have put your finger on the *Mail's* key trading problem.'

I was taken aback. 'What do you mean, Clive?' I asked.

'Well, what looks so good politically is precisely what is making it difficult to sell advertising in the *Mail*. You don't have a proper readership profile.'

'But that is our readership profile,' I protested. 'Those are our supporters. Like-minded people across the colour line. All part of an emerging multiracial middle class with the same needs, all buying the same kind of things.'

'Well, the industry doesn't see it that way,' Kinsley replied, as he turned to leave. I presumed that by 'the industry' he meant the advertising agencies, all run by white managers and predominantly staffed by whites. He was telling me, in his oblique way, that in the eyes of the ad agencies our black readers, consumers, were not the same as white consumers. That they didn't count when selling advertising space. Which implied that our multiracialism was the reason for our trading problems, that for a newspaper to succeed in South Africa it had to be an apartheid newspaper, with a readership that was predominantly either white or black.

The implications hit me like a bombshell. If that were Kinsley's firm belief, it meant there was an inherent incompatibility between him and what the *Rand Daily Mail* stood for.

From there the conflict grew. We continued to lose white readers and gain black readers, and Kinsley, backed by his advertising manager, Nigel Twidale, kept urging me to reverse the trend. But how? Did they want me to lose the black readers? Did they want to dump the special Extra Edition that was targeted specifically at Johannesburg's big black townships, Soweto and Alexandra? 'No, no,' Kinsley replied. 'But we must get more white readers, particularly white women readers.'

That quest for white women readers became an obsession with him. He came back to it, again and again, every time we had a discussion. *The Star*, our afternoon rival, was dominant in attracting white women readers, he pointed out, and it was white women who made the key household purchasing decisions. We had to get more white women readers to be competitive.

Frankly, I didn't know how to do that. My own research told me that morning newspapers worldwide tended to have fewer women readers than afternoon newspapers. The rhythm of women's days, especially married women, mothers, determined that. Their early mornings tended to be heavily committed to such activities as getting the children ready and off to school, often driving them there, then attending to daily household chores, grocery shopping and the like, so that by the time they are through the morning is done. They then have time to sit down and read early editions of an afternoon paper. Hence *The Star*'s entrenched advantage in this particular sector. Single women and working women lived to a somewhat different rhythm, but South Africa at that time was still far behind the developed world when it came to the feminist revolution. Their numbers didn't correct the imbalance.

Too much politics, was the insistent cry. Women weren't interested in politics. Too much news about black people and black issues. That was turning white readers off. Too much space being given to the emerging black trade union movement. The white business community didn't like that; it was turning them off.

I knew all this, but what was a newspaper editor to do about

it? As I had anticipated when I took the job, the whole political landscape was changing. Black people were re-emerging
from the years of silence and giving voice to their grievances and
demands. The legalising of black trade unionism was providing that
voice with an organisational framework, and with the ability to
negotiate and strike as weapons to exert pressure on the white
establishment.

So black politics was back, which meant the whole basis of
our national discourse was changing. Politics was no longer a
whites-only thing; now it was becoming an interracial thing. The
black revolution, interrupted in 1960, was about to resume. I had
anticipated this as I took the editorial seat, for all the signs were there
with the upsurge of Black Consciousness and the establishment of
the Wiehahn Commission, which was why I had restructured and
strengthened our political and labour teams. It was a huge story in
the making, and the Mail was right on top of it.

White South Africa was alarmed by it. Alarmed by the news of
what was happening. Because of our honeycomb society, whites
in their isolated social cells were not in touch with the blacks
in theirs. In their secluded lives they saw little of the mounting
turmoil in the townships, but the Mail was telling them about it,
day after day, and they didn't like it. They didn't want to read
about it; it was too scary. They thought it was sensationalising the
news, stirring things up, encouraging blacks to be troublesome.
And the government and the Afrikaans press were telling them
that, day after day. The Mail was a troublemaker.

No wonder we were losing some white readers, although our
loyal readers, those informed enough to realise the importance
of what we were reporting, which included a remarkable number of Afrikaners who knew their own language newspapers,
all committed supporters of the Nationalist government, were
giving them a heavily sanitised version of events. They were
propaganda sheets, and serious Afrikaners who wanted to know
what was going on knew that they could get that best from the
Rand Daily Mail.

And no wonder we were gaining black readers so rapidly,
because with the main black newspapers shut down, the Mail was

giving them the best coverage of events that were of the most intense concern to them.

So how was I to reverse the trend of our readership profile? Stop reporting the news of an impending revolution because whites didn't want to read about it? Stop monitoring the growth of potential black political power through the new labour unions? As an editor committed to journalism's code that a newspaper's job is to report the news as fairly and as accurately as possible, without fear or favour, and never to bow to extraneous factors that hide or distort the truth, I couldn't do that. And Kinsley kept telling me he didn't want me to. He just wanted more white readers. Particularly more white women readers.

What made matters doubly stressful was that the apartheid government was also berating us for publishing what it called 'negative' news giving South Africa a bad name overseas. We were an 'anti-South African' newspaper, siding with the country's enemies (meaning mainly the Soviet Union). We would respond editorially saying it was not our news reports that were harming South Africa's reputation abroad, but the government's inhumane policies. But it cut no ice. The demand was for more 'patriotic' news reporting. And the pressure and threats and new items of restrictive legislation kept mounting, increasing the risks the press faced. I remember a remark that Ben Bradlee, executive editor of *The Washington Post*, made during a visit to the Mail newsroom. As he flipped through a book by our lawyer, Kelsey Stuart, listing the 120 restrictive press laws we had to navigate, he shook his head. 'You guys have to make decisions every day of a kind that we in the US might have to make once in our careers,' he marvelled.

The threats and the pressure from the government side were immense. One way and another I wound up in court six times, fortunately all successfully thanks to our brilliant legal team of Stuart and Sydney Kentridge. But it was tough. Now here were Kinsley and Twidale piling it on from within my own management. I recall Ray Louw, who had been through it all himself, once saying to me in a moment of sympathy: 'It's like being knocked around the boxing ring by a tough opponent, and then having your own seconds coming out of your corner hitting you over the head with the water bucket.'

* * *

JAMMED BETWEEN this rock and a hard place, I found myself struggling more and more with the concept that our black readers were of no value to advertisers. Nigel Twidale referred to their numbers as 'the black take-off'. By that he didn't mean the rocket that was about to take off in less than a decade and that has advertising managers scrambling for the black readers and audiences today. He meant the number that he had to 'take off' of the Mail's audited circulation figures when he and his team sold advertising in the Mail. In other words, they were worthless.

This not only puzzled me, it angered me. Here we were, a newspaper that had been arguing the case for racial integration, presenting the vision of a multiracial society for 20 years, while our advertising department considered our black readers of no value. Political differences aside, this was hardly likely to make for good teamwork. I never heard Kinsley use that objectionable phrase, but nor did I hear him contest it even though it was used many times in his presence. What was obvious, though, was that if the advertising sales staff believed that, and were backed up by management, we were hardly likely to see a boom in the Mail's advertising revenue.

Part of Kinsley's complaint about our readership profile was that it didn't match those of other papers in the group, which made selling advertising on a group basis difficult. We didn't fit the package, as he put it. The advertising team had developed what he considered to be a skilfully developed sales pitch, and the Mail's readership profile was out of kilter with it. This was hampering the group sales effort, so we were holding back the other papers as well. Clearly he wanted a change to get us back in line with the others. But he never called it a political change. Always an 'image change', the difference being something I found hard to decipher.

The more I thought about all this, the more convinced I became that we had things arse about face, in newsroom parlance, that instead of wanting to change the product to match the sales pitch, we should be developing a sales pitch to match the product. This became my new enterprise.

First, I gathered information from a body called the Central Business District (CBD) organisation, established to study conditions in the centre of Johannesburg, a city that had grown from a honky-tonk mining camp to a burgeoning megalopolis in just over a hundred years. Among other things, they were studying patterns of demographic change and economic activity in the city. What struck my eye as I waded through their reports and talked to their officials was that 60 per cent, and growing, of retail trade done in the CBD was with black customers. So much for Twidale's 'black take-off'.

I also recalled a series of lectures that Raymond Louw had organised for the company while he was still editor of the Mail, to prepare us for the advent of television. One of the many peculiarities of South Africa was that the apartheid government had refused to allow television into the country for a quarter of a century, a peculiar phobia on the part of Albert Hertzog, the long-serving Minister of Posts and Telecommunications, who feared TV's modernising and liberalising influences. Eventually his successors woke up to the fact that they could control it and turn it into a powerful propaganda machine. That meant this powerful medium didn't creep up on us in the newspaper industry gradually, as it had elsewhere. It came with a bang, in its most modern, full-colour form and to a population long hungering for it. Foreseeing its implication for the print media, Louw had brought a number of specialists from the United States to advise us how best to meet this new competition.

Their advice was fairly simple. You can't beat TV with breaking news, which had always been the Mail's strength, so focus on more interpretative news. Use TV as a news appetiser: it will tell people what has happened, you in the print media must tell them why and how it happened and what its implications may be. On the advertising side, these media specialists warned that TV would go primarily for national advertising, meaning the adverts of big national and multinational corporations, which had the nation-wide audiences they wanted. So, while newspapers should still try to retain a share of this big-money market, they should protect themselves from TV by strengthening their retail advertising – in other words, local advertising, all the way down to the shop on the corner – which national TV would not be pursuing.

I don't know how much of this was passed on to Kinsley in the course of the managerial transition. I suspect nothing. He certainly revealed no recognition of it. But I decided to combine the advice of the specialists with the information I had gleaned from the CBD association to draft a proposal for Kinsley.

Firstly, I suggested that our loss of white readers was surely due in part to the big-bang arrival of television only the year before I assumed the editorship of the Mail, since whites constituted the majority of initial TV subscribers. Secondly, I urged that our advertising pitch should be reshaped to include the black readers, pointing out that blacks were the main purchasers in the retail stores in the heart of our main circulation area. I wrote a memo proposing this to Kinsley. His reaction was indifference. He seemed to disapprove of my venturing into his domain.

Undaunted, I went further and discussed the idea with the country's leading sociologist at the time, Professor Lawrence Schlemmer. He was enthusiastic, to the point of offering to undertake a major research project within the Johannesburg CBD to assess the potential success of my idea. So keen was he that he offered to do this for us cost-free. Kinsley showed no interest. I suggested that our black readers were leading opinion-formers in the townships, and that their influence would extend far beyond their own numbers. A sales pitch developed specifically for the Mail should emphasise that as well. Kinsley remained unimpressed. The Mail needed more white readers, he insisted, especially white women readers, to fit into the group sales pitch. He never took up Professor Schlemmer's offer of a cost-free survey. His mind was closed on the subject.

* * *

FRUSTRATING though this was, Kinsley's most fatal error was his decision to centralise all management responsibilities on a single, centralised unit serving all the papers, with himself in command. It deprived the *Rand Daily Mail* of its own management team, with whom we in the editorial department had worked harmoniously as a team for years. We could have liaised with them in working out the kind of sales presentation Professor Schlemmer had in mind, which I believe would have enabled the Mail to survive these troubled transition years and enter the new South Africa triumphantly as the flagship of the new country's media.

As it turned out, the loss of our own sales team was the paper's death knell. Nor was Kinsley totally unaware of this possibility. On the day he announced his decision, Roy Paulson, then the Mail's manager, walked into Kinsley's office and told him: 'Clive, this is a bad decision. As of this day you have killed the *Rand Daily Mail*.'[2] It is worth noting that Paulson gave this bold prediction to Kinsley despite the fact that the rearrangement involved his own promotion to group administrative manager.

To this day, Paulson believes the Mail could have been saved. 'Look, it was a hard sell,' he admits, 'but our sales team tried hard, they cared about the Mail, and they succeeded. But once they were absorbed into a company pool of sales people, that team spirit diffused. Then everyone's chief concern was to fulfil his quota, which they did most easily on the powerful *Sunday Times*, which almost sold itself, all to the detriment of the other publications. They weren't going to waste too much time on the hard sell of the *Rand Daily Mail*.'

Not only that, Paulson pointed out that the Mail was different from the other papers in the group and that the group sales presentation would not work for it. It needed its own team presenting its own particular merits. But Kinsley remained adamant in the face of Paulson's warnings, 'You're talking rubbish,' he told the Mail's departing manager.[3]

In fairness, it must be noted that Kinsley and Twidale were taking their cue from 'the industry', as they called the managers and staff members of the advertising agencies, and indeed the advertisers themselves, the owners and managers of the businesses with whom the ad agencies were dealing. The vast majority of them were white South Africans, sharing the same anxieties and prejudices of the general population. They didn't like the Mail and some said so openly in the op-ed columns of other newspapers.

Paulson believes he and his staff could have saved the paper if they had stayed with the Mail and not been appointed to the centralised management. And where, aside from his disagreement over the *Rand Daily Mail*, he was not impressed with his boss's capabilities.

'Kinsley was inefficient,' says Paulson. 'Sloppy. He didn't attend to detail. I used to come in to work early and go into his office, where I would riffle through documents piled on his desk and take out those that had been lying there unattended for days, and deal with them myself. And the worst of it was, he never noticed.'

Finally, Paulson decided to leave. 'I went into his office and said bluntly to Kinsley: "Clive, I know you don't like me and I don't like you. So let's talk severance."'[4]

Paulson went from there to be general manager of Caxton, a rival printing and publishing company. Later he was to return to the reincarnated SAAN, then called Times Media, to help resuscitate the company after the death of the Mail and the near demise of the company. He is now retired.

* * *

TO ADD TO our woes, Kinsley told me on one of his visits to my office in August 1980 that the English-language newspapers were going to increase their cover prices from 15 cents a copy to 20 cents. The newspaper industry had long had a collusion agreement on the selling price of papers, which meant we would have to follow suit. This was obviously going to knock our circulation figures back somewhat, as it always did with these periodic price increases, only for sales to recover gradually over a few months.

Under the constant pressure to 'do something' editorially about our declining advertising sales, my mind flashed back to a bold suggestion Ray Louw had made while he was editor, which had proved remarkably successful. Instead of trying to compete with *The Star* on advertising rates, Louw suggested to then MD Walton that the Mail should charge a higher rate. That would bring in more revenue, and since there would be fewer ads per page Mail ads would be more visible than *The Star*'s, which would please advertisers. Fewer ads would also mean more editorial space, thus more news, leading to higher circulation, which would also please advertisers. It sounded wacky but it worked like a dream. Circulation and revenue increased considerably.

Prompted by this recollection, and desperate to find a way other than those unattainable white women readers, I asked Kinsley what the economic impact would be if we seized the moment when all dailies were increasing their cover prices and took the Mail ahead of the field to 25 cents. Kinsley's eyes lit up. 'What an interesting idea,' he said. 'It would knock circulation, of course, but it would bring in a lot more revenue. This could be the answer. Let me do some calculations.'

I never saw those calculations, but I was swept along by Kinsley's enthusiasm for the idea. We had a series of discussions about it, always just he and I: Kinsley hated big meetings, always preferring one on one, never more than three. So wider input on any idea was minimal. My chief concern was how, editorially, we could justify being the most expensive daily newspaper in the country. I stressed that this meant we would have to sell ourselves as more of an upmarket paper. Kinsley liked the idea. He obviously believed this would shake out a lot of black readers who wouldn't be able to afford the higher price. I insisted that it meant selling our high-quality news coverage more vigorously. Kinsley had been warning me that he would want me to retrench at least 20 editorial staff members in the coming year's budget: I now argued that this would be unthinkable with a higher cover price. Indeed I argued that, if we adopted such a strategy, not only would I want to retain our full editorial staff, I would also want 15 extra columns of editorial space a week to carry more news to justify our higher price.

When Kinsley came back to me, he was all smiles. 'We can do it,' he said. 'With that higher cover price we can come close to breaking even in next year's budget.' He pointed out that our anticipated loss for the current year, 1980, was in the region of R2 250 000 and the price increase would bring in about R2 million.

What a relief. I called a staff meeting and told them what we were going to do. I told them management believed we could

418

almost break even with the higher cover price, but we would have to work harder to maintain our lead in news coverage. The challenge would be to retain our most loyal readers. I believed our white constituency was growing, since the Progressive Party, which we had supported since Gandar's day, had grown from having only one MP to becoming the official opposition in Parliament. The Saturday edition, once derided as the 'Egghead' edition, had grown from the weakest to the largest circulation of the week. Serious analytical news and comment seemed to be selling. I was more uncertain about our black readership, all poorer people, but it was growing so fast I hoped the setback would not be too severe.

We planned a campaign to launch what we called the new 'premier Mail', telling readers we were going to give them a bigger, better, more newsy and more informative newspaper for their extra five cents.

But it was a disaster. The public was angry and circulation plunged. I must take my share of the blame for this. It was my idea. But Kinsley had backed it and I had not reckoned with the fact that we still did not have a sales team of our own with a specific sales pitch to market the new 'premier Mail'. It was still the same group team under Twidale, selling advertising for the group as a whole. The justification for our higher cover price seemingly didn't get through to 'the industry', for advertising fell along with circulation.

But I was not aware of the full story. As always, communication between editorial and management was sporadic, and after launching the 'premier Mail' there was a long silence from the management floor. Although I knew the circulation figures had plunged, as we had anticipated, I had no idea what the overall financial situation was.

Come 16 February 1981, budgeting time, Kinsley asked me to come up to his office. He was looking gloomy. 'We are budgeting for a loss of R4 380 000 this year,' he said. 'It's bad.'

'But how can that be, Clive?' I asked, astonished. 'You told me that with the new cover price we would come close to breaking even.'

'Well it hasn't worked out that way,' he replied. 'There have been a few miscalculations.' He explained that the 25-cent cover price hadn't brought in the extra R2 million he had told me it would, but only R900 000. Furthermore, the cost of the paper for the extra paging he had given me for the 'premier Mail' hadn't been budgeted for.

'But how could that come about?' I asked, flabbergasted. 'Who screwed up?'

'I don't really know,' Kinsley replied. 'But I'm afraid the extra 40 to 60 pages a week for the 'Punter's Friend' weren't budgeted for either.'

'Punter's Friend' was a long-standing editorial attraction that involved week-by-week computerised predictions of the country's horse races. It was astonishingly accurate and was by far our single most successful circulation booster. Yet here was our management failing to budget for its inclusion in the paper, or for the additional editorial space the MD had agreed to provide for it, and Kinsley couldn't tell me how any of this had come about or who was to blame for such a grotesque blunder. And why had I not been informed of any of this?

Nor had I been told that Kinsley's decision, taken in October, to sever a partnership scheme with the *Sunday Times* had cost the Mail R2 200 000.

I was incredulous. I seethed with rage, but with a massive effort managed to restrain myself there in his office. Instead, I returned to mine and wrote him a 21-page memo, in which I said:

> I am sure you will appreciate that I have found this news, coming upon me so unexpectedly and belatedly, disconcerting and de-moralising. The new 'premium' *Rand Daily Mail* was my idea, and something to which I felt personally committed. I put a tre-mendous amount of effort and emotional energy into it, realising that it was a high-risk exercise but believing that if we could pull it off it would be the answer to the chronic problem of the Mail's trading position.
>
> I now find that all these beliefs and expectations were never really on in the first place. It is a great let-down. My feeling of demoralisation is intensified by the fact that I was not kept

informed about the position; and also by the fact that there appear to have been some quite amazing lapses in budgeting.

I never received a reply.

After another two months of silence from the management floor, I attended a lunch at the Rand Club, a favourite watering hole for Johannesburg's business elite, where I found myself in company with Kinsley. We chatted amiably, not mentioning the Mail's problems. As the lunch ended Kinsley suggested we share a company car back to the office. Still the atmosphere was relaxed as we sat in the back together. As the car drew up at the SAAN building, Kinsley glanced at his watch. 'Oh my goodness,' he said, 'I'm running late for the board meeting.'

'Oh, I didn't know there was a board meeting today,' I said. 'What's it about?'

'They have to decide on the future of the *Rand Daily Mail*,' Kinsley replied as he scrambled out of the car.

I was startled. 'Clive,' I said, speaking to him through the open back door, 'is my job on the line at this meeting?'

'Yes, I suppose it may be,' he shot back over his shoulder, 'but I must hurry, I'm running late.'

A few days passed and I heard nothing. Then I happened to bump into Kinsley in the lift. 'Did the board come to a decision about the Mail the other day?' I asked.

'Yes,' he said, 'they want a change.'

'Do you mean a change of editor?'

'Yes,' he replied, getting out of the lift. I got out with him.

'I think I should have a right to address the board before they reach a final decision,' I said.

'I'll arrange that,' came the reply.

Before meeting with the board I got in touch with Max Borkum, whom I knew to be close to all the power figures at the Anglo American Corporation, the ultimate but studiously detached owners of SAAN. Borkum, being Helen Suzman's election manager and the Progressive Party's chief Mr Fixit, had always been very close to the Mail, a friend and a confidant. He was appalled at what I told him.

'I'll arrange a meeting with Gordon Waddell,' he said. Waddell, a former Scottish rugby player and captain who had been capped 18 times as a British and Irish Lions flyhalf, had been working for the Oppenheimer empire for some time, during which he won the favour of Harry Oppenheimer himself. He had come to South Africa to join the headquarters staff, was married briefly to Mary Oppenheimer, the heiress, and became chairman of Johannesburg Consolidated Investments (JCI), the Anglo subsidiary that held the major shares in SAAN. He also joined the Progressive Party, which Harry Oppenheimer funded liberally, and became a Member of Parliament. So I knew him well and had come to like him. When we met at Borkum's home, Waddell asked me to draw up a memo setting out my proposals for the salvation of the *Rand Daily Mail*. This I did, a detailed document setting out the arguments I had been putting to Kinsley: that I believed our black readers were of growing value to advertisers, and that the survey offered cost-free by Professor Schlemmer could give us the information needed to develop a strong sales story about their value to advertisers.

I also took the opportunity to present some strong criticisms of the management. I noted the appalling budget lapses, and repeated a point Ray Louw had often made, that he believed the Mail carried an unfair bulk of the cost allocations arising from the company's joint operations.

A few days later, I had another meeting with Waddell at Borkum's home. It was brief. He tossed my memo across the table back at me. 'This is no good,' he snapped. 'It contains nothing new. You've said it all before.' With that he left. Borkum, looking nonplussed and agitated, quickly poured me half a glass of neat whisky to calm my surge of distress and anger. He was solicitous, but I knew the game was over. Kinsley and MacPherson had told Anglo American they had to get rid of me, and Oppenheimer, reluctant as always to get involved in the newspapers he owned, had passed the message on to Waddell.

My presentation to the board was a farce. I had prepared it carefully, telling the directors I believed strongly that we should follow the Schlemmer route and build a strong case showing advertisers that black readers were the market of the future and that it would be wise to start building up their brand names among those readers now. I told them that one could obviously not be absolutely certain of the success of such a strategy, but I believed a trial run with it would soon indicate its potential. 'Give me six months,' I said, playing on a recent quip by Prime Minister Vorster that in six months he would be able to show that his 'outward-looking' policy to black Africa could bear fruit. It raised a few chuckles from the otherwise stony-faced board members.

'Give me six months,' I said, 'and if there are no results, I'll resign.'

I knew as I left that my words had fallen on deaf ears. The decision had been made by Kinsley and MacPherson (the rest of the board were of no account) and cleared with Oppenheimer. There was nothing more to be done.

My dismissal notice arrived at the end of May 1981. I was to leave at the end of June.

Who was to succeed me was never discussed with me, which I suppose was not surprising given my fraught relationship with Kinsley, but when I heard that it was to be Tertius Myburgh, I was dismayed. My memory flashed back to the warnings I had been given by Eschel Rhoodie and David Abrahamson – that General van den Bergh had assured them that Myburgh was a BOSS agent and would warn them if I got close to breaking the Muldergate scandal. And that someone else higher up the SAAN hierarchy was also on BOSS's books. Was it MacPherson? I wondered. One of the boards he chaired was Hortors Stationery, while David Abrahamson had been its CEO.

Moreover, Myburgh was not going to leave the *Sunday Times*; he would remain there as well. Kinsley's brainwave was that Myburgh should be editor-in-chief of both papers, with a managing editor working under him on each to handle its daily operations. It struck me as being a cockeyed idea. Rex Gibson, then still editor of the *Sunday Express*, thought so too when Kinsley told him of the arrangement. 'Congratulations, Clive,' was his response. 'People say that editing the *Rand Daily Mail* is too big for one man, so now you're giving it to someone part-time.'[5]

I was even more dismayed to hear that Ken Owen, then an

assistant editor at the *Sunday Times*, was going to be the new man-aging editor at the Mail. I had known Owen for years and admired him as a talented journalist with an eloquent pen. But I also knew him to be a moody, irascible and intolerant personality. I knew instinctively that he would be a misfit at the Mail, with its proud and assertive staff. I telephoned Gordon Waddell immediately.

'Gordon,' I said, 'I accept that I'm on my way out, so this is not about me, but I seriously believe Ken Owen is the wrong person for the *Rand Daily Mail*. For the sake of the paper, I beg you to reconsider.'

Waddell was outraged. 'I don't have to listen to this,' he de-clared and slammed down the phone. But I was not wrong: Owen's reputation preceded him. As Gibson was later to observe: 'A firestorm greeted Owen in his first weeks … he [Owen] found that the staff was hostile to the point of enmity.'[6] A fine journalist on the wrong paper at the wrong time. The newsroom became a deeply demoralised place, which only increased Owen's contempt for the Mail's journalists as a 'dysfunctional, disloyal bunch', as he declared openly.

There was a public outcry at the changeover. Public protest meetings were held, the Black Sash and the Institute of Race Relations issued angry statements, and full-page advertisements with reams of names of disenchanted readers were placed in newspapers, including the Mail. An avalanche of letters descended on both the paper and me personally, expressing shock, sympathy and outrage − a great many from our black readers, including Archbishop Desmond Tutu and Dr Nthato Motlana, chairman of the Soweto Committee of Ten, the two most influential black figures in the country at the time. Joel Mervis made a press state-ment saying my departure from the Mail 'will be received with regret not only by his colleagues in South Africa but by journalists around the world. He is internationally known around the world.'[7]

But I guess the tribute I cherished most was from my old editor and mentor, Laurence Gandar: 'As a former editor,' he said in a press statement, 'I greatly admired the insight shown by Allister Sparks into the role a newspaper should play in a multiracial, segregated society. He recognised that, in the public interest, a special responsibility fell upon the press to act as a channel of communication between the groups – in my view a critical factor in the tense and anxious times in which we live.'[8]

Myburgh and Owen left the *Rand Daily Mail* after only eight months. Myburgh told the board he couldn't handle both papers and wanted to return to the *Sunday Times*, so the crackpot arrangement was called off and the two managing editors also returned to their old jobs. By that time the Mail's losses had ballooned to R8 million for the 1981 financial year, four times what it had been under my editorship the previous year and double Kinsley's budget for the new regime.

During his eight months at the Mail, Myburgh had compiled a report ostensibly analysing what was needed to save the Mail, a proposal involving massive new capital expenditure, which he must have known would never be accepted. He was a little more explicit about his real reasons for quitting the Mail in an interview with Joel Mervis: 'I knew that if they did not accept my proposal the Mail was destined for one end, and that if someone was going to close the Mail they weren't going to catch a smart Dutchman like me doing it.'[9]

So the one they chose to go down with the ship was Rex Gibson, who performed the task with grace and no small degree of nobility. Those three courageous years are his story, and he told it well in a book of his own, *Final Deadline: The Last Days of the Rand Daily Mail*, which I commend to all who want to follow the story of the death of the country's greatest daily newspaper to its end in 1985.

* * *

THERE WAS A fascinating coda to the board's decision, taken in December 1982, to close the *Rand Daily Mail* by converting it into a specialist financial daily on the lines of the London *Financial Times*. It would have a much smaller staff and a circulation of only 40 000, but a cover price of 30 cents. Kinsley believed it could make a small profit. Before going ahead with this project, however, he decided to engage the *Financial Times* consultancy division to undertake a

The Journalist

FEB-MARCH 1987   Journal of the Southern African Society of Journalists

Former Mail editors react to Waddell's remarks

MAIL: WHAT NOW?

By DENYSE ARMOUR

THE *Rand Daily Mail* is dead.

Saan blundered in closing it down.

Where to now?

In the wake of former JCI chairman Gordon Waddell's admission that the closure was wrong, a former editor of the *RDM* has suggested the best way of putting things right could be to revive the paper.

Waddell said, in an inter-

GANDAR ON THE MAIL

See Page 24

view with *Leadership* published this month, that he viewed his part in the closure of the paper with "the greatest possible regret".

"I say that because I have no doubt that the *Rand Daily Mail*, run by the present management of Saan, would not have died. To the extent that I have failed, given that I had a voice and a say which could, if all of us had agreed earlier to instal that management, I must accept a degree of guilt.

"I think the problem with Saan was always seen as the style of the editors. I don't think the problem lay there at all. The problem lay with the management of the business as opposed to the editorial side.

"To the extent that I failed to carry that point of view, then I must have been guilty," Waddell said.

These, and other of Waddell's statements during the interview, at long last publicly vindicate the editors and journalists of the *RDM* who, for at least two years, have been blamed for Saan's financial woes.

Clive Kinsley, former MD of Saan, said he did not wish to comment on Waddell's remarks.

But Raymond Louw, former *RDM* editor asked: "The question now is, what will be done now that the mistake

● To Page 23

*I was infuriated by Gordon Waddell's admission that the closure of the
Rand Daily Mail was a regrettable error, that the paper should not have
died. It was ultimately he who killed it.*

426

research project, at a hefty fee of £250 000. Part of the terms of reference were that the consultants would look into every aspect of the *Rand Daily Mail*'s operation. Kinsley was obviously looking for an authoritative backup for his decision.

Five months later, Financial Times Business Enterprises delivered their report, listing a series of 'negative aspects' they had found in the management of the Mail and what should be done to rectify them. The consultants' key findings were explicit:

> The fact that marketing of the *Rand Daily Mail* was carried out in conjunction with the group's other newspapers tended to put the Mail at a disadvantage. It also appeared that in the marketing field, agencies were not made aware of the strengths of the newspaper and were, therefore, unable to reach a conclusion as to what type of advertising, if any, should be used in the *Rand Daily Mail* ... As far as marketing was concerned the strengths of the newspaper were not in fact acted upon.

After noting the tremendous advantage of the staff's exceptional loyalty to the Mail, the report observed that 'the poor management structure' of the company meant there was little relationship between its departments and the Mail. This had given rise to 'a great deal of mistrust on the part of the staff'. The *Financial Times* team went on to express some doubts about the feasibility of publishing a daily financial newspaper in South Africa. Instead it recommended what it felt could be done to save the *Rand Daily Mail* over the next three years:

> The *Rand Daily Mail* should have its own manager and a task force dedicated to the paper. The publication should be directed towards opinion makers within the community, but with no distinction between race or class, and this direction should be utilised to obtain advertising for that particular market.

All exactly what I had pleaded for in my many memos to Kinsley. As Mervis notes: 'In the major conflict between Sparks and Kinsley, the consultants came out firmly on the side of Sparks.'[10]

Not surprisingly, Kinsley dismissed the consultants' report as

replied 6/7/81

230 PARK AVENUE • NEW YORK. N.Y. 10017 • (212) 697-6162

Published by The Stanley Foundation   Telex: WPRNY62342   Cable: PRESSWORLD

ALFRED BALK, Editor and Publisher

June 10, 1981

Dear Allister:

     I was shocked and saddened
to hear of your dismissal, and frustrated,
too, because one feels so utterly helpless.

     Enclosed are copies of near-
deadline inserts on the matter. The
issue will go into the mail next week.
We will, of course, follow up.

     If you come to New York please
consider using our guest room for several
days. We are at 50 E. 89th Street now.

     In any event, do let me know
your plans. Persevere. You are an extremely gifted and valuable member of
human society, and channels will open
for many contributions, I am sure.
Perhaps beginning with a book.

               All best,

Of the hundreds of letters I received after my dismissal from the
Rand Daily Mail, *this one from Al Balk, editor and publisher of*
World Press Review, *was one of the most meaningful. Only a few*
months before, he had named Rex Gibson and myself joint International
Editors of the Year at a ceremony in New York.

worthless, despite the huge fee he had paid to engage them.

Two years after the death of the Mail, there was another intriguing coda, this time an admission of guilt. Kinsley had left SAAN by then and the company had a new management team. A former Mail staffer, Hugh Murray, who had founded a new glossy magazine, *Leadership*, interviewed Gordon Waddell about his reflections on the death of the Mail. Waddell, who had left Anglo American and returned to Britain, was contrite, saying he now viewed his part in the paper's closure with 'the greatest possible regret'. Improvements under the new management had persuaded him that the Mail need not have died. Thus his *mea culpa*:

> To the extent that I have failed, given that I had a voice and a say which could, if all of us had agreed earlier to install this new management, I must accept a degree of guilt. I think the problem with SAAN was always seen as the style of the editors. I don't think the problem lay there at all. The problem lay with the management of the business as opposed to the editorial side. To the extent that I failed to carry that point of view, then I must have been guilty.[11]

A bit like the hangman saying 'Oops!' after the execution.

CHAPTER TWENTY-FOUR

A Foot Soldier Again

AS I WALKED out of that familiar newsroom for the last time, I had no thoughts about what I might do next. I had been there for 23 years and the emotional turmoil of my departure had blotted out all such thoughts. But as the realisation sank in, I became aware that my future looked bleak. I was 48 years old, with a wife and four children, three of them approaching university age, and no visible prospect of getting a job on another South African newspaper. Having been fired from SAAN, I couldn't imagine any rival company offering me a senior job: their Mahogany Rows were all filled with their own best people. Nor would any other editor feel comfortable having me in his reporters' room. I was struck by the sobering thought that I was unemployable in South African journalism, that I would either have to leave my profession or leave my country — and I didn't want to do either.

In a curious final twist I received an invitation to have lunch with Harry Oppenheimer at Brenthurst, his baronial mansion on a vast estate in the heart of Johannesburg. It was like a royal command: one didn't decline such an invitation. I wondered what it was about. Was he thinking of ordering a review of my dismissal? Was he going to offer me a job somewhere else in his vast empire?

Oppenheimer received me with his characteristic quiet charm. He was a warm, undemonstrative man with a modesty that belied

430

his great power. To my surprise he had almost his entire board of directors present, all of whom greeted me in the same manner. It has always intrigued me the way underlings of powerful people tend to take on the mannerisms, sometimes even the tone of voice, of the chief. We were seated at a long table with Oppenheimer at the head and me on his right.

As the meal began he asked me to give my account of what had gone wrong at the Mail. This I did, in effect repeating the presentation I had given to the SAAN board. Oppenheimer offered a few sage remarks during my presentation, which I thought indicated agreement with my points, and he asked a few questions. The other board members said nothing and remained stony-faced throughout. At the end of the meal Oppenheimer thanked me for coming, and after I had shaken hands with all the others he ushered me out to my car.

'If you find yourself in any difficulty, please give me a call,' he said as he shook my hand. I looked into his eyes and said nothing, but in my mind a small voice was saying to myself: 'Whatever happens to me, I'm damned if I'll ever do that.' A small flame of anger, even contempt, burned inside me. Here was this man with the power to save our great newspaper, which I knew he recognised was on the right side of a great moral crisis afflicting our country, yet he didn't want to get involved by exercising that power. He didn't want his vast corporation to be seen getting involved in the controversial politics that would incur. 'Damn you,' I thought. 'Freedom of expression is what newspapers are all about. If it is my professional duty as an editor to fight for it, then it is also yours as an owner. If you don't want to dirty your hands doing that, then don't own a newspaper.'

A day or so later I received a phone call from Andrew Wilson, news editor at *The Observer* in London. Colin Legum, their renowned Africa correspondent, was retiring, he told me, and having read the news of my dismissal he wondered whether I might be interested in a freelance contract to cover southern Africa for *The Observer.*

My spirits took a leap. I had long been a great admirer of *The Observer*, which at that time had some of the finest writers in journalism whose work I had followed for years. I told Wilson I most certainly was interested, and that I intended coming to London shortly so that we could meet and discuss the terms of the job. Suddenly I could see a whole new career opportunity opening up for me. I could set myself up as a professional foreign correspondent covering South Africa and · its neighbouring countries, which were all involved in the struggle against apartheid, not only for *The Observer* but possibly for other newspapers as well. Maybe I would not have to choose between leaving either my country or my profession after all. I promptly telephoned a fellow journalist and friend, Peter Younghusband, who was doing exactly that with great success.

'Absolutely,' he replied, when I asked him whether he thought I could build a viable new career in this way. 'What you need is a central pillar, a paper that will give you a contract and a salary and which will pay your basic costs, and then you can use the information you gather for that paper to write and broadcast for other media in other countries that are not in competition with your contracted paper. You've already got your central pillar with *The Observer*, so all you've got to do now is pick up a few more outside the UK.'

Here was my opportunity. The life of a foreign correspondent had always fascinated me, now here was an opportunity to have the best of both worlds. Based in my own country, what's more, one I knew thoroughly and which was in the throes of a mounting crisis that was surely going to escalate into a major world story. Out of desolation and despair had come the vision of a dream job.

* * *

MY DISMISSAL from the Mail coincided with the date on which my three months' long leave fell due. Despite the disruption of our lives, Sue and I decided to go ahead with our plans to take a three-month holiday in France with our son, Julian. We flew first to London, leaving a close lawyer friend, Ernest Wentzel, to handle severance negotiations with SAAN's management on my behalf. It turned out to be a parsimonious settlement in light of my 23 years' service to the company – a vengeful one, I suppose, since I had not gone quietly. 'They were the meanest bunch of bastards I've ever had to deal with,' Ernie told me on my return.

On arrival in Britain I called at *The Observer* offices, just off Fleet Street, where I was warmly welcomed by the editor, Donald Trelford, and news editor Andrew Wilson. The negotiations were brief and satisfactory. They wanted me and I wanted the job. Colin Legum, the legendary figure I would be partly replacing, wished me well.

Later that day I received a call from Stanley Uys, SAAN's London editor and my old Press Gallery colleague. He was giving a dinner for some friends at his home that evening, and would Sue and I like to join them. Among the guests would be a Dutch journalist, André Spoor, who was about to become editor of a new high-quality daily newspaper in Rotterdam that was being established by merging two other dailies, the *Nuwe Rotterdamse Courant* and *Die Handelsblad*. The new paper was to be called the *NRC Handelsblad* and Spoor wanted to make it the top daily in the Netherlands.

It was purely fortuitous. Spoor, an elegant, silver-haired man in his sixties, told me he regarded South Africa as one of the biggest foreign stories for his Dutch readers, but he was having difficulty getting a work permit to base a staff correspondent there. The South African authorities were turning him down. Because of the historical connections between the two countries, the apartheid regime was particularly sensitive to the critical stance taken by Dutch journalists, and indeed by the generally liberal Dutch public. They were shutting out Dutch journalists. Would I, Spoor wondered, be prepared to do the job for them? When I protested that although I spoke Afrikaans I couldn't possibly write in Dutch, he brushed that aside. All his staff were multilingual, he told me in his excellent English, and they would translate my reports with ease.

So within a few days I had two exciting jobs to replace the one I had lost. 'I told you,' my always positive wife remarked, 'the doors are opening. There'll be more.'

While in Britain Sue, Julian and I stayed at the country estate of one of my most remarkable friends. Boris Wilson had progressed from a Jewish kid in a shtetl in the Balkans to become a fruit-market

In the comfortable and well-equipped office I eventually built for myself at home, where I have now been working for 32 years.

salesman in Johannesburg, then a millionaire businessman, a medical doctor and finally a liberal politician and Member of Parliament. It was through Boris and his limitless contacts that the widow of another liberal South African exile offered us free use of her holiday home in the Dordogne valley of southwestern France.

It was the ideal spot for a bruised little family seeking escape. The holiday home was a seventeenth-century stone house on a farm near the small towns of Belvès and Sarlat in what the French call the Périgord Noir. This is the region of *pâté de fois gras*, truffles and goat's-milk cheese, set in a landscape of rolling hills, valleys and old castles, with the sleepy Dordogne River flowing through it to join the Garonne and form the broad Gironde estuary, along which for centuries ships have carried some of the world's finest wines from Bordeaux to the appreciative palates of connoisseurs around the globe.

Come 14 July, Bastille Day, Sue and I, together with little Julian, joined the colourful celebrations in the nearby small town of Belvès. I was seated at the mayor's side, and we quickly fell into animated conversation. The mayor, a working-class man, told us he was chairman of the local branch of the Communist Party, making him the first practising communist I had ever met, since the party was banned in South Africa. That made him as much of a curiosity to me as I was to him. But the conversation soon moved beyond ideological territory as we reflected on the historical importance of the day, of how the storming of the Bastille by the ordinary citizens of Paris back in 1789 had marked the beginning of the French Revolution, which in turn had marked the beginning of the global struggle for democracy that had now reached South Africa.

We talked of the events leading up to the storming of that fortress-prison, and of the philosophies of Voltaire and Jean-Jacques Rousseau. I was struck by the depth of knowledge that this ordinary man, deep in rural France, had of his country's history and of the philosophers who had shaped that history. It drove home for me the importance of education, and of history in particular, in building a stable democratic society, and of how poorly endowed our people in South Africa were because of Verwoerd's separate Bantu education system for blacks.

We danced, too, on the town's cobblestone square that night, Sue and I with Julian on my shoulders, while fireworks lit up the night sky. All in celebration of the birth of democracy. A healing moment for this bruised campaigner.

I did one more important thing during that time of spiritual convalescence in the Dordogne. I penned a letter to Ben Bradlee, executive editor of *The Washington Post*, unsure whether he would remember me from that visit he had made to the *Rand Daily Mail* newsroom some years before. I knew he had a staff correspondent based in South Africa, but would he, I asked, be interested in occasional op-ed articles from me analysing the unfolding racial crisis in my country? The reply came swiftly and decisively, as befitted a man of his renowned dynamism. Yes, he wrote, but he wasn't just interested in op-ed articles; the Post's correspondent in Johannesburg was about to return to the United States and

Receiving the British Order of Christian Unity's Valiant for Truth Award, 1982. The award was presented to me at the London Press Club by Lady Mary Soames (on my right), Winston Churchill's daughter and wife of Lord Soames, the Governor of Zimbabwe during its transition to majority rule.

he wanted me to take her place. He sensed there was a big story building up there and he wanted someone who knew the country thoroughly to cover it for the Post. Would I be prepared to fly to Washington to discuss this with him?

Indeed I was. The three of us flew to Washington Dulles International Airport and into the throbbing heart of one of the world's most powerful newsrooms. The sheer size of it was daunting. It seemed to me at first glance to be the size of a city block, and the air was filled with the continuous chatter of computer keyboards and ringing telephones – a place of ceaseless 24/7 activity. In the midst of it all was Bradlee, with his creased face and booming voice, ensconced in a glass cubicle from which his short-sleeved figure would emerge periodically to roam the floor like an ever-vigilant commander surveying his troops. He waved me inside for a back-slapping greeting and an expression of sympathy for what 'those stupid bastards have done to you down there in Joburg'.

Again, the details of an agreement were concluded in a matter of minutes. I explained that I had already reached agreements with *The Observer* and the nascent *NRC Handelsblad*. 'That's fine,' Bradlee responded. 'We'll be able to share expenses with them so you'll be able to get around more.' He explained that although he had a staff correspondent based in Nairobi to cover the rest of Africa, he would like me to keep in touch with the ANC leaders in exile, mostly based in the Zambian capital of Lusaka. He wanted me to cover both ends of the South African story, the apartheid regime and the insurgent ANC.

This opened up an exciting new prospect for me. Other South African journalists were unable to do that, for the government's censorship laws made reporting on the liberation movements impossible. Those laws, which had applied to me when I worked for the Mail, made it a crime to publish anything said by the ANC or any of its members, so their side of the story remained untold inside South Africa. Now I would be freed from that restriction. For the first time I would be able to report the full story, from both sides, which is what good journalism is supposed to be about. Of course this would be for foreign readers only, but what a sense of freedom I would have being able to do it.

As we flew back via London, I decided to make contact with the ANC office there to clear the way for this new journalistic opportunity. I made arrangements to meet with a still young Thabo Mbeki, then the key envoy and political adviser to Oliver Tambo, the movement's exiled leader. We had a long meeting in the lounge of a London hotel, beginning a relationship that was to grow into a friendship that still endures.

There was a sobering twist to the meeting, however. The ANC, plagued by the infiltration of BOSS spies, had ruled that no such meeting could take place one on one. The ANC person attending such a meeting had to be accompanied by a colleague to ensure that all was above board. At this meeting Mbeki was accompanied by a senior member at the ANC's London office named Solly Smith. It later turned out that Smith himself was a spy. Clearly, escaping the long arm of the apartheid regime was not going to be as easy as I thought.

437

* * *

I SETTLED INTO my new job immediately upon our return to South Africa, attaching myself to an operation in downtown Johannesburg run by a remarkable telex operator known simply as 'Fingers' van der Merwe. I don't think any of the foreign correspondents located there knew Fingers' real name, only that his moniker came from his ability to punch out telex tapes at astonishing speed in whatever languages they were written, whether he understood them or not. He was a Franz Liszt of the telex keyboard.

Fingers had begun his career working for a pittance at the Post Office. I first met him when, because of his speed, the Post Office transferred him to Parliament to transmit copy for the Press Gallery correspondents. Then his entrepreneurial instincts flowered and Fingers established his own communications business with branches in Johannesburg and Cape Town, transmitting copy for nearly all of the country's foreign correspondents. By the time I joined his establishment he was a millionaire, employing a team of the country's fastest telex operators.

My decision to locate myself there was in due course to have interesting consequences. But more of that later.

I slipped quickly and easily into my new role. Writing for *The Observer* and the *NRC Handelsblad* was straightforward; both countries had historic links to South Africa, and readers had an adequate knowledge of where South Africa was and what its key issues were. *The Washington Post* was more challenging. The city's inhabitants span an exceptionally wide spectrum of social levels. With its veritable army of politicians, diplomats, journalists, lobbyists and think-tank specialists, Washington, DC, has arguably the highest percentage of well-informed political eggheads of any city in the world. But it is also a Southern city with a large number of poorly educated people. In my numerous visits there I have encountered many who barely know where South Africa is. Some envisage Africa vaguely as a single country like the US, with South Africa as the Dixie end of it.

Knowing this, *The Washington Post* was a stickler for explanatory detail. Most of its readers had heard of apartheid, but the nomenclature of its race classification required constant explanation. Who were the Afrikaners? And the coloureds: anyone with a touch of melatonin in the skin is considered black in the US, so who were these people of colour if they weren't blacks? And what about those called the Bantu? And, omigod, the Indians? One couldn't clutter every story with lengthy explanations, but with time I managed to evolve a kind of shorthand vocabulary that eased the task.

These details became particularly important since the first phase of my new career coincided with the attempt by Prime Minister PW Botha to reform apartheid by establishing a tri-cameral Parliament, with separate chambers for white, coloured and Indian members. Each of these legislatures was intended to govern its particular race group, but with the dominant white chamber having an overriding say in joint sittings and on what were euphemistically called 'general affairs' − meaning matters of concern to all.

Many white South Africans were taken in by the new consti-tutional dispensation, seeing it as a breach in the political colour bar that was giving the country such a bad image abroad, and Foreign minister Roelof (Pik) Botha worked hard trying to sell it in the international marketplace. Tertius Myburgh's *Sunday Times* supported the new measures enthusiastically, and when PW called a whites-only referendum two-thirds of the white voters endorsed the new constitution.

But in my reports I focused on the fact that the majority black population were neither included in nor consulted about the new dispensation. They were simply shut out, and they felt insulted and outraged. All they could expect was a small degree of self-rule in the black townships, while for the rest they were supposed to be accommodated politically in their impover-ished tribal Bantustans. My reports pointed out that the magic year 1978, when the tidal flow of black migrant workers to the industrial cities was supposed to have begun turning, had come and gone and the urban influx was flowing stronger than ever. This, I contended, and as Laurence Gandar had foretold two decades earlier, meant the fantasy of racial separation was fast disappearing and the National Party would soon have to confront Verwoerd's recognition that the only alternative to his policies was racial integration. My reports appeared to have some influence overseas as other foreign correspondents began following that line. *The Economist*, whose senior editor, Simon Jenkins, had earlier been influenced by Myburgh, dismissed PW's reforms as 'neo-apartheid'.

In fact, though, the reforms had major consequences. The outrage it aroused in the black community triggered the first organised black response to the regime's actions since the banning of black political movements 23 years earlier. The Reverend Allan Boesak, leader of the coloured branch of the racially segregated Dutch Reformed Church, suggested, in an impromptu remark during a speech in Johannesburg, that a united front of churches, civil associations, trade unions, student organisations and sports bodies should be formed to oppose the constitutional proposals.

Seven months later, in July 1983, such a body, calling itself the United Democratic Front (UDF), encompassing 565 affiliate bodies, was formed at a mass rally in the Cape Town township of Mitchells Plain. The UDF's initial focus was to organise a nationwide boycott of black township council elections. It was stunningly successful. There was a 5 per cent poll in Soweto, 11 per cent in the Port Elizabeth townships, 15 per cent in the Vaal Triangle townships south of Johannesburg and 19 per cent in Durban. By the end of the year the UDF had 700 affiliates, representing 3 million people.

The UDF then ran a boycott campaign against elections to the new coloured and Indian parliamentary chambers with equal success, thus effectively stripping the new constitutional system of any legitimacy. The regime went ahead and installed the discredited parliamentarians anyway — one of them on the strength of a paltry 154 votes — but the most significant outcome of Botha's ploy was that it had put black politics back in business, with the UDF established as a powerful new organisation capable of mobilising the black community. It was a turning point in the black struggle against apartheid.

* * *

FOR THE NEXT several years I was essentially a war correspondent. The UDF campaign against the tricameral Parliament swelled into a full-scale insurrection, and as the government declared repeated states of emergency and mobilised the police and the military, the country became locked in what was a drawn-out, low-level civil war.

It began just five days after the elections for the tricameral Parliament. The starting point, fortuitously, was Sharpeville, thrusting that modest Vaal Triangle township into world headlines for the second time. There had been a long build-up of grievances following the township's council elections the year before, which was symptomatic of what was happening countrywide. The elections had been heavily boycotted, which meant the black councillors who were elected were branded as apartheid collaborators, which in the heated atmosphere of the time was swiftly becoming regarded as a capital offence. The Sharpeville councillors had further increased their unpopularity by raising house rents, privatising for themselves the extremely profitable local beer halls and dividing ownership of the township's liquor stores among themselves and their relatives. They built themselves grand homes while the people struggled to pay the higher rents.

As anger built up, an Anglican priest, Father Geoffrey Moselane, called his congregation together to discuss the issues. It turned into a mass meeting of residents, at which it was decided to march to the council offices next morning to tell the despised councillors the people were not prepared to pay the increased rents.

That night, a Sunday, tensions were running high in Sharpeville. Some rioting broke out in various spots and the police were jumpy. A policeman spotted a shadowy figure in the dark and fired a shot. Reuben Twala, the popular captain of the local soccer team, fell dead. It was the spark that set fire to the whole nation.

That night, enraged black youths roamed the streets of Sharpeville crying vengeance. 'Twala is dead, we are going to get them!' they cried. They converged on the fancy homes of the councillors, demanding that they come out. Sam Dlamini, the mayor, was the first to die as he emerged from his front door, to be cut down by hand-made machetes. His mutilated body was flung into a car and set ablaze. Someone filled a tyre with petrol, set it on fire and rolled it down Dlamini's hallway. It hit a wall at the end, splashing the blazing petrol into an eruption of fire. Two more councillors died that night, one of them incinerated with his bodyguard in his own torched home.

I leapt into my car and raced to Sharpeville at daybreak as I picked up news of the trouble on radio. As I was driving the 75 km to Sharpeville, Father Moselane and his group, now numbering nearly 5000, were marching, unaware of what had happened during the night, towards the council offices to make their protest – only to find a large body of police blocking their way. The township was on fire, three councillors were dead, the rest had fled for their lives, and now here was a mob marching on the council offices. The police panicked and opened fire with shotguns, rubber bullets and teargas canisters. That was the scene I encountered as I arrived at the council offices: gunfire, dust, screams and the chaos of fleeing humanity and falling bodies. I abandoned my car and managed to scramble behind the police line.

Later I was able to locate a dazed and bewildered Father Moselane and get his account of events, then track down other witnesses to piece together a picture of what the young 'comrades' – as they called themselves – had done during the night. The fires and chaos in Sharpeville raged on for another two days, during which the angry youths stoned the police, burned automobiles and torched every council building in sight, while the police in turn fired at anything that moved. Thirty people were killed. But what was more serious was that rioting flared across the country, from the Vaal Triangle to the East Rand to the squatter camps of Cape Town, the townships of the eastern Cape and Durban and back to Soweto. The insurrection raged for three years, resulting in more than 3000 deaths, 30000 detentions and much damage to property and the national economy.

It was a testing time for us journalists, whose job it was to convey the news of these fast-moving events to the rest of the world. South Africa quickly developed into a major world news story, and with that came an influx of foreign reporters and television crews. I was fortunate in that I knew the country, spoke its most important languages and had a wide range of contacts. I was also well known in the black communities through the *Rand Daily Mail*'s long stand on issues close to their hearts, with the result that on several occasions I was hustled to safety when my white skin put me in danger of the wrath of angry crowds. The people I felt most sympathy for in those hectic days were the television crews, whose work required them to get as close to the action as possible, and who then often had to flee for their lives with their heavy equipment.

What I came to realise, as these dramatic events unfolded, was that the role I was now playing, of telling this story to the world, was as important, if not more so, than my role had been as editor of the *Rand Daily Mail*. The Mail's role had been to help prevent all white attitudes in South Africa from congealing into unanimous support for the apartheid regime, as had happened in Ian Smith's Rhodesia, while at the same time reassuring the black majority that there were whites on their side in the moral struggle. Now my reports were contributing to the mobilising of foreign pressure to force the Nationalist government to abandon apartheid – which in the end turned out to be the most potent of the many pressures on the regime through the 1980s. The regime, of course, regarded this as tantamount to treason, so I encountered even greater hostility than before.

As the civil war intensified it assumed an almost ritualistic form. There would be a huge funeral rally each Sunday to bury the casualties of the previous weekend's conflict. Tens of thousands of people would turn up for these rallies, usually in some big sports stadium. The coffins would be set out in rows on the playing field, with a podium behind them where the priests, usually including Desmond Tutu, then Bishop of Johannesburg, and sometimes members of the UDF committee, would conduct proceedings. The atmosphere was electric, a potent blend of grief, anger and solidarity expressed through the chanting of political slogans and the singing of struggle songs – some with lovely, haunting melodies but violent words – all punctuated by prayers, angry

443

oratory and the high-pitched voices of ululating women. They were blatantly political events at which orthodox religious rituals featured hardly at all, yet they were spiritually powerful.

To reach one of these events was akin to crossing an international border. The venue would be encircled by a ring of steel, military vehicles, including the hated Hippos – big, cumbersome armoured personnel carriers – packed with troops and police, waiting for the trouble that would inevitably break out when the rally ended and the crowd began to disperse. You would have to show your press pass to a senior police officer in order to pass through that outer cordon.

Once through it, you would be confronted by a young comrade, the equivalent of an immigration officer, wearing the insignia of the UDF, who would demand to know your credentials. What was your name? Which country were you from? Which newspaper or other media organisation did you represent? You would then be allowed to enter the stadium, the equivalent of passing into another country, with its animated crowd and vastly different culture, language and political ethos.

The rally would last for hours, and end with entreaties by the speakers – usually Bishop Tutu in his intensely passionate way – to disperse peacefully and not give the waiting armed forces cause to attack them. But to no avail. Even as the young comrades began moving towards the exits they would begin singing their revolutionary songs and start taunting the police, while the Hippos would start up their engines. There was an awful inevitability about what followed, as though it was driven by some kind of sado-masochistic impulse on both sides. It was always a one-sided conflict between the heavily armed police and the comrades hurling stones and sometimes petrol bombs, at the end of which there would be more bodies for the following Sunday's funeral rally.

Two things struck me about this terrible ritual that went on week after week. One was that the comrades seemed oblivious to the casualties they suffered. As Tutu put it to me at the time: 'These young people frighten me. They think their lives are not worth living, so they might as well die for the sake of liberation.' The other thing that troubled me was that the vast majority of white South Africans knew nothing of what was happening right next door to them. I had always been contemptuous of Germans who said they knew nothing of the Nazi atrocities, but here was a recurrence of that phenomenon before my eyes. Apartheid was part of it. Whites didn't know about it because it happened in black areas and they didn't see it. But they also didn't know because they didn't want to know about it. This had been the *Rand Daily Mail*'s problem: many of its readers didn't want to read about the truth because they didn't want to know about it.

* * *

AS THE STRUGGLE intensified in the mid-1980s, PW Botha – by now executive President – declared a second and more stringent state of emergency, in which he prohibited open-air marches and rallies. So the venues for political protest events shifted to churches, particularly St George's Anglican cathedral in Cape Town and the Regina Mundi Roman Catholic church in Soweto. It was at the latter that I was to have my scariest experience of those tempestuous times.

Regina Mundi is not a beautiful building like the graceful Gothic edifice of St George's. But it is bigger. A large, cavernous structure that from outside looks like a cross between an aircraft hanger and a warehouse, capable of accommodating up to 7000 people. The only item of beauty is a large modernist painting called 'Madonna and Child of Soweto' by renowned South African artist Larry Scully gracing a wall to one side of the chancel. The building also has some bullet holes in the roof, testifying to its role in the struggle.

For the most part, the apartheid regime respected the sanctity of holy places. So churches were safe havens for political gatherings. The police would wait outside, and the action would take place as the rallies ended and the activists emerged.

It was on 16 June 1986, the tenth anniversary of the Soweto student uprising and just four days after a new state of emergency had been declared, that I attended the first such rally in Regina Mundi. Preachers from all denominations participated, with Desmond Tutu, by then the Archbishop of Cape Town, prelate of the Anglican Church in southern Africa and a Nobel peace laureate, as the central figure. Some leaders of the UDF also addressed the rally, but with the main ANC leaders either in prison or in exile, Tutu had become the most prominent spokesperson for the internal resistance movement.

The service-cum-rally lasted several hours, and was a powerful, emotional affair with all the usual struggle songs and chants, mixed in with hymns, prayers, sermons and rousing political speeches, during which a phalanx of armed police took up positions on an open space some 75 metres from the front entrance to the church. The occasion ended with Tutu issuing his usual appeal to the young comrades to leave in peace and not provoke the police into attacking them. And they, as usual, ignored him. As the first comrades emerged they ran forward and began throwing stones at the police, who in turn unleashed a barrage of rubber bullets, shotgun fire and teargas canisters.

I came out with the body of the crowd into the midst of this maelstrom. People were screaming and running and falling all around me. I spotted a large rock on a patch of lawn and dived behind it, pinning myself to the ground. I could hear rubber bullets and shotgun pellets pinging off the rock but for the moment I felt reasonably safe, although getting away from there was going to be problematic. Then came a nasty surprise.

A large, ungainly vehicle was making its way towards me. It was disgorging teargas. Vast quantities of the stuff. And it was heading straight towards me from the side. I couldn't get out of its way without exposing myself to the gunfire. So I lay there as the vehicle, known to the comrades as a 'sneeze machine', circled around my rock and deposited a ton of the stuff directly upon me.

There are few things more frightening than finding yourself unable to breathe. I gasped and spluttered, but I could not take in air. With my face streaming with tears and burning from the gas, I staggered to my feet, but I could neither see nor breathe. There was nothing I could do, and as a sense of panic and desperation

446

rose in me I fell to the ground and began to lose consciousness. Then, from a hazy distance, I heard someone calling my name. 'It's Allister! Let's fetch him, guys.' The voice was that of Jon Qwelane, one of the *Rand Daily Mail*'s black reporters, who was trying to make a getaway in a battered old Volkswagen Golf with about half a dozen others piled in and on top of it.

I have only a vague recollection of what happened immediately after that. I felt myself being picked up by my arms and legs and carried forward at a run. Four black men carried me into a nearby house, where a group of women set about dousing my face with water and urging me to blow my nose into drenched cloths and to try to inhale through them. They were obviously experienced at treating teargas asphyxia, because as I regained my breath I saw buckets of water outside every home on the block, with groups of women attending to affected people like myself. They had all made advance preparations for what was now happening. It was a striking example of the collective spirit of the African people in the struggle against apartheid, and of their ready acceptance of a white victim in need of help.

Those women clucked and fussed over me for two hours, soaking and wiping my face continuously and refusing to let me go until they were sure I was fully recovered. There was a second patient in that house with me, a young black nurse from the nearby Baragwanath Hospital who had also been teargassed, though not as badly as me. When at last my carers felt assured I was fit to go, they asked if I would drive the young nurse back to her residence at the hospital, which I did.

I managed, though still bleary-eyed, to drive myself back to my home in the whites-only suburb of Rivonia. As I walked into my garden I saw Sue hitting up on the tennis court with Julian. 'Hi,' she called out cheerfully. 'How was your day?'

Two worlds in one country – a universe apart.

CHAPTER TWENTY-FIVE

The Power of Washington

PERSONALITIES make news, and in the 1980s two of the most vivid personalities in South Africa were Winnie Mandela, the banned, banished and persecuted wife of Nelson Mandela, and Mamphela Ramphele, the close comrade of the murdered Steve Biko. Winnie Mandela was confined to a small town called Brandfort in the heart of the Orange Free State, and Ramphele to a remote village called Lenyenye in the far north of the country, where soon after Biko's death she gave birth to his son, whom she appropriately named Hlumelo – isiXhosa for 'the living shoot of a dead tree'.

Both made powerful human stories, which my newspapers displayed prominently. Ramphele's was about how, as a medical doctor and proselytiser of Black Consciousness, she had done a remarkable job of teaching the local rural folk, mainly the women, to be self-sufficient in everything from child care to brickmaking and building.

But it was Winnie's story that landed me in trouble. I had visited her in Brandfort several times. She was a strong personality and her impact on the white citizenry of that small and deeply conservative Afrikaner country town was considerable, as she swept into its local liquor store to order champagne, and into the local dress shop to try on their latest fashions. It made great copy for my overseas readers. Brandfort's white citizens were accustomed to the black people of the local township showing them deference at all times, and they didn't know how to handle this tall, confident woman of striking beauty, who ignored all the apartheid conventions of black subservience and confronted them as an equal. She did so with elegance and charm, which confused them even more. Winnie had a great fashion sense, and she took pains whenever she entered the white town to look her sartorial best. It was a subtle form of provocation that turned her years of internal exile there into a constant act of political defiance.

Sometimes I visited Winnie with my family, and once with Katharine Graham, the owner of *The Washington Post*, during a tour she made of South Africa in the company of the paper's editorial page editor, Meg Greenfield. We met with Winnie in the home of the town's only lawyer, Piet de Waal, a group of four which technically constituted a criminal offence since Winnie's banning order prohibited her from being in the company of more than one person at a time. Kay Graham was captivated by Winnie's personality, and when I told her afterwards that Winnie could possibly face a term of imprisonment for having met with us as a group, I think she was more horrified by that than by anything else she had seen in the land of apartheid.

One of the stories I wrote around that time was about the tortuous process Winnie Mandela had to undergo to visit Nelson Mandela on Robben Island. Her movements were closely monitored by the police all the way there and back. She was not allowed to travel to Cape Town by train or car, which meant incurring air and taxi expenses. It was so costly she could afford to see her husband only twice a year.

My story elicited a flood of sympathetic readers' letters to all my newspapers. One reader, an elderly English widow named Marjory Ruck, wrote to the editor of *The Observer*, enclosing a cheque and expressing her compassion, as she put it, 'from one who knows the pain of being separated from a beloved husband'.

Donald Trelford phoned me. 'What should we do with this money?' he asked.

My response was instinctive. 'Let's use it to pay for Winnie to make an extra visit to Nelson, courtesy of dear Marjory Ruck, and I'll accompany her and write a detailed story about having to go through the same monitoring process she has to endure. It will make a good story and I'm sure it will please Marjory Ruck and all the other letter writers.'

Trelford liked the idea. So did Winnie. Thus began an assignment that was to have consequences over the next two years that echoed through four countries, involved the White House, and embarrassed a newly appointed member of the South African judiciary.

* * *

I DROVE TO Brandfort and picked up Winnie from her Spartan cottage in the black township. We called at the local police station, where she had to check in with the station commander and inform him she was leaving for Cape Town to visit her imprisoned husband. From there we drove 55 km to Bloemfontein airport, escorted all the way by a police car with two armed men aboard. There was no communication with these men as they stood by watching us as we checked in. They followed us to the boarding point, and only then were we left alone.

At the airport in Cape Town the procedure was reversed. Police met us as we exited the plane, followed us to the baggage hall, then tailed us as I picked up a hire car and drove Winnie to an assigned house in the coloured township of Athlone, where she spent the night. Next morning I collected her there, drove to Cape Town's Caledon Square police station, where again she had to check in with the station commander.

From there things took a different course from Winnie's previous visits. Nelson Mandela had recently been moved from Robben Island to Pollsmoor prison, in the city's Constantia valley.

'I've been coming here for 20 years,' Winnie told me as we set out from the police station, 'but I've never seen Cape Town. I've always had to go straight to the harbour to board the ferry to the island, and then back again. So I've never actually seen this famous city. You must show it to me now.'

A little warning bell rang in my head. I knew Winnie could be reckless in her provocative political activities. I knew, too, that the law required that I take her by the most direct route to the prison. But I figured that if I diverted a little I could plead that, since I was not a Capetonian, I was uncertain of the shortest route. So we made a few diversions, among others passing by the Houses of Parliament, where I pointed out the spot to which young Philip Kgosana had led his column of marchers 25 years earlier. I soon noticed that we were being followed by a dirty-brown Toyota. It was not a marked police car, as the others on this trip had been, but I had little doubt the two coloured men in it were security police spooks.

I took the scenic route along the lower slopes of Table Mountain, which went past the entrance to the stately Groote Schuur manor house, which Cecil John Rhodes had bequeathed to all future South African prime ministers. I pointed it out to Winnie. 'That's where PW Botha has his official residence,' I told her.[1]

Her response was instantaneous. 'Oh, take me there,' she said. 'I can ask Elize to let me measure the curtains' – Elize being President Botha's wife. This was Winnie at her mischievous best, and, as any journalist will appreciate, it was an irresistible quote that I embedded in my memory for use in the story I would write of this venture.

We drove on, winding through some of the world's most beautiful scenery until we arrived at the forbidding gates of Pollsmoor prison. There were formalities and forms to fill in, but finally we entered the grounds and I parked the hire car. The brown Toyota had followed us all the way, and I noticed it had managed to pass the entrance gates without any formalities.

I accompanied Winnie to the visitors' entrance to the prison. She had promised to try to persuade the prison authorities to let me accompany her to see Nelson, which would have given me a major scoop. I was shown to a small waiting room while an officer took Winnie's request to a senior official. It took some time, causing my hopes to rise, but in the end the answer came back negative. I walked back to the hire car and sat there, watching the two spooks sitting slouched in the front seats of the Toyota, chain-smoking. Slowly a sense of indignation rose in me.

By the time Winnie emerged from the prison, after about an hour, I had worked myself into a state of petulance. I strode over to the Toyota, noticing as I approached that its dashboard was fitted with lots of electronic apparatus, presumably tracking devices. The two men sat up, startled. 'I know who you are and you know who I am,' I said, 'so let's stop playing games. The fact is, I don't know the quickest way back to Caledon Square, so instead of you following me why don't you go ahead and I'll follow you there?'

With that I went back to our car and waited a moment to see if the brown car would move. It didn't. So I started the engine and drove out of the gate.

'They're not coming,' Winnie cried, as she looked back. I swung into a narrow side street, pulled over and parked behind a tree. We waited a moment and saw the Toyota emerge and head off at speed along the road back to town.

'We've lost them,' Winnie said excitedly. 'Now you can really show me around.'

It was a critical moment, the kind where one can easily be swept along by the enthusiasm of a reckless companion without giving enough thought to possible consequences. I knew that what she wanted to do was foolish, but she was insistent and the adrenaline was flowing in my system.

'Where do you want to go?' I asked.

'To Simon's Town,' she replied promptly. 'I want to see the place that all the diplomatic fuss has been about.'

Simon's Town? It was crazy. This had been a British naval base for years, and under the terms of the Simon's Town Agreement had been transferred to South African control in 1957. There had been some wrangling between the two countries over the terms of the agreement, and Britain had cancelled it in 1975 – to the annoyance of the ANC, which wanted to see Britain take a strong stand against the apartheid state on all issues.

So we headed for Simon's Town. This was foolish because it was now the main base for the South African Navy and had been declared a 'key point' in security legislation, meaning the media were prohibited from reporting anything about it. For a journalist to take a banned person there, particularly such a high-profile revolutionary figure as Winnie Mandela, was the height of folly. Yet it was typical of the impulsive bravado of this extraordinary woman that she didn't give a damn if we were caught or not. Consequences didn't count when her blood was up.

There wasn't much to be seen in Simon's Town, as it turned out, aside from a few sailors strolling about, but for Winnie what counted was that she had been there; she had broken the apartheid regime's rules; she had triumphed.

As we drove away Winnie spotted a roadside sign bearing the name of the naval base. 'Stop,' she ordered, 'You must take a picture of that.'

She leapt from the car and posed before the sign with an arm stretched across it. The scene as I looked through the viewfinder of my camera was as incriminating a piece of evidence as any security cop could ever wish for: Winnie Mandela standing there with her arm across a sign announcing she was in the 'key point' of Simon's Town, and in the background a panoramic view of the naval base itself with warships in harbour.

We made our way safely back to Caledon Square, where no questions were asked about our having shaken off our tail. I imagine our tailers were too scared to report that they had lost us.

The return trip to Brandfort was a repeat, in reverse, of the tedious outward journey, with all its security surveillance. In the story I wrote, I omitted any reference to the Simon's Town visit. But I included that vivid quote about measuring the curtains in the presidential residence. The story was a hit in all my papers, and Marjory Ruck sent a letter of appreciation to Donald Trelford.

I had taken one further precaution. I had the roll of film with Winnie's picture processed, but not printed. I couldn't use that picture, for it would have had Winnie facing an array of serious charges – although in retrospect I suspect she may have revelled in that, too. She was a glutton for high-publicity punishment. But I didn't destroy the picture. I simply tossed the whole sheet of negatives into a drawer in my desk in Fingers' offices.

* * *

EIGHTEEN MONTHS later, I was coming down my driveway at the end of my morning jog. It was 7 am and I saw Sue outside the front door waiting for me. 'The security police are here,' she told me. 'Four of them. They've been here about an hour and they want to go through all your documents in your little upstairs office.'

'What on earth are they looking for?' I asked.

'I don't know, they won't say,' Sue replied, 'but they look very stern. The head guy, a Captain Pitout, has narrow eyes. He looks like a nasty piece of work.'

I went upstairs and introduced myself to the narrow-eyed Pitout. 'What do you guys want?' I asked.

'Mr Sparks, we believe you have violated security laws in some of the reports you have written, and we need to search through all your manuscripts. I hope you will cooperate so that we don't have to disrupt your home too much.'

He was polite enough, but I felt my blood rise. 'This is outrageous!' I exploded. 'This is nothing but political harassment. I write only for overseas newspapers and your security laws don't apply outside this country. So I refuse to cooperate with you. You'll have to get on with whatever dirty work you've been ordered to do, but I'm afraid my wife and I have to get on with our business of the day.'

'I'm afraid you cannot leave this house until we have finished searching it,' Pitout replied.

'And what about me?' Sue chipped in. 'I have to take my son to school.'

'Yes, you may do that,' Pitout said, 'but Mr Sparks will have to stay here until we have finished.'

'Well, I've got to take a shower,' I said, still standing there in my sweaty tracksuit. Pitout didn't respond, so I moved into our main bedroom, catching Sue's eye as I went to indicate that she should follow me. I led her into the en-suite bathroom and shut the door. A terrible thought had just struck me: when the security police had finished going through all my papers here at home,

454

they would surely move on to my office at Fingers' establishment – and there, in a drawer in my desk, was that sheet of negatives containing the picture of Winnie Mandela in Simon's Town.

'When you drop off Julian at school,' I said to Sue in the softest of whispers, which I hoped couldn't be heard by the four men still in my little office, 'please stop by my parents' home and call Bernard Simon, who's in the office next door to mine. Ask him to go into my office and take a sheet of negatives out of the bottom-left drawer of my desk, and destroy it. He can just flush it down the toilet. Ask him also to look in my filing cabinet, in the drawer marked M, and to take out my Mandela file and destroy everything in it too.'

Sue agreed and slipped away, but not before reminding me that she had a difficult day ahead of her, too. It was Julian's fifth birthday and she had invited 14 of his kindergarten classmates to a party at our home. What if the police were still there when all these children arrived?

I noticed that the four men going through my files were paying particular attention to sheets of telex copy, at which point my memory clicked in. I recalled that, some years before, Patrick Lawrence, a senior reporter at the *Rand Daily Mail*, had been charged and found guilty of quoting a banned person in a report for *The Guardian* in London. The key to his prosecution was that the security police had been able to bully the telex operator who had transmitted the copy into testifying against Patrick. The court held that Patrick had therefore published the quote to one person in South Africa. That meant the judgment stood as case law and could be used against me. Which explained why Pitout and his men were scanning all my old telex messages. They were looking for one in which I had quoted a banned person.

Which one? Ah yes, of course, the one about Winnie Mandela wanting to measure the curtains in the presidential residence. PW Botha was a petulant man, ill-tempered and petty, and the cheek of that quote must have stung him. He was probably irked anyway by my reports about accompanying Winnie to Pollsmoor. As I was to learn much later, the President was beginning to establish some highly sensitive indirect contacts with Nelson Mandela in

Pollsmoor — which was why he had been transferred there from Robben Island — and the thought of a journalist nosing around the prison with Mandela's wife at that time probably disconcerted him. I had to be taught a lesson, so the cops were dispatched to my home on a fishing expedition.

I sped to my city office as soon as the cops left our home — empty-handed, I was pleased to see — and got there shortly before they did. I greeted Pitout when he arrived with a single companion. 'Go ahead,' I said, gesturing towards the various cabinets around the room. But their presence in that building, among all those foreign correspondents, soon had the wires buzzing. My phone began to ring incessantly, as journalists across the county as well as some from abroad phoned to ask if it were true that I was being raided by the police, and did I have anything to say about it. I had plenty to say, giving angry statements over the phone, in the hearing of my persecutors, about being subjected to political harassment by the security police.

Next came calls from radio stations, and I took delight in taking on the style of a sports reporter giving a live commentary on a game. 'I have Captain Pitout in front of my desk right now,' I said, 'and he's moving over towards my filing cabinet on the right. I see him checking the labels on the filing drawers; I suppose he's looking for the letter M, I'm sure he wants the Mandela file; and, yes, he's opening the M drawer now and he's taking out the Mandela file ...'

By this time Pitout's face was purple with rage. He stormed out of the room and went to the telephone exchange where he ordered the unplugging of all phones. All the foreign correspondents were cut off.

But my moment of enjoyment was short-lived. I heard heavy boots stomping down the corridor, then saw a posse of police pass my open door. I heard them enter Bernard Simon's office next door, and a few moments later saw them re-emerge with a hand-cuffed Bernard accompanying them. Pitout looked at me with a satisfied smile curling his lips.

All that remained, after Pitout and his colleague had left and the telephones were reconnected, was to phone Sue and warn her that she should expect to be arrested at any moment; her phone call from my parents' home had obviously been intercepted. When she came on the line she, too, sounded harassed. Fourteen alarmed mothers were turning up at the door to snatch their little darlings to safety from a home where some dreadful crime must have been committed, for the radio was telling them the host couple were being raided and arrested.

* * *

MY THREE EDITORS rallied immediately to my defence, with Ben Bradlee taking the initiative. The veteran of the Watergate scandal and publication of the Pentagon Papers, which revealed secrets of the Vietnam War, was not going to stand aside and let his South African correspondent be harassed in this way. Besides which, he reckoned that if I could be charged with publishing material to a telex operator, it meant South Africa was aiming to apply its censorship laws to newspapers worldwide, since all news out of the country was transmitted by telex. That was unacceptable. It had to be fought. So Bradlee got Trelford at *The Observer* and Spoor at the *NRC Handelsblad* to agree to share costs for Sue and I to engage South Africa's two top defence lawyers to represent us at our impending trials. I engaged Sydney Kentridge, and Sue engaged Johann Kriegler. Both later became justices of the new South Africa's first Constitutional Court.

To the three editors' great credit, they also agreed to foot Bernard Simon's defence costs. Although he did not write for any of them, they accepted that he had intervened at my behest and was now charged jointly with Sue for allegedly 'defeating the ends of justice'. A nice touch, that charge. I would have thought defeating the ends of injustice would have been more appropriate. I must also give Bernard credit. He had good reason to feel resentful of me for having dragged him into this unpleasant affair, but he stood with us like a true warrior for the cause of free speech.

Bradlee's first instruction was for Sue and I to fly to Washington. He wanted to discuss strategy. On arrival we were ushered into a small war room, just off the Post's newsroom, where

Bradlee introduced us to the company's counsellor, Boisfeuillet Jones, known simply as 'Bo' to his colleagues, who he said would be keeping a close eye on our court cases. Bo was both charming and smart, a former Rhodes Scholar and Harvard Law School graduate. He wanted to be briefed on South African court procedures and given details of the charges Sue, Bernard and I would be facing. 'Bo will be your contact person here,' Bradlee told me. 'Please keep him informed about everything. He'll go to South Africa when the trials begin.'

We met again the next morning, and I sensed that Bradlee was all charged up. He was enjoying the challenge of confronting the South African system. 'We need some bright ideas,' he said, and almost in the same breath called for his secretary. 'Is Lou Cannon around?' he asked her, referring to the Post's senior White House correspondent. 'See if you can find him and tell him I want to see him.'

Cannon appeared soon afterwards. 'Lou, do you think you could arrange for Allister here to see the President,' Bradlee said by way of introducing me. 'He's our correspondent in South Africa and he and his wife are having some problems with the government there. It would be good if he could tell the President about them.'

'I'll go over to the White House and see what I can do,' Cannon replied.

'Lou is very close to Reagan,' Bradlee explained as the correspondent disappeared. 'He covered him for many years when Reagan was Governor of California, and probably knows him better than any other journalist in the country. That's why I brought him here to cover the White House for us.'

I was startled. 'But Ben, what do I say to the President if I get to see him?'

'Oh, we'll think about that later,' he replied, with a dismissive wave of the hand.

It was a couple of hours before Cannon returned. 'I'm sorry, but the President's really tied up for the next few days,' he told us. 'But I can get Allister to see Judge Clark.'

'That's great!' Bradlee declared. 'Maybe even better.' He

458

explained that William P Clark, the President's national security adviser, had been a long-time rancher friend of Ronald Reagan's in California, and had become an aide to him when Reagan was elected Governor of that state. Bill Clark had also become a judge of the Supreme Court of California, and then had followed Reagan to Washington.

'He's not very bright,' Bradlee told me. 'He is said to have dropped out of law school and then had to sit his Bar exams twice. But he's closer to Reagan than anyone else, other than Nancy. He's also the most right-wing guy in the whole administration. Which I reckon will serve our purposes just fine.'

Then turning to Cannon: 'When can Allister see him?'

'Right now,' came the reply.

'Hey wait,' I cut in. 'What do I say when I see him?'

'Never mind,' said Bradlee, waving us to the door. 'Just see him.'

It was not a long walk from the *Washington Post* offices to the White House, and Cannon and I had little to say as we headed there. I asked him a few questions about Clark. What was he like?

'Oh, he's really a cowboy,' Cannon replied. 'He loved life on the ranch, which is where he met Reagan and they became buddies. He hates it here in Washington. Too many liberals around for his liking. He can't wait to get back to his ranch, but he'll stay here as long as Reagan wants him.'

We whipped through the security barriers at the White House as Cannon flashed his press card; he was obviously a familiar figure there. We arrived at Clark's office and Cannon handed me over to Clark's secretary. 'I'll wait here till you're through,' he said.

I felt like crying out: 'No, no, I need your help! I don't know what I'm doing here.' But the secretary was already holding open Clark's door, ready to introduce me.

Clark rose from his desk, a tall, loose-limbed man and I noticed he was wearing cowboy boots. He greeted me with a country drawl and gestured to me to take a seat at his desk. I faced him across the desk and for a moment we stared at each other in silence. He eventually broke it. 'I hear you're having a few problems down there in South Africa,' he said.

'Yes,' I replied, 'I've had some problems as a result of a report I wrote for the Post.'

'Have you spoken to our ambassador down there?'

'Yes.'

'Well, that was the right thing to do.'

Silence again. 'Your Mister Botha (he pronounced the consonants as in 'the') seems to be doing a good job down there,' he ventured after the uncomfortable break.

I felt trapped. It was at the time PW was implementing his tricameral Parliament, which I strongly opposed. What the hell could I say to this man whom I was supposedly meeting to win over and get his help?

'Some people feel that way, but I'm afraid I disagree with his policies,' was my cautious response.

A longer silence this time. I felt I could read what was ticking over in his mind. Another damn liberal − these press people are all the same.

He rose and thrust out his hand. 'Well, thank you for coming. I hope things work out right for you down there in South Africa.'

With that he ushered me to his door.

I walked back in silence with Lou Cannon. He didn't ask what had transpired in that office and I didn't tell. I was too embarrassed. What a cock-up I had made of such a rare meeting with a high-powered figure in the Reagan administration.

Back in Ben's office, he leapt up from his desk and clutched me by the shoulders. 'How did it go?' he asked, eyes gleaming.

'Terrible,' I replied. 'I'm sorry, Ben, I just didn't know how to handle it.'

'Tell me what happened.'

I gave him a detailed − indeed verbatim − account of the brief exchange of empty phrases between Clark and myself. But when I reached the last phrase, Bradlee gave a yelp of delight and slapped me on the back.

'He really said that? He said, "I hope things work out right for you in South Africa"? Allister, that's all we need. Well done. Great stuff. We can work with that. Sit down, here's what we're going to do.'

460

As I slumped, bewildered, into a chair, Bradlee outlined his plan of action. 'Tomorrow morning we'll have breakfast here and I'll invite James Symington, South Africa's lobbyist here in Washington. I know it's a bit late to invite him, but he's been trying to see me for ages, so he'll come running. And when he's here and we're all having breakfast together, you can mention in the course of the conversation — you must just drop it in subtly, you understand — that you had a meeting with Judge Clark at the White House about your problems with the court actions against you and Sue, and that he had said he hoped things would work out right for you.

'Then I'll ask Kay Graham to give a dinner at her home tomorrow evening,' Bradlee went on. 'She can invite some high-powered guests. I'll make sure you are seated next to Mrs Graham, and that John Chettle is seated on her other side.' Chettle was the US representative of the South Africa Foundation, a body set up by the South African business community to counter the bad publicity the country was getting abroad because of apartheid.

'Mrs Graham will ask you about the court charges and you can explain everything to her so that Chettle can hear it all,' Bradlee went on. 'Then, when the dinner's over, I'll ask Chettle to drive you and Sue back to your hotel, and on the way you can just mention casually that you saw Judge Clark at the White House yesterday.'

Subtlety, as I came to realise, was not Ben Bradlee's strong point. We were still busy decanting the orange juice and had not yet taken our seats at the breakfast table next morning, when Bradlee blurted out: 'Allister, tell Jim how you went to see Judge Clark at the White House yesterday and what he said to you about the court cases you and Sue are facing in South Africa.'

I saw Symington flinch. 'You were at the White House?' he asked incredulously.

'Oh yes,' I replied, trying to sound casual as I began to slip at last into the mode of Bradlee's war games, 'Ben arranged it. We are very concerned about the implications of the South African government's attempts to apply its censorship laws to

461

the world media.' Symington looked concerned, so I suggested ever so tactfully that it might be a good idea for him to let the Department of Foreign Affairs back home know how seriously the matter was being regarded in the US.

The dinner was a grand affair, with some officials from the State Department present as well as Don Graham, the great lady's son, who was soon to take over from her as publisher of the *Washington Post*. I had met Kay Graham before, of course, during her visit to South Africa, but sitting next to her at the table and being able to have a more intimate conversation, I found her a deeply interesting person. People at the Post liked to describe her as the most powerful woman in the world. But what struck me most was that she was obviously intensely shy. She spoke to me frankly about how she had struggled to cope with the limelight after being thrust into the public role of chairperson of The Washington Post Company after the suicide of her husband, Philip Graham. 'It was a struggle, but I think I made it,' she said with the gentlest of smiles. She was hugely admired by her staff.

We did our duty, as required by Ben Bradlee, at our table that night. Kay Graham asked me how the charges had come about, and I told her about Winnie's irresistible remark on our drive to Pollsmoor prison, of how that must have irked PW, and of how the police had ransacked our home and my office searching for the telex copy of my story. She expressed shock at how the security police had tapped my parents' home to intercept Sue's phone call to Bernard Simon, and how Bernard had been marched out of his office in handcuffs. For free-press America this was shocking stuff, and I noted that John Chettle was taking it all in.

Right on cue, Chettle, accompanied by his wife, offered to drive Sue and I back to our hotel. They were a charming couple and we chatted easily on the way, mostly about the personality of Kay Graham. Then Chettle chipped in with something about her intense interest in the charges Sue and I were facing. 'Yes,' I responded, 'she and Ben have taken a really serious view of it. Ben arranged for me to go down to the White House yesterday to see Judge Clark—'

'What!' Chettle exclaimed, almost wrenching his neck out of

joint as he turned to look at me in the back seat. 'You saw Judge Clark about this?'

'Yeah,' I replied, trying to affect a casual tone. 'Lou Cannon took me down there to talk to Judge Clark, and Clark said he hoped things would turn out okay for us.'

* * *

WHAT INFLUENCE all this had on the eventual outcome of our cases I cannot say, but it was certainly an eye-opening experience for me on how Washington operates. The capital is a veritable cobweb of networks across which thousands of lobbyists are constantly peddling influence. It is a city engaged in the manufacture of a single product, words. The words of politicians, diplomats, lobbyists and lawyers, journalists, academics, civil servants and pontificators, millions upon millions of words churned out every day. It conjures up for me the image of a city floating like a hovercraft on a cushion of hot air. But the fact is, words have impact.

Not long after our return from Washington, Sue and Bernard were summoned to appear in the Johannesburg Magistrates' Court. It was a routine appearance intended only to set a date for their trial, which would take place in the Transvaal Supreme Court. But to my consternation Bo Jones had flown in from Washington that morning.

'Why did you come just for this brief appearance?' I asked him. 'What a waste. There'll be no evidence, no argument, they won't even have the charges put to them, or be asked to plead.'

'I know,' Bo replied. 'You explained all that to me when we first met. But you see, we've got to wrap the flag around you.'

He did more than that. He had been in touch with the US Embassy in Pretoria and arranged for several members of the diplomatic staff, as well as some from other embassies, to attend the brief hearing. At Bo's request they had all used their diplomatic immunity to park their official cars, with national pennants flying, right outside the main entrance to the squat, gloomy magistrates' court building in downtown Johannesburg. Naturally this attracted attention, so the press gallery in our courtroom quickly filled with reporters. Suddenly this two-minute formal appearance of the two accused had become something of a media event. Photographers began snapping pictures and reporters began interviewing Bo. '*The Washington Post*, and indeed the whole of the United States, is taking great interest in this case,' Bo told them.

There was, of course, a court roll to be gone through, which meant we all had to sit in the public gallery listening to cases of petty crime as we waited for Sue and Bernard's case to be called. Teatime came and the magistrate, a small weed of a man, adjourned the court. Bo Jones promptly left us to go backstage and introduce himself to the magistrate, who invited him to share a cup of tea with him. I don't know what sort of conversation passed between them, probably no more than Bo explaining his interest in Bernard and Sue's case, but what transpired after that tea break was remarkable.

A case of petty theft had to be heard, the last before Sue and Bernard were to appear in the dock. A black teenager was accused of robbery, of snatching a white woman's handbag in a Johannesburg street. Some people had chased after the youngster and caught him. The handbag was returned, but the aggrieved woman had pressed charges.

The teenager denied guilt. There had been a scuffle when several men had tackled the thief, he said. He had joined the scuffling mob to see what was happening, and the men had wrongly accused him of being the one who had grabbed the handbag. A case of mistaken identity. The boy's mother gave evidence for him. 'My son is a good boy,' she said. 'He is attending school and he would never do a thing like that.'

I had attended scores of such petty cases in magistrates' courts as a young reporter, and I never knew of one to last more than five minutes. The petty criminals with their improbable stories were rubber-stamped off to jail for a week or two without so much as a comment from the beak.

But this one turned out to be different. To our astonishment the magistrate adjourned the court, announcing that he would reconvene in half an hour to deliver a written judgment. It must have been the first time in South African judicial history that a presiding officer had felt the need to deliver a written judgment in such a petty case.

When the judge returned, he adopted a pompous air as he began reading his judgment. 'In South Africa we practise Roman-Dutch law,' he began, 'in which an accused person is considered innocent until proven guilty. In this case …'

I stopped listening to him and switched my attention to the interpreter. The case was being conducted in English, but the accused was a Xhosa youth, so an interpreter was translating the magistrate's words into isiXhosa, which I could follow. When the judgment reached the point where the magistrate was talking about the need for a guilty verdict to be 'beyond reasonable doubt', and that in this case it was just the word of the complainant against that of the accused, with no corroborative evidence on either side, I could see a puzzled expression on the interpreter's face and his interpreting began to dry up. When the final 'not guilty' verdict was announced, I heard the interpreter say to the teenager: 'You are very lucky, you'd better get out of here fast.'

Bo Jones flew back to Washington that same night. In and out with just 12 hours in Johannesburg. First class each way, so that he could get a good night's sleep and be ready for work the next morning.

* * *

A FEW WEEKS later I received a telephone call from Bo. His message was brief and cryptic. 'Tell your lawyers to go see the Minister of Justice in Pretoria. All the charges will then be dropped.'

I called Sydney Kentridge first. He gave a chuckle. 'Well done,' he said. I had kept him informed of the activities in Washington.

Johann Kriegler was less enchanted. 'I can't do that,' he exclaimed. 'This is most improper.'

I responded cautiously. I knew Kriegler to be a stickler for correctness. As an Afrikaner whose conscience had made him distance himself from Nationalist politics, I realised he would be reluctant to be involved in anything irregular. 'I know you may find this difficult,

Johann,' I said, 'but as Sue and Bernard's defence lawyer, isn't your first duty to them? To get them off these outrageous charges?'

I heard a slight grunt at the end of the line. But I knew he would do it.

A week later it was announced that Justice Minister Jacobus (Kobie) Coetsee had appointed Johann Kriegler a judge of the Supreme Court. I felt a twinge of guilt as I realised how uncomfortable that meeting with the minister must have been for Johann.

CHAPTER TWENTY-SIX

Seeing All Sides

THROUGHOUT the 1980s I was engaged in what I called 'shuttle journalism'. I shuttled between the civil war raging in the black townships of South Africa, as the young UDF comrades sought to make them ungovernable, and the relative peace and calm of the ANC headquarters in Lusaka; between the more formal wars being waged in the frontline states, Angola and Mozambique, and contacts with foreign diplomats concerned with the rising intensity of the racial conflict on all these fronts.

I was also trying to monitor the shifts beginning to take place within the Afrikaner community, not only with the emergence of the *verligte* (enlightened) wing of the National Party but also in the religious community of the Dutch Reformed Church, where the moral revolt launched by the Reverend Beyers Naudé and the Reverend Allan Boesak was gathering momentum.

Not least, my wife Sue had become actively involved as a member of the Black Sash women's movement, which was engaged in both protest demonstrations and advice counselling, giving legal and other advice to the many black people who got caught up daily in the tangled web of apartheid laws.

Sue had begun her married life with me as the politically innocent young wife of an editor, who committed the *faux pas* of asking the President's wife at a formal dinner what her husband did for

467

a living. But she grew rapidly in awareness, 'doing her own thing', as she put it, by joining the Black Sash and becoming intensely involved in its campaigns. Not only did she become a valuable news source for me with information from the black townships where she spent much of her time, but I also found myself sometimes reporting on events in which she was involved as a protester.

The first time I found myself in that uncomfortable role was when Sue joined a sizeable group of her Black Sash colleagues to stage a march on the Moroka police station in Soweto protesting against the detention without trial of a large number of black activists held there.

I stood at the roadside with other reporters and TV cameramen, feeling acutely anxious as I watched Sue and her companions march down the road towards a line of heavily armed police in riot gear blocking their way to the police station. The commander of the police unit stepped forward and ordered the women to halt, but they marched on. He ordered his men to get ready with their shotguns and teargas canisters, but he didn't give the order to fire as the women continued their approach. It was a tense moment, but then some primitive sense of chivalry must have caused him to baulk at firing on a group of women. Instead he ordered his men to arrest them, which they did, running forward to grab the women and hoist them bodily into a police van − which promptly took off for police headquarters at John Vorster Square in the heart of the city, where they were kept overnight in those forbidding cells.

* * *

THE SHUTTLING back and forth between Lusaka and the township battles across the country was the most illuminating feature of this phase of my life. These battles would begin spontaneously, triggered usually by a clash between the police and a single comrade, then rage through the township in an incoherent way that was difficult to follow. As the struggle intensified and the scope of events widened, *The Washington Post* realised it was developing into a major world story and moved its Central

African correspondent, Glenn Frankel, to join me in Johannesburg. We worked closely together for many months, often producing two front-page stories a day — one being what we called a 'day story', reporting the breaking events of the day, and the other a 'news analysis', explaining the significance of new developments and trying to project a sense of where the whole revolutionary upheaval might be headed. It was both stressful and stimulating work, day after day, weekends included, for which the Post nominated us jointly for a Pulitzer Prize — and for which my reports in *The Observer* won the top British press award for foreign reporting.

It was also dangerous work, being white in a maelstrom of black fury, but for the most part the rampaging comrades seemed to recognise the journalists in their midst as being on their side. Publicity was certainly to their advantage. But there were mishaps. Ken Oosterbroek, a brilliant photographer who did courageous work for *The Star*, was shot and killed and a colleague wounded, during a skirmish in Thokoza township, east of Johannesburg, in April 1994.

In Athlone, outside Cape Town, I landed up, together with my student son Michael, in the midst of a fierce battle between armed police and coloured protesters, some of whom were Muslims shouting *Allah Akhbar!* (God is Great!) as they hurled stones and sometimes fired pistols at the police. Michael, who was studying politics at the University of Cape Town, had asked to accompany me, partly for the adventure and partly to gather some real-life material for his studies. We met up with Michael Hornsby, the correspondent for *The Times* of London, and for a time found shelter behind a broken wall as the battle raged around us. But a moment came when we were in danger of being cornered there and we decided to make a break for safer ground. The three of us sprinted through the milling crowd and headed down the street, with the police firing shotguns from behind us. A shot hit Michael Hornsby in the back, shredding his shirt and ripping the flesh beneath it. He staggered from the force of the shot but kept going. People from nearby houses shouted to us and pointed to a house where they said we could get help.

It turned out to be a doctor's home, where the front door was swiftly opened to let us in. A grim scene met our eyes. Wounded people, many groaning in pain and some unconscious, possibly dead, were lying in a tangled mess on the sitting room floor. Two doctors, the one whose house it was and another who had joined him, were frantically attending to the more serious cases. One of the doctors took a quick look at Michael's back. It was pock-marked with shotgun pellets – 69 of them as he later learned – and was bleeding. 'I'm sorry I can't attend to you,' the doctor said, 'but you're going to be okay and there are people here who are seriously injured. I must attend to them. Go to a doctor in town and he can clean you up, but I advise you not to have the pellets removed. They'll come out in time.'

He apologised once more, then as we turned to leave he enjoined us to go out by a back door and try to slip away unnoticed. 'If the police discover that we are here helping these people, they'll come and arrest everyone for attending a prohibited gathering,' he said. It was only then that I noticed that all the blinds on the windows of that house were closed to preserve the secrecy of urgent medical attention being conducted inside.

As the war dragged on, the Post transferred Glenn Frankel to become its correspondent in Israel. He was replaced first by David Ottaway, then by Paul Taylor. It was Taylor's misfortune to run into serious trouble on his very first foray into a black township. Phillip van Niekerk, who had been one of my star reporters on the *Rand Daily Mail* and had now also become a free-lance correspondent, drove with Taylor into Sebokeng township, in the volatile Vaal Triangle, south of Johannesburg. A group of belligerent comrades forced them to a halt and ordered them out of the car. Without warning the leader of the group drew a pistol and fired two shots. One struck Taylor in the chest, the other hit Van Niekerk in the head, a terrible wound, with the bullet entering at the point of Phillip's right jaw and exiting beside his left ear.

Fortunately the bullet that went into Paul's chest had first struck his arm, which reduced its velocity so that it did not penetrate deeply. He was still able to stay on his feet. But Phillip's wound was grievous. He had been shot right through the head, the bullet shattering his jaw on both sides and missing the carotid artery by a millimetre. He fell to the ground, and lay conscious but bleeding profusely while the wounded Taylor walked groggily down the road seeking help from the terrified township dwellers, most of whom fled indoors.

Taylor eventually found help and Phillip was helicoptered to a Johannesburg hospital where he underwent complex surgery. I was at the hospital that night as his life hung on a thread, but slowly Phillip recovered. The maxillofacial surgeon who fixed up his shattered face was the same specialist who had attended to Hendrik Verwoerd after his first assassination attempt. He told Phillip his wound was almost identical to the now deceased Prime Minister's.

I had a lucky escape myself soon after that, also in Sebokeng. Again a crowd of hyped-up comrades forced my car to a stop and ordered me out. The crowd swarmed around me and the mood soon became hostile. Who was I? What was I doing there? I responded in isiXhosa, which is understandable to Zulus, who seemed to be the dominant element in that group. Suddenly someone in the crowd cried out: 'Hey, it's Joe Slovo!' I have no idea why, for I bore no physical resemblance to that leading Communist Party figure who was a senior commander in the ANC's guerrilla army. Except perhaps that we both had grey hair. Whatever it was, I found myself suddenly hoisted shoulder high and carried down the road as a hero until I was able to plead with them to put me down and let me get on with my revolutionary business. On my next visit to Lusaka I thanked Joe Slovo, and the mutual ravages of age on our hirsute condition, for saving my life. He laughed heartily.

The contrast between the battles in the South African townships and the ANC's exile headquarters in Lusaka, 1 600 km away, was striking. Although the ANC premises in Lusaka were rudimentary, things were orderly. People went about their business quietly and one had to make appointments to see key figures. This was supposedly the headquarters of a revolutionary war against apartheid, yet there was no sense of military activity, or even much awareness of it, here. There were no easy means of communication between the war front and the military headquarters that was supposedly directing it. The leaders of the military wing, Umkhonto we Sizwe, pretended to be closely in touch with events on the ground, but it took only a few moments of conversation to realise that I knew more than they did about what was going on in the South African townships.

In later years, after the ANC had taken power, this pretence that it was fully aware and in control of what was happening inside South Africa was not only maintained but also magnified. The myth was established, and the history of the transition re-written accordingly, that it was the heroic MK army that forced the apartheid regime to the negotiating table. The roles of all other participants in the struggle have been marginalised, if not brushed aside altogether. The 'insiles', as those who fought the war at home rather sarcastically call themselves today, the UDF, the young comrades who fought those furious township battles, the religious leaders who raised the moral doubts in Afrikaner minds, and other players, have all been airbrushed out of the great story of the liberation struggle. To the extent that the UDF is even acknowledged today, it is portrayed as having been established by the ANC leaders in exile and its activities directed from Lusaka. The truth is that, except for a handful of attacks within South Africa, the ANC's exiled forces fought most of their battles outside the country, in the frontline states of Angola, Namibia and Mozambique, mostly in tandem with civil wars being fought in those countries. Those were important contributing factors, but they were minor compared with the township battles, the pressure of international sanctions and the erosion of the moral and theological underpinning of the apart-heid doctrine in Afrikaner minds.

* * *

NONE OF THIS is to imply that my trips to Lusaka were not worthwhile. They were extremely so. That was where the ANC had its headquarters, which meant that was where its political de-cisions were made – and South Africa's transition to democracy was a political, not a military, achievement.

The one positive thing I will concede about the ANC's military wing was the psychological effect its mere existence had on those young comrades who waged the real war in the townships. The notion that there was an army out there waiting to join them in their struggle sustained and energised them and kept up the morale of millions of ordinary black South Africans. Even small children took to running about the township streets with hand-made wooden replicas of the romanticised AK-47 automatic rifle.

But the real value of the Lusaka headquarters was its political brains trust. Oliver Tambo was the leader of the exiles, but he was a peripatetic figure based primarily in London, from where he travelled the world keeping in touch with ANC supporters. He visited Lusaka only when necessary. I met him there only twice, once for an interview when I was taken to his safe house blindfolded, an indication of the movement's security jitters. The second time was at his request, when he asked me to speak to a group of his key lieutenants about the shift in thinking taking place in some quarters of the Afrikaner community that I had written about and which he had read in *The Observer*. He also gave me a taped message to give to Winnie Mandela to pass on to Nelson Mandela when next she visited him in prison.

I found Tambo to be a quiet, thoughtful and essentially a gentle person. I sensed he was privately uncomfortable about the armed struggle, but he was a loyal and disciplined member of the movement and he defended it whenever required to do so. His role and his skills were in diplomacy.

The real political brains trust at headquarters, the strategic thinkers, were Thabo Mbeki, Chris Hani and Joe Slovo. And they, I soon realised, were not of the same mind. Indeed the more time I spent in Lusaka, the more aware I became that the organisation was riddled with factions. This was not surprising: the ANC was a coalition of people with many different political ideas, but with one uniting factor in their desire to overthrow apartheid. But these strategic and ideological differences were to manifest themselves in a more problematic way when eventually the ANC came to power.

Mbeki was the most personable. I had warmed to him when

I first met him in London, and now that developed into a close friendship. I would put out the word when I checked in at Lusaka's Pamodzi Hotel, and at some point in the evening I would get a message that he, too, had checked in there. I would make my way to his room clutching a bottle of Scotch, and we would talk about our respective perceptions of the state of the nation, either till sunrise or until the Scotch was finished. Mbeki was well educated, with an MA in economics and development from the University of Sussex, highly sophisticated, warm and articulate. He was the key thinker in the ANC and very close to Tambo, and I soon realised that he had become convinced that negotiation was the only way to resolve South Africa's race conflict, and that he was bound to play a lead role in trying to achieve it.

Chris Hani was the polar opposite to Mbeki, also well educated and articulate, with a degree in modern and classical literature from the University of Fort Hare, but, as the commander of Umkhonto we Sizwe, inevitably committed to a military solution. I never got to know him as well as the other leading figures; I sensed a remoteness between us, which I suspect stemmed from criticisms I had written of the ANC's strategic decision to launch its armed struggle and my friendship with his rival, Mbeki. But it was clear he had a popular following, and as events unfolded he joined the negotiating process under Nelson Mandela and played a unifying role until he was assassinated at a critical moment during the negotiations in April 1993.

I have to rate Joe Slovo as one of the most interesting people I have ever met. He was a dyed-in-the-wool communist and a committed revolutionary, which made him the apartheid government's most wanted man. They would have killed him on sight given the opportunity, but he was cunning and elusive. He never slept in the same place two nights running, and when he agreed to let me write a profile of him he would call me 15 minutes ahead of the agreed time to name a venue, then never stay for more than 30 minutes of interviewing before disappearing again. It took a week to complete the assignment. During one of those interviews, he tripped on a step and an automatic pistol fell from a concealed ankle holster. 'Oops,' he said lightly as he stooped to pick up the weapon and replace it in the holster, 'you weren't supposed to see that.'

I liked Slovo despite his politics. Unlike most ideologists, he had a streak of pragmatism and a great sense of humour. He also had a remarkable brain. Slovo had left Lithuania for South Africa with his parents at the age of ten. He did not complete primary school, taking his first job at age 14, yet after serving in the South African Army during the Second World War he was able to get an ex-serviceman's dispensation to study law at the University of the Witwatersrand, graduating top of his class with an LLB degree in five years instead of the normal seven. He practised as an advocate for several years, but after the Communist Party was banned he went into exile with the ANC to become the best-known figure in its military wing. Slovo married an equally bright and committed woman, Ruth First, who was also hounded by the security police and eventually assassinated by a letter bomb in 1982 while teaching at the Eduardo Mondlane University in Mozambique.

When I first met Slovo in Lusaka he greeted me warmly. 'I've always enjoyed your writing,' he told me, 'you've done some really good stuff.' I expressed surprise, noting that communists seemed often to dislike liberals even more than far-right conservatives, a phenomenon Freud described as 'the narcissism of minor differences'.

'Oh no,' Slovo responded with a hearty laugh, 'the only difference between you and I is that you want the revolution to stop at February and I want it to go on to October.' I suggested that maybe we could cut a deal and end it in June.

Joe Slovo went on to play a vital role during the negotiations that brought an end to apartheid, when he showed a sense of realism well beyond many of his ANC colleagues in helping to bring about agreement. In a private conversation during those years he confessed to having been a dedicated Stalinist for much of his life, but that his late wife Ruth had exercised a 'humanitarian influence' on him and that he had ended up as an admirer of Mikhail Gorbachev's *perestroika* reforms in the Soviet Union. Slovo became Minister of Housing in the government of Nelson Mandela, but sadly contracted bone cancer and died in 1995, aged 69. It was a great loss to the country; he could have been an invaluable influence in the faction-ridden Jacob Zuma era.

My trips to Lusaka were not my only exposure to influential ANC figures. In July 1987 Frederik van Zyl Slabbert, a leading Afrikaner intellectual, invited me to join a group of 52 mainly Afrikaans-speaking people of note to accompany him to a meeting with a group of ANC exiles led by Thabo Mbeki in Dakar, Senegal. Slabbert had been leader of the opposition Progressive Federal Party in Parliament, but had resigned in despair at the prospect of the all-white legislature ever achieving a breakthrough. He and a fellow liberal MP, Alex Boraine, had founded an organisation they called the Institute for a Democratic Alternative for South Africa (Idasa). Dakar was their first big venture.

The meeting was held in French-speaking Senegal because of the intercession of the Afrikaner poet, Breyten Breytenbach, who had exiled himself in Paris after violating South Africa's mixed-marriages law by wedding a Vietnamese woman. Breytenbach had befriended French President François Mitterand and his wife, Danielle, whose foundation funded the Dakar venture.

For a week I was a fascinated listener, and occasional participant, as the two sides batted around the key differences between them — the ANC's commitment to a violent struggle, the notion of power-sharing between the races, and whether or not there should be constitutional protection for minorities in a new, democratic South Africa. What impressed me most about the exchanges was the intellectual rigour with which the ANC members marshalled their arguments, and the disarming diplomatic skills of Mbeki. He managed, with a combination of charm, reassurances and political toughness, to ensure that the ANC group did not concede a single point of importance in the joint agreement, called the Dakar Declaration, that was finally adopted unanimously by both sides.

From Dakar, Slabbert's group, accompanied by some of the ANC members, moved to Ouagadougou, capital of another former French colony, Burkina Faso. There we were hosted by President Thomas Sankara, a charismatic revolutionary figure popularly known as the 'Che Guevara of Africa', who was assassinated by his deputy, Blaise Compaoré, in a coup just three months after our visit — giving us some food for thought about the realities of Africa.

From Burkina Faso to Ghana and its capital city of Accra, where, those many years before, I had been arrested by Kwame Nkrumah's security men. The highlight for me on this occasion was a meeting our group had with a group of Ghanaian students. The students immediately tackled Mbeki. Why, they demanded, when African countries were helping to fund the ANC's war against white oppression in South Africa, was he here talking to these white South Africans instead of killing them?

It was a key moment for Mbeki, calling for all his diplomatic skills. Quietly, tactfully, Mbeki explained that while the ANC greatly appreciated the support it was getting from Ghana and other African countries, its objective in seeking to liberate South Africa was not the same as their own had been in liberating Ghana from colonialism. The ANC accepted that the white population of South Africa, especially the Afrikaners such as this group accompanying him, would stay in the country after apartheid was dismantled. They had no metropolitan 'home' to return to; they had been in South Africa for centuries and it was their only home. 'That is why the ANC has always advocated a non-racial future for our country,' he said. 'Our aim is to end apartheid and build a nation where all South Africans are equal, black and white.'

Mbeki's target audience was not so much the Ghanaian students as his white companions. And he hit a bullseye. Slabbert in particular was deeply impressed, regarding it as a statement of great courage before such an audience. 'I could die for that bugger,' he said of Mbeki afterwards.

In the years since then, the Dakar expedition has become somewhat controversial. Was it the ground-breaking event Slabbert had hoped for, or were the Idasa brigade simply a naive group taken in by Mbeki's charm and clever diplomacy?

Looking back, I rate it as an event of notable value. Not a breakthrough in itself, but, seen in context with other contacts that followed, some again organised by Idasa and others by the government's own intelligence services, I do think it contributed valuably to mutual understanding and eventual agreement. To my mind the only disappointing aspect was that Mbeki, having established a close and trusting relationship with Slabbert, bringing two major intellectuals from opposite sides of the ethnic divide together, who could have worked constructively in tandem during the early years of democracy, did not follow up when the ANC came to power. And particularly when Mbeki himself became president. It was a great opportunity lost for no apparent reason.

* * *

IN ADDITION TO these political and diplomatic contacts, I also made my way to the battlefields of the key frontline states, Angola and Mozambique. What drew me to these war zones was an awareness of the strategic threat the apartheid regime faced when the revolutionary overthrow of the Salazar-Caetano dictatorship in Portugal in 1974 led to that country pulling out of its war-torn African colonies.

This meant the apartheid regime faced the threat of the ANC being able to use those countries, now in the hands of friendly black governments, as springboards from which to launch attacks on South Africa from both east and west. However, the threat from Angola in the west would first have to penetrate South West Africa, a former German colony controlled by South Africa since the end of the First World War under a League of Nations mandate, to reach the South African border. That brought the mandated territory's own liberation movement, the South West African People's Organisation (Swapo), into the picture as well.

Angola was the most brutal of those two war fronts. A 14-year war of independence there morphed into a 27-year civil war between a cluster of liberation movements. The Popular Movement for the Liberation of Angola (MPLA), led first by Agostinho Neto, then, on his death, by José Eduardo dos Santos, seized power in the capital, Luanda, as the Portuguese withdrew, but was promptly challenged by Jonas Savimbi's National Union for the Total Liberation of Angola (Unita), which controlled the southern provinces.

The struggle was then internationalised. Apartheid South

478

Africa, with the covert backing of the United States, intervened in support of Savimbi's anti-communist Unita. Cuba had established four training bases in Angola to help train MPLA and ANC forces. When Fidel Castro learned of South Africa's support for Unita, he decided to protect his bases from being overrun by making a large-scale commitment of special forces and 35000 Cuban infantry to support the MPLA. The Soviet Union flew in the Cubans and provided the financial, logistical and military support to keep the MPLA government in business. The ANC's military wing, which was dependent on the Soviet bloc for military training and equipment, supported the MPLA and was engaged in some of the fighting.

I visited the Angolan battlefronts on four occasions, twice courtesy of Savimbi's Unita and twice to Dos Santos's capital, Luanda, where I became the first South African civilian to visit that city since the Portuguese withdrawal.

The first invitation from Savimbi came to the foreign press corps via the South African Defence Force. It was wrapped in mystery. We had to gather at a rural airfield north of Pretoria, sign indemnity forms, and board an ancient, twin-engined DC-3 Dakota aircraft that purported to belong to an outfit called Wonder Air. We took off early in the morning and after crossing the Botswana border droned slowly over the shimmering wastes of the Kalahari Desert. During the flight I made my way forward to chat to the pilot, where I noticed an array of modern navigational equipment that was clearly not standard to the original model of this old plane. It was obviously not a private charter plane.

For five hours we flew over hundreds of square kilometres of nothing. There was not a town to be seen, not a building even. No roads or railways, not a sign of a human being. Just occasional herds of game scattering at the sound of engines overhead. What a place to fight a war. It was, of course, also a convenient place to hide an army, which is what Savimbi did with his headquarters base at Jamba in the southeastern corner of Angola.

As we stepped out of the Dakota on to a dirt airstrip that had been hacked out of the surrounding bush, we were greeted by a choir of young girls dressed in Unita's red-and-green colours and gyrating to the accompaniment of tom-tom drums as they sang songs in praise of their rebel leader, whose huge portrait was planted there like a billboard. A banner bade us welcome to 'The Liberated Territory of Angola'. We were taken to a table beside a thorn tree, which turned out to be an immigration checkpoint. The formalising of make-believe.

We climbed aboard camouflaged trucks, made in Czechoslovakia and captured from the MPLA, where we were joined by guards with captured Russian AK-47 rifles, and began a nightmare four-hour journey along bumpy sand roads that wound through thick tsetse-fly-infested bush. The worst of it was that the Czech trucks appeared to have lost their springs at some point in their exchange of ownership, so that we jolted about painfully in the back. The bone-crushing journey also had several interruptions: once when one of the trucks overturned, spilling the choristers out, two of whom were injured and were hauled, moaning, into our truck; again when a guard was swept overboard by the branch of a tree which struck him like a gybing boom; and finally when one of the trucks developed engine trouble.

It was dark when we reached Jamba, but the place was a revelation. Savimbi may have borne the mark of Cain for collaborating with apartheid South Africa, but Jamba showed him to be a remarkable man. It was a makeshift camp of reed huts to which the Unita leader had brought all the accoutrements of a modern town. There was a well-equipped hospital where surgeons performed sophisticated operations; a vehicle workshop; a munitions plant where captured weapons were repaired; and a tailoring establishment where seamstresses made the uniforms that everyone wore. Savimbi's soldiers and workers were paid nothing, but all were accommodated, clothed, fed, educated, trained and cared for medically for free. Perhaps the ultimate socialist society founded by a man fighting against communism.

We correspondents were billeted in reed camps, each with its own small bathroom, and where the beds were made up with freshly ironed linen. Young, well-educated soldiers (the camp also had its own school) attended to our every need with the discreet efficiency of trained staff at a safari camp.

After showing us around his camp next morning, Savimbi briefed us in polished English, sketching out the main positions of his and the MPLA's forces on a blackboard. I took an immediate liking to Savimbi, a man of high intelligence, wit and obvious organisational skills. Looking back, I lament the fact that this remarkable man never came to play a role in the governing of his country or in the affairs of the continent as a whole. He was certainly one of the most capable African leaders I ever encountered. But although Dos Santos could never defeat Savimbi, he refused ever to negotiate with him, drawing the other liberation movements into his national government. Savimbi was eventually killed in a battle with MPLA forces on 22 February 2002. He was 68 years old.

* * *

A YEAR LATER I was back in southern Angola, this time to go to the scene of the biggest battle of the war between the MPLA and Unita, on the banks of the Lomba River. Again I flew with a group of foreign correspondents in that same 42-year-old Dakota, but this time to the town of Mavinga, some 250 km north of Jamba, from where we travelled another 250 km to the Lomba River in the same old Czech trucks, making it the deepest any journalists had gone into the southern war zone and the closest to the fighting front.

This time the flight was a good deal scarier than the first one. We crossed the border into Angola at night and the pilot immediately dropped to treetop height to keep below the MPLA radar network, which he told us could have alerted Russian MiG fighters based within easy range at Lubango and Menongue. Flying at 50 metres above the ground, which I had done before in Namibia and Rhodesia, was scary enough, but doing so at night was doubly so. Moreover the pilot switched off his navigation lights as well as the cabin lights and ordered us not to show any illumination inside the lumbering old crate: no matches, no cigarettes, no nothing. 'If they see us we're sitting ducks,' he warned.

He put the Dakota down between paraffin-flame flares on

a bush runway that finished in the main street of Mavinga, a shattered shell of a town in Angola's Cuando-Cubango province.

After spending the night in underground bunkers as a safeguard against frequent MPLA air attacks on the town, a Unita patrol took us in those springless trucks on another long trip to the Lomba River battlefield, where a massive attempt by the MPLA to break through to Savimbi's headquarters at Jamba had been stopped and turned back.

It was the most ghastly scene I have ever beheld. The smell of death was everywhere. This was no gentleman's war in which the enemy's dead get buried. They were lying there in the blazing tropical sun, hundreds of them. The air was thick with flies and the trees heavy with vultures, nature's gloomy undertakers waiting to do their work. The battlefield was also strewn with the burnt-out hulks of Russian armoured cars and troop carriers, one with a 'Stalin Organ' rocket launcher mounted on it. Nearby there was also the wreck of a big Russian Mi-25 helicopter gunship, which Savimbi's troops claimed had been brought down by a mortar bomb fired from the ground.

Trees had been smashed down by heavy vehicles and stripped by shells, and there were hundreds of foxholes, slit trenches and underground bunkers, making the scene look like a First World War battlefield. The earth was scarred with shell craters and scorched areas where explosions had started bush fires. It was obvious that a major conventional battle had been fought there in what until then had been a guerrilla war.

Moreover the battle was not yet over. We could hear the occasional crump of mortar fire across the Lomba River. Savimbi, speaking to us in an underground bunker, told us the retreating MPLA army was only about 30 km away, heading for the town of Cuito Cuanavale.

The large number of unburied bodies and all the destroyed Russian military hardware indicated to me that the MPLA forces had been caught in a heavy surprise attack. This made me suspect that South African commandos with air support had intervened to rescue Savimbi. It was a nauseating feeling, as I gazed at the scorched and rotting bodies still slumped in their slit trenches, to think that my countrymen, perhaps even some relatives of mine, were probably responsible for this scene out of a horror movie. And all to defend the evil system of apartheid. Inhumanity compounded. And I was part of it, for much as I despised apartheid, South Africa was my country.

My suspicions were reinforced by the claim of the helicopter gunship having being brought down by a mortar shell, which struck me as improbable. But when I asked Savimbi whether there had been South African involvement, he denied it. 'There was not a single South African soldier here,' he said. 'We didn't need it and we didn't request it. I didn't want South African troops here. If one were killed or captured it would cause too many problems.'

True enough. But when I later contacted a Portuguese journalist friend, Benjamin Formigo, who was covering the war out of Luanda, he told me the government there claimed South African forces had been involved and had carried out three air raids on MPLA positions on the Lomba River.

* * *

MY FIRST VISIT to Luanda was to join a press party accompanying the black American politician, the Reverend Jesse Jackson, on a tour of African countries in March 1987. *The Washington Post* believed Jackson intended making a run for the Democratic presidential nomination the following year, which indeed he did. The foreign desk asked me to link up with him in Luanda, where he was due to arrive from Nigeria, and cover the rest of his tour.

I flew to Luanda via Lusaka and happened to land at the same time as Jackson's party, which meant I was able to join the tour at the airport. It was my personal introduction to African political ostentation. President Dos Santos was at the airport to meet Jackson, who was given a welcome akin to that of a head of state – some of which was extended to his entourage. I found myself ushered into the back of a big black Mercedes-Benz, which took off at high speed in a cavalcade of cars with flashing blue lights, wailing sirens and motorcycle outriders. I felt like royalty sitting there, alone in the back seat of my splendid car, wondering whether I should wave to the cheering crowds lining the streets.

But as is often the case in Africa, all this ostentation was against a backdrop of visible economic decline and poverty. Before Angola's protracted wars, Luanda had been a lovely seaside city, with tropical palms lining the Marginal esplanade, which curves around its crescent-shaped bay. But as our cavalcade sped through the city's crowded streets I could see it was a shell. The cafés were abandoned, the shops shuttered and empty. There were no taxis, no buses, no hire cars.

We pulled up at our hotel, a five-star island of luxury in a sea of ruin. I was quickly summoned to Jackson's room, where he wanted me to brief him on the country. This was to become a regular event on our arrival in each new city on his tour. Even by American political standards, Jackson's appetite for publicity was insatiable and I was the guy from *The Washington Post*, the one to publicise him where it mattered most. He could never remember my name, calling me Alex throughout the tour, but he wanted my company constantly, as an adviser and sometimes as a sounding board on whom to practise his latest rhetorical turns of phrase. But most of all when he was meeting heads of state. Alex had to be there to record his every activity.

I found myself approving of Jackson's liberal stance on American politics, particularly his concept of a 'rainbow coalition' embracing all races, an image later to be used to describe the new South Africa. But I didn't warm to him personally. There was just too much hubris and too much godliness in his political speeches. I also sensed a superficiality. When I saw him again a year later while he was campaigning in the US, he didn't remember me. Alex had been but a temporary tool of convenience.

I was back in Luanda on a more hard-news mission 18 months later. It was at a time when the US was trying to broker peace between President Dos Santos and Jonas Savimbi. Things were changing on the global front: Mikhail Gorbachev was reorientating the Soviet Union's foreign ventures, while the US, embarrassed by disclosures of its support for South Africa in Angola, also wanted out so that it could help stabilise the country in which American oil companies had a big stake. With the Russians and Cubans becoming eager to leave, South Africa also began to think of ending its border war and allowing South West Africa to become independent after free elections.

The only snag in this was the ongoing war between Dos Santos and Savimbi. The US had managed to persuade the two to shake hands at a meeting in President Mobutu Sese Seko's gaudy palace at Gbadolite in northern Zaire (now the Democratic Republic of Congo). But after only three months, fighting had broken out again and *The Washington Post* sent me to Angola to assess the situation. This time I spent ten days travelling across some of the central and southern provinces with Dos Santos's troops.

But before heading southwards I had an encounter that illustrated the complexity of this drawn-out, multinational struggle. I met a young Cuban soldier who spoke a little English in a Luanda bar one evening. He was waiting to be evacuated back home, and as we chatted I asked him what his military role had been in Angola. His had been a fairly easy stint, he told me, he had been posted in Cabinda, the oil-rich enclave separated from the main body of Angola by the mouth of the Congo River and a narrow strip of territory belonging to Zaire. His job, he said, had been to guard a Gulf Oil plant from possible attack by South African troops who had penetrated into Cabinda.

'I was very mixed up,' he said. 'I was here to help Angola but I was defending an American oil company from being attacked by South Africans. I didn't know who was my friend and who was my enemy.'

I flew to the central city of Huambo, Angola's second city 600 km south of Luanda. This was the main hub of the 1 344-km Benguela Railway, built in 1902 to connect the copper mines of Zambia and the Congo's Katanga province to the Angolan port of Lobito. The railway had lain unused since 1975, the track disrupted in many places and the station at Huambo cluttered with derelict locomotives covered in cobwebs. The city itself was a ruin. It had been the centre of many brutal battles between MPLA and Unita forces, during which large numbers of people had been massacred and others had fled. At one point Savimbi

485

had gained control of the city and claimed the province of Huambo to be an independent republic, only for the MPLA, with Cuban help, to recapture it a year later.

It was in that shattered city that I saw one of the most distressing scenes of my journalistic experience. Legless children. One of the cruellest features of this and other southern African wars was the large-scale use of anti-personnel landmines. These were planted in the pathways and agricultural fields where the peasants walked and on the riverbanks where they fished and fetched water. The mines wrought havoc among the rural populations, particularly in Angola, which at that time had the highest amputee rate in the world, with 18 000 victims in a population of 19 million. The International Red Cross had established an artificial limb factory in Huambo and another in nearby Cuito, mostly using timber from the surrounding bush, where together they were fitting an average of 80 feet and legs a month — and still they couldn't keep pace with the need.

As I moved through that makeshift hospital in Huambo, talking to those mutilated survivors and the weary doctors attending to them, I felt a surge of anger at the injustice of these hapless victims being the pawns in a proxy war being waged between two superpowers half a world away, a war over power and influence and ideology, issues in which these innocent victims had neither knowledge nor interest. Their only role was to do the suffering and the dying. A war which the power-mongers waging it from a distance called a Cold War, but which for the peasants and women and children walking these paths and riverbanks of central Angola was hot and hellish.

* * *

MOZAMBIQUE, on the eastern side of the southern African subcontinent, was the other battlefront I visited in the 1980s. It, too, had been a Portuguese colony until the revolution in Lisbon. Mozambique then became the staging ground from which ANC guerrillas could infiltrate South Africa from the east. The organisation located its intelligence chief, Jacob Zuma, in Maputo, the capital, to organise this front of its liberation struggle.

That meant South Africa frequently launched attacks on what it perceived to be ANC bases or hideouts in Mozambique, some overtly by aerial bombardment and others surreptitiously by its intelligence agents. Thus the letter bomb that killed Ruth First, and the 1988 car-bomb explosion in which the ANC's leading legal scholar, Albie Sachs, later to become a Justice of South Africa's first Constitutional Court, lost an arm and an eye and very nearly his life.

But while the main ANC operations were out of the south of the country, the main war front was to the north of Maputo, between the forces of the ruling Frelimo movement and those of a rebel outfit called Mozambican National Resistance (Renamo). Another African civil war following independence.

Frelimo had taken power unopposed in 1975 when the Portuguese withdrew, but Ian Smith's Rhodesia had set up Renamo as an anti-Frelimo movement in the northern provinces of Mozambique. Smith was able to do so not so much by exploiting tribal differences, which were less acute in Mozambique than in Angola, but by playing on northern resentment that they had been neglected while the south had been developed under Portuguese colonial rule. And they saw no prospect of the Frelimo regime redressing that imbalance.

Smith's purpose in establishing Renamo was to have a small group informing him about the activities of Robert Mugabe's liberation army, which was based in Mozambique. But the movement grew quickly, and when Rhodesia finally succumbed to black rule and became Zimbabwe, South Africa inherited Renamo as a kind of orphan child, but a child that became singularly robust.

My purpose in plunging into northern Mozambique in 1987 was that Renamo was giving independent Zimbabwe a hard time. As South Africa faced an imminent threat of international sanctions, the fear in landlocked countries to the north, such as Zimbabwe and Zambia, was that the apartheid regime would retaliate by closing their links to the sea. As a safeguard, Zambia had enlisted Chinese help in the 1970s to build a rail link northwards to the port of Dar es Salaam, the Tanzanian capital. But

Zimbabwe faced a more problematic situation. Its only links to the ocean, other than via the South African rail network, were through Mozambique, and then even the line to the port of Maputo passed through South African territory. That left only a road-rail link to Beira, Mozambique's second port city, 1 200 km north of Maputo – in the very heartland of the civil war raging between Renamo and Frelimo.

The Beira Corridor, as it was called, also carried an oil pipeline that was Zimbabwe's only source of fuel at the time, and was constantly under Renamo attack. I undertook my own investigation of this vulnerable lifeline, which would make a good story for my papers. While on a trip to Zimbabwe to interview President Mugabe, I learned that Renamo guerrillas had disrupted the oil flow for the umpteenth time, by sabotaging the pumping station in Beira. I called at the Harare offices of Lonrho, the company that built and maintained the pipeline, to ask whether I could accompany their repair team when they went to fix it. After much hesitation and many warnings that it would be a perilous journey, a senior official agreed that I could accompany a truck that would be leaving the border town of Mutare in a few days' time to transport spare parts for the pumping station in Beira.

I duly met up with the truck driver in Mutare. He turned out to be a lively young black Zimbabwean, aged about 18. The truck was an old Toyota, on the back of which were the spares for the pumping station, as well as a machine gun mounted on a tripod and manned by four uniformed Zimbabwean soldiers. As we approached the heavily guarded border gate, the young driver sought to assure me that all would be well on the journey. 'Don't worry,' he said. 'I know how to beat these terrs. The trick is to drive so fast that you can bust through their roadblocks before they even realise you are coming. I got through a group of them waiting in the bush alongside the road on my last trip. Man, I went through there so fast they never even fired a shot.'

So we set off at high speed along a narrow dirt road with two tarmac strips intended for the wheels, but which were broken in many places. The truck bucked and lurched, repeatedly flinging the soldiers on the back off their feet and making them grab hold of the machine gun as its tripod lost its footing. They shouted to the driver to slow down, but he just grinned. 'I know what I'm doing,' he shouted above the roar of the engine.

We drove like that for an hour, bringing us to a heavily fenced and guarded halfway station on the 250-km drive to Beira. It was only about 10 am, but the driver said we would stop there overnight. 'It's not good to drive in the afternoon,' he explained. 'That's when the terrs come out. They don't like attacking in the morning, because then our soldiers have time to track them down. But in the afternoon they can get away and hide in the dark.'

It was a Frelimo military camp, and I was given a meal and shown to a bunk for the night. I didn't sleep well. Throughout the night there was the periodic sound of gunfire from the surrounding bush, sometimes distant and sometimes alarmingly close. I had no idea whether this indicated night-time skirmishes, or whether Renamo guerrillas were hunting for food among the plentiful game in the bush.

I had a different driver for the second leg of the journey. The young Zimbabwean had returned to Mutare and my new companion was a weather-beaten white Rhodesian in his mid-sixties. 'Some of these young chaps think the way to beat the terrs along this road is to drive like hell,' he told me as we set out. 'It's the worst thing you can do. All the terrs have to do is open up with one AK-47 burst and you'll lose control of the truck. Then they'll come to where you've crashed and finish you off.

'Look,' he went on, 'I survived the whole Rhodesian bush war, and I tell you the only way to survive in this situation is to drive at a slow, steady speed and keep your eyes skinned on the bush each side of the road watching for any movement.'

I didn't know whether to feel comforted or alarmed. As we tootled along at 60 km per hour I couldn't help feeling we were sitting ducks if we were to encounter a bunch of Renamo guerrillas. On the other hand, the older man sounded wiser and he was certainly more experienced. It was also more comfortable and our Zimbabwe guards with their machine gun were able to keep their footing on the back of the truck. I thought that meant they would be better able to retaliate if we came under attack.

Interviewing President Kenneth Kaunda in the grounds of State House, Lusaka, together with Financial Times *correspondent Michael Holman.*

A landmine crater we passed on my hell-run to Beira in 1987.

As we entered Beira the older man suggested I have dinner with him at his apartment. 'You won't get any food at the Dom Carlos,' he said, naming the only functioning hotel in the shattered city. 'There's no water there either, and they don't have any electricity.'

That was indeed the case when the old man dropped me off at the hotel after hosting me to a dinner of supplies provided by Lonrho, which he kept in a small refrigerator and cooked over a stove powered by a generator. At the Dom Carlos I found two men behind a reception desk lit by three candles. I checked in and they gave me a key for my room on the second floor, together with a candle to find my way there. The elevator wasn't working so I had to use the stairway. Midway up the stairs a gust of wind came through broken windows and blew out my candle, leaving me to grope my way to my room feeling the numbers with my fingertips like a blind man reading Braille.

Next morning, after another bad night disturbed by loud bursts of gunfire within the city, I paid a hotel worker to fetch a bucket of water from the sea so I could wash and flush the toilet. The city was a depressing sight. Beira had been without electricity for 165 days, so the whole city and its port were running on auxiliary power. The vital pipeline on which Zimbabwe was dependent was operating on three diesel engines, which had to run non-stop. All three had broken down.

No cafés, restaurants or food shops were functioning. I entered the shell of the once-luxurious President Hotel, where I found squatters living in the lounge and using the parquet flooring blocks as firewood. There were no taxis, few buses and the handful of rattletrap cars were rationed to 7.5 litres of petrol a week. A hundred thousand peasants had flocked to the city to escape the depredations of the guerrilla war in the countryside and for easier access to a United Nations food aid distribution centre. Many had brought goats and other livestock with them, leaving them to wander about the traffic-free streets and graze on a disused golf course. Some were tethered to parking meters.

* * *

IT WAS A relief to get back to Zimbabwe, returning the way I had come. I made my way to Harare, where I called on my long-time friend Judith Todd. Judy and I happened to be art collectors, and at that time Zimbabwe had a colony of wonderful stone carvers. At his studio, one sculptor named Henry Munyaradzi showed us around his fine collection and we each bought a piece. The one I chose was an exquisitely chiselled face, but it was heavy. Having bought it, I realised it was going to cost me a fortune in excess baggage on my flight home. Better to go by train.

I had phoned Sue from Harare asking her to meet me at Johannesburg's Park Station. But when I arrived she wasn't there. Other passengers disembarked and melted away, while I sat with my luggage and that heavy stone sculpture. As time slipped by, up to nearly an hour, my level of irritation increased.

When Sue eventually pitched up she was looking smart in her best suit. 'So sorry to be late,' she said in a light tone. 'I got held up.' I don't remember how I responded, but I was none too amused and there was little conversation as we drove home.

Once there she offered me a cup of tea and I followed her into the kitchen, hoping for more of an explanation.

I looked at her and saw tears begin to well up in her eyes. 'I'm so sorry,' she said. 'I've been at the doctor. I have breast cancer.'

Then, throwing herself into my arms, she sobbed: 'I'm too young to die.' She was 41.

CHAPTER TWENTY-SEVEN

Life with Sue

SUE NEVER SHED another tear throughout her long struggle with cancer. Instead she threw herself at life with increased vigour, as though to savour every moment of whatever time she had left. She underwent one mastectomy, then another, but the cancer metastasised into her bones. Sue did have chemotherapy, numerous courses of it, causing her to lose her hair, which re-emerged grey, only to be lost again. But she never lost the shine in her eyes or the flash of her smile. Her innate *joie de vivre*, which is what had initially attracted me to her, remained undiminished.

That was Sue's defence mechanism; she never shrank from it, requiring her oncologist to hide nothing from her, to the point of insisting that he tell her when there was no point in having any further chemo treatment, until 'management' was all he could offer, at which point she blanched for only a moment. Sue even volunteered to be a guinea pig for a young researcher working with her oncologist in an experiment to test the effects of a positive attitude of mind on patients with terminal cancer. Her cancer was more advanced than all other members of the group when the test began, but she outlived them all — and attended the funerals to console their families.

As for me, I was shattered when Sue broke her news at the end of my train trip home. As I recall, my first instinct was one of denial: No, it can't be true, lightning doesn't strike in the same place twice. But of course there is no celestial law to prevent that, nor is there one that says a spouse cannot be widowed twice. Life delivers its blows indiscriminately. But it was Sue's lively positiveness that drew me, our son Julian and the rest of our family along in her slipstream.

In line with Sue's frank approach to her illness, I accompanied her to every one of her consultations with her oncologist and to every one of her chemotherapy treatments. I thus became an honorary citizen of what the writer Christopher Hitchens called Tumortown.[1] The treatment itself is part of the bitter irony of cancer: you need to be poisoned to get better. As Sue's oncologist explained: 'Oh yes, we can cure cancer. The problem is to enable the patient to survive the treatment.'

Our lives became bifurcated the moment Sue's cancer diagnosis was delivered, as we both shuttled between Tumortown and Wellville, trying to fight off the shadow of death in the one and savour the fullness of life in the other. It is not easy to keep the one from shadowing the other, but Sue managed it through a ferocious determination to paint Wellville as brightly as she could. There were times when I felt I sank deeper into depression than she did, but who knows what she went through during those private moments when I was away from home? So much of her courage was for the sake of Julian and I.

Sue's social work for the Black Sash was the key to her positive attitude, and this, too, she shared with me. Aside from participating in the organisation's frequent demonstrations against some monstrous new apartheid intrusion into black life, she ran an advice desk in a squatter community called Ennerdale, south of Johannesburg. She would be there every weekend, facing a line of black people caught up in the spiderweb of regulations designed to keep them out of the major cities. It was an activity that brought her face to face with the everyday cruelty of what was referred to as 'petty apartheid'. It was also a job that revealed some of the ironies wrought by abject poverty in a land of plenty.

One Sunday, as Sue sat at her desk facing a long queue of these hapless people, she saw an elderly woman in the queue collapse.

Hurrying to the scene, she found the woman gasping for breath and obviously in serious distress. Begging those waiting for help to excuse her for abandoning her desk, Sue managed with some help from bystanders to ease the distressed woman into her car and race to the big Johannesburg General Hospital, some 50 km away.

After getting her patient admitted, Sue waited to speak with the medical specialists examining her. When they reported to her, it was to explain that the woman had a chronic heart condition for which a pacemaker had been fitted some years before, but unfortunately the pacemaker had not been serviced and the battery had run flat. But all would be well, the doctors assured Sue, they would service the pacemaker, fit a new battery, and she would be okay to go home in a few days. But it had been touch and go, they added. If Sue had not been at hand to bring her in, the woman would surely have died that day.

When Sue collected her patient to take her back to Ennerdale, she asked her why she hadn't been regularly to the hospital, as the doctors had advised, for the pacemaker to be serviced. 'I'm too poor,' the woman explained. 'I didn't have money for the bus fare.'

My story about this little cameo of life in South Africa made the front page of *The Washington Post* — the story of a country that could fit this black woman with a life-saving piece of First-World medical equipment, then send her back to a Third-World slum so poverty-stricken she didn't have the bus fare to keep it functioning.

* * *

BY FAR THE most important of Sue's roles during those cancer years was to act as the Black Sash's monitor of the country's longest and most controversial treason trial, at which 22 leading members of the United Democratic Front were put on trial for their lives in the small town of Delmas, 85 km east of Johannesburg. The apartheid regime's reason for holding such a major trial at such an insignificant venue was to prevent large protest demonstrations taking place at the courthouse. The Black Sash, under the presidency of the indefatigable Sheena Duncan, decided it needed to be closely monitored and she chose Sue for the job.

It was one of two treason trials ordered by the PW Botha administration, which was determined to smash this internal organisation that had arisen to campaign against his tricameral Parliament, then gone on to whip up the wave of township battles now tearing the country apart. The first trial, which I covered for all my papers, was in Pietermaritzburg, where 16 UDF members were charged with treason and murder. All were acquitted after a brilliant defence by the country's leading black lawyer, Ismail Mahomed, who was later to become the new South Africa's first Chief Justice. This was swiftly followed by the Delmas trial, where the defence team was led by another great civil rights lawyer, Arthur Chaskalson, who later succeeded Mahomed as Chief Justice upon the latter's untimely death soon after the transition. Appearing with Chaskalson for the defence was another pillar of our legal fraternity, George Bizos, who was the imprisoned Nelson Mandela's close friend and legal adviser. A formidable team.

The Delmas trial lasted just over three years, from October 1985 to December 1988, and for every one of the court's 437 sitting days Sue drove the 170-km round trip in her little rattletrap two-seater car to attend and report on the proceedings. I travelled to Delmas with her on many occasions, for again it rated as a major overseas story. Western governments were growing more and more concerned at South Africa's vicious response to activists, whose demand for democratic rights struck them as being eminently reasonable. My reports were prominently displayed, often on front pages, and I felt a sense of satisfaction that my work was helping to build foreign pressure on South Africa to end apartheid – perhaps every bit as important as whatever domestic influence I'd had while editing the *Rand Daily Mail*.

I took pride, too, in the role Sue was playing at that trial despite her illness. Hers was an immense and important achievement, for she did more, much more, than merely submit her reports to the Black Sash about the unusual judicial proceedings that unfolded during that long trial. Sue also organised her own negotiations across the apartheid battle lines between the UDF leaders in the prisoners' dock and key apartheid doubters in the Afrikaner community – the *verligtes*. She enabled them to meet one another in the courtroom during lunch breaks.

The three UDF leaders in the dock, Mosiuoa Lekota, Popo Molefe and Moss Chikane, would give Sue the names of such people they wished to meet; she would then contact them and persuade them to accompany her, after which she would drive them to the Delmas court for their lunchtime discussions, then deliver them back to their homes before returning to hers. I never kept count of the number of these consultative missions she undertook, but they were many. It was not as grand a discussion series as Van Zyl Slabbert's Dakar expedition, but, as an effort by a solitary individual, I believe it played a role in the miracle of our transition.

But fun and affection were always the larger part of Sue's personality. When she learned that one of the younger trialists was distressed at the thought that he might be executed or sentenced to life imprisonment before being able to marry his girlfriend, Sue became the central figure in a plan to arrange the wedding then and there. She had established a close enough relationship with the rather forbidding judge, Kees van Dijkhorst, to persuade him to allow an extended lunch adjournment on an agreed day. The next step was to persuade Desmond Tutu, then the Anglican Bishop of Johannesburg, to conduct the marriage ceremony. Tutu carefully transformed the judge's bench into an altar, complete with altar cloth, candles, a cross and a bowl of white flowers.

The final step was to persuade two of her stepsons, my teenage boys who were students at the University of Cape Town, to arrange a wedding reception. That involved using their youthful skills to replace the contents of several five-litre cartons of fruit juice with wine, which they carried boldly into the courtroom during the break and served in paper cups to the wedding guests. I attended the service and remember it vividly, with Tutu delivering a powerful address on the injustice of apartheid and the importance of love, justice and freedom, after which it was time for the trial to resume.

But Sue was not done with the fun part yet. True to form, she had not only befriended all the court orderlies, but also the driver of the Black Maria that transported the prisoners back and forth each day between the courthouse and Modder B Prison. I watched her slip out of the courtroom towards the end of the wedding proceedings and persuade the driver to take the remaining litres of 'fruit juice' back to Modder B for the prisoners.

Sadly, the young couple were unable to consummate their nuptials that wedding night, for the bride had to return to her home and the groom to his cell. But I gathered later that there was one helluva party in the prison that night. As Lekota confessed to me: 'After nearly three years without a drink, I had the worst hangover of my life the next morning. But, man, it was worth it.'

Not long after that, Tutu was enthroned as Archbishop of Cape Town. Sue and I travelled to Cape Town for the grand two-and-a-half-hour ceremony in St George's Cathedral, attended by the Archbishop of Canterbury, Robert Runcie, his envoy, Terry Waite, and clergy from all parts of Europe and the United States.

After the service, the congregants adjourned to the city's Goodwood sports stadium for three hours of celebration, with a vast crowd of singing, dancing supporters, during which Sue slipped among the great and the good, recording messages from them to be played to the treason trialists in Delmas. It made for an extraordinary anthology – messages of support and encouragement from Tutu himself, as well as from Runcie, Waite, Coretta Scott King (widow of the Reverend Martin Luther King, Jnr) and even, illegally, from Winnie Mandela, who had committed multiple violations of her banning order by travelling to Cape Town, joining the great crowd and effectively delivering a political speech through Sue's tape recorder, and getting away with it all. Again the recordings were a huge morale-booster in the grim cells of Modder B.

As befitted so much investment in the cause of lightening the burdens of oppression, the Delmas case turned out to be a triumph for the twin causes of liberty and forgiveness. Judge van Dijkhorst found four of the accused guilty of treason and 11 others guilty of lesser offences. Lekota was sentenced to 12 years' imprisonment and Molefe to ten years. But all charges were overturned on appeal a year later, the Appeal Court finding that Judge van Dijkhorst had dismissed one of his two assessors improperly. The judge had claimed that by signing a petition against apartheid four years before the case arose, the assessor, Professor Willem Joubert, had shown himself to be biased in favour of the accused.

But in the dirty washing that got hung out in court over this affair, it was the judge whose objectivity emerged looking the more questionable. The juicy bit Sue managed to glean from the acrimonious exchange of affidavits that took place was that at an early stage in the trial Van Dijkhorst had privately bet the dissenting professor a bottle of whisky that the accused were so compromised that their lawyers would surely not risk submitting any of them to cross-examination in the witness box. When 11 of them did in fact testify, the judge reluctantly paid up. That, too, made a front-page story in *The Washington Post*.

The cherry on top came another year later when, following South Africa's first all-race general election, Lekota and Molefe became premiers of the Free State and Northern Province, respectively. They decided to hold a joint celebration to which they invited all the Delmas trialists, together with their defence lawyers, Sue and I — with Judge van Dijkhorst as their guest of honour. Graciously he came and made a little speech wishing them all well in the new South Africa.

* * *

SUE AND I travelled frequently, to Switzerland to visit her relatives, to Britain to visit old friends, across most of Western Europe and, at her encouragement, to the United States for me to take up several teaching and writing fellowships at Duke University and the University of North Carolina. During the fascinating phase of Mikhail Gorbachev's *perestroika* reforms we also made two visits to the Soviet Union. Despite the particularly dense apartheid curtain dividing the two countries, we went deep into that vast country, to the republics of Georgia and Uzbekistan, right down to the northern border of Afghanistan, where the Red Army was winding down its brutal war against the mujahedin.

Travel, as the hoary old saying goes, broadens the mind, but I think this is particularly true for South Africans. We tend to become obsessive about our racial conflicts, imagining our issues to be unique in the world, understandable only to those of us who live there. We imagine the whole world to be watching us with breathless anxiety, wondering what will happen when our unique racial conflict erupts with cataclysmic implications for all humanity. Yet when we get abroad we discover that our affairs are barely a blip on other people's radar screens. Viewed from the distant cities of Tashkent, Bukhara or Samarkand, or even from Durham, North Carolina, South Africa is barely visible.

This is not to suggest that our problems are not serious, or that South Africa is not in some way a social laboratory or testing ground for the problems of racial integration, the full impact of which the rest of the world is only just beginning to face. But we are not unique. We are not special. And I am indebted to Sue, as well as to the foreign newspapers for which I wrote for 13 years, for enabling me to acquire more of an international perspective on my own country that I believe was an important corrective influence.

* * *

OUR TWO VISITS to the Soviet Union had a strong influence on my thinking about the political future of South Africa. I had long regarded myself as a liberal in the classical Lockean sense, which meant being instinctively on the side of the underdog in our racist society. But during my later years at the *Rand Daily Mail* I found myself increasingly at odds with the business community's lack of interest in the politics of apartheid. Big business was largely in the hands of the English-speaking community, while Afrikaners dominated the political arena. Most business leaders, with some notable exceptions, seemed content to have it that way; they would utter ritual criticisms of apartheid but declined to get involved in politics or even speak out collectively against it. Only as the South African economy became more complex and they found their businesses running out of skilled labour, thanks to poor apartheid education for blacks, did they begin to complain a bit more audibly.

I guess my contempt for this *mea non culpa* attitude increased when management pressure on me for sticking to the *Rand Daily Mail*'s strong anti-apartheid policy began to intensify. When I challenged captains of industry about this, telling them I believed the business community's perceived indifference to the plight of our black population might drive them into the communist camp, they pooh-poohed the idea. Business was about making money, it was not in the bleeding-hearts game, they would say. Some would call me naive and preach to me about Joseph Schumpeter's concept of 'creative destruction', meaning the process of constantly destroying old economic structures to create new and better ones to the advantage of all. Blacks, too, would eventually benefit.

I felt sickened by this, the ultimate, unbridled *laissez-faire*, and it made me realise that this kind of liberalism, later to be called neo-liberalism, was not for me. And I guess the shutting down of the *Rand Daily Mail*, by the biggest and supposedly most liberal company in the country, had a further impact on my political outlook.

I didn't become a Marxist, even though many good friends of mine were, because communism was by definition a dictatorship. I had read Isaiah Berlin on the fine but critical difference between idealism and Utopianism. Idealism had brought about much that is good in the world, he wrote, but Utopianism crossed a fine line from there into the disastrous. If you believe that you have the formula for the creation of the perfect society, in which all members live in pure harmony for evermore, then in the name of humanity you cannot allow anyone to oppose such perfection. You have to stamp out all opposition, even kill the dissenters who resist the attainment of such perfect harmony.[2]

So communism was not for me. I was above all a democrat. Nevertheless I felt myself move to the left at that emotionally vulnerable time of my life. I was not sure where or how far. Then came Gorbachev with his reform policies of *glasnost* and *perestroika*, openness and reform. I was fascinated. Was this the opening up of a new way, to some sort of democratic communism?

It was in that frame of mind that I flew with Sue from the United States to Moscow. The trip had been made possible through a meeting in the US with a Russian professor, Apollon Davidson, who had specialised in South African history at Moscow State University. He and his assistant, Irina Filatova, were excellent guides, translators and educators on the realities of Soviet life. The state travel agency, Intourist, had booked us into a fine-looking hotel right on Red Square, with a room containing a grand piano, where we were told Lenin had once slept. At dinner on our first night we were presented with a splendid menu containing a long list of exotic-looking dishes. But as we tried to place our orders the gloomy waiter told us over and over, 'Is finish!' Eventually I asked in exasperation: 'Well, what have you got?'

'Bifstek,' the waiter replied.

'Is that all?' I asked.

'Yes.'

The steak turned out to be dry, tough and barely edible. After three days of this enforced diet, we decided to cross Red Square to another hotel, the Rossiya, for lunch. It was more cheerful and better frequented, but although the menu was more extensive we were told there was no wine. So we ordered vodka. At which point we were asked to show our passports to prove we were foreign tourists. This was at a time when Gorbachev was trying to cut down on the national consumption of vodka. As I discovered, this was easily done in a country run on a system called 'democratic centralism'. If you want your citizens to drink less vodka, you simply order the state distilleries to stop making the stuff. So while we were there vodka was almost unobtainable in Russia — except in tourist hotels like the Rossiya.

As Sue and I received our little carafes of vodka, two boisterous workmen came in off the street and sat at our table. They were dressed in overalls, true members of the proletariat. And they ordered, not food but ... vodka. Obviously they had either bribed someone or, more likely, had comrades inside the establishment who could pull strings for them. A one-litre flagon arrived for each of them, which the two men proceeded to down with gusto. We fell into a clumsy, raucous and largely incomprehensible conversation with them, punctuated by many toasts to our respective countries (I don't think they knew where South Africa was), and down with Gorbachev for cutting back on the supply of vodka. After half an hour they had finished their vodka – as well as the remains of ours – and with glasses raised to us in a final toast, reeled out of the dining room, thoroughly sozzled.

Great fun, but for me it drove home a stark lesson in how easy it is for a totalitarian government, even a reformist one like Gorbachev's, to control people's lives, to determine what they may eat and drink, read and ultimately even think. All you need is control of the means of production. If you, Big Brother, however reformist and well-meaning, think your people are drinking too much vodka, you simply tell the state distilleries to stop making it. The end of individual choice. The end of freedom.

We kept seeing instances of this. A camera shop with rows and rows of a single type of camera in the window. Shoe shops the same. No choice. And empty shops. Shortages of all manner of everyday things. And queues everywhere. Early one morning, before the shops opened, I saw a long queue of people lined up outside a bookshop that had not yet opened. I asked someone in the queue why they were lining up so early. He explained that word had got out that there was a new book by a politically controversial author and that only a restricted number of copies were likely to be printed. If you wanted to buy one, you had to get there early. He had joined the queue at 5 am.

Sue and I happened to be in Moscow the day the first McDonald's restaurant opened on Pushkin Square. We saw a queue wrapped around the square that must have been at least a kilometre long, like an enraptured crowd waiting to pay homage to some holy relic. I sought out a young man near the back who spoke a little English. 'How long do you think it will be before you to get to the restaurant?' I asked him.

'Maybe two hours,' he replied.

'What is it that you want to buy that is worth such a long wait?'

'A hamburger,' he said. 'I've never tasted one and I want to find out what they are like.'

Life without choices. State control of the means of production is what communism claims is needed to liberate people from the exploitation of profit-seeking capitalism. As I saw it in operation during those two visits, it seemed to me to be the centralised control of people's everyday lifestyles. That struck me as being a form of tyranny. But then so did the crass indifference of South Africa's business community to the grotesque inequalities of our own society. The answer had to be somewhere else, and I am still groping towards that.

* * *

SUE AND I had two sojourns at Duke University, one for a full academic year and another two years later for a single semester, during which I taught courses on the racial conflict in South Africa and wrote the first two of what later became a trilogy of books on the subject. I also taught in the excellent journalism department at the University of North Carolina at Chapel Hill, where we lived. These were joyful and intellectually stimulating interludes in our lives together. I enjoyed teaching, particularly the interaction with bright students, some of whom have kept in touch with me to this day. But if I found the experience stimulating, it was even more so for Sue. With the help of friends connected to the university, she was able to undertake a series of courses at UNC given by Professor William Peck under the rubric of 'The Psychology of Religion'. She and Peck developed a lifelong friendship as a result. He regarded her as one of his best students.

I must stress that Sue's choice of subject was not connected in any way to the fact that she was a cancer sufferer. It stemmed from her deep interest in humanity, especially as a result of her work in South Africa's black townships. She was fascinated by the evolution of different cultures, of what shapes people's beliefs and mores in different parts of the world and so often puts them at odds with one another. She felt this was fundamental to a deeper understanding of what would face the future South Africa as it set about the challenges of integrating its many different races and cultures. Peck's course, she believed, went to the very heart of that, and as her studies and readings on the subject deepened she became my educator as well.

As for the spiritual aspect of her studies, they greatly liberalised her. Although never a devout observer, Sue had been brought up a member of the Swiss Reformed Church: the stern John Calvin had, after all, been a towering historical figure in French-speaking Geneva. Her studies of the many common psychological factors that had shaped not only the precepts of the dominant Western religions but also all others, ranging from the Incas of Peru, the Gypsies of Eastern Europe, to the Hindus and Buddhists of the East, changed all that. Sue jettisoned Calvin's notions of pre-destination and the fearful divide between salvation and eternal damnation and settled for a more holistic faith of her own that I can only describe as a form of universal ecumenicism. An incor-poration of all faiths that echoed some of the theological beliefs of Archbishop Desmond Tutu, with whom both she and I devel-oped a great admiration and friendship. As Tutu puts it: 'God is not a Christian. Christianity is a relatively new kid on the religious block. What faith you belong to is very largely an accident of birth and geography ... It is not the faith that comes first, it is the fact of being human together.'[3]

It was a belief system that was to have a strong influence on me as it evolved in Sue's mind and as she shared it with me over the remaining years we spent together. A belief system that not only shaped my own spiritual outlook on life, but also has pro-foundly influenced my political thinking as well. It is the basis of Tutu's concept of a 'Rainbow Nation', later adopted by Nelson Mandela. Just as Tutu felt all religions were reaching for the same spiritual truth, each in its own way, so too does the Rainbow Nation idea hold that each human group should take pride in its own race and cultural heritage, while at the same time embracing all other groups as fellow citizens in a common humanity. It is not a melting pot of all blending into a single cultural, linguistic and political national entity, but of each embracing 'the others' in all their differences.

To that considerable extent, the spirit of Sue still lives within me and in my writings.

CHAPTER TWENTY-EIGHT

Moments with Mandela

THE FIRST TIME I saw Nelson Mandela was the day after his release from prison. *The Washington Post* had sent staffer David Ottaway to cover his emergence from Victor Verster prison, outside Paarl, and assigned me to handle his arrival at his home in Soweto. Day one had been a messy affair. Winnie had arrived at the prison nearly an hour late, as was her habit, by which time the crowds were so dense that Mandela's driver took a back road, which extended the time it took to reach Cape Town.

Mandela was to address the country from the balcony of the Mother City's old City Hall, but when their car eventually arrived there the crowd on the Grand Parade out front had grown so vast and impatient that they swarmed around the car, clambered over it and began rocking it. The panicky driver turned about and fled. Mandela directed him to the home of a lawyer friend, Dullah Omar, where they rested to regather their composure. The result was that it was growing dusk when the Mandelas reached the City Hall, by which time some rioting and looting had taken place and the police had even opened fire, wounding a few people. It was not, as it turned out, a stirring speech. Not surprisingly, Mandela looked a bit disorientated. As he told me afterwards, 'People kept shoving a strange, furry object in front of me that I thought was some new kind of weapon that had

An embrace with ANC stalwart Walter Sisulu. My family became particularly close to the Sisulu family, a relationship I still cherish.

been invented while I was in prison.' They were, of course, TV microphones: South Africa had not had television when Mandela went to prison, and now suddenly he was being required to appear on this strange new medium. Complicating matters further, he had left his glasses in the prison and had to borrow Winnie's, which didn't fit and kept slipping down his nose. All of which made his delivery halting.

The speech itself was also too cautious to be inspiring. Mandela was aware that the ANC leaders in Lusaka knew he had been having secret talks with government ministers and intelligence agents while in prison, so his chief concern was to reassure them that he had not made any concessions as terms for his release. The result was that what should have been a great historic speech was addressed

507

more to that distant audience than to the wildly excited crowd before him. 'I wish to stress that I myself have at no time entered into negotiations about the future of our country, except to insist on a meeting between the ANC and the Government,' he told them. Then adding for further reassurance: 'I am a loyal and disciplined member of the African National Congress. I am therefore in full agreement with all its objectives, strategies and tactics.'

Day two in Soweto was different. It was the people's day; it was also my day for covering this historic moment. The whole huge township was in a fever of excitement with boisterous crowds singing and dancing and ululating everywhere. I had difficulty driving through the thronging crowds, made doubly so as help-yourself passengers wrenched open the doors of my car and piled in, while others found seating on the roof and bonnet. Bit by bit I made my way towards the Mandelas' matchbox house in Vilakazi Street, where I knew he would be staying.

I found myself in the midst of a great throng outside the one-bedroom brick house. I spotted Zwelakhe Sisulu, the son of Mandela's soulmate and fellow prisoner, Walter Sisulu, performing the tough job of trying to prevent the crowd from overwhelming the fence surrounding the house. Zwelakhe had been on my staff when I was editor of the *Rand Daily Mail*. I caught his eye and he signalled to me to go around to the back of the house where the crowd was thinner. With the help of some, I was lifted over their heads and over the fence into the grounds of the Mandela house, from where Zwelakhe took me inside.

There, in a tiny sitting room, I met the Great Man for the first time. I remember being startled at how tall and lean he was. Publishing pictures of prisoners had been prohibited under the security laws, and the only clandestine one that had circulated during his incarceration had been of a strong, muscular heavy-weight boxer. Even the one official picture of him released after his meeting with PW Botha, and the TV shots of him leaving the prison the previous day, somehow didn't convey the extent to which my mental image of him had differed.

He greeted me with that famous smile and gestured to me to sit beside him on a cramped little settee, where he began telling me how much my reporting and columns had meant to him and his fellow prisoners over the years. 'You and Laurence Gandar and the *Rand Daily Mail* kept our spirits up during the darkest days,' he said — making me feel as though I had just been awarded the world's greatest prize for journalism.

But no sooner had our conversation begun — which I later realised was probably the first one-on-one interview he had given since his release, indeed for the past 27 years — than a small boy poked his head around the doorway to tell Mandela some people had arrived to see him. The child mentioned some names that meant nothing to me. 'Please excuse me,' Mandela said as he rose from the settee. 'This is very important.'

Three elderly men entered the room, bowing and shaking his hand solemnly, after which a fascinating conversation followed in their isiXhosa language, which I was able to follow. It became clear they were elders from the village of Qunu in the Transkei, where he had spent his youth and where he has now been buried. The conversation was about the minutiae of village life: who had married whom, and what name had so-and-so given her new baby. So it went for about half an hour, during which the lives and doings of just about everyone in that tiny community were analysed, the state of the rains and crops debated, and fraternal greetings exchanged. Only when the three old men left did Mandela return to the little settee to talk to the journalist about high matters of state. But even then he was charmed to know that I could speak his home language, so that the conversation had to deal with the details of my own personal background before turning to what for him seemed to be secondary matters.

I learned more about Mandela in that first hour of our acquaintanceship than in all the many meetings and conversations I had with him in the years that followed. Here he was, with the focus of the whole world upon him to a degree that has seldom been equalled, devoting his undivided attention to the smallest details of life in a tiny community that he had not seen or communicated with for three or four decades. And of the details of my own life, rather than what important messages he might have wanted to convey to the world through me as a journalist.

It was an aspect of his character, the secret of his natural leadership quality, that I was to see throughout that first week of a schedule so pressured as to be nightmarish. Again and again Mandela would pause to make these little acknowledgments to people below the rank of the major activists, whose modest contributions to the anti-apartheid cause he had observed and noted on some inner personal honours list. It was a key aspect of his charisma: the omniscient leader who paid attention to the least of his flock.

Mandela went public on day three, with a massive rally in Johannesburg's Soccer City stadium. As Nadine Gordimer, soon to be a Nobel literature laureate, was to write, it was the moment of a lifetime for everyone there. They formed 'a joyous, gyrating mass that filled the stadium and clung to retaining structures like swarming bees'. Mandela had been in prison nearly three decades, she noted, yet absolutely everyone there knew him. 'In all that time there was no black child in whose face, at the mention of his name, there was not instant recognition. And there were no whites – enemies of the cause of black freedom as well as supporters – who did not know who this man was. His body was hidden behind walls; his presence was never obliterated by them.'[1]

As with his first speech in Cape Town, having to address such a large and expectant crowd after so many years of silence must have been daunting. But Mandela did a better job this time, although still insisting that he was not the leader but just an ordinary member of the ANC, subject to the leadership of the party in Lusaka. He was not a rousing orator, but he spoke in a dignified, senatorial style that commanded attention. The crowd responded with roars of acceptance. Despite his words of deference, as far as they were concerned he was their leader – and indeed the President-in-waiting of a new South Africa.

* * *

SHORTLY BEFORE Mandela's release, word leaked out that he had told a senior Western diplomat who had visited him in prison that he still believed a future ANC government should nationalise 'the commanding heights of the economy', including

510

the mining industry and the major banks. This understandably caused a flutter in the dovecote of business, who saw it as a road to economic disaster. This anxiety extended to alarm when, immediately after his release, Shaun Johnson, then political editor of *The Star*, asked Mandela if that were indeed his view.

'Yes,' Mandela told him bluntly, 'that has always been the view of the ANC ever since we adopted the Freedom Charter, and I see no reason why we should change it.' Which, strictly speaking, was not correct. The ANC had indeed adopted the Freedom Charter at the 1955 Congress of the People in Kliptown, Soweto. But the Freedom Charter, still a lodestar document for the ANC, does not explicitly call for nationalising privately-held financial institutions. Most of it was drafted by Rusty Bernstein, a leading intellectual of the Communist Party of South Africa, who had followed the instructions of then ANC leader, Chief Albert Luthuli, to avoid any direct reference to nationalisation or other aspects of communist dogma that might scare off otherwise sympathetic whites from attending the rally, which Luthuli wanted to be as broad-based as possible. So Bernstein worded the Charter carefully, the relevant clause reading: 'The mineral wealth of the country, the banks and monopoly industry, shall be transferred to the ownership of the people.'

The intended ambiguity lies in Bernstein's use of the phase, 'the people'. For while communists have claimed it to mean the nationalisation of the commanding heights of the country's economy, it can, and has, been argued that 'the people' and 'the state' are not one and the same, that indeed state ownership would deprive ordinary people of the right to ownership. This escape hatch for anti-communists was widened by another paragraph in the Charter which reads: 'All people shall have equal rights to trade where they choose, to manufacture and enter all trades, crafts and professions.' That sounds awfully like the right to be a capitalist.

With the business community all of a flutter as a result of Johnson's report, I wrote in my weekly column in *The Star* — I had resumed it there at the kind invitation of the editor, Harvey Tyson, after the closure of the *Rand Daily Mail* — that Mandela was making a grievous mistake. The essence of my column was to point out that Zambian President Kenneth Kaunda had followed that route with disastrous consequences after his country had gained independence in 1960. He had nationalised Zambia's copper mines, the mainstay of the nation's economy, but had neither the finances to compensate the holding company, essentially Oppenheimer's Anglo American Corporation, nor the ability to operate the mines as a state corporation. So he had not only been forced to raise a huge loan to compensate Anglo, but also had to pay the company a stiff management fee to continue operating the mines. The result was that, while the Zambian economy was impoverished, Anglo American walked away from the deal with a cash bonanza that enabled it to form an offshore branch called Minorco, which turned the South African company into a multinational giant.

The phone rang early on the day my column appeared. 'It's Nelson Mandela here,' the voice said, nearly knocking me over in surprise. I was later to become accustomed to the way that, even after becoming president, Mandela often made phone calls himself rather than have a secretary or aide make them for him. Once again, his instinct for the personal touch.

'Why did you write that column this morning?' he demanded, sounding quite cross.

'Because, Mr Mandela, I believe in what I have written,' I replied. 'I believe that nationalising the central pillars of our economy would be a disaster for the country.'

'Why do you say that?' he asked.

I recounted to him what I had written in the column, about how Kaunda's decision to nationalise the copper mines had ruined the Zambian economy.

There was a long silence on the line, then Mandela's voice again in a softer tone: 'Won't you come and have lunch with me today? I'd like to talk to you more about this.'

So I made my way to Soweto, not this time to the small house in Vilakazi Street where he had lived before his imprisonment, but to a more grandiose one a few blocks away that Winnie had built. He met me at the front door. When I asked him how he felt about their new house, he gave a scowl.

He led me into the dining room where a serve-yourself lunch had been laid out. We helped ourselves and took our seats at a large central table. Mandela wasted no time getting to the subject on his mind. 'I am surprised that you don't approve of the idea of nationalisation,' he began. 'I have always admired the way the Afrikaners helped their people out of the Great Depression by starting their own businesses. That uplifted them, and I felt we should do the same.'

'Yes that's true,' I replied. 'But they did that through the *Reddingsdaadbond*.[2] They collected money from their own people to start their own institutions, like Volkskas bank, the insurance company Sanlam, and even their own burial society. That's very different from taking over big existing banks and mining companies and having to pay the owners huge sums in compensation – only to find, as Kaunda did, that you don't have the trained people to run them, so that you have to enter into management contracts with the previous owners to run them for you. So you end up paying them twice. And if the price of the commodity you are mining falls, as copper did for poor KK, you are in big trouble. He's never been able to get out of that trouble.'

Mandela was quiet for a long time. Deeply pensive. When he spoke again it was in a soft tone: 'Yes, I see that. You see, Allister, the trouble is I really don't know much about economics. I must go and talk to some of our business people.'

I marvelled at the admission. How unusual for a politician so obviously headed for great things. I remember thinking to myself that Africa would be a far better place if more of its leaders would have the humility to admit their shortcomings and seek specialist advice before acting. But I guess only those humans who are truly great can do that.

True to his word, Mandela did consult some leading businessmen on the issue, most notably Chris Liebenberg, then chief executive of Nedcor, a major banking corporation, whom he later appointed as his Minister of Finance.

Indeed, as I learned later, Mandela also pursued the matter further when he attended the World Economic Forum in Davos, in February 1992. There he found himself questioned repeatedly about what economic policy he would follow when he became president. When he mentioned the word 'nationalisation', the response was always the same: if he did that there was no way South Africa would be able to attract foreign investment. The decisive moment came when the Dutch Minister of Industry and leaders from Vietnam and China told him the world had changed during his years in prison, and that, following the collapse of the Soviet Union and with globalisation making all economies interdependent, they were themselves now having to accept private enterprise.

As Mandela confided to his close friend and biographer, Anthony Sampson, on his return from Davos he summoned other ANC leaders and told them: 'Chaps, we have to choose. We either keep nationalisation and get no investment, or we modify our attitude and get investment.'[3]

But while Mandela himself was persuaded to accept that modern economic reality, it is sadly not something that has yet entered the soul of the ANC.

From there our conversation that day drifted off to other things, mainly about events during the last phase of Mandela's imprisonment, when he was moved from Robben Island, first to Pollsmoor then to Victor Verster. What was the purpose of moving him around like that? I knew from earlier discussions with Justice minister Kobie Coetsee that the minister had met with Winnie at the recommendation of his lawyer friend in Brandfort, Piet de Waal, and that Coetsee had also met with Mandela when the latter was in hospital undergoing prostate gland treatment.

I sensed I was on the verge of a major story here about the details of what had changed the government's thinking about releasing Mandela. So I began questioning him about it.

'Well, you see, they wanted to release me but they didn't know how to go about it, or what might happen if they did. They wanted to bargain with me, but I wouldn't bargain. I kept telling them they couldn't bargain with someone who wasn't free. I would have to talk to the leadership in Lusaka before there could be any bargaining. But they kept coming to see me. They couldn't do that while I was on the island because it would soon become known. So they moved me to Pollsmoor. Then they worried because I was there with the other leadership group, so they moved me to Victor Verster where I would be on my own.'

'How often did they meet with you?' I asked.

'Oh, many times. At first it was just Kobie Coetsee, then they formed a whole committee headed by Niël Barnard, the chief of the National Intelligence Service. I can't remember how often I met with that committee, but I think it was about 27 times.'[4]

I realised instantly that I was on to a major scoop and asked Mandela if I could have a longer interview with him on these lines.

'You'll have to ask my minders,' he replied with a chuckle. 'You see, my time is not my own any more. I thought I was coming out to freedom, but it seems that is not the case.'

* * *

I PUT IN my request for that interview to Mandela's aide, Barbara Masekela, right away, but a couple of months passed without a response. Then early one morning Barbara called me. 'We've had a security alert for Mr Mandela from our intelligence people, and I'm wondering whether you could have him for the day?' she asked. 'I'll send two security guards with him, and I thought you could maybe use the time for that interview you wanted.'

Two birds with one stone, as it were. But for me it was an absolute bonanza. I could have Mandela's undivided attention for an entire day in the intimacy of my own home.

He arrived about an hour later and ordered his two security men to stay with the car in the street outside my property. Mandela was notoriously indifferent to security considerations. On his first visit to New York he had horrified his security detail by going jogging down Fifth Avenue alone at five in the morning. He apologised to his bodyguards for alarming them, explaining that he had awakened at 4.30 every morning for 27 years in prison, then spent an hour doing exercises. He hadn't broken out of that routine yet, so he thought going for a run would be okay.

Sue's mother, Yvonne Matthey, was visiting us from Switzer-land when Mandela arrived. He greeted her first, with great courtesy, then embraced Sue, Julian and I. After which he strode briskly into the kitchen and introduced himself to our house-keeper, Meriam Nzimande. 'Good morning,' he said, 'I'm Nelson Mandela.' Meriam let out a gasp of undisguised astonishment and pleasure, after which Mandela had quite a long conversation with her about her family and her place of origin, before stepping outside to greet the elderly gardener, Joseph Makhanya. This I came to know later was standard practice for Mandela wherever he went, whether to private homes or public functions: the black workers, from waiters to cooks and cleaners, were always greeted personally, often before VIPs at the function.

Yvonne offered him breakfast. 'Oh yes, please,' he said with a broad smile. 'But since you are from Switzerland I don't sup-pose you know how to cook mealie-meal porridge, which is my favourite breakfast.'

'Yes, of course I do,' she replied. 'I lived in South Africa for many years.'

So mealie-meal, or corn-meal, porridge it was, which Mandela proclaimed to be the best he had ever tasted – giving Yvonne something to dine out on within her Swiss circle for the rest of her life.

Thus what became popularly known as 'Madiba Magic', the personal touch of this gracious old man that led to his clan name becoming attached to his ability to enchant all who met him – and to make good things happen besides. Watching him here in my home called to mind Minister Coetsee's description of his impression of Mandela on meeting him for the first time in a Cape Town hospital ward five years earlier. 'I had studied Latin and Roman culture,' Coetsee said to me, 'and I remember thinking, this man has all the qualifications of an old Roman citizen, *dignitas, gravitas, honestas, simplicitas.*' More specifically, he struck me as being in the mould of Marcus Aurelius, the Stoic Roman emperor whose life of self-sacrifice made him into an exacting, lofty spirit who lived in a simple, unostentatious manner but exuded an aura of imperial dignity. Mandela was a patriarch with a common touch.

The interview took place on my sunlit veranda and lasted several hours. It was a comprehensive account of his life and thoughts during all that time in prison. I asked few questions; I just let it flow out in an effortless stream. He told me of the harsh first years when the warders had been abusive and brutal. 'We had to stand up to them right from the beginning and not let them intimidate us,' he said. 'But I also realised that we would have to try to improve our relationship with them. You see, Allister, it gets very cold on that island in winter, and when you are freezing in your cell at night it's no good writing a letter to the Commissioner of Prisons about it. All you can do is to ask a warder to bring you another blanket.'

Being a lawyer was the key to Mandela's strategising. Prison warders were from the poorest elements of white Afrikaner society, poorly educated and poorly paid. So Mandela made a point of inquiring about their personal circumstances. He found that most were in financial difficulties, many with domestic problems as well. There wasn't enough money to go around, so wives were also working in menial jobs. The children were ill-disciplined and doing poorly at school, some of them on drugs. Home lives were turbulent, with too much alcohol; there were divorces and separations and the crippling burden of maintenance payments, garnishee orders and court cases for defaulters.

It was a small investment for Mandela to make to give some of the hardest-pressed of these white warders free legal advice. The rewards came in the form of more blankets on cold nights and a steadily improved relationship between warders and prisoners, which made prison life a little less onerous. So it was that the prisoner became the legal adviser to his jailers.

There was an even more important dividend that came from these contacts in the form of a social insight that I believe had a major influence on the strategies Mandela was to follow after his release.

'I realised then,' Mandela explained to me, 'why those warders were so vicious towards us when we first arrived. I realised that they were actually afraid of us. We were the black majority. They were from the poorest and therefore the most vulnerable elements of white South African society, and they knew that if we the ANC, representing the black majority, ever came to power they would be the first to lose their jobs. So they were afraid of us, and that's what made them act so violently towards us.

'Then I also realised that if we were ever going to be able to reach a deal around a negotiating table, we would have to reduce that level of fear that they had of us.'

A negotiating table? This from the man who launched the armed struggle and founded the ANC's armed wing, believing that to be the only way to achieve freedom for his people after Verwoerd had banned the ANC and all other black nationalist movements back in 1960? A silence settled over us as Mandela pondered my questioning. 'Yes, that is how I felt at the time,' he murmured with a slight shaking of his head. 'There seemed no other way to move forward at that time. But even then I saw the armed struggle as a weapon, a tactical weapon. I don't think I ever believed that we could overthrow the military might of the South African Defence Force. The aim was to put so much pressure on the apartheid government that it would be forced to come to the negotiating table.'

So much for the fantasy propagated by returned exiles – particularly those that did little or no actual fighting – that the objective of the armed struggle was 'the seizure of power', a phrase that has caused much confusion in the minds of some of today's young radicals whose knowledge of the anti-apartheid struggle and criticism of the decision to reach a negotiated settlement is derived from mythologised history. The blunt assessment of the former chief of the South African Defence Force, General Jannie Geldenhuys, was that 'Umkhonto we Sizwe, the ANC's military wing, was never a significant military factor. It had no impact on the struggle of the 1980s.'[5]

As Mandela later also told the South African generals during the negotiations: 'We know we can never defeat you militarily, and you know that you can never kill all of us.' I have always regarded that as the crispest summing-up of the South African conflict ever uttered. It was a stalemate, or what the mediation specialists call 'a violent equilibrium', which meant the only way it could ever be ended was at a negotiating table.

518

Indeed, so committed did Mandela become to gaining greater insight into the national psyche of the Afrikaner *volk* that he sought out Afrikaans literature in the prison library. He told me that in doing so he was dismayed to find there were no works of the celebrated Afrikaans poet, DJ Opperman, so he wrote to the Commissioner of Prisons pointing this out. I was fascinated to hear this, and could only imagine how dumbfounded the commissioner must have been to receive this complaint from his most notorious political prisoner, regarded as a 'terrorist' by the Afrikaner establishment. Even more remarkably, Mandela went on to tell me that the commissioner sent a request to the leading Afrikaans publishing house asking them to send not only a volume of Opperman's poems but also an anthology of other Afrikaans poetry to Mandela on Robben Island.

'Yes,' Mandela said. 'I received this big bundle of books from the publishers. Opperman's poems and others. So I wrote to the manager of the publishing house thanking him, and asked him very delicately, without mentioning names for the prison censors to see, to thank the commissioner for the gift.'

So intrigued was I by this gem of a disclosure, which I felt gave wonderful insight into the perceptiveness of Mandela's intelligence and of his intrinsic humanitarianism – not only must you know your enemy but also you must understand the most intimate aspects of his humanity – that I resolved to explore this remarkable exchange further. In doing so I found a copy of that letter of thanks Mandela wrote to the manager of the publishing house, Tafelberg, dated 27 February 1975. To my further astonishment I found it was written by hand in elegant Afrikaans.

'Thank you heartily for the beautiful gift of books I received from you today,' it reads. 'DJ Opperman's anthology is of exceptional value and I treasure it more than I can express in words. The Big Book of Verse contains a comprehensive collection of poems from a substantial cross-section of our people.'

Our people! What an astonishingly inclusive phrase for an imprisoned revolutionary to use about the people with whom he was at war.

I managed eventually to draw Mandela around to the subject

of my most immediate interest, which was those secret meetings, the detail of how they unfolded, and how they led eventually to his release and thus to the impending transformation of apartheid South Africa. The story he told me was rich in detail and colour, of how and where the meetings had taken place, what the sticking points were, what his anxieties were, and how difficult he had found it not to be able to communicate with his colleagues, particularly Tambo and the other leaders in Lusaka, but also with his comrades among the imprisoned leadership group from whom he had been separated when they moved him to Victor Verster.

It was an astonishing piece of real-life history, told to me by the man who was at the very centre of it, of how for four years, before the rest of the world knew anything about it, South Africa's future was being discussed in a series of secret meetings in hospitals, prisons and a Cabinet minister's home (Kobie Coetsee had once had Mandela brought from Pollsmoor to his official residence in Cape Town). And how, at the same time, government officials had slowly and carefully begun getting Mandela ready for release, taking him for drives in the countryside, and once for a walk along a remote beach up the Atlantic coast, to accustom him to the world from which he had been cut off for a quarter of a century.

Seldom can a journalist have been given such a vivid world scoop in such a relaxed atmosphere in his own home as Mandela gave me that day, while Sue and her mother served us endless cups of coffee. It was a story that not only made headlines in my own newspapers, but also enabled me to stitch together a 20 000-word cover story for *The New Yorker* magazine, under the title, 'The Secret Revolution', which won a Citation for Excellence from the Overseas Press Club of America. It went on to form the core of my second book, *Tomorrow is Another Country*, which was translated into six languages. That, in turn, caught the eye of a British television producer, Brian Lapping, who commissioned me to work with his company to make a three-part documentary series, titled *Death of Apartheid*, for the BBC and the Discovery Channel in the US. That meant interviewing all the key characters in the drama, including Mandela, all over again on camera, which they all did most graciously. I did most of the interviewing and spent

GEVANGENIS
ROBBENEILAND
Robben- Eiland.
27 Februarie 1975.
ROBBEN ISLAND
PRISON

Geagte Heer,

Graag wil ek u hartlik bedank vir die pragtige boekgeskenk wat ek vandag van u ontvang het.

D.J. Opperman se bloemlesings is van besondere waarde en ek waardeer hulle meer as wat ek in woorde kan stel. Die Groot Verseboek bevat 'n omvattende aantal uiteenlopende gedigte van 'n substansiële deursnee van ons volk. Die biografiese besonderhede in die Junior- en Senior Verseboek gee 'n verteenwoordigende deursnee van die figure wat 'n belangrike rol gespeel het in die bou van die Afrikaanse literatuur. Miskien sal ek eendag die geleentheid kry om my dankbaarheid aan u te betuig.

In verband hiermee, wil ek graag noem dat ek baie onlangs my begeerte om Opperman se poësie te hê teenoor 'n vooraanstaande en welbekende figuur in ons land se openbare sake, bekend gemaak het. Miskien dra u daarvan kennis. As dit die geval is, mag ek u vra om my dankbaarheid aan hom oor te dra?

Die uwe,
NRMandela.
N. R. MANDELA.

10 MAR 1975

Die Bestuurder.
Tafelberg Uitgewers
Posbus 879
Waalstraat 28,
Kaapstad.

Nelson Mandela's letter, written from Robben Island prison in elegant Afrikaans, to Tafelberg Publishers thanking them for sending volumes of Afrikaans poetry that he had requested from the Minister of Prisons. Mandela was eager to study the mind and soul of his people's oppressors.

several months in London helping with the editing and doing the narration for the series. The series was also broadcast by SABC-TV as well as in the Netherlands and Japan. It was also named runner-up for an Emmy award.

All told, I have to rate that as the single most successful story – and certainly the most lucrative – of my journalistic career. All due, no doubt, to the mellowing influence of that excellent plate of mealie-meal porridge. At least my mother-in-law claimed it to be so.

* * *

BUT THERE WAS more to that day of Mandela's visit than just the interview. After a light lunch, he told us politely that he would appreciate a brief rest. It turned out that, like Winston Churchill, he had the blessed ability of being able to lie back, close his eyes and catnap for ten or twenty minutes and waken completely refreshed. So it was early afternoon when he was back with me on the veranda.

'Is this home of yours in Rivonia?' he asked, looking a little puzzled. I told him that indeed it was, but that Rivonia had grown considerably in recent years, that it had been a mere village beyond Johannesburg's northern suburbia when I moved here, and that my home had been out in the countryside when I'd had it built on a portion of a smallholding farm that had been subdivided.

I saw Mandela's face light up with interest. 'Really,' he said. 'How far is Liliesleaf from here?'

Liliesleaf was the name of the smallholding where the security police had arrested the ANC high command on 11 July 1963. Mandela had himself hidden out there for many months while operating underground, but had been captured in Natal before the raid.

'Oh, it's only a few kilometres down the road,' I told him. 'But it's not a smallholding any longer. It's all part of a suburb now, but the original house is still there.'

'I'd like you to take me there,' he said. It was more of a command than a request.

I was a bit hesitant. Wasn't I supposed to be taking care of him here at my home because of the security alert? But Mandela was not to be denied. He wanted to visit that spot that was so embedded in the history of the ANC. So we got in my car and I drove out of my property, pausing briefly to let the surprised security guards know where we were going. They followed in their car. No sirens, no blue lights, just two ordinary passenger cars.

When we reached the house, a long, thatched structure with a string of outbuildings behind it, the entrance gate was locked. I rang the buzzer and a black woman, obviously the housekeeper, appeared at the front door to tell me the owner, Helmut Schroeder and his family, were not at home. Then she spotted Mandela, let out a shriek of delight and ran to the gate to unlock and open it for us. Mandela greeted her warmly, asked her name, and gravely inquired whether it might be possible to look over the house even though the owner was not there. The excited woman brushed aside any such hesitation and urged us to come in.

It was like watching someone enter a time warp as I accompanied Mandela into that property. He walked about the grounds in something like a trance of revived memories, recalling small details of an earlier life there when his name had been David Motsamayi, and he had posed as a gardener for Arthur Goldreich, an artist whose real role was as a key figure in the ANC's military wing. Mandela reminisced to himself, and sometimes aloud to me and to the housekeeper who accompanied us, while the two bodyguards waited beside the cars in the street.

'That's where I slept,' I heard Mandela murmur, half to himself, as he gestured to one of the rooms in an outbuilding intended to accommodate black domestic staff. 'You see, I had to pretend to be an ordinary black workman here so that I would not stand out and attract attention,' he explained. 'There were other ordinary black workers here as well, not members of the movement, and my place was to be junior to them. I had to cook for them and serve them food. They even ordered me about and called me "boy". This had to look like a normal South African home in a white area.'

As we walked under a tall tree, Mandela looked up. 'I shot a bird there once,' he said, pointing high into the branches. 'I had a pellet gun that I was supposed to use for target practice. I saw this sparrow up there and I took aim and shot it. It fell at my feet and Arthur Goldreich's little boy, Paul, who was with me, he was only about five, burst into tears. "David, why did you kill that bird? Its mother will be sad." You know, I felt terrible about it. In fact I was never able to kill anything again, not even insects in my cell on the island. Isn't that strange for the leader of a military organisation?'

He was deep in thought as we walked a little further, then he stopped dead in his tracks. Turning to the housekeeper he asked: 'Please show me where the kitchen is.' She led us around to the back of the house and indicated the kitchen door.

'I buried some weapons here, 50 paces from the kitchen,' he said, looking directly at me. So I positioned myself against the kitchen door and began striding across the back garden, counting the paces as I went. When I reached 20 I came up against a garden wall. Beyond was another property with a house directly in the line I had taken from the kitchen wall.

'It must be in the next property,' I called to Mandela, who was still standing beside the housekeeper at the kitchen door. 'I'll go there tomorrow and ask if I can pace out the rest in their grounds.'

Mandela did not explain what kind of weapons these were, but recounted in detail how they had been buried. 'We dug a hole deep enough so that any plough that dug up the soil there would not disturb the weapons. Then we wrapped them in cellophane and I put a metal plate over them and we filled in the hole.'

He had used the plural 'we'. Which meant he had not undertaken this little burial ceremony alone. Someone had helped him. Regrettably, I didn't ask who, which might have enabled us to solve the riddle. For a major riddle it has become. My story about those buried weapons has turned into a saga, culminating as I write this 25 years later, in the making of a movie about the great search that still continues. The people next door, when I called on them, were unable to help. Since then, Liliesleaf has been turned into a museum whose curator, Nicholas Wolpe, son of Goldreich's fellow escapee, Harold Wolpe, has engaged specialists from around the world to try to locate this hidden historical treasure. What Wolpe has established, however, is that the cache consisted

With Mandela on his first visit to Liliesleaf Farm since his release from prison, with a solitary bodyguard in the background. Mandela is explaining where he 'buried some weapons' on his return from a clandestine tour of Africa to establish the ANC's armed wing, Umkhonto we Sizwe.

of a single weapon, a ceremonial pistol and about 500 rounds of ammunition, given to Mandela by Emperor Haile Selassie of Ethiopia in 1962 during the ANC leader's tour of Africa to solicit aid for the armed struggle. So it remains a sacred political relic still to be uncovered.

The visit to Liliesleaf completed, it was time to return Mandela to his minders back at ANC headquarters in downtown Johannesburg. But we had reckoned without the magnetism of the man. By the time we reached the cars, word had got around the neighbourhood that Mandela was there and domestic workers were streaming out of every property to see him, creating an excited hubbub of cries and ululations. And Mandela, despite the growing agitation of his bodyguards, was determined to wait in the street to greet each one of them with a great big smile.

It seemed to take forever for him to hug each of these overjoyed women. And then, just as the crowd began to thin, a final disciple emerged from a property at the very end of a long slope down towards a stream at the end of the road. She was a large woman, heavy and slow, and it was going to take a while for her to make it up the 300 metres of incline to where Mandela was standing, in the middle of the street, beaming encouragement.

'Please, Mr Sparks, you must get Mr Mandela into your car right now,' one of the bodyguards pleaded. 'He can't stand here like this any longer.' But there was no moving him. Mandela just stood there, beaming, waiting, while this solid woman trundled heavily up the long slope, ululating as she came and the crowd cheering her on. Until at last she arrived, gasping for breath, and flung herself into Mandela's arms. After which he had to thank her for coming, ask her name, wish her and all her extended family well, and give her a final hug before condescending to get into my car and be driven away.

Thus ended a truly extraordinary day.

* * *

I SAW MANY different facets of Mandela's personality in the stormy phase that followed, leading up to the toughly contested negotiations, the majestic moment of his inauguration as South Africa's first black president and the exercise of racial reconciliation throughout his first and only term of office.

After the warmth of that day spent at my home, I saw him display cold, controlled anger towards FW de Klerk when he felt the President had stolen a march on him at the opening of the Convention for a Democratic South Africa (Codesa) in a cavernous exhibition hall alongside a highway near Johannesburg airport. De Klerk had been the last speaker at the introductory phase of the first plenary session, and, after the usual bland utterances wishing the negotiators well, had accused the ANC of dishonouring an agreement to dismantle its guerrilla force, saying this called into question its ability to enter into binding agreements at the convention.

Mandela requested time to respond. He strode to the podium and turned on the President with ice-cold fury that chilled the audience. Speaking in slow, measured tones and referring to De Klerk in the third person without looking at him, though he sat only two or three metres away, Mandela declared: 'He thought I would not be able to respond. He was mistaken. I respond now.' He then went on to lambaste De Klerk for playing dirty politics, saying: 'Even the head of an illegitimate, discredited minority regime, as his is, has certain moral standards to uphold.'

Some thought it was a reckless way to start what were obviously going to be delicate negotiations, but Mandela had made two essential points. One was to warn his opponents that he was going to be no pushover; the other, perhaps even more important, was to reassure his followers, most of whom didn't yet know him, that he was indeed a tough customer and had come out of jail fighting fit.

I also saw him nonplussed and thrown into confusion by his own people. As the civil war raged throughout Natal province between ANC supporters and followers of Chief Mangosuthu Buthelezi's Inkatha Freedom Party, Mandela travelled to Natal to call for peace at an ANC rally. A huge crowd had gathered to hear him speak, perhaps expecting him to champion their cause, but when he called instead for them to 'take your guns, your knives and your pangas and throw them into the sea', an angry hiss ran through the mob. Perhaps it was the first time Mandela had ever experienced such an adverse reaction from his own followers, for he was taken aback and fell silent for a while. He had lost his audience. They listened to the rest of his speech in a sullen mood. And sadly the war between ANC and Inkatha continued unabated.

That, too, was a moment replete with meaning, for it signalled that black South Africans would not be easily dictated to by a strong personality such as Mandela. Today, pessimists often suggest that South Africa may be following Zimbabwe on the road to becoming a failed state. I cite that moment when Mandela's own people hissed him to silence to argue that, unlike Zimbabweans who have allowed Robert Mugabe to cow them into silent submissiveness, black South Africans are too robust to allow that to happen.

Most strikingly of all, I saw Mandela rise to the level of statesmanship following the cold-blooded murder of Chris Hani on 10 April 1993. Hani had become a folk hero among black South Africans, especially the radical youth. Not only was he the leader of the South African Communist Party (SACP) and chief of staff of Umkhonto we Sizwe, but he was also one of the few who had acquired the reputation of a war hero for his exploits in battle. Now he had been shot to death in broad daylight by a white racist, a Polish immigrant named Janusz Waluś, as he stepped out of his car outside his own home.

The country could have gone up in flames that day, such was the fury that swept the land. It was probably the single most perilous moment in our recent history as we teetered on the brink of disaster. But it was Mandela who saved the day. He went on television that night to address the nation in a speech widely acclaimed as presidential − even though he was not yet President. De Klerk was still in that supreme position, but he had the intelligence and insight to realise that Mandela was the only one who could steady the ship of state on that stormy night when it could so easily have foundered in a wave of black wrath. Mandela delivered that broadcast in sonorous, statesmanlike tones:

> Tonight I am reaching out to every single South African, black and white, from the very depths of my being. A white man, full of

528

prejudice and hate, came to our country and committed a deed so foul that our whole nation now teeters on the brink of disaster. A white woman, of Afrikaner origin, risked her life so that we may know, and bring to justice, the assassin. The cold-blooded murder of Chris Hani has sent shock waves throughout the country and the world ... Now is the time for all South Africans to stand together against those who, from any quarter, wish to destroy what Chris Hani gave his life for – the freedom of all of us.

I have listened to many speeches by many political leaders in many parts of the world during my long career as a journalist, but the thing that always struck me about the impact Mandela was able to make was not that he was a great orator. His use of language was excellent but his delivery was too slow and monotone to be called oratorical. No, what made him great was that he was a master of the essential gesture to deal with the situation at hand. He had an exquisite sense of how to touch the right emotional buttons of his audience or the country as a whole.

In the case of the Hani speech, it was his delicately noting that it was a foreigner, not a white South African, who had committed the foul deed, and a white Afrikaner woman whose brave actions had led to the killer's arrest. So, too, the symbolic gesture of reconciliation when he visited Hendrik Verwoerd's widow, Betsie, and had tea with her in the tiny Afrikaner community of Orania, and, of course, his famous appearance at the Rugby World Cup final in 1995 when he presented the Webb Ellis Cup to the captain of the Springbok team, François Pienaar, wearing the captain's Number Six jersey – a gesture of identification with the Afrikaner captain of the triumphant team of what is essentially the national sport of the Afrikaner people.

That amounts to political genius in my book.

* * *

THESE WERE difficult days as I watched the transitional phase of our history unfold. Not only were there frequent breakdowns in the negotiations, but also the country was aboil with the black civil war and white right-wingers were doing their damndest to derail the talks and establish a power base of their own in one of the black Bantustans, the territory of Bophuthatswana, from where they hoped to be able to launch a counter-revolution. The country was awash with foreign correspondents, many of them writing doomsday scenarios about how South Africa was finally going to expire in the bloodbath that puritanical idealists abroad had long predicted and, I sometimes suspected, felt ought to happen. Yet I had the advantage of knowing the country and having contacts on all sides of the multiple conflicts, which helped me keep track of events and maintain a steady confidence that it would end in success.

But there were certainly tense moments, and once again I found myself shuttling between reporting on the intense debates in the Codesa negotiations and being a war correspondent covering the battles raging in the two civil wars outside. On a crisp midwinter day in 1993 the two came together, as I watched a raucous mob of some 3000 Afrikaner right-wingers make their way towards the Kempton Park exhibition centre where the Codesa negotiations were taking place. There were farmers in floppy hats, women with children in tow and young men in khaki carrying placards bearing the swastika-like emblem of the *Afrikaner Weerstandsbeweging* (AWB), the Afrikaner Resistance Movement, which opposed the negotiations. Some wore the black uniforms of the AWB's *Ystergarde*, or Iron Guard, with SS-type shoulder flashes and cap badges. Many had holstered pistols on their hips, long hunting knives hanging from their belts and shotguns and hunting rifles sheathed in quilted bags. An altogether dangerous-looking lot.

I quaked as I watched them storm through the gates and begin rocking cars and ripping off rear-view mirrors as they passed through the parking lot to surround the building where the talks were taking place. Then a yellow armoured car edged its way through the crowd to crash through the plate-glass frontage into the foyer of the building. Men in AWB uniforms raced up the stairway, scrambled over balustrades looking for delegates and shouting that they were going to shoot any blacks they saw. They made their way into the negotiating chamber and sat in the seats. They emptied the delegates' bar, poured fruit juice on the carpets and urinated on the desks. Their leader, the burly, bearded Eugene Terre'Blanche, marched into their midst to deliver a fiery address – and then the mob withdrew to light their braai fires on a stretch of open ground near the exhibition centre, open their picnic hampers and quaff gallons of beer.

In a sharply contrasting experience, as the Codesa talks got under way Sue and I, together with 11-year-old Julian, were caught in a lethal outbreak of black violence in the township of Boipatong, south of Johannesburg. The warfare between Inkatha and the ANC had spread north from Natal to the migrant worker communities of the Witwatersrand. A posse of Inkatha warriors crept out of their workers' hostel one night and hacked, stabbed and shot 38 township residents to death in their homes, presuming Boipatong to be an ANC stronghold. The outraged residents were convinced that state security forces were behind the attack. To counter this, President de Klerk decided to make a conciliatory visit to Boipatong.

It was a Saturday and we had gone first to Ennerdale, where Sue had her advisory desk. When she had finished there, we decided to stop by Boipatong to see how De Klerk was coping with his unaccustomed mission. We arrived just in time to see him beating a hasty retreat out of the township. The angry residents were in no mood for a visit from the President whose forces they believed were responsible for the attack on them. They began rocking and bouncing his car. The alarmed driver slammed it into reverse and, with engine screaming and wheels spinning in the dirt, backed out of a narrow alley and sped away.

A symbolic sight in itself, but more drama awaited us. As we were about to leave, I noticed some of the big Hippo armoured personnel carriers that had accompanied De Klerk heading deeper into the township. 'What's going on down there?' I asked a bystander.

'I think someone has been killed down there,' the man replied, pointing to a stretch of marshy ground on the far side of the township. We began following the stream of people heading that way along with the Hippos, which were packed with armed police. On the way, we were joined by a Nigerian journalist friend, Dele Olojede, the recently arrived correspondent for New York *Newsday*. It was his first venture into a turbulent township and he was scared.

'Don't worry, Dele,' I told him, half in jest. 'These cops won't shoot a whitey, so you just stick close to me and you'll be alright.'

At the bottom of a long slope we saw a line of police armed with shotguns on a shallow bank at the edge of the marsh. I led Dele towards the police, moving in behind them as they faced towards the reed-filled marsh, while Sue told me she and Julian were going to join the crowd of onlookers further behind us.

A young man told me the body of a black youth was lying among the reeds. He said the police had shot the youth, then placed a panga beside his body to make it look as though they had shot him in self-defence. The people wanted to retrieve the body, the man said, but the police were keeping them away while an ambulance tried to reach the body. But the ambulance had become stuck in the mud.

Suddenly a shot rang out. In a flash the police line spun around and opened fire on the crowd. I flung myself to the ground at the feet of the policeman closest to me, who was firing repeatedly over my prone body. I could see people running and falling as they were hit, and the air was filled with screaming and shouting. To my horror, I realised Sue and Julian were in that fleeing mob being fired upon, but there was nothing I could do except remain pinned to the ground.

Then, as suddenly as it had started, the shooting stopped. I heard an officer screaming: 'Who told you to shoot? I never gave an order to fire!' Much later, I learned that the ambulance driver, upset at being stuck in the mud, had slipped while trying to climb out of the vehicle and accidentally discharged his own firearm, which the jittery line of police mistook for a signal to open fire.

The agitated officer ordered his men to withdraw and board the fleet of Hippos waiting nearby. As they did so, shots rang out from township houses behind me and I heard the angry zip-zip-zip of bullets passing overhead. Activists with crude but effective pipe-guns, made from water piping, were opening up on the police as they ran for the Hippos. As this became a barrage, I realised I was in a predicament. I had no idea where Sue and Julian were, except that the main body of the crowd had disappeared among some houses. If I were to stand up, my white skin would make me a target. But I couldn't continue lying there indefinitely.

A few metres ahead, I could see the bodies of several dead and wounded black people. Beside me were two black men, both unhurt. 'Let's try to move those wounded people to safety,' I said to them. It sounded like a charitable offer, but I had self-preservation very much in mind. Alongside my black helpers I would be safer. That is how I got out of that ugly situation. After carrying the wounded to safety, I was able to find Sue and Julian, who had been plucked to safety by a black family.

But we still faced the problem of walking, as a white family, through this very angry black township, to the spot where we had left our car. It seemed a perilous prospect. But as I pondered our dilemma I heard a car pull up and a familiar voice call out. 'Get in quick,' Dele called, holding open a door.

'Don't worry, Allister,' he said mockingly as he drove away. 'These folk won't shoot a darkie, so you just stick close to me and you'll be alright.'

* * *

NELSON MANDELA'S inauguration as President in May 1994, following the ANC's election victory, was one of the emotional highlights of my life. Sue and I were given seats in the amphitheatre of the splendid Union Buildings in Pretoria. That meant we were seated immediately behind the largest array of royals and other heads of state ever to gather in South Africa – in itself symbolising the scale of our transition from a country that only a few years before had been an international pariah.

Nearly every country on earth was represented, making for a vibrant sartorial mix, from ornate Latin American military uniforms to colourful African cloaks and headwraps and silk Asian saris. The political mix was equally striking, and symbolic as old enemies encountered each other. US Vice-President Al Gore, his wife Tipper and US First Lady Hillary Clinton were there along with their country's nemesis, Fidel Castro of Cuba. Palestinian leader Yasser Arafat was there along with Israeli President Ezer Weizman. Castro shook hands with the South African military generals his men had fought against in Angola. Mandela himself invited three of his former jailers to attend the ceremony as honoured guests.

There was a delightful, if somewhat alarming, moment when Sue ran after Castro as he headed towards his seat. She was clutching a commemorative first-day cover we had each been given and banged him on the shoulder with it. As he turned his great bearded head and glared angrily at Sue, she thrust the envelope before him and asked, in what I took to be an attempt at Spanish, for him to sign it. His glare turned slowly into a grin, then a chuckle at her presumptuousness as he took her ballpoint and signed it. 'I got it!' she called out triumphantly to me.

There were ceremonial moments as the old South African flag was lowered and the new one hoisted, and as a military band struck up with the new national anthem, a blend of the old and the new sung in four of our new official languages.

But for me the most stirring moments came with Mandela's speech, delivered in his now familiar slow, measured voice emphasising the most compelling phrases, each of which sent a shiver down my spine:

> The time for the healing of the wounds has come. The moment to bridge the chasms that divide us has come. The time to build is upon us.

Then, towards the end, the most noble pledge of all:

> We enter into a covenant that we shall build a society in which all South Africans, black and white, will be able to walk tall, without any fear in their hearts, assured of their inalienable right to human dignity − a rainbow nation at peace with itself and the world ... Never, never and never again shall it be that this beautiful land will again experience the oppression of one by another and suffer the indignity of being the skunk of the world.

A covenant! What a mighty thing is that. It bears the connotation of a sacred vow. I felt a surge of emotion. Of national pride for the first time in my life. And with that a personal sense that all those many thousands of words I had written over the years had played a role and at last been justified.

LONG WALK
TO FREEDOM

To Allister,

Best wishes to one of
South africa's eminent
journalists, & whose
outspoken views have
served the cause of
democracy in this country
magnificently.

NMandela
24 · 1 · 97

A treasured inscription in the copy of Mandela's autobiography
that he gave to me.

* * *

BUT MY MOST cherished memory of Mandela was of when
he came to our home one more time to bid farewell to Sue shortly
before she died.

He knew she had cancer and had asked me, when we met at
a public function a few weeks earlier, how she was doing. Sadly, I
told him I thought the end was near.

Sue and Mandela on our veranda during his last visit before she died.

'Oh, I'm so sorry to hear that,' he said. 'Then I must come and see her soon.'

A week later our phone rang and Julian answered. 'Hello, is that Julian?' Mandela asked, again demonstrating his remarkable memory for people's names. 'Please tell your mother that I am coming to see her today.'

He arrived about an hour later. He was actually on his way to Johannesburg airport to board a plane for a state visit to Saudi Arabia, but he broke his journey to visit Sue. Again, there was no presidential cavalcade of cars with wailing sirens and motorcycle outriders, as became the fashion with his successors. Just two cars, with his bodyguards following behind. And again, as with his previous visit, he made the bodyguards wait in the street outside our property while he came into our home to see Sue.

He spent two hours there with the three of us. A joyful time of warm, intimate conversation during which Sue glowed with happiness. He thanked her for the work she had done with the Black Sash and for her role in arranging those negotiating sessions during the Delmas treason trial. It was like a healing touch of recognition and I know Sue cherished every moment of it.

CHAPTER TWENTY-NINE

WHAM

THAT SUBLIME feeling of triumph, of having the dream of a lifetime come true against all the odds, stayed with me throughout Nelson Mandela's term of office, and a bit beyond as Thabo Mbeki seemed to carry the baton for a while. But, as with all dreams, there comes an awakening to reality. Remoulding three centuries of racial domination and exploitation, and the shattering of black family life through generation upon generation of migrant labour, was never going to be a quick fix. Nor was there going to be any swift reincarnation of more such great souls as Nelson Mandela.

So decline was inevitable. But even so, the speed and extent of it has been a surprise and a huge disappointment.

Some voices of scepticism were raised even as the world applauded Mandela's gestures of reconciliation and canonised the man to the level of a living saint. To the doubters it all seemed too good to be true, that all those generations of oppression and exploitation could be so easily forgiven. But I dismissed the doubters. I felt confident because I knew all the key players personally and I had watched them come together in a remarkable spirit of unity at Codesa. Moreover, the mood within the country was jubilant; a new spirit of cross-cultural fellowship seemed to infuse everyone. A sense of hope and optimism filled the air.

As the badly crippled apartheid economy began to recover, then to surge, the pessimists shifted their line of argument to pose the question of what would happen when the magic of Mandela's term of office came to an end. He had indicated from the outset that he would hold office for only one term, although the Constitution allowed him two. He wanted to signal to the world, and to his own people, that the desire to remain in power indefinitely, which had been so prevalent in the rest of Africa, would not apply to South Africa. We were going to be different: a true democracy with none of that destructive 'Big Man' syndrome.

So the sceptics began raising the question of what would happen after Mandela left office. The 'WHAM' question, as it was quickly labelled. Again I was dismissive of the scepticism, putting it down to a knee-jerk response. To me the future looked secure. I had no reason to doubt that there would continue to be progressive improvement in our national circumstances after Mandela left office. I had faith in his deputy, Thabo Mbeki, who I had come to know so well and greatly admired during my contacts with him in exile and after his return. An extraordinarily well-educated, worldly-wise and sophisticated man, who had effectively become the engine-room manager of the country during the Mandela presidency. Indeed I had come to regard Mbeki in the role of a prime minister under a Mandela monarchy. In that role Mbeki had shown himself not only to be efficient but also pragmatic. Though he had been steeped in Marxist philosophy all his life, on coming to power he recognised that the world had changed and he had crafted for Mandela the business-friendly Growth, Employment and Redistribution (Gear) macroeconomic policy. In his own words, this was 'a pragmatic balance struck between our domestic demands and the realities of the international context'. Such flexibility, I felt, was exactly what the new South Africa needed. So my answer to the WHAM question was that there would continue to be plain sailing.

But I was wrong. As I came to realise after he became President, Thabo Mbeki was a conflicted personality, trapped between the two worlds of his political inheritance and the one in which he now found himself. He was also, like Jan Smuts, a philosophical visionary who allowed his idealistic dreams of an African Renaissance to distract him from the political realities of the here and now.

* * *

I FIRST SENSED a shift in the political air when, shortly after Mbeki's inauguration, I encountered him walking through Cape Town's Company's Garden towards the Houses of Parliament. I stopped to wish him well for the new session that was about to open, and to chat with Sheila Sisulu, a personal friend, who was part of a small group accompanying him. It was a casual moment, but I could see Mbeki was miffed. He stood stiffly to one side as I exchanged a few words with Sheila. I sensed immediately that times had changed. The era of informal relationships with Mandela were over, as were the days of chewing the fat over a bottle of whisky with Mbeki. He was Mr President now, and one would have to make formal appointments to see him.

A short while later I bumped into a journalist colleague, John Battersby, who had shared in some of those encounters in Lusaka's Pamodzi Hotel. 'Have you seen Thabo?' he asked with a sardonic grin. When I replied that I had, he confided that he had seen Mbeki arrive from Cape Town airport in a presidential cavalcade. 'I guess things are going to be different now,' he said.

Indeed they were. Mbeki as president was a very different person from the smart but easy-going friend we had known in exile. He became formal and remote. 'Aloof' was a word one heard with increasing frequency among the rank and file of the ANC. Mbeki could still turn on the charm when he chose to, but one sensed that the responsibility of stepping into the presidency weighed heavily upon him. Assuming office after such a giant as Mandela could not have been easy, but even more burdensome, I imagine, was the weight of expectations. He had been groomed for this role virtually from childhood, and now he was there and expected to perform with both his formidable parents watching from the sidelines.

Add to that the factional rivalries and frustrations that plagued the ANC in exile, which meant that leaders of different factions tended to surround themselves with trusted loyalists. The armed wing particularly had been prone to infiltration by South African agents, which generated an atmosphere of pervasive suspicion and opened the way for the planting of smears against rival factions. Mbeki, as a bright and favoured son, had always been close to the unchallenged leader of the exiles, Oliver Tambo, but he engendered animosity from the militarists under Chris Hani and other rival groups. Given all these factors, it is not surprising that this capable man developed what seemed to me, as an admirer, to be a paradoxical sense of insecurity that drove him to be overly watchful and to choose a Cabinet of proven loyalists rather than the most capable team available to advise on the daunting road ahead.

I recall that the first public criticism of Mbeki, while he was still viewed publicly as the ANC's brightest star, came from Professor Robert Schrire, then head of the political science department at the University of Cape Town. In a remarkably prescient article, as Mbeki was about to take over from Mandela, Schrire noted that Mbeki hated open conflict and tended to avoid confrontation with opponents. Therefore he would surround himself with 'courtiers' who would never challenge him. 'Not for Mbeki the Kennedy and Roosevelt style of leadership,' Schrire wrote, 'where strong and independent personalities are brought into the presidential team and the President, through strength of personality, resolves the inevitable conflicts.'[1]

Schrire likened Mbeki more to Richard Nixon, a man with a complex mix of beliefs and values who was impossible to categorise either politically or ideologically, but whose dislike of conflict and opposition would lead him to isolate critics, centralise power upon himself and his chosen team, and impose 'an imperial presidency':

We could thus script the following scenario: a powerful but unloved leader, surrounded by loyal but mediocre staff, seeks to control the vast apparatus of government. His manipulative style leads to his gradual isolation from both the public and the political elite ... He views politics as a struggle between enemies rather than a competition between opponents. Policy failures are attributed to conspiracies and dark hidden forces. Ultimately this

540

combination of character flaws and the excesses of the imperial presidency bring about the inevitable tragedy.[2]

To that I might add my own view that some of the complexities of Mbeki's personality were due to a distorted upbringing. As his father, Govan, once explained to me, he and his wife, Epainette, both key members of the Communist Party, were so involved in the liberation struggle that they felt certain they would both end up with long terms of imprisonment. Therefore they had decided to sever ties of affection with their children, sending them away to live with friends and relatives at a very young age, so that they would not pine when their parents went to jail. They had to grow up as strong, disciplined comrades in the struggle. A case, I would say, of a lack of parental love in a time of national phobia.

Personality factors aside, I would say Mbeki got off to a reasonably good start, continuing effectively what he had been doing as Mandela's chief operating officer. The task was daunting, amounting to what I called at the time a three-in-one revolution. The first was the political task of democratising the most deeply entrenched and institutionalised system of segregation the modern world had seen, which involved merging all segregated institutions, from the state education and health systems to incorporating the ten tribal Bantustans, into the main body of the country. The second was to transform South Africa from an isolated siege economy into a player in the new globalised marketplace. The country had to change from being a highly protected, inward-looking economy into an open, internationally competitive one. And the third, and most difficult, was to try to narrow the yawning wealth gap between the white and black populations.

But in dealing with these issues Mbeki also sowed the seeds of some of the deep structural problems that have become largely responsible for the socio-political and economic decline the country is now experiencing under his egregiously inadequate successor, Jacob Zuma.

* * *

IN A SPEECH early in his first term, Mbeki referred to South Africa as having two economies, one black and one white, an observation I likened in one of my columns to a double-decker bus with a comfortable upper deck and a crowded, uncomfortable lower deck – and no stairway between. Mbeki picked up on that imagery, turning it into a metaphorical house that needed to have that stairway installed. Thus the birth of his controversial policy of Black Economic Empowerment, or BEE, later to be expanded into Broad-Based Black Economic Empowerment, or B-BBEE. I sought an interview for him to elaborate on his thinking, during which he told me bluntly: 'Too many whites think that getting rid of political segregation and giving black people the vote is all that needs to be done. Everything else can stay the same. But we have to have economic integration too.'

Indeed. But how? BEE is more than just affirmative action, although it includes that. It is a complex set of requirements that businesses must comply with to enable more black people not only to get better jobs but also to own and manage enterprises. The need is obvious. Under colonialism and apartheid black people were prohibited from doing skilled work, and they were denied the right to form companies or establish their own enterprises beyond the level of what was termed 'providing the basic necessities of life' – such as fresh produce stalls and wood and coal merchants.

But simply removing these obstacles was not enough. White businesses had to be compelled to open their doors to black partners, as well as help these previously disadvantaged people acquire skills to enable them to advance economically. This requires every private business to keep a scorecard of compliance with a set of BEE laws, to show that it has met with the requirements of the system's Codes of Good Practice – without which it can do no business with the government or any of its state agencies.

Fine in theory, but a bureaucratic nightmare in practice. Nonetheless, the local business community not only cooperated with the system, but also broadly welcomed it. The rationale was that the rapid emergence of a black middle class would serve as an insurance against the leftist tendencies within the ANC that they so feared. They would have black middle-class allies in the business community.

What they did not foresee, and I feel sure Mbeki didn't either, is that the system would quickly, and inevitably, morph into a patronage system, which has become so pervasive now within the Zuma administration that it has turned South Africa into a country of corruption as notorious as Nigeria. Zuma, himself corrupt beyond measure, sits atop a pyramid of loyal recipients of his political patronage.

Equally serious, the system has not narrowed the wealth gap, as Mbeki intended. Indeed the gap has widened in an ugly fashion, with a wealthy upper strata of black society with the right political connections leading lives of conspicuous consumption to a degree that can only be described as obscene.

The result – and this is where the white business community got it so wrong – is that it is the working class and the poorest of the poor who feel alienated from and resentful of the ANC regime. As shack-dwellers watch what are derisorily referred to as 'black diamonds', living in grand mansions in what used to be whites-only suburbs and driving around in top-of-the-range Mercedes-Benzes, a feeling of betrayal arises among those whom the ANC promised 'a better life for all'. And it is the imminent emergence of populist parties on the left who stand to profit from that.

Another misstep during the Mbeki era has compounded this problem by pitching the national economy into a long downward slide, which, together with a woeful education system, has increased unemployment, especially youth unemployment, to the point where nearly half the population under the age of 35 are unemployed – indeed many of them unemployable.

How did it come about that this long economic decline began under the presidency of the most highly qualified economist in the ruling party?

I believe a clue to this conundrum can be found in a document entitled, 'Towards a Ten Year Review', authored in 2004 by an Mbeki acolyte, Joel Netshitenzhe, as head of the ANC's Policy Co-ordination and Advisory Services, which reviewed the government's policy achievements during its first ten years in office and assessed their appropriateness for the future.

There one finds one of the major causes of our economic decline. It is contained in the doctrine of democratic centralism, which holds that the state should be at the controlling centre of all economic activity in the country. It is a concept derived initially from the Soviet model, but modified by the southeast Asian 'Tigers' – Singapore, South Korea, Hong Kong and Taiwan – to involve a high level of state coordination of the private sector as well as state-run enterprises.

It is not surprising that the ANC was attracted by this model, for the Asian Tigers achieved exceptionally high growth rates, above 7 per cent, from the 1960s through the 1990s. By the turn of the century they had become advanced, high-income economies.

The problem with this concept, so attractive on paper, is that in practice it can succeed only in a situation where the state has access to a very high level of skills, especially technical skills. Which the Asian Tigers had, but which South Africa most certainly does not have.

For a government to coordinate the activities of the private sector, it must have civil servants who are as skilled in business management, if not more so, than the CEOs of the country's most successful big corporations. They must understand each other and be able to coordinate their roles in a creative way. Indeed in the case of the Asian Tigers, Singapore especially, these individuals were largely interchangeable, often shuttling between civil service and top business management roles.

Without that, the system becomes a disaster. For a government with a poorly skilled civil service to set about trying to lead and coordinate private sector activities can only result in a mismatch that will strangle the country's economy. This is happening in South Africa. We are a country that has never had an efficient civil service, and now with large-scale affirmative action it has been lowered still further as it passes through a long learning curve. In his review, Netshitenzhe noted that a mere ten years after the advent of democracy, three-quarters of the civil service were Africans, and therefore new in the job.

That no one took notice of the inevitable consequences of this mismatch tells its own tale. During their years in exile, today's ANC policymakers derived their ideas in an environment of 'progressive' theories rather than one of practical reality. They read and they attended lectures and they debated. Life was akin to a students' common room. They wrote position papers, but they never actually managed anything in the real world. Then, when the moment came to take over and run a complex, modern industrial economy, their entire intellectual universe collapsed along with the Berlin Wall and the Soviet empire. They have had to learn the realities of governing, from local to national level, on the job and from scratch. The result is there to be seen in the failure of every one of South Africa's parastatal corporations. If the state cannot run those, then it is in no position to lead or co-ordinate the country's economic activities. The persistent attempt to do so is what in my columns I have called 'the centralising of inefficiency'. That is at the heart of our declining economy.

* * *

THESE STRUCTURAL misjudgments were seeds that were only to germinate later, reaching full flower under the Zuma administration. What wrecked Thabo Mbeki's international reputation and tarnished the image of our national rebirth had nothing whatever to do with policy choices. It was the result of a personal aberration. Mbeki's AIDS denialism.

I was in Washington on a scholarship at the Woodrow Wilson International Center for Scholars when the news broke in the US that the newly elected South African President was in denial about the AIDS epidemic beginning to ravage his country. I couldn't believe it. Not this bright young man I knew so well. There had to be a mistake. So I went to the South African Embassy to have lunch with my friend Sheila Sisulu, who was now ambassador to the US. Knowing that Mbeki was about to visit Washington, I urged her to arrange for him to address the National Press Club so that he could clear the air of this terrible misunderstanding.

Sheila looked uncomfortable at my suggestion. 'I'm sure it's a bit late, isn't it? These things have got to be arranged a long time in advance, and we've got a whole programme already prepared for him.'

I told Sisulu I thought it was such a big and important issue that the Press Club would be only too pleased to fit Mbeki in – and that the press would come running. But if that wasn't possible, I was sure *The Washington Post* would be pleased to have Mbeki meet with their senior editors – and since I knew people at the Post I could put the idea to them.

The Post lunch duly took place – and I was horrified to learn afterwards from my friends who had attended that it had made things worse. They told me Mbeki had gone into a harangue about the falsehood being spread that the new democratic South Africa was facing destruction from a virus that either didn't exist or was harmless. These cases of the weakening of the immune system, Mbeki had told them, were not due to AIDS but to conditions linked to poverty, such as kwashiorkor, and diseases such as tuberculosis, widely prevalent in Africa. The response had to be in providing better nutrition, not expensive new drugs that were in fact seriously harmful.

There had been no mistake or misunderstanding. I had to face the fact that my President was in denial.

To this day I am still baffled by Mbeki's response to the AIDS crisis. How could this intelligent man, so modern and rational in every other way, run off the rails into a morass of irrationality on this issue? I have tried hard to understand it, but still don't. Not fully, anyway. And why could such a consummate politician not see the huge damage he was doing to himself, his presidency and his country? To say nothing of the thousands of young people, particularly young women and their babies, who died or had their futures ruined by his denialism. A research unit at the University of Cape Town eventually estimated that more than 300 000 South Africans had died prematurely as a result of Mbeki's denialism.

What I ultimately had to acknowledge, with great regret, for I had really liked and admired this man, was that, for all his brilliance, Thabo Mbeki was a flawed personality. I can only imagine that somewhere deep in his psyche, the psychological effect of an exceptionally gifted young man being subjected to the humiliations of apartheid, of having crude white yobbos, not ankle high to him in human worth, treat him as an inferior human being, may have left some deep emotional scars.

But the ultimate irony is that this huge AIDS blot on Mbeki's record was not what led to his downfall. That came about because of a revolt within his party against his pro-business Gear policy, which I still regard as his most successful achievement.

* * *

AS THE COUNTRY underwent change while moving into the post-Mandela era, so did the pattern of my life, although it remained anchored in journalism. The first inkling that I might want to shift my focus on events came when, out of the blue, I found myself on the ANC's list of candidates for the first parliamentary election. I was dumbfounded. At first I thought someone was playing a practical joke on me. I was not a member of the ANC; I have always regarded it as a matter of principle that a journalist should not belong to a political party, for anyone who does faces the irresolvable conflict of either slanting his or her political reports in its favour, or being disloyal to the party whose aims and objectives you have pledged to support. But I soon discovered that, regardless of not being a member, the ANC members in the voting area where I lived had nominated me, and the party's nominating committee had put me on the list.

What is more, I was in an electable position on the ANC's proportional representation list, one ahead of the celebrated singer Miriam Makeba, who was ultimately elected. So had I remained on the list I would have become a member of that first democratic Parliament led by President Nelson Mandela.

I must admit I was flattered – and intrigued. It would be a great honour and a wonderful experience to be a member of that historic assembly. I discussed it with several ANC friends, including Thabo Mbeki, and they were encouraging. But they made it clear that I would have to join the ANC, which of course was obvious. Mbeki had asked me to give him time to think about it.

547

'You seem to be a different kind of liberal,' he remarked cryptically, which I thought probably meant he saw me as being somewhat to the left, or perhaps closer to African people, than most white liberals because of my origins among the amaXhosa of the eastern Cape. As I pondered the prospect it became, in Hamlet's words, 'sicklied o'er with the pale cast of thought'. I recalled my years of sitting in the Press Gallery, listening to all those hours of dreary speeches and wondered about the life of a backbencher, which I would surely be, waiting for days, weeks, for a few minutes of glory at the podium.

But most of all I was chilled by the thought of having to give up journalism. I loved it. It had become the very core of my being, and I couldn't image life without its constant challenges and variety — and I couldn't be unfaithful to my own code of not practising it while being a member of a political party. So I sent the ANC's election list committee a message saying thanks, but no thanks. Later Mbeki admonished me for not waiting for him to come back to me, but I have no regrets. Only, in retrospect, an increasing sense of thankfulness for not having taken that course and become a spin doctor having to deal with the great decline.

What that interlude of inner reflection did, however, was instil in me a wish to be more closely involved in the affairs of my country. For the past 13 years, since my dismissal from the *Rand Daily Mail*, I had been a foreign correspondent reporting and analysing the dramatic events taking place in my country for foreigners. I felt my coverage had played a role in the transformation, because I believed international pressure from the US, Britain and the Netherlands, where most of my reports had appeared, had contributed significantly to the transition. But now the change had taken place and I felt a need to become involved more directly in the shaping of the new South Africa.

Since I had put my commitment to journalism ahead of an opportunity to become a legislator, I realised that role should logically be within my profession. During my many visits to the United States, I had made contact with the Poynter Institute, a remarkable training organisation in St Petersburg, Florida. Owned and funded by the immensely wealthy *St Petersburg Times*, it had established a record for giving excellent short, mid-career courses for journalists. So I went to Florida to see the institute in operation. I found it stimulating and exciting, and that is when I conceived the idea of starting something similar in South Africa. I knew we had a number of excellent black reporters in the country – many had worked for me on the Mail – but I knew, too, that because of apartheid's job reservation laws none had any experience in mid-level and senior executive positions in newsrooms. Clearly there was going to be pressure for rapid black advancement in all sectors of journalism, which meant those talented reporters were going to be shot up swiftly into those positions, right up to editor level, without having had any mid-management experience in how to deal with and inspire excellence in staff members under them. There was a need to fill that gap, and a local version of the Poynter Institute seemed the way to provide it.

So I embarked on such a project. I didn't realise what a task it would be, because you can't just wish such a thing into existence. It required money, it required staffing, and it required support – and I had no experience in any of those fields. Like the newly freed black people, I would have to learn on the job.

To begin with, I obtained the enthusiastic support of the Poynter Institute, which pledged to send some of its best trainers to South Africa to train our trainers. They put me through such a course in St Petersburg to get a sense of what was needed. I informed all of my foreign newspapers of my plans, explaining that I would soon have to stop writing for them to devote myself full time to my project. Then I began trying to raise money, by far the most difficult task of all. My first success was at *The Washington Post*, where Katharine Graham promised to give me $33 300. But it was conditional on my being able to raise an equivalent sum elsewhere.

So the search went on, turning me into what I called an 'upper-class beggar'. Everyone I spoke to liked my idea, but, as I was to discover, individuals, and particularly governments, don't readily give away money to something so insubstantial as an idea, something that exists only as a dream in an enthusiast's mind. I did manage to scrape up some modest sums from those ever-generous

Scandinavian countries and the Netherlands. But nothing from the US to match and unlock Katharine Graham's offer.

I was still working for the Post at the time, along with staffer David Ottaway, who had been my partner in covering Nelson Mandela's release. Giving him a lift home after an assignment one evening, I poured out my woes to him as we sat in my car outside his house and asked whether he knew of any source I might approach in the US that might be able to match Kay Graham's offer.

'How much do you need?' David asked.

'Thirty-three and a third thousand dollars,' I replied. 'With Kay's money that would be about R150 000. I think I could risk launching with that, in the hope that when I have the institute up and running, something that actually exists and isn't just a figment of my imagination, I may be able to raise more.'

David didn't say anything. He simply reached into his pocket, drew out a chequebook, wrote a cheque for $33 300 and gave it to me.

'Good luck,' he said quietly as he slipped out of the car and went into his house – leaving me speechless.

Only later did I learn that David came from a wealthy family that owned a chain of small-town newspapers, but that he wanted nothing to do with the family business. His only ambition was to be a reporter on a great newspaper like *The Washington Post*, where he had repeatedly turned down offers of promotion. All he wanted was to be a reporter – and he was a great one. What money he had acquired from the family business he had placed in a trust – and it was from there that the cheque had come, which made the founding of the Institute for the Advancement of Journalism (IAJ) possible.

I ran the IAJ as its director for seven years, with a close friend, Govin Reddy, as my deputy. It was a success from the start, and I am proud to say that it helped equip a string of those fine black reporters to become successful editors and maintain a high standard of robust journalism that is a distinguishing feature of South Africa to this day. A number of illustrious journalists followed me as its director, including Hugh Lewin, the former political prisoner who became a successful author, and the legendary Donald Woods.

*President Mandela as the guest of honour at the tenth anniversary
of the Institute for the Advancement of Journalism, which I founded
in Johannesburg. With us is Professor Anton Harber, head of Wits
University's Journalism department.*

Nelson Mandela came to honour us when the IAJ celebrated its tenth anniversary, identifying himself in a celebratory speech with Thomas Jefferson's famous words of support for a free press: 'Were it left to me to decide whether we should have a government without newspapers, or newspapers without a government, I should not hesitate for a moment to prefer the latter.' It was an important pledge and a moment to remember.

The IAJ has expanded its training activities across the whole African continent since then. It is still operating after 23 years, during which more than 100 000 journalists have attended its courses. I am still a member of its board of directors, but I am no longer involved in running the institute, for it opened up an unexpected new experience for me.

* * *

NO SOONER had I got the IAJ up and running than I realised that the most urgent media challenge the new South Africa was going to face would be the need to transform the South African Broadcasting Corporation (SABC) – and that the IAJ should play a role in it. Since 1948 the SABC had dominated the airwaves as an explicit and unashamed propaganda machine. It was controlled and directed by an extreme right-wing Afrikaner intellectual, Dr Piet Meyer, who was chairman of the Broederbond and one of the key architects of the apartheid ideology. So pervasive was Meyer's influence that the corporation's ostentatious head office building, which dominated Johannesburg's western skyline, was named after him. Moreover, the SABC was not only the state broadcaster but also the broadcast licensing authority and, except for a few small radio stations operating in the Bantustans, had preserved its own monopoly position. As a result there were almost no journalists or media administrators in the country with broadcasting experience other than those who had been trained (and seriously tainted) by the SABC.

It became clear to me that there was no way the ANC and other anti-apartheid parties would be prepared to compete in a democratic election campaign with this powerful propaganda machine still in the hands of the National Party. The matter had not yet arisen at the Codesa negotiations, which were still bogged down with structural and procedural disputes, but I felt the IAJ should take a lead in putting the issue on the national agenda before the negotiators found themselves running out of time.

It also became clear that change at the SABC would have to begin at the top, with a completely new board of directors. Through a good contact in the Australian labour organisation, Apheda, I was able to raise funding to invite a group of two dozen interested people whom we at the IAJ thought might be potential members of a new SABC board, to participate in a week-long workshop with some top broadcasters from the Australian Broadcasting Corporation (ABC), the BBC and the American public television programme *Frontline*. It was a fascinating and instructive week, but the most important outcome was a commitment by the ABC to send a team of journalism trainers to the IAJ over the next several years to run courses for SABC journalists and print journalists who might seek jobs at the public broadcaster.

552

Publicity around this quickly established the IAJ's reputation as a centre for broadcast training. It also alerted the negotiating parties to the importance of transforming the SABC before the election. The result was that, after some intense negotiating, an agreement was hammered out for the selection of a new board of directors. At the ANC's insistence, it had to be done through a democratic process, which turned out to be elaborate but fascinating.

Public bodies across the country were invited to submit nominations, resulting in more than 500 names from all walks of life being nominated. From these, 45 were shortlisted to appear for interviews before an eight-person selection panel. The panel comprised five blacks and three whites, seven men and one woman. It was to be chaired by two Supreme Court judges, Ismail Mahomed, known to be supportive of the ANC, and Piet Schabort, known to be pro-National Party. Of these, Mahomed was by far the most interesting and dominating personality. I had come to know him well while covering the Pietermaritzburg treason trial, where he had successfully defended the UDF accused. He was the first black lawyer to be appointed to the Bench by the apartheid regime in its dying days, and became the new South Africa's first Chief Justice – only, tragically, to die of cancer shortly after that.

The wonderful, democratic novelty about the whole procedure was that the interviews of the shortlisted candidates – of which I was one – were to be televised live by the SABC.

So it was that in May 1993 I arrived with the other 44 candidates in a cavernous hall alongside the negotiating centre, to be interviewed individually by the selection panel. I was seated alone in a hard-backed chair in the middle of that vast hall, where I felt like a prisoner at the bar as I faced those legal eagles lined up on a stage before me, with TV cameras hovering around me. I had to make a presentation to the panel on the role I believed a true national broadcaster should play, then face cross-examination by members of the panel. 'Intimidating' is the word that springs to mind. There was a packed audience behind me, and I knew there were millions more watching on TV in their homes and offices across the country. In fact those audiences attracted the highest audience ratings the SABC had ever achieved – an indication of what one journalist described as the 'voyeuristic fascination' members of the public felt in watching members of the old regime, once so all-powerful and arrogant, face cross-examination, especially from the tough Judge Mahomed, who seemed to relish every moment of it.

Eventually the panel named a 25-member board, consisting of 12 Africans, ten whites (of which I was one), two coloureds and one Indian. Eight were women. The chairman was the highly respected writer Njabulo Ndebele, with Ivy Matsepe-Casaburri, a champion of rural women's causes with a PhD from Rutgers University in New Jersey, as his deputy. As I wrote at the time, seldom can a governing board of any media organisation anywhere in the world have been chosen so publicly and so democratically. I was proud to be among them.

Then came the shock. President De Klerk refused to accept the board as chosen. He rejected Ndebele as chairman on the spurious ground that he could not speak Afrikaans; De Klerk himself could not speak a word of any of the nine African languages Codesa had accepted as official. He also vetoed seven others chosen by the selection panel, myself included, claiming that the group as a whole was loaded in favour of the ANC. He replaced us with seven others of his own choosing. It was a blatant violation of the process agreed to by the Negotiating Council, but De Klerk was still President of the country and so had the legal, if not the moral, authority to do so. I remember feeling outraged by his action, not only because of the personal insult to myself, but also because of the recklessness of establishing such a precedent of government interference right at the outset of an attempt to establish an independent public broadcaster. I felt it didn't bode well for the future, which turned out to be the case.

I returned to the IAJ, but only briefly. Redemption was at hand. Once Mandela became President and after he had appointed some of the chosen board members to ambassadorial posts, I was among those who filled the gaps and so became a member of the board of directors of the SABC.

So it was that I came to spend the next four years in the belly of that beast, giving me an insider's view of the challenging, ego-driven, power-laden, racially stressed and politically charged transformation of this huge state-owned corporation – a micro-cosm of the transformation of the country as a whole. A fascinating experience, but in the end, like its larger equivalent, disappointing.

My first two years were as a board member, helping to draft a mission statement that I felt spelt out the proper role of a public broadcaster committed to bringing the news to the public without fear or favour, but also without any commitment to a ruling or opposition political party. Then the new CEO, Zwelakhe Sisulu, asked me if I wouldn't consider stepping down from the board to take over as editor-in-chief of television news. He felt the news-room wasn't dynamic enough and wanted me to energise it. 'I want you to make it like the newsroom we had at the *Rand Daily Mail*,' he said. I was reluctant. The post was already occupied by a respected black journalist who was a long-time friend, and I felt it would not look good for a white guy to take over from him. But Zwelakhe was insistent, saying he would take care of the personal and political aspects of the change, and I have to admit that the challenge was appealing.

Eventually I agreed, on condition that I would do the job for only one year, during which I would try to invigorate the newsroom and develop a new team of young black newsroom executives to take over when I left. I have written in detail about my time in that newsroom, in a chapter called 'A Prague Spring' in my book *Beyond the Miracle*, and I do not wish to repeat the details here. It is enough to note, as the chapter heading implies, that I think my year at the SABC was a success, but that things changed rapidly after my departure.

A phase of destructive factionalism and rabid greed emerged around who would get my job when I left, which undermined the culture of professionalism I had tried to implant. This quickly reduced the SABC to what it had been before, only this time pro-pagandising for the ANC rather than the NP. A recidivism that came about because there was never again a democratic process to elect a truly independent board of directors, who in turn would appoint competent professionals to the key editorial positions. The nomination process fell into the hands of the ANC-dominated parliamentary select committee on communications, which routinely appointed a reliable ANC supporter as CEO. From then on promotions in all branches of the public broadcaster depended on those who had the powers of appointment. Understanding of the role of the media counted for little or nothing. Toadying to the politically connected became endemic. Anyone who showed the slightest tendency towards independence would be summarily removed, resulting in a remarkable sequence of comings and goings in all the top positions throughout the post-Mandela years – a process that has been hugely destructive.

And so we are back at the beginning. My only satisfaction is that I still encounter black SABC journalists who remember me from my brief era in that newsroom and who say to me, *sotto voce*: 'I wish you were still there. It was so good in those days.' I take courage from that. It means the culture of professionalism I tried to implant is still there, buried but hopefully able to bloom again one day.

* * *

MY DEPARTURE from the SABC, followed by Sue's death soon afterwards, left me in a state of emptiness. The fact that Sue had lived with her cancer for so long – half our 25 years of marriage – meant her passing didn't have the same shattering impact on our lives that Mary's did. The children and I were prepared for it; we'd had time, as it were, to do some of the grieving in advance. But losing a second soulmate is a hard thing to bear, and this time I didn't have the emotional escape route of being able to immerse myself in work. Sue and I had shared so much in the passionate bonding of the anti-apartheid struggle that her sudden departure left me feeling as though there was a void in my life. It had lost its purpose.

The moment of her peaceful death is still engraved in my memory. I woke up early that morning to hear her shallow breathing in the bed beside me. I listened to it grow shallower, and then slipped quietly out of bed to call Julian, then 20 years old. 'I think the moment has come,' I whispered to him. Julian joined me as we knelt at Sue's bedside, each holding one of her hands. The breathing became shallower, and shallower – and then it stopped. Just like that. One moment she was there with us, a wife and a mother, and a second later she was gone, leaving a widower and a motherless son looking at each other across a chasm of silence. What an immense moment that single second is that separates the living from the dead, and how hard it is for one's emotions to straddle it. Sue had been such a vibrant influence for so long that I felt as though my life spirit had been drained away. I carried on writing my syndicated column, which has always been a therapeutic distraction in times of stress. And I was still on the board of the IAJ. But there was a hiatus.

Then, out of the blue, came an invitation from a former US diplomat named Richard Hurt, who had high-level connections in Qatar, to be part of an international Board of Visitors to advise the Arab state's Al Jazeera television station on its plans to launch an English-language service. The station had been running an Arabic channel for several years, but the ruling Emir, Sheikh Hamad bin Khalifa Al Thani, wanted to put his tiny desert country on the map as a rich and influential Middle Eastern Switzerland, and he thought a top-quality global TV service was the way to do it. And he had the money, from the country's huge natural gas resources.

Al Jazeera had its own board of directors and the decision to launch the English service had already been taken. Our job on the Board of Visitors was to advise it on editorial policies and journalistic practices.

So for the next three years I flew to Qatar regularly to take part in meetings of this board with a dozen other journalists from Europe and the Middle East. It was a wonderful professional experience, but even more fascinating for me, with my South African interest in multicultural conflicts, was to get a close-up view of the convoluted politics of the Middle East. In addition to my role on the Board of Visitors, I became friends with Al Jazeera's managing director, Wadah Khanfar, a Palestinian who, by coincidence, had taken a course in African studies at Rand Afrikaans University (now the University of Johannesburg). He invited me to participate in annual meetings of his Al Jazeera Forum, attended by Middle East specialists from across the world.

Working with the Al Jazeera planners was a wonderful professional experience, but with my South African interest in the politics of cultural conflicts I found the opportunity to get close-up insights into the complexities of the Middle East to be even more enthralling.

I was in Qatar on 25 January 2006, the day Palestinians went to the polls to vote for members of the Palestinian Legislative Council. It was only the second such election to have been held, and the militant Hamas organisation was competing for the first time. It had boycotted all attempts at peaceful settlement as pointless, opting instead for a policy of armed resistance.

There was great excitement in the Arab community, and in the Al Jazeera newsroom, as the results came in showing Hamas to be in the lead. Many of the people I spoke to felt that a Hamas victory could be a game-changer, that the very fact the organisation had agreed to participate in the election indicated that its more moderate wing, under Ismail Haniyeh, had gained influence. If they won they might be able to come in from the cold to unite Palestinians in a joint push for a negotiated settlement with Israel.

Hamas did win, handsomely, by 74 seats to Fatah's 45. Western election monitors, including the Carter Center and a European team of observers, declared the election to have been free and fair. Haniyeh was named Prime Minister. But the Western powers refused to recognise the elected regime, saying Hamas was a terrorist organisation not to be trusted.

Was an historic opportunity lost here? I think so. Maybe not a great opportunity, but certainly one to try something new to test the outcome, rather than to continue with the same old dead-end strategy that is never going to get anywhere. Who knows what may have happened if the Haniyeh wing's influence had been able to expand significantly. By rejecting them, the democratic West killed off whatever influence they had and entrenched the violent status quo.

Fascinated by all this, by the region's passions and its complexity, I decided to explore further on my own. With the help of some of my new Middle East contacts, I managed to make my way to Baghdad for face-to-face meetings with Hamas's leaders exiled there. I spent three days talking with them in a house that served as their headquarters, mostly with the deputy leader, Mousa Abu Marzook. I found him an urbane and erudite man, with a PhD in engineering from the University of Colorado. He told me he had spent 11 years in the US. I questioned him hard about Hamas's odious anti-Semitic charter, and Marzook agreed it was bad. 'But nobody changes their founding charters even when they are out of date,' he said, noting that the charter of Israel's ruling Likud Party claims all land from the Nile to the Euphrates (in Iraq) to be part of Eretz Israel.

Marzook also argued that Hamas did not deny Israel's right to exist. 'Israel is a reality. Of course it exists,' he said. 'But we are also not going to recognise its right to exist as an exclusively Jewish state.'

The answer, he contended, was to declare a ten-year *hudna*, or ceasefire, during which Israel would withdraw its forces from the occupied territories. 'Then we can start negotiating our differences. We can't negotiate while we are under occupation and killing each other.'

It made me think of Nelson Mandela's response to PW Botha's early overtures to release him conditionally. 'Prisoners can't negotiate if they are not free,' he had said.

Was Marzook having me on? Was this terrorist leader trying to sucker the naive journalist from South Africa? Maybe. But I've been around the block a few times and I'm not easily suckered. I found some of his points thought-provoking. As a journalist, I've always believed in the old Roman legal dictum of *audi alterem partem* – hear the other side.

Marzook invited me to break bread with him and his colleagues on my last night in Baghdad. A visitor from Hezbollah, who had arrived with a message from Lebanon, joined us. The furnishings were sparse. We sat at a long, narrow dining table, Marzook directly opposite me. A picture of the Al-Aqsa Mosque hung on a wall. The food was spicy and we ate with our fingers. The atmosphere was relaxed. When we were finished, Marzook wished me well and gave me a gift of dates.

* * *

ANOTHER CHANGE that took place in my life was that I got married again. From when I first worked for him at the *Rand Daily Mail*, I had not only admired but also developed a close friendship with Laurence Gandar. He probably had a greater influence on my development as a journalist than anyone else. Laurence was shy and reclusive, but within the small circle of close friends he drew around him he was great company, warm and witty. I was fortunate to be drawn into that circle at a young age.

We became family friends. Laurence's wife, Isobel, was a fun extrovert. Their only son Mark, like his father, was quiet and withdrawn, a naturalist and scientist who was drawn to the outdoors. We visited each other often, and after Isobel died of cancer, Laurence drew particularly close to the cancer-stricken Sue.

Then Mark married Jenny, a highly qualified nurse with two daughters from a previous marriage. So she became part of the circle. They had a son, Owen, the spitting image of his grandfather. Mark and Jenny enjoyed cycling in the forests around Pietermaritzburg, and it was there that Mark one morning suffered a fatal heart attack.

It was shortly before Sue died. We attended each others' grief-stricken memorial services. We drew closer. We married. I took Jenny and young Owen with me to America for another semester of teaching and writing at Duke University and the University of North Carolina.

But it didn't work out. We tried. For nine years we tried. But we were too different, in interests and personalities and even in life-styles. So we did the sensible thing and decided to part company so that we could remain good friends. Had we stayed together it would have ruined that possibility.

One learns something from even the saddest errors in life. In this instance, that mutual grief and sympathy are not in themselves sufficient grounds for a happy marriage.

CHAPTER THIRTY

Killers of the Dream

AS MY CONTRACT with the SABC drew to a close, I began wondering what I might do next. I mentioned this casually in conversation one day with Chris Gibbons, a top broadcaster I had engaged to launch a successful news-hour television programme. 'Oh, if I were you I'd offer my services as a political analyst to some investment house,' he responded. It was an off-the-cuff suggestion but it set me thinking. Why not? I'd been analysing South African politics all my life and I had plenty of contacts in government. And although I was just three years short of my allotted three score years and ten, the idea of retirement held no appeal. After letting the idea germinate in my mind for a while, I called a stockbroker friend, Peter Jardine, with whom I had made a few modest investments, and asked whether he knew of any institution that might be interested in such a service.

'What a coincidence,' Peter replied. 'The Standard Bank has just decided to launch a stockbroking branch and has asked me to head it. I'd love to have you provide that kind of service. Let's talk about it.'

So I underwent another career change. Well, let's say a career mutation, for the new job was essentially the same as journalism. I was required to provide written reports on any political, social and industrial relations developments that I felt might affect investment markets. These reports were circulated to the new brokerage's clients domestically and abroad. I was also required to make periodic presentations to the asset managers of all the country's major investment houses. At the same time I decided to maintain my passion for journalism proper by reviving the column I had written while on the *Rand Daily Mail*; it has appeared as a syndicated column in a number of South African newspapers ever since.

It was a satisfying package of activities that turned out to be successful. The country's leading financial newspaper, the *Financial Mail*, ran a rating system to rank investment analysts, and I was rated first in my category of political analysts for ten successive years. This enhanced my market value as an analyst to the point where I found my services in demand and was able to earn some quite serious money for the first time in my life, which helped compensate for the miserable pension I received from SAAN after 23 years' service with two editorships. It also enabled me to enhance my investment skills. As I came to know and befriend the asset managers who attended my presentations, I quite shamelessly picked their brains on Johannesburg Stock Exchange trends, to the advantage of my own portfolio.

More importantly, having to look at political events from an economic perspective added a new dimension to my analytical abilities. Not only did the experience increase my understanding of economics, it also sharpened my awareness of the difficult economic choices facing the ANC administration as it came to power, and the political implications of those choices.

To begin with, I came to realise the full extent to which apartheid had distorted the national economy. It had, as Mbeki categorised it, produced two separate economies in one country, with whites living in a developed First World economy and the black majority in what at the time was called a Third World economy. In one of my early analytical reports, I wrote that introducing socio-economic mobility between the two economies was the primary challenge facing the new administration.

But if that were the core challenge, the core problem was that the economic distortions were so many and so varied that the new government couldn't possibly deal with them all at once. Yet the expectations within the long oppressed and exploited black community were that it should do so. Therefore a crisis of expectations seemed inevitable. A careful selection of priority issues and effective action dealing with them was surely essential.

Unfortunately that didn't happen. As I became increasingly aware, the ANC was neither an efficient nor a decisive organisation, especially after power shifted from Mbeki to Jacob Zuma. It had many smart people in its leadership and they had done some clever strategic and diplomatic work in bringing the liberation struggle to fruition, but in all those years of exile they had done nothing to prepare themselves to become a government. They never learned how to run any kind of business enterprise. They had devoted themselves to ideological studies instead, many of them at the Lenin Institute in Moscow. They were all at sea in a capitalist world of globalisation and the 'Washington consensus'. Nelson Mandela was able to steady the ship, and Thabo Mbeki, the educated economist, had held it on course for a while. Then came Jacob Zuma.

* * *

I DIDN'T GET to know Zuma in exile as I did the other ANC leaders, since he was based in Mozambique while I was visiting the movement's headquarters in Lusaka. In fact, the first time I met him was at the ANC's first national conference after its return to South Africa. Zuma came up to me and introduced himself as I stood among the press corps. My immediate impression was of a warm and affable man. I knew he had been the organisation's head of intelligence, but that was about all. As I watched him during the conference, held in the Durban suburb of Westville, I noticed he didn't participate much in the debates but that he had an easy relationship with the rural and working-class black delegates. He was clearly a man of the people.

Only later did I discover that Zuma had had no formal schooling and that he remained a Zulu traditionalist with open contempt for what he called 'smart blacks', the rapidly emerging educated black middle class. I also learned that he had a reputation within the ANC for being what one member called 'a stallion', a womaniser with an excessive sexual appetite who had four wives and had fathered some 27 children in and out of wedlock.

Beyond that I knew nothing until the end of Mandela's five-year term, when Mbeki became President and named Zuma as his deputy. I was astonished at Mbeki's choice. From its earliest days, when a Columbia law school graduate named Pixley ka Isaka Seme had founded the organisation nearly a century before, the ANC had always elected well-educated people, mostly university graduates, to its leadership. Now here was Mbeki, himself an MA graduate, putting someone with no schooling in pole position to succeed him.

The contrariness of it led me to inquire about Zuma's early life, to find out what might be considered special about him. I learned that he was born in a remote region of northeast Natal called Nkandla, that he had never known his father, who had died when the boy was four, and that his mother had been a domestic worker. Jacob had grown up under the tutelage of a stern grandfather who had required him to herd his cattle. The family were so poor they couldn't afford school fees, which is why Jacob never went to school.

Yet the youngster was so eager to learn that, during school vacations, he persuaded more fortunate kids who were attending school to tell him what they were learning. They showed him how to scratch out the letters of the alphabet in the dust of Nkandla. Then, as a teenager, Zuma joined the ANC Youth League, leading to his eventual arrest as a member of the senior body after it was banned. He was sentenced to ten years' imprisonment on Robben Island, and it was there that he completed what education he had in what became known as the 'island university' where those political prisoners who were educated tutored those who were not. That is where Jacob Zuma learned to read and write and to speak English. I was moved by this story of his early life and came to respect him as a man of courage and dedication. I also liked him personally. But I still felt that his not having had any formal education meant he was not equipped to become President of South Africa.

There is another aspect of Zuma's role in the peaceful transition of our country that deserves to be noted before he is thrown into the trash can of history. With the civil war still raging throughout KwaZulu-Natal province, President Mandela asked Zuma to take a job in the coalition government of that province and use his influence to end the war. This he did. The war dried up as most Zulus joined the party of their charismatic fellow tribal nationalist, and Buthelezi at last led his diminished party into the national Parliament.

But Zuma's deployment also meant that, while other senior ANC members got Cabinet jobs in the national government worth R100 000 a month, Zuma's salary as a provincial MEC was only R25 000. It was nowhere near enough to support his huge family as well as his own expensive lifestyle.

* * *

ZUMA WAS NOT alone in finding himself short of money. The entire ANC faced an acute financial crisis as it returned to South Africa. All its assets had been seized when it was banned back in 1960, and although sympathetic governments, notably the Scandinavian countries, had helped sustain it in exile, it had no resources or even premises to return to in 1990 – only the daunting need to find some R40 million to establish itself as a political party ready to fight the election of its life.

Thousands of exiles were streaming back into the country without jobs and often without homes or even families to whom they could return. This dilemma was partly eased after the first election in 1994, when many jobs opened up for them in the national and provincial legislatures, in municipal councils and, more gradually, in the civil service.

But Zuma's money problem was more acute than most. He quickly found himself slipping into debt, and as he did so he turned for help to a sharp young Indian businessman named Schabir Shaik, who had worked for him as an underground intelligence agent during the struggle years. It was a fateful decision for both Zuma and Shaik – and for South Africa.

565

But I am moving ahead too fast. The Shaik-Zuma relationship evolved in the context of a highly controversial deal undertaken by the government, apparently at the behest of Deputy President Mbeki, to whom Mandela had delegated wide administrative powers while he himself concentrated on the urgent task of racial reconciliation.

I first heard of this deal when it came before Parliament for ratification, and as a political analyst I was astonished by its irrationality. The ANC had come to power with its black electorate abuzz with anticipation. They had been oppressed and exploited for generations, and now this new liberation movement had come to power promising 'a better life for all'. There were so many priorities – housing, health, education, jobs, electricity, water. The list seemed endless, the costs daunting and the expectations extreme.

Yet the new regime chose to make its first major expenditure project the re-equipping of the South African National Defence Force (SANDF).

I was flabbergasted. But my role was to try to explain to investors why the new regime, under such intense delivery pressure, was prioritising this hugely expensive and seemingly unnecessary project. What was in their minds? So I went to Parliament to listen to the debate. The main opposition, a mutation of the old Progressive Party now called the Democratic Party (later the Democratic Alliance) and consisting of only seven MPs, was asking exactly that question. Why this huge expenditure of some R48 billion on armaments when the new South Africa had no potential enemies in sight?

What struck me particularly as the debate heated up was that in some instances the items being purchased were more costly than others on offer and actually in conflict with the recommendations of the military units concerned. The most striking example was a decision to buy Gripen fighter jets and Hawk jet trainers from a British-Swedish consortium, BAe/Saab, in preference to similar planes on offer from Italy's Aermacchi, which were half the price and which the South African Air Force had recommended. This smelled fishy. I knew the arms industry had a notorious reputation for paying kickbacks, and I became more and more suspicious that the real purpose of the arms deal was simply to fill the ANC's depleted coffers, that it had made its need for money priority number one, ahead of the needs of its people.

I sat there listening to the Minister of Trade and Industry, Alec Erwin, argue that the so-called offset deals – the amounts the arms suppliers agreed to invest in South Africa in return for being granted tenders – would almost cover the cost of the purchases. I listened to the Deputy Minister of Defence, Ronnie Kasrils, wax lyrical about these 'offsets'. They would bring in new investment and create jobs, he said. 'Far from being a drain on our resources, it [the arms deal] will provide a tremendous boost to our economy and Treasury. It will delight the Minister of Defence.'

I was sceptical. I had read a book by a journalist friend, Anthony Sampson, called *The Arms Bazaar*, in which he warned that off-sets were a lure arms suppliers often used to secure sales, but that penalties for non-delivery were often either built into the tender price, or the offsets were simply not fully honoured.[1] My scepticism was intensified when the feisty Patricia de Lille, of the PAC, told Parliament, in September 1999, that two ANC MPs on the defence portfolio committee had given her a memorandum with detailed allegations of corruption in the arms deal.[2] This imme-diately set every investigative journalist in the country on to the story. I joined the pack.

The arms deal inevitably came before Parliament's Standing Committee on Public Accounts, known by its acronym, Scopa, an important body containing MPs of all parties whose job was to keep a close eye on government expenditures and investigate any that seemed suspect. It had begun life in the new Parliament by working as a strictly non-partisan group, with an opposition party chairman, Gavin Woods of the IFP, and an ANC member, Andrew Feinstein, as deputy chairman. I knew Feinstein, and when I questioned him about the arms deal he was at first ad-amant that Scopa would investigate it thoroughly, but soon I noticed he was becoming more reticent and agitated.

Eventually Feinstein confessed to me, in a high state of agitation, that the ANC leadership was blocking Scopa from investigating the deal. First the chief whip, Tony Yengeni, had told him he didn't think a public investigation into the deal was a good idea; it should rather be dealt with internally. Feinstein was distressed. He had seen a preliminary report from the Auditor-General that contained what he called 'a litany of irregularities', and he realised Yengeni's proposal was an obvious attempt to cover up any scandal.

Worse was to come. Scopa drafted a resolution calling for a forensic investigation into the arms deal, to be undertaken by a group of key investigative bodies, including one headed by a High Court judge, Willem Heath. The government baulked at this. President Mbeki went on television to denounce what he called attempts to discredit the government by making 'unfounded and unsubstantiated allegations of corruption'. That done, Woods received a letter signed by Zuma, but later revealed to have been drafted by Mbeki, excoriating Scopa's inquiries into the arms deal as being 'tantamount to a fishing expedition'. This was followed by an ANC announcement that it was 'strengthening Scopa' by taking control of the committee. An ANC loyalist was named to replace Woods as chairman and Feinstein was removed as deputy.

Disillusioned, Feinstein resigned from the ANC and went to Britain, where he set about probing the role of the European manufacturers who had been involved in the deal. His indefatigable work culminated in an explosive book exposing the details of both the scandal and the cover-up.[3]

As it turned out, the cost of the arms deal escalated from an initial estimate of R30 billion to R52.3 billion.[4] A sizeable feeding trough for the well-connected. The late Joe Modise, who was Minister of Defence at the time and a key driver of the deal, is reputed to have pocketed a cool R30 million for himself. His adviser, Fana Hlongwane, is alleged to have entered into a consultancy agreement with British Aerospace on a retainer of R1 million a year – and to have eventually received an R8 million settlement for his help.

Then came a twist in the tail of the saga. Tony Yengeni, the ANC chief whip, who had hounded Feinstein and Woods and eventually squelched the Scopa investigation, was himself found guilty of accepting a substantial discount for a luxury

Mercedes-Benz 4x4 from DaimlerChrysler Aeronautic Defence and Space, which had been awarded a R220-million contract to provide tracking radars for a fleet of frigates acquired in the arms deal. Yengeni was sentenced to four years' imprisonment after pleading guilty in a plea bargain. He served only four months of his sentence.

In a show of comradeship, top ANC parliamentarians carried Yengeni shoulder-high to the prison to begin his sentence, and were there again to give him a hero's welcome on his release. I saw that, and Mbeki's pardon, as an ominous sign that the ANC top brass saw corruption as a condonable offence.

Yet I also have a glimmer of understanding of this collective response to Yengeni's imprisonment. I believe generations of being the victims of unjust apartheid laws had degraded the sense of respect for the law in the minds of many black people. Indeed, to have defied those laws and gone to prison had become a badge of honour in the black community. Moreover, Yengeni had been a genuine struggle hero. He had been detained without trial and subjected to particularly severe torture in a case that had been vividly demonstrated – and televised – during a hearing of the Truth and Reconciliation Commission.

As the scandal expanded, with the newspapers digging up more and more details and the government's explanations sounding increasingly unconvincing, I found it a distressing time. Having been so supportive of the ANC and of Mandela's vision for the new South Africa, I couldn't understand this sudden downward turn of events. The new regime seemed to be stumbling into errors with no idea of how to extricate themselves. So, in my new role as a political analyst, I offered to give them some advice on damage control. What to do when something goes badly wrong?

My offer was accepted and I addressed several groups of leading ANC and Cosatu figures. My message was simple: the basic lesson, I told them, is to have a thorough investigation to unearth every detail of the scandal, then disclose everything at once. Don't leave a single item to be unearthed later. Have one bad day at the office – and then it will all be over. The public memory is short. But if you try to cover it up, the scandal will continue to suppurate in the dark, with bits of it constantly being dug up by relentless investigative journalists, and each new disclosure will cause the whole scandal to flare up anew.

I told them of my experiences working for *The Washington Post*, where that paper's handling of the Watergate scandal had become a legend. I pointed out that it was the cover-up rather than the petty burglary at the Democratic National Committee's headquarters in the Watergate office complex to get hold of the party's campaign secrets that had destroyed President Richard Nixon and his administration. And I told them how editor Ben Bradlee had handled a scandal of his own, when a *Washington Post* reporter's Pulitzer Prize-winning story turned out to be a fabrication. Bradlee had commissioned the paper's autonomous ombudsman to undertake a comprehensive investigation into who, from the editor downwards, had slipped up or not been vigilant enough in the handling of the story. The Post had then published every word of the ombudsman's findings across the front page and four full inside pages. With nothing left for anyone else to uncover, the scandal died in a single day.

I drew my audiences' attention to Bradlee's pithy comment on this affair in his autobiography. 'Thanks to Watergate,' he wrote, 'I had learned a vitally important lesson: The truth is the best defence, and the whole truth is the very best defence.'[5]

Remember that, I told them.

Alas, they didn't. Not then, nor since. So the arms deal scandal suppurates on, continuously re-emerging and re-infecting the body politic with new and bigger scandals. It is the primary cancer afflicting the new South Africa, and under the Zuma administration particularly, metastasising into every limb and organ of both the party and the state. It is threatening to kill Nelson Mandela's rainbow nation dream.

* * *

THE STORY of how Jacob Zuma became embroiled in the arms deal goes back to the contacts he made during the struggle years. After his release from Robben Island in 1973, Zuma became a member of the military wing of the ANC, and soon afterwards was sent first to Swaziland, and then Mozambique, to deal with the massive flow of young people leaving South Africa in the wake of the Soweto uprising. From there his role evolved into an attempt to get an armed struggle going across the borders in his home province of Natal. Because of his familiarity with the tribal structures of the region, Zuma's job was to organise an underground network in Natal to which guerrilla fighters could be infiltrated. That required a reception committee on the Natal side of the border to meet the arriving guerrillas and link them to the network. Zuma found the opportunistic young Schabir Shaik to set this up for him.

The Shaik family, Durban Indians will tell you, were sharp operators. They were 'fixers' with contacts, which is exactly what Zuma required. The cadres he was filtering across those borders needed money, false identity documents, safe houses, stuff like that, and Schabir Shaik had the contacts to provide them. So a relationship developed between him and Zuma – a relationship that was to evolve into personal friendship.

It was not surprising, therefore, that when Zuma found himself in financial difficulties after his redeployment to KwaZulu-Natal a dozen years later, he turned to his old collaborator for help. As Schabir Shaik was later to testify at his corruption trial in the Durban High Court, Zuma came to him one day and confessed that he could not come out on his meagre income.

'He told me he was going to have to leave politics and get a job,' Shaik told the court. 'I told him: "You can't do that, comrade. You're too important. Why don't you leave it to me. I'll help manage things for you."'

I followed reports of the Shaik trial in the Durban High Court closely, checked key aspects of the court record and read the excellent books by Andrew Feinstein, Paul Holden and others to try to piece together the relationship between the two men. It was obviously friendly as well as mercenary. Shaik admired Zuma and admitted to helping him financially out of a spirit of friendship, but as he effectively became the manager of all Zuma's financial affairs it clearly expanded well beyond that.

The relationship began at a modest level, with Shaik giving Zuma interest-free loans with no date for repayment. He paid the children's school fees and the family's clothing and food bills. Family members would simply call at food and clothing stores, take what they wanted and Shaik would settle the bills. But, as Judge Hilary Squires was to find at Shaik's trial, Shaik's generosity towards his friend was not motivated entirely by charity. He expected favours in return. Zuma was MEC for Economic Affairs in the provincial administration, as well as being national chairman of the ANC, so Shaik saw an opportunity to use his friend's political influence to leverage valuable contracts for his own company, Nkobi Holdings. As Judge Squires put it, the relationship between Shaik and Zuma amounted to a 'mutually beneficial symbiosis that the evidence shows existed'. In other words, you scratch my back and I'll scratch yours.

That, too, began modestly. Shaik managed, with Zuma's influence, to land some beneficial projects for Nkobi Holdings in the province, to do with upgrading Durban Airport, building roads and setting up a cellular telephone network.

Then both sides of the symbiotic relationship began to expand. Schabir's brother, Chippy Shaik, happened to be in charge of arms acquisitions for the SANDF as the arms deal got under way. With that connection, and using the political influence of Zuma, Shaik was able to present Nkobi Holdings as a suitable black economic empowerment partner to a French arms company, Thomson-CSF, which then won a lucrative contract to provide the electronic technology to arm the combat suites of the frigates to be acquired as part of the arms deal.

Shaik also managed to hustle Thomson-CSF into agreeing to pay Zuma a R500000 a year bribe – expected to run over two years – to protect the French arms company from any investigation into the arms deal, and to use his influence to further Thomson's interests in procuring additional investment opportunities in South Africa. The French company required Zuma to confirm by encrypted code that he was prepared to do this, which Zuma duly did.

However, it appears that Shaik had difficulty getting Thomson-

CSF to cough up on the bribe agreement. While at the same time Zuma was beginning to incur some serious new expenses, putting the hard-pressed Shaik in an awkward situation. Zuma had ordered work to begin on building a fine new cluster of mansions for himself and his family on trust land at Nkandla, where he had been born. The tender cost for this was a cool R1 340 000.

Shaik was appalled. He tried to stop the development going ahead, but Zuma overruled him. Zuma managed to raise a bond, for which another Durban businessman, Vathasallum (Vivian) Reddy, stood surety, whereupon Zuma wrote a R1-million cheque for the contractor in the name of a company called Development Africa, in which he, Shaik and Reddy were directors.

Again Shaik intervened to stop the cheque, waiting instead until he received half of the first tranche of Zuma's bribe money from Thomson-CSF so that he could use that to pay the Nkandla contractor. Shaik followed this up with three more post-dated cheques for R250 000, presumably in anticipation of receiving a further R750 000 from Thomson-CSF. But Thomson-CSF never paid that money, leaving Shaik to make two more payments of R135 000 from the account of Development Africa, which meant that he, Reddy and the contractor all lost out on the Nkandla deal.[6]

But that was only the beginning. In the years that followed, public expenditure on Nkandla was to balloon into the greatest of all the Zuma scandals.

There were also smaller scandals. In the course of the Shaik trial, the state ordered a forensic audit of both Shaik and Zuma's financial records, which were then presented to the court in a 259-page report. They presented a picture of Zuma maintaining a lifestyle well beyond his means, making purchases without regard to the costs involved, and leaving the hapless Shaik scrambling to cope with the financial mess.

That mountain of evidence proved Shaik's guilt on all charges, for which Judge Squires sentenced him to 15 years' imprisonment on each of two corruption charges, and three years on a lesser charge, all to run concurrently. It also exposed Zuma's involvement in these criminal activities.

573

A few days later Mbeki fired Zuma as Deputy President. He had little option, given the extent to which Judge Squires had implicated Zuma in his judgment against Shaik. But it meant Mbeki had not only made an enemy of Zuma, but also a martyr in the eyes of his supporters.

The unfortunate thing for the future of South Africa is that Zuma was never charged together with Shaik. Had that been done, I believe the future course of our country would have been very different.

For that lapse of judgment, the blame must fall on the then Director of the National Prosecuting Authority (NPA), Bulelani Ngcuka. I came to know Bulelani well during the struggle years, when he was a brave and effective civil rights lawyer and a member of the UDF. I liked him. He was a good lawyer, but he made a terrible mistake. In August 2003 he announced, as the Scorpions investigative unit wrapped up their investigation into the financial affairs of both Zuma and Shaik, that he believed the state had a *prima facie* case against Zuma but that he was not going to charge him because he didn't think the case was winnable.

That, I'm afraid, was not a decision for the chief of prosecutions to make. If there is a *prima facie* case against someone, it means the state has established a case for such an individual to answer. Such a person should then be charged to answer the case, and it is for a court to decide whether the individual is guilty or not. To state publicly that the state has a *prima facie* case against an individual and not put it to the test, is unfair to both the individual and to society at large, for the accusation is made, staining the individual's reputation, but never tested to clear the air.

I can understand Ngcuka's dilemma. If you are going to commit regicide you had better make sure you kill the king, otherwise you are going to be dead meat yourself. But those are the challenges one must face when one takes on a top job, and I'm afraid Ngcuka failed the test, to the great detriment of his country.

But even with that legal escape, Zuma's immediate problems were not over. Some time later I picked up word that the police were investigating a case of alleged rape against Zuma. The complainant was a 31-year-old woman, the daughter of one of

Zuma's closest friends who had died in exile, after which the young woman looked to Zuma as a paternal figure, addressing him affectionately as 'uncle'. She claimed she had gone to Zuma's Johannesburg home for advice, and that it was there, in his home, that he had raped her. Zuma vehemently denied the charge. He admitted having sex with the woman (whose name the court withheld) but insisted it was consensual. He also admitted that he knew she was HIV-positive and that she was an AIDS activist working in the townships to combat the disease. When asked whether he had used a condom as a precaution against transmission of the disease, Zuma, the husband of four wives, admitted he had not, but added under further questioning that he had taken a shower afterwards to minimise the risk of transmission. It was a claim that has subjected Zuma to endless ridicule, with the country's leading cartoonist, Zapiro, depicting him ever since with a shower spray permanently attached to his head.[7]

Judge Willem van Heerden found Zuma not guilty, citing the evidence of other ANC members who said the complainant had made false allegations of rape against other congress members while in exile. He also took into account the fact that she had not reported the case immediately. Eight years later, a Constitutional Court judge, Justice Zak Yacoob, speaking at a human rights workshop, criticised the judgment, saying he thought Van Heerden had given undue weight to those issues and not enough to the intimidation the young woman had felt at the hands of someone she regarded as a father figure.

What repelled me particularly about this case was the sight of large crowds, including many women, crowding around the courthouse each day to sing Zuma's praises. He joined them, dancing and giving voice to his machine-gun song. The crowd yelled abuse at the young woman accuser whenever she arrived at the court, and at one point women in the pro-Zuma mob hurled stones at someone they mistook for a friend of the accuser. After the case, the young woman and her mother fled the country to settle in the Netherlands, which gave them asylum.

A few years after the rape case, by which time Zuma had been elected President of the country, the news broke that he had fathered another child out of wedlock, this time with a young woman named Sonono Khoza, daughter of another close friend, Irvin Khoza. He seemed unperturbed by these scandals, claiming that, in accordance with African tradition, he was open about his sexual relationships and took responsibility for them, whereas white men were secretive about their affairs.

* * *

THE CHARGE SHEET that has hung intermittently over Zuma's head for almost a decade is formidable. There are 16 major charges, covering corruption, fraud, money laundering and racketeering. It is the corruption charges that are truly mind-blowing, covering 783 payments from Shaik to Zuma totalling R4072499.85. They include everything from the Zuma children's school fees to household costs, travel costs, legal costs, traffic fines and medical costs, all the way to packets of cash that Zuma allegedly picked up from time to time. They also include R400 000 allegedly paid for Zuma's Nkandla homestead, as well as Zuma's failure to declare these payments to the revenue service and to Parliament as unearned 'gifts'.

Faced with this daunting barrage, Zuma chose a legal strategist with the improbable name of Kemp J Kemp to lead his defence team. Kemp, a slightly rumpled figure who evokes recollections of the TV detective Columbo, had a reputation for winning cases against the odds. This he certainly burnished with his defence of Zuma by pursuing what became known as a 'Stalingrad strategy'. The sobriquet stemmed from an early exchange between himself and a judge when Kemp sought a court order to block an attempt by the state to retrieve documents that Thomson-CSF, now renamed Thint, had lodged in Mauritius.

Judge Jan Hugo intervened. 'If a person professes his innocence,' he asked, 'then why go to all these lengths to prevent this evidence from being obtained?'

'We think it is important,' Kemp replied. 'This is not like a fight between two champion fighters. This is more like Stalingrad. It's burning house to burning house.'

576

By which he meant the defence saw the case as a fight for Zuma's survival, and that he intended fighting this drawn-out war street by street, house by house, until the enemy was exhausted and would begin its long retreat. It was a strategy he followed to the letter, challenging every issue raised by the state, appealing every verdict all the way to the Constitutional Court, then finding new legal issues to start the process all over again. The state, of course, was required to foot all of Zuma's defence costs.

The delays caused by the 'Stalingrad strategy' led eventually, in September 2006, to an exasperated KwaZulu-Natal judge, Herbert Msimang, striking the case from the Pietermaritzburg High Court roll. That meant Zuma no longer faced any charges, but it was still open for the state to recharge him. Mistaking the outcome, thousands of Zulus burst into celebration and marched through the streets carrying a coffin with Mbeki's face on the lid, obviously implying that he was behind a malicious conspiracy.

The next day Zuma addressed a massive Cosatu rally in Johannesburg, where General Secretary Zwelinzima Vavi, the country's leading trade unionist, effectively pledged the organisation's support for Zuma. 'The overwhelming majority of working people, of the working class, the poor, the marginalised, should be very happy today,' Vavi told the crowd. 'This was all a politically-inspired case to prevent him from advancing his political career.'[8]

It was the beginning of Zuma's remarkable surge towards power. From that moment onward, Vavi's powerful trade union federation, backed by the SACP, became an open campaigner for Zuma, leading a left-wing revolt to oust Mbeki as president of the ANC at its upcoming national conference in December 2007. Mbeki was already shedding support because of his authoritarian leadership style and his AIDS denialism, but it was his pro-business economic policy, Gear, that was the clincher for the leftists. Vavi in particular raged against it, portraying Gear, modest as it was, as falling in line with the so-called Washington consensus and amounting to a betrayal of the revolution's socialist ideals. He was quickly joined in this by a wild young demagogue, Julius Malema, later to become leader of the ANC Youth League, who declared himself ready to 'kill for Zuma'.

It soon became clear to me that a major transformation was in the offing. For all his many shortcomings, Zuma had a natural talent for electioneering, and that is what he had clearly begun to do, beginning with the supportive crowds that had gathered at each of his court appearances. I had watched his support grow steadily from those early signs, but now, with Vavi's support and that of the rambunctious Malema, it really began to roll.

* * *

THREE WEEKS before the ANC was due to hold its national conference in the northern city of Polokwane, I wrote an analytical article boldly predicting that Mbeki was heading for defeat as leader of the party. I had not only sniffed the air, I had also done the maths. I had checked the number of delegates that would be coming from the various provinces, and calculated what their likely voting strengths would be. From this I predicted that Zuma would get 61 per cent of the votes and Mbeki 38 per cent.

The article caused a sensation. I had written it for the Standard Bank's Emerging Markets Research Unit, to which I was then contracted, for them to distribute on their email service to a select list of clients. It was thus written for a relatively small and private audience, and a notation stated clearly that the views expressed were mine and not necessarily the bank's. But such was its impact, since I was the first established political analyst to predict so emphatically that the President of South Africa was headed for defeat with a purported left-winger replacing him, that the article went viral. Both the bank and I were inundated with phone calls and emails from news reporters, foreign diplomats, risk analysts and anxious investors from all parts of the world. Such is the way of the internet.

In the article I set out three possible scenarios. The first analysed what would likely happen if Mbeki remained determined to take the issue to a vote. This, I said, would lead to a bitter fight on the conference floor, with Mbeki losing amid triumphant calls from the Zuma camp for a clean-out of Mbeki's closest and most senior lieutenants from the administration. There could even be a call, backed by a motion of no-confidence in Mbeki as President of the country, for him to resign immediately so that Zuma could take over.

This could result in the departure of some of the most able people in the Cabinet, resulting in a sharp change of direction in social and economic policies and a general rupturing of the party and the county. This, I wrote, was the worst-case scenario.

My second scenario was for Mbeki to realise he was on a losing track and to decide, in order to avoid the humiliation of defeat on the conference floor, to announce that he was withdrawing from the contest in the interest of national unity, and to invite Zuma to do likewise. There could then be a deal allowing a compromise candidate to take over the leadership of the party, someone acceptable to the left, such as ANC secretary-general Kgalema Motlanthe, whose role would be to reunite the party and its alliance partners.

My third scenario was for Mbeki to realise he was going to lose, announce his withdrawal from the race in the interests of party and national unity, while at the same time approaching Zuma in a spirit of magnanimity and offering to join with him in healing the rift and bringing the two warring sides together. Mbeki could then serve out his second and last term as President of the country, with Zuma waiting in the wings as president of the party to take over the national presidency after the next election, in 18 months' time.

Sadly, Mbeki's advisers remained convinced they could deliver him a majority by some energetic lobbying over those final three weeks. But they were wrong. Hopelessly so. At Polokwane Zuma received 2 329 votes to 1 505 – 60.67 per cent to 39.25 per cent, almost exactly the figures I had calculated.

The political consequences were likewise as I had predicted – a clean-out of Mbeki supporters, a demand that the President resign immediately, and a split in the party to form a new group called the Congress of the People (Cope), which, as it turned out, promptly wrecked what might have become a major movement by descending into a destructive internal leadership conflict.

My only omission was that Zuma didn't take over immediately, deciding instead that Motlanthe should serve out the rest of Mbeki's presidential term. The modest, thoughtful Motlanthe did a sterling job, applying himself with quiet dignity and efficiency. He did much to soothe the seriously divided ANC and the country prospered. But after him, the decline.

* * *

TWO YEARS into Jacob Zuma's second term, I find myself observing a country in trouble, a South Africa in a maelstrom of political discontent and economic distress. People are fuming politically because of Zuma's failure to deliver on any of his promises. The economy is suffering from weak commodity prices, budget and trade deficits, a stagnant industrial economy combined with a declining currency, a swelling population and a low growth rate, a high rate of strikes and a low rate of productivity, widespread corruption, poor service delivery, the widest wealth gap in the world – wider even than during apartheid – a high crime rate, and a failed education system feeding into a 38 per cent unemployment rate alongside a serious skills shortage.[9]

I don't believe any of these faults can be rectified as long as Zuma remains President; he is too focused on his own security and self-interest to pay sufficient attention to them, and too lacking in understanding even if he had the will. He is a skilled manipulator, not a leader, and he has used his manipulative skills to build a patronage system around himself for protection. The result is that the country is badly governed. It is a reductionist administration that deals in slogans and buck-passing. Fundamental problems go unattended, if not unnoticed.

Worse still, not only has the stench of the arms deal scandal followed Zuma into the presidency, but it has been compounded by an even greater scandal involving his private housing complex at Nkandla. On becoming President, the law required the security facilities at the property to be upgraded to secure his safety. The original estimate for the upgrading was R27 million, but, as newspapers were the first to reveal, the actual expenditure turned out to be a staggering R246 million.

The Public Protector, Thuli Madonsela, whose job is akin to that of an ombudsman appointed under the Constitution to hear public complaints, carried out an investigation into the matter. In a 444-page report, Madonsela described the cost overruns as an 'unconscionable misappropriation of public funds', from which Zuma had benefited improperly.

Among the items Madonsela cited as constituting improper benefits were a swimming pool, a visitor's centre, an amphitheatre, a tuck shop, a cattle kraal and a chicken run, which she reckoned had nothing to do with security. She recommended that Zuma should refund the state the excessive amount spent, and that the South African Police Service (SAPS), who are responsible for the President's security, should determine the amount.

But Zuma has refused to pay a cent. And the Minister of Police, Nathi Nhleko, obligingly determined that all the alterations were essential for the President's safety. Cattle had a religious connotation in African tradition, Nhleko contended, therefore their safe kraaling was justified; the swimming pool was really a fire pool necessary to douse any flames that might spring up among the complex's thatched buildings; the amphitheatre was a reinforcement against flooding. As for the chicken run, it was vital to prevent the chickens from running free and setting off Nkandla's security sirens. Therefore the President owed nothing.

This provided rich material for the cynics and the cartoonists and the stand-up comedians. It also provoked some explosive moments in Parliament as the Speaker, Baleka Mbete, abandoned all pretence of objectivity and intervened to protect the President from opposition outrage. In the first and worst of these conflicts, Julius Malema, now at the head of a new party, the Economic Freedom Fighters (EFF), led his 12 MPs, all clad in red workers' overalls, in a chorused chant: 'Pay back the money!' When they defied the Speaker's order to be seated, she summoned armed security police to evict them from the House, resulting in a wrestling melee with not a few fists flying.

Hardly an edifying scene in the Parliament for which so many had struggled for so long to vote. The High Court later declared the entry of armed police into Parliament to be improper, and the forcible eviction of MPs from the debating chamber to be a violation of democratic rights.

People ask me whether I am disillusioned at this state of affairs, having been so supportive of the ANC and its efforts in the early years of the transition. I tell them that 'disillusionment' is too strong a word, for it would imply that I believe the new South Africa is doomed to fail, which I do not. I believe what we are undergoing is an aberration. Many countries go through bad phases under bad leadership, but they recover and learn from what went wrong. I believe the Zuma era is such a phase, and with our long history of stepping back from oft-predicted disaster, I believe we shall do so again.

I am disappointed, certainly. When I think back to the uplifting sight of those long queues at our first democratic election and the surge of patriotic emotion that I experienced at Mandela's inauguration, the feeling of a great letdown verges on anger. It had begun so well, how could they have messed it up so badly, so quickly? It is at such times that I thank God I never accepted that opportunity to join the ANC and become a member of the first democratic Parliament. Where would I have been now had I done so? I could never have remained loyal to such a corrupted movement, never have remained silent. It could only have ended in bitterness.

Thank goodness I decided to remain an independent journalist. Which always brings me back to reality after those spasms of clotted anger. Journalism requires a degree of detachment in order to be objective, or at least fair in one's assessments. Which I believe has enabled me to track the course of the decline under Zuma more dispassionately than would otherwise have been possible.

So in the interests of fairness let me note that despite Mbeki's errors of judgment and Zuma's multiple defects, South Africa is still a much better place than it was under apartheid. Firstly, it is no longer a country where it is a crime *not* to be a racist. It is not headed towards becoming a failed state, as some of the dinner-table chatterati in white suburbia contend. It is not another Zimbabwe in the making. It still has many inner strengths. The central pillars of our political and economic establishment are intact. The Constitution is in place, the courts are functioning, as are Parliament and most of the provincial legislatures. The Treasury is in good hands, as is the Reserve Bank. Our major commercial banks are rock solid and the efficiency of the revenue service is widely recognised.

The media, with some exceptions, are still free and outspoken to a degree not equalled outside the Western world. The exceptions are, firstly, the SABC, which, to my great dismay, has reverted to being a poorly-run state propaganda broadcaster, as it was under apartheid. But new independent broadcasters have come on air to provide excellent alternatives, and the ubiquitous social media cannot be silenced. Some new newspapers, surreptitiously backed by government agencies, have come on the market in response to Zuma's call to 'tell the good news' of ANC rule, but there are still good, critically outspoken publications being produced under black editors and lively columns written by black columnists. I am proud of the role the IAJ has played in sustaining this tradition. Its foundation is probably the most important contribution I have made.

The most heartening feature of the new South Africa, which I believe will eventually save it from the Zuma decline, is the robustness of its civil society, which in turn is largely due to the vigorous media. The majority of the black population support the ANC, but it is not a placid, submissive support. They support it because they see it as 'their' party, the party that liberated them from apartheid and whose struggle songs and slogans they have grown up with from childhood. But, unlike their Zimbabwean counterparts, they have not been crushed into quiescence. When the ANC government does something they disapprove of, black South Africans speak out. Strikes and protest demonstrations against poor delivery of services, or other disagreements, are frequent and often disruptive.

The ANC is weakening as discontent spreads. Its major partner, Cosatu, has split, with half its member unions breaking away, including a deeply disillusioned Zwelinzima Vavi, who was so instrumental in hoisting Zuma onto the throne. The breakaway group plan to form a rival labour federation, and maybe a political party as well. Julius Malema, once a vociferous Zuma supporter, is now intent on bringing about his old master's demise with an EFF assault from the left. The main opposition party, the liberal Democratic Alliance (DA), continues to grow steadily and has increased its appeal to the black community by electing the charismatic Mmusi Maimane as its leader. Thus a pincer movement is forming to squeeze the ruling party in the middle. With our proportional representation electoral system, I foresee the ANC steadily losing outright control of more and more municipal and provincial legislatures, and eventually the national Parliament. Which will compel the ANC to seek coalition partners.

That holds out the prospect of incremental change. It has long been my observation, often shared with my liberal Afrikaner friend, the late Frederik van Zyl Slabbert, as we criss-crossed this tortured continent, that the most perilous moment for an emergent African country was not the moment when it became independent under black majority rule, but when the party of liberation first faces the prospect of defeat. That is when coups take place and dictatorships take root – until the oppressed people reassert themselves once again to demand a proper democracy.

I believe we are approaching that moment. Some in the ANC believe that because of their long struggle they have a right to rule indefinitely, indeed a duty, since they regard themselves as the custodians of their people's freedom. As Jacob Zuma said in 2008, the ANC will rule 'until Jesus comes back' – which I suppose means until eternity.

But I don't believe the end of ANC rule will come in a single shock defeat. I believe it is more likely to come incrementally, gradually, city by city, province by province, each change softened by coalitions before reaching national level. Indeed the process has begun already: the DA is firmly in control of the Western Cape province, as well as some 28 municipalities.

That is what gives me hope that we shall have a soft passage through our second transition into the fulfilment of the rainbow nation dream, which is of a nation of great diversity that can live together in harmony and periodically change its government peacefully.

584

Afterword

Gracias a la vida
par que me ha dado tanto.

SO MIGHT I sing along with the Argentine singer Mercedes Sosa: 'Thank you Life, for what you have given me.' What an extraordinary privilege to have been born on the stage of one of history's great morality plays, and to spend a long life as a journalist recording and analysing and sometimes being a player in the unfolding drama. A drama that goes to the centre of the human condition, where people of all colours and cultures and faiths and ideologies have been thrown together onto this stage to clash and fight one another in 11 civil wars spanning three centuries, and then try to bind together into a single nation, which the great liberal philosopher, John Stuart Mill, said would not be possible – not as long as a dominant minority felt itself superior to the majority.

It is a play that has portrayed the worst of human nature and the best. It has played out the agony of black disinheritance and exploitation, the identity crisis of the white Afrikaners and the connivance of the English-speaking South Africans. It has witnessed great cruelty and wickedness – and one of humanity's great acts of forgiveness.

What a privilege to have been part of it all. Thank you Life.

But as I enter the evening of my life, the play is not over. I have tried in my final chapter to express my views on how the great drama may unfold in South Africa, but I also believe it is of wider importance, a drama with many acts still to be played out on a global stage.

I am indebted to that fine Afrikaner historian, Hermann Giliomee, for drawing my attention to a remarkable exchange of correspondence between two very different individuals on this subject. In 1951, just three years after the National Party's unexpected victory in the post-war election, a young Afrikaner Nationalist intellectual, Piet Meyer, who was one of the party's most fanatical apartheid ideologists, wrote to the distinguished English historian, Arnold Toynbee, who had just published a single-volume abridgment of his 12-volume *A Study of History*. 'What special intellectual or spiritual task,' Meyer asked, 'do you suggest to the Afrikaner nation, which, as a young West European nation, is only now reaching its spiritual maturity?'

I have no doubt Meyer was looking for some kind of validation from Toynbee of the Afrikaner people's right to exist as a distinctive *volk*, or nation, in the midst of the 'non-European' black majority of South Africa. Meyer was deeply influenced by the philosophers of the German Romantic movement, particularly Johann Herder, who believed that culture, heritage and language were what defined a *volk* – which the South African Dutch Reformed Church then transmuted into a declaration that such a *volk* had a divine right to exist.

That became the basis for the church's theological justification for apartheid, which I suspect Meyer wanted Toynbee, at the high point of his fame, to endorse.

But Toynbee's reply must have come as a shock to him – and stands as a lesson for all humanity today. 'My personal feeling,' the historian wrote, 'is that the Afrikaner nation is confronted with a most difficult and at the same time most important spiritual task, which it is bound to undertake without having any choice of refusing. It seems to me that, in South Africa, you are faced already with a situation that is going very soon to be the common situation of the whole world as a result of the "annihilation of distance" through the progress of our Western technology … There will never be room in the world for the different fractions of mankind to retire into isolation from one another again.'[1]

What foresight! Toynbee wrote those words as the first experimental computers were being constructed, more than a decade before Marshall McLuhan coined the phrase 'the global village', and 40 years before the full-blown digital revolution burst upon the world. Meanwhile, jet travel has also become commonplace, completing Toynbee's 'annihilation of distance'.

What Toynbee tried to tell Meyer was that apartheid could never work in a rapidly integrating society. It took the National Party half a century to recognise that, after inflicting enormous social damage with its long denial. Mercifully, we have undertaken the difficult task of coming to terms with that reality. Now we face the equally difficult task of learning to live with 'the other', to build a single nation out of a multitude of different ethnic entities – *volkere*, as Herder would call them – who have been in bitter conflict for more than three centuries.

When I look at the Israelis and Palestinians, the Protestants and Catholics of Northern Ireland, the Greeks and Turks of Cyprus, the disintegration of Yugoslavia and of the former Soviet Union, even the difficulty the ethnically identical East Germans had in reuniting with West Germany after a mere 45 years of separation, I become aware of what a daunting task it is we have undertaken. But problematic though it is, we have made a start and it is vital that we succeed, because, as Toynbee noted, we are the first to confront the challenge that awaits the whole world. We are the test case. As I watch the constant stream of migrants moving inexorably from the poorer parts of the world to the lands of development and opportunity, I see a repeat of the unstoppable flow from tribal lands to the cities of South Africa. And in the increasing attempts to restrict the flow through tough visa controls, arrests and talk of building border walls and fences to keep them out, I see a replication of apartheid's influx control regulations, pass laws and forced removals.

'Send them back to their Bantustans,' is the cry in many lands.

'They are flooding our country, threatening our national identity.'

True. But I'm afraid they will keep coming. The only way to deal with that reality is to come to terms with it. All of us in this shrinking world have to learn to live in harmony with 'the other'. Nelson Mandela and Archbishop Desmond Tutu, both Nobel Peace Prize winners, have given South Africans the vision of a 'rainbow nation' at peace with itself and the world. Now we have to conjure up the vision of a 'rainbow world'.

Not easy. It's going to require instilling a great deal of tolerance, empathy and human understanding. And we South Africans have been assigned the role of showing the way. The polecat of the world has become the pathfinder.

ACKNOWLEDGEMENTS

WRITING about my own life and experiences has been the most difficult task I have ever undertaken. Journalists are trained to report and analyse events as they occur and to keep themselves in the background, so my minders had to keep calling me to order: 'It's about you, stupid!' Two people in particular helped keep me on that straight and narrow, and indeed coached me throughout the writing process, and to whom I am profoundly indebted for their advice and guidance. They are Hugh Lewin, himself a fine journalist and successful author, with whom I worked closely in founding the Institute for the Advancement of Journalism (IAJ) in Johannesburg; and my long-time friend Caroline Millington, a former senior executive at the BBC and now an artist, who lives in London and is at once my strongest supporter and sharpest critic. How fortunate I am to have had such skilled advisers.

Memory was another problem with this book. As an only surviving child on an isolated farm, I had no siblings to jog recollections of my early life, which psychologists tell us is when our personalities are formed. Having experienced widowhood twice didn't help either. So my greatest thanks on this issue must go to my four sons, Simon, Michael, Andrew and Julian, who were my closest fact-checkers. They scrutinised my manuscript and drew my attention to errors and omissions. They also provided

589

me with some of the anecdotal material about my childhood that they had heard from their grandparents. Beyond that, Michael and Andrew, both now living in England, helped me with internet research into aspects of our ancestral history, especially in the search for my mysterious German great-grandfather, Otto Robert Stephan. Both undertook missions on my behalf to Colchester, in East Anglia, where the German Legion of which Robert was a member was encamped for military training in the 1850s, where he met his young wife, Charlotte, at the church door and wedded her in a hasty mass marriage, then took her to the war-torn eastern Cape frontier – where he vanished from the family history. My thanks to two independent historical researchers, Nolene Lossau of Lanseria and the late Dr Keith Tankard of East London, for being the first to put me on track to rediscover the life and fate of that poor lost forebear.

For vital details about these and other events on that early frontier, I am indebted particularly to Professor Jeff Peires, director of Rhodes University's Cory Library in Grahamstown, who helped me solve the mystery of the battle sword I inherited. And to Andrew Phillips, a historian at the University of Essex in Colchester, who linked me to the history of the German legionnaires when they were based in that city and provided me with a unique picture of their garrison camp. I received wonderful help from a distant cousin, the late Margaret Lloyd, who kept a detailed record of family relationships, and from the staff of both the Western Cape provincial archives in Cape Town and the Frontier Museum in King William's Town. A special thanks, too, to Monika Sommer, counsellor at the German Embassy in Pretoria, who drove me from Berlin to the village of Berggießhübel, near Dresden, to serve as my interpreter and help me find Otto Robert Stephan's birth records in the small Lutheran church there.

Raymond Louw, my predecessor as editor of the *Rand Daily Mail*, Rex Gibson, who became its final editor, and Roy Paulson, its last business manager, all read specific chapters of the book dealing with my years on that great newspaper, and I thank them for their input. I also drew on Joel Mervis's official history of the newspaper's parent company, South African Associated

Newspapers (SAAN), and from Gerald Shaw's history of the *Cape Times*. An interview with Henry Kuiper, the former MD of SAAN, who plucked the relatively unknown Laurence Gandar out of a business job to make him the inspirational editor of the Mail, so beginning an epic phase in South African journalistic history, was also instructive.

As for the Mail's role in exposing the Muldergate scandal, one of the greatest newspaper stories ever published in South Africa, my thanks and congratulations must go to the paper's exceptional investigative team, led by Chris Day and the late Mervyn Rees, and to the paper's managing editor, the late David Hazelhurst, who put those bombshell front pages together through an unforgettable week that brought down an apartheid Prime Minister and his putative successor. The Mervyn Rees archives, now lodged at the IAJ, were an invaluable source for details of his sleuthing – and of his meetings with the still anonymous Myrtle.

Finally, my thanks to my publishers, particularly Jonathan Ball himself and his publishing director, Jeremy Boraine, for their faith in backing me to produce what would inevitably be a long book, because of the stretch of time it had to cover – from the era of DF Malan to that of Jacob Zuma. Thanks, too, to their excellent editor, Alfred LeMaitre, who had to suffer hearing me wince as he wielded his trimming knife. Funny how editors who have done that to others all their lives hate having it done to themselves. *C'est la vie.*

NOTES

PREFACE

1   For detailed accounts of the death of Hintsa, see Noël Mostert, *Frontiers*, Jonathan Cape, London, 1992, pp. 712–726; and Jeff Peires, *The House of Phalo*, Jonathan Ball Publishers, Cape Town, 2003, pp. 123–126.

CHAPTER TWO

1   Andrew Phillips, 'When the Germans came to Colchester', *Essex County Standard*, 1 March 1991.

2   ELG Schnell, *For Men Must Work: an account of German immigration to the Cape, with special reference to the German military settlers of 1857 and the German immigrants of 1858*, Maskew Miller, Cape Town, 1954.

3   *Ibid*, p. 148.

4   *Ibid*, p. 53.

CHAPTER FOUR

1   *Time*, 17 April 1952.

CHAPTER SEVEN

1   The expression was used by Robert Baden-Powell, founder of the Boy Scouts, who was a regular contributor to *The Boy's Own Paper*.

CHAPTER EIGHT

1   An anthology of Wallace's wartime dispatches can be found in *Unofficial Dispatches of the Anglo-Boer War*, second edition, Struik, Cape Town, 1975. The story of Wallace's peace treaty scoop is told in Joel Mervis's vivid history of the company that founded the *Rand Daily Mail* and the *Sunday Times*: Joel Mervis, *The Fourth Estate*, Jonathan Ball, Johannesburg, 1989, pp. 1–20.

2   Mervis, *op. cit.*, pp. 1–20.

3   *Ibid*, p. 12.

4   Wallace, *op. cit.*, pp. 261–266.

5   Mervis, *op. cit.*, p. 59.

6   *Ibid*, pp. 195–196.

7   *Ibid*.

CHAPTER NINE

1   Douglas Hurd, 'Great Speeches of the 20th Century', *The Guardian*, 24 April 2004. Hurd served as Foreign Secretary under both Margaret Thatcher and John Major.

2   Personal interview, 10 March 1989.

3   Lewis Sowden, *The Land of Afternoon: The Story of a White South*

African, Elek Books, London, 1968, p. 201.

CHAPTER TEN

1   *Die Burger*, 14 June 1957, cited by Hermann Giliomee, *The Last Afrikaner Leaders*, Tafelberg, Cape Town, 2012, p. 45.
2   Giliomee, *op. cit.*, p. 65.
3   Schalk Pienaar, 'Safeguarding the Nations of South Africa', in Schalk Pienaar and Anthony Sampson, *Two Views of Separate Development*, Oxford University Press, Cape Town, 1960.
4   Allister Sparks, *The Mind of South Africa*, Heinemann, London, 1990, pp. 210–211.

CHAPTER TWELVE

1   See Sparks, *op. cit.*
2   WJ Cash, *The Mind of the South*, Vintage Books, New York, 1991, p. ix.
3   *Ibid*, p. x.
4   Crane Brinton, *The Anatomy of Revolution*, Vintage, New York, 1965, pp. 215–250.
5   *Ibid*, p. 185.
6   JRM Butler, *A History of England, 1815–1918*, Thornton Butterworth Ltd, London, 1928, p. 70.
7   JRM Butler, *The Passing of the Great Reform Bill*, Longmans, Green & Co, London, 1914, pp. 240–241.
8   *Morning Chronicle*, 2 August 1830.
9   Élie Halévy, *A History of the English People in the Nineteenth Century, Vol 3: The Triumph of Reform, 1830–1841*, Ernest Benn, London, 1965.

CHAPTER THIRTEEN

1   Steenkamp was a descendant of the small group of Boer Trekkers who reached Kenya, where they joined a farming community around the Highlands town of Eldoret. He thus grew up a British subject and joined the British colonial service.
2   Recorded interview by Andre Croucamp for archive files of the Liliesleaf Trust, Rivonia, 1990.

CHAPTER FOURTEEN

1   Hugh Lewin, *Bandiet: Seven Years in a South African Prison*, Heinemann, London, 1981, p. 28.
2   *Ibid*, p. 48.
3   *Ibid*, p. 34.
4   Benjamin Pogrund, *War of Words*, Seven Stories Press, New York, 2000, pp. 160–161.
5   *Ibid*, pp. 162–164.

6   *Ibid*, pp. 162–163.
7   *Ibid*, p. 168.
8   *Ibid*, p. 149.
9   *Ibid*, p. 175.
10   Mervis, *op. cit.*, p. 353.

CHAPTER FIFTEEN

1   The Morning Group was a collaborative arrangement by all the country's morning newspapers to pool services and exchange news.

CHAPTER SIXTEEN

1   The biblical enemies of the Israelites.
2   Giliomee, *op. cit.*, p. 58.
3   Mervis, *op. cit.*, p. 338.
4   *Ibid*, p. 357.
5   *Ibid*.
6   Clive Corder, *A Coat of Many Colours*, private publication, 1977, p. 59.
7   Gerald Shaw, *The Cape Times: An Informal History*, David Philip, Cape Town, 1999, p. 201.

CHAPTER EIGHTEEN

1   The full expression in isiXhosa is *Ubuntu ungamntu ngabanye abantu*, or 'People are people through other people'.

CHAPTER NINETEEN

1   The Black Sash was a white women's resistance movement founded in 1955 to protest against the removal of coloured voters from the common roll in the Cape Province. Members wore black sashes as a sign of mourning for the violation of the Constitution. As the apartheid system expanded into every aspect of black people's lives, so, too, did the range of Black Sash activities. These included the establishment of advice offices in which members acted as volunteer advocates to black families affected by the apartheid laws.

CHAPTER TWENTY

1   The photographer who took the picture, Sam Nzima, was working for *The World*, a predominantly black newspaper. When the government shut down *The World* in 1978, I invited Nzima to join the *Rand Daily Mail*, but he declined, saying he feared the security police would kill him.
2   Mervis, *op. cit.*, pp. 412–423.
3   *Ibid*, p. 474.

CHAPTER TWENTY-ONE

1   Mervis, *op. cit.*, p. 434.
2   Mervyn Rees and Chris Day, *Muldergate: The Story of the Info Scandal*, Macmillan South Africa, Johannesburg, 1980, p. 164.
3   *Ibid*, pp. 4–5.

CHAPTER TWENTY-TWO

1   *Report of the Commission of Inquiry into Alleged Irregularities in the Department of Information*, Government Printer, Pretoria, 1979, paras 1.286 and 12.437.

CHAPTER TWENTY-THREE

1   Mervis, *op. cit.*, p. 477. In his account of the clash between Kinsley and myself, Mervis writes: 'After the storm came the calm, Sparks got his reporter, and a good story as well.' That is incorrect.
2   Roy Paulson, personal interview, 14 April 2015.
3   Mervis, *op. cit.*, p. 477.
4   Paulson, personal interview, *op. cit.*
5   Rex Gibson, *Final Deadline: The Last Days of the Rand Daily Mail*, David Philip, Cape Town, 2007, p. 143.
6   *Ibid*, pp. 144–145.
7   *Rand Daily Mail*, 1 June 1981.
8   *Ibid.*
9   Mervis, *op. cit.*, p. 508.
10 *Ibid*, p. 508.
11 *Leadership*, March 1987.

CHAPTER TWENTY-FIVE

1   I was incorrect. While Groote Schuur was for many years the official residence of South Africa's prime ministers, PW Botha chose to live in neighbouring Westbrooke, the former residence of the country's Governors General. The Groote Schuur manor house is today a museum.

CHAPTER TWENTY-SEVEN

1   Christopher Hitchens, *Mortality*, Atlantic Books, London, 2012.
2   This theme occurs frequently in Berlin's many essays, but for the most comprehensive expression of it see *The Crooked Timber of Humanity*, edited by Henry Harvey, Pimlico, London, 2003, pp. 20–48.
3   Allister Sparks and Mpho M Tutu, *Tutu: The Authorised Portrait*, Macmillan, London, 2011, p. 245.

CHAPTER TWENTY-EIGHT

1   *The Observer*, 18 February 1990.

2   Literally 'Rescue-deed Association'. The organisation was launched by the Broederbond.
3   Anthony Sampson, *Mandela: The Authorised Biography*, HarperCollins, London, 1999, p. 435.
4   In *The Secret Revolution* (Jonathan Ball, Cape Town, 2015), Niël Barnard writes that they met 50 times.
5   Giliomee, *op. cit.*, p. 265.

CHAPTER TWENTY-NINE
1   Robert Schrire, 'Thabo's Republic', *Leadership*, November 1998.
2   *Ibid.*

CHAPTER THIRTY
1   Anthony Sampson, *The Arms Bazaar: From Lebanon to Lockheed*, Hodder & Stoughton, London, 1977.
2   De Lille later joined the Democratic Alliance and became Mayor of Cape Town.
3   Andrew Feinstein, *After the Party: A Personal and Political Journey Inside the ANC*, Jonathan Ball, Cape Town, 2007, p. 189.
4   Paul Holden, *The Arms Deal in Your Pocket*, Jonathan Ball, Johannesburg, 2008, p. 26.
5   Benjamin Bradlee, *A Good Life: Newspapering and Other Adventures*, Simon & Schuster, New York, 1995, p. 438.
6   Holden, *op. cit.*, pp. 142–143.
7   Zapiro's real name is Jonathan Shapiro, a former architecture student who became an anti-apartheid activist, and then studied at the School of Visual Arts in New York.
8   *Mail & Guardian*, 21 September 2006.
9   That unemployment figure includes people who have ceased looking for jobs – a figure deleted from official statistics for reasons I don't understand, for they certainly are not working.

AFTERWORD
1   Hermann Giliomee, *The Last Afrikaner Leaders*, Tafelberg, Cape Town, 2012, p. 17. Quoted from P Meyer, *Nog nie ver genoeg nie*, Perskor, Cape Town, 1984, p. 64.

INDEX

Note: 'AS' indicates Allister Sparks. Page numbers in *italics* refer to photographs.

605